CONTENTS

LIST OF FIGURES,
TABLES, AND MAPS

FIGURES

TABLES

MAPS

ABBREVIATIONS

BEFEO   *Bulletin de l'école française d'extrême orient*

BIHP   *Chung-yang yen-chiu-yüan li-shih yü-yen yen-chiu-so chi-k'an* 中央研究院歷史語言研究所集刊 (Bulletin of the Institute of History and Philology, Academia Sinica)

BK   Pei-ching (Beijing) ta-hsüeh, Li-shih-hsi k'ao-ku (kaogu) chuan-yeh, t'an-14 shih-yen-shih 北京大學, 歷史系考古專業, 碳-14實驗室 (C-14 laboratory of the archaeology specialty, history department, Peking University)

BMFEA   *Bulletin of the Museum of Far Eastern Antiquities*

CKKH   Chung-kuo k'o-hsüeh-yüan k'ao-ku yen-chiu-so 中國科學院 考古研究所 (Chinese Academy of Sciences, Institute of Archaeology). After May 1977: Chung-kuo she-hui 社會 k'o-hsüeh-yüan . . . (Chinese Academy of Social Sciences . . .)

DFLW   Damon, P. E., Ferguson, C. W., Long, A., and Wallick, E. I. "Dendrochronologic Calibration of the Radiocarbon Time Scale," *American Antiquity* 39.2(1974): 350–366

H   *hui-k'eng* 灰坑 (pit)

KK   *K'ao-ku* 考古

KKHP   *K'ao-ku hsüeh-pao* 考古學報

M   *mu* 墓 (burial)

NTU   Radiocarbon Laboratory, National Taiwan University, Taipei

PS   *Palaeontologica Sinica (Ti-chih tiao-ch'a-so Chung-kuo ku-sheng-wu-chih* 地質調查所中國古生物志)

SI   Smithsonian Institution, Radiation Biology Laboratory, C^{14} Laboratory, Rockville, Maryland

WW   *Wen-wu* 文物

ZK   Chung-kuo (Zhong'guo) k'o-hsüeh-yüan (kexueyuan), K'ao-ku yen-chiu-so, t'an-14 shih-yen-shih 中國科學院, 考古研究所, 碳-14實驗室 (C-14 laboratory of the Institute of Archaeology, Chinese Academy of Sciences). After 1977: Chung-kuo she-hui 社會 k'o-hsüeh-yüan . . . (Chinese Academy of Social Sciences . . .)

CONTRIBUTORS

Noel Barnard is a Senior Fellow in the Department of Far Eastern History of the School of Pacific Studies at the Australian National University. He specializes in ancient Chinese paleography, metallurgy, the history of technology, and the application of science in archaeological studies. Among his books are *Bronze Casting and Bronze Alloys in Ancient China* and, co-authored with Satō Tamotsu, *Metallurgical Remains of Ancient China.*

K. C. Chang was born in Peking and educated in Taiwan; he received his Ph.D. from Harvard University, where he is now a Professor in the Department of Anthropology. Chang is the author of numerous articles about early Chinese culture; his most recent books include *The Archaeology of Ancient China* and *Shang Civilization.*

Te-tzu Chang is a geneticist and leader of the genetic resources program at the International Rice Research Institute, Los Baños, Philippines. His main research has involved the development of high-yielding rices and the global conservation of rice germ plasm, but he also has a strong interest in retracing the ancient history of Asian crop plants through multidisciplinary analysis and synthesis.

Cheung Kwong-yue is a Senior Research Officer in the Department of Far Eastern History, Australian National University. He specializes in ancient Chinese inscriptions and has worked on the problem of the forgery of inscribed bronzes. He has traveled extensively in China, the United States, Europe, and Japan in connection with his research on Chinese bronzes and has participated in several international symposia.

Wayne H. Fogg is presently a Visiting Professor in the Department of Geography at the University of Oregon. His primary research interests are biogeography, swidden agriculture, and the geography of China.

Ursula Martius Franklin is a Professor of Metallurgy and Materials Science at the University of Toronto, a Research Associate of the Royal Ontario Museum, and an Affiliate of the University of Toronto's Institute for the

History and Philosophy of Science and Technology. Her research has centered on the characterization of ancient materials in general and on the development of bronze technology in China in particular.

Morton H. Fried is a Professor of Anthropology at Columbia University, where he has taught since 1949. He first visited mainland China in 1947, and he was there most recently in 1977. He has also worked in Taiwan. Among his recent books is *The Problem of Tribe*.

W. W. Howells has taught at Harvard University since 1954 and has been Professor Emeritus since 1974. His research interests include human evolution and human variation in the living, as well as the analysis of recent human crania to specify the nature of racial or population differences in terms of multivariate analysis. His books include *Mankind in the Making*, *Cranial Variation in Man*, *Evolution of the Genus Homo*, and *The Pacific Islanders*. He was a member of the Paleoanthropology Delegation to the People's Republic of China in 1975.

Louisa G. Fitzgerald Huber served as Assistant Professor of Fine Arts at Harvard University from 1975–1980. Her dissertation on the traditions of Chinese Neolithic ceramics will be published in the *Bulletin of the Museum of Far Eastern Antiquities*.

Karl Jettmar is a member of the Heidelberg Academy of Sciences and the German Archaeological Institute and he is Head of the Department of Anthropology at the University of Heidelberg, where he has taught since 1964. Jettmar, the author of five books and numerous articles, has participated in ethnographic expeditions to Pakistan, Afghanistan, India, and Thailand.

David N. Keightley is a Professor of History at the University of California, Berkeley, where he has taught since 1969. Keightley, the author of *Sources of Shang History: The Oracle-Bone Inscriptions of Bronze Age China*, is currently at work on a study of temperament and mentality in Late Shang China. He is one of the editors of the journal *Early China*.

Fang Kuei Li is Professor Emeritus at the University of Washington and at the University of Hawaii. A member of the Academia Sinica, he has made numerous contributions to the study of Athapaskan and Tai languages and to Tibetan and Chinese linguistics.

Hui-lin Li is John Bartram Professor of Botany and Horticulture at the University of Pennsylvania. Born in China and educated there and in the United States, he holds degrees from Soochow, Yenching, and Harvard universities. A member of the Academia Sinica, he has published numerous articles on the natural vegetation and cultivated floras of China.

William Meacham is editor of the *Journal of the Hong Kong Archaeological Society* and Research Fellow at the Centre of Asian Studies, University of Hong Kong. He has directed several major excavations of prehistoric sites in Hong Kong and has served as an adviser on archaeological exhibits to the Hong Kong Museum of History.

Richard Pearson specializes in the prehistory of China, Japan, and Korea; he has conducted fieldwork in Taiwan, Okinawa, Korea, and the Hawaiian Islands. He is currently a Professor of Anthropology at the University of British Columbia.

E. G. Pulleyblank is a Professor of Chinese in the Department of Asian Studies, University of British Columbia. He is the author of *The Background of the Rebellion of An Lu-shan* and of articles on the history of the T'ang dynasty and earlier periods. His work has focused recently on the history of the Chinese language, including the reconstruction of the sound system of Chinese and investigations into its relation to other languages.

Robert Orr Whyte was a Visiting Fellow at the Institute of Southeast Asian Studies in Singapore when he contributed his chapter of this volume. For the past thirty years he has worked on several aspects of applied ecology in monsoonal Asia and has produced a series of papers presenting an environmental interpretation of the origin of Asian cereal and grain legumes during a botanical Neolithic revolution. He is now engaged on a longer-term study of the evolving biogeography of China since the mid-Tertiary, at the Centre of Asian Studies, University of Hong Kong.

PREFACE

The origins of Chinese civilization is a complex and noble theme that has its own history. Chinese myths tell of sage emperors who rapidly invented the strategic elements of culture in relatively recent times. Fu Hsi (traditional dates, 2852–2738 B.C.), for example, introduced hunting, fishing, animal husbandry, and the eight trigrams used in the *Yi-ching*. Shen Nung, the divine farmer (2737–2698 B.C.), invented agriculture and discovered the medicinal properties of plants. Living in a golden age, the sages and their ministers were thought to have created Chinese civilization by what we might call "the immaculate conception of culture traits"; they were certainly the analogues, and probably the creations, of the culture-bearing *chün-tzu* (noble man) of later times.

Such a rationalized and foreshortened view of prehistory, combined with a comfortable assurance about the priority and superiority of Western culture, persuaded many Western scholars that early China lacked any culture of its own. Joseph de Guignes, for example, claimed (1759) that the Chinese had originally come from Egypt. Terrien de Lacouperie, in a series of works written over a hundred years later, became increasingly convinced that the Chinese "are themselves intruders in China proper" (1887:4), "that the early civilisation and writing of the Chinese were simply derivations from those of Elam and Chaldaea," and that Chinese civilization was "a loan, a derivation, an extension eastward from a much older form of culture in the west" (1894:1). Such works as these were characterized by a lack of archaeological evidence, a great trust in Chinese texts of a far later date than the period under discussion, a reliance on the assumption of *post hoc, ergo propter hoc*, an inability to distinguish between significant genetic connection and trivial coincidence, and, not infrequently, the tendentious assumption "that in all investigated cases, culture is the result of an introduction from abroad, and not of a spontaneous development" (de Lacouperie 1894:x).

Berthold Laufer was far better informed about the Chinese evidence, but even he assumed that "as far as the present state of our archaeological knowledge and the literary records point out, the Chinese have never passed through an epoch which for other cultures has been designated as a stone age" (1912:29, cf. p. 55). Laufer omitted all mention of a Shang dynasty and started his account of Chinese jade with the Chou. Lauriston Ward found it "impossible to escape the conviction," less than thirty years ago, that "many of the fundamental elements of Chinese culture had their origin in the countries near the Mediterranean sea" (1954:130). And the hypothesis that ceramics, the idea of a script, and the technique of bronze casting were originally transmitted to China from such regions as Iran or south Russia is still to be found in the latest *Encyclopaedia Britannica* (Loehr 1979:300–301).

On the basis of "the present state of our archaeological knowledge"— and those words must be emphasized—there is now little doubt that, whatever the origin of a few particular elements, the complex of culture traits that we refer to as Chinese civilization developed in China. It possesses a respectable antiquity and an indigenous, documented pedigree. The golden age now beginning is that of Chinese archaeology which, despite the political and social turmoil of the twentieth century, has amply demonstrated the existence of a Chinese Neolithic, a Neolithic which has begun to make its mark on the study of human prehistory just as China is making its mark on the modern world. We have immeasurably more data to work with than did scholars who wrote only fifty years ago; and, thanks to the development of archaeology, anthropology, and related disciplines and ancillary techniques, we are able to ask, as in the pages that follow, more precise and sophisticated questions about the origins of Chinese civilization.

The value of this book stems, in fact, not only from the importance of its subject but also from the way in which the different but overlapping methods of the archaeologist, art historian, botanist, climatologist, cultural anthropologist, ethnographer, epigrapher, linguist, metallurgist, physical anthropologist, and political and social historian are all brought to bear on the topic of early cultural development in China. Time after time we benefit not just from "thick description" but, to adapt Clifford Geertz's phrase, "thick analysis" as scholars from various complementary disciplines make their contributions to the discussion of a specific issue.

This sense of reinforcement and complexity helps to create a spirit of intellectual excitement and thus even of optimism, but the mood of the contributors is also one appropriate to continuing exploration rather than definitive conclusion. Despite the thousands of Neolithic and early Bronze

Age sites already known, the startling number of new archaeological finds that continue to be reported indicates that few if any large, final answers should be expected in the following chapters. The move from specific artifact assemblages, decor analyses, linguistic reconstructions, and so on, to a reconstruction of the social realities that produced them is still, in many cases, premature if not impossible. Further, it must be acknowledged that the study of early China is still too specialized and fragmented in its research concerns and disciplines for a comprehensive synthesis to be established. Volumes like this one, together with the conferences that produce them, may eventually lead to such a synthesis, but what emerges here—in addition, of course, to the factual data and analytical schemes that lie at the heart of the individual chapters—are primarily some considerations of methodology and conceptualization, some major hypotheses, and some crucial disagreements.

The basic methodological issue is, for the Chinese case as for all others, how should the archaeological evidence be gathered and interpreted so as to best satisfy the concerns with which we approach it? For the contributors to this volume it is clear that the question of origins needs to be dealt with, not in terms of first events and achievements, but in terms of processes of intensification and cultural exchange, in terms of the development of the social and political organism, and in terms of continually expanding areas of settlement and the changing natural environment.

Historiographical or even epistemological questions are fundamentally important. In archaeological terms this involves the developmental models, Marxist or otherwise, the political or patriotic biases we bring to China, and the ways these considerations influence research designs and interpretations. There is always the possibility that a primary concern with chronology, typology, and stratigraphy, for example, will lead to a selection of data unsuited to the study of interassemblage variability or the reconstruction of settlement patterns and the environment. The need for a terminology that will advance beyond the current practice—which is both narrow and, because not standardized, potentially confusing—of naming Chinese cultures and phases after type-sites is another source of concern. Overemphasis on class structure and property relations, as well as the natural desire to publish the more glamorous finds, could lead to a disproportionate interest in elite burials as compared with, for example, more mundane lithic technology, domestic architecture, and refuse heaps. Questions of data retrieval and selection also involve technical competence and training, as well as ideological predispositions. The striking absence of plant remains in most Chinese archaeological reports, for example, may well be attributed to the shortage of paleobotanists rather than to a lack of interest in the data.

The conceptions and influences that shape the published Chinese archaeological record, in short, have a historical character of their own, and they are, of course, not unique to China—where, as elsewhere, the ancient material culture is the product of the archaeologist's eye. All the contributors share the concern of their Chinese colleagues to reconstruct the full range of early Chinese society and to discover how this can best be done.

In anthropological terms, the assumptions underlying the title of this volume need to be questioned. Should "origins" be considered as history or as process? Should "Chinese" and "culture" be defined in terms of ethnic, racial, linguistic, geographical, social, technological, or other considerations? Some of the chapters below address such theoretical issues explicitly. Fried, for example, discusses the nature of the tribe and its creation by the emerging state. Pearson considers the limitations of the present archaeological data, particularly in terms of patterns of adaptation, for the Ch'ing-lien-kang culture. The chapters by K. C. Chang and by me bear on the issue of how states function. In questions of these sorts, the Chinese case has as much to offer scholars of other cultures as it has to learn from them.

The contributors employ a remarkably wide range of methods: Whyte's comprehensive reconstruction of the paleoclimate (not presented at the conference, but graciously submitted for the volume); Hui-lin Li's meticulous definition of the three ecogeographical zones; T. T. Chang's botanical and historical study of the way cereal grains developed from wild phenotypes; Fogg's imaginative use of ethnographic analogy to provide a scenario for the domestication of millet (as well as to capture a sense of the natural color and religious excitement involved); Franklin's thoughtful reflections about the social implications of large-scale metal production; Howells' preliminary but highly significant multivariate analysis of skulls; Fang Kuei Li's valuable introduction to the reconstruction of Archaic Chinese; Pulleyblank's wide-ranging use of linguistic and historical data, and so on.

One of the contributions of the volume is to delineate problems of definition, problems of inadequate data, and the kinds of research strategies (in terms of both excavation and reporting techniques) and the use of analytical models that future scholars may wish to pursue. I have termed all these considerations of evidence and intention historiographical and epistemological because they are finally concerned not just with what we know, but with how we know what we know, why others want us to know it, and why we want to know it. They should, in the Chinese case as elsewhere, be constantly borne in mind.

In addition to these methodological considerations, several chapters propose a series of hypotheses about the origins of certain aspects of Chinese culture. These include, to cite some examples, the interaction between the east coast and Chung Yüan cultures (Huber), the contribution of non-Chinese populations, especially from the west (Pulleyblank), the origins of Chinese writing (Cheung), the origins of Chinese metal winning, metal production (Franklin), and metal-working (Barnard), the links between Hsia, Shang, and Chou (K. C. Chang), and the extent and nature of the Shang state (Keightley).

Numerous questions—rhetorical, perhaps, at present, but well worth bearing in mind for the future—were raised during the conference: If *Setaria italica* is poor fodder for horses, is it possible that *Panicum miliaceum* appeared in China at the same time as the horse? What consequences do climatic conditions and the quality of edibles have for social organization? What cultural effect, for example, does the need for greater storability of the northern food crops imply by contrast with the perishability but readier availability of the southern crops? What kind of archaeological evidence can document a transition from (open membership) clan to (closed membership) lineage organization? Is evidence of social stratification greater for the east coast than for other areas of neolithic development, and to what ecological features, if any, should such differences be related? To what extent is interaction between a number of diverse societies a precondition for the rise of the pristine state? Do archaeological remains indicate increasing exploitation during the Chinese Neolithic? Does exploitation arise from competition between groups or does it develop within single communities? To what extent were linguistic groups and tribes coterminous? Does the ablaut relationship suggest common origins between Indo-European and Sino-Tibetan? How can the art historian's analysis of individual motif development be integrated with considerations of overall design to illustrate patterns of social interaction?—a particularly important question for both the ceramic vessels of the Chinese Neolithic and the ritual bronzes of early historic times. What criteria—racial, social, political, economic, territorial, ideological—should be used to define early populations in China? Would it be more appropriate to speak of a Lung-shan tradition than a Lung-shan culture? It is not surprising that, at this stage of our knowledge, there are more questions than answers. But the high probability that the extraordinarily rich evidence will eventually permit some of these questions to be answered confirms the importance the Chinese case has and will have in helping us to understand the origins of civilization in general.

The conference was particularly fortunate in the participation of Karl

Jettmar, who presented two wide-ranging talks of extraordinary interest on the cultures and ethnic groups to the north and west of China in Neolithic and early historic times. His review article (ch. 8) gives a tantalizing indication of the richness, complexity, and immense scale of the archaeological data to be found in such areas as Cis- and Trans-Baikalia, the Mongolian People's Republic, the Amur Basin, and the Maritime Province of the USSR. Whatever conclusions are finally reached about the influences that entered China from these areas, or vice versa—and the conclusions have their political dimension (see, e.g., Price 1976)—the origins of Chinese civilization will not be fully understood until the Neolithic and Bronze Age context of the Eurasian steppe as a whole is clarified. When and where does the "Neolithic revolution" appear in these areas? Is there evidence for iron casting in the second millennium B.C.? What significance should be attached to the rock engravings in the Karatau range which depict chariots in a style similar to that of Shang oracle-bone graphs?

Soviet archaeology presents its own methodological problems. Readers of Jettmar's contribution will note, for example, how Cheboksarov's conclusions drawn from the analysis of An-yang skulls differ from those of Howells (ch. 11). But, as Jettmar makes clear, Soviet archaeology is a field that scholars of early China ignore at their peril. Similar considerations, of course, apply to the potential significance of Southeast Asia, which, apart from the discussions in Meacham's presentation (ch. 6), is not well represented in this volume.

Such matters as the place of production of the southern variants of Miao-ti-kou ware (ch. 7), the origins of written Chinese (ch. 12), the distinction between Hsia and Early Shang sites (ch. 16), and the nature and location of the Late Shang capital (ch. 17), also need to be considered. One of the most important issues involves the question of whether China was a primary area for the development of metallurgy. The art historians (such as Huber, ch. 7) generally argue for the existence of wrought sheet-metal prototypes, reflected in the metallic-looking shapes of Ch'i-chia ceramics and the appearance of rivet-like knobs on both Erh-li-t'ou pots and Middle Shang *li-ho* bronzes. The existence of such a sheet-metal tradition, strongly implied but not yet demonstrated, would suggest that knowledge of metal working had been imported into China from cultures to the west.

The archaeologists, by contrast (represented in this volume by Barnard, ch. 9), pointing to the absence of actual metallic prototypes and the indifference to and ignorance of smithy techniques of the Shang and early and middle Chou bronze industry, argue for the indigenous development of a piece-mold metal-casting industry, deriving naturally from ceramic prototypes and the highly developed technical skills of the Neolithic potters. Unless the actual sheet-metal prototypes are discovered, this issue will be difficult to resolve with finality. (The debate continues. The claims of the wrought-metal advocates are forcefully argued by Robert W. Bagley in Fong 1980: 74, 103–104. Barnard [in press] provides a rebuttal on behalf of those favoring the cast-metal hypothesis.)

A second key issue involves stimulus diffusion versus independent invention. The origins of metallurgy, of the written script, of ceramic designs, of tribal organization—all have to be considered in these terms. It seems likely that the main thrust of future research will be toward identifying, in the Neolithic, various nuclear areas rather than one North China Nuclear Area and to explaining their mutual influences. Whether one nuclear area proves more nuclear than others remains to be seen. The role of nuclear areas is also crucial to our understanding of the formation and interaction of the early Bronze Age states, the Hsia, Shang, and Chou, in the Chung Yüan area. The identification of strategic culture traits and complexes and of their transmission will teach us much about the processes involved. So will carbon-14 dates.

The use of thermoluminescent techniques is still in its infancy (Barnard 1979: x–xiv; Wang Wei-ta 1979), but carbon-14 dating has already made contributions of major significance, particularly in demonstrating the contemporaneity and cultural diversity of the early nuclear areas of the Neolithic in the Pan-p'o, Ch'ing-lien-kang, and Ta-p'en-keng regions (K. C. Chang 1977: 84, fig. 31), and with regard to the whole question of the relation between the Chung Yüan, east coast, and southeast coastal cultures. The carbon-14 dates cited (see finding list) are taken from the latest, invaluable survey of Barnard (1980); as a result they may differ, but generally not significantly, from the dates given in the original archaeological reports. So far as possible, the carbon-14 dates are cited according to the dendrochronological calibrations of Damon, Ferguson, Long, and Wallick (1974), referred to hereafter as DFLW. (On the problems involved, see Barnard 1980: 7–9). When specific dates are being discussed, all corrected dates below are recorded as B.C. or B.P.; the uncorrected ones are recorded as b.c. or b.p. The raw dates and other calibrations can readily be consulted in Barnard's pages; his book also provides, as does his previous survey (1975), an excellent introduction to the considerable cautions to be exercised when dealing with radiocarbon dates. There is no doubt, as techniques become more refined and as large numbers of dates become available, that scientific dating will aid in the formulation and testing of hypotheses about the development of Chinese culture, not only within the territories of modern China but also in such areas as Siberia, Central Asia, and Southeast Asia.

Geography is as important as chronology to our understanding of the development and interaction of cultures in early China. In addition to the maps that accompany some chapters below, a general map of China, placed at the end of the preface, shows the major sites discussed. Since no units smaller than the *hsien* are given on this map, readers looking for a particular site should locate it at the *hsien* level; Sian (Shensi), for example, represents Pan-p'o, Ch'ing-chiang (Kiangsi) represents Wu-ch'eng, and so on.

A word should be said about various other conventions used herein. In the interests of consistency, modern Chinese characters are, so far as possible, given in their full forms, regardless of whether simplified characters were used in the original publication (on the problems involved, see Barnard and Satō 1975:xxvi). The Wade-Giles system of romanization given in *Mathews' Chinese-English Dictionary*, pp. xviii–xxi, is used throughout (with three exceptions: the use of *yi* instead of *i*; the use of post office spellings for many provinces and large cities; and K. C. Chang's preference [ch. 16] for Sandai rather than San tai). The romanization of Chinese place names follows that used in Chang's *Archaeology of Ancient China* (1977). The names of Chinese and Japanese authors are treated in two ways. No comma is used when one or more of the works cited is in Chinese and Japanese, thus: Chang Kwang-chih. If all the works by a Chinese or Japanese author are in Western languages, then the name is treated in Western style, thus: Chang, Kwang-chih. But when an author has written in both Oriental and western languages, then the Oriental form is followed: Chang Kwang-chih. Russian names are transliterated according to the Library of Congress system. Chinese research institutes, museums, and their committees are treated as authors in the bibliographical citations, but, to avoid excessively unwieldy citations, work groups and university departments are not; their articles are referred to by journal title and date.

The Conference on the Origins of Chinese Civilization, at which original versions of the chapters in this volume were presented, was held in Berkeley from June 26 to 30, 1978. Though some revisions have taken account of more recent archaeological publications—K. C. Chang's "Concluding Remarks," for example, was written in the spring of 1979—the volume should generally be considered to represent our understanding at that time. New discoveries and new hypotheses continue to appear. To take but one example, Tsou Heng (1979) has recently argued, on the basis of stratigraphical considerations and traditional texts, that the domed *ho* 盉 that he believes was characteristic of the Erh-li-t'ou sites in the Cheng-chou area was a ritual vessel that identifies Hsia culture. It is precisely the *li-ho* 鬲盉 form that proponents of the wrought-metal hypothesis cite as ceramic evidence of a wrought-metal culture and which, in the view of one of the discussants, may have been an import. Huber's view (ch. 7) that the Hsia was indeed such a metal-working culture thus receives explicit support from Tsou Heng's attempt to identify the repertoire of Hsia vessel types.

The Berkeley conference was funded by the Committee for the Study of Chinese Civilization of the American Council of Learned Societies and by the Wenner-Gren Foundation for Anthropological Research. Additional grants from the American Council of Learned Societies and the Association for Asian Studies paid for the editorial assistance involved in revising the original papers for publication. The willingness of these institutions to support our work is deeply appreciated and gratefully acknowledged. I am particularly glad to acknowledge the generous assistance of K. C. Chang, who was an invaluable source of practical guidance and scholarly inspiration during the planning of both the conference and this volume and who generously supplied a chapter of Concluding Remarks. I owe a great debt to Noel Barnard, Nancy Price, and E.G. Pulleyblank, who also provided much valuable advice in the planning stages. Essential logistic support, provided by the Center for Chinese Studies of the University of California at Berkeley, left the participants free to read, discuss, and reflect while the conference was in progress. Special thanks is also due W. Thomas Chase, Clarence F. Shangraw, Hsio-yen Shih, and Henry Stewart, whose papers, which added much to the breadth of our discussions, are not included in this volume because they did not bear directly on the question of origins. (For a list of the institutions where the original papers, together with a record of the discussions, should be on deposit, see *Early China* 4 [1978–79]: 89–90.) Their work, when published, will add still further to our knowledge of China's early culture. I should also like to express gratitude to Robert Bagley, Virginia Kane, John LaPlante, Nancy Price, and Dorothy Washburn, who provided informed and stimulating commentary for some of the discussion sessions. I am grateful to Constance Cook, Mary Garrett, and Meryl Lanning for indefatigable assistance in editing the manuscript and to Anne Holmes and David J. Pauleen for their painstaking care in helping prepare the index and glossary. Lynn Mally's help with Russian transliteration and Adrienne Morgan's preparation of most of the maps are deeply appreciated. Finally, my thanks must go to the conference rapporteurs, Dessa P. Bucksbaum, John Ewell, and David Goodrich, whose transcripts of the panel discussions provide a valuable record of the issues raised; their numerous acts of assistance, well beyond the call of duty, did much to make the conference memorable.

DAVID N. KEIGHTLEY

April 1980

REFERENCES

Barnard, Noel

1975   *The First Radiocarbon Dates from China*. Rev. and enl. Monographs on Far Eastern History 8. Canberra.

1979   *Radiocarbon Dates and Their Significance in the Chinese Archaeological Scene: A List of 280 Entries Compiled from Chinese Sources Published up to close of 1978*. Canberra.

1980   *Radiocarbon Dates and Their Significance in the Chinese Archaeological Scene: A List of 420 Entries Compiled from Chinese Sources Published up to Close of 1979*. Canberra.

in press   "Wrought Metal-Working Prior to Middle Shang (?)—A Problem in Archaeological and Art-Historical Research Approaches." *Early China* 6 (1980–81).

Barnard, Noel, and Satō, Tamotsu

1975   *Metallurgical Remains of Ancient China*. Tokyo

Chang, K. C.

1977   *The Archaeology of Ancient China*. 3d ed., rev. and enl. New Haven.

Damon, P. E., Ferguson, C. W., Long, A., and Wallick, E. I.

1974   "Dendrochronologic Calibration of the Radiocarbon Time Scale." *American Antiquity* 39.2:350–366.

Fong, Wen, ed.

1980   *The Great Bronze Age of China: An Exhibition from the People's Republic of China*. New York.

de Guignes, Joseph

1759   *Mémoire dans lequel on prouve que les Chinois sont une colonie Egyptienne*. Paris.

de Lacouperie, Terrien
1887   *The Languages of China Before the Chinese: Researches on the Languages Spoken by the Pre-Chinese Races of China Proper Previously to the Chinese Occupation.* London.
1894   *Western Origin of the Early Chinese Civilisation from 2,300 B.C. to 200 A.D.* London.

Laufer, Berthold
1912   *Jade: A Study in Chinese Archaeology and Religion.* Field Museum of Natural History Publication 154. Anthropology ser., vol. 10. Chicago.

Loehr, Max
1979   "History of China: Prehistory and Archaeology." In *The New Encyclopaedia Britannica: Macropaedia*, vol. 4:297–301.

Mathews, R. H.
1956   *Mathews' Chinese-English Dictionary.* Rev. ed. Cambridge, Mass.

Price, Don C.
1976   "The Origins of Chinese Culture: Some Russian and Chinese Views." *Early China* 2:60–67.

Tsou Heng 鄒衡
1979   "Kuan-yü t'an-t'ao Hsia wen-hua ti chi-ke wen-t'i 關于探討夏文化的幾個問題." *WW* 1979.3:64–69.

Wang Wei-ta 王維達
1979   "Ku-tai t'ao-ch'i ti je-shih-kuang nien-tai 古代陶器的熱釋光年代." *KK* 1979.1:82–88.

Ward, Lauriston
1954   "The Relative Chronology of China through the Han Period." In *Relative Chronologies in Old World Archeology*, edited by Robert W. Ehrich: pp. 130–144. Chicago.

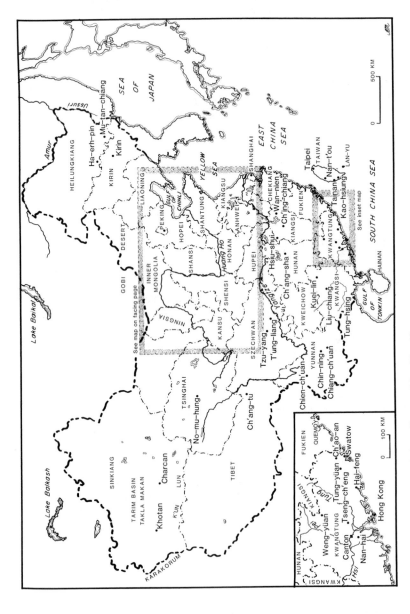

The major archaeological sites discussed in this volume.

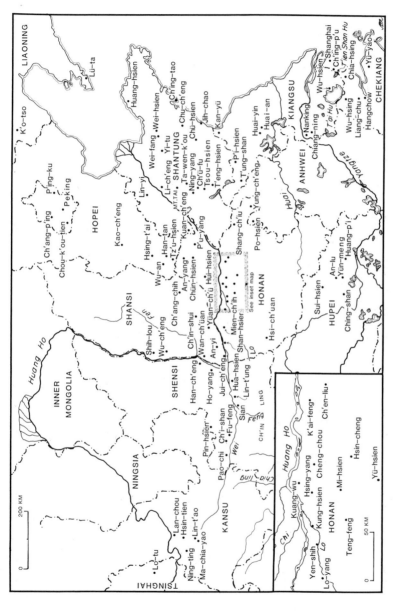

Central area (enlarged) of the map on the facing page.

I ENVIRONMENT AND AGRICULTURE

1

The Evolution of
the Chinese Environment

ROBERT ORR WHYTE

An analysis of the progressive effect upon the environment of the geological events and consequent climatic changes which started in innermost Asia in the late Tertiary is crucial to an understanding of the origins of civilization in China. How had the environment in which Upper Cave man lived at Chou-k'ou-tien (16,922 ± 410 b.c. [ZK–136-0]) evolved over the preceding millennia, and what further changes occurred between then and the period 5000 to 500 B.C.? Such a study cannot yet be based on adequate empirical data, but must depend rather on scientific deductions not previously made, bringing together accepted facts from the study of mountain uplift or orogeny, plate tectonics, paleoclimatic conditions and changes, and the evolution of associated biological ecosystems, as indicated by studies of paleobotany, palynology, paleontology and the subsequent histories of floras and faunas (Lamb 1977). For this purpose, it is necessary first to review not the sequence of events within the populated and cultivated eastern part of what is now called China, but rather the great changes in land form and associated ecosystems which have occurred in the lands lying immediately to the west, in what came to be called innermost Asia (Stein 1925) or the (political) heartland of Asia (Mackinder 1904). This lies between 75° and 115° longitude and between 27° and 50° latitude.

This chapter is presented in the relatively general terms applicable to a volume representing a wide range of disciplines; a more precise consideration of the geological, paleoclimatic and biological factors involved during the initial formative period and up to the present will appear

3

elsewhere (Whyte and Williams, forthcoming). The climatic conditions in which the Yang-shao and Lung-shan developed have been described in a recent study of the natural environment in China during the last ten thousand years (Kweiyang Institute of Geochemistry 1978).

SIGNIFICANCE OF CLIMATE

Our concern here is with the relative biological and anthropological significance of three types of climate, which may operate individually or together in different situations. These are: (1) cyclic patterns and changes in the upper atmosphere; (2) climates induced by major changes in land form following tectonic movements and orogeny which may in turn have had considerable influence on or have been associated with the climates of the high atmosphere; and (3) the microclimate at and immediately above ground level in the biosphere, in which the component species of biological ecosystems and man and his cultivated crops and domestic animals live, in an environment much reduced from its potential optimum by man's use and misuse of land and of its protective plant cover, wild and cultivated. On any particular site, it must be the task of the ecologist and the meteorologist to decide which types of climate are predominant in their effect on plant and animal life, and on the water resources upon which they and ultimately man depend.

Although there were probably major paleoclimatic periods in innermost Asia in earlier geological ages, our concern is with the two most recent periods, here called Paleoclimates One and Two. Between these two contrasting paleoclimatic periods occurred the great changes in land form which caused the marked differences in environment of the two periods.

PALEOCLIMATE ONE

In the early Tertiary, at least up to the late Eocene, the climate of Laurasia, the land mass of Asia, was characterized by very warm and wet conditions up to latitudes beyond 45° north (Frakes and Kemp 1972). These climates at high latitudes are confirmed by the distribution of fossil plants and animals and by climatically significant rock types. They can be explained at least in part by the global temperature distribution derived from calculations based on oxygen isotope data for the oceans.

Because of the absence in the early tertiary of any marked mountain impediments along the southern fringe of Laurasia, the winds from the still present Tethys Sea carried tropical and subtropical conditions far north, to encompass the whole of modern China, including Tibet, Sinkiang, Inner Mongolia, and Manchuria.

During the first half of the Oligocene, conditions changed. The presence of colder Oligocene waters in high latitudes led to less evaporation and therefore to decreased precipitation and colder air temperatures (ibid.). These factors operated before those discussed in the next section. The process of poleward heat transport by the oceans operates even less effectively today, and the consequences are seen in the still lower temperatures and rates of precipitation.

PLATE TECTONICS AND OROGENY

The situation on the land surface of Laurasia in the early Tertiary, when there were no high altitudes or mountain ranges between the northern shores of the Tethys Sea and about 50° north latitude, was dramatically changed during the latter part of the Tertiary by two major geological events.

Periodic and progressive uplift or orogeny of the high plateaus of Tibet to four to five thousand meters elevation, of the Karakorum, and of the Himalaya and associated ranges was roughly synchronous with the arrival of the South Asian Plate (Hallam 1973:32, 84). Following the final phase in the disruption of Gondwana (Jurassic), and the opening of the Indian Ocean by a mechanism of sea-floor spreading and continental drift (Hiertzler et al. 1973), the Plate was rafted from its original position along the eastern edge of Madagascar, northward over fifty degrees of latitude in fifty million years (McElhinny 1968; Blow and Hamilton 1975; Molnar and Tapponnier 1975) to conjoin Laurasia during the Miocene. The Tethys Sea in these parts was eliminated by the arrival of this new land mass, which met Laurasia along the Indus/Brahmaputra suture. This has been confirmed recently by Chinese workers (Chang and Chong 1973; Yin and Kuo 1978) and by the Wadia Institute of Himalayan Geology, and in earlier studies by many other specialists.

The 1973 expedition to Tibet of the Chinese Academy of Sciences involved four hundred scientists in surveys in the fields of geophysics, stratigraphy, paleontology, petrology, tectonic geology, geomorphology, geothermics, and in surveys of the Quaternary period. Fossil evidence led to the conclusion that in the early and middle Jurassic, the Ch'ang-tu region in the eastern part of the Tsinghai-Tibet Plateau was covered by a shallow sea or was a depression and had a hot, humid environment. During the Pliocene, although Tibet was uplifted and rose above sea level, the terrain was still not high, and its environment was sub-tropical. Only in the ensuing period did the Tsinghai-Tibet Plateau reach its present altitude (New China News Agency 2 July 1977, monitored by British Broadcasting Corporation/Summary of World Broadcasts 20 July 1977). For the uplift within inner Asia itself, see the map of Molnar and Tapponnier (1975).

PALEOCLIMATE TWO

Innermost Asia

Careful analysis of the factors which induced the establishment of the rain shadow north of the Himalayan and Tibetan mountain mass is necessary before the sequence of events can be fully understood. With the arrival of the Plate and the closing of the Tethys, a new monsoonal pattern evolved. Rains driven by the southwest monsoon up the Bay of Bengal had their greatest force of impact at the lower eastern end of the Himalayan range, as witnessed by the very heavy precipitation along the southern face of the Meghalaya mountain mass (Cherrapunji) and other mountains in the vicinity. The southern slopes of the Himalayas to the west received their rains following the passage of the monsoon up the Gangetic Plain, and hence their rains were much reduced in force.

Up to the present limits of the monsoonal vegetation—about thirty-five hundred to four thousand meters—the warm, wet winds would have progressed into innermost Asia, but for a lesser distance with every increase in altitude of the mountain mass. Above four thousand meters such cold rain and snow as could still pass over the range northward were out of tune with the former humid tropical vegetation but suitable for the high-altitude cold-temperate vegetation now present in Tibet (apart from the Tsinghai Plateau and the eastern valleys still within reach of the southwest monsoon).

Thus, through a sequence of climatic changes which requires more accurate definition, Paleoclimate One in innermost Asia gradually changed from the humid tropical and subtropical climates of the early Tertiary. These changes were associated in time with, and were also partly related to, the increasing differences between polar and equatorial temperatures and concomitant falls in sea surface temperatures. Over a long period, and starting from the northern latitudes southward, the climates and their associated biological ecosystems changed through all the intermediate stages to humid-temperate, to semi-arid, and to arid conditions in which rain never falls. One may ask whether and how far north in the heartland of inner Asia we have a combination of a climate induced by geological uplift which has become superimposed upon or integrated with a climate governed by the upper atmosphere.

The history of vegetation in northern Eurasia during the Pleistocene described and mapped by Frenzel (1968) was one of repeated changes, corresponding to the advance and retreat of glaciation, between (1) huge steppe areas generally with some loess depositions, governed by extremely cold and dry climates, and (2) widespread forest areas whose most characteristic elements were warmth- and moisture-loving trees, perhaps the "tediously monotonous evergreen forest flora" of Kryshtofovich (1929). Aigner (1977a; 1977b) has used Frenzel's "highly speculative reconstruction of Würm-maximum vegetation," consisting of twelve mainland geographic-vegetational regions plus several formed by regression of the sea, to show that the whole picture was as complex then as it is now. For the region of primary interest in this study, that which lies between the northern Eurasia of Frenzel and the northern slopes of the K'un Lun and the Himalayan range, including the great Eurasian steppe reaching from southern Russia across Turkestan to Mongolia (Butzer 1961), data are inadequate. One notes, however, that the lands on the south of Frenzel's Eurasian zone remained under steppe during both the glacial and the interglacial periods, perhaps indicating the greater power of the Himalayan rain shadow.

Within innermost Asia, or more specifically between the Caspian Sea on the west and the China Sea on the east, three arid cores can be recognized, at least one and perhaps two of which have been of great significance in the origin and evolution of Asian annual crop plants (cereals and grain legumes): the Kara Kum and Kyzyl Kum, the Taklamakan, and the Gobi (Whyte 1977). And far to the north of innermost Asia, the prevailing northwest winds brought the aeolian dust from the retreating glaciers into China to create the loess lands, burying a vegetation and its associated fauna of which we as yet know little. Stein (1925) was concerned whether progressive or advancing desiccation of the environment in the Taklamakan in particular could have been the cause of the state of the land as he found it; that is, of the occurrence of dry irrigation channels now beyond the reach of water and the abandonment of outlying oases. He considered that these could have resulted just as well from successive intrusions of migrating tribes from the grasslands of the north. These tribes—the Wusun, Sakas, Yüeh-chih, Huns, Turks, Mongols, and others—driven by recurrent droughts and the destruction of their usual grazing resources, periodically swept through the lands of inner Asia and on to the west, into southeast Asia and southern Europe. Colonel Sir Sydney Burrard, former surveyor-general of India, suggested (Stein 1925:489–90) that the diminished volume of the rivers used for irrigation in the oases of Yarkand, Qarghaliq, Khotan, and Charchan, for example, was due to the progressive shrinkage of the fossil ice which had been left from the last Pleistocene glaciation as relict glaciers which are still present under masses of detritus high in the K'un Lun ranges. If this is so, it would not be necessary to propose a continuance of progressive desiccation of the total environment as the cause of abandoned dwellings and derelict irrigation channels, at least within the relatively short time span involved.

In one of many writings on the history of the northern (Mongolian) part of inner Asia, Lattimore (1951:329–34) refers to the theory of climatic variation put forth by Arnold Toynbee to explain the alternating periods of encroachment of nomads upon settled lands (during periods of aridity) and of settled peoples on nomad steppes (during periods of greater rainfall). Toynbee believed that the "paroxysm" of aridity which occurred in the thirteenth century in inner Asia coincided with Mongol unrest and the rise of Genghis Khan; the reverse trend toward greater humidity in the fourteenth century corresponded with the rapid ebb of Mongol power. These are, according to Lattimore, tempting and dangerous assumptions which do not take into account real developments within nomadic societies and the growth of commerce.

Eastern China

Although the environment of the eastern, now densely populated part of China was probably not directly affected by the mountain uplift in the southern parts of innermost Asia, there can be no doubt that the presence from the late Tertiary onward of such a vast block of newly established aridity had a marked secondary effect. Superimposed on any effects on the original tropical/subtropical environment caused by the sea surface cooling in northern latitudes, the prevailing northwest winds entering eastern China from the region of the Gobi and Kansu were a major contributory factor in the evolution of the environment of eastern China and so of Chinese civilization. The Tertiary uplift of the lesser mountain chains in Yunnan and Szechwan may also have contributed to some extent. Aridity progressed toward the coastal regions of the southeast in arcs of decreasing intensity. There was probably a fluctuating sequence of short- or long-term pulsations between arid and humid conditions; this is still evident today.

BIOGEOGRAPHICAL EVOLUTION

Biogeography can be defined as the study of the distribution of living components, plants and animals, wild and domestic, and their associated beneficent or maleficent bacteria, fungi, and insects, as governed by the factors of the physical environment: geomorphology, geology (Lee 1939; a new geological map is being produced by the Academy of Geological Sciences, Peking), soils, climate, and above all the availability of water. In the study of the evolution of the Chinese environment, factors of both time and space are important. If we know the nature and geographical range of any one of the elements, flora, fauna, or climate, in any part of China, it should be possible to deduce the nature and range of the others.

If the fossil record shows that certain types of fauna occurred in a particular region, it can be assumed that the natural vegetation provided feed which was adapted to their dietary requirements and dentition and that the climate would have promoted the growth of such vegetation. Thus, in the study of early fauna, it is not so much the taxonomy and bone structure that are important in the ecosystem approach as a knowledge of the kind of terrain the animals preferred and what they ate.

Vegetation and flora

When the mountain uplift began first in Tibet, the vegetation became the first in this part of Asia to evolve through the stages of ecological succession from lowland tropical to, ultimately, highland arid continental. The component genera and species changed from high-temperature-adapted mesophytes to cold-tolerant xerophytes. It will be necessary to decide whether the forests of the early humid tropical periods in the Tertiary were composed predominantly of gymnosperms or angiosperms, and when the transition from one to the other might have taken place. Students will need to study sources such as the reports of the Sino-Swedish expedition to the northwestern provinces of China under the leaderhip of Sven Hedin, especially those on paleobotany (Bohlin 1971) and botany (Bohlin 1949; Norlindh 1949).

An expedition of the Chinese Academy of Sciences in 1977 reports "plants left over from the Tertiary period" in the Tsinghai-Tibet Plateau (New China News Agency broadcast of 2 July 1977; BBC/SWB 20 July 1977). These may be Laurasian relicts pushed south by aridity or, alternatively, species of Gondwanian origin which entered the Northern Hemisphere on the South Asian Plate and which later became associated in communities with Laurasian species along the Brahmaputra suture. The Chinese expedition finds that Tibet has at least a thousand species of trees from more than a hundred families, with almost every major species of the Northern Hemisphere represented. This may be evidence of the telescoping of a number of former latitudinal floras within a now restricted relict area or refugium under the influence of aridity advancing from the north. The Chinese explain the occurrence of Tertiary species as evidence that Tibet was not affected by glaciers during the Quaternary period and could therefore give continued shelter to Tertiary plants.

Although the vegetation of eastern China was not directly influenced by the actual creation of the rain shadow within innermost Asia to the west, it did become exposed to the subsequent secondary effects of the proximity of this new arid region. Maps showing a theoretical reconstruction of climax types of vegetation before denudation of the land have been published by Wang Chi-wu (1961), Aigner (1977a), and others. They indicate the present location of an original or derived form of tropical rain forest which has been pushed by the pulsations of the new climate to a relict area far to the south in Yunnan, Kwangsi, Szechwan, Kwangtung, and Hainan Island. The various forest zones shown on present maps to the north of the northern borders of the rain forest represent gradations toward a cold temperate environment in the north and to the arid environment of inner-most Asia to the west and northwest. In passing, it can be suggested that groups of genera and species of differing adaptation within one plant family might be more accurate indicators of environment than the rather broad physiognomic types of mixed vegetation now used for the purpose. The Gramineae could be adopted with profit as botanical criteria for change in environment.

It then becomes desirable to discover what types of vegetation extended up to the forty-fifth or fiftieth parallel when the factor of aridity first began to operate in the Oligocene, and whether any of the types now present within the rain forest in eastern China existed to the north of the Tertiary rain forest. Further, because of the significance of the nuclear area to current interpretations of the origins of agriculture and civilization, it will be desirable to attempt to define what the flora and fauna on the ground surface of this region might have been before the deposition of loess.

Current emphasis on the significance of *Artemisia* (Ho 1975:28–30; Pearson 1976) in pollen cores as an indication of a climax community would not appear to be justified. Elsewhere in the world, for example in the Anatolian Plateau, communities dominated by *Artemisia* are a seral stage in regression in a degraded forest environment. The *Artemisia* stage in succession does, however, tend to become fixed, and progression upward to a higher rank of plant community generally seems difficult. The regressive stages of vegetation in northern China which, according to palynological evidence, ultimately became dominated by *Artemisia* need not have been caused by the activities of man or his animals, as some have suggested, but perhaps by the destructive action of the dry, loess-laden winds.

Fauna and domestic livestock

Evidence from the fossil record is becoming available from different parts of China, which makes it possible to speculate on the causes of the extinction of the animals concerned. The South China "Redbeds" Research Group (1977) has found fossils of many Paleocene (early Tertiary) mammals in five redbed basins in South China (Kwangtung, Kiangsi, Anhwei, and Hunan). These fossils have been compared in age with those reported for Gashato in the southern part of Mongolia (Szalay and McKenna 1971) and also for roughly corresponding horizons in Sinkiang (Turfan) and Inner Mongolia. The South China fauna is roughly contemporaneous with that from the sites in innermost Asia.

The South China provinces had at that time (and still potentially have) a plant cover of tropical rain forest (tropical wet evergreen) or a closely associated forest type. If it is correct to correlate fauna with vegetation, then the vegetation in innermost Asia would also have been some form of mesophytic tropical or subtropical forest. The characteristic fauna would have become progressively extinct or would have been obliged to move elsewhere in the face of advancing desiccation and lower temperatures. A similar interpretation can be applied to the recent discovery of tropical or subtropical fauna (rhinoceros, salamanders, snakes, turtles, deer, tapir, pig) and flora (a forest of broad-leaved deciduous trees including banyan— *Ficus sp.?*) of a mid-Miocene period in the mountain village of Shan-wang in Shantung province (New China News Agency broadcast 20 December 1978; BBC/SWB 7 February 1979).

Since these adverse climatic conditions did not reach South China, the comparable fauna there must have been eliminated, much later, by the destruction of their habitat by man or by hunting.

For the early Tertiary periods, for the later Pleistocene period, and for Chou-k'ou-tien in particular, Andersson (1934) quotes the observations of Zdansky (1923; 1928) regarding the fauna discovered at various sites. At Chou-k'ou-tien, fossils of dog, bear, tiger, cat the size of lions, rhinoceros, horse, pig, deer, ape, and a type of buffalo, *Bibos geron*, were found. Andersson concludes that on the whole the Chou-k'ou-tien fauna reveals many features which place it in the earliest part of the Pleistocene. In the loess formation was found a fauna belonging to the middle Pleistocene. Chang (1977 : 23–28) also describes the animal and plant (especially pollen) fossils from the Pleistocene formations throughout China in river terraces and cave fissure deposits. These are particularly useful for chronological purposes as indicators of the climatic conditions in which they occurred. According to recent studies, the Chinese Pleistocene can be divided into early, middle, and late. Chang (1977 : 32–33) describes the fauna and flora of the Upper Cave of Chou-k'ou-tien, extending from latest Pleistocene to earliest Holocene. Considerable fluctuations in tree flora occurred during these periods, from cold temperate to warm temperate and back again, rather similar to trends noted over a longer period in the Holocene in Liaoning province (Kweiyang Institute of Geochemistry 1978).

It will be necessary to analyze whatever information exists from archaeological sites regarding the faunal components of the biological ecosystems, the species involved, their zones of distribution, their dietary habits and preferences, their reaction to advancing aridity and their adoption in early and modern Chinese animal husbandry (Watson 1969). In order to recreate the Tertiary and later biological ecosystems in which plants and animals co-existed in restless forms of symbiosis or even antagonism, it seems desirable to make a start by mapping the distribution of wild animals from evidence available from early archaeological sites. These data could be discussed with specialists in animal ecology, evolution, and nutrition, and with climatologists, to see whether any parallelism exists between past and present zones of vegetation and flora and past and present distribution of fauna. Reference may again be made to the reports of the expedition of Sven Hedin, especially those volumes dealing with the vertebrate paleontology of Tsaidam, western Kansu and Mongolia (Bohlin 1937a; 1937b; 1942; 1946; 1951).

The surveys made by the 1973 Chinese Academy of Sciences expedition to the Tsinghai-Tibet Plateau relate to fauna which may have become extinct for reasons associated with change in environment, dentition, and/or loss or change of feed resources. The extinct hipparion, for example, was a three-toed mammal related to but not now considered a direct ancestor of the horse; it was characteristic of fauna up to the Miocene and Pliocene. Fossils were discovered on the northern slopes of the Himalayas and other ranges, areas to which these animals may have retreated from a much wider zone of distribution and availability of appropriate feed in the face of advancing desiccation.

The fauna of eastern China, present, ancient and extinct, can be visualized as falling into two main categories, wild and domesticated. The former would comprise two major groups: (1) the truly indigenous components of ecosystems which may have evolved steadily and/or moved elsewhere along with their associated vegetation under the influence of advancing aridity, but before the advent of man in effective numbers, and (2) the adventitious faunal complexes which evolved in the new environments created by the clearing of vegetation.

CROP GENETIC RESOURCES AND EVOLVING VEGETATION

This picture of the evolution of the Chinese environment in recent times in terms of geological history is one of ever-increasing stress on its biological occupants, the wild plants and animals, and later on man, his crops, and his domestic animals. A fundamental problem which arises regarding the physiological effects of this stress on plants is related to the origin of the annual gramineous and leguminous crops which are man's main source of food. Most botanists agree that annuals are derived from perennials. In the search for the key to the evolution of annuals from perennials, the most important question in the whole of agricultural botany, it has been proposed that stress involving the operative factors of aridity combined with high and fluctuating temperatures for at least part of every year has an important effect on the proportion of annual plants in hitherto predominantly perennial species of Gramineae and Legumiosae in particular. This has already been demonstrated in the fringes of the westernmost arid core of Asia (Kyzyl Kum and Kara Kum). There, the annual progenitors or prototype annuals of the major cereals, wheat, rye, oats, and barley, and also (at a greater distance from the arid core) of many important grain legumes arose from ancestral perennials in an explosion of annuality which provided the botanical basis for the Neolithic revolution of southwest Asia (Whyte 1977).

Whether and to what extent this environmental interpretation of the origin and evolution of annuality may apply to the cereals and grain legumes of eastern monsoon Asia, and especially of China, must be considered. It appears that annuals of subsequent economic significance became available in large number and variety in different plant communities exposed to similar environmental factors over a remarkably short period of time, over one or two post-Pleistocene millennia, some ten thousand years ago. This has to be related to the time sequence of the climatic and vegetation sequence discussed above, of the earliest appearance of man, and of the change from a hunting and gathering to a cultivating economy.

Although in China rice was slightly later in the time scale than millets, rice will be considered first. It is proposed that perennial species of *Oryza*, a Gondwanian genus, came from Africa on the South Asian Plate and entered, at the northeastern corner of the Plate, into the already established plant ecosystems in Laurasia. These perennial species took up positions in forest climax vegetation throughout the zone accepted by rice geneticists as the place of origin of Asian rice, from Assam/Meghalaya in the west to the coast of the South China Sea in the east, which provided ecological niches suitable to their autecology (see Chang, ch. 3, below). This would mean that, in China, the wild perennial species of *Oryza* could have extended northward to what are now the northern limits of double-crop rice or of a vegetation zone to be specified. Beyond that line subtropical perennials could not have passed because they would have been killed by the winters.

During a period yet to be determined, again some ten thousand years ago, the operative factors of stress extended far down from the Gobi in a pulsating manner, of which the 1976–1978 east Asian drought is an example, over one or two millennia. This caused annual types to arise from the resident perennials, which may themselves have been eliminated by the recurrent periods of drought. Man recognized the significance of these new larger-seeded prototype annuals in his search for food grains to replace those he had formerly obtained by hand-stripping ancestral perennials. He took the new grains north into zones where perennial rice had never grown—that is, as far north as Sapporo in Hokkaido—and he therefore had to learn to cultivate and domesticate them in the warm, humid summers to which as annuals they were now adapted.

The situation regarding the two older millets, *Setaria italica* and *Panicum miliaceum*, the original cereals of Chinese crop farming in the Ordos region, is not so clear-cut. Apart from philological confusion, the problem is complicated by the fact that taxonomists do not yet appear to have indicated what the perennial ancestors of these two millets might have been or, in agreement with ecologists, in what type of plant communities they might have occurred at the time of their supposed domestication. Everything now depends on better knowledge of the taxonomic relations and genecology of the perennials and annuals (extant or extinct) in these two genera.

At this stage, three alternatives can be proposed for these millets.

(1) The annuals arose from perennials which already existed in the natural vegetation of the northwest nearest the area in which cultivation of

the millets is first reported, an interpretation considered unlikely because the environment would by that time have become too arid for perennial species of *Setaria* and *Panicum*.

(2) Perennial, relatively mesophytic species of *Setaria* and *Panicum* (both originally Gondwanian genera of tropical or subtropical adaptation) came across on the Plate in the company of the perennial *Oryza*. Because some species of these two genera are less mesophytic than perennial rice, they were able to advance further north than the *Oryza* belt in southern China and so would have come under the influence of the operative annual-inducing factors before perennial *Oryza*, thus becoming the first to enter Chinese agriculture.

(3) The prototype annuals arose from ancestral perennials somewhere far to the west and the two millets arrived in China as already established crops via the oases of the heartland of Asia, which are relicts of the Tertiary continuous zone of vegetation but now of quite different botanical composition. (This route would best agree with the view that the cool temperate *Setaria viridis* is the immediate ancestor or prototype annual of *Setaria italica*.)

CONCLUSION

When agreement has been reached regarding the past rates and continuity of uplift of the Himalayan range and its associated ranges and plateaus, it would be interesting to attempt to calibrate this with significant events in the evolution of the Chinese environment: the advent of aridity first in the higher latitudes (Gobi 45° north latitude) and then progressively extending to the lower (Taklamakan 38° north latitude), the associated extinction of primitive types of fauna and the change in types of natural vegetation, the pushing of tropical forests southeastward across eastern China, the advent of man associated with the progressive opening of the forest canopies and the establishment of a herbaceous and gramineous ground cover, and the evolution of annual types of millets and rice as the basis of subsequent agriculture.

In the subsequent steadily evolving climatic and biological scene, early man developed first as another component of the biological ecosystem, with the flora he collected and the fauna he hunted, and later as an initiator and progressive refiner of economic land ecosystems. It has to be considered up to what stage in human evolution in China man adapted or had to move away in accordance with the ecological changes induced in his habitat by advancing aridity, and at what stage he began to advance in the technology of land management and in social structure and so became static in an environment which had already become relatively stabilized. In which of the earlier bioclimatic and vegetation zones of increasing aridity did he evolve from a biological to an economic status, and why and when?

It will be necessary for archaeologists and anthropologists to decide on the extent to which they are able to accept the interpretation that environment determined the behavior of early man in his selection of appropriate habitats for settlement, in his ability to manipulate the manipulation of these environments as evidence of his change from a biological to an economic status, and in his choice of crops, livestock, and methods of husbandry. The environmentalist considering the Chinese situation in prehistory and history would regard aridity as the predominant factor in such an interpretation. We need to know, in relation to the evolution and geographical location in China of early economic man and his domestic crops and livestock, if and when this whole situation became stabilized. If it did not or has not become stabilized, was the rate of increase in aridity greater or lesser in the first five millennia which are the concern of this volume, when major changes in human social structure and technology occurred, than in preceding ages? It may be necessary to search for some of the answers to these questions in areas now well beyond the modern limits of successful dry-land cultivation.

REFERENCES

Aigner, J. S.
   1977a   "Comment on Meacham's Local Evolution in South China Neolithic." *Current Anthropology* 18:427–430.
   1977b   "The Hoabinhian in China." In *Festschrift in Honour of Hallam Movius Jr.*, edited by A. K. Ghosh: Calcutta.

Andersson, J. G.
   1934   *Children of the Yellow Earth: Studies in Prehistoric China.* London.

Blow, R. A., and Hamilton, N.
   1975   "Palaeomagnetic Evidence from DSDP Cores of Northward Drift of India." *Nature* 257:570–572.

Bohlin, B.
   1937a   "Eine tertiäre Säugetier. Fauna aus Tsaidam." *PS* ser. C, vol. 14, fasc. 1.

1937b	"Oberoligozäne Säugetiere aus den Shargaltein-Tal (Western Kansu)." *PS* n.s. C, no. 3.
1942	"The Fossil Mammals from the Tertiary Deposit of Taben-buluk, Western Kansu. P.1. Insectivora and Lagomorpha." *PS* n.s. C, no. 8a.
1946	"The Fossil Mammals from the Tertiary Deposit of Taben-buluk, Western Kansu. P.2. Simplicidentata, Carnivora, Artiodactyla, Pterissodactyla and Primates." *PS* n.s. C, no. 8b.
1949	*A Contribution to Our Knowledge of the Distribution of Vegetation in Inner Mongolia, Kansu and Ching-hai.* Sino-Swedish Expedition Publication 33.11. Botany.
1951	"Some Mammalian Remains from Shih-erh-ma-ch'eng, Hui-hui-p'u Area, Western Kansu." Sino-Swedish Expedition Publication 35.6. Vertebrate Palaeontology.
1971	*Late Palaeozoic Plants from Yüerhhung, Kansu, China.* Sino-Swedish Expedition Publication 51.4. Palaeobotany.

Butzer, K. W.

1961	"Climactic Change in Arid Regions Since the Pliocene." In *A History of Land Use in Arid Regions*: pp. 31–56. Arid Zone Research Series 17, UNESCO. Paris.

Chang, Cheng-fa, and Chong, Hsi-lan

1973	"Some Tectonic Features of the Mt. Jolmo Lungma Area, Southern Tibet, China." *Scientia Sinica* 16:257–265.

Chang, Kwang-chih

1977	*The Archaeology of Ancient China.* 3d ed., rev. and enl. New Haven.

Frakes, L. A., and Kemp, E. M.

1972	"Influence of Continental Positions on Early Tertiary Climates." *Nature* 240:97–100.

Frenzel, B.

1968	"The Pleistocene Vegetation of Northern Eurasia." *Science* 161:637–649.

Hallam, A.

1973	*A Revolution in the Earth Sciences: From Continental Drift to Plate Tectonics.* London.

Hiertzler et al. Hiertzler, J. R., Veevers, J. V., Bolli, H. M., Carter, A. N., Cook, P. J., Krashenjinnikov, V. A., McKnight, B. K., Proto-Decima, F., Renz, G. W., Robinson, P. O., Rocker, K., and Thayer, P. A.

1973   "Age of the Floor of the Indian Ocean." *Science*
             180:952–954.

Ho, Ping-ti
1975   *The Cradle of the East: An Inquiry into the Indigenous
             Origins of Techniques and Ideas of Neolithic and Early
             Historic China, 5000–1000 B.C.* Hong Kong and Chicago.

Kryshtofovich, A. N.
1929   "Evolution of the Tertiary Flora in Asia." *New
             Phytologist* 28:303–312.

Kweiyang Institute of Geochemistry
1978   "Development of Natural Environment in the Southern
             Part of Liaoning Province During the Last 10,000 Years."
             Scientia Sinica 21:516–532.

Lamb, H. H.
1977   *Climate: Present, Past and Future.* Vol. 2: *Climatic History
             and the Future.* London.

Lattimore, O.
1951   *Inner Asian Frontiers of China.* New York.

Lee, J. S.
1939   *The Geology of China.* London.

McElhinny, M. W.
1968   "Northward Drift of India—Examination of Recent
             Palaeomagnetic Records." *Nature* 217:342–344.

Mackinder, H. J.
1904   "The Geographical Pivot of History." *Geographical
             Journal* 23:421–437.

Molnar, P., and Tapponnier, P.
1975   "Cenozoic Tectonics of Asia: Effects of a Continental
             Collision." *Science* 189:419–426.

Norlindh, T.
1949   *Flora of the Mongolian Steppe and Desert Areas. 1.* Sino-
             Swedish Expedition Publication 31.11. Botany.

Pearson, R.
1976   "[Review of] Ping-ti Ho, *The Cradle of the East.*" *Science*
             193:395–396.

South China "Redbeds" Research Group
1977   "Palaeocene Vertebrate Horizons and Mammalian Faunas
             of South China." *Scientia Sinica* 20:665–678.

Stein, A.
1925   "Innermost Asia. Its Geography as a Factor in History."
         Geographical Journal 65:377–403, 473–498.

Szalay, F. S., and McKenna, M. C.
1971   "Beginning of the Age of Mammalia in Asia: The Late
         Palaeocene Gashato Fauna, Mongolia." *Bulletin of the
         American Museum of Natural History* 144:269–318.

Wang, Chi-wu
1961   *The Forests of China: With a Survey of Grassland and
         Desert Vegetation.* Maria Moors Cabot Foundation
         Publication 5. Cambridge, Mass.

Watson, W.
1969   "Early Animal Domestication in China." In *The
         Domestication and Exploitation of Plants and Animals*,
         edited by P. J. Ucko and G. W. Dimbleby: pp. 391–395.
         London.

Whyte, R. O.
1977   "The Botanical Neolithic Revolution." *Human Ecology*
         5:209–222.

Yin, Chi-hsiang, and Kuo, Shih-tseng
1978   "Stratigraphy of the Mount Jolmo Lungma and Its North
         Slope." *Scientia Sinica* 21:629–644.

Zdansky, O.
1923   "Uber ein Säugerknochenlager in Chou K'ou T'ien."
         Bulletin of the Geological Survey of China 5:83–89.
1928   "Die Säugetiere der Quartärfauna von Chou K'ou T'ien."
         PS ser. C, vol. 5, fasc. 4.

2

The Domestication of Plants in China: Ecogeographical Considerations

HUI-LIN LI

The idea of a Neolithic Revolution, implying a sudden and dramatic change in human history, is misleading. Evidence has been accumulated to show that the transition from food gathering to food producing was very gradual; from a biological point of view, it can be regarded as an evolutionary sequence of adaption by man to a particular environment.

The geographical origin of agriculture has also been a subject of reappraisal. A single point of origin, a zone including Anatolia, Iran, and Syria, was once believed to have given rise to plant domestication sometime before 7000 B.C. From there, agriculture was supposed to have spread to other parts of the world. Now, however, independent origins in many different parts of the world are considered probable, and the centers are no longer confined to the Northern Hemisphere. Different agricultural systems were developed in response to each environment, seed cultures in the north and "vegecultures" in tropical areas.

Alphonse de Candolle, the first authority on the origin of cultivated plants, postulated (1884:17) that agriculture arose independently in three regions: "China, the southwest of Asia (with Egypt), and intertropical America." The geneticist Nicholai I. Vavilov later expanded the number of centers of origin of cultivated plants to five (Vavilov 1926) and then to eleven (Vavilov 1949–1950). Although his "centers" were really wide geographical or political areas rather than environmental ranges (Burkill 1953:17), Vavilov's genetic and ecological approaches stimulated further study along these lines.

THE NATURAL ENVIRONMENT

Three Phytogeographical Zones

Both de Candolle and Vavilov regarded China as a center of origin of cultivated plants. The immense size of the country, stretching from approximately 70° to 134° east longitude and from 18° to 53° north latitude, encompasses very varied geographical features and climatic conditions; it cannot in any sense be considered a single floristic region. Just as the natural flora of China must be divided into several distinct areas, the origin of cultivated plants developed from the indigenous flora also requires the recognition of regional diversity.

Various schemes of classification of the natural vegetation of China, such as those by me (Li Hui-lin 1944) and by Keng Po-chieh (1958), Wang (1961), and others, provide a phytogeographical basis for the investigation of the origins of cultivated flora. Using this background, I have delineated three broad latitudinal zones in eastern China (Li 1970) where agriculture has been practiced since protohistoric times. Recent archaeological finds seem to corroborate these phytogeographically determined zones and, further, suggest the nuclear areas of agricultural origin within each.

The three zones, the North China belt, the South China belt, and the South Asia belt, are distinguishable physiographically as well as phytogeographically. The Ch'in Ling mountain range and its eastern extensions form a boundary between the North and South China belts, roughly along the line of the thirty-fourth parallel. Topography, climate, and soil, as well as natural vegetation, are sharply different to the north and south of the Ch'in Ling. To the east, where the mountain ranges are not as high, the floristic differences are less distinct. The southern limit of the North China belt is generally considered to run even further east, between the Yangtze and Huai rivers. Essentially, the North China belt includes the Huang Ho basin, the loess highlands and plains of North China.

Climatically, the cold-winter wheat-growing region of North China, with its limited precipitation, can be contrasted with the moist, rice-growing climate of South China. The boundary between the South China belt, which includes the Yangtze river basin, and the South Asia belt falls roughly along the twenty-fifth parallel, a few degrees north of the Tropic of Cancer, along the Nan Ling mountain range. Southern Yunnan and the Hsi Chiang basin, a multiple rice-crop area with a tropical climate, fall within the South Asia belt. Further south, the South Asia belt also includes Burma, Thailand and the Indochinese peninsula exclusive of the southern extension of the Malay Peninsula.

Grassland and Woodland

In order to understand the natural environments of these three belts, we must take a closer look at the ecogeography of Asia. The largest land mass in the world, the Asiatic continent has a vast, arid heartland fringed by moist areas facing the oceans. Differential heating of the dry hinterland and the oceans causes air pressure differences which create a seasonal reversal of surface air flow, the Asiatic monsoon system. Mountain ranges inhibit this air flow.

The monsoons are the dominant factor in creating the precipitation distribution patterns of China, which lies at the eastern edge of Asia facing the ocean. Moisture-laden winds from the Pacific blow in the summer, while cold, dry desert winds flow in from arid Central Asia in the winter. The climates of North and South China are, however, very different. During winter, central Asia is dominated by cold air masses producing high-pressure systems, in contrast to the lower air pressure over the warm surface of the Pacific. In North China, close to the high-pressure system center, the winds are the strongest and coldest. South China, on the other hand, lies farther from the high-pressure center and is also shielded by the Ch'in Ling range, and its winters are more moderate.

A diagonal gradient in climate and vegetation runs from the forests of the humid regions of the southeastern coastal areas across the central grasslands, ending in the arid deserts of the northwest. As Wang pointed out (1961:2), the ecogeography of China is thus founded on two great natural plant formations, the woodland to the east and the grassland-desert complex inland to the north and west.

The Environmental Setting of Agricultural Origins

The three regional belts under consideration comprise the eastern woodland half of the country; the western half is made up of grasslands and deserts including the Tibetan plateau and the Sinkiang-Mongolian deserts. The relation between woodland and grassland played a crucial role in the initiation of agriculture. Neither environment separately provides a conducive setting for beginning cultivation. Forests are a close environment, better suited for concealment than travel. Early man in his food-gathering stage lived there, but agriculture did not begin until he moved away. The forest does not offer the kind of heliophilous, herbaceous plants which are man's staple crops. Important staple crops are all sun-loving, high-energy-producing plants; in the north they are mostly annuals (Ames 1939), while in the south they are either perennial herbs or woody plants.

The right kind of plants for cultivation are found in the open grassland environments, but the grasslands themselves were not the home of food-gathering primitive man. Shelter could not be found there, nor were the meager resources sufficient to support him. It was at the boundary between woodland and grassland, in an intermediate savanna environment, that cultivation began. The vegetation here is varied, providing both helio-philous herbaceous plants and scattered trees and shrubs for shelter. While agriculture was incipient, man could live in this intermediate zone for prolonged periods, finding both natural plants and animal resources in the transitional environment. Starting usually from the forest's edge, the earliest stages of agriculture all over the world have required that man break down the woodland, his original home (Sears 1967).

Human activities since prehistoric times have greatly altered the original grassland and woodland environments. Eastern China, once essentially woodland, has been largely cleared for intensive cultivation. It is densely populated except for the underdeveloped frontiers and montane-boreal areas. The western plains are used primarily for grazing. Nomadic peoples sparsely populate the west, with heavier populations only in limited irri-gated arable sections.

Botanists have searched for clues to reconstruct the original natural environment. Remnants of natural forests have been preserved in many areas, and in remote, less accessible places extensive primeval forests are still found. Even in densely populated and cultivated areas, the observant botanist will note "scattered trees among fields and along roadsides, or an occasional grove in or near a village. Striking cases of luxuriant vegetation hide the temples and monasteries scattered about the countryside or nested in mountain valleys" (Walker 1944:334).

These scattered hints, in addition to climatic and soil conditions, have been used by botanists to reconstruct the natural environment which existed before agriculture (Wang 1961:5). Recently, a number of archae-ological, paleontological, and palynological studies have helped to more definitely ascertain the chronology of past vegetation in certain areas.

Chu (1972), using animal remains unearthed at An-yang and Pan-p'o and phenological records from oracle bones, concludes that the mean annual temperature in China some five thousand to three thousand years ago was approximately two degrees centigrade higher than at present. Climatically, therefore, prehistoric and protohistoric China was generally milder and moister. Vegetation was correspondingly different but also exhibited the regional differences which can be seen today. Topogra-phically, we can safely assume that there have been no major changes during the past five thousand or more years except for disturbances, usually local in effect, due to erosion, alluviation, or earthquakes.

THE NORTH CHINA BELT

Temperate North China consists of the basin of the Huang Ho and its tributaries. The western part, the loess highland, embraces Kansu, Shensi, most of Shansi, a large part of Honan, and parts of Hopei. Loess, which has a low humus content and a high water-holding capacity, covers this upland region to a considerable depth. A series of high, broad parallel ridges running in a northeast-southeast direction alternates with wide valleys.

Northeastern China consists of level plains through most of Hopei, eastern Honan, northern Anhwei, northern Kiangsu, and western Shantung. The wide-open flat, fertile plains are covered with loess carried by wind and rivers. Farther to the east are the rugged Shantung highlands.

Strongly influenced by its proximity to the arid central Asia hinterlands, North China has a harsh climate. Annual precipitation, falling mostly in summer, is only 250–500 millimeters in the western highlands and 400–750 millimeters in the eastern plains. Winter is severe, with little precipitation, mostly snow. The mean temperature in the winter ranges around minus six degrees centigrade. Due to the vagaries of the monsoon, both droughts and floods are common.

Despite the harshness of its climate, the North China plain is now the largest agricultural center of China. Part of the loess highlands is also under cultivation, but most of the highland area is covered by barren slopes. Historical and prehistorical evidence indicates that one of the nuclear areas of Chinese civilization was in the southern part of the loess highlands. Agriculture seems to have begun immediately to the north of this area, in the northern part of the highland.

The Natural Vegetation
The Loess Highlands

Great controversy surrounds the matter of North China's original vegetation. Diametrically opposed theories have been expounded: for example, Chang Kwang-chih (1968:32, 35; 1977:35) believes that the western loess highlands were originally forest-clad and the eastern plains wet, marshy, and thickly forested; Ho (1969a; 1969b:12; 1975:34) concludes that North China as a whole, including both the western highlands and eastern plains, was a semi-arid steppe.

Plant geographers such as Keng Po-chieh (1958), Wang (1961), and others seem generally to agree that while the major mountain ranges of North China were originally covered at the higher levels by extensive coniferous forests, the eastern part, including the plains and the eastern mountains of the highland region, was largely or partially covered by mixed deciduous hardwood forests. They also agree that the western part, which is most of the loess highland region, was covered by a savanna-type vegetation between grassland and woodland.

Both Keng (1958:79) and Wang (1961:79) consider the eastern loess highland to belong to the great eastern woodland complex of China; the western loess highlands are believed to be transitional between woodland and grassland. Keng breaks the woodland part of North China into two subregions: mountains—the eastern loess highland—and plains, the great North China plains.

Remnant forests suggest that mountainous vegetation, coniferous and mixed mesophytic forests with exposed areas of semi-arid vegetation or grassland and alpine forests above tree line, was prevalent throughout mountainous North China when the climate was slightly moister and milder. Seedlings of forest trees still grow concealed among bushes and grasses which now cover huge expanses of the slopes and foothills (Wang 1961:79). The original vegetation has mostly been replaced by these bushes and grasses, including *Corylus heterophylla*, *Vitex incisa*, *Themeda triandra*, and *Bothriochloa* (*Andropogon*) *ischaenum* and xerophytic thorny shrubs like *Zizyphus spinosa*.

Recent palynological studies have largely borne out this picture of the original vegetations as constructed by phytogeographical methods. Pollen and spores from peat bogs and the plains near Peking were studied by Chou (1963), who concluded that a mixture of forest and grassland existed. He also found indications of marshy or aquatic vegetation from low, wet areas. Another study from the southern slopes of the Yen Shan, northwest of Peking, by Liu et al. (1965) reported similar findings. *Artemisia* was one of the grassland plants found in these palynological studies.

The main part of the loess highland lies to the west of this mountainous area, in western Shansi, Shensi, and Kansu. Its climate is harsher and vegetation more sparse. Northern Shensi and Kansu are grassland and desert. To the southwest the vegetation is savanna. Forest remnants are rare, growing only on some high mountains.

Five thousand years ago, with a slightly higher temperature, the vegetation must have been slightly more luxuriant than now. The coniferous and broad-leaved forests would have extended to lower elevations, and naturally growing trees would have been more common even at lower levels. This reconstruction is supported by a number of pollen studies, including one at Liu-shu-kou, Wu-ch'eng-hsien, Shansi (Liu and Chang 1962), which lies closest to the area under consideration. Liu-shu-kou is about 115 kilometers east of Yen-an, just across the Huang Ho from

Huang-lung-shan. Pollen finds from an entire loess profile were analyzed by Ho (1975:28). His finds for the stratum dating from the period of incipient agriculture (the upper 20 out of 121 total meters) were tabulated as follows: (a) Woody plants: *Abies* 2, *Pinus* 15, Cupressaceae 3, *Quercus* 2, *Morus* 2, *Salix* 7, *Corylus* 2; (b) Herbaceous plants: *Typha* 1, Gramineae 56, Cyperaceae 3, *Humulus* 3, Chenopodiaceae 18, Caryophyllaceae 1, *Clematis* 48, *Convolvulus* 14, *Artemisia* 722, Compositae 32, other Dicotyledons 72. There were 33 pollen grains from woody plants and 970 from herbaceous, totalling 1,003. His conclusion was that the paleo-environment of the loess highlands was a semi-arid steppe little if at all forested. He pointed especially to the large proportion of *Artemisia* as substantiation of his hypothesis. The pollen finds, however, can be interpreted to represent quite a different ecology: they seem to me to indicate a vegetation similar to that of the present, but slightly more luxuriant. This was a transitional environment between grassland and woodland. Conifer forests (*Abies*, *Pinus*, Cupressaceae) grew at high levels, and other trees (*Quercus*, *Morus*, *Salix*, *Corylus*) occurred at lower levels more commonly than they do now. Grasslands with scattered shrubs were extensive in drier areas.

Pearson (1974) considered the very small amount and sparse distribution of pollen grain of the profile as insufficient evidence to support the viewpoint of Ho and the palynologists of a non-wooded steppe for the entire loess highland. He questioned the validity of their conclusion based on "raw" pollen counts, which failed to take account of the amounts of pollen produced by each group of genera; he noted especially that oak is usually under-represented in pollen spectra because of its limited pollen production; he also suggested that the relatively high preservation of *Artemisia* pollen in alkaline loess deposits could be explained by its particularly thick exine. It should be mentioned further that *Artemisia* plants produce abundant pollen continuously and successively for several months during the growing season, whereas trees such as oak and pine shed all their pollen within a few days.

Ho thought that the sharp increase in *Artemisia* shows that the climate in the late Pleistocene was becoming cooler and drier. *Artemisia* species, however, vary in habitat from xerophytic to mesophytic and therefore are not confined to arid environments. Rather, the significant fact about *Artemisia* is that nearly all its species are "weedy" in nature; they are characteristically among the most aggressive plants in taking over abandoned, formerly cultivated fields in temperate climates. The noticeable increase in *Artemisia* during this period seems strongly to indicate the beginning of primitive swidden or slash-and-burn, the first stage of Chinese agriculture. Pearson (1974) also noted *Artemisia* as a successional species and thus considered its occurrence as evidence of human disturbance of the forests.

Somewhat to the south, pollen from the Neolithic Yang-shao sites at Pan-p'o near Sian yielded results (Chou 1963) similar to those of Liu-shu-kou. Chou's conclusion was that the vegetation was a sparse grassland with scattered broad-leaved trees such as willow, walnut, birch, hornbeam, oak, elm, and persimmon. The climate was similar to that of the present. More trees were represented at this site than at the more northern one.

Agriculture would have begun in this open grassland-woodland semi-arid setting. Natural flora provided a number of annual heliophilous her-baceous plants, as well as some woody plants which were especially well-adapted to this environment and suited to domestication. Loess soil must have greatly facilitated early cultivation. Furthermore, varied ecospaces such as the mesophytic forests and marshes were available for human exploitation, providing other components for what was to become a complete crop complex, the physical basis of an agricultural civilization.

In the beginning agriculture was of the slash-and-burn variety, a waste-ful practice which destroyed the natural vegetation and exhausted the land. Population pressure contributed to the dispersion of people away from the original center of plant domestication. Migration eventually brought men, with their cultivated crops, to the river valleys south and east of the loess highlands, environments favorable to further developments in agriculture and in civilization.

The Great Plain

The great alluvial plain of North China has been so extensively cultivated that its original vegetation has been the subject of much dispute among historians and plant geographers. Although Chang Kwang-chih (1968:32, 35; 1977:35) felt it was wet, marshy, and thickly forested, and Ho (1969a; 1969b:12) that it was a semi-arid steppe, other theories have held that it was grassland (Schimper 1898), wooded steppe (Huang 1940–41), or deciduous summer-green forest (Schimper and Faber 1935; Lundegarch 1957). The last view has been generally accepted in recent years by plant geographers with extensive field experience. After studying existing vegetation and historical evidence, Wang, in his survey of the phytogeography of China (1961:86), concludes that, except for the saline coast and alkaline depressions, the greater part of the plain was in pre- and protohistorical times covered by deciduous broad-leaved forest.

Considering the present severe climate of the great plain, the relative abundance of tree species is impressive. They appear to represent a flora which once had an extensive range over North China but which is now confined to the foothills. Judging from the remnant forests in the foothills, it seems as though the original woods were composed of oaks (*Quercus aliena, Q. dentata, Q. variabilis*) with an admixture of *Celtis, Ulmus, Pistacia*, and many other deciduous trees which occasionally still grow on the plains. This mixed hardwood forest is equivalent to the broad-leaved forest of Keng Po-chieh (1958:7) and other authors.

Chang Kwang-chih's archaeological study (1959:263) generally corroborates the dominant interpretation of the plant geographers. His belief is that during the postglacial era down to several thousand years ago the North China plain was warmer and moister than at present. It was covered by forests and shrubberies with scattered marshes, as evidenced by the abundance of timber remains in Neolithic and Bronze Age sites, numerous discoveries of well-scaled woodcutting tools, and finds of warmth- and moisture-loving animals and some aquatic plants. Since Neolithic times, the forest has been almost completely obliterated by the action of man as well as by the gradual desiccation and cooling of the climate.

The Cultivated Flora
Cereals

The principal staple crop of Neolithic North China is generally considered to have been the millets. Although wheat or barley was usually included among the few choice grains named in the ancient classics, Ho maintains (1969a:160–166; 1969b:26–27; 1975:74–76) that there have been no verified prehistoric finds of wheat or barley in China.

Chinese millets consist of plants belonging to two genera: *Setaria* and *Panicum*. It is now generally accepted that the traditional name *su* 粟 refers to the species *Setaria italica*, the foxtail millet, whereas *shu* 黍 and *chi* 稷 refer to two varieties of the species *Panicum miliaceum* (the broom-corn millet), namely, var. *glutinosum*, the glutinous kind, and var. *effusum*, the non-glutinous kind, respectively.

There is, however, some confusion in the nomenclature of Chinese millets found in the ancient literature, a confusion compounded by the interpretations of later authors; this situation remains to be clarified (Liu Yü-chüan 1960; Tsou 1960). Such a clarification might be achieved through a critical examination of the ancient records of the graphs *su*, *shu*, and *chi* and by combining philological studies with phytotaxonomy. *Shu, chi*, and *su* are the three most frequently mentioned staples in the *Shih-ching* (Book of Odes), indicating that they were the primary food crops of Chou China (Ts'ao 1960).

Actual remains identified as *Setaria italica* have been found in a number of Yang-shao sites which show that the species, if correctly identified, was then extensively grown. Only one find each of *Panicum miliaceum*, kaoliang (*Andropogon sorghum*), and wheat has been reported. These unique occurrences are considered by Chang Kwang-chih (1977:95) to be suspect, or, if the identification or stratigraphy is reliable, to reflect the species' rarity.

There are various hypotheses as to the origin of *Setaria italica*. It is generally believed to have been derived from *Setaria viridis*, a weedy wild millet widely distributed in the warm regions of the Old World. Both *Panicum miliaceum* and *Setaria italica* are known for being highly drought-resistant (Ho 1975:58). Ho notes particularly that botanists have shown by experiment that among common cereal plants *Setaria italica* has the "highest" efficiency of transpiration and that it is best suited to dry situations. This quality, together with the mention of a number of varieties in the *Shih-ching*, the occurrence of wild millets in the loess area, and the antiquity of their cultivation, lead Ho to believe that these two millets are indigenous to North China.

The Soybean

The soybean (*Glycine max*) is one of the most valuable food crops ever discovered and domesticated by man. The combination of a rich and complete protein content and an abundant amount of oil within the same seed is unique. Domestication of the soybean has had a profound and lasting effect upon Chinese agriculture and nutrition.

The origin of cultivation of this important crop occurred in North China. The genus *Glycine* comprises some ten species widely distributed in the tropical and warm-temperate parts of the Old World (Hermann 1962). The subgenus Soja, occupying the most northern part of the range of the genus, temperate eastern Asia, contains only two species, the widely distributed *G. ussuriensis* and the cultigen *G. max*. *Glycine max* is supposed to be a derivative of either *G. ussuriensis* or some other closely related species. While all the other species are perennials and twining or climbing plants, *G. max* stands alone as an annual and an erect plant.

There have as yet been no prehistoric finds of the soybean. Evidence of its antiquity depends on the analysis of the character *shu* 叔 found on a Shang bronze studied by Hu Tao-ching (1963), who believes the lower half of the character represents the nodules formed on soybean roots by symbiotic nitrogen-fixing bacteria which are found in all legume plants. Ho

(1969b:29; 1975:79) considers the domestication of the soybean rather recent and suggests that it probably first occurred successfully in the eastern half of North China not too much earlier than the eleventh century B.C.

Because the soybean is extensively grown in northeast China, Fukuda (1933) strongly argues that a soybean gene center exists there and that this is where soybeans were first domesticated. He points to the fact that many varieties are growing there, most of which appear to have primitive characteristics, and that a weedy form, *G. gracilis*, is found there. Hymowitz (1970) rightly refutes this, as historical records prove definitely that the cultivation of soybeans in northeast China is a recent phenomenon. *Glycine gracilis* is a weed formed as a result of outcrossing between *G. max* and *G. ussuriensis*, and Hermann (1962) reduces it to synonymy under *G. max*.

In a review of the cultivation and utilization of soybeans in Chinese literature, Li Ch'ang-nien (1958a; 1958b) points to the occurrence of the crop in pre-Ch'in China in Shensi, Shansi, Honan, Hopei, and Shantung, and to its cultivation there at least in the Chou period if not earlier. He suggests that there was originally a black-seeded form growing in the western part of North China and that later a yellow-seeded form was introduced from northwestern Hopei. This dual origin theory corresponds somewhat to the present distribution of the primarily black-seeded form in Shensi and Shansi and the yellow-seeded form in Northeast China.

Hemp

Cannabis sativa, hemp, was used in ancient China as a major fiber plant and as one of the leading grains. Long believed to be an Asiatic plant, its origin has been pinpointed to North China (Li Hui-lin 1974b; 1974c).

The first archaeological record was found in Neolithic remains discovered at Yang-shao by Andersson in 1921 (Andersson 1923). Some pottery artifacts were decorated with clear impressions of cloth, the thread of which was believed to be hemp. Many pottery spinning whorls and numerous finely made bone needles were also unearthed at the Yang-shao site at Hua-hsien, Shensi (*KK* 1959.2). Fragmentary but distinct impressions in the dirt in one grave were, according to the discoverers, probably made by hemp cloth. Spinning whorls, pottery with textile markings, and other traces of hemp have also been located at the Yang-shao site of Pan-p'o near Sian (CKKH and Shen-hsi 1963) and the Lung-shan site at Hsi-ch'uan, Honan (Ho-nan-sheng, Ch'ang-chiang, and Wen-wu 1972:10).

The character *ma* 麻 has not been found among the deciphered logographs of the oracle bones, but there is one archaeological find dating back to the Shang period relating to hemp. In 1931 Li, reporting on excavations at An-yang (Li Chi 1931), mentioned conspicuous cloth patterns on some of the *ku*-type bronze weapons. Although no statement was made about the actual material of the cloth, hemp was the most likely fiber, as it was the only plant textile fiber known in ancient North China.

The first actual find of hemp cloth was a fragment in a grave of the Western Chou in Shansi (Ko 1972). The weave was quite tight, indicating that weaving techniques had by then reached a relatively high standard.

In the early classics of the Chou period appear a considerable number of records pertaining to hemp both as a textile fiber and as a food grain. Hemp's dioecious nature was recognized early, as different logographs were assigned to the male and female plants, as well as to the flowers, fruiting clusters, and seeds; the specialized names show the antiquity of its cultivation. In the *Shih-ching* hemp is mentioned no less than seven times, mostly as a fiber but also as a grain. The growing of hemp is briefly mentioned, as well as the preparation of the fibers and the use of the textile in making ropes.

Another feature of the hemp plant, its use as a drug and its stupefying effect, detailed in the *Pen-ts'ao ching* (compiled in the first or second century A.D.), seems to have been known to the ancients much earlier. I have demonstrated (Li Hui-lin 1974b) that the character *ma* since early times has had two connotations, one of "numerous and chaotic," derived from the nature of the fibers, and the other of "numbness or senseless," derived apparently from the properties of the fruits and leaves used as infusions for medicinal purposes.

Cannabis is a plant of sunny, semi-arid habitat. The species seems native to the loess highland area and has been used there since early times as a fiber, food grain, and medicinal plant. It thrives best in a rich soil and is thus a natural follower of human migration, as human habitats provide a favorable environment for it. Nomad tribes in the north, practitioners of shamanism, apparently used the plant as a drug and carried it west to central and western Asia and India, where it was used primarily as a hallucinogen and not as a textile fiber (Li Hui-lin 1974b; 1974c).

Fruits

A distinctive aspect of plant cultivation in North China is the significant role played by fruit and nut trees. The eastern mountainous part of the loess highland is at present renowned for its great production of temperate fruits, some introduced but most indigenous. Both orchard trees and many wild species with edible fruits grow in this region.

The leading fruit trees, in terms of great economic importance and great antiquity in cultivation, are the jujube, peach, apricot, and persimmon. All are highly nutritious and can be dried and preserved for long periods; they were apparently used as staple foods for the ancient residents of the region.

The Jujube. The Chinese jujube, *Zizyphus jujuba*, is closely related to the common spiny shrub *Z. spinosa*, which is widespread in drier situations throughout North China. The latter is sometimes treated as a variety of the former and is considered the wild ancestor of the cultivated jujube. The close relation between the two plants has long been reflected in classical tradition, as the character *tsao* 棗 (the jujube) is a vertical arrangement of the same two radicals which horizontally form *chi* 棘 (the wild jujube).

Zizyphus jujuba, in the past called *Z. vulgaris* and *Z. sativa*, is a name used incorrectly to include the Indian jujube, a similar but distinct species: *Z. maratiana*. *Zizyphus jujuba* is regarded by botanists as a species indigenous to China, whence it was introduced in both wild and cultivated forms to central Asia, the Mediterranean, and northern India several hundred years ago; there it became naturalized (de Candolle 1884; Thomas 1924).

Pollen studies reveal the presence of *Zizyphus* during the early Neolithic in North China, but it is not ascertainable whether it was wild or cultivated. Fruit stones found along with millet at the Pan-p'o site near Sian indicate early cultivation of this or some other fruit trees. Jujube was mentioned in the *Shih-ching*, apparently as a cultivated tree. Jujube, chestnut and hazelnut were specifically designated in the *Chou-li* (Rites of Chou) as appropriate gifts at the first meeting of a prospective bride and groom. Its use and cultivation must have spread to more southern regions quite early, but, as pointed out in the *Shih-chi*, "Huo-chih lieh-chuan," the best orchards in early Han times were still found at An-yi in southern Shansi. The jujube has been the most extensively and intensively cultivated fruit tree in China, with increasing numbers of varieties recorded in literature through the ages up to development of the several hundred current varieties, which grow largely in North China.

The Chinese jujube has a high food value and can be eaten fresh or dried. Analysis of its composition (Church 1924) shows that it compares favorably with the fig in terms of edible matter, total sugars, and acid. The date has similar values except for a considerably lower protein content. Figs and dates are the two most important fruits of western Asia and, together with olives and grapes, are regarded as the first important horticultural additions to the Mediterranean grain culture in the fourth and third centuries

B.C. (Zohary and Spiegel-Roy 1975). The jujube, together with the peach, the apricot, and the persimmon, played a comparable role in the origin of cultivation in North China.

The Peach. Next in importance is the peach (*t'ao* 桃), *Prunus persica.* Ever since de Candolle in 1884 asserted positively that the peach originated in China, there seems to have been no dissension from this view. It has been reported from time to time that wild peach trees have been collected from mountains of North China, but these may be only naturalized escapees from cultivation and not truly indigenous trees. Suggestions have also been made that the peach is a cultigen derived from the closely related species, *Prunus davidiana*, which grows in the mountains of Hopei, Honan, Shansi, and Shensi and which is often used as a graft stock for the cultivated peach.

Many varieties of the peach are cultivated in China for their ornamental flower or edible fruit. There are many legends ascribed to the plant, some preserved in tradition and custom. Since ancient times it has been known as the fruit of longevity, and mythical powers are credited to the fruit and other parts of the tree. The peach fruit is eaten fresh and is also used extensively dried.

Although at present there is no definite archaeological or palynological evidence to determine the antiquity of the cultivated peach and apricot, their frequent mention as common orchard trees in the *Shih-ching* points to their domestication long before the Chou period.

The Apricot. The apricot (*hsing* 杏), *Prunus armeniaca*, a congener of the peach, was again ascertained as of Chinese origin by de Candolle; its cultivation must be as early as that of the peach. As with the peach, many legends were associated with the tree, and mythical powers were attributed to the fruit and other parts of the plant. The fruit, fleshy and sugary, is used extensively dried and preserved.

The Persimmon. The Chinese persimmon (*shih* 柿), *Diospyros kaki*, now extensively cultivated in North China and Japan, is a species of Chinese origin. Large quantities of the fruit are produced each year in North China, where hundreds of varieties of the tree are grown. The dried fruit, which can be preserved for a long time, is highly nutritious, like the jujube. Once the fruit is dried, a crystalline sugar is deposited on the outside.

Cultivation began in North China at an early date. Pollen of *Diospyros* has been reported from Neolithic sites in the loess highland. Wild or cultivated, its fruit was available then as a supplemental food.

The wild prototype of the cultivated persimmon, var. *sylvestris*, still grows in the hills of North China and Korea. The only other species of the genus in North China, *D. lotus*, which grows wild but is sometimes also cultivated for the edible but smaller fruit, may have also contributed to the origin of the cultivated persimmon.

The Chestnut and Hazelnut. The above four fruits together with two nut trees, *li* 栗, chestnut, *Castanea mollissima*, and *chen* 榛, hazelnut, *Corylus heterophylla*, are the most important fruit trees of ancient North China. The nut trees were mentioned frequently together in the *Shih-ching.* Carbonized hazelnut found at the Sian Pan-p'o site has been carbon-dated at 4300 ± 200 B.C. (CKKH shih-yen-shih 1972; Hsia 1977). Both were highly valued in ancient times; the hazelnut subsequently became less important and the chestnut more widespread in cultivation and use.

Other Fruits. Many other fruit trees originated in North China, perhaps at later times than those discussed above. Both the eastern loess highland and the hills and mountains of northern Hopei and western Shantung were sites of origin. Among the fruit trees involved are *li* 李, Chinese plum, *Prunus salicina*; *ying-t'ao* 櫻桃, Chinese cherry, *Prunus pseudocerasus*; *sha-li* 沙梨, sand pear, *Pyrus serotina*; *pai-li* 白梨, white pear, *Pyrus bret-schneideri*; *lin-ch'in* 林檎, Chinese apple, *Malus asiatica*; *hai-t'ang* 海棠, Chinese crab apple, *Malus spectabilis*; *shan-cha* 山樝, Chinese hawthorn, *Crataegus pinnatifida*; *shan-li-hung* 山裏紅, large hawthorn, *C. pinnatifida* var. *major*; *mu-kua* 木瓜, Chinese quince, *Chaenomeles sinensis*; and *chih-chü* 枳椇, raisin tree, *Hovenia dulcis*. With the exception of the last, all belong to the rose family, Rosaceae.

Vegetables

So far the earliest vegetable known to have been used in North China is the *Brassica* (Chinese cabbage), whose seeds were found along with those of millet at the Pan-p'o site (CKKH and Shen-hsi 1963). The plant was by then already being cultivated. Many plants are known to have been gathered and used as vegetables in ancient times, but their status, wild or cultivated, is not always discernible from the literature. Among such plants mentioned in the *Shih-ching*, the following are the most important which appear to have been under cultivation, at least during Chou times: *fei* 菲, radish, *Raphanus sativus*; *feng* 葑, turnip, *Brassica rapa*; *chiu*, 韭, Chinese chive, *Allium odorum* (*A. tuberosum*); *ts'ung* 葱, Welsh onion, *Allium fistulosum*; *hsieh* 薤, scallion, *Allium bakeri*; *kua* 瓜, melon, *Cucumis melo*; and *k'uei* 葵, mallow, *Malva verticillata* (Lu 1958; Keng Hsüan 1974).

Among these, mallow was mentioned also in the *Chou-li* as the leading leafy vegetable. It remained in this position at least until the fifth to sixth centuries A.D., for Chia Ssu-hsieh 賈思勰 treated it as the most important leafy vegetable in his *Ch'i-min yao-shu* 齊民要術, an agricultural treatise on North China of the later Wei of the Northern Dynasties. Following that, however, it was gradually superseded by the Chinese cabbage, *Brassica chinensis*. Its fall from favor was probably due to changing food habits. In ancient times vegetable oils were not available, so mucilaginous vegetables like mallow were a required part of the diet; later, when technological advancement enabled people to extract oil from vegetable seeds, they became unnecessary. The mallow, a perennial, was gradually replaced by more easily cultivated annual or biennial vegetables until it was forgotten as a vegetable and, recently became a weed (Li Hui-lin 1969).

That man's consumption of leafy vegetables in earlier times included both cultivated and wild plants can be shown by the fact that *lai* 菜 or *li* 藜, the pigweed, *Chenopodium album*, and *ho* 藿, the leaves of the soybean, were frequently mentioned together as a food, used especially by the poor. *Chenopodium album* is now a weed widely distributed over the country.

Besides the major vegetables, the *Shih-ching* mentions many other plants gathered for use as vegetables. These include both wild and cultivated plants and plants then under cultivation but which have since, like the mallow, become de-domesticated. The *Ch'i-min yao-shu* describes a number of such plants. Three mentioned earlier, in the *Shih-ching*, are *liao* 蓼, common smartweed, *Polygonum hydropiper*; *chü* 苣, a wild lettuce, *Lactuca denticulata*; and *chüan-erh* 卷耳, cocklebur, *Xanthium strumarium*. All three are at present weeds, but all were cultivated at the time of Chia Ssu-hsieh (in the fifth to sixth centuries A.D.), who gave detailed instructions for their cultivation and preparation. *Polygonum hydropiper* was regarded as a cultivated vegetable of great importance, the other two as of lesser importance. This indicates that at the time of the *Shih-ching* these plants were most likely already cultivated. Their subsequent decline was similar to that of the mallow.

The Mulberry

The mulberry and the lacquer tree demonstrate more than any other plants the distinctiveness and originality of the agriculture and the cultivated flora of North China. The mulberry tree, *Morus nigra*, is unique among forage plants; it is a tree rather than an herb, and the animal its leaves feed is a domesticated worm. The earliest record of this domestication, which came about in the loess highland of North China, has been dated 2600 to 2300 B.C. by the discovery of half of a silk cocoon unearthed at Hsi-yin, Hsia-hsien, in southern Shansi by Li Chi (1927). Mulberry and silk are referred to in the Shang oracle-bone inscriptions, and remnants of textiles found on Shang bronzes have been identified as silk (Ho 1969b:30; 1975:82; Hu Hou-hsüan 1972).

Sang 桑, the mulberry tree, *Morus alba*, is one of several species of the widespread genus *Morus* native to North China. It grows in mixed mesophytic forests. Under cultivation it has developed many forms and varieties. The mostly highly domesticated variety is the *lu-sang* 魯桑, var. *multicaulis*, a low shrubby form with large, dark, unlobed leaves with blunt teeth along the margins. The leaves of other cultivated varieties and of the wild form are deeply lobed and sharp-toothed along the margins.

In the *Shih-ching* the mulberry tree is mentioned twenty times, more than any other tree, and always described as a domesticated plant. Clearly, it was already cultivated in extensive plantations in North China. The gradual migration of mulberry cultivation and the silk industry from North China to the Yangtze valley seems to have begun in the Warring States period or shortly thereafter (Chang K'ai 1960; Hsia 1972).

The Lacquer tree

The *ch'i* 漆, lacquer tree, *Rhus verniciflua*, yielding its famous varnish or lacquer, is another distinctive cultivated tree of North China. In the wild it grows widely in China in exposed, sunny situations. Natural forest trees were probably selected and protected in the loess region at first and later domesticated.

Poisonous juice from the stem produces a lustrous protective coating superior to any other natural varnish known. The fact that the water radical is present in the character *ch'i* indicates the early recognition of the use of the juice. In ancient times lacquer was used for writing on bamboo slips, wooden tablets, and silk. Its earliest known use was for painting patterns on pottery such as those at An-yang sites (*KK* 1976.4). Whether the tree was already in cultivation then cannot be determined. In the *Shih-ching* it is mentioned three times, undoubtedly as a cultivated tree. It is also said that Chuang-tzu was once the official keeper of a lacquer garden, indicating that lacquer tree plantations, official and private, were well established by the Warring States period.

The discovery and development of the use of this unique product demonstrated great ingenuity, for not only is the juice poisonous, but its drying from a clear liquid into a permanent coating requires a long, slow process of oxidation in a moist atmosphere. Perhaps the need for a substance with its qualities encouraged a search among the rather limited flora.

The resultant product proved not only a superior protective material but eventually an important artistic medium.

Other cultivated plants

To conclude this account of the cultivated flora of North China, plants of two additional categories can be mentioned briefly. One category is that of plants used as condiments. The *mei* 梅, Japanese apricot, *Prunus mume*, was used originally as a condiment rather than as a fruit. The *Shu-ching* (Book of History) mentions two products, salt and *mei*, as the chief seasonings for food. *Prunus mume* is a cultigen, probably originating in the southern part of North China. Another important early condiment was the pungent *chiao* 椒, Chinese prickly ash, *Zanthoxylum simulans*, which grows in northern and central China and was first cultivated in the loess highland area. The use of both fruits is mentioned in the *Shih-ching*.

The other group is plants used as dyes. Two herbs were used as dyestuffs from at least the Chou period, as they are mentioned in the *Shih-ching*. One is *liao-lan* 蓼藍, Chinese indigo, *Polygonum tinctorium*, the leaves of which, upon fermentation, yield a fast blue dye. It is still commonly cultivated in North China. The second is *ch'ien* 茜, Chinese madder, *Rubia cordiflora*, a common plant in North China, the root of which produces a reddish dye. The *Shih-ching* refers to the first as *lan* and to the second as *ju-lou* 茹藘.

Characteristics of the Cultivated Flora

Although the natural flora of the North China belt was relatively sparse, a remarkably well-rounded crop complex was developed here. As is typical of relatively cold climates, this was and is predominantly a seed culture. The gathering of nutritious fruits and seeds led to haphazard planting and, eventually, to intensive cultivation of selected species.

The core of the North China crop complex consists of semi-arid species found in the woodland-grassland transition ecospace. The large number of fruit trees, especially of the rose family, is a distinctive feature of this crop complex, as is the inclusion of the mulberry and lacquer tree, with their unique and original human applications.

THE SOUTH CHINA BELT

Lying roughly between the Ch'in Ling and Nan Ling ranges, the South China belt encompasses the vast Yangtze provinces. It includes the extensive lake country of the middle and lower Yangtze with its hills and alluvial plains, the hilly region of southeastern China, and the plateaus in the west, including the upper Yangtze valley. Topographically it is quite distinct from North China; the landscape is much more diverse than the relatively uniform broad plateaus and wide plains of the North China belt. Mountain ridges and narrow valleys alternate. The large plain areas are essentially expanded valley basins, often associated with lakes of all sizes.

Although South China is subject to the effects of the monsoon, its climate is more stable than that of the north, and droughts and floods are much less frequent. Total precipitation is heavier, with a pronounced summer maximum and a heavier winter precipitation. Lower latitudes and higher precipitation allow the growth of a more luxuriant and varied vegetation.

Natural Vegetation

Originally, South China was entirely covered by dense, temperate forests. Cultivation and human habitation have completely altered the aspect of the lower slopes and plains, where secondary growths of planted pines, bamboo, oaks, and other hardwoods now stand. Remnants of natural forest persist, however, especially around Buddhist and Taoist establishments secluded in the mountains. Most of the less accessible regions and higher elevations, particularly in the western highlands, are still covered by natural forests. South China's original vegetation is therefore more readily reconstructed than that of the north.

The Yangtze Valley

Along the middle and lower course of the Yangtze lie the southern part of Kiangsu, northern Chekiang, Anhwei, northern Kiangsi, northern Hunan, and Hupei. The region has a mild, damp climate. Total precipitation is between 100 and 150 centimeters, nearly twice as much as North China's. Although nearly half of the total precipitation is concentrated in three summer months, no month goes without rainfall. With the exception of higher elevations, the temperature does not fall below zero in mean temperature, although temperatures as low as minus fourteen degrees centigrade have been recorded. Average frost-free seasons last from 230 to 280 days.

The main soil types of the extensive Yangtze watershed area are brown forest soils in northern Hupei and Anhwei and yellow earth and red earth in the valleys and hills south of the river. Lower and delta regions of the lower Yangtze are essentially of non-calcareous alluvial soil, now extensively cultivated and highly productive (Wang 1961:96).

Paleobotanical evidence shows that many of the broad-leaved genera were wide spread through the Northern Hemisphere during the Tertiary but survived glaciation mainly in temperate eastern Asia and eastern North America. The floristic composition of the mesophytic forests of the Yangtze valley is especially close to those of Japan and eastern North America (Li Hui-lin 1952). Its richness in endemism, monotypic genera, and archaic plants in the ligneous flora is distinctive in plant distribution patterns (Li 1953).

The Yangtze valley is extensively covered by bodies of water of all sizes and descriptions. The middle and lower course of the river and the lower delta basin is a continuous series of lakes large and small, connected by rivers and canals and interspersed with flood plains or hills; together they form an extensive freshwater environmental system unique in the temperate world. This vast wetland has a long geological history. Shallow epicontinental seas covered the area during the Mesozoic. In the same period the gradual uplifting of the Asiatic continent began (Liu and Chang 1962), which resulted in the formation of numerous lakes and wetlands in central China. Barbour (1935) demonstrated that the middle and lower course of the Yangtze was formed beginning in the late Mesozoic by the linear connection of a series of swamps.

With most of South China covered by dense forest, this huge wetland was the largest open area in prehistoric times. Rich in plant and animal resources, it provided a congenial home to Neolithic man and conditions favorable to his initiation of plant manipulation and domestication.

The Southeastern Provinces

From southern Chekiang and northern and western Fukien through southern Kiangsi and southern Hunan to northern Kwangsi, the hilly southeastern provinces have a warmer and more humid climate than the Yangtze valley. They were originally heavily clothed in evergreen sclerophyllous broad-leaved forests growing primarily from the red earth which covers the rolling hills. An area transitional to the swampy Yangtze basin lies in the north and expanded river valleys are also found there.

Throughout most of the region the original forest cover has been removed and replaced by secondary groves of hardwoods, bamboo, and pines, the latter often in open, parklike stands. *Pinus massioniana* forms the most extensive type of secondary forest, either in pure stands or mixed with xerophytic deciduous hardwoods (Wang 1961:136).

The Southwestern Plateau

Sometimes called the Yunnan-Kweichow highland, the southwestern plateau includes these two provinces except for the southernmost, more tropical part of Yunnan. It shows a great diversity in topography, climate, and vegetation. Most of the area has an altitude of 1,000 to 2,800 meters and is covered primarily by sclerophyllous evergreen broad-leaved forest which is dominated by various species of oaks, especially on the moister slopes and in humid valleys. Pure stands of *Pinus yunnanensis* or mixed stands of pine and oak originally grew on the drier slopes; they are now the most common vegetation.

Montane-boreal coniferous forests are highly developed in north-western Yunnan and adjacent western Szechuan and eastern Tibet, where the average altitude is above 4,000 meters. Situated along the eastern periphery of the Tibetan plateau, the area is traversed by high mountain ridges and deep river valleys. Distinct altitudinal zonation is characteristic of the vegetation.

The Szechwan Basin

The Szechwan Basin includes the greater part of Szechwan, north-western Kweichow, western Hupei, and a small part of northwestern Yunnan in the area around the upper course of the Yangtze. It is a large highland of red sandstone divided into a number of uplands and broad valleys, including the expanded valley basin, the Red Basin, and its en-circling high mountains. Although the soils are very fertile, little level land can be found. High mountains shelter the Red Basin, permitting it a mild and almost frostless winter, unlike the rest of the South China belt at the same latitude. Its growing season lasts the whole year.

Although now a rich agricultural region, the Szechwan Basin was originally heavily forested and was thus unfavorable for primitive cul-tivation. Agriculture and domesticated crops were introduced later; the indigenous flora have contributed only a few cultivated species dating from more recent times.

All the major vegetation types of South China thus converge in the Szechwan Basin at different altitudes. Extensions of the evergreen sclero-phyllous broad-leaved forest of southeastern China grow at lower eleva-tions, extensions of the mixed mesophytic forests of the lower Yangtze valley grow at middle elevations, and montane coniferous forests occur at high altitudes.

At present, with the land cultivated extensively in terraced fields, the original forest cover has been destroyed. Forest remnants occur only in some hill and marginal areas. Subtropical rain forests with *Ficus lacor* and the bamboo *Sinocalamus affinis* occur along rivers at 200–400 meters, especially in the southwest. Cultivation of sugar cane, bananas, oranges, lychees, and longan is possible in the warm, humid climate.

The Cultivated Flora

Rice (tao 稻), *Oryza sativa*, has been the staple cereal for the people of South China since prehistoric times. The consensus is that it is southern Asiatic in origin. According to Te-tzu Chang's summary (1976a : 143), the cultivated species evolved from an annual progenitor over a broad area that extended from the Ganges plains across Upper Burma, northern Thailand and Laos to North Vietnam and southern China. Domestication is thought to have occurred independently and concurrently at many sites inside or bordering this belt (Chang 1976a; 1976b).

In a thorough review of the Chinese literature, Ch'en Tsu-kuei (1958; 1960) comes to the conclusion that rice culture originated in southern China and was introduced to the Honan area of the Huang Ho valley in prehistory. Ho believes comparative archaeological data shows that rice culture in China antedated rice culture in India by at least a thousand years. His review of archaeological and historical records led him to believe that China was one of the original homes of rice and the first area in the world where it was cultivated (Ho 1969b : 20, 24; 1975 : 64).

Neolithic rice remains have been discovered repeatedly in sites along the middle and lower Yangtze basin in recent years, each find pushing back the age of rice culture. Ting (1959) reported the discovery of large quantities of rice husks in baked clay at three sites in Hupei belonging to the Ch'ü-chia-ling culture and dated by both the cultural assemblage and carbon dates to around 2000 B.C. (CKKH shih-yen-shih 1974; Hsia 1977). Later at Chu-chia-chü, Ching-shan-hsien, Hupei, similar rice remains in baked clay were found; and the cultural assemblage there indicated a more primitive early phase of the Ch'ü-chia-ling culture (Hu-pei-sheng 1964). Carbonized rice found at Ch'ien-shan-yang, Wu-hsing, Chekiang (Che-chiang-sheng 1960) was dated to 3310 ± 135 B.C. (CKKH shih-yen-shih 1972; Hsia 1977). The latest significant find at Ho-mu-tu, Yü-yao, Chekiang, where there were rice remains among a rich cultural assemblage (Che-chiang-sheng wen-kuan-hui and Po-wu-kuan 1976; *WW* 1976.8; Che-chiang-sheng and Po-wu-kuan 1978; *KKHP* 1978.1), is carbon-14 dated to 4410 ± 140–5005 ± 130 B.C. (CKKH shih-yen-shih 1977; Hsia 1977). This discovery has given archaeologists (*WW* 1976.8) strong evidence to disprove the theory that the rice of China came from either India or Japan, and it has firmly established South China as the earliest center of origin of rice culture. This early date of domestication is comparable to that of millet culture in North China.

Rice, however, could serve in the formation of an agricultural system only in conjunction with other crops. It is thus necessary to reconstruct the Neolithic complex developed in this southern region.

Aquatic Flora

The site of Ho-mu-tu is located at a very low altitude (Che-chiang-sheng wen-kuan-hui and Po-wu-kuan 1976). At the third and fourth levels of the site, the animal remains are mostly those of aquatic and hilly species. Plant remains are mostly plains grasses together with aquatic plants like *Trapa* and *Phragmites*. There are also sub-tropical hillside trees like *Cinnamomum*, *Choerospondias* (*Spondias*), and *Ficus* and trees of higher, colder climates like pines and hemlocks. These remains indicate that the original environment must have been that of a coastal plain densely covered with lakes and ponds with scattered low hills. The climate was warm and moist, subtropical in nature.

Such a site would be a typical abode for Neolithic man along the Yangtze basin. Diverse adjacent environments were available for him to explore and exploit in his efforts to gather and manipulate plants and plant materials. The outstanding and most prevalent ecological situation was that of the wetlands, where aquatic plants abounded and where rice grew or was being cultivated.

Besides rice, a number of aquatic flowering plants were cultivated extensively for food. Little known to people elsewhere, these are crop plants of a distinct system of farming, a wetland agriculture developed only in the special environment peculiar to the Yangtze basin. Aquaculture (farming of aquatic animals and plants, a term recently coming into general use) has been practiced in China since Neolithic times. The Ho-mu-tu site reveals the presence of *Trapa*, preserved because of its hard fruit shell, and *Phragmites*, a common plant of the Yangtze delta which apparently has sometimes also been cultivated. Other aquatic crops of the Yangtze basin may be of equally early cultivation:

Fruit or seed

Chih 芰, Water-caltrop	*Trapa natans*
Ling 菱, Water-caltrop	*Trapa bicornis*
Ch'ien 芡, Fox nut	*Euryale ferox*
Lien 蓮, Lotus seed	*Nelumbo nucifera*

Rhizome

Ou 藕, Lotus root	*Nelumbo nucifera*
Tz'u-ku 慈姑, Arrowhead	*Sagittaria sagittifolia*
Po-ch'i 荸薺, Water chestnut	*Eleocharis tuberosa*

Cereal (and vegetable)

Ku 菰, Wild rice	*Zizania caduciflora*

Vegetable

Ch'in 芹, Water dropwort	*Oenanthe javanica*
Ch'un 蓴, Water-shield	*Brasenia schreberi*
Yung 蕹, Water spinach	*Ipomoea aquatica*
P'u 蒲, Cattail	*Typha latifolia*

Fiber

Teng-hsin-ts'ao 燈心草, Rush	*Juncus effusus*

The plants that furnished fruits, seeds, or fleshy underground stems rich in starch and sugar and sometimes in protein are still used as staple crops today. These plant parts must be among the food materials, along with fish and other aquatic animals, that were originally gathered by Neolithic man. Long familiarity with these plants eventually led to their cultivation.

Two species of *Trapa*, the two-horned *Trapa bicornis* and the two- or four-horned *T. natans*, with their numerous varieties, are still extensively cultivated in China, especially in the lower Yangtze basin.

The seeds of *Nelumbo* have been frequently discovered in peat bogs of eastern Asia, but these were probably all from wild plants. On the other hand, the finding of two lotus seeds together with millet in pottery jars at a Yang-shao site at Ta-ho-ts'un, Cheng-chou, undoubtedly represents cultivation (Cheng-chou-shih 1973). *Nelumbo* was one of the earliest cultivated plants in China, and both the seed and tuberous rhizome were used as food. The assignment of different logographs to all parts of the plant, flower, seed, rhizome, and even the plumule inside the seed, also attests to its great antiquity.

Sagittaria sagittifolia is widely distributed in the Northern Hemisphere, but its cultivation occurred only in China. The cultivated form is designated either as var. *sinensis* or as a distinct species, *S. sinensis* (Glück 1942). *Eleocharis tuberosa* is a species of long cultivation because it is a cultigen. It is apparently derived from one of the many species of the genus distributed in eastern Asia.

Zizania is unusual among food crops, its use shifting from cereal to vegetable. It is a grass genus with three species, one in eastern Asia and two in North America. One of the North American species, *Z. aquatica*, is the wild rice used by the American aborigines as food but not cultivated. The Chinese species, *Z. caduciflora*, was used originally in ancient China as a cereal, *ku* (also *chiang* 蔣), one of the six grains, *liu ku* 六穀, mentioned in the *Li-chi* (Book of Rites). The stem vegetable was first recorded in the herbals of the Sung dynasty; but in one of them, the *Pen-ts'ao t'u-ching*

(A.D. 1062) an attempt was made to identify this fungus-infested edible stem with the *ch'ü-shu* 蘧蔬 mentioned in the *Erh-ya* (compiled by an unknown author probably in the second century B.C.). It is likely that it was never extensively or intensively cultivated as a grain. It gradually lost significance as a grain when the cultivated plant was infected by the fungus *Ustilago esculentum*, which causes swelling of the young stem. The enlarged stem becomes succulent and sweet during the early stage of infection. Known as *chiao pai* 茭白 or *chiao sun* 茭筍, the infected stem became used as a delectable vegetable and was extensively cultivated in the Yangtze basin for that purpose.

The several leafy vegetables on the list are also cultivated plants of long standing. *Oenanthe* was a common vegetable in ancient China, named both in the *Shih-ching* and the *Chou-li*. In the *Lü-shih ch'un-ch'iu* (third century B.C.) mention is made of the *ch'i* 葟 (*ch'in* 芹) plant of Yün-meng, Hupei, as the greatest delicacy of the vegetable world. *Brasenia* is also mentioned in the *Shih-ching* as *mao* 茆. The antiquity of *Ipomoea* is shown by the fact that it is a cultigen species. *Typha*, mentioned in the *Shih-ching*, grows widely in China and is still cultivated in some parts of the country. Its tender shoots are used as a vegetable just as they were in ancient times.

In addition to the food plants, there was one other economically important plant in ancient times, *Juncus effusus*, formerly cultivated in paddy fields; its slender stems were used in mat and basket making, and the pith of the stem was used as a wick for vegetable oil lamps. According to the great Ming naturalist Li Shih-chen, in his *Pen-ts'ao kang-mu* (A.D. 1560), the earliest record of this plant is found in the *Kuang-chih*, by Kuo Yi-kung, of the late third century A.D.

These aquatic crops are annual or perennial heliophilous herbs that grow naturally in marshlands or lakes. As cultivated plants they are raised as annuals or biennials in ponds or paddy fields, frequently in rotation with rice. The large number of bone spades found at the Ho-mu-tu site (Che-chiang-sheng wen-kuan-hui and Po-wu-kuan 1976:8; Che-chiang-sheng and Po-wu-kuan 1978; *KKHP* 1978.1) shows that agriculture was then already well-developed beyond the slash-and-burn stage and was entering the stage of sedentary farming with rice cultivation and crop rotation. The significance of aquatic or wetland agriculture in the Yangtze basin is demonstrated further by the geography of aquatic plants. Freshwater plant species, unlike most terrestrial ones, characteristically have wide geographical ranges, often extending beyond continental boundaries. All the species considered here occur in countries and continents beyond China, but they are not cultivated anywhere but in China. It is only in the special ecospace of the Yangtze basin that these wide-ranging species of diverse botanical sources evolved coincidentally into a unique agricultural system.

Fruits

Though the flora of South China was far richer than that of North China, it is noteworthy that relatively few fruit trees were domesticated in the south. Furthermore, the southern fruits are juicier and more watery than the northern ones, but none are as nutritious as the jujube, persimmon, peach, and so on, so that they can be used as staple foods. The role of fruits in the north was in the south played by the aquatic fruit and tuber crops closely associated with rice.

The fruits which originated in South China are those of warm-temperate evergreen rather than deciduous trees. They do not indicate great antiquity and appear to have been developed in the hilly districts after agriculture spread from the wetlands to these areas in protohistoric times.

The family Rosaceae, so well developed in the north, is represented only by p'i-p'a 枇杷, the loquat, *Eriobotrya japonica*, an evergreen tree at present extensively cultivated in the lower Yangtze basin. It also grows both wild and cultivated in the hills of western Hupei and Szechwan, where its culture probably first originated (Wilson 1913:29).

Another well-known fruit tree, *yang-mei* 楊梅, *Myrica rubra*, extensively cultivated in the southeastern provinces, probably originated in the hills of northern Chekiang, as wild trees of the species, var. *sylvestris*, are still found in the region, growing in rather poor, rocky soils in semi-shaded areas (Meyer 1911).

Many species of citrus fruits are grown in the warmer parts of southeastern Asia, but because of the prevalent hybridization and apomixis in the genus *Citrus*, it is difficult to ascertain the botanical and geographical origins of the numerous cultivated forms or varieties. Many such variations are known to have originated in the warmer parts of South China, but difficulties in tracing their histories are compounded by confusion in ancient nomenclature and the uncertainty of their botanical identities.

The orange species or varieties known more definitely to be of South Chinese origin are the more cold-resistant ones. The *chü* 橘 of ancient China, later also called *kan* 柑, is undoubtedly *Citrus reticulata*. This is the species that is extensively cultivated in the provinces of South China as far north as the Yangtze basin, with numerous varieties (Hu Hsien-su 1957:834, 838). The northernmost and hardiest variety is the tangerine,

C. reticulata var. *deliciosa*, sometimes treated as a distinct species, *C. deliciosa*.

A review of the history of the orange in ancient Chinese literature by Yeh (1958a : 1958b) shows that the earliest records of the orange in the "Yü-kung" (ca. third century B.C.) and the *Erh-ya* (ca. second century B.C.) refer to it as *Chü-yu* 柚 and *chü*, respectively. *Yu* is now specifically identified with *C. grandis*, a tropical species which was not introduced into South China until later.

A closely related genus of *Citrus*, *Fortunella*, the kumquat, originated in South China, but its cultivation appears to be not earlier than T'ang and Sung times (Yeh 1958b). According to the *Chü-lu* by Han Yen-chih (A.D. 1178), *chin-kan* 金柑, the common species of kumquat, *F. crassifolia*, originated in Kiangsi and was at first unknown to northerners until introduced to the capital, K'ai-feng, around A.D. 1035.

Nut trees are even less developed in South China than other fruit trees. Only two species, both gymnospermous trees native to the mountains of western Chekiang and adjacent Anhwei, are used for their edible nuts. Their cultivation and production is limited geographically and cannot be traced to any great antiquity. Ginkgo (*yin-hsing* 銀杏), *Ginkgo biloba*, whose nut is commonly called *pai-kuo* 白果, was first introduced to K'ai-feng from the southeastern provinces in Sung times (Li Hui-lin 1956). Another nut tree, *fei* 榧, *Torreya nucifera*, also known to have been in cultivation since Sung times, is still cultivated, with several varieties, but only in northern Chekiang (Hu Hsien-su 1927). Both are slow-growing forest trees which are difficult and uneconomical to cultivate, which accounts for their limited cultivation and use.

Legumes

Cultivated beans of the genus *Phaseolus* originated in the warmer regions of both the New and Old Worlds. Several of the species cultivated in eastern Asia from China to India are confused in nomenclature, in their Chinese vernacular as well as in their scientific names. Three species seem to have originated in South China. One is *hsiao-tou* 小豆 or *ch'ih-hsiao-tou* 赤小豆, the rice bean, *Ph. calcaratus*, which grows both cultivated and wild in South China. The earliest records of *hsiao-tou* appear in the *Ta-tai Li-chi* and the *Li-chi* of the first century B.C. (Li Ch'ang-nien 1958a; 1958b). *Ch'ih-tou* 赤豆, the adzuki bean, *Ph. angularis*, a cultigen, is now extensively cultivated in China and Japan. Records of the species, however, can be traced only as far back as the sixth century A.D. to the *Ch'i-min yao-shu*.

Another bean, *lü-tou* 綠豆, the mung bean, *Ph. radiatus*, can also be traced only to the *Ch'i-min yao-shu* (Li Ch'ang-nien 1958a; 1958b). The mung bean is a cultigen, widely cultivated in India as well as in South China; both countries have been suggested as its geographical origin.

Fibers

Three plants cultivated for textile fibers originated in South China. *Ko* 葛, *Pueraria thunbergiana*, commonly called kudzu vine, is mentioned in the *Shih-ching* and was used by the ancient Chinese for making fine fabrics. It grows wild and is cultivated over most of the country but especially in the lower Yangtze provinces of Kiangsu and Chekiang. Its enlarged root is a source of starch. Another fiber plant cultivated since ancient times is *chu-ma* 苧麻, ramie, *Boehmeria nivea*, which yields the famous *hsia-pu* or summer cloth so extensively used in China. In the *Shih-ching* and other classics, the character *chu* 苧 is given as *chu* 紵 (Lu 1958). The plant is cultivated especially along the Yangtze valley, and there are many distinct varieties grown in different areas, each suitable to the particular local climatic and soil conditions.

Vegetables

Apart from the aquatic crops, South China produces only one tuber crop of importance. The *shu-yü* 薯蕷, Chinese yam, *Dioscorea opposita* (long known incorrectly as *D. batatas* or *D. esculenta*), is widely grown and is a native of South China (Ting and Ch'i 1948). Some researchers, however, consider it southern Asiatic in origin.

A number of leafy vegetables are of early South China origin. Some appear as cultigens and are mentioned in ancient literature. These include *hsien* 莧, the edible amaranth, *Amaranthus mangostanus*, and various kinds of mustards: *ch'ing-ts'ai* 青菜, *Brassica chinensis*; *yu-ts'ai*, 油菜, *B. campestris*; and *chieh* 芥, *B. juncea*.

The gourd, *Lagenaria siceraria*, has been used both as a vegetable and as a vessel or container in both North and South China since prehistoric times. The species is of particular interest to students of ethnobotany because it is one of the few plants definitely present in both the Old and the New Worlds in prehistory. Recently, discovery of gourd seeds at the Neolithic site of Ho-mu-tu, Chekiang, establishes without doubt its presence in eastern China seven thousand years ago (Che-chiang-sheng wen-kuan-hui and Po-wu-kuan 1976; *WW* 1976:8; Che-chiang-sheng and Po-wu-kuan 1978; *KKHP* 1978.1). It was apparently an indispensable aid in the everyday life of Neolithic man there, used for implements and as floats for crossing streams before the invention of boats. Many pots found at the Ho-mu-tu site are shaped like the gourd.

A few vegetables which originated in South China represent unique examples of plant exploitation peculiar to the cultivated flora of China. They are luxury foods of low nutritive value but high productive cost. The flower buds of *hsüan* 萱, the day lily, *Hemerocallis fulva*, an ornamental mentioned in the *Shih-ching*, are used as a vegetable called *chin chen ts'ai* 金針菜. The earliest records of this plant as a food can be traced, according to the Ming naturalist Li Shih-chen, to the *Pen-ts'ao t'u-ching* of the Sung period. The bulb scales of *pai-ho* 百合, lilies, *Lilium brownii* and some other species of the genus, are similarly used. *Lilium brownii* is a cultigen. The earliest mention of *pai-ho* as food is found in the *Pen-ts'ao ching* of the second century A.D. Another unique and original use of plant materials as food is that of young bamboo sprouts, a food of very low nutritive value. Bamboos abound in South China, and a number of species are cultivated for the culms as well as for the edible sprouts. These include *k'u-chu* 苦竹, *Sinoarundinaria reticulata* (*Phyllostachys reticulata*), and *mao-chu* 毛竹, *S. pubescens* (*Ph. edulis*), both extensively cultivated south of the Yangtze. It is uncertain how long early bamboos have been in cultivation, but as the culms are useful for many purposes and are an indispensable article for the everyday life of the South Chinese (Li Hui-lin 1942), presumably they were first cultivated for the culms rather than the sprouts. The earliest archaeological find of bamboo is cords made of bamboo fibers at the Ch'ien-shan-yang site in Chekiang (Che-chiang-sheng 1960) carbon-14-dated 2627 ± 133 B.C. (ZK–50; CKKH shih-yen-shih 1977; Hsia 1977).

The culture of the tea plant and the use of tea leaves for a beverage started in China. In tracing the origin of tea, it is first necessary to clarify the taxonomy of the species, *Camellia sinensis*. According to the monographer of the genus *Camellia* (Sealy 1958), there are two varieties in the species, var. *sinensis*, a shrub or small tree, and var. *assamica*, a tall tree with larger, usually thinner leaves. The Chinese variety is a hardier plant cultivated throughout southern China; the Assam variety is indigenous to southern Assam-Burma-Thailand-Indochina-South China. The original tea plant used as a beverage is var. *sinensis*.

The plant has been cultivated so long and so widely in South China that at present it is difficult to ascertain its geographical origin from wild plants in the natural vegetation. Ancient Chinese records indicate widespread spontaneous growth of the tea plant throughout the provinces of South China. When and where tea culture originated seems most clearly elucidated by Ku Yen-wu (in his *Jih-chih lu* ch. 7), who concluded, after reviewing ancient records, that the use of tea started in Shu (Szechwan) and was introduced to central China after the Ch'in conquered Shu, in the fourth century B.C.

Sealy (1958) calls attention to the fact that although var. *assamica* was used in southern Asia as a pickle, for chewing, and for infusion, it was not used as a beverage. Tea drinking and the cultivation of the tea plant definitely started in Szechwan sometime before Ch'in unified the country.

Industrial Plants

Several woody plants, cultivated for various industrial uses, originated in certain regions of South China. No archaeological or historical data indicate the antiquity of their culture, but it can be surmised that they were developed in hilly regions after agriculture was extended from the wetlands to these originally forested lands. Such trees include *wu-chiu* 烏桕, the Chinese tallow tree, *Sapium sebiferum*; *yu-ch'a* 油茶, the tea-oil tree, *Camellia oleifera*; and *t'ung* 桐, the tung-oil trees, *Aleurites montana* and *A. fordii*. *Sapium sebiferum* is cultivated for the oil from the seed and for the fatty matter surrounding the seeds. It grows well and is cultivated throughout South China, especially in the eastern provinces of Kiangsu, Anhwei and Chekiang. *Camellia oleifera* is cultivated throughout South China for the oil from the seeds. The two species of *Aleurites*, also cultivated for the oil from the seeds, are grown in the more southerly and warmer parts of South China.

Characteristics of the Cultivated Flora

Botanical and phytogeographical evidence of the great differences between the environments of North and South China points to the existence of two separate centers of plant domestication (Li Hui-lin 1966). Each center produced a well-rounded complex of crops independently capable of nurturing human culture. Recent archaeological discoveries support this dual-origin thesis. Hsia (1960) was one of the first to note that recently discovered sites along the Yangtze and the southeastern coastal region reveal an economic level comparable to that of the Neolithic sites of the Huang Ho area, but a dissimilar cultural pattern. After studying the notable find at Ho-mu-tu in Yü-yao, Chekiang, and comparing it to the Sian Pan-p'o site in Shensi, he questioned the generally accepted premise of the unilateral origin of Chinese Neolithic culture (Hsia 1977). These two sites are among the earliest dated Neolithic sites in China, carbon-14 dated to before 5000 B.C. They revealed different cultures, each at a similar stage of economic development, depending upon primitive agriculture together with fishing, hunting, food-gathering, and some domesticated animals, but responding to vast differences in natural environment in their own ways.

Rice, already in cultivation during Neolithic times, appears to have been the staple food and the product of the wetland farming which is unique to South China. Lacking the open, transitional grassland-woodland kind of environment which was the site of the origin of cultivation in northern China, the south afforded instead the vast swampland of the middle and lower Yangtze basin. This swampy area provided both the relatively clear spaces and the abundance of heliophilous herbs which encourage crop domestication. In addition to rice, the main cultivated plants included another cereal (*Zizania*), starchy fruit staples (*Trapa*), seeds (*Nelumbo, Euryale*), and tubers (*Nelumbo, Sagittaria*), together with a number of vegetables.

Added to animal resources, these wetland plant foods provided Neolithic man with a readily available, highly nutritious diet. Land plants supplying fibers, protein-rich beans, fruits, and vegetables were introduced into cultivation from the surrounding hilly regions to supplement the wetland core crops. Vegetative propagation was used for a number of tuber plants, in sharp contrast to the predominantly seed-propagated culture of North China.

Comparing the crops of the south and the north today, it is interesting that those of the south are of much less economic and cultural importance. The soybean of the north is more nutritious and versatile than the several southern beans and has largely supplanted the use of other beans through-out China. Southern fruits, such as oranges, loquats, and *Myrica*, are less nutritious than the northern jujube, persimmon, peach, and others; and again, the northern fruits have been adopted in the south. Instead of more staples, southern agriculture tended to produce luxury foods such as tea as a beverage and delicacies like bamboo shoots, day lily buds, and lily bud scales.

THE SOUTH ASIA BELT

The extreme southern part of China belongs phytogeographically to the South Asia belt, which includes Burma, Thailand, and the Indochinese peninsula with the exception of the Malay peninsula, which penetrates into the equatorial South Island belt (Li Hui-lin 1966; 1970). This is the area where rice is generally considered to have originated, perhaps preceded by the more primitive cereal Job's tears, *Coix lachryma-jobi*. Vegetatively propagated tuber crops like yams, *Dioscorea* spp., become important.

Citrus fruits like *Citrus grandis* and *C. limon* probably originated here. Adjunct crops like the cinnamon tree, *Cinnamomum cassia*, the betel nut, *Piper betle*, and the betel palm, *Areca catechu*, are undoubtedly indigenous.

The study of the origin of cultivated plants in this region is complicated by the fact that it is more or less continuous with the important regions of South China in the north, India in the west, and Malaysia in the south. Because this belt is largely beyond the geographical scope of this volume, our discussion will be limited to the Chinese portion. This is the part of China lying south of the Nan Ling mountain range, including Kwangtung and Kwangsi and extending northeast to include coastal Fukien and west to include the southern part of the Yunnan-Kweichow plateau. The land lies mostly south of the Tropic of Cancer. It is practically frost-free and has a year-long growing season. It is largely a dissected highland with rugged topography. The Hsi Chiang, Tung Chiang, and Pei Chiang converge to form a rich alluvial plain, the Canton delta.

The major type of natural vegetation of the hill country and mountains is a sclerophyllous evergreen broad-leaved forest comprised chiefly of oaks (*Quercus, Castanopsis,* and *Pasania*) with an admixture of laurels (Lauraceae) and other trees. In warm and humid valleys and lowlands there is the rain forest, a mixed evergreen broad-leaved forest of the tropics. Most of the lowland is cleared, but areas of well-preserved rain forest still exist in parts of Hainan, Yunnan, and Kwangsi (Wang 1961:155).

The cultivated plants domesticated in this area are primarily indigenous tropical fruit trees. The most famous fruit of southern China is *li chih* 荔枝, the lychee, *Litchi chinensis*. Its cultivation must have started quite early, as it was introduced to the northern Chinese around the first century B.C., when Emperor Wu Ti of Han conquered Nan-yüeh. By the time of Ts'ai Hsiang 蔡襄, who wrote the *Li-chih p'u* 荔枝譜 (A.D. 1059), the first monograph on a fruit tree by a Chinese writer, over thirty varieties were known and recorded. Probably of equal antiquity is *lung-yen* 龍眼, the longan, *Dimocarpus longan* (*Euphoria longan*), a related and similarly well-known fruit tree. Both trees are known only in cultivation (Groff 1921).

Another fruit tree which originated here is the *kan-lan* 橄欖, "Chinese olive", *Canarium album*, used extensively in China as a preserved fruit. It is widely cultivated in Kwangtung today, and wild plants are still to be found in the mountains of Hainan Island. A related species, *wu-lan* 烏欖, *C. pimela* of Kwangtung, is also cultivated for its fruit.

The culture of several citrus fruits probably originated in this area, including the well-known *suan-ch'eng* 酸橙, sour orange, *Citrus aurantium*, and *t'ien-ch'eng* 甜橙, the sweet orange, *C. sinensis*.

In addition to fruit trees, a palm, *p'u-k'uei* 蒲葵, the fan palm, *Livistona chinensis*, has been cultivated in Kwangtung since ancient times for its leaves, which are made into fans used all over the country (Ch'en Yung 1937).

It is impossible to extend the cultivation of trees originating in this tropical region to the north, with the exception of the Red Basin of Szechwan, which enjoys a milder climate than other regions of the same latitude because it is encircled and protected by mountain ranges. The fruits and products of these trees, however, are widely known and used all over China. Most northern plant products are also commonly used in this extreme southern portion of China, which is culturally Chinese and phyto-geographically southern Asiatic.

CONCLUSION

From the phytogeographical evidence, it appears that the earliest cultivated crops upon which Chinese agriculture was founded evolved from the domestication of indigenous plants. The characteristics of this indigenous flora, as well as the natural environment, climate, and geography, have all influenced the evolution of the crucial process of plant domestication. No clear indications of any importation of crops or other outside influence have yet been documented, although the possibility that some cereals were introduced from elsewhere during the early Neolithic age has been raised.

Within this existing flora, early men found the progenitors of a well-rounded crop complex which could provide for the needs of life and their evolving civilization. Although this crop complex is characteristically Chinese, close analysis reveals that not one, but two distinct sets of ancient crops with distinct geographical origins are involved, so that it is appropriate to speak of the dual origin of Chinese agriculture.

The northern area of origin apparently lies in the semi-arid southern part of the loess highland. Here the core of the cultivated flora includes such drought- and cold-resistant food plants as millets, possibly seed-hemp, and fruit trees like jujube, persimmon, chestnut, and hazelnut. In the ecospaces adjacent to the semi-arid core area, more mesophytic but still cold-resistant plants were introduced into cultivation for diverse uses, including many other fruit trees and vegetables, soybeans, the mulberry, and the lacquer tree. The northern crop set was developed from a relatively sparse natural flora, and in most cases the domesticated plants are taxonomically isolated species hardy enough to survive in the harsh environment.

In sharp contrast, the southern site of origin is found in the lower

Yangtze basin, a wet setting of marshes, lakes, and rivers. Aquatic food plants, including rice, possibly seed-*Zizania*, such tuberous plants as the water chestnut, the arrowhead, and the lotus and such fruits as *Trapa* make up the core crops. When wetland farming spread to upland situations, warm, temperate land plants including different kinds of legumes, fruits, and vegetables, and beverage plants such as tea, were introduced into cultivation. Most of these were adjunct or luxury foods. Interestingly enough, despite its much more luxuriant native vegetation and easier climate, the south did not produce a greater number of domesticated plants than the north.

Ssu-ma Ch'ien in his *Shih-chi* ("Huo-chih lieh-chuan") of the first century B.C. described the Yangtze basin as a land low and wet, where man died young, a rich land abounding in plant and animal foods easy to gather, where the incentive for hard work was lacking and humans tended to be lazy and unproductive. Without the compulsion to manipulate his surroundings, southern man developed only a relatively small number of important crops, despite the exceedingly rich and varied natural flora available to him. Living in the cold, dry, rather harsh climate of the loess highland, on the other hand, northern man had to struggle for survival and, out of a sparse natural flora, domesticated a number of crops of great merit.

At present, the two earliest known centers of Neolithic village farming are at Pan-p'o, Hsi-an, in the north and Ho-mu-tu, Yü-yao, in the south. Both have been carbon-14-dated to around 4700–5000 B.C. (Hsia 1977). Incipient agriculture must be at least several millennia older, dating into the early Neolithic period.

Several barriers kept the early northern and southern crop complexes distinct to varying degrees. The lofty Ch'in Ling range, rising between North and South China, was one of the most effective. Not only did it sharply demarcate the different floras of the north and south, but it barred human migration until protohistoric times. To its east, in Honan, lower mountain ranges eventually permitted limited contact in the late Neolithic between northern dryland and southern wetland farming. Farther east in the Huang Ho-Huai Ho plain there are no geographical barriers other than differences in climate; consequently, during the late Neolithic, more agricultural contact and exchange took place there.

The extension of the range of cultivation of plants depends on a number of factors, but for woody plants and perennial herbs, temperature is cardinal. Perennial herbs and woody plants from warm regions are not hardy enough to grow in colder climates, but northern woody plants and perennials are more likely to tolerate a southward move. The effect of northern agriculture on the south has therefore been greater than vice versa. In time the cultivation of northern trees like the mulberry, lacquer tree, peach, apricot, and many others was extended to the south, but southern plants such as tea, oranges, and loquats have not proved hardy enough to survive in the north. Tropical plants such as the lychee, longan, and canarium have been restricted to the warmest parts of South China. Tropical agriculture therefore has had no direct influence on the development of the essentially temperate agriculture of China.

Aside from temperature, other factors such as soil, moisture, disease, and photoperiodism determine whether the ranges of plants which are not woody or perennial can be extended. Since the important annual crops of the north such as soybeans and millet do not find these aspects of the southern environment congenial, they have remained distinctly northern domesticates. Similarly, rice has always been primarily a southern crop.

These barriers, although effective in preventing the extension of cultivation of many plants, have not forestalled the eventual transportation of the end product of cultivation. Though Chinese agriculture can accurately be described as dual in origin as well as in current practice, the use of the products of soybeans, tea, mulberries, hemp, and lacquer, to name only a few, has become a universal and unifying force in the culture that is typically "Chinese."

REFERENCES

Ames, O.
   1939   *Economic Annuals and Human Culture*. Cambridge, Mass.

Andersson, J. G.
   1923   "An Early Chinese Culture." *Bulletin of the Geological Survey of China* 5.1:26.

Barbour, G. B.
   1935   "The Physiographic History of the Yangtze." *Memoirs of the Geological Survey of China*, ser. A, 14:1–112.

Burkill, I. H.
   1953   "Habits of Man and the Origin of the Cultivated Plants of the Old World." *Proceedings of the Linnean Society of London*. 164:12–42.

Chang K'ai 章楷
   1960   "Wo-kuo ts'an-yeh fa-chan kai-shu 我國蠶業發展概述." *Nung-shih yen-chiu chi-k'an* 農史研究集刊 2:109–138.

Chang Kwang-chih 張光直
1959   "Chung-kuo hsin-shih-ch'i shih-tai wen-hua tuan-tai
           中國新石器時代文化斷代." *BIHP* 30.1:259–309.
1968   *The Archeology of Ancient China.* Rev. and enl. ed. New
           Haven.
1977   *The Archaeology of Ancient China.* 3d ed., rev. and enl.
           New Haven.

Chang, Te-tzu
1976a   "The Rice Cultures." *Philosophical Transactions of the
           Royal Society of London* ser. B, 175:143–157.
1976b   "The Origin, Evolution, Cultivation, Dissemination, and
           Diversification of Asian and African rices." *Euphytica*
           15:425–441.

Che-chiang-sheng   Che-chiang-sheng wen-wu kuan-li wei-yüan-hui
           浙江省文物管理委員會
1960   "Wu-hsing Ch'ien-shan-yang yi-chih 1956, 1958 nien fa-
           chüeh pao-kao 吳興錢山漾遺址1956, 1958年發掘報告."
           KKHP 1960.2:73–93.

Che-chiang-sheng and Po-wu-kuan   Che-chiang-sheng wen-wu kuan-li
           wei-yüan-hui 浙江省文物管理委員會 and Che-chiang-
           sheng po-wu-kuan 浙江省博物館
1978   "Ho-mu-tu yi-chih ti-yi-ch'i fa-chüeh pao-kao 河姆渡
           遺址第一期發掘報告." *KKHP* 1978.1:39–94.

Che-chiang-sheng wen-kuan-hui and Po-wu-kuan   Che-chiang-sheng
           wen-kuan-hui 浙江省文管會 and Che-chiang-sheng po-
           wu-kuan 浙江省博物館
1976   "Ho-mu-tu fa-hsien yüan-shih she-hui chung-yao yi-chih
           河姆渡發現原始社會重要遺址." *WW* 1976.8:6–14.

Ch'en Tsu-kuei 陳祖槼
1958   *Tao (shang-p'ien)* 稻(上篇). Chung-kuo nung-hsüeh yi-
           ch'an hsüan-chi chia-lei ti-yi-chung 中國農學遺產選集
           甲類第一種. Peking.
1960   "Chung-kuo wen-hsien shang ti shui-tao ts'ai-p'ei
           中國文獻上的水稻栽培." *Nung-shih yen-chiu chi-k'an*
           農史研究集刊2:64–93.

Ch'en Yung 陳嶸
1937   *Chung-kuo shu-mu fen-lei-hsüeh* 中國樹木分類學.
           Nanking.

Cheng-chou-shih   Cheng-chou-shih po-wu-kuan 鄭州市博物館
1973   "Cheng-chou Ta-ho-ts'un Yang-shao wen-hua ti fang-chi

yi-chih 鄭州大河村仰韶文化的房基遺址." *KK* 1973.6: 330–336.

Chou K'un-shu 周昆叔
1963   "Hsi-an Pan-p'o hsin-shih-ch'i shih-tai yi-chih ti p'ao-fen fen-hsi 西安半坡新石器時代遺址的孢粉分析." *KK* 1963.9: 520–522.

Chu K'o-chen 竺可楨
1972   "Chung-kuo chin wu-ch'ien-nien lai ch'i-hou pien-ch'ien ti ch'u-pu yen-chiu 中國近五千年來氣候變遷的初步研究." *KKHP* 1972.1: 15–38.

Church, C. G.
1924   "Composition of the Chinese Jujube." *United States Department of Agriculture Bulletin* 1215: 24–29.

CKKH and Shen-hsi   CKKH and Shen-hsi-sheng Hsi-an Pan-p'o po-wu-kuan 陝西省西安半坡博物館
1963   *Hsi-an Pan-p'o* 西安半坡. Chung-kuo t'ien-yeh k'ao-ku pao-kao-chi k'ao-ku-hsüeh chuan-k'an ting chung ti-shih-ssu-hao 中國田野考古報告集考古學專刊丁種第十四號. Peking.

CKKH shih-yen-shih   CKKH shih-yen-shih 實驗室
1972   "Fang-she-hsing t'an-su ts'e-ting nien-tai pao-kao (erh) 放射性碳素測定年代報告(二)." *KK* 1972.5: 56–58.
1974   "Fang-she-hsing t'an-su ts'e-ting nien-tai pao-kao (san) 放射性碳素測定年代報告(三)." *KK* 1974.5: 333–338.
1977   "Fang-she-hsing t'an-su ts'e-ting nien-tai pao-kao (ssu) 放射性碳素測定年代報告(四)." *KK* 1977.3: 200–204.

de Candolle, A.
1884   *Origin of Cultivated Plants.* London.

Fukuda, Y.
1933   "Cytogenetical Studies on the Wild and Cultivated Manchurian Soybeans." *Japanese Journal of Botany* 6: 489–509.

Glück, H.
1942   "Critical Research Concerning the Indian Arrowhead (Sagittaria sinensis = S. sagittifolia Auct.)." *150th Anniversary Volume, Botanic Garden Calcutta*: pp. 59–90.

Groff, G. W.
1921   *The Lychee and Longan.* Canton.

Hermann, J. F.
1962　"A Revision of the Genus Glycine and Its Immediate Allies." *United States Department of Agriculture Technical Bulletin* 1268:1–81.

Ho-nan-sheng, Ch'ang-chiang, and Wen-wu　Ho-nan-sheng po-wu-kuan 河南省博物館, Ch'ang-chiang Liu-ch'eng kuei-hua-pien kung-shih 長江流域規劃辦公室, and Wen-wu k'ao-ku-tui Ho-nan fen-tui 文物考古隊河南分隊
1972　"Ho-nan Hsi-ch'uan Hsia-wang-kang yi-chih ti shih-chüeh 河南淅川下王崗遺址的試掘." *WW* 1972.10:6–19, 28.

Ho Ping-ti 何炳棣
1969a　*Huang-t'u yü Chung-kuo nung-yeh ti ch'i-yüan* 黃土與中國農業的起源. *Hong Kong.*
1969b　"The Loess and the Origin of Chinese Agriculture." *American Historical Review* 75:1–36.
1975　*The Cradle of the East: An Inquiry into the Indigenous Origins of Techniques and Ideas of Neolithic and Early Historic China, 5000–1000 B.C.* Hong Kong and Chicago.

Hsia Nai 夏鼐
1960　"Ch'ang-chiang liu-yü k'ao-ku wen-t'i 長江流域考古問題." *KK* 1960.2:1–3.
1972　"Wo-kuo ku-tai ts'an-sang ssu-ch'ou ti li-shih 我國古代蠶桑絲綢的歷史." *KK* 1972.2:12–27.
1977　"T'an-14 ts'e-ting nien-tai ho Chung-kuo shih-ch'ien k'ao-ku-hsüeh 碳-14測定年代和中國史前考古學."*KK* 1977.4:217–232. (Partially translated by Nancy Price in *Early China* 3 [Fall 1977]: 87–93.)

Hu Hou-hsüan 胡厚宣
1972　"Yin-tai ti ts'an-sang ho ssu-chih 殷代的蠶桑和絲織." *WW* 1972.11:2–7, 36.

Hu Hsien-su (Hsien-hsü) 胡先驌
1927　"Synoptical Study of Chinese Torreyas. With Supplemental Notes on the Distribution and Habitat by R. C. China." *Contributions of the Botanical Laboratory Science Society of China* 3.5:1–37.
1957　*Ching-chi chih-wu shou-ts'e* 經濟植物手冊 vol. 2, pt. 1. Peking.

Hu-pei-sheng　Hu-pei-sheng wen-wu kuan-li wei-yüan-hui 湖北省文物管理委員會

1964   "Hu-pei Ching-shan Chu-chia-chü hsin-shih-ch'i yi-chih ti-
        yi-tz'u fa-chüeh 湖北京山朱家咀新石器遺址第一次發掘."
        KK 1964.5:215–219.

Hu Tao-ching 胡道靜
1963   "Shih shu p'ien 釋菽篇." *Chung-hua wen-shih lun-ts'ung*
        中華文史論叢 3:111–120.

Huang Ping-wei 黃秉維
1940–41 "Chung-kuo chih chih-wu ch'ü-yü 中國之植物區域."
        Shih-ti tsa-chih, Kuo-li Che-kiang ta-hsüeh.
        史地雜誌國立浙江大學 1(3):19–20, 1(4):38–52.

Hymowitz, T.
1970   "On the Domestication of the Soybean." *Economic Botany*
        24:408–421.

Keng, Hsüan
1974   "Economic Plants of Ancient North China as Mentioned
        in *Shih Ching* (Book of Poetry)." *Economic Botany*
        28:391–410.

Keng Po-chieh 耿伯介
1958   *Chung-kuo chih-wu ti-li ch'ü-yü* 中國植物地理區域.
        Shanghai.

KK
1959.2 "Shen-hsi Hua-hsien Liu-tzu-chen k'ao-ku fa-chüeh chien-
        pao 陝西華縣柳子鎮考古發掘簡報":71–75.
1972.3 "1971-nien An-yang Hou-kang fa-chüeh chien-pao 1971年
        安陽后岡發掘簡報":14–25.
1976.4 "1975-nien An-yang Yin-hsü ti hsin fa-hsien 1975年安陽
        殷墟的新發現":264–272.

KKHP
1978.1 "Ho-mu-tu yi-chih tung-chih-wu yi-ts'un ti chien-ting yen-
        chiu" 河姆渡遺址動植物遺存的鑒定研究": pp. 95–107.

Ko Chin 葛今
1972   "Ching-yang Kao-chia-pao tsao-Chou mu-tsang fa-chüeh
        chi 涇陽高家堡早周墓葬發掘記." *WW* 1972.7:5–8.

Li Ch'ang-nien 李長年
1958a   *Tou-lei (shang-p'ien)* 豆類(上篇). Chung-kuo nung-hsüeh
        yi-ch'an hsüan-chi chia-lei ti-ssu-chung 中國農學遺產選集
        甲類第四種. Peking.

1958b   "Chung-kuo wen-hsien shang ti ta-tou ts'ai-p'ei ho li-yung
               中國文獻上的大豆栽培和利用." *Nung-yeh yi-ch'an yen-
               chiu chi-k'an* 農業遺產研究集刊 1:77–107.

Li Chi 李濟

1927   *Hsi-yin-ts'un shih-ch'ien ti yi-ts'un* 西陰村史前的遺存.
               Peking.

1931   *An-yang fa-chüeh pao-kao: ti-san-ch'i* 安陽發掘報告:
               第三期. Nanking.

Li Hui-lin 李惠林

1942   "Bamboo and Chinese Civilization." *Journal of the New
               York Botanical Garden* 43:213–223.

1944   "The Phytogeographic Divisions of China: With Special
               Reference to the Araliaceae." *Proceedings of the Academy
               of Natural Sciences of Philadelphia* 96:249–277.

1952   "Floristic Relationships Between Eastern Asia and
               Eastern North America." *Transactions of the American
               Philosophical Society*, n.s. 42.2:371–429.

1953   "Endemism in the Lingneous Flora of Eastern Asia."
               Proceedings of the 7th Pacific Science Congress 5:212–216.

1956   "A Horticultural and Botanical history of Ginkgo."
               Morris Arboretum Bulletin 7:3–12.

1966   *Tung-nan-ya ts'ai-p'ei chih-wu chih ch'i-yüan* 東南亞栽培
               植物之起源. Hong Kong.

1969   "The Vegetables of Ancient China." *Economic Botany*
               23:253–260.

1970   "The Origin of Cultivated Plants in Southeastern Asia."
               Economic Botany 24:3–19.

1974a   "Plant Taxonomy and the Origin of Cultivated Plants."
               Taxon 23:715–724.

1974b   "The Origin and Use of Cannabis in Eastern Asia:
               Linguistic-Cultural Implications." *Economic Botany*
               28:293–301.

1974c   "An Archaeological and Historical Account of Cannabis
               in China." *Economic Botany* 28:437–448.

**Liu Chin-ling 劉金陵, Li Wen-yi 李文漪, Sun Meng-jung 孫孟蓉, and
Liu Mu-ling 劉牧靈**

1965   "Yen-shan nan-lu ni t'an ti pao-fen tsu-ho 燕山南麓泥炭
               的孢粉組合." *Chung-kuo ti-ssu-chi yen-chiu* 中國第四紀
               研究 1.1.

Liu Tung-sheng 劉東生 and Chang Tsung-yü 張宗裕

1962   "Chung-kuo ti huang-t'u 中國的黃土." *Ti-li hsüeh-pao*
               地理學報 *42.*

Liu Yü-ch'üan 劉毓璩
1960   "Shih-ching shih-tai chi su pien 詩經時代稷粟辨." *Nung-shih yen-chiu chi-k'an* 農史研究集刊 2:38–47.

Lu Wen-yü 陸文郁
1958   *Shih ts'ao-mu chin-shih* 詩草木今釋. Tientsin.

Lundegarch, H.
1957   *Klima und Boden in ihrer Wirkung auf das Pflanzenleben.* Jena.

Meyer, F. N.
1911   "Agricultural Explorations in the Fruit and Nut Orchards of China." *United States Department of Agriculture Bureau of Plant Industry Bulletin* 204:1–62.

Pearson, R.
1974   "Pollen Counts in North China." *Antiquity* 48:226–228.

Schimper, A. F. W.
1898   *Pflanzengeographie auf physiologischer Grundlage.* Jena. (English ed.: *Plant Geography upon a Physiological Basis.* Oxford, 1903.)

Schimper, A. F. W., and Faber, F. C.
1935   *Pflanzengeographie auf physiologischer Grundlage*, rev. ed. Jena.

Sealy, J. R.
1958   *A Revision of the Genus Camellia.* London.

Sears, P. B.
1967   "Beyond the Forest." *American Scientist* 55:338–346.

Thomas, C. C.
1924   "The Chinese Jujube." *United States Department of Agriculture Department Bulletin* 1215.

Ting Ying 丁穎
1959   "Chiang-Han-p'ing-yüan hsin-shih-ch'i shih-tai hung-shao-t'u chung ti tao-ku-k'o k'ao-ch'a 江漢平原新石器時代紅燒土中的稻穀殼考查." *KKHP* 4:31–34.

Ting Ying 丁穎 **and Ch'i Ching-wen** 戚經文
1948   "Chung-kuo chih kan-shu 中國之甘藷." *Chung-hua nung-hsüeh hui-pao* 中華農學會報 186:23–33.

Ts'ao Lung-kung 曹隆恭
1960   "Chung-kuo nung-shih wen-hsien shang shu ti ts'ai-p'ei

中國農史文獻上粟的栽培." *Nung-shih yen-chiu chi-k'an*
農史研究集刊 2:94–107.

Tsou Shu-wen 鄒樹文
1960   "Shih-ching shu chi pien 詩經黍稷辨." *Nung-shih yen-chiu chi-k'an* 農史研究集刊 2:18–34.

Vavilov, N. I.
1926   "Studies on the Origin of Cultivated Plants." *Trudy po prikladnoi botanike, genetike i selektsii [Bulletin of applied botany, genetics and plant breeding]* 16.2:139–248.
1949–1950   "The Origin, Variation, Immunity and Breeding of Cultivated Plants." Translated by K. S. Chester. *Chronica Botanica* 13:1–336.

Walker, E. H.
1944   "The Plants of China and Their Usefulness to Man." *Annual Report of the Smithsonian Institution*: pp. 334–339.

Wang Chi-wu
1961   *The Forests of China: With a Survey of Grassland and Desert Vegetation*. Maria Moors Cabot Foundation Publication 5. Cambridge, Mass.

Whitaker, T. W., Cutler, H. C., and MacNeish, R. S.
1957   "Cucurbit Materials From Caves Near Ocampo, Tamaulipas." *American Antiquity* 22:353–358.

Wilson, E. H.
1913   *A Naturalist in Western China*. 2 vols. London.

WW
1976.8   "Ho-mu-tu yi-chih ti-yi-chi fa-chüeh kung-tso tso-t'an-hui chi-yao 河姆渡遺址第一期發掘工作座談會紀要":
          15–17, 37.

Yeh Ching-yüan 葉靜淵
1958a   *Kan-chü (shang-p'ien)* 柑橘(上篇). Chung-kuo nung-hsüeh yi-ch'an hsüan-chi chia-lei ti-shih-ssu-chung 中國農學遺產選集甲類第十四種. Peking.
1958b   "Chung-kuo wen-hsien-shang ti kan-chü ts'ai-p'ei 中國文獻上的柑橘栽培." *Nung-yeh yi-ch'an yen-chiu chi-k'an* 農業遺產研究集刊 1:109–163.

Yu Hsiu-ling 游修齡
1976   "Tui-Ho-mu-tu yi-chih ti-ssu wen-hua-ts'eng ch'u-t'u tao-ku ho ku-ssu ti chi-tien k'an-fa 對河姆渡遺址第四文化層出土稻谷和骨耜的幾點看法." *WW* 1976.8:20–23.

1977   "Hu-lu ti chia-shih—ts'ung Ho-mu-tu ch'u-t'u ti hu-lu chung-tzu t'an-ch'i 葫蘆的家世—從河姆渡出土的葫蘆種子談起." *WW* 1977.8:63–64.

Zohary, D., and Spiegel-Roy, P.
1975   "Beginnings of Fruit Growing in the Old World." *Science* 187:319–326.

3

The Origins and Early Cultures of the Cereal Grains and Food Legumes

TE-TZU CHANG

Productive agriculture is the backbone of all flourishing civilizations. Prehistoric civilization in China began to bloom and spread when concurrent progress in crop production was made in the central plain, in areas bordering the southern banks of the lower Yangtze Chiang basin, and probably in the adjoining areas. *Shu* 黍 (millet), *chi* 稷 (millet), *tao* 稻 (rice), *mai* 麥 (barley and wheat), and *shu* 菽 (soybeans)—the five cereals mentioned in mythological writings—provided the basic necessities for the eventual expansion and development of Chinese civilization.

This chapter synthesizes the early history of the major food crops based on information drawn from several disciplines. The ecological, edaphic, and biotic environments are also discussed to provide additional perspectives.

MILLETS

Taxonomy and nomenclature

Among the five cereals mentioned in the Chou classics, *shu* 黍 and *chi* 稷 undoubtedly referred to the millets. But at the species level, Chinese and Japanese scholars have not been able to agree on which of these Chinese

NOTE: I am particularly indebted to Amano Motonosuke, Chang Kwang-chih, Theodore Hymowitz, Kao Ch'ü-hsün, and Robert Orr Whyte for providing me with articles that would not otherwise have been accessible. I am also grateful to Lloyd T. Evans and R. O. Whyte for their critical review of the manuscript.

characters should be identified with *Panicum miliaceum* L. and which with *Setaria italica* (L.) Beauv. Appearance of names such as *su* 粟 and *liang* 梁 at later dates has added confusion.

The problems of nomenclature stem from a lack of botanical description of *shu* and *chi* in the early writings. The two species, in any event, have rather few distinctive features: *S. italica* has a spike-like panicle, simple and loose spikes, an involucre of bristles below each spikelet, and lemmas and paleas adhering to the grain, while *P. miliaceum* has a slender, drooping panicle and is awnless (Purseglove 1972: 198, 257; Rachie 1975: 3–4). After threshing, the grains of the two species are rather difficult to distinguish (Robbins 1917: 212–218) except for the high glans in *miliaceum*, the mat in *italica*, and the longer and more slender embryo of *italica* (Krishnaswamy 1938). Studies by Tsou (1960) and Liu Yü-ch'üan (1960) have, therefore, failed to relate *shu* and *chi* to the appropriate botanical species or to one of the three botanical varieties under *P. miliaceum: effusum, contractum,* and *compactum* (Robbins 1917: 215).

On the other hand, all scholars of China and Japan have agreed that *shu* was used to indicate *P. miliaceum*. But *chi* was either considered as the starchy (non-glutinous) type of *miliaceum* (Kishimoto 1941; Liu 1960; Ho 1969a; 1975; Li Hui-lin 1970) or as *S. italica* (Yü Ching-jang 1956, 1958; Tsou 1960; Hsü Cho-yün 1971). *Su* and *liang* have invariably been interpreted as *S. italica* (Kishimoto 1941; Kitamura 1950; Yü 1956, 1958; Tsou 1960; Ho 1969b). It is thought that *liang* could have been a superior type of *su* (Hsü 1971).

Antiquity and Importance

Both *shu* and *chi* were recorded in the Shang bone oracles (Liu 1960: 39; Li Hsiao-ting 1965: 2315–2351). In the *Shih-ching*, *shu* and *chi* appeared as separate names twenty-eight and sixteen times respectively and were mentioned jointly sixteen times (Liu 1960). Therefore, the importance of both millets as food in the Chung Yüan, the central plains area, is beyond dispute. The finding of millet grains later identified as *S. italica* at the Pan-p'o site near Sian (CKKH and Shen-hsi 1963: 46, 215) dated to between 4773 and 4294 B.C. (ZK–38; ZK–127) (Hsia 1977b: 229) have confirmed its predominance since the beginning of the Yang-shao period, around 5000 B.C. (K. C. Chang 1975). *Panicum miliaceum* was found at Ching-ts'un, southern Shansi (Bishop 1933; cited by Ho 1975: 58), but the same sample has also been interpreted as a weedy form (Chang 1977: 95). Remains of millets were also found at the P'ao-ma-ling site in Kiangsi

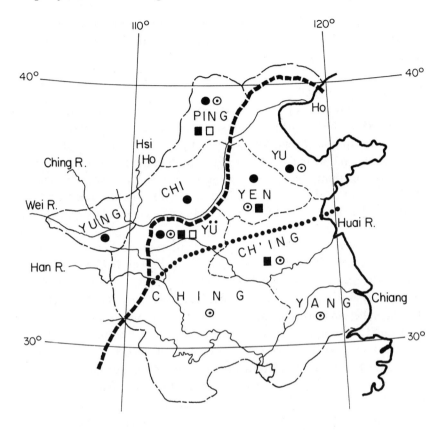

MAP 3.1. **Geographic distribution of the cereals and of soybeans in the nine** *chou* **(districts) during Chou, showing the eastward shift of rice cultivation later. (Adapted from Herrmann 1966:7, 12.)**

province (Chang 1973), which is dated to 2807 B.C. (ZK–51) (Hsia 1977b:230).

During the Chou dynasty, millets comprised the staple crop of Yung-chou and Chi-chou; two of the three staple crops in Yu-chou; two of the four major crops in Yen-chou; and two of the five crops in Ping-chou and

Yü-chou (map 3.1). From the Spring and Autumn to the Warring States periods (722–256 B.C.), millets and soybeans were the staples of the north (Liu 1960).

Origin and Evolution

The nearest relative of *S. italica* is probably *S. viridis* L. (Koernicke and Werner 1885). The two taxa have the same chromosome number (2n = 18). Normal metaphase chromosomes in the F_1 hybrid, high F_1 pollen, and seed fertility and normal character segregation in the F_2 indicate that the two taxa apparently have the same genome A (Kihara and Kishimoto 1942; C. H. Li et al. 1942; H. W. Li et al. 1945). Another weed species, *S. faberii* Herrm., collected from Ch'eng-tu in Szechwan, has genomes A and B (Li et al. 1942).

Setaria viridis is an Old World species that grows wild from the northeast provinces to the southwest of China (H. W. Li et al. 1945; K. C. Chang 1977). Because it was also found in India, Africa, and southern Europe and its diversity was considerable in India, Krishnaswamy (1938) concluded that the millets in Europe came from North China. *Setaria italica* has also been found at the sites of the Lake Dwellers in Western Europe (ca. 500 B.C.) but is unknown in Iran, Syria, and Greece (Laufer 1919:565; Purseglove 1972:257). Ho has reviewed the relative chronology of the millets in China, India, Persia, Europe, and Africa (1969a:133; 1975:57–60) and concluded that millet cultivation in China preceeded that in the other areas.

Panicum miliaceum is generally considered indigenous to North China (Krishnaswamy 1938; 1951; Vavilov 1951; Zeven and Zhukovsky 1975), though de Candolle (1884) and Watt (1891) viewed it as native to Egypt and Arabia and as an early introduction into India. A weedy type, *P. spontaneum* Lysev., may be the closest relative of *P. miliaceum*. The weedy race is found in Afghanistan, Kazakhstan, and Mongolia (Mansfeld 1959; cited by Zeven and Zhukovsky 1975). Another millet found in India and Southeast Asia is *P. sumatrense* (little millet), which has the same chromosome number as *miliaceum* (2n = 36) and can thrive under adverse conditions (Purseglove 1972:201). It would be worthwhile to examine the genetic relationship between *P. miliaceum* and *P. sumatrense* to determine whether *sumatrense* is a close relative of *miliaceum*.

Changes During Domestication

The domestication process from *S. viridis* to *S. italica* probably involved the following changes: prostrate to erect growth habit; increase in plant height and panicle length; extension of growth duration; loss of pigments on vegetative organs, anthers, bristles, pericarp, and endosperm; decrease in shattering; and increase in grain weight (Kihara and Kishimoto 1942; H. W. Li et al. 1945).

Culture of Millets

Both *P. miliaceum* and *S. italica* are adapted to semi-arid climates and infertile soils. The former probably matures earlier and is more resistant to prolonged drought than the latter (Purseglove 1972:199). They are adaptable to many soils, including alkali soils (Liu Yü-ch'üan 1960).

The millets require less intensive care than other cereals and probably fitted well into the primitive agriculture of the prehistoric era. At the Pan-p'o site, stone tools for cultivation (e.g., axes, spades, shovels, knives)—primarily for digging—were found along with stone instruments for grinding and pounding grain. Excavated areas for storing grain were also found at the sites. The houses had walls, roofs, and fireplaces. There were pigs and dogs, probably confined by fences. The presence of animal hide and of bone fish hooks suggests a combination of hunting and fishing, along with crop cultivation (millets and *Brassica* species). Some of the land may have been cleared by burning the natural vegetation (CKKH and Shen-hsi 1963:46, 59). At Miao-ti-kou (Honan) and Pan-p'o (Shensi), the early settlements appear to have involved shifting and repetitive occupations (K. C. Chang 1977:97). Some earlier scholars have considered the Yang-shao villages large, sedentary communities (Cheng 1959:69).

During the Shang dynasty, crop cultivation was largely outside the settlements, as inferred from the archaic characters *k'en-t'ien* 墾田 on the bone oracles (Yü Hsing-wu 1972). Stone hoes, spades, and probably wooden digging sticks were used during the Yang-shao period (Chang 1977:91). Bronze and wooden tools came into use during the Chou dynasty (Liu 1960). In the ideal administration depicted by the *Chou-li*, numerous officials were appointed to direct the tillage, planting, and irrigation (Lee 1921:44).

Alternate cultivation and fallowing in three-year cycles was described before the third century B.C. (in the *Chou-li*; see Ho 1975:52). Fallowing was intended for conserving soil moisture rather than fertility (ibid., p. 51). The use of draft animals and manure probably began during the Shang (Ts'ao 1960; Hsü Cho-yün 1971) and was widely used in the Spring and Autumn period (Hsia 1977a). About the same time, weeding, mid-season tillage, and hilling around plants appeared in writings (Liu 1960). Iron tools came into use during the Warring States period (Hsü 1971).

Early cultivators recognized the drawbacks of continuously planting millets on the same piece of land. Soybeans entered into a rotation system with millets during a period from the fifth to the third century B.C. (Li Ch'ang-nien 1958). Soon wheat and barley entered into rotation with the millets (Ts'ao 1960).

From the dawn of agriculture in the central plain down to the Spring and Autumn period, *chi* and *shu* were two dominant crops. *Chi* was such an important crop in the loess highlands that the people of the Chou dynasty gave the name Hou Chi 后稷 (Lord of millet) to their legendary ancestor. *Su* (millet) and soybeans were predominant crops during the Warring States period. *Su* and *mai* (barley and wheat) were the principal cereals through the Han period (Liu 1960; Hsü 1971).

Odes in the *Shih-ching* suggest a large-scale community type of farming, although family farms are also indicated. Farming, weaving, and hunting were concurrently practiced up to the early Spring and Autumn period (Hsü 1971). Family-unit farms probably replaced community farms from the end of the Western Chou (Lee 1921; Amano 1962).

RICE

Origin of the Chinese Rices

Rice (*Oryza sativa* L.) was also among the five cereals mentioned in Chinese myths about ancient times, though until recently the validity of the inference that it originated in China has been questioned by Indian, British, and Russian botanists and historians. China was not considered a primary habitat for the evolution of cultivated rices because of the dearth of wild species there (Vavilov 1932; 1951; Zukovskij 1962; Ramiah and Ghose 1951; Richharia 1960; Darlington 1963; Nayar 1966; Buth and Saraswat 1972). The water supply in Shensi and southern Shansi provinces appears to have posed difficulties for growing flooded rice (Watson 1969). The implications have been that cultivated rice was introduced from southern and southeastern Asia less than four to five millennia ago (Watt 1891; Watson 1969; 1971). On the other hand, de Candolle (1884:387) argued that rice cultivation in China preceded that in India.

It is now known that the immediate wild relatives of the cultigen—*O. rufipogon* Griff., *O. nivara* Sharma *et* Shastry, and the *spontanea* forms of *O. sativa*—have been found to exist in Kwangtung, Kwangsi, Yunnan, Taiwan, and Kiangsu and on Hainan island (Ting 1933; T. T. Chang 1975; Nan 1975; Kuang-tung 1975). The character for wild rice (*ni* 秜) and other characters (*li* 離, *lü* 穭, 秞) appeared in early historical records (Ting 1957). The occurrence of self-perpetuating wild rices in South China was described in the *Shan-hai-ching* around 207 B.C. (ibid). The northernmost

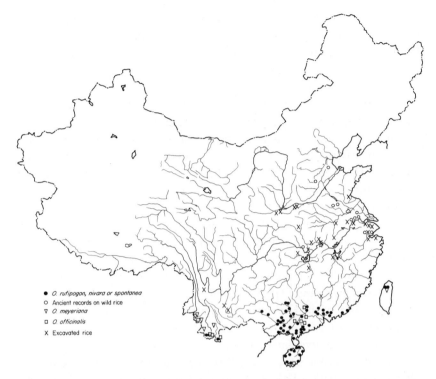

MAP 3.2. **Geographic distribution of (a) wild rices recorded in ancient writings, (b) the wild species of *Oryza* found during the twentieth century, and (c) excavated rice remains.**

distribution reached about 38° north latitude, near the gulf of Chihli (Ting 1961). As recently as 1950, *spontanea* rices of the *keng* 粳 type were found in Tung-hai-hsien, Kiangsu province (Nan 1975). Other wild species found in China are *O. officinalis* Wall. *ex* Watt and *O. meyeriana* Baill. (Ting 1961). The geographic distribution of the wild rices in southern and southwestern China is shown in map 3.2.

According to my hypothesis of the Gondwanian origin of the genus *Oryza*, the progenitors of about half of the twenty species in the genus would probably have been present on the South Asian Plate (the Indian Plate and its associated portion of mainland Southeast Asia) before the fracture of the supercontinent beginning in the early Cretaceous. The Asian species of *Oryza* would have spread to adjacent areas following the drift and subsequent union of the South Asian Plate with the Asian mainland (Chang 1976a; 1976b; 1976c; 1976d). (Recent geological findings on the northern slope of Mount Everest reveal the presence of Gondwanian facies and fossil remains of four plant genera [Yin and Kuo 1978], which suggests that fragments of the Indian Plate extend into the Chinese side of the Himalayan mountain range.) Another implication is that contacts between the people of China and those in southern and southeastern Asia may have taken place in prehistoric times.

The northward dissemination of rices, both cultivated and wild-annual, was likely a slow-moving process largely from one homestead or clan to another. The cultivation and domestication processes could have taken place concurrently and independently at many sites along the route of dispersal. Early traders could also have carried rice as both food and merchandise (Lu and Chang 1980).

Most rice researchers now agree that the area of the greatest diversity of *O. sativa* is located in a belt that extends from the Assam-Meghalaya area in India to mountain ranges in mainland Southeast Asia and southwest China (Chang 1976b; 1976c). Many of the early-maturing and drought-escaping annual forms probably emerged during the Neothermal period (about fifteen thousand to ten thousand years B.P.) along the southern and northern slopes of the Himalaya (Whyte 1972; Chang 1976b).

The temperate race of *O. sativa*, *keng* 稉, 粳 (also known as Japonica), probably became differentiated from the tropical race Indica (known as *hsien* 秈, 籼, in China since A.D. 121) in Yunnan and Kweichow provinces when it was distributed along the hilly slopes (Ting 1957; Liu Tzu-ming 1975; Chang 1976c). The *keng* race was brought into the central plain along the ancient overland trade route that passed through Yunnan, Szechwan, and Shensi (Herrmann 1966:9). *Keng* rices also spread to the T'ai Hu 太湖 area and the elevated areas in the south and southwest (Ting 1949; Chang 1976b; 1976c).

The Antiquity of *hsien* and *keng* Rices

The *hsien* rices could have dispersed via two primary routes. In and around the triangle bordering northeast India, northern Burma, northern Thailand, and southwestern China, the *hsien* type became markedly diversified (T. T. Chang 1976b). *Hsien*, mixtures of *hsien* and *keng*, and *keng* types can still be found at the lower, middle, and higher elevations, respectively, in the hills of Yunnan (Ting 1961; Kuang-tung and Yün-nan 1974). The *hsien* type and its wild relatives could also have been brought from Indochina and dispersed along the seacoast up to Hupei (Chang 1976b).

Hsien later became the predominant race in China, covering most of the production areas south of the Yangtze Chiang (Ting 1949). The oldest sample of *hsien* rice found in the lower Yangtze delta to date is from the

Ho-mu-tu site in Yü-yao-hsien, Chekiang (Che-chiang-sheng and Po-wu-kuan 1976). The rice grains, hulls, straw, and stems excavated from Ho-mu-tu are dated to 5008 ± 117 B.C. (BK–75057) (Hsia 1977b). The rice grains found at the site were identified as the *hsien* type (Yu 1976). The dimensions of the carbonized grains vary considerably in length and width, ranging, in my judgment, between those of the *spontanea* rices and modern cultivars. On the other hand, the grains unearthed at Sung-tse, Ch'ing-p'u-hsien, near Shanghai (Shang-hai-shih 1962), dated to about 4042 ± 149 B.C. (ZK–55) (Hsia 1977b), fall within the range of present-day cultivars. The samples from Ho-mu-tu preceded the Chalcolithic sample found in India dated to 4,530 b.c. (Vishnu-Mittre 1976), as well as the Non Nok Tha sample of Thailand estimated as of about 3500 b.c. (Bayard 1970; Solheim 1972). The Non Nok Tha specimen has been identified as an essentially wild form (Chang 1976b; 1976c).

The oldest finding of remains of *keng* rice in North China still belongs to the site at Yang-shao excavated by Andersson and others (Edman and Söderberg 1929; Andersson 1934), estimated at between 3200 and 2500 b.c. (K. C. Chang personal communication, 1978). By the Chou dynasty, rice cultivation was well established in North China, particularly in the lower Huang Ho valley (Ting 1949; Amano 1962; Nan 1975).

The oldest specimens of *keng* rice in the Yangtze Chiang basin were found at Ch'ien-shan-yang, Chekiang province (ZK–49, 3311 ± 136 B.C.), and Ch'ü-chia-ling, Hupei (ZK–125, 2696 ± 190 B.C.) (Ting 1959; Che-chiang-sheng 1960; Hsia 1977b). A carbonized specimen found at Hai-men-k'ou in Yunnan is estimated at 1308 ± 105 B.C. (Yün-nan-sheng 1958; ZK–10, Hsia 1977b).

Domestication and Ecological Diversification

The true domestication process probably first took place in China because the cooler weather and shorter crop season there exerted great selection pressure on the early cultivars and made them more dependent on human care for perpetuation than were their tropical counterparts. The quantities of rice remains (grains, hulls, stems, and leaves) found at Ho-mu-tu were not only large, but they also predated similar findings in southern and southeastern Asia.

Northward dispersal of the *keng* type resulted in varietal types that were shorter in growth duration, less sensitive to the photoperiod, thriftier in vegetative growth, tolerant to cool night temperatures, longer in the grain-ripening period, and heavier in grain weight than their tropical prototype, the Indica race. Concurrent changes involved increases in grain thickness and grain weight, decrease in the amylose-to-amylopectin ratio, and decreases in (or losses of) primitive characteristics such as shattering, grain dormancy, and internode elongation ability (T. T. Chang 1976c). Because these changes took place in China long before cultivation began in Japan, the temperate race is more accurately designated as Sinica (Chang 1976b; 1976c) than by the widely used name of Japonica (Kato et al. 1930).

The *hsien* (Indica) rices of China were also earlier in maturity and thriftier in vegetative growth than the tropical cultivars of the same ecogeographic race. But the grains were generally smaller and lighter than some of the big-and-bold-grained varieties of Southeast Asia.

A distinct feature of the ecological diversification of both Indica and Sinica races in China is the lack of varietal types strongly adapted to deep water or dryland cultivation—a strong contrast to the diverse ecotypes found in southern and southeastern Asia (Chang 1976c; Chang and Oka 1976). Although the planting of rice in deep water or on floating wooden frames was mentioned in writings of later periods (Amano 1962), such plantings were of insignificant acreage and were largely discontinued in later years.

The predominantly lowland type of rice adapted to shallow water also indicates that Chinese cultivators exercised great care in water control (irrigation and drainage) from the early days of rice cultivation. Thus, the rice cultivars of prehistoric China were true domesticates in the context of Helbaek (1969) long before rice cultivation began in many areas to the south.

Cultivation Practices

Rice was probably a minor food, supplementing the millets and legumes, in the central plain prior to the Chou dynasty. It was grown on marshy but flood-free sites around river bends of the Huang Ho tributaries in Honan and Shensi provinces (Ho 1969a: 155). The sites were generally between small rivers and wooded hills (K. C. Chang 1977: 174). The total area of rain-fed rice was small.

The rice crop was directly seeded, probably by broadcasting (Ting 1949; T. T. Chang 1976b). The varieties were predominantly awned and early-maturing (Ting 1957).

Much of the skepticism about growing rice in the central plain stemmed from the mistaken notion that it grows only in a continuously flooded field (Watson 1969; 1971). The early sites of rice cultivation probably had high water tables or were occasionally covered by flood water or both. The climate of the area was more humid than at present (K. C. Chang 1968; Ho

1969a). Indeed, the rice cultivars have become so diversified that the hill rices of southern and southeastern Asia are frequently interplanted with corn in dryland culture, depending on rainfall as slight as five to seven hundred millimeters in the crop season (O'Toole and Chang 1978).

Archaeological findings in earlier sites in Chekiang and Kiangsu provinces indicate that rice, shellfish, other fish, pigs, fruits, and legumes constituted the main diet from the dawn of agriculture. Spades or hoe blades (*ssu* 耜) made of stones or the bones of large animals were probably used in preparing the fields (Che-chiang-sheng and Po-wu-kuan 1976). A wooden spade was found at the second layer of the Ho-mu-tu site, dated to 3718 ± 135 B.C. (Yu 1976; BK–75058). Pigs, dogs, and probably water buffalo were the domesticated animals. The rice growers lived in houses made of cut timber joined by mortise and tenon. Clay pots served as cooking utensils (Che-chiang-sheng and Po-wu-kuan 1976).

It is conceivable that the relatively warm climate and swampy habitat south of the Yangtze Chiang allowed wild rices to be readily self-perpetuated by the shattering grains and therefore made possible the gathering of grains from wild populations in low-lying areas for several millennia prior to the estimated 5008 B.C. date (BK–75057) of the Ho-mu-tu site.

Agricultural technology in the north is likely to have been relatively more advanced than that in the Yangtze basins prior to the Chou dynasty. But the culture in those areas later known as Ch'u 楚 and Yüeh 越 was not as primitive as many traditional historians have generally held, based solely on the writings of historians who resided in the north and rarely traveled. An example of traditional historians' impressions can be found in Ho (1975:55, 374).

Findings from the Sung-tse and Ch'ien-shan-yang sites indicate differences in wealth and signs of private ownership between 4042 and 3311 B.C. (Wu 1975; ZK–55, ZK–49). Moreover, as the production of rice began to expand, much of the refined technique in the complicated process of rice culture and post-harvest processing was developed south of the central plain, probably in the Han, Huai, and middle and lower Yangtze basins (T. T. Chang 1976b). The people of Ch'u and of Wu 吳 were skillful in making iron implements (K. C. Chang 1968), some of which might have been used for rice tillage.

Planting by broadcasting seeds into low-lying areas was probably the initial method of cultivation. The slash-and-burn approach predominated in the forested areas of the Yangtze valley. On elevated grounds, seeding was probably done by the dibbling method (T. T. Chang 1976b).

Transplanting is first mentioned in Eastern Han (A.D. 23–220) writings (Amano 1962:183); no description of its evolution is available. I surmise that transplanting came about from efforts to fill in spots of missing stand with plants taken from densely sown spots in a broadcast crop. Success with the replanting process and recognition of its benefits led to the widespread practice of transplanting, the advantages of which have been enumerated by Nishiyama (1949) and T. T. Chang (1976b).

Waterworks began about 700 B.C., initially for flood control (mentioned in the *Shih-ching* ["Pai hua," Mao 229]). Irrigation projects are recorded in Honan as early as 563 B.C. and in the central Yangtze valley in 548 B.C. (Ting 1961; Ho 1969b).

Writings in the *Chou-li* indicate that by the Chou dynasty rice was extensively grown in the districts (*chou*) of Yang (southern Kiangsu) and Ching (Hunan and Kiangsi) as well as Yu, Ping, Yen, Ch'ing, and Yü (map 3.1). The appointment of "rice men" (*tao-jen* 稻人) to supervise the planting and irrigation of rice fields (third century B.C.) indicates the desire to organize rice cultivation in the community. The combined use of burning and flooding to control weeds is also mentioned in the *Chou-li*.

The Impact of Rice Cultivation

Rice is easier to cook than other cereals. This tasty and productive grain gradually replaced other cereals in all areas where it could be grown.

As the climate in North China became increasingly semi-arid following extensive deforestation in the northwest (K. C. Chang 1968), rice cultivation moved east and south to more humid areas (see map 3.1) (T. T. Chang 1976b). Rice cultivation began in the Korean peninsula at least before the sixth century B.C. (Kim 1977; Won-Yong Kim personal communication, 1978). Japan acquired its rices from the lower Yangtze Chiang basin (Andō 1959) or from Korea or both (T. T. Chang 1976b; 1976c). The earliest finding of rice in Japan dates to the third century B.C. (Morinaga 1967).

Although no information is available concerning the size of the human population and rice production statistics in prehistory, it can be inferred that the spread of rice cultivation generally led to larger population increases than was the case with other food crops because rice has the highest digestible energy (96.3 percent, versus 86.4 percent for wheat and 87.2 percent for millet; Eggum, 1979) and is labor-intensive.

The mass migration of people from the north to the Yangtze valley and to points further south during the Chin and Sung dynasties (A.D. 317–1279) was not only largely supported by rice production in the southern areas but also provided impetus for the dramatic expansion later of the irrigated rice area in the middle and lower Yangtze Chiang basins (Ting 1961; Amano 1962). Rapid population increase in China following the spread of the Champa rices (Ho 1956) further suggests that such a trend was highly probable, though to a lesser extent, in prehistory.

BARLEY AND WHEAT

Antiquity and origin

Mai 麥 was one of the five cereals mentioned in the Chou classics. The archaic character for *mai* was found in the bone oracles of the Shang ruins. Also found in Shang oracles was the character *lai* 乘, 來. *Lai* has frequently been interpreted to represent wheat (Shinoda 1951; Yü-Hsing-wu 1957; Hu Hsi-wen 1958; Li Hsiao-ting 1965), while *mai* has been taken as referring to barley (Kitamura 1950; Shinoda 1951; Yü 1957). It is also thought that another character, *mou* 牟, found in Chou texts, may have referred to barley (Shinoda 1951; Yü 1957).

Mai was one of the frequently mentioned cereals of the Shang dynasty, next in frequency to *shu*. But the production of *mai* in North China appears to have been limited during the Shang period (Yü 1957).

Because *lai* means "come" and the characters *lai*, *mai*, and *mou* all lack the *ho* 禾 radical, the origin of these grains has been interpreted as foreign. The period of introduction from the Near East has been estimated as in the second millennium B.C. or slightly earlier (Ho 1975; Harlan 1976). On the other hand, the recent finding of wild taxa, *H. spontaneum* C. Koch and *H. langunculiforme* Bacht., in Szechwan and Tibet has led some to postulate that *H. spontaneum* and the cultivated two- and six-row barleys were indigenous to the plateau of southwest China (Shao, Li, and Baschan 1975; Hsü T'ing-wen 1975). Cultivation of the barleys in the plateau area prior to their introduction into North China seems probable.

The oldest finding of carbonized wheat kernels comes from Tiao-yü-t'ai, Po-hsien, Anhwei Province. The sample resembles *T. antiquorum* Heer. Chin (1962) estimated that its age was early Hsia, but a carbon-14 dating, based on an insufficient sample of the wheat, yielded 504 ± 138 B.C. (ZK–252; Barnard 1980:3). A semi-wild wheat (*T. aestivum* ssp. *Junannensis*) has been found recently in Tibet (Shao, Li, and Baschan 1979).

Barley

The genus *Hordeum* has a diffused pattern of genetic diversity. The origin and evolution of the cultivated barleys (*Hordeum vulgare* L.) has been reviewed by Takahashi (1955), Helbaek (1966), and Harlan (1968;

1976). Among the wild species, the six-row and brittle-eared *H. agriocrit-hon* E. Aberg has been found in eastern Tibet, in Szechwan province, and in Nepal. However, this taxon has recently been considered a weed race arising from the crosses of *H. spontaneum* (two-row, brittle-eared) and the cultivated six-row barley (Harlan 1968). *Hordeum spontaneum* was formerly considered indigenous to Mesopotamia (ibid.), but recent surveys have shown its widespread distribution in Tibet and Szechwan (Shao, Li, and Baschan 1975; Hsü T'ing-wen 1975), as well as in northwestern India (Witcombe 1978).

The six-row barley varieties of China mostly have naked grains, hooded lemmas or brittle awns, black or purple chaff, non-brittle rachises, and dense spikes (Harlan 1968). Other common characteristics are small seeds, short awns or none, and quick-ripening grain (Vavilov 1957). The differences between two-row and six-row forms, as well as between covered and naked barleys, are controlled by a single gene or not more than two genes in each case (Harlan 1976).

People in North China probably acquired the naked barleys from the plateau in the southwest, with barley and wheat coming to the central plain in mixtures. Later, China became a secondary center of diversity for the naked barleys (Harlan 1968). Because barley was easier to cook (boil or steam), its consumption probably preceded that of wheat in China, as was the case in ancient Mesopotamia and dynastic Egypt (Harlan 1976).

Wheat

Indications that wheat and barley were two different cereals began to appear during the Shang dynasty (Yü Hsing-wu 1957). The bread wheats (*Triticum aestivum* L.) came by way of Mongolia and Yunnan (Yü Ching-jang 1972). Wheat, along with rice and millet, has been found at Chien-ch'uan in northwest Yunnan, dated at 1308 ± 105 B.C. (K. C. Chang 1977:455; ZK–10, Hsia 1977b).

Cultural Practices and Production

Little was written about barley and wheat until the Eastern Chou. Timely seeding and harvesting of the maturing crop were considered critical. The removal of weeds was also emphasized (Hu Hsi-wen 1958).

Up to the third century B.C., the *Chou-li* records that *mai* was planted in the districts of Yü, Ch'ing, Yen, and Ping (map. 3.1). The planting time appears to have been in the fall. Barley and wheat were included in some of the sacrificial rituals. Damage by flood was mentioned in the *Ch'un-ch'iu Tso-chuan* of the Eastern Chou, circa fifth century B.C. (Hu Hsi-wen 1958).

From the beginning of the Warring States period, *shu* (the soybean) began to overtake the millets in predominance, as indicated by various writings. Between the Ch'in and the Western Han, however, *mai* and *ho* (millets) still dominated *shu* (Liu Yü-ch'üan 1960).

Wheat later gained dominance over barley in both production and economic value. The widespread cultivation of wheat can be ascribed partly to a lower water requirement than that of barley (Altman and Dittmer 1973:906) and partly to its higher yield under favorable conditions. Chinese wheats were characterized by short plant stature, early maturity, compact and mostly awnless spikes, and small grains (Vavilov 1957).

OTHER CEREALS

Because Chinese sorghums (*Andropogon sorghum* var. *vulgaris*, or *Sorghum nervosum* of *S. bicolor* ssp. *bicolor*, or *S. nervosum* Bess *ex* Schult. for kaoliang) carried *shu* in their older name, *shu-shu* 秫黍, 蜀黍 (the millet of Szechwan), of about A.D. 300, they were sometimes confused with the millets (de Candolle 1884; Kishimoto 1941). The dates of the earliest sites that probably contained sorghum grains range between late Shang and the time of Christ (Ho 1975:380). *Shu-shu* has not been found in the Shang oracle inscriptions, however.

Doggett (1970) hypothesized that when cultivated sorghum reached South China between 1500 and 1000 B.P., it hybridized with the diploid S. *propinquum*, and further introgression led to the distinct characteristics of the kaoliang group in race *Nervosum*. Other scholars have considered the above dates too early for the introduction of sorghum into China; in their view it came from India, probably via Yunnan and Szechwan (de Candolle 1884; Hagerty 1940; Shinoda 1948; Yü Ching-jang 1958; Amano 1962). The more probable date of introduction is between the twelfth (Hagerty 1940) and thirteenth (Shinoda 1948) centuries.

Maize (*Zea mays* L.) also carries *shu* 黍 in its Chinese name: *yü-shu-shu* 御蜀黍, 玉蜀黍 (imperial sorghum or jade sorghum). It was also called *yü-mai* 玉麥 (imperial wheat) or *yü-mi* 玉米 (imperial rice). Ho (1955) has proposed that maize was first brought to the Ming court as a tribute by tribesmen in the southwest. Another theory is that it came to China by way of Tibet (Anonymous 1934).

Other cereals mentioned in various writings that were probably of minor importance are (1) *pai* 稗 or *shan* 穇 —*Eichinochloa crusgalli* var. *frumentacea* [Roxb.] Trin (Kitamura 1950); (2) *ku* 菰, 苽 —Manchurian water-rice, *Zizania latifolia* Truc. (Li Hui-lin 1970); and (3) *yi-yi* 薏苡 —Job's tears or adlay, *Coix lacryma-jobi* L. (K. C. Chang 1970; Li 1970).

THE SOYBEAN AND OTHER LEGUMES

The Origin and Domestication of Soybeans

The soybean (*Glycine max* [L.] Merr.) belongs to subgenus *Soja* (Moench) F. J. Herm. Its closest wild relative in the same subgenus is *G. soja* Sieb. *et* Zucc. (formerly known as *G. ussuriensis* Regel *et* Maack). This wild species grows in South China, Taiwan, the Yangtze basin, the northeastern provinces of China, Korea, Japan, and adjoining Siberia (Hermann 1962), largely in wet lowlands or on the banks of rivers and lakes (Ho 1975). The two species have chromosomes similar in size, and they hybridize readily. Their hybrids have high fertility, normal meiotic behavior in the F_1, and character segregation similar to those of intra-specific crosses. Another taxon, *G. gracilis* Skvortz., has been proposed as a third member of the subgenus, but the three taxa apparently belong to the same species complex (Hymowitz 1970; Hadley and Hymowitz 1973). *Glycine soja* appears to be the most likely progenitor of the cultigen (Karasawa 1936), and introgressive hybridization between the two species in areas where they overlapped presumably led to the appearance of *G. gracilis* (Hadley and Hymowitz 1973).

Among the six species in subgenus *Glycine*, *G. tomentalla* Hayata (2n = 40, 80) and *G. tabacina* (Labill.) Benth (2n = 40, 80) have been found in Taiwan, South China, and Oceania. But attempts to cross either one with *G. max* on the diploid or tetraploid level were unsuccessful (Palmer and Hadley 1968). Crosses within the subgenus *Glycine* were likewise unfruitful (Newell and Hymowitz 1978).

The domestication process from *G. soja* to *G. max* involved the following changes: more erect growth habit, larger plant size, increased seed size, less shattering of mature seeds from the pod, increased oil level, decreased protein content of seed, and loss of photoperiod sensitivity (Hymowitz 1976; Lü 1978).

Based on the wild strains and cultivars collected from different geographic areas of China, the samples within one region showed similar traits, and samples of different regions showed a parallel trend in variability. Domestication appears to have taken place in several areas of China (Lü 1978).

Antiquity of the Soybean

References to the soybean in Chou and Han works about the mythological past have led many scholars to believe that it was among the food crops grown during the period of Emperor Shen Nung (ca. 2700 B.C.). But this inference lacks substantial evidence.

A reliable clue to the antiquity of the soybean can be drawn from the archaic character for it, *shu* 菽, which appeared both in the odes of the *Shih-ching* and on bronze inscriptions of the Western Chou. The *shu* pictograph can be traced back to approximately the eleventh century B.C. (Hu Tao-ching 1963). Both *shu* and *jung-shu* 戎菽 appeared in the odes several times (Ho 1975:78).

The soybean probably emerged as a domesticate during the Chou dynasty (Ho 1969a:168; Hymowitz 1970:416). The proto-Tungusic people in the northeast plains could have brought the seeds to the early Chou court. It became widely disseminated in the Chou culture area only after 664 B.C., following the expedition of Lord Huan of Ch'i, who brought seed from the Mountain Jung tribe (Ho 1975:77–79). As the Ch'in dynasty expanded and trade increased, the legume spread to the south (Li Ch'ang-nien 1958), to Korea, Japan, and southeast China. The northeastern provinces became a center of diversity (Hymowitz 1970). The soybean thrives better in mesophytic regions than in arid zones (see King 1966:180 for comparative data on efficiency of transpiration).

Millet and soybeans became important crops grown in rotation in about the fourth century B.C. The long lapse between the first domestication of millet and that of the soybean indicates a prolonged process of trial and error by people who were probably of different tribes (Ho 1975:80).

Impact of the Soybean

Soon after domestication and dissemination during the Chou dynasty, the soybean became an important source of plant protein. Because its root nodules fix nitrogen, it entered into the widely practiced millet and soybean rotation system (this is mentioned in the *Kuan-tzu* 管子 of the fifth to third century B.C.; Li Ch'ang-nien 1958). Within three centuries, millet and soybeans became the major crops in areas north of the Huai river.

Other Grain Legumes

The adzuki bean (*Phaseolus angularis*) appears to be the only other legume indigenous to China. It has been called *hsiao-tou* 小豆 ever since the Eastern Chou (Li Ch'ang-nien 1958). Its primary center of diversity is in South China (Li Hui-lin 1970). Because some varieties of adzuki bean have red seed coats, they were named red beans and later became confounded with the species complex of black gram and green gram (*P. mungo* L. and *P. aureus* Roxb.). The grams, broad beans (*Vicia faba* L.), asparagus beans (*P. vulgaris* L.), cowpeas (*Vigna unguiculata* [L.] Walp.), and peanuts (*Arachis hypogaea* L.) were all foreign introductions.

PERSPECTIVES FOR FUTURE STUDIES

This survey of cereals and grain legumes in China reveals that, in spite of the continuous compilation of historical records since Shang times and recent archaeological finds, many gaps, uncertainties, and discrepancies about the origins of the important food crops remain to be resolved. It is now certain, however, that about seven thousand years ago two fairly well-established crops were cultivated and served as mainstays: millets in the central plain and rice in the southern portion of the lower Yangtze basin. It is difficult to speculate on the relation between the two important cultured and agricultural nuclei, but contacts between them and the places between them probably occurred much earlier than recorded history has indicated. Similarly, the dispersal and cultivation of barley, wheat, and soybeans indicate that contacts and exchange of commodities, including crop seeds, between the Chinese in the central plain and those to the west and north might also have taken place before recorded history. Early contacts with people in southern Asia and mainland Southeast Asia are also probable.

The Gondwanian theory about the origin and dispersal of species in the genus *Oryza* not only reconciles past controversies on the origin of Asian cultivated rice and the evolution of the Chinese rices but also emphasizes the importance of a center of diversification over that of a center of origin. Since the plant materials that man had observed and described several millennia ago were only relics of the truly wild progenitors, man's role in molding the cultivated forms was as important as his role in dispersing the crops over land and sea. The multi-disciplinary analysis used in retracing the geographic dispersal of the species in *Oryza* (T. T. Chang 1976c; 1976d) can be used to study the other crops with rewarding results. The millets, barley, and wheat appear to have followed man's tracks along the routes of travel in the supercontinent Laurasia, whereas the genus *Glycine* seems to have had its roots in the eastern half of Gondwana Land.

Archaeologists, ethnobotanists, anthropologists, and evolutionary geneticists also need to search beyond the present borders of China to find some of the missing links. The southwest region of China and its adjoining areas may offer great potentials for exploration and the survey of botanical specimens. Within China proper, the extreme south region around the Pearl river has not been fully explored for archaeological evidence. This region may furnish information of vast importance concerning the cereals and legumes, as well as the probable role of root crops in that humid subtropical region. Concurrent studies on paleometeorology and paleobotany may also provide valuable background information.

Even as we anticipate new knowledge emerging in the future, we cannot help marveling at the detailed accounts about Chinese agriculture in the early historical records. The ancient writings not only provide descriptions of the innovations of the early Chinese cultivators who were scattered over several regions of the country, documenting the rich ecogenetic diversification emerging from such efforts, they also record the recognition by both government-franchised historians and individual writers that plant cultivation has been a vital force since the dawn of Chinese civilization.

The contributions of Chinese rice farmers had great impact on rice cultivation in other parts of eastern Asia, Southeast Asia, parts of western Asia, and Europe (T. T. Chang 1976b; Lu and Chang 1980). Several civilizations adjacent to China have largely derived their agricultural economy from the innovations of China's early cultivators. The combined efforts of historians, archaeologists, ethnobotanists, anthropologists, and geneticists will undoubtedly continue to reveal how the early Chinese civilization developed, flourished, and expanded.

REFERENCES

Altman, P. C., and Dittmer, D. S.
1973   *Biology Data Book*, vol. 2. 2d ed. Bethesda, Md.

Amano Motonosuke 天野元之助
1962   *Chūgoku nōgyōshi kenkyū* 中国農業史研究. Tokyo.

Andersson, J. G.
1934   *Children of the Yellow Earth: Studies in Prehistoric China.* London.

Andō Hirotaro 安籐広太郎
1959   *Nihon kodai inasaku shi kenkyū* 日本古代稲作史研究. Tokyo.

Anonymous
1934   "Maize in China." *Nature* 133:420.

Barnard, Noel
1980   *Radiocarbon Dates and Their Significance in the Chinese Archaeological Scene: A List of 280 Entries Compiled from Chinese Sources Published up to Close of 1978.* Canberra.

Bayard, D. T.
1970   "Excavation of Non Nok Tha, Northeastern Thailand, 1968." *Asian Perspectives* 13:109–143.

Bishop, Carl W.
1933   "The Neolithic Age in Northern China." *Antiquity*
            7:389–404.

Buth, G. M., and Saraswat, K. S.
1972   "Antiquity of Rice Cultivation." In *Research Trends in
            Plant Anatomy*, edited by A. K. M. Ghouse and Mohd.
            Yunus: pp. 33–38. New Delhi.

Chang Kwang-chih 張光直
1968   *The Archaeology of Ancient China*. Rev. and enl. ed. New
            Haven.
1970   "The Beginnings of Agriculture in the Far East." *Antiquity*
            44:175–185.
1973   "Radiocarbon Dates from China: Some Initial Inter-
            pretations." *Current Anthropology* 14:525–528.
1975   "Chung-kuo k'ao-ku-hsüeh shang ti fang-she-hsing t'an-su
            nien-tai chi yi-yi 中國考古學上的放射性碳素年代及意義."
            Kuo-li T'ai-wan ta-hsüeh k'ao-ku jen-lei hsüeh-k'an
            國立臺灣大學考古人類學刊 37/38:29–43.

1977   *The Archaeology of Ancient China*. 3d ed., rev. and enl.
            New Haven.

Chang, Te-tzu
1975   "Exploration and Survey in Rice." In *Crop Genetic
            Resources for Today and Tomorrow*, edited by O. H.
            Frankel and J. G. Hawkes: pp. 159–165. Cambridge, Eng.
1976a   "Rice." In *Evolution of Crop Plants*, edited by N. W.
            Simmonds: pp. 98–104. London.
1976b   "The Rice Cultures." In *The Early History of Agriculture*,
            a discussion of the Royal Society and the British
            Academy. *Philosophical Transactions of the Society,
            London* B275:143–157.
1976c   "The Origin, Evolution, Cultivation, Dissemination, and
            Diversification of Asian and African Rices." *Euphytica*
            25:425–441.
1976d   "Paleogeographic Origin of the Wild Taxa in the Genus
            Oryza and Their Genomic Relationships." *International
            Rice Research Newsletter*. 1.2:4.

Chang, Te-tzu, and Oka, Hiko-ichi
1976   "Genetic Variousness in the Climatic Adaptation of Rice
            Cultivars." In *Climate and Rice*: pp. 87–111. Los Baños,
            Philippines.

Che-chiang-sheng   Che-chiang-sheng wen-wu kuan-li wei-yüan-hui
浙江省文物管理委員會
1960   "Wu-hsing Ch'ien-shan-yang yi-chih ti-yi, erh tz'u fa-
chüeh pao-kao 吳興錢山漾遺址第一、二次發掘報告."
KKHP 2:73–91.

Che-chiang-sheng and Po-wu-kuan   Che-chiang-sheng wen-kuan-hui
浙江省文管會 and Che-chiang-sheng po-wu-kuan 浙江省
博物館
1976   "Ho-mu-tu fa-hsien yüan-shih she-hui chung-yao yi-chih
河姆渡發現原始社會重要遺址." *WW* 8:6–13.

Cheng Te-k'un
1959   *Archaeology in China, vol. 1: Prehistoric China.*
Cambridge, Eng.

Ch'en Tsu-kuei, ed. 陳祖槼
1958   *Tao (shang-p'ien)* 稻(上篇). Chung-kuo nung-hsüeh yi-
ch'an hsüan-chi chia-lei ti-yi-chung 中國農學遺產選集
甲類第一種. Peking.
1960   "Chung-kuo wen-hsien shang ti shui-tao ts'ai-p'ei
中國文獻上的水稻栽培." *Nung-shih yen-chiu chi-k'an*
農史研究集刊 2:64–93.

Chin Shan-pao 金善寶
1962   "Huai-pei p'ing-yüan ti hsin-shih-ch'i shih-tai hsiao-mai
准北平原的新石器時代小麥." *Tso-wu hsüeh-pao* 作物學報
1.1:67–72.

CKKH and Shen-hsi   CKKH and Shen-hsi-sheng Hsi-an Pan-p'o po-
wu-kuan 陝西省西安半坡博物館
1963   *Hsi-an Pan-p'o* 西安半坡. Chung-kuo t'ien-yeh k'ao-ku
pao-kao-chi k'ao-ku-hsüeh chuan-k'an ting chung ti-shih-
ssu-hao 中國田野考古報告集考古學專刊丁種第十四號.
Peking.

Darlington, C. D.
1963   *Chromosome Botany and the Origin of Cultivated Plants.*
New York.

de Candolle, A.
1884   *Origin of Cultivated Plants.* London.

Doggett, H.
1970   *Sorghum.* London.

Edman, G., and Söderberg, E.
1929   "Auffindung von Reis in einer Tonscherbe aus einer etwa

Fünftausend-jährigen Chinesischen Siedlung." *Bulletin of the Geological Society of China* 8.4:363–368.

Eggum, B. O.
1979   "The Nutritive Value of Rice in Comparison With Other Cereals." In *Chemical Aspects of Grain Quality Workshop*: pp. 91–111. Los Baños, Philippines.

Hadley, H. H., and Hymowitz, T.
1973   "Speciation and Cytogenetics." In *Soybeans: Improvement, Production and Uses*, edited by B. E. Caldwell: pp. 97–116. Madison, Wis.

Hagerty, M
1940   "Comments on Writings Concerning Chinese Sorghums." *Harvard Journal of Asiatic Studies* 5:259–260.

Harlan, J. R.
1968   "On the Origin of Barley." In *Barley: Origin, Botany, Culture, Winter Hardiness, Genetics, Utilization, Pests.* Agricultural Handbook 338, pp. 9–31. U.S. Department of Agriculture.
1976   "Barley." In *Evolution of Crop Plants*, edited by N. W. Simmonds: pp. 93–98. London.

Helbaek, H.
1966   "Commentary on the Phylogenesis of *Triticum* and *Hordeum*." *Economic Botany* 20:350–360.
1969   "Plant Collecting, Dry-farming and Irrigation Agriculture in Prehistoric Deh Luran." In *Prehistoric and Human Ecology of the Deh Luran Plain*, edited by F. Hole, K. V. Flannery, and J. A. Neely: pp. 383–426. Memoirs of the Museum of Anthropology no. 1. Ann Arbor.

Hermann, F. J.
1962   "A Revision of the Genus *Glycine* and Its Immediate Allies." U.S. Department of Agriculture Technical Bulletin 1268.

Herrmann, A.
1966   *An Historical Atlas of China*, edited by N. Ginsburg. Chicago.

Ho Ping-ti 何炳棣
1955   "The Introduction of American Food Plants into China." *American Anthropologist* 57.2:191–201.

1956   "Early-ripening Rice in Chinese history." *Economic History Review* 9:200–218.
1969a   *"Huang-t'u yü Chung-kuo nung-yeh ti ch'i-yüan* 黃土與中國農業的起源." Hong Kong.
1969b   "The Loess and the Origin of Chinese Agriculture." *American Historical Review* 75:1–36.
1975   *The Cradle of the East: An Inquiry into the Indigenous Origins of Techniques and Ideas of Neolithic and Early Historic China, 5000–1000 B.C.* Hong Kong and Chicago.

Hsia Nai 夏鼐
1977a   "K'ao-ku-hsüeh ho k'o-chi-shu—tsui-chin wo-kuo yu-kuan k'o-chi-shih ti k'ao-ku hsin fa-hsien 考古學和科技術—最近我國有關科技史的考古新發現." *KK* 1977.2:81–91.
1977b   "T'an shih-ssu ts'e-ting nien-tai ho Chung-kuo shih-ch'ien k'ao-ku shih 碳-14測定年代和中國史前考古史." *KK* 1977.4:217–232. (Partially translated by Nancy Price in *Early China* 3 [Fall 1977]:87–93.)

Hsü Cho-yün 許倬雲
1971   "Liang-Chou nung-tso chi-shu 兩周農作技術." *BIHP* 42.4:803–842.

Hsü T'ing-wen 徐廷文
1975   "Ts'ung Kan-tzu yeh-sheng erh-leng ta-mai ti fa-hsien lun ts'ai-p'ei ta-mai ti ch'i-yüan ho chung-hsi fa-sheng 從甘孜野生二稜大麥的發現論栽培大麥的起源和種系發生." *Yi-ch'uan hsüeh-pao* 遺傳學報 (*Acta Genetica Sinica*) 2.2:129–137.

Hu Hsi-wen, ed. 胡錫文
1958   *Mai (shang-p'ien)* 麥(上篇). Chung-kuo nung-hsüeh yi-ch'an hsüan-chi chia-lei ti-erh-chung 中國農學遺產選集甲類第二種 Peking.

Hu Tao-ching 胡道靜
1963   "Shih-shu p'ien 釋菽篇." *Chung-hua wen-shih lun-ts'ung* 中華文史論叢 3:111–120.

Hymowitz, T.
1970   "On the Domestication of the Soybean." *Economic Botany* 24:408–421.
1976   "Soybeans." In *Evolution of Crop Plants*, edited by N. W. Simmonds: pp. 159–162. London.

Karasawa, K.
1936   "Crossing Experiments with *Glycine max* and *G. ussuriensis*." *Nihon shokubutsu-gaku shūhō* 日本植物学輯報 [*The Japanese journal of botany*] 8.2:113–117.

Karlgren, B.
1944   "The Book of Odes, *Kuo feng* and *Siao ya*." *BMFEA* 16:171–256.
1945   "The Book of Odes, *Ta Ya* and *Sung*." *BMFEA* 17:65–99.

Kato, S., Kosaka, H., Hara, S., Maruyama, Y., and Takigushi, Y.
1930   "On the Affinity of the Cultivated Varieties of Rice Plants, *Oryza sativa* L." *Kyūshū teikoku daigaku nōgakubu kiyō* 九州帝国大学農学部紀要 [*Journal of the Department of Agriculture*, Kyushu Imperial University] 2.9:241–276.

Kihara Hitoshi 木原均 and Kishimoto Enko 岸本艷
1942   "Awa to enokoro-gusa no za-shu あはトえのころぐさ の雑種." *Shokubutsu-gaku zasshi* 植物學雜誌 [*The botanical magazine*] 56.662:62–67.

Kim Wong-yong 金元龍
1977   *Han-guck go-go-hack yoeun-bo* 韓國考古學年報, 4:1–33; pl. 1–23. Seoul.

King, L. J.
1966   *Weeds of the World. Biology and Control.* New York.

Kishimoto Enko 岸本艷
1941   "Awa, kibi, hie, morokoshi rui no kigen to rekishi 粟、黍、稗、蜀黍類の起源と歴史." *Idengaku zasshi* 遺伝学雑誌 [*Japanese journal of genetics*] 17:310–321.

Kitamura Shiro 北村四郎
1950   "Chūgoku saibai shokubutsu no kigen 中国栽培 植物の起源" *Tōhō gakuhō* 東方学報 19:76–101.

Koernicke, F.,\and Werner, H.
1885   *Handbuch des Getreidesbaues.* 2 vols. Berlin.

Krishnaswamy, N.
1938   "Geography and History of Millets." *Current Science* 6:355–358.
1951   "Origin and Distribution of Cultivated Plants of South Asia: Millets." *Indian Journal of Genetics and Plant Breeding* 11:67–74.

Kuang-tung   Kuang-tung nung-lin hsüeh-yüan 廣東農林學院
1975   "Wo-kuo yeh-sheng-tao ti chung-lei chi ch'i ti-li fen-pu
            我國野生稻的種類及其地理分布." *Yi-ch'uan hsüeh-pao*
            遺傳學報 (*Acta Genetica Sinica*) 2.1:31–35.

Kuang-tung and Yün-nan   Kuang-tung nung-lin hsüeh-yüan 廣東農林
            學院 and Yün-nan ta-hsüeh 雲南大學
1974   "Yün-nan-sheng ssu-mao ti-ch'ü hsien-ching tao ch'ui-
            chih fen-pu tiao-ch'a pao-kao 雲南省思茅地區籼粳稻
            垂直分布調查報告." *Chih-wu hsüeh-pao* 植物學報 (*Acta
            Botanica Sinica*) 16.3:208–222.

Laufer, B.
1919   *Sino-Iranica*. Chicago.

Lee, Mabel Ping-hua
1921   *The Economic History of China*. Columbia University
            Studies in History, Economics and Public Law 99.1. New
            York.

Li, C. H., Pao, W. K., and Li, H. W.
1942   "Interspecific Crosses in *Setaria*, II: Cytological Studies of
            Interspecific Hybrids Involving: 1. *S. faberii* and *S. italica*,
            and 2. a three way cross, F_2 of *S. italica* × *S. viridis* and
            S. faberii." *Journal of Heredity* 33:351–355.

Li Ch'ang-nien, ed. 李長年
1958   *Tou lei (shang p'ien)* 豆類(上篇). Chung-kuo nung-hsüeh
            yi-ch'an hsüan-chi chia-lei ti-ssu-chung 中國農學遺產選集
            甲類第四種. Peking.

Li Hsiao-ting 李孝定
1965   *Chia-ku wen-tzu chi-shih* 甲骨文字集釋. Chung-yang yen-
            chiu-yüan li-shih yü-yen yen-chiu-so chuan-k'an chih wu-
            shih 中央研究院歷史語言研究所專刊之五十. 8 vols.
            Nankang.

Li, H. W., Li, C.H., and Pao, W. K.
1945   "Cytological and Genetical Studies of the Interspecific
            Cross of the Cultivated Foxtail Millet, *Setaria italica* (L.)
            Beauv., and the Green Foxtail Millet, *S. viridis* L." *Journal
            of the American Society of Agronomy*. 37:32–54.

Li, Hui-lin
1970   "The origin of cultivated plants in Southeast Asia."
            Economic Botany 24:3–19.

Liu Tzu-ming 柳子明
1975   "Chung-kuo t'sai-p'ei-tao ti ch'i-yüan chi ch'i fa-chan
            中國栽培稻的起源及其發展." *Yi-ch'uan hsüeh-pao*
            遺傳學報 (*Acta Genetica Sinica*) 2.1:23–30.

Liu Yü-ch'üan 劉毓瑔
1960   "Shih-ching shih-tai chi su pien 詩經時代稷粟辨." *Nung-
            shih yen-chiu chi-k'an* 農史研究集刊 2:38–47.

Lu, Jonathan, and Chang, Te-tzu
1980   "Rice in Its Temporal and Spatial Perspectives." In *Rice:
            Production and Utilization*, edited by B. S. Luh: pp. 1–74.
            Westport, Conn.

Lü Shih-lin 呂世霖
1978   "Kuan-yü wo-kuo ts'ai-p'ei ta-tou yüan-ch'an ti wen-t'i ti
            t'an-t'ao 關於我國栽培大豆原產地問題的探討." *Chung-
            kuo nung-yeh k'o-hsüeh* 中國農業科學 (*Scientia
            Agricultura Sinica*) 4:90–96.

Mansfeld, R.
1959   *Vorlaufige Verzeichnis landwirtschaftlich oder gärtnerisch
            kultivierter Pflanzenarten: Kulturpflanze Suppl.* vol. 2.
            Berlin.

Morinaga Toshitaro 盛永俊太郎
1967   "Nihon no ine 日本の稲." *Nōgyō* 農業 988:1–10.

Nan Po 南波
1975   "Chiang-su-sheng Tung-hai-hsien Chiao-chuang ku yi-
            chih 江蘇省東海縣焦莊古遺址." *WW* 8:45–56, 60.

Nayer, N. M.
1966   "Spatial and Temporal Aspects of Origin of Rice."
            Proceedings of the Academy of Science 63B:297–303.

Newell, C. A., and Hymowitz, T.
1978   "A Reappraisal of the Subgenus *Glycine*." *American
            Journal of Botany* 65:168–179.

Nishiyama Takeichi 西山武一
1949   "Chūgoku suitō nōgyō no hattatsu 中国水稲農業の発達."
            Nōgyō sōgō kenkyū 農業綜合研究 3.1:118–159.

O'Toole, J. C., and Chang, T. T.
1978   "Drought and Rice Improvement in Perspective."
            International Research Institute Research Paper Series, 14.

Palmer, R. G., and Hadley, H. H.
1968   "Interspecific Hybridization in *Glycine*, Subgenus *Leptocyamus*." *Crop Science* 8:557–563.

Purseglove, J. W.
1972   *Tropical Crops: Monocotyledons*, vol. 1. New York.

Rachie, K. O.
1975   *The Millets: Importance, Utilization and Outlook.* Hyderabad.

Ramiah, K., and Ghose, R. L. M.
1951   "Origin and Distribution of Rice." *Indian Journal of Genetics and Plant Breeding* 11:7–13.

Richharia, R. H.
1960   "Origins of Cultivated Rices." *Indian Journal of Genetics and Plant Breeding* 20:1–14.

Robbins, W. W.
1917   *Botany of Crop Plants.* Philadelphia.

Shang-hai-shih   Shang-hai-shih wen-wu pao-kuan wei-yüan-hui 上海市文物保管委員會
1962   "Shang-hai-shih Ch'ing-pu-hsien Sung-tse yi-chih ti shih-chüeh 上海市青浦縣崧澤遺址的試掘." *KKHP* 2:1–29.

Shao Ch'i-ch'üan 邵啓全, Li Ch'ang-sang 李長桑, and Baschan Chiren (Pa-sen Tz'u-jen) 巴森次仁
1975   "Ts'ai-p'ei ta-mai ti ch'i-yüan yü chin-hua 栽培大麥的起源與進化." *Yi-ch'uan hsüeh-pao* 遺傳學報 (*Acta Genetica Sinica*) 2.2:123–128.
1979   "Hsi-ts'ang ti pan-yeh-sheng hsiao-mai 西藏的半野生小麥." *Yi-ch'uan hsüeh-pao* 遺傳學報 (*Acta Genetica Sinica*) 6:34.

Shinoda Osamu 篠田統
1948   "Pai-kan-chiu 白乾酒." *Gakugei* 学芸 39:24–31.
1951   "Gokoku no kigen 五穀の起源." *Shizen to bunka* 自然与文化 2:37–70.

Solheim, W. G., II
1972   "An earlier Agricultural Revolution." *Scientific American* 226.4:34–41.

Takahashi, R.
1955   "The Origin and Evolution of Cultivated Barley." *Advances in Genetics* 7:227–266.

Ting Ying 丁穎

1933   "Wild Rice of Kwangtung and New Variety Bred From the Hybrids of Wild Rice with Cultivated Rice." *Sun Yatsen University College of Agriculture Agronomy Bulletin* 3 : 1–24.

1949   "Chung-kuo ku-lai ching-hsien tao-chung ts'ai-p'ei chi ch'i fen-pu chih t'an-t'ao yü hsien-tsai tao-chung fen-lei yü-pao 中國古來粳籼稻種栽培及其分佈之探討與現在稻種分類預報." *Sun Yatsen University College of Agriculture Agronomy Bulletin* 6 : 1–32.

1957   "Chung-kuo ts'ai-p'ei tao-chung ti ch'i-yüan chi ch'i yen pien 中國栽培稻種的起源及其演變." *Nung-yeh hsüeh-pao* 農業學報 8 : 243–260.

1959   "Chiang-Han-p'ing-yüan hsin-shih-ch'i shih-tai hung-shao-t'u chung ti tao-ku-k'o k'ao-ch'a 江漢平原新石器時代紅燒土中的稻穀殼考查." *KKHP* 4 : 31–34.

Ting Ying, ed.

1961   *Chung-kuo shui-tao ts'ai-p'ei hsüeh* 中國水稻栽培學. Peking.

Ts'ao Lung-kung 曹隆恭

1960   "Chung-kuo nung-yeh shih wen-hsien shang su ti ts'ai-p'ei 中國農業史文獻上粟的栽培." *Nung-shih yen-chiu chi-k'an* 農史研究集刊 2 : 94–108.

Tsou Shu-wen 鄒樹文

1960   "Shih-ching shu chi pien 詩經黍稷辨." *Nung-shih yen-chiu chi-k'an* 農史研究集刊 2 : 18–34.

Tuan Hsi-chung 段熙仲

1960   "Chü san Li shuo shu fei chi 據三禮說黍非稷." *Nung-shih yen-chiu chi-k'an* 農史研究集刊 2 : 35–37.

Vavilov, N. I.

1932   "The Process of Evolution in Cultivated Plants." *Proceedings of the 6th International Congress of Genetics* 1 : 331–342. Ithaca, N.Y.

1951   *The Origin, Variation, Immunity and Breeding of Cultivated Plants.* Translated by K. S. Chester. Chronica Botanica 13. New York.

1957   *World Resources of Cereals, Leguminous Seed Crops and Flax, and Their Utilization in Plant Breeding.* Translated by M. Paenson and Z. S. Cole. Washington, D.C.

Vishnu-Mittre

1976   "Discussion." In *The Early History of Agriculture.*

Philosophical Transactions of the Royal Society, London
B275:141.

Watson, W.
1969   "Early Cereal Cultivation in China." In *The Domestica-
tiona and Exploitation of Plants and Animals*, edited by
P. J. Ucko and G. W. Dimbleby: pp. 397–402. London.
1971   *Cultural Frontiers in Ancient East Asia.* Edinburgh.

Watt, G.
1891   *"Oryza."* In *Dictionary of the Economic Products of India*
5:498–654. New Delhi.

Whyte, R. O.
1972   "The Gramineae, Wild and Cultivated of Monsoonal and
Equatorial Asia, I: Southeast Asia." *Asian Perspectives*
15:127–151.

Witcombe, J. R.
1978   "Two-rowed and Six-rowed Wild Barley from the Western
Himalaya." *Euphytica* 27:601–604.

Wu Ju-tsu 吳汝祚
1975   "Ts'ung Ch'ien-shan-yang teng yüan-shih wen-hua yi-chih
k'an she-hui fen-kung yü ssu-yu-chih ti ch'an-sheng
從錢山漾等原始文化遺址看社會分工與私有制的產生."
KK 5:271–273.

Yin, Chi-hsiang, and Kuo, Shih-tseng
1978   "Stratigraphy of the Mount Jolmo Lungma and Its North
Slope." *Scientia Sinica* 21:629–644.

Yu Hsiu-ling 游修齡
1976   "Tui Ho-mu-tu yi-chih ti-ssu wen-hua-ts'eng ch'u-t'u tao-
ku ho ku-ssu ti chi-tien k'an-fa 對河姆渡遺址第四文化層
出土稻谷和骨耜的幾點看法." *WW* 8:20–23.

Yü Ching-jang 于景讓
1956   "Shu 黍." *Ta-lu tsa-chih* 大陸雜誌 13.7:201–204.

Yü Ching-jang, ed.
1958   *Ts'ai-p'ei chih-wu k'ao: ti yi chi* 栽培植物考:第一輯. Kuo-
li T'ai-wan ta-hsüeh nung-hsüeh-yüan ts'ung-shu 國立臺灣
大學農學院叢書 no. 6. Taipei.
1972   *Ts'ai-p'ei chih-wu k'ao: ti erh chi* 栽培植物考:第二集.
Taipei.

Yü Hsing-wu 于省吾
1957   "Shang-tai ti ku-lei tso-wu 商代的穀類作物." *Tung-pei*

jen-min ta-hsüeh jen-wen k'o-hsüeh hsüeh-pao 東北人民
大學人文科學學報 1:81–107.

1972   "Ts'ung chia-ku-wen k'an Shang-tai ti nung-tien k'en-chih
從甲骨文看商代的農田墾殖." *KK* 4:40–41, 45.

Yün-nan-sheng   Yün-nan-sheng po-wu-kuan 雲南省博物舘

1958   "Chien-ch'uan Hai-men-k'ou ku wen-hua yi-chih ch'ing-li
chien-pao 劍川海門口古文化遺址清理簡報." *KK* 6:5–12.

Zeven, A. C., and Zhukovsky, P. M.

1975   *Dictionary of Cultivated Plants and Their Centres of
Diversity.* Wageningen, Netherlands.

Zukovskij, P. M.

1962   *Cultivated Plants and Their Wild Relatives.* Abridged
translation by P. S. Hudson. Farnham Royal, England.

4

Swidden Cultivation of Foxtail Millet by Taiwan Aborigines: A Cultural Analogue of the Domestication of *Setaria italica* in China

WAYNE H. FOGG

Foxtail millet, *Setaria italica* (L.) Beauv., was an important dietary staple of the prehistoric Yang-shao culture and of the people of the historic Shang and Chou of North China. The same cereal also played a central role in the ritual life of these peoples. Although the actual place and time origins for the domestication of *S. italica* will most likely remain obscure, the processes and techniques necessary for the creation of the cultivar from its wild ancestral grass, *Setaria viridis* (L.) Beauv., can be approximated through field study and cultural analogue. The following reconstruction of the evolutionary history of the *S. italica* cultigen will add to our understanding of the way of life and ancient civilization of the North China region.

The process of selecting accumulative genetic changes in the wild *S. viridis* to evolve the cultivar *S. italica* must have occurred over several millennia. Only sophisticated techniques permit maintenance for highly domesticated cultivars of *S. italica*. In order to identify the farming techniques that were crucial in the domestication processes of selection, maintenance, and dispersal of new phenotypes caused by genetic changes, it is necessary to note the differences between primitive and advanced forms of the cultivar.

Primitive varieties of foxtail millet are short, usually less than one hundred centimeters, and multi-tillered with thin stems, narrow leaf blades,

NOTE: A Summer Stipend from the National Endowment for the Humanities supported part of my research for the summer of 1977.

TABLE 4.1 *Setaria italica* **Varieties from the Bunun Village of Tung-Pu, Hsin-Yi-Hsiang, Nan-t'ou-hsien, 1977**

Non-glutinous starch varieties (14)

Hanevalval	Named for the rainbow. The glumes and bristles as they approach maturity in the field turn red. After harvest and drying they turn buff yellow. The panicle shape is cylindrical, with a round distal end.
Pishpish	The panicle is like a squirrel's tail, open and bushy. The shape is wide near the base and pointed at the distal end. The seed coat is yellow, glumes a deep crimson-purple. When cooked the grain is white, very tender, and easily digested. It is given to young children and the elderly.
Masunglab	Named for green. The seed coat and endosperm are a distinct waxy green. The panicle shape is long, narrow, and bi-forked at the distal end, and the lobes are dense and tightly packed.
Havit	Named for the one-hundred-pacer snake *Agistrodon acutus*, which the panicle shape resembles: it is pointed but wider at the distal end than at the base and has an extended appearance like that of the snake with raised head—caused by the outer layer of seeds at the tip of the bristles. The bristle tips have a fertile floret, hence this cultivar in Lukai tribal areas is called *thagathaga*, which means two layers. Could this type of cultivar be the double-kerneled millet mentioned in the *Shih-ching*?
Banode	A long panicle, with densely packed lobes and a branching distal end. The lobe shape is round. Considered one of their best varieties. When cooked it congeals like the glutinous starch type and has a good flavor.
Ishleshe	A long panicle, with a branching distal end. The lobes are beaked or hooked at their tips. The glumes are deep red and the seed coat is tan.
Hadloh	Named for the color white. This is the whitest panicle among their cultivars. The shape is long and narrow and has a branching distal end. Lobe spacing is dense. It is the most tender variety and is served to guests.
Lobonoku	A Bunun clan name, which could represent either the originator of the variety, a ritual group leader, or a hamlet place name. The panicle shape is narrow, with a pointed distal end. The glumes are red and the seed coat is tan. Except for the panicle shape it resembles the *hanevalval* variety.
Dahigh	A Bunun clan name. This is considered the most ancient variety. The panicle shape has a rounded distal end and is dense and firm. It feels heavier in the hand than other cultivars. The glumes are brown and the seed coat is tan.
Madanhas	Named for the color red. The panicle is brick red with a rounded distal end. This is considered one of the most ancient cultivars and it is very difficult to thresh.
Modlohalo	The panicle shape is wider at the base than at the pointed distal end.
Ishbougha	The panicle shape is rounded, the color a dull yellow. The lobes are elongated, narrow, and loosely spaced.

TABLE 4.1 (*cont.*)

Banga	Named for a V or a bi-forking shape like that of a tree limb joining a trunk. The distal end of the panicle is forked. The panicle is pink when ripening in the field.
Lochlasad	The panicle is pointed with a light tan color.

Glutinous-starch varieties (4)

Coulevungath	A Bunun clan name. The panicle is deep yellow and has a wide bushy shape, with the distal end round and wider than at the base.
Cungsavesad	The panicle is yellow with a pointed tip and has small lobes and short bristles.
Eval	A Bunun clan name. The yellow-tan panicle has a pointed distal end and thin, elongated lobes.
Savungath	Similar to Coulevungath, except that the panicle is pointed and contains long bristles.

and short panicles of two to twelve centimeters. The panicle and seed is generally limited to a brown-purple or straw-white color. Only non-glutinous starch types are maintained. Side tillers do not ripen simultaneously with the more central ones. The maturation period is shorter than that for the advanced cultivars, while the lemma and palea tightly enclose the caryopsis and are relatively difficult to thresh for food.

Highly domesticated cultivars of *S. italica* are tall, equal to the height of a man, single-tillered, and have stout, robust stems, wide leaf blades, and a long panicle length of from ten to more than fifty centimeters. Varieties are maintained for different combinations of panicle shapes, lobe forms, coloration of panicle imparted by the glumes, lemma-palea, seed coats, bristles, and stem color (table 4.1). Selection over thousands of years has created a wide array of varieties of both non-glutinous and glutinous starch types. The lemma and palea do not enclose the caryopsis tightly and are easily removed during threshing.

The sticky starch varieties of *S. italica* are recessive mutants of the non-sticky starch type. The glutinous starch endosperm is caused by a single recessive characteristic that differentiates it from the non-glutinous type (Watabe 1967:5). The difference between the two is in the quantitative ratio of the main constituents of starch: amylose and amylopectin. Non-glutinous types consist of approximately 20 percent amylose and 80 percent amylopectin. The glutinous varieties consist of almost 100 percent amylopectin (ibid., p. 4). When cooked the grains of the glutinous type become viscous, hence the name "sticky millet." Although both glutinous and non-glutinous types are used for porridge, only the sticky starch cultivars of *S. italica* are used for brewing wine and steaming millet cakes. Foxtail millet wine was important to the ancient Chinese, and it remains an important item for social and ceremonial uses among the Austronesian groups of Taiwan's Central Mountains. Unfortunately, this sticky starch type of foxtail millet has not been recognized by Western taxonomists (de Witt, Oestry-Stidd, and Cubero, in press; Hubbard 1915; Krishnaswamy 1951; Rominger 1962; Werth 1937). Waley (1954: 158–159) admits his difficulty in understanding references to glutinous millet in ancient Chinese texts:

> It is very likely that excavation of tombs will before long settle exactly what crops the Chou people grew . . . It is clear that there were two kinds of millet, one used for eating and one chiefly for making wine. The two terms are generally translated "common millet" and "glutinous millet." I am, however, informed at Kew that this distinction, though applicable to rice, has no meaning when applied to millet.

In fact, for thousands of years glutinous and non-glutinous varieties of *S. italica* and *Panicum miliaceum*, broomcorn millet, were maintained by the Central Mountain aborigines. They were maintained probably by the Yang-shao farmers on the mainland, and certainly during the Shang and Chou dynasties.

Of special significance during a primitive stage of selection is the absence of glutinous starch types. Only when cultivators intensified efforts in cereal domestication did they evolve techniques that permitted them to maintain the glutinous varieties of foxtail millet. Whenever the ethnic or archaeologic group under investigation is able to maintain the glutinous type, we can conclude that it is at an advanced stage of cereal farming and is able to maintain any variety that is a result of some stable genetic change.

FIELD RESEARCH

In order to study the process of domestication, to gain insights into swidden techniques, and to understand the probable evolution of *S. italica*, I conducted field research among five Austronesian tribes of Taiwan during 1974–75 (Fogg 1976) and the summer of 1977. The Taiwan aborigines more than any other group in Asia have preserved traces of a way of life in which the sacred *S. italica* cultigen was an intregal part. Their history and farming techniques are assumed to be similar to prehistoric traditions in mainland Southeast Asia and North China. The aboriginal swidden cultivation of foxtail millet provides insights into the domestication process of the cultigen and into spiritual attitudes toward the ancestral grain spirit.

Early in my field research I realized that the foxtail millet cultivars of the Central Mountain tribes, the Taiyal, Bunun, Paiwan, and Lukai, were highly advanced; whereas those of the Yami, located on Lanyu Island (Botel Tobago), east of Taiwan proper, were primitive. Further, the Central Mountain tribes are able to maintain the glutinous starch cultivars, while the Yami were unable to maintain them even when provided with seed of this type.

For analysis, the cycle of swidden cultivation of foxtail millet by the Taiwan aborigines is divided into eight steps: (1) site selection, (2) preparation of seed and sowing, (3) weeding, (4) protection from predators, (5) harvesting, (6) seed selection, (7) storage, and (8) dispersal of varieties. In the following discussion the more complex techniques observed among the Central Mountain tribes in each of the eight steps of the swidden cycle are presented first, followed by those of the Yami. Comparisons are made between the two groups when the differences in swidden procedure are important to an understanding of the domestication process. The Yami methods of swidden cultivation and their cultivars of *S. italica* provide an analogue from which to reconstruct the steps necessary for the initial domestication and maintenance of primitive phenotypes of the cultigen. The Central Mountain tribes of Taiwan provide the techniques which were probably necessary for the steps in the domestication process for maintenance of advanced varieties. Crucial steps for the maintenance of advanced cultivars are weeding and roguing of primitive phenotypes, seed selection, and the concept of separating varieties during selection and sowing.

Swidden Site Selection

The major considerations for site selection by the Central Mountain tribes are for aspect, soils, precipitation patterns, and vegetation growth. The amount of land set aside for the millet swidden depends on the number of persons sharing the work and harvest. For a family of six members a square of approximately one hundred meters on each side is cleared, although some swiddens are several times larger. Sunny, south-facing slopes with loose, friable soils are preferred. Slopes with angles up to sixty degrees are farmed. According to informants, it is a simpler task to fell trees, hoe, and pull soil down-slope than on level ground; and fire burns hotter up-slope with the same amount of fuel. Fully regenerated forests are generally avoided. Sites that have approximately twenty to twenty-five years of regrowth are considered optimum. After felling and firing, lopped branches and other debris are piled behind stumps on the swidden slope to form irregular terraces. These function to prevent erosion, break the fall of rolling stones, and accumulate organic matter for leaching into the field during the growing season. Once cleared, the field is left until time for sowing, which varies from December to May depending on elevation, habitat, and precipitation patterns. Swidden sites often remain in cultivation, with intermittent fallow periods and various traditional crop rotations, for as long as twenty years.

The Yami select their swidden locations for identical reasons, although their fields are much smaller and require some additional protection from strong sea breezes. Yami sites have a greater grass and herbaceous ground cover and are often sown on former dry taro or sweet potato clearings. On such sites the Yami use a dibble stick to break the sod and root systems of plants; then they turn clumps of earth over by hand to expose the roots to the sun. They do not terrace their foxtail millet fields, although they maintain elaborate terraces and drainage systems for their wet taro. In addition to sowing on hillsides, the Yami also broadcast *S. italica* on flat land near the seashore that is protected by windbreaks of *Pandanus*.

Seed Preparation, Sowing, and Hoeing to Cover Seed

In the Central Mountains preparation of seed, sowing, and hoeing are performed on the same day. The timing of the early spring rains is important. If seed is broadcast before adequate precipitation, the young *S. italica* seedlings with their shallow, branching root system wither in the hot sun. Only one variety of *S. italica* is sown in a given swidden on any given day; other varieties are sown in different sections of the swidden on separate days. The seed sheaf of the variety selected for sowing is taken down from its storage place and carried to a work site in front of the home or field hut. The stems are cut short and the sheaf placed in a winnowing basket. The seed is threshed from the panicles by rubbing them between the hands or feet, then winnowed. One to two liters of *S. italica* seed along with a handful of *Phaseolus radiatus* (L.) and *Chenopodium album* (L.) seeds are mixed for sowing a square some fifty meters on a side. Only one person sows, usually the leader of the "union of households" or ritual group. Broadcasting begins at the bottom of the field and quickly progresses upslope. Immediately on completion of sowing, the other members of the cultivating group align themselves at the bottom of the field and begin hoeing earth over the seed. Care is taken not to retrace steps back down-slope and not to bury the seed too deeply. The blade of the hoe is thrust into the soil no more than five centimeters and pulled down-slope. Hoeing also functions to loosen the soil and to clear weeds. On completion of hoeing, crops such as *Zea mays* (L.), *Coix lachryma-jobi* (L.), and *Sorghum* are dibbled in the sown area to

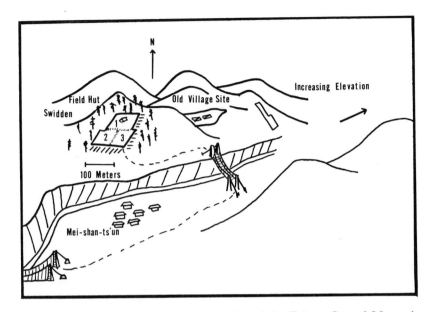

FIGURE 4.1. The swidden pattern of *S. italica* of the Taiwan Central Mountain tribes, represented by the Bunun village of Mei-shan. Numbers 1, 2, and 3 represent different varieties of *S. italica*. Variety 1 is sown first, followed by variety 2 one week later and 3 at the end of that week. Different varieties are not sown on the same day. Spatial separation between varieties is maintained within the same swidden site; it is not generally maintained by separate swiddens. The inner boundaries between varieties follow a natural feature, such as a depression or change in slope. Ideally, varieties in the field are delimited and marked by dibbling a row of *Zea mays* (in ancient times *Coix lacryma-jobi*).

furnish a few individuals of these plants. On subsequent days up to a month later, the same techniques are employed to sow different varieties of *S. italica* in other areas of the swidden. Within the swidden, natural features such as an alignment of depressions, rocks, or stumps are used to delineate boundaries between different varieties that will be sown on different days. In former times a row of *Coix* was dibbled by some farmers between areas with different varieties of *S. italica* to separate these varieties (fig. 4.1).

In these steps of swidden cultivation the Yami differ in several important ways from the Central Mountain folk. The Yami mix together the seed of all their foxtail millet varieties, sow them in the same field on the same day, and after sowing leave the seed exposed on the surface of the ground. A few weeks later the site is checked, and if necessary the seed is broadcast a second time. The major farming tool of the Central Mountain people is a narrow-bladed hoe, while that of the Yami is a dibble stick. I never witnessed a Yami using a hoe during any phase of foxtail millet cultivation. The Yami do not sow or dibble other seed crops in their *S. italica* swidden, although they do polycrop vegetatively reproduced plants with foxtail millet. Solitary individuals of taro, *Colocasia esculenta* (Schott.), sweet potatoes, *Ipomoea batatas* (Lamk.), and formerly yams, *Dioscorea* spp., remain in the swidden. Around the edges of the field, *Pandanus*, *Musa*, and wild berries are encouraged, and they furnish snack food for workers in the swidden.

Weeding

The Central Mountain tribes begin weeding and thinning of *S. italica* seedlings four to eight weeks after broadcasting, when the plants are ten to forty centimeters tall. One weeding is sufficient unless consecutive days of rain follow the initial weeding; then the uprooted weeds re-establish themselves and a second weeding becomes necessary. On 25 March 1975 I carefully observed a Bunun couple weed their swidden that had been sown late in January. The site was near Tung-pu, Nan-t'ou-hsien (ca. 23°33′ north, 120°56′ east) at an elevation of eleven hundred meters. Few weeds occupied the site. The *S. italica* seedling stand was uniform in height, averaging forty centimeters, and lush and dense. Weeds were uprooted by hand and seedlings were culled from areas of density and when necessary transplanted onto patches of bare ground. Culled weeds and seedlings were placed in piles to the sides of the swidden and behind terraces in the field. Concern in weeding is for uniform height and for spacing of a hand's width between each plant. The result is that, although there are no rows, after weeding the foxtail millet plants have even spacing, height, and density.

A study of the Central Mountain seedlings seemed to verify that they all consisted of the single-tillered phenotype. However, a minute inspection of the several thousand culled seedlings set aside in piles revealed that a handful of multi-tillered seedlings had been culled from the swidden. Measurement for seedling height, length, and width of leaf blade proved that without exception, given equal habitats, the multi-tillered seedlings were always shorter and had narrower leaf blades than the single-tillered ones. Culling during weeding is key process in domestication techniques. The Central Mountain aborigines remove a primitive genotype during the weeding process by removing its phenotype. By uprooting them at this stage, no possible contamination of the primitive genotype can occur with the advanced form because it is rogued before it flowers. The reason given for culling is not because the aborigine does not like the multi-tillered seedling, but because shortness and narrow leaf blades are perceived homoeopathically as unhealthy and weak. Plants with these characteristics are culled to preserve the healthy plants. The result is maintenance of tall, single-stemmed varieties.

The Yami weed their foxtail millet field only once. No seedlings are intentionally culled or transplanted, and no attempt is made to maintain even spacing and height. The result is that the appearance of the Yami field after weeding is uneven and irregular. Whenever wild *S. viridis* or primitive phenotypes of *S. italica* occur in the field, they are not culled. This results in the continual introgression of wild genotypes into *S. italica*.

Protection from Predators

Just before the long, nodding panicles begin to mature, the Central Mountain aborigines erect devices in the swiddens to prevent crop losses to predators. Noisemakers constructed from old tin cans, pieces of bamboo, or slate are strung through the field. Connecting lines are led back to the field hut located near the upper central quadrant of the swidden. From this time until harvest, someone usually lives in the field hut. An occasional shout and yank of the noisemakers aids in protecting the crop from the rats and birds who enjoy the feast of tender seed.

The Yami have had no effective protection for their millet crop, and have resorted only to magical devices. A miniature wooden boat was placed in the field. Around the boat were implanted four stems of the sago palm *Arenga englari* (Beccari) or *Miscanthus* reed, then two stones were placed on the boat. This device was supposed to eradicate the rats as effectively as plant poisons kill or stun fish in the river or sea (Kano 1946).

Harvesting

The Central Mountain groups harvest by hand the panicle of each plant, one by one. The culm is easily snapped in two at any node of the stem below the panicle. The stem at the base of the panicle is grasped with the left hand as the thumb and first finger of the right hand slide down the stem separating the leaf blade from the stem. At a node some forty centimeters below the panicle the stem is broken with a snap of the wrist. Generally no harvesting tool is employed. Some individuals use a small bamboo knife which fits into the palm of the right hand. The back edge of the blade extends along the first finger. Stems are easily broken between the blade edge and the thumb. After harvest the bamboo tool is abandoned in the field.

As panicles are harvested they are put into one's back basket. When enough have been collected to form a sheaf, the basket is set on the ground and the panicles are removed and tied into a sheaf. The stems are bound at two places, below the panicles and at the cut end of the stems. The bound sheaf is then passed down-slope along the line of harvesters to pre-selected sites in the swidden. After completion of the harvest, the sheaves are picked up and carried to the field hut or home site for further seed selection and preparation for drying and storage. On the following day or as time permits, the other crops in the swidden are collected. Iron knives are commonly used to harvest them.

The Yami harvest kit includes an iron knife, fiber stripped from the bark of *Pandanus* for tying the sheaves, and a net bag for carrying the millet home. Unlike the cultivars of the Central Mountain tribes, those of the Yami have thin and supple culms. The stems do not break easily at the node and some harvesting tool is necessary. The Yami harvest by grasping the stems at the base of the panicle with the left hand, pulling it taught, then severing the stem with a knife held in the right hand. Harvesting in this manner, the Yami proceed through their swidden collecting panicles of the largest size. These are carefully placed in a neat pile. The same procedure is repeated for each size range. After the harvest is completed, the "varieties" based on size categories are tied into sheaves and carried home. Because the Yams' multi-tillered millet does not ripen simultaneously, they return one or two weeks later to harvest side tillers as they reach maturity. Panicles on side tillers less than three centimeters in length are left in the field and become part of the mulch in the same site when the earth is turned for the sweet potato crop.

Seed Selection

The Central Mountain tribes select the next year's seed during harvest. As the panicles are harvested one by one, they are carefully observed for desired qualities. When one with exceptional qualities is noted, it is passed to a person in the middle of the harvesting line, who places it in a back basket. At the home site a second study is made of the seed panicles in the basket, a re-examination is made of the harvested sheaves, and a few more panicles from the latter are added to the former. Those with undesirable characteristics or damage from insects or disease are removed for immediate consumption. The best and longest seed heads are then woven into a long-stemmed sheaf and designated "the beautiful millet," which is set aside for next year's seed. With this important selection process completed, the stems of the remaining sheaves are cut short for storage and food. Because only one variety is harvested on any one day and the seed sheaf is selected on the same day, there is no mixing from different varieties; thus the genetic purity of each is maintained.

Selection pressure is almost totally focused on increasing the length of the panicle and does not result in an appreciable increase in seed size. Selection also is for diversification of varieties, beauty, and adaptation to local environmental conditions. For example, the Lukai cultivators who live near the southeastern coastal region of Taiwan, where a humid climate prevails, select panicles for length and fairly wide lobe spacing along the seed head. This aids in drying and in the prevention of damage from mildew and fungal diseases. The Taiyal of Li-hsing-ts'un (ca. 24°9′ north, 121°12′ east), at eighteen hundred meters above sea level where a cooler climate exists, select for panicles with densely packed lobes. A reason given is that dense lobe spacing makes it more difficult for birds to get at the grain.

The Yami lack any procedure for selecting a seed sheaf.

Storage

After drying in the sun, the sheaves are placed in storage. Grain is threshed from stored sheaves as needed. Most tribal groups in the past kept sheaves in outdoor granaries, although some had storage places inside their dwellings. The granaries were built some one and a half meters above ground level and supported on posts. The walls were made of thatch, planks, or bamboo; the roofs of thatch. The most important protective device, set on top of each post, was the rat guard, made from a circular piece of wood or slate and about sixty centimeters in diameter. Today all aborigines except the Taiyal store their millet sheaves inside their homes, usually in large wooden cabinets that line a wall located near the hearth fire so that the grain stays dry. A tight enclosure is necessary to keep out mice, rats, and other predators. Once or twice a year, on sunny days, the sheaves are removed from storage and taken outside to dry in the sun. Seed sheaves and individual panicles of new forms that have been selected from the field are kept on a shelf or peg located above the food sheaves to prevent possible contamination and mixing of seeds.

The Yami once had storage granaries with rat guards. Today sheaves are kept in the home, usually near the hearth fire.

Dispersal of Foxtail Millet Varieties

Patterns of seed dispersal that must have occurred over and over since prehistoric times can be illustrated by examples from Taiwan. Besides exchanges of varieties between individual farmers, there were customary ways for exchanging varieties of *S. italica* between hamlets and even tribal groups. Because it was an item of great concern and prestige, one was usually anxious to have others try his best millet. When different groups met for rituals or peaceful meetings, a common practice was to exchange foxtail millet cultivars by giving away side lobes from panicles. A Bunun informant from Mei-shan-ts'un (ca. 23°17′ north, 120°49′ east), Kao-hsiung-hsien, reported in 1975 that a new form of foxtail millet had appeared in his swidden four years earlier. The panicle lobes were wide and branching. He thought it was interesting, saved the panicle, and cultivated a patch of it the following year. That harvest year he gave some panicles of this new form to a brother who lived in the village of T'ao-yüan-ts'un (ca. 23°9′ north, 120°46′ east), some fifteen kilometers southwest down the river valley from Mei-shan-ts'un. A Taiyal informant from Li-hsing-ts'un reported in 1975 that in the recent past visiting aborigine missionaries tasted foxtail millet varieties from Li-hsing and asked for some seed samples to take home. On a return visit the missionaries brought seed panicles of their own "tasty" varieties for the people of Li-hsing to plant.

It should be noted that in former times as many as twenty distinct cultivars of foxtail millet were maintained year after year on any given mountain slope (table 4.1). No single farmer maintained all twenty cultivars in one season. Because stored seed remains viable for three or four years, varieties not sown could be saved for another year. If a family did not have seed of a desired variety they could obtain it from a neighbor or other hamlet. Cultivars were sometimes stolen from the fields of other tribes.

ANALYSIS

Swidden Techniques of Foxtail Millet Cultivation

Table 4.2 compares the swidden techniques of the Central Mountain tribes and the Yami. The explanation of the different abilities of the two groups in maintaining *S. italica* cultivars lies in their respective cultivating techniques, rather than in physical environment. The climate on Lanyu is not significantly different from that of tribal villages near the lowlands of southeastern and southwestern Taiwan. The Yami techniques provide a hypothetical model for incipient *S. italica* domestication; the Central Mountain techniques serve as a model for advanced domestication. I believe the same model can be extended back in time to mirror similar developments that occurred in mainland southeastern and eastern Asia in prehistory, especially prior to the use of the plow. A brief note concerning harvesting techniques: although today the Yami use an iron harvesting knife, in prehistory during incipient domestication of *S. italica*, bamboo, stone, bone, or shell probably provided the material for harvesting tools.

The Central Mountain people are able to select and maintain any phenotype that is a result of some stable genetic change. Each foxtail millet

TABLE 4.2 **Comparison of the Foxtail Millet Swidden Cultivation Cycle**

	Central Mountain aborigines	Yami
1. Site selection and land preparation	Large-scale Terracing and erosion control	Small-scale No terracing or erosion control
2. Preparation of seed for sowing	Keep each variety separate	Mix seed of all varieties
3. Sowing and planting	Mix *S. italica* seed with *Chenopodium* and *Phaseolus* Cover millet seed by hoeing Interplant *Coix*, maize, and sorghum Sow each millet variety in a separate area Sow different varieties on separate days	*S. italica* is the only sown cereal Do not cover the seed Do not plant other cereal crops with millet Sow seed of all varieties in the same field area Mix varieties and sow at the same time
4. Weeding	Rogue weak and short millet seedlings Transplant to achieve even spacing	Do not rogue millet seedlings Do not transplant millet seedlings
5. Protective devices	Field hut occupied as crop reaches maturity; noise-makers, scarecrows erected	Use magical devices only
6. Harvesting	Do not use iron knife (taboo), use bamboo knife or hand for breaking of stem Complete harvest in one or two days for each variety	Use iron knife Return for multiple harvesting of the same field
7. Seed selection	Carefully select seed sheaf	Do not select seed sheaf
8. Storage	Keep seed sheaf separate	Do not keep a distinct seed sheaf
9. Dispersal of new varieties	Select and disperse new varieties	Do not select new varieties
10. Maintenance of varieties	Maintain both glutinous and non-glutinous starch varieties; brew millet wine	Maintain only the non-glutinous variety; do not brew millet wine

plant is observed in its life cycle at least three times: during weeding, harvesting, and selection for the seed sheaf. A distinct seed sheaf is maintained for each variety and is sown on different days in different areas of the swidden. Both temporal and spatial separations therefore assure maintenance of genetic lines. The seed of the cultivars is not tightly enclosed by its palea and lemma, and moisture and heat reach all sown seed at the same time. Covering the seed by hoeing helps creat optimum conditions for the simultaneous germination of *S. italica* and the elimination of wild *Setaria* species. Foxtail millet seedlings of the sown variety rapidly occupy the swidden site with a dense, even stand. The practice of culling for height eliminates primitive genotypes of *S. italica* that might cross with the single-stemmed cultivars.

The Yami lack the concept of maintenance of pure seed for each variety and the procedure for spatial and temporal separation of cultivars. As a result, they cannot maintain highly evolved varieties. Further, they do not cull primitive phenotypes during weeding. Their cultivation techniques favor survival of the primitive phenotype which resembles the wild *S. viridis* in its many-tillered and prostrate growth form.

Folk Perceptions and Beliefs

Folk perceptions and beliefs are important to the domestication process. Techniques, once successful, probably remained conservative and controlled by religion, taboo, and rituals to guarantee continued success. The ancient patterns of taboo codified the empirically learned techniques and may reflect the original stages of domestication.

Among the Taiwan aborigines, human relations have been considered very much over shadowed by a magico-spiritual balance or imbalance resulting from the "soul spirit" of persons, living and dead. The world at large contained wandering spirits of deceased ancestors. The feared intervention of such beings or ancestors with the living was expected if ritual life was neglected. The soul spirit, *quanito* or *xianito* in Bunun and *anito* in Yami, could put itself in motion by its own feeling and will or could be called by its human owner. For example, the Taiyal of Li-hsing-ts'un maintained a cultivar of *S. italica* called *noadan* that had red leaves and was used specifically for head-hunting rites. Cooked grains were placed in the mouth of the victim and his soul-spirit initiated to the community. Among all the Mountain aborigines and Yami, ancestral spirits were associated with *S. italica*. Such a belief in ancestral spirits must be founded in the remote past and preserved in rituals that interweave with custom.

In the swidden rituals, the people had direct transactions with the foxtail millet plant, which they treated as if it were a being equipped with human sense organs and which was very susceptible to external influences of human sickness and abuse. Good or ill fortune in swidden cultivation was interpreted in terms of the pleasure or anger of the ancestors and soul spirit of the millet (Mabuchi 1974:292). Violations of taboo were believed to anger the ancestral spirits and to endanger the millet crop and the community. To mistreat *S. italica* plants demonstrated disrespect toward the ancestral spirits. For this reason it was taboo to beat the foxtail with a stick or flail, harvest en masse as with a sickle, or use such innovations as iron knives, rice, or rice wine that postdate the cultivation of *S. italica*.

Folk Classification of Foxtail Millet Cultivars

Over thousands of years, the Central Mountain tribes have selected out and maintained a wide array of foxtail millet cultivars. When in 1975 I asked an elder Bunun informant from Mei-shan-ts'un, T'ao-yüan-hsiang, Kao-hsiung-hsien, why they had so many varieties, he said that whenever a new and different plant appeared it was considered a gift from the ancestral spirits. It was carefully picked and set aside, and the next season a special plot was cleared for sowing seed from that panicle. If it did well it was kept for cultivation. The prehistoric farmers of North China probably had as many different cultivars as those of the Central Mountain tribes. It is also likely that the Yang-shao farmers and later Chinese of the Shang and Chou had a complex name and classification system for their varieties of *S. italica* that was analogous to that of the Taiwan aborigine. Among the Central Mountain aborigines, I have had the opportunity to compare cultivars of both *S. italica* and *P. miliaceum*. Glutinous and non-glutinous cultivars are maintained for each species, but the diversity among foxtail millet is far greater than for broomcorn millet. The millet cultivars attributed to Hou Chi in *Shih-ching* (Mao 245) are probably *S. italica*:

> . . . he sowed it with the yellow riches . . .
> there was black millet, double-kernelled black millet,
> millet with red sprouts, with white sprouts.
> (Karlgren 1950:201.)

> . . . he planted the yellow crop . . .
> It was heavy, it was tall . . .
> It nodded, it hung . . .
> The black millet, the double-kernelled,
> Millet pink-sprouted and white.
> (Waley 1954:242.)

The imagery recalls that of the maturing foxtail millet in the swiddens of Taiwan. The fields become alive with color, and an excitement begins to fill the mountainside as the nodding panicles of yellow, red, purple, brown, black, and white cultivars ripen against the interspersed brilliant crimson sprays of *Chenopodium album* and the greens of taros. Each variety is named after some qualifying characteristic, such as resemblance to a natural object, surname, color, or panicle shape. Each tribe has a generic term for *S. italica*, a separate name for the sticky starch type of the cultivar, and distinct names for each variety, whether the sticky or non-sticky type. The generic term for *S. italica* in the five tribal languages, Taiyal, Bunun, Paiwan, Lukai, and Yami, is (respectively) *tarakkesi, maxloch, vau, buchun*, and *karai*. Hence the reason why it is often difficult to clearly ascertain the millet species referred to in ancient texts. An example of folk classification is given in table 4.1. Eighteen varieties of *S. italica* were collected from the Bunun swiddens near Tung-pu, in Hsin-yi-hsiang, Nan-t'ou-hsien during the summer of 1977.

This information reveals the extraordinary energy that subsistence cultivators put into elaborating their sacred cultigen. It also reflects a sophisticated swidden farming technique. Among the Taiwan aborigines, the Bunun have had the most dispersed settlement pattern and the most complex array of *S. italica* cultivars. Their home sites often consisted of no more than two or three family units on the flanks of mountain slopes. This settlement pattern is more primitive than that of the known Yang-shao or Lung-shan sites. But the Bunun swidden techniques are probably similar to those of early Yang-shao and Lungshanoid cultures. The early domestication history of the cultivar probably occurred among groups of even simpler cultures.

Historic and Evolutionary Overview

Three cultures known to archaeology in southeastern and eastern Asia, the Hoabinhian, Lung-shan, and Yang-shao, are known to have been associated with the beginnings of agriculture. Their boundaries in space and time tend to overlap and follow the sequence from Hoabinhian to early Yang-shao and Lungshanoid cultures, but there is much controversy over their relationships (Chang 1968:83–85, 146–147; 1973:528; also Meacham 1977; Solheim 1972; Yen 1977:595–596). Known Hoabinhian cultures are associated with the northern mountain region of Southeast Asia (Spirit Cave, Non Nok Tha) from Thailand to South China and perhaps Japan. The Yang-shao is primarily a cultural development of the Wei river tributary system and North China, the Lung-shan an evolution into farming villages with many cultural variants located among and between the two cultures—that is, in the central Yangtze region and the piedmont or adjacent flatlands bordering the North China Plain and south coastal China. Probably *S. italica* evolved from the horticultural swiddens of culture groups that had similarities to late Hoabinhian and the early phases of Yang-shao and Lung-shan development.

Between 20,000 b.p. and 6000 b.p., half of the land area of Southeast Asia was submerged as sea levels rose more than fifty meters (Agrawal and Kusumgar 1974:50; Fairbridge 1968:134, 152). The emergence and submergence of former land areas and land bridges in Asia probably stimulated groups of people to migrate. As they withdrew from the diminishing shore, there would have been a great deal of cultural contact, stimulus diffusion, and increasing population pressure on the resources of the land for sustenance. Some cultures probably had to withdraw onto higher ground and began to exploit more intensively the greater diversity of flora and fauna available on the mountain slopes. It was probably due to this process and during this time that the domestication of cereals in China and Southeast Asia occurred. It is significant to note that cereals, primarily *S. italica*, supplied 50 percent of the farmed food staple for the Central Mountain tribes and yams (the latter now replaced by *Ipomoea*) and tubers of taros, the other half. Among the Yami (who rely for food primarily on tubers and resources from the sea) foxtail millet, although important for prestige and ceremony, is a minor item of diet.

Very likely, evolving Hoabinhian farming groups merged into proto-Yang-shao/Lungshanoid culture levels in Asia with taro as a major staple. In new environments where taro was more difficult to maintain, increased efforts were probably invested in foxtail millet domestication to supplement the diet. Surely efforts and experimentation involved several different interspecific grasses, but it appears that *S. italica* was amenable to changes and phenotypic plasticity caused by domestication pressures. During this period of initial domestication the wild foxtail, *S. viridis*, was a weed in swiddens throughout the region. It was probably collected in the wild or from the garden as an edible weed. The continuing occurrence of the weedy cereal in the tuber swiddens probably led to some selective weeding. Genetic changes may have resulted in new phenotypes that had larger panicle heads, or taller stems. Because of its self-pollinating nature, individuals of such plants, if tolerated as a weed in the swidden, would have shed some seed in the garden before harvest, assuring that subsequent generations of the genotype would repeatedly occur in the disturbed garden plot. Because of the long viability of the buried seed (ten to twenty years), these more robust wild foxtail millets would have persisted over several years. Somewhere cultivators probably began to protect individuals with tall stems and longer seed heads and to uproot the smaller phenotypes in the garden. Once a cultivator had the idea of spreading seed of these protected types, initial steps toward domestication, selection, and planting could have resulted in the domestication of this millet. With continued selective weeding and sowing of larger forms, it would have been possible to maintain and create a new plant with a new genotype, *S. italica*, from *S. viridis*. I suggest that so long as man was not forced into intensifying his food production, *S. italica* remained at this primitive maintenance level of cultivation. The phenotypes of *S. italica* during this phase of domestication would have been relatively short, with many tillers and small seed heads. They would have resembled the Yami type of cultigen. As some culture groups increased their use of foxtail millet and other cereals, the domestication processes intensified. Perception of new phenotypes resulting from genetic changes and intensification in seed selection, sowing, hoeing, weeding, harvesting, and maintenance techniques probably permitted groups to cultivate and maintain the single-stemmed cultivars and glutinous varieties of the millet. These new phenotypes could have seemed like a gift from the gods and ancestors.

In the initial stages of foxtail millet domestication other millets, such as *Eleusine, Panicum,* and *Echinochloa,* were also probably cultivated or brought into domestication. However, it appears that through time the length of the panicle head on these millets did not change as greatly as that of the foxtail millet under domestication. The difference in size of panicle between the wild foxtail millet and the single-stemmed cultivated *S. italica* is remarkable. The panicles of *S. viridis* and primitive forms of *S. italica* are usually three to six centimeters long. In the Central Mountains of Taiwan I observed panicles that were forty to sixty centimeters long. The height of the plant in the single, non-tillered forms equals that of a man. Important to an understanding of the probable belief, spirit associations, and operational processes in domestication is the fact that primitive people at that time were animists. Such an evolved *S. italica* plant with a long seed head and height almost double that of primitive foxtail millet phenotypes and other cultivated millet species must have been an exciting event to the mixed tuber and cereal horticulturists. This might be a reason for the great ritual importance of foxtail millet. The tall and single-stemmed black, white, pink, red, yellow, brown, bush-tailed, bi-forked, and double-kerneled panicle forms and glutinous varieties of *S. italica* were probably viewed as gifts from the ancestors. Subsequently, perhaps, the ritual significance for foxtail millet eclipsed that of the other, shorter millet cereals. When recording the origin myths of the Bunun from informants (in the village of Tung-pu, 1977) I asked why *S. italica* was ritually more important than other millet cereals. One informant became excited and raised her hand repeatedly in a spiral motion upward. She responded, "Maxloch (*S. italica*) became different from all the others when it became tall."

The primacy of origins between rice and foxtail millet is an open and controversial question. I propose that foxtail millet domestication could have preceded rice domestication. According to Brookfield's premise (1972:37), in agricultural evolution the system that offers the best returns for labor inputs is selected. Simpler choices will be selected first, and advancement up the hierarchy of difficulty will encounter increasing resistance. A shift from vegeculture to foxtail millet, foxtail millet to hill rice, and hill rice to paddy rice appears to involve increasing efforts. Dry rice and paddy rice, according to my informants, take considerably more labor than foxtail millet. Some Taiwan aborigines have had experience with both foxtail millet and dry rice, and some with paddy rice. They invariably told me that foxtail millet is easier to cultivate because: (1) the foxtail millet swidden needs only one weeding; whereas hill rice requires two; (2) foxtail millet is less demanding of soil requirements than hill rice; and (3) foxtail millet requires less protection from predators as the grain reaches maturity.

Whatever the case, it seems logical that the initial stages of domestication for tubers and cereals in Asia evolved from a garden and horticultural technique based on hoe tillage and the individual tending of plants. This technique and the association of a soul spirit to individual plants is common to the region. The domestication of *S. italica* began when man was close to the natural world around him, when he saw, felt, and tasted the differences among individual plants. Any study of plant domestication as a cultural phenomenon, especially in Asia, must take these considerations into account.

REFERENCES

Agrawal, D. P., and Kusumgar, Sheela
  1974   *Prehistoric Chronology and Radiocarbon Dating in India.* New Delhi.

Brookfield, H. C.
  1972   "Intensification and Disintensification in Pacific Agriculture; A Theoretical Approach." *Pacific Viewpoint* 13.1:30–48.

Chang, Kwang-chih
  1968   *The Archaeology of Ancient China.* Rev. and enl. ed. New Haven.
  1973   "Radiocarbon Dates from China: Some Initial Interpretations." *Current Anthropology* 14.5:525–528.

de Witt, J. M. J., Oestry-Stidd, L. L., and Cubero, J. I.
  in press   "Origins and Evolution of Foxtail Millets (*Setaria italica*)." *Economic Botany.*

Fairbridge, Rhodes W.
  1968   *Encyclopedia of Geomorphology.* New York.

Fogg, Wayne H.
1976   "Setaria italica: Its Origins and Process of Cereal Domestication in Asia." Ph.D. dissertation, University of Oregon.

Hubbard, F. T.
1915   "A Taxonomic Study of *Setaria italica* and Its Immediate Allies." *American Journal of Botany* 2:169–198.

Kano Tadao 鹿野忠雄
1946   "Kōtōsho Yamizoku no awa ni kansuru nōkō girei 紅頭嶼やミ族の粟に関する農耕儀礼." In Kano, *Tōnan Ajia minzokugaku senshigaku kenkyū* 東南亜細亜民族学先史学研究 1:380–397. Tokyo.

Karlgren, Bernhard
1950   *The Book of Odes.* Stockholm.

Krishnaswamy, N.
1951   "Origin and Distribution of Cultivated Plants of South Asia: Millets." *Indian Journal of Genetics and Plant Breeding* 11:67–74.

Mabuchi Toichi 馬渕東一
1953   "Awa o meguru Takasago-zoku no nōkō girei 要をめぐる高砂族の農耕儀礼." *Niiname no kenkyū* 新嘗の研究 1:108–144.
1974   *Ethnology of the Southwestern Pacific. The Ryukyus-Taiwan-Insular Southeast Asia.* Taipei.

Meacham, William
1977   "Continuity and Local Evolution in the Neolithic of South China." *Current Anthropology* 18.3:419–440.

Rominger, J. M.
1962   *Taxonomy of Setaria (Gramineae) in North America.* Illinois Botanical Monographs, no. 29, Urbana.

Solheim, Wilhelm G.
1972   "An Earlier Agricultural Revolution." *Scientific American* 226.4:34–41.

Waley, Arthur
1954   *The Book of Songs.* London.

Watabe, Tadayo
1967   *Glutinous Rice in Northern Thailand.* Kyoto.

Werth, E.
1937   "Zur Geographie und Geschichte der Hirsen." *Angewandte Botanik* 19:42–88.

Yen, D. E.
1977   "Hoabinhian Horticulture? The Evidence and the Question From Northwest Thailand." In *Sunda and Sahul: Prehistoric Studies in Southeast Asia, Melanesia and Australia*, edited by J. Allen, J. Golson, and R. Jones: pp. 567–599. New York.

II CULTURES AND PEOPLES

5

The Ch'ing-lien-kang Culture
and the Chinese Neolithic

RICHARD PEARSON
with the assistance of Shyh-charng Lo

CHINESE NEOLITHIC CULTURES

Chinese Neolithic cultures were the foundation for the development of civilization, the state, and urbanism. It was in the Neolithic that sedentary communities initiated the cultivation of such staple Chinese crops as millet and rice, and that styles of artifacts (particularly ceramics) which were uniquely Chinese came into being. The Neolithic in China has been shown, from recent excavations, to consist of several sequences of different cultures in different regions. Because the cultures of first Kansu and then the North China Plain, the Chung Yüan, are the best known, it was once common to see these areas as primary cultural hearth lands affecting all of China. However, with the reporting of new dated excavations in the south and along the eastern coast the picture has changed, so that no discussion of the origins of Chinese civilization can be based solely on the Huang Ho basin.

> New archaeological data unearthed in the last decade or so and the newly available radiocarbon dates suggest that the early Postglacial inhabitants of at least two or possibly three regions in China crossed the threshhold to agricultural ways of life. They centered in the Middle Yellow River of North China, the southeastern coastal areas, and the lower Yangtze and Huai River areas, and they are known respectively as Yang-shao, Ta-p'en-k'eng, and Ch'ing-lien-kang (Chang 1977b: 153).

Recent Chinese archaeological research has identified two early food-producing cultures, the millet-farming Yang-shao culture of the Huang Ho and the rice-growing culture of the lower Yangtze. A third, along the southeast coast of China, remains hypothetical in the absence of plant

119

remains. It is thought to have relied heavily on root crops (Chang 1977a:87).

Although there are many questions unresolved, data concerning the postclimatic optimum are now appearing in Chinese sources (Chang 1977b:144). In the northern area, cultivation appears to have begun in an ecotonal situation of steppe and oak forest along the water courses of the Fen, Wei, and Huang rivers. There is debate about the climate and vegetation at this time (Ho 1969; Chang 1977a:33–35; Pearson 1974). I believe there is clear evidence to support the idea that Yang-shao farmers practiced slash-and-burn cultivation on the forested terraces of the Huang Ho. Dog and pig bones have been found in Yang-shao sites, while cattle are known from two sites, sheep and goats from two others; and silk worms, with the cocoon cut, from yet another (Chang 1977a:95).

The process by which populations settled down and began farming has not been extensively elucidated in China. Only a few sites from the late Pleistocene have been conclusively dated:

ZK–109–0 Chih-yü, Shuo-hsien, Shansi (112°17': 39°25'). Fossilized ox bones (*Bubalus ef.* Wansijocki) from Palaeolithic remains, layer 2.
28,945 ± 1370 b.p. (5,730 years half-life).
(Barnard 1980:73; CKKH shih-yen-shih and Chung-kuo 1976:30.)

ZK–417   Hsia-ch'uan, Ch'in-shui, Shansi (112°10': 35°43'). Charcoal from layer no. 2 square 8, 76SCXIT8 ②. [Microlithic culture context?]
23,900 ± 1000 b.p.
Three other dates obtained from this site have been published: ZK–384, 21,700 ± 1000 b.p.; ZK–393, 21,700 ± 1000 b.p.; and ZK–385, 16,400 ± 900 b.p. ZK–384 and ZK–85 appear definitely to be from microlithic culture contexts.
(Barnard 1980:77; Chung-kuo she-hui 1978:285–286.)

BK–76050 Hsi-k'uo Reservoir, T'ung-liang, Szechwan (106/107°: 29/30°). Ebony from deposit formed at juncture of river and lake at base of reservoir, S.T.X. ①. Paleolithic stone implements and fossilized animal bones in same layer.
21,550 ± 310 b.p.
(Barnard 1980:59; *WW* 1978.5:75.)

BK–77022 Huang-shan, Ha-erh-pin, Heilungkiang (126/128°: 44/46°). Fossilized wood from hillside.
30,000 ± 700 b.p.
(Barnard 1980:136; *WW* 1978.5:76.)

ZK–118–0 Mu-tan-chiang-shih (?), Heilungkiang (129°35': 44°35'). Mammoth tooth (*Mammuthus primigenius* B.). Late Pleistocene-Holocene.
21,540 ± 1000 b.p.
(Barnard 1980:136; Chung-kuo she-hui 1978:284.)

Although there are some tantalizing mentions of microlithic remains at some of these sites, no full reports are available. Dated post-Pleistocene sites, with the exception of Hsien-jen-tung in Kiangsi province, discussed below, are not fully published.

The earliest sites, which the Chinese have termed Incipient Neolithic are those from south of the Yangtze. Three different types of site location are found (P'eng 1976: 16–18). First there are cave sites, such as Hsien-jen-tung in Kiangsi Province and Weng-yüan in Kwangtung province. The second type is shell midden sites, such as Tung-hsing in Kwangsi and Shih-wei-shan in Kwangtung. The third site location type is on relatively flat plateaus, such as the Hsi-chiao-shan site in the Pearl river delta, Kwangtung. The basic artifacts from these sites are abundant chipped stone pebble tools and rare polished stone tools, both used for fishing and gathering. Pottery occurs at many of these sites. It is of a coarse cord-marked pattern, and the vessel forms are *kuan* 罐 and *ying* 缶 jars with constricted necks, shallow *p'an* 盤 bowls, straight-sided *po* 鉢 jars, and footed *tou* 豆 stands.

The lowest layer of the Hsien-jen-tung site produced chipped pebble choppers, flakes and polished stone discs, points, and chisels, along with cord-marked pottery, bone points and harpoons, and animal bones. The Tseng-p'i-yen site, south of Kuei-lin (*KK* 1976.3), has yielded an assemblage which appears to be similar.

We do not know which plants and animals, if any, were domesticated by the Incipient Neolithic peoples. As K. C. Chang (1977a: 513) has pointed out, many of these sites were once considered Mesolithic and have only recently been designated Incipient Neolithic. They bear many characteristics of the Hoabinhian sites of Southeast Asia and were probably left by people with subsistence patterns and a yearly round similar to those of the Hoabinhian populations.

These sites are distinguished as a group from the Ch'ing-lien-kang sites, which have reddish sandy pottery, polished stone tools (chipped stone tools seem completely lacking), and the bones of pigs, dogs, goats, and bovids.

There is considerable chronological overlap between the Incipient Neolithic sites and the earliest sites of the Ch'ing-lien-kang, suggesting that in favorable areas domestication may have appeared earlier than in other areas. Only the vaguest picture of the relations between these two kinds of sites emerges at this point because of the paucity of detailed site reports, the very low level of sophistication of reporting on subsistence patterns, and the almost total lack of paleo-environmental data.

TABLE 5.1 **Radiocarbon dates for the Ch'ing-lien-kang culture and other early sites in the lower and middle Yangtze area**

Laboratory Number	Site	Sample	Associated Culture; Sources of Publication	b.p. (before 1950), half life 5730 ± 40	b.c., half life 5730 ± 40	Re-calibrated B.C. (DFLW)
			A. Incipient Neolithic			
ZK–92–0	Hsien-jen-tung, Wan-nien, Kiangsi, lower stratum	Fossilized animal bone	Incipient Neolithic (Chiang-hsi-sheng 1976:35; Barnard 1980:53)	8823 ± 235	6873 ± 235	—
BK–75057	Ho-mu-tu, Yü-yao, Chekiang	Wood from YMT 16; 4:13, layer 4	Incipient Neolithic (*WW* 1976.12:84; Barnard 1980:86)	6310 ± 100	4360 ± 100	5008 ± 117
ZK–279–1	Tseng-p'i-yen, Kuei-lin, Kwangsi, 73KjDT5③	Mollusk shell	South China, Incipient Neolithic (Hsia 1977:220; Barnard 1980:39)	11,310 ± 180	9360 ± 180	—
ZK–280–0	Tseng-p'i-yen, Kuei-lin, Kwangsi, rear half of cave interior, layer 3 73KJDT5③	Fossilized bone	Neolithic, with coarse red pottery (Chung-kuo she-hui 1978:283; Barnard 1980:39)	7580 ± 410	5630 ± 410	—
ZK–263 (2)	Ho-mu-tu, Yü-yao, Chekiang, layer 4	Acorns, T-21 4	Incipient Neolithic (Chung-kuo she-hui 1978:287; Barnard 1980:86)	6085 ± 100	4135 ± 100	4793 ± 133
			B. Neolithic			
BK–75058	Ho-mu-tu, Yü-yao, Chekiang, layer 2, YMF1:13	Wood	Ma-chia-pang phase, Ch'ing-lien-kang (*WW* 1976.12:84; Barnard 1980:86)	5050 ± 100	3100 ± 100	3718 ± 135
ZK–315	Yü-tun, Ch'ang-chou, layer 4, 74; chw IT1310④:1	Charcoal	Ch'ing-lien-kang (Chung-kuo she-hui 1978:283; Barnard 1980:57)	5000 ± 120	3050 ± 120	3657 ± 150
ZK–316	Yü-tun, Ch'ang-chou, layer 5, 74; chwIT1310⑤:1	Charcoal	Ch'ing-lien-kang (Chung-kuo she-hui 1978:283; Barnard 1980:57)	5020 ± 120	3070 ± 120	3683 ± 150

Lab No.	Site	Material	Culture			
ZK–343–1	Lin-chia-ts'ao, Shanghai, 2 m. below surface of old shoreline at T'ai Hu	Oyster shells	Late Neolithic (Chung-kuo she-hui 1978:284; Barnard 1980:59)	5875 ± 185	3925 ± 185	4587 ± 205
ZK–344–1	Ma-ch'iao, Shanghai old shoreline; lower level of Liang-chu culture layer	Clam shell fragments, accumulated by wave action	Liang-chu culture (Chung-kuo she-hui 1978:284; Barnard 1980:60)	5680 ± 180	3730 ± 180	4391 ± 254
ZK–292	Ch'ing-p'u, Feng-hsi, 4th layer, stratum of green ashy soil	Wood	No culture assigned (Chung-kuo she-hui 1978:287; Barnard 1980:59)	4080 ± 100	2130 ± 100	2551 ± 137
ZK–90	Ta-tun-tzu, P'i-hsien, Kiangsu	Charcoal	Ch'ing-lien-kang (CKKH shih-yen-shih 1974:334; Barnard 1980:58)	5785 ± 105	3835 ± 105	4497 ± 208
ZK–55	Sung-tse, Ch'ing-p'u, Shanghai	Wood	Ch'ing-lien-kang (CKKH shih-yen-shih 1972:57; Barnard 1980:58)	5345 ± 105	3395 ± 105	4042 ± 149
BK–76022	Ts'ao-hsieh-shan, Wu-hsien, Kiangsu, layer 5, 10.45 m. below surface, WCT 703	Fossilized wood	Early Ch'ing-lien-kang (Hsia 1977:220; Barnard 1980:59)	5370 ± 110	3420 ± 110	4069 ± 168
BK–76023	Yü-tun, Ch'ang-chou, Kiangsu, layer 5, 4.5 m. below surface, CHWIT1310	Charred wood	Middle Ch'ing-lien-kang (Hsia 1977:220; Barnard 1980:57)	5300 ± 110	3350 ± 110	3993 ± 115

SOURCE: Chang 1977a: 486, 511, 512.
NOTE: The dates from Tseng-p'i-yen, Kuei-lin, are included for comparison.

The Ho-mu-tu site at Yü-yao-hsien, Chekiang, (Che-chiang-sheng and Po-wu-kuan 1976), is the most important discovery for elucidating the origins of Ch'ing-lien-kang culture. With a recalibrated dating of about 5000 B.C. (table 5.1), this site has firmly established rice cultivation in the Yangtze delta at an early period. Abundant rice remains, which have been identified as *Oryza sativa indica* (Chang 1977a: 513), have been recovered; other plant remains include water caltrop, gourd, sour date, and other fruits and nuts. The remains of pig, dogs, and (probably) water buffalo, as well as the bones of deer, turtles, rhinoceroses, and elephants have also been recovered. Animal shoulder blades were used as tilling implements (Hua 1977). Some of the pottery forms seem similar to those of the Ch'ing-lien-kang period. The site gives the first concrete evidence of early rice cultivation in the Yangtze river valley and seems to be the forerunner of the Ch'ing-lien-kang culture in terms of general adaptation and pottery styles.

Because of the geological conditions of Kiangsu and northern Chekiang, it is doubtful that very early sites will be found in the same locations as later ones. T'an (1973: 7) has recommended further survey in the southeast corner of Kiangsu along the north coast of Hangchow bay. The coastal areas of other parts of the region were not developed, and the land surrounding the T'ai Hu may have been dry land in early prehistory but may have sunk below water level in the more recent past. Therefore I do not believe that the absence of pre-Ch'ing-lien-kang sites in the area necessarily means that the culture was first derived from some other part of the country. It may have stemmed from people living at the edges of the Yangtze delta or in the middle reaches of the Yangtze Chiang.

The Ch'ing-lien-kang culture represents an adaptation to a different environment from that of North China: to the moist, marshy region of the lower Yangtze. Its development appears to be intimately linked to the buildup of alluvium along the coast of Kiangsu and at the mouth of the Yangtze Chiang. It is based on rice cultivation. The development is of comparable date to the Yang-shao, and there are broad similarities in the presence of painting on pottery and vessel shapes (particularly the distinctive tripod forms); at the same time, however, there are sharp differences in the forms of vessels and stone tools, and of painting styles. Although there are few faunal analyses available, and some of the most imposing sites are cemeteries, the general locations of the sites indicate that the inhabitants were using both fresh water and marine resources, often at the same time. The recently discovered Ho-mu-tu site in Chekiang province may be ancestral to the Ch'ing-lien-kang culture, but there are not enough artifacts yet to make a detailed stylistic comparison.

Although there are no skeletal remains from the Ta-p'en-k'eng culture of the southeast coast, there are some 296 individuals known from the Yang-shao sites of Pan-p'o (61), Pao-chi (136), and Hua-hsien (99), all in Shensi. Chang Kwang-chih (1977b:153) states that all three populations bear striking resemblances; they seem closest to such modern populations as southern Chinese, some Indochinese peoples, and Indonesians, according to Yen Yen, a physical anthropologist of the Institute of Archaeology, who studied them. In the 1970s, three populations totaling 219 individuals from the northern region of the Ch'ing-lien-kang culture were recovered, from Ta-wen-k'ou, Shantung (79 individuals), Hsi-hsia-hou, Shantung (27), and Ta-tun-tzu, Kiangsu (113) (Chang 1977b:153–154). These three populations show some statistical separation from Yang-shao cranial measurements. Of the modern populations with which they have been compared, Polynesian samples have been closest.

Racial characteristics of the Hsi-hsia-hou skeletons resemble those of the Ta-wen-k'ou specimens. The basis for this comparison is the application of the "t" and "k" tests on the cranial data. At both the Ta-wen-k'ou and Hsi-hsia-hou sites the lateral incisors were removed, probably in initiation rites. The incidence of this practice at Hsi-hsia-hou was 33 percent among the males and 67 percent among the females (Yen 1973:126).

The Yang-shao culture is comparatively well known from abundant reports in Chinese and English. The Ch'ing-lien-kang culture is less well known, as many of the discoveries have been made only within the last decade. Terminological confusion concerning the latter is rife; nevertheless, there is clear evidence of a second Neolithic breakthrough in China, occurring roughly contemporaneously with the Yang-shao, in the lower Yangtze region, based on rice. It is this culture, or groups of tightly related cultures, with which I shall deal. The third postulated beginning of cultivation, along the southeast coast, remains unsubstantiated, with problems of dating and a lack of excavated food remains (Reed 1977:911).

DESCRIPTION OF THE CH'ING-LIEN-KANG CULTURE

The Ch'ing-lien-kang culture was first identified in an excavation in 1951 at the Ch'ing-lien-kang site in northern Kiangsu. As a result of intensive survey by the Shanghai and Nanking museums and other local organizations, over sixty-five sites are currently known in Kiangsu, which appears to be the center of the distribution. About five hundred Neolithic sites are known in the coastal provinces such as Shantung, Kiangsu, Anhwei, and Chekiang, and there are about sixty sites in the lower Yangtze valley. Other sites have been found north into the middle portion of Shantung, south to the T'ai Hu, west to Anhwei, and east to the Tien Shan Hu, in an area of about one hundred thousand square kilometers. Sites such as Ta-wen-k'ou in Shantung, Sung-tse in Shanghai, and Ma-chia-pang in Chekiang have been classified as Ch'ing-lien-kang although they are relatively widely spread. The site of Ch'ing-lien-kang has not undergone a large excavation—only four test areas, each five meters by five meters—and the ceramic sample included only forty-three specimens, which were more or less complete, plus two fragments of grindstones and two fragments of stone chisels (Chu Chiang 1977). This has led to some criticism that the original site does not represent what has come to be known as the Ch'ing-lien-kang culture (ibid.). Yet the main criteria for defining a new culture, as outlined by Hsia Nai (1959), seem to be covered: a well-defined group of associated traits, distribution in a number of residential and burial sites, and a group of diagnostic traits which include characteristics of everyday living. A great deal of emphasis has been placed on the characteristics of the burials and pottery styles, however, so that we have little idea of residential and settlement patterns. Chu Chiang (1977) has made these criticisms of Wu Shan-ching's (1973) comprehensive formulation of the Ch'ing-lien-kang culture. Chang Kwang-chih (1977a : 136) has stated that there is still no working definition which applies to the whole cultural unit, north and south of the Yangtze. But an article published by the Nanking Museum (Nan-ching 1978) shows that many of the artifact categories are clearly shared by both groups (see figs. 5.1, 5.2). An important conference in which the Yangtze Neolithic was discussed took place in Nanking in 1977 and was sponsored by the Nanking Museum and the Wen Wu Publishing House.

As early as 1957, authors such as Tung Ch'u-chen noted that the Ch'ing-lien-kang culture possessed a number of characteristics which set it apart from other Neolithic cultures in China. Tung noted that sites such as Pei-yin-yang-ying in Nanking and Ch'ing-lien-kang showed, in their painted ceramics, characteristics of Yang-shao. At the same time, he mentioned the variation in Neolithic stone tools in China—the stone plow and flat shovel of Shansi, the long, large, thick, and heavy shovels of Sian, the long, flat shovels from Honan, the flat, grooved axes of Chi-nan, the perforated axes from southern Kiangsu and northern Chekiang, and the triangular stone tools from Chekiang. At one point, the Ch'ing-lien-kang culture was called the Kiangsu Lung-shan culture, and its relation to the Lung-shan was one of the major problems in the early research.

At the time of excavation of the Pei-yin-yang-ying site (Nan-ching

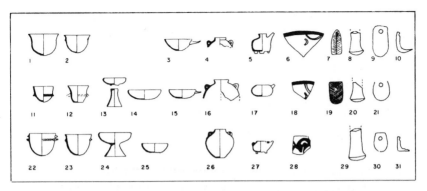

FIGURE 5.1. **Comparison of artifacts from the Hsü-Hai area (northern coast of Kiangsu, Huai-an-hsien, and south of the Yangtze) in the earliest period of the Ch'ing-lien-kang. (Nan-ching 1978:47.) Upper row: objects from the Hsü-Hai area, earliest (initial) period, Ch'ing-lien-kang culture. Middle row: objects from the Ch'ing-lien-kang site, Huai-an-hsien. Lower row: objects from the earliest (initial) period, Ch'ing-lien-kang culture, south of the Yangtze. 1, 3, 4, 6, 7, 8, Ta-tun-tzu; 2, 5, Erh-chien-ts'un; 9, 10, Lien-yün-kang; 11–21, Ch'ing-lien-kang; 22–25, 27, 28, Ts'ao-hsieh-shan; 26, Pei-yin-yang-ying, Nanking; 29, Ma-chia-pang; 30, 31, Yü-tun-ts'un, Ch'ang-chou.**

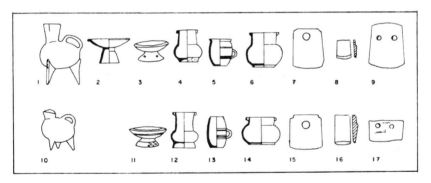

FIGURE 5.2. **Comparison of artifacts from north and south of the Yangtze in the latest period of the Ch'ing-lien-kang culture. (Nan-ching 1978:53, 54.) Upper row: north of the Yangtze. Lower row: south of the Yangtze. 1, 2, 4, 5, 8, 9, Ta-tun-tzu; 3, 6, 7, Hua-t'ing; 10, Kuang-fu-lin; 11, 12, 16, Yüeh-ch'eng; 13, 14, 15, 17, Chang-ling-shan.**

1958), it was considered that Ch'ing-lien-kang belonged to the later Neolithic and that it had received influence from both Lung-shan and Yang-shao. It was thought of as later than Lung-shan but earlier than the Han dynasty. Excavation at a number of sites in Kiangsu, including Ta-tun-tzu (Nan-ching 1964), showed that the Ch'ing-lien-kang strata lay *under* the Lung-shan remains.

Survey and excavation at Kan-yü, in northeast Kiangsu, yielded three sites with Lung-shan remains. These sites are close to the Shantung border and are about ten kilometers from such other Lung-shan sites as Jih-chao and Ta-t'ai-tzu in Shantung (Nan-ching 1962b). The excavation of the site of Erh-chien-ts'un at Lien-yün-kang in November 1959 uncovered three cultural layers: Han dynasty on top, Lung-shan in the middle, and Ch'ing-lien-kang in the lower layer. The second excavation, in 1960, showed two different situations below the Han layers. In the first case, the Lung-shan and Ch'ing-lien-kang remains were found in two different parts of the site in the same relative stratigraphic position, without superimposition. But in most parts of the site, the Ch'ing-lien-kang were found beneath the Lung-shan remains.

Radiocarbon dating has confirmed that the Ch'ing-lien-kang culture is early (table 5.1). The dates from Ta-tun-tzu are almost as early as those for Pan-p'o-ts'un, and the other recalibrated dates range from the fifth millennium to the early fourth millennium B.C. Wu Shan-ching (1973) has stated that the dating for the later Ch'ing-lien-kang culture, both north and south of the Yangtze, should fall between 5800 and 4275 b.p. (The corrected range would be about 4500 to 2600 B.C) Chang Kwang-chih has acknowledged that the

> possible establishment of the Ch'ing-lien-kang culture in northern Kiangsu as a third early Neolithic center in China parallel to the Yang-shao and Ta-p'en-k'eng is an important event in the history of Chinese archaeology, but it brings to the fore a number of questions that cannot be answered (1977a:134).

Chang has classified only the earliest manifestation of the Ch'ing-lien-kang as the type, grouping the later remains under the Lungshanoid cultures. Wu Shan-ching, on the other hand, has created a broader category of Ch'ing-lien-kang culture (see figs. 5.1, 5.2), embracing four periods north of the Yangtze river and three periods to the south. For our purposes of attempting to focus on local ecological development rather than on stylistic influences, the broader category, based on successive layers at a number of key sites, seems more useful.

There appears to be strong local continuity in ceramics and stone tools from the early Ch'ing-lien-kang to later periods (figs. 5.3, 5.4). Wu mentions that the *fu* 釜 shaped *ting* 鼎 and the *po* 缽 shaped *ting* of the Liu-lin period appear to have developed from the *fu* and *po* of the Ch'ing-lien-kang period through the addition of tripods. The *tou* 豆 without cutouts of the Ch'ing-lien-kang period developed into the *tou* with cutouts in the ring foot of the Liu-lin period and the *tou* with large cutout ring feet of the Hua-t'ing

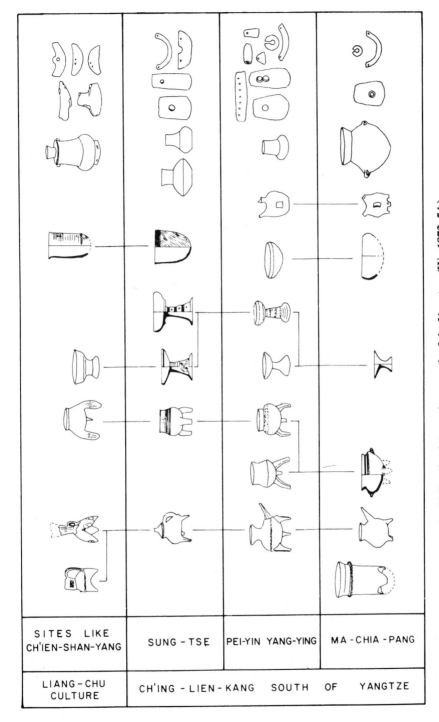

SITES LIKE CH'IEN-SHAN-YANG	SUNG - TSE	PEI-YIN YANG-YING	MA - CHIA - PANG
LIANG - CHU CULTURE	CH'ING - LIEN - KANG SOUTH OF YANGTZE		

FIGURE 5.3. Ceramic sequence for the Ch'ing-lien-kang culture south of the Yangtze. (Wu 1973:54.)

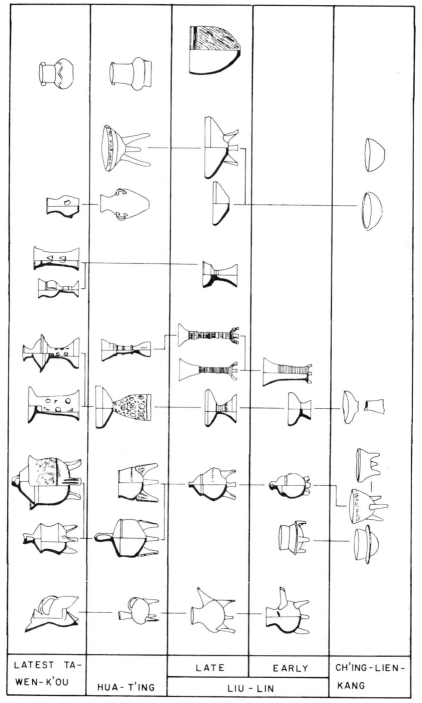

LATEST TA-WEN-K'OU	HUA-T'ING	LATE	EARLY	CH'ING-LIEN-KANG
		LIU - LIN		

FIGURE 5.4. Ceramic sequence for the Ch'ing-lien-kang culture north of the Yangtze. (Wu 1973:50.)

花廳 period. The tripod *ku* 觚 shaped cup and the small mouthed *kuan* with handles of the Liu-lin period developed into the *ku*-shaped cup with ring foot, and into the *kuei* 鬹 with solid legs in the Hua-t'ing period. All three periods used flat, perforated stone axes, stone adzes, and deer-jaw cutting tools, with less emphasis on stone reaping knives than in the sites north of the Yangtze. It is also of interest that the jade objects from the Chiang-nan sites are the earliest examples found of the Chinese Neolithic. The jade must have come from Chekiang and Anhwei provinces.

Subsistence Patterns of the Ch'ing-lien-kang

It is unfortunate that most of the work on the Ch'ing-lien-kang culture has focused on stylistic similarities of ceramic types (without attention to sampling strategies or quantitative techniques) and on burial sites. The shell deposits and waterlogged sites would appear to be favorable places for ecological analyses; little of this type of research has been forthcoming, however, beyond the level of noting the presence and absence of different kinds of food remains.

Wu (1973:57) notes that remains of pigs, dogs, goats, cattle, fish, turtles, oysters, deer, and rabbits and, south of the Yangtze from the Mei-yen site, great numbers of water buffalo bones, have been found. Rice grains have been recovered from the Sung-tse site (lower stratum) and from Ts'ao-hsieh-shan in Wu-hsien (Chang 1977a:140). Bones of cattle, deer, boar, fish, and fox, and turtle shells, fragments of bamboo and wood, and a carbonized water caltrop shell (*Trapa* sp.) were found at Ma-chia-pang (Chang 1977a:140). Abundant bones of water buffalo (*Bubalus* spp.) were found among the cattle bones.

Data for Environmental Reconstruction

Evidence cited by Chu K'o-cheng (1972), which is based on a very limited number of pollen analyses and the presence of certain animals in archaeological deposits, indicates that from five thousand to three thousand years ago the yearly average temperature was about three to five degrees centigrade higher than now. One line of evidence is provided by the bamboo rat, whose northern limit has moved south by one to three degrees of latitude since the Yang-shao period.

At the same time, according to evidence in Japan and Southeast Asia, sea levels were higher; the peak of post-Pleistocene levels was reached between seven thousand and five thousand years ago. One might expect that the low-lying areas of Kiangsu province and the mouth of the Yangtze would have been submerged during the post-Pleistocene maximum sea levels and would have emerged gradually with the buildup of alluvium and the lowering of the sea. Although this process did take place in the broadest sense, local subsidence at the mouth of the Yangtze and round the T'ai Hu and the effects of currents and tides have complicated the picture. No simple rate of buildup based on a constant rate of deposition per year can be used with any reliability. T'an Ch'i-hsiang postulates four zones of buildup in the Shanghai area based on different processes (map 5.1).

The most important geological unit is the Kang-shen zone, which is composed of broken shell and sand. The literal name of this zone, "hill body," refers to the slight rise created by an ancient beach line. In 1959, the Ma-ch'iao archaeological site was found in the Kang-shen zone. Ma-ch'iao has four layers: the top is T'ang and Sung, the second is Warring States, the third is Shang and Chou, and the fourth is Neolithic. This zone was thus in existence five to six thousand years ago. The process of formation is thought to have been very slow, with probably between five hundred and three thousand years required to extend the zone one kilometer. The reason for the slow buildup is that the amount of sediment, contained as it was by forests and marshes, was slight compared to later times, and the rate of sedimentation is thought to have been in equilibrium with the rate of sinking. At this time the T'ai Hu was protected from the sea by two sandy spits, one which curved southwest and another which extended from the mouth of the Ch'ien-t'ang river. The seawater outside this sand spit region was much deeper and cleaner than in later times. The second zone, a vast, shallow sea connecting with the T'ai Hu to the west and the Pacific to the east, lay inside the Kang-shen zone. After the formation of the Kang-shen zone, the land of the second zone was protected and became the earliest inhabitable area in the Shanghai region. This area, which appears to have been composed of fine alluvium from the Yangtze, formed more rapidly than the Kang-shen zone, and it was consolidated in its southern portion faster than in the north. More than ten Neolithic sites have been found in the area. Several deeper areas became freshwater lakes. Other freshwater lakes here have a different origin, derived as they are from sinking in the T'ai Hu area (the lowest in the Shanghai region) in later times. The third and fourth zones, which do not concern us here, were formed in the first few centuries A.D. and in post-Sung times, respectively.

The buildup of the second zone was from the south first. Thus, T'an suggests it is the southeast corner, near Chekiang province, which might yield sites earlier than Sung-tse. With the formation of the Kang-shen zone, the second zone could be inhabited easily.

The tentative conclusions which can be drawn from these brief points

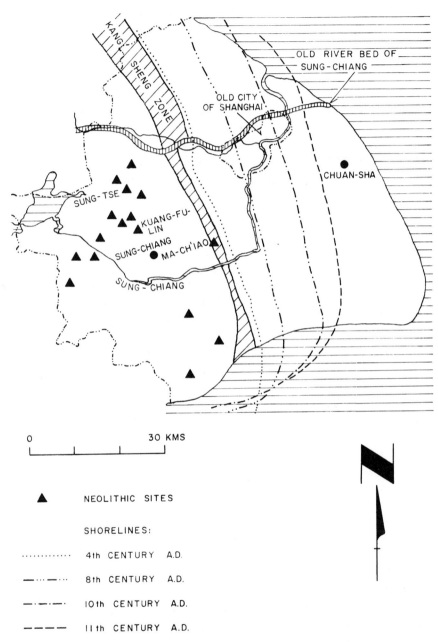

MAP 5.1. **Land and sea level changes in the Shanghai area. (T'an 1973:6.)**

are that the climate at the time of the early periods of Ch'ing-lien-kang culture was warmer and moister than at present and that the lowland terrain around the T'ai Hu was extensive. It appears to have been a kind of ecotone, comprised of the mesophytic forests mentioned by Wang (1961:95–129), strand vegetation and marshes, clean unsilted bays, and freshwater lakes. People also lived on the shoals extending out from the river mouth. Yin and Chang (1962) reported that they discovered many sites in the T'ai Hu which were covered with peat built up by flooding as the land sank after the Neolithic occupations. One site at K'un-shan was deposited in the lake-bottom silt, showing that in this case the prehistoric people lived directly at the edge of the lake. Later buildup has occurred with the accumulated sediment of recent times and of reclamation schemes carried on since the T'ang dynasty.

How did the people of the Ch'ing-lien-kang culture use the land on which they lived? Some slight indications can be gained from the locations of the sites. In the 1950s the Nanking Museum undertook a number of regional surveys, finding 15 mound-shaped sites at Hu-shu near the Ch'in-huai river and 139 sites in an area of some four thousand square kilometers in the Ning-chen mountains of Kiangsu and Anhwei (Yin and Chang 1959). Some examples of these mound-shaped sites (characterized as *t'ai* 台) follow in the Ch'in-huai area (Nan-ching 1962a).

T'ai 161	Hu-kuo-an. Three to 7 meters above the flat plain, flat top, greyish soil, 90 meters long east-west, 80 meters wide north-south, 7200 square meters in area.
T'ai 165	Chu-ch'in ta-shan. Oval in shape, about 7 meters above the surrounding flat terrain, about 120 meters east-west, 80 meters north-south, greyish soil.
T'ai 166	Chiang-ch'eng-tzu. Small river in the southwest side, mound on both north and west side, flat plain on the south. Site is about 8 meters above the surface of the surrounding terrain, ovaloid with a flat top, 90 meters long east-west, 70 meters north-south.

Many of these sites contain Liang-chu culture remains on the surface, with Ch'ing-lien-kang remains in their deeper layers. The Ch'ing-lien-kang sites appear to have been on high ground. It is not clear whether the surrounding land was dry at the time of occupation.

In the Huai-yin-hsien region, the vicinity of the original Ch'ing-lien-kang, the Nanking Museum has worked on the distribution and relationships of the Ch'ing-lien-kang, Lung-shan, Liang-chu, and Hu-shu cultures (Yin and Chao 1963) (map 5.2). The largest Ch'ing-lien-kang site found was 150,000 square meters in area, the smallest 250 square meters. Generally the sites seemed to fall between 2,000 and 7,000 square meters.

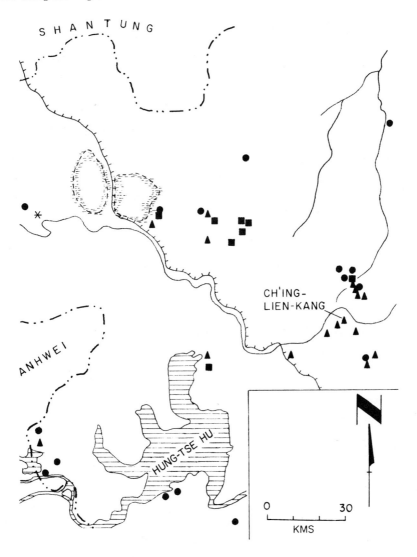

▲   NEOLITHIC PERIOD   ■   CHOU DYNASTY SITES
    SITES
✳   SHANG DYNASTY SITES   ●   HAN DYNASTY SITES

MAP 5.2. **Sites in the vicinity of Huai-yin-hsien, Kiangsu. (Yin and Chao 1963:1.)**

The sites were found in a number of type locations, the first group on the
north and south banks of the Fei-huang river, on low mounds covered by a
layer of sandy yellowish soil 1 to 3 meters thick. The yellowish overburden,
which made the sites difficult to locate, was deposited by flooding of the
Huang Ho and the Huai in the Ming and Ch'ing dynasties. Beneath the
yellowish soil, the predominant soil type is grey silt. At the Yen-chia-ma-
t'ou site, located on the west side of the high land at Ch'ing-lien-kang, the
cultural layer is composed of hard greyish soil 1.1 meters thick, underlaid
by yellowish grey soil about 20 centimeters thick, with fewer remains. The
lowest layer of the site, which is reddish sand, is sterile. The second location
type is on the plain near the lakes. These sites are larger in area than the
previous ones and are composed of greyish soil. In the summer and
autumn, the low-lying areas near the lakes are submerged, creating islands.
Some of these sites are near small rivers. The third settlement location is on
mounds, in which case the cultural materials are found in a yellowish grey
soil.

Sites identified as Lung-shan in the survey are found on mounds, but
also on what the authors describe as flat areas a little higher than their
surroundings. Although the t'ai are shared by the two overlapping cultures, sites on the flat plains are not specifically mentioned for the Ch'ing-
lien-kang culture.

Long occupation of the same place, as seen in the deep deposits and
relatively large number of sites with several superimposed cultural layers,
seems to be the general rule for Ch'ing-lien-kang sites. Examples are Pei-
yin-yang-ying, Ta-tun-tzu, Ts'ao-hsieh-shan, and Sung-tse. This stability
of settlement seems to indicate a slowly developing settlement and subsistence pattern in which the general form of land use changed gradually if
at all. The stone tool inventory in particular seems to remain the same. The
perforated stone tools appear to have been used as hoes, similarly to
wooden examples found much later in the Yayoi in Japan. They would
seem to be suitable for turning soft, alluvial soils. It is also interesting that
these tools appear from the early Ch'ing-lien-kang, in such sites as the Yü-
tun-ts'un (fig. 5.5).

There appear to be few sites among those which are well published which
show pioneering of new ecotypes or changing subsistence strategies. This
may be a matter of sampling or reporting, however. The sites which have
been chosen for excavation are the deepest, best stratified examples. Very
small sites have been listed in survey reports, and these and other marginal
categories should be sampled in future fieldwork. The Liang-chu sites on
the slopes around the edge of the Yangtze delta may indicate a change of

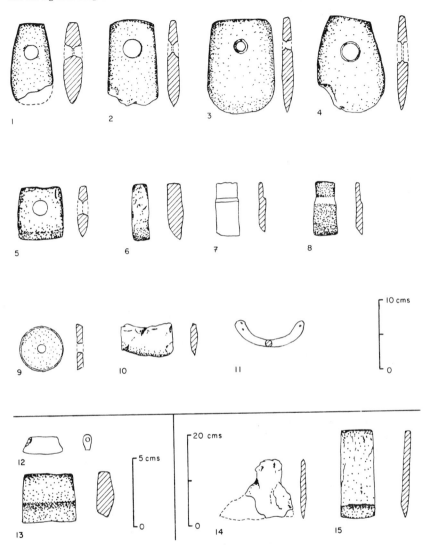

FIGURE 5.5. **Stone tools, early Ch'ing-lien-kang, from Yü-tun-ts'un, Ch'ang-chou, Kiangsu. (Ch'ang-chou-shih 1974:113.) 1, 2, 3, 4, 5, perforated stone axes; 6, 13, bevelled adzes; 7, 8, stepped adzes; 9, stone spindle whorl; 10, stone knife; 11, semi-circular jade ornament; 12, jade tubular bead; 14, "battle axe" (*yüeh*); 15, adze.**

subsistence or a broadening of land-use patterns to accommodate a population increase (map 5.3).

NORTHERN AND SOUTHERN VARIANTS OF THE CH'ING-LIEN-KANG CULTURE

The Nanking Museum group has expressed strong conviction that the Ch'ing-lien-kang culture is a single cultural unit which extends from the Kiangsu-Shantung border to Chekiang Province (figs. 5.1, 5.2). Some participants in the 1978 Berkeley Conference on the Origins of Chinese Civilization expressed the opinion that rice may have been grown in the southern regions occupied by the Ch'ing-lien-kang and millet in the north. But there is no direct evidence of millet from the northern Ch'ing-lien-kang culture area at this time.

Differences in the mode of burial have been noted between the north and the south (Nan-ching 1978). Northerners were buried in the extended position lying on their back; some were also interred in a flexed position. In the south, few individuals were buried in a dorsal position—most were buried lying face down. The stone tools are noted to be more elaborate in the southern region; there are stone triangular knives, stone tools for paddy cultivation, and stone knives with handles.

Cultivation equipment appears to have developed earlier in the south and then spread to the north. During the fourth period, the Liang-chu culture in the south had rather advanced cultivating tools compared to those found in the northern Ta-wen-k'ou culture. The Ta-wen-k'ou culture, however, had rather elaborate bone and tusk tools not known in Liang-chu.

Throughout this chapter, I have assumed a kind of local continuous evolution of culture, which seems to be favored in the site reports. I believe this is clearest in the stone tool assemblages and in what appears to be utilitarian pottery. In pottery found in the burial sites the Lungshanoid component seems stronger. But I have not yet done enough analysis of the raw data presented in the site reports to present this as anything more than a strong impression. I am convinced of the utility of careful plotting and tabulation of correspondences between site assemblages, something which has not been done to any degree in the available literature. The data are available and can easily be reduced with quantitative techniques. I should like to know, for instance, if the burial assemblages favor the same kinds of vessels in the northern site of Ta-tun-tzu (which would appear to have heavier Lung-shan influence), the Nanking site of Pei-yin-yang-ying, and

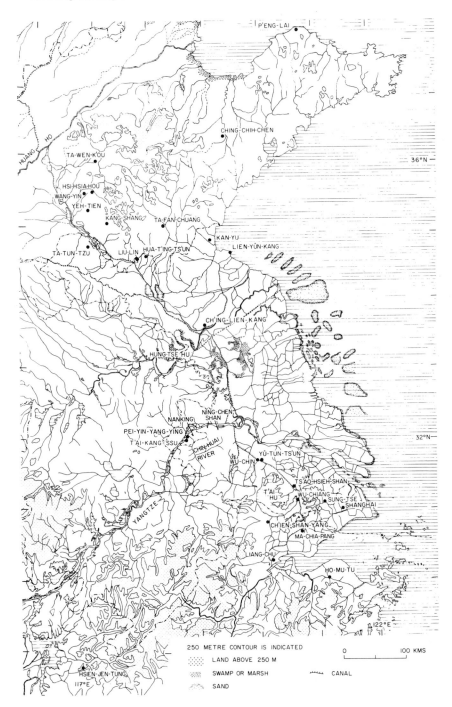

MAP 5.3. **Major Neolithic sites, Yangtze delta and coastal region, Kiangsu and northern Chekiang.**

the Shanghai site of Sung-tse. I should also like to separate the pottery found in contexts clearly *not* associated with the burials, since this pottery is often presented within the reports.

SIGNIFICANCE OF THE CH'ING-LIEN-KANG CULTURE

The Ch'ing-lien-kang culture and the early site of Ho-mu-tu provide data on the early development of the most important subsistence mode for monsoonal eastern Asia: the cultivation of rice. The evidence is clear, as early as 5,000 B.C., and it is impeccable—identifiable plant remains in stratigraphic context. In addition to the remains of rice, abundant tools thought to have been used for cultivation, and wooden house remains which suggest permanent occupation, show the development of what has been considered a short fallow system of cultivation (Yu 1976). In the later sites, increasing wealth, evident in the burial methods and accoutrements, must have involved intensification of cultivation practices, which would permit a surplus to feed a growing population and an emerging administrative hierarchy. In sites of the final stage of the Ch'ing-lien-kang cultural tradition, such as Ta-wen-k'ou (Shan-tung-sheng 1978) and Hsi-hsia-hou (CKKH Shan-tung tui 1964), the great wealth of some burials (which are not, however, given clear spatial segregation) suggests the emergence of chiefs. In particular, the proliferation of jade objects in a variety of badge-like forms which bear little relation to utilitarian artifacts seems to provide evidence of social ranking.

Although there are general similarities between the Ch'ing-lien-kang culture and the Yang-shao and Lung-shan, there are clear divergences in artifact types, such as ornaments and stone tools, and pottery styles. The Ch'ing-lien-kang culture constitutes a third Neolithic stream of development. Although not all archaeologists would attribute such late sites as Ta-wen-k'ou to the Ch'ing-lien-kang culture, the social differentiation apparent at these sites, as well as the occurrence of animal effigy burial vessels, albeit of clay, in high-status burials, suggest that strands from the Yangtze and coastal Neolithic are woven into the fabric of the Chinese Bronze Age.

This chapter has dealt primarily with the description of these sites and their ecological contexts. Future studies should be concerned with the cultural contribution of the recently discovered Ch'ing-lien-kang culture to later periods of Chinese archaeology and cultural history.

REFERENCES

Barnard, Noel
 1980   *Radiocarbon Dates and Their Significance in the Chinese Archaeological Scene: A List of 420 Entries Compiled from Chinese Sources Published up to Close of 1979.* Canberra.

Chang, Kwang-chih
 1977a   *The Archaeology of Ancient China.* 3rd ed., rev. and enl. New Haven.
 1977b   "Chinese Palaeoanthropology." *Annual Review of Anthropology* 6 : 137–159.

Ch'ang-chou-shih   Ch'ang-chou-shih po-wu-kuan 常州市博物舘
 1974   "Chiang-su Ch'ang-chou Yü-tun-ts'un hsin-shih-ch'i shih-tai yi-chih ti tiao-ch'a ho shih-chüeh 江蘇常州圩墩村新石器時代遺址的調查和試掘." *KK* 1974.2 : 109–115.

Che-chiang-sheng   Che-chiang-sheng wen-wu kuan-li wei-yüan-hui 浙江省文物管理委員會
 1960   "Wu-hsing Ch'ien-shan-yang yi-chih 1956, 1958 nien fa-chüeh pao-kao 吳興錢山漾遺址1956,1958年發掘報告." *KKHP* 1960.2 : 73–93.

Che-chiang-sheng and Po-wu-kuan   Che-chiang-sheng wen-kuan-hui 浙江省文管會 and Che-chiang-sheng po-wu-kuan 浙江省博物舘
 1976   "Ho-mu-tu fa-hsien yüan-shih she-hui chung-yao yi-chih 河姆渡發現原始社會重要遺址." *WW* 1976.8 : 6–14.

Chiang-hsi-sheng   Chiang-hsi-sheng po-wu-kuan 江西省博物舘
 1976   "Chiang-hsi-sheng Wan-nien Ta-yüan Hsien-jen-tung tung-hsüeh yi-chih ti-erh-tz'u fa-chüeh pao-kao 江西省萬年大源仙人洞洞穴遺址第二次發掘報告." *WW* 1976.12 : 23–35.

Chu Chiang 朱江
 1977   "Kuan-yü 'Ch'ing-lien-kang yi-chih' ho 'Ch'ing-lien-kang wen-hua' wen-t'i 關于'青蓮崗'遺址和'青蓮崗文化'問題." *KK* 1977.3 : 189–192.

Chu K'o-chen 竺可楨
 1972   "Chung-kuo chin-wu-ch'ien-nien lai ch'i-hou pien-ch'ien ti ch'u-pu yen-chiu 中國近五千年來氣候變遷的初步研究." *KKHP* 1972.1 : 15–38.

Chung-kuo she-hui   Chung-kuo she-hui k'o-hsüeh-yüan k'ao-ku yen-
          chiu-so shih-yen-shih 中國社會科學院考古研究所實驗室
1978   "Fang-she-hsing t'an-su ts'e-ting nien-tai pao-kao (wu)
          放射性碳素測定年代報告(五)." *KK* 1978.4 : 280–287.

CKKH Shan-tung tui   CKKH Shan-tung tui 山東隊
1964   "Shan-tung Ch'ü-fu Hsi-hsia-hou yi-chih ti-yi-tz'u fa-
          chüeh pao-kao 山東曲阜西夏侯遺址第一次發掘報告."
          KKHP 1964.2 : 57–107.

CKKH shih-yen-shih   CKKH shih-yen-shih 實驗室
1972   "Fang-she-hsing t'an-su ts'e-ting nien-tai pao-kao (erh)
          放射性碳素測定年代報告(二)." *KK* 1972.5 : 56–58.
1974   "Fang-she-hsing t'an-su ts'e-ting nien-tai pao-kao (san)
          放射性碳素測定年代報告(三)." *KK* 1974.5 : 333–338.

CKKH shih-yen-shih and Chung-kuo   CKKH shih-yen-shih 實驗室 and
          Chung-kuo k'o-hsüeh-yüan ku chi-chui tung-wu yü ku-
          jen-lei yen-chiu-so shih-yen-shih 中國科學院古脊椎動物
          與古人類研究所實驗室
1976   "Ku-chih piao-pen ti t'an–14 nien-tai ts'e-ting fang-fa
          骨質標本的碳 - 14年代測定方法." *KK* 1976.1 : 28–30, 58.

Ho, Ping-ti
1969   "The Loess and the Origin of Chinese Agriculture."
          American Historical Review 75.1 : 1–36.
1975   *The Cradle of the East: An Inquiry into the Indigenous*
          Origins of Techniques and Ideas of Neolithic and Early
          Historic China, 5000–1000 B.C. Hong Kong and Chicago.

Hsia Nai 夏鼐
1959   "Kuan-yü k'ao-ku-hsüeh shang wen-hua ti ting-ming wen-
          t'i 關於考古學上文化的定名問題." *KK* 1959.4 : 169–172.
1960   "Ch'ang-chiang liu-yü k'ao-ku wen-t'i 長江流域考古
          問題." *KK* 1960.2 : 1–8.
1977   "T'an–14 ts'e-ting nien-tai ho Chung-kuo shih-ch'ien
          k'ao-ku-hsüeh 碳 - 14測定年代和中國史前考古學." *KK*
          1977.4 : 217–232.

Hua Ch'üan 華泉
1977   "Tui Ho-mu-tu yi-chih ku-chih keng-chü ti chi-tien k'an-
          fa 對河姆渡遺址骨制耕具的幾點看法." *WW* 1977.7 :
          51–33.

Huang Hsüan-p'ei 黃宣佩, **Wu Kuei-fang** 吳貴芳, **and Yang Chia-yu**
          楊嘉祐

1976   "Ts'ung k'ao-ku fa-hsien t'an Shang-hai ch'eng-lu nien-tai
               chi kang-k'ou fa-chan 從考古發現談上海成陸年代及
               港口發展." *WW* 1976.11:45–55.

KK
1962.3a   "Chiang-su Lien-yün-kang-shih Erh-chien-ts'un yi-chih ti-
               erh-tz'u fa-chüeh 江蘇連雲港市二澗村遺址第二次發掘 ":
               pp. 111–116.
1962.3b   "Nan-ching Hsi-shan-ch'iao T'ai-kang-ssu yi-chih ti fa-
               chüeh 南京西善橋太崗寺遺址的發掘 ": pp. 117–124.
1963.6   "Chiang-su Wu-chiang Mei-yen hsin-shih-ch'i shih-tai yi-
               chih 江蘇吳江梅堰新石器時代遺址 ": pp. 308–318.
1976.3   "Kuang-hsi Kuei-lin Tseng-p'i-yen tung-hsüeh yi-chih ti
               shih-chüeh 廣西桂林甑皮岩洞穴遺址的試掘 ": pp. 175–
               179.

Nan-ching Nan-ching po-wu-yüan 南京博物院
1958   "Nan-ching-shih Pei-yin-yang-ying ti-yi, erh-tz'u ti fa-
               chüeh 南京市北陰陽營第一、二次的發掘." *KKHP*
               1958.1:7–24.
1962a   "Chiang-su Yi-liu ti-ch'ü Hu-shu wen-hua yi-chih tiao-
               ch'a 江蘇儀六地區湖熟文化遺址調查." *KK* 1962.3:125–
               128.
1962b   "Chiang-su Kan-yü hsin-shih-ch'i shih-tai chih Han-tai yi-
               chih ho mu-tsang 江蘇贛榆新石器時代至漢代遺址和
               墓葬." *KK* 1962.3:129–132.
1964   "Chiang-su P'i-hsien Ssu-hu-chen Ta-tun-tzu yi-chih t'an-
               chüeh pao-kao 江蘇邳縣四戶鎮大墩子遺址探掘報告." *KK*
               1964.2:9–56.
1978   "Ch'ang-chiang hsia-yu hsin-shih-ch'i shih-tai wen-hua jo-
               kan wen-t'i ti t'an-hsi 長江下游新石器時代文化若干問題
               的探析." *WW* 1978.4:46–57.

Pearson, R.
1974   "Pollen Counts in North China." *Antiquity* 48.191:
               226–228.

P'eng Shih-fan 彭適凡
1976   "Shih-lun Hua-nan ti-ch'ü hsin-shih-ch'i shih-tai tsao-ch'i
               wen-hua—Chien-lun yu-kuan ti chi-ko wen-t'i 試論華南
               地區新石器時代早期文化—兼論有關的幾個問題." *WW*
               1976.12:15–22.

Reed, Charles A.
1977   "Origins of Agriculture: Discussions and Some

Conclusions." In *Origins of Agriculture*, edited by C. A.
Reed: pp. 879–953. The Hague.

Shang-hai-shih   Shang-hai-shih wen-wu pao-kuan wei-yüan-hui 上海市
文物保管委員會
  1962a   "Shang-hai-shih Ch'ing-p'u-hsien Sung-tse yi-chih ti shih-
chüeh 上海市青浦縣崧澤遺址的試掘." *KKHP* 1962.2:
1–31.
  1962b   "Shang-hai-shih Sung-chiang-hsien Kuang-fu-lin hsin-
shih-ch'i shih-tai yi-chih shih-t'an 上海市松江縣廣富林
新石器時代遺址試探." *KK* 1962.9:465–469.

Shan-tung-sheng   Shan-tung-sheng po-wu-kuan 山東省博物舘
  1978   "T'an-t'an Ta-wen-k'ou wen-hua 談談大汶口文化." *WW*
1978.4:58–66.

T'an Ch'i-hsiang 譚其驤
  1973   'Shang-hai-shih ta-lu pu-fen ti hai-lu pien-ch'ien ho k'ai-fa
kuo-ch'eng 上海市大陸部分的海陸變遷和開發過程." *KK*
1973.1:2–10.

T'ung Chu-ch'en 佟柱臣
  1957   "Huang-ho Ch'ang-chiang chung-hsia-yu hsin-shih-ch'i
wen-hua ti fen-pu yü fen-ch'i 黃河長江中下游新石器
文化的分佈與分期." *KKHP* 1957.2:7–21.

Wang, Chi-wu
  1961   *The Forests of China: With a Survey of Grassland and
Desert Vegetation*. Maria Cabot Moors Foundation
Publication 5. Cambridge, Mass.

Wu Shan-ching 吳山菁
  1973   "Lüeh-lun Ch'ing-lien-kang wen-hua 略論青蓮崗文化."
WW 1973.6:45–61.

WW
  1976.12   "Yeh-t'i shan-shuo-fa t'an-14 nien-tai ts'e-ting kung-tso
ch'u-pu pao-kao 液體閃爍法碳14年代測定工作初步
報告": pp. 80–84.
  1978.5   "T'an-shih-ssu nien-tai ts'e-ting pao-kao (hsü-yi)
碳十四年代測定報告(續一)": pp. 75–76.

Yen Yen 顏誾
  1973   "Hsi-hsia-hou hsin-shih-ch'i shih-tai jen-ku ti yen-chiu
pao-kao 西夏侯新石器時代人骨的研究報告." *KKHP*
1973.2:91–144.

Yin Huan-chang 尹煥章 and Chang Cheng-hsiang 張正祥

1959   "Ning-chen shan-mai chi Ch'in-Huai-ho ti-ch'ü hsin-shih-
        ch'i shih-tai yi-chih p'u-ch'a pao-kao 寧鎮山脈及
        秦淮河地區新石器時代遺址普查報告." *KKHP* 1959.1:
        13–40.

1962   "Tui Chiang-su T'ai-hu ti-ch'ü hsin-shih-ch'i wen-hua ti
        yi-hsieh jen-shih 對江蘇太湖地區新石器文化的一些認識."
        KK 1962.3:147–157.

Yin Huan-chang 尹煥章 and Chao Ch'ing-fang 趙青芳

1963   "Huai-yin ti-ch'ü k'ao-ku tiao-ch'a 淮陰地區考古調查."
        KK 1963.1:1–9.

Yu Hsiu-ling 游修齡

1976   "Tui Ho-mu-tu yi-chih ti-ssu wen-hua-ts'eng ch'u-t'u tao-
        ku ku-ssu ti chi-tien k'an-fa 對河姆渡遺址第四文化層
        出土稻谷骨耜的幾點看法." *WW* 1976.8:20–23.

6

Origins and Development
of the Yüeh Coastal Neolithic:
A Microcosm of Culture Change
on the Mainland of East Asia

WILLIAM MEACHAM

In this chapter, a description will be presented of the Yüeh cultural horizon from its possible emergence in the early Holocene to its ultimate incorporation in Han civilization, with an emphasis on the earlier periods. A few preliminary remarks are in order on the points at which this development does, and does not, relate to the "origins of Chinese civilization." If by the latter is meant the cumulative historical entity, then of course the prehistory and incorporation of any of its integral parts is of direct relevance. As I shall endeavor to demonstrate, the prehistoric inhabitants of the southeast coastal area designated as Yüeh 越 (both peoples and area) have an ancestral link with the present population of the same area, and their descendants have of course made an enormous contribution to Chinese civilization since the Han era.

But even if we confine our inquiry to the roots and first causes of the earliest manifestation of a literate, urban-centered, bronze-working, class-structured society, there is much to be learned from a consideration of the culture processes and developments occurring in peripheral areas and peoples. The process by which these peoples moved from Paleolithic through Neolithic and often to the brink of civilization is in many, perhaps most, significant aspects similar to the process through which the populations of the Central Plains (Chung Yüan) also passed in their own evolution. This continuity and shared cultural process between regions has often been obscured in the "nuclear area" interpretation of Chinese prehistory, especially in the establishment of a nuclear-orbital or donor-receptor relation between the Central Plains and other populations. If we are to see (as surely we must) the rise of early Chinese civilization as part of a much larger development than that transpiring solely in the nuclear area or, better, "genesis area," then the evolution of the Yüeh and other contiguous peoples may shed considerable light on the cultural origins and processes from which early Chinese civilization developed.

Up until the last few years, when the data have made such a position almost untenable, the pattern of cultural relations in prehistoric China has been modeled on that thought to have prevailed beginning with the rise of Shang civilization. Such remote regions as the southeast coast were said to have felt the impact of Neolithic developments in the nuclear area, often coming in waves of ideas, or even of settlers, penetrating a primordial tropical jungle sparsely inhabited by hunter-gatherers little changed since the Pleistocene. This tendency to view the area where Shang civilization first appeared as the hub of the "Chinese" universe in even earlier times as well—and as a *centrum ab quem* artifacts, ideas, and people spread into peripheral regions—was a transplant (into the extremely fertile soil of the traditional North-China-centered world view) of the diffusion/migration hypotheses associated with early Near Eastern civilization. The new nucleus of development in the Far East was seen in the loess region of the Huang Ho basin, and the qualities and characteristics of this region were held to account for the spectacularly rapid pace of development there. A by-product of this intensive cultural activity was the setting off of explosive tremors radiating out from the nuclear area and stimulating similar though minor developments in the orbital areas.

Although it must be admitted that the nuclear area model was a very attractive and elegant synthesis of the data and hypothesis of development, the cultures and peoples distant from the nucleus were obviously relegated to a secondary position not theoretically justifiable, or in accord with the data available, as a few writers did note. It is ironic that the emphasis on the local origins and independent evolution of Chinese civilization which was put forward as a counter-model to the "western origins" theory should lead to a comparable nuclear scheme within China. While there are still a number of proponents of the nuclear model, including some (Ho 1975; Cheng 1976) who take the concept to extreme and often ludicrous conclusions, recent data (above all, the carbon-14 dates) clearly require abandonment of the nuclear area model for prehistoric China and a new and vigorous inquiry into how and by what mechanisms the Central Plains became the genesis area (if indeed it was) for the complex of traits defined as civilization. I can find no common ground here with Noel Barnard (1977) and Ho (1975:20, 167–168), who see in the carbon-14 dates an *increased* possibility of the primacy of the nuclear area six thousand years ago.

A small number of carbon-14 dates has opened up new and virtually undreamed-of horizons in Neolithic China, and we should not be unprepared for similar openings in the Bronze Age (if, indeed, they have not already occurred). If the Central Plains is to be seen as any kind of nucleus in late prehistory, it is now distinctly possible that it was in many respects a *centrum ad quem*, perhaps more akin to the eye of a whirlpool created by an *implosive* movement of culture traits than to the explosively fissionable nucleus so frequently described in recent decades. If so, the role of areas around the genesis area would take on a wholly new character, and their contribution to the rise of Shang may be much greater than previously supposed. There are, however, many theoretical and practical problems with this model as well, to be discussed below.

The foregoing notwithstanding, it can still be argued with some justification that Shang civilization emerged at the end of a unique, geographically and perhaps ethnically limited cultural chain of events. It is only at the final stages of this development that an entity comes into focus which can be called "Chinese," "Chinese culture," or "Chinese civilization." The Yüeh and most other ancient populations in the territory of modern China were not directly involved in this birth of civilization, which may have involved no more than a few centuries and an area smaller than the present Honan province. There is a sense in which the traditional view of ancient Chinese history is correct (and perhaps it originated ultimately in the first appearance of dynastic civilization): those on the fringes and outside this esoteric event were "barbarians" in that they did not enjoy (or suffer from) the fruit of civilization until they were brought into close contact with it by an imperial expansion of the civilization itself. Though the Yüeh of the pre-Han era may have acquired on occasion some of the trappings of Chinese civilization, most of the Yüeh peoples (including the inhabitants of the state/territory of Yüeh in the Spring and Autumn and Warring States periods) should not be considered "Chinese"—if, that is, the term is to be defined by cultural content, which seems the only meaningful definition for anthropological-historical purposes. The most compelling data that could be advanced in support of the barbarian status of the Yüeh is the fact that their contemporaries of the central states considered them so. It was a very gradual process of assimilation that finally conferred on them Chinese status (Creel 1970:194–241).

Any use of the word "Chinese" in an anthropological sense encounters a number of difficulties. It seems that we shall never have sufficient physical anthropological criteria to distinguish Chinese from non-Chinese within the broad category of southern Mongoloid. The problem is not only with the inadequacy of skeletal remains; there are virtually no distinguishing sub-racial differences between, for example, Cantonese, Chuang, and Vietnamese (see the discussion by Howells, ch. 11, below). Nor will linguistics alone provide a criterion, owing to the obvious lack of evidence regarding the spoken language. The fact that written Chinese was in use in the state of Yüeh (probably composed largely of Austronesian or Thai-Kadai speakers, following Benedict [1967–1968]), rather than indicating that its people were Sinitic, is evidence of the presence of Chinese cultural elements in the Yüeh sphere.

A definition of "Chinese" based on modern or historical political realities, though convenient and consistent with the noun "China," tends to rob the word of the content it ought to carry. To label, as Chang suggests (1977:640), "all local cultures in prehistoric China that, in their entirety or in large part, became part of the historical Chinese civilization" as Chinese or proto-Chinese would tend to deny that these cultures might more accurately be described as Tai, Mon-Khmer, Malayo-Polynesian, and so on.[1] The Yüeh probably arose from a Tai cultural sub-stratum (Eberhard 1968), and they did become culturally Chinese at some stage in their history. It is useful to attempt to describe this transition, but to assign a "Chineseness" to the prehistoric inhabitants of Kwangtung, Tibet, and Manchuria would blur the true cultural affiliations of these peoples. On the other hand, there may well be, as described above, a close relation between the way these widely distant peoples evolved in Neolithic times. We must, however, use "prehistoric China" in its geographical sense only, avoiding extrapolations backward in time of later cultural phenomena.

An area population will be examined here with a view to eliciting which elements of its cultural evolution may be representative of a broader macrocosmic development, but without attempting to establish a cultural identity among the various units. That is, whereas the culture content of the Yüeh, Lungshanoid, Yang-shao, and other peoples was diverse, their cultural origins and pattern of development may have been highly similar and attributable in part to certain shared catalysts. Finally, it may be possible to suggest priorities of assumptions and theoretical perspectives,

---

1. Chang offered another, perhaps more useful definition elsewhere: "Before [the Ch'in unification], the ancient Chinese were but one of the local peoples of China. After, the Chinese were to become the people of China" (1976:v). The former definition is presumably cultural, while the latter reverts (apparently) to the geographical. It might be best to avoid the use of the word altogether to designate any single group of people prior to the Shang.

derived from common stimuli, which would better frame the archaeological data and give rise to new hypotheses regarding the relationships of peripheral areas to the genesis area.

THE EMERGENCE OF THE NEOLITHIC IN COASTAL SOUTH CHINA

An assumption and modus operandi in what follows will be that late Pleistocene and Holocene prehistory can best be investigated without direct reference to the culture history of contiguous regions. There is clearly no need to postulate migrations into the area to populate it, or to invoke diffusions of ideas to explain many or most of the innovations which took place there. While there certainly was broad inter-regional exchange of certain traits, the sources of most cultural development should, I believe, be sought primarily in internal rather than external stimuli. I have elaborated on this theme elsewhere (Meacham 1977), and there is no need to list yet again the many instances in which the assumption of local evolution and continuity has been vindicated (sometimes in the face of considerable opposition). Rather, I shall attempt here a reconstruction of the emergence and development of the Neolithic of the southern coast, focusing on the Yüeh but with occasional reference to the southern "Lungshanoid," which has been much more extensively investigated. The aim will be quite simply to operationalize the local evolution model by presenting a synthesis of data and formulating a plausible early scenario for developments documented in their later stages only.

This section will be of necessity highly speculative, not only because of the paucity of data and sites known to date from this earliest "Neolithic" period (which featured pottery, polished stone tools, and possibly incipient animal and plant domestication). It is probable that much of the development in this "Crystallitic Period" (Solheim 1972) took place on the then exposed continental shelf of South China. The fact that this area is now under up to one hundred meters of sea, and that any cultural deposits not destroyed by the marine transgression are probably well overlaid by silt and may never see the light of day, should nonetheless not result in the neglect of this area in schemes dealing with the early Neolithic. On the contrary, the important ecological, topographic, and cultural changes associated with this vast continental plain may have been of supreme importance in the spread and overlapping of traits into Neolithic cultures which come into focus by 4000 B.C.

Before attempting to bridge this void in the archaeological record, data relating to the early Neolithic should be briefly reviewed. The upper Paleolithic of late Pleistocene South China is known from a number of upland sites (mainly caves) yielding chipped pebble tools and faunal remains (Aigner 1979). It is now virtually certain that the Mesolithic Hoabinhian and the early Neolithic Bacsonian (following the terminology of the Vietnamese) are inter-grading stages in a gradual evolution of pottery and ground (then polished) stone industries on a Paleolithic base. All sites of this important transitional stage are cave sites in the mountainous interior, and those which have been dated (notably Bo-nam and Con Moong in North Vietnam, Tseng-p'i-yen in Kwangsi, Hsien-jen-tung in Kiangsi, and, still further afield, Spirit Cave in Thailand) fall within the 10,000–5000 B.C. range. The North Vietnam sites are the best dated (*Khao Co Hoc* 1976.2:18), and a total of eight carbon-14 dates indicate an overlapping range of 9000–5600 B.C. for Hoabinhian and 8300–5900 B.C. for Bacsonian—the latter associated with crudely polished stone axes and corded pottery and possibly with domesticated water buffalo, root crops, and hill rice (Davidson 1975; Long 1975).

The two carbon-14-dated sites from South China accord with the general pattern of evidence from Vietnam. While the stratigraphy at Hsien-jen-tung is very complicated and will require greater care when dating samples are taken, there is no reason to question the validity of the date (as Hsia 1977:219 has done).[2] Both dated samples (8920 and 6873 b.c.; ZK–39, ZK–92–0) probably derive from the early assemblage (discussed in detail in Meacham 1976:207–208), which in the opinion of the excavators "belongs to the earliest Neolithic period in China dating to at least eight thousand years ago." Similarly, the carbon-14 date of 9360 b.c. (ZK–279–1) from Tseng-p'i-yen (which Hsia again finds "too early") may come from the lower portion of the prehistoric stratum which yielded material of clearly late Neolithic affinity, as well as chipped pebble and polished bone tools similar to those of Hsien-jen-tung.

In brief, there is evidence of an upland population advancing steadily in pottery and stone technology, and probably also in domestication. Solheim

---

2. Hsia (1977) notes that both sites are in limestone caves, and the ground water contains "old" carbonates which may contaminate the shells, "making the carbon-14 a little older". While theoretically possible, such a backward contamination is very rarely seen. Exchanges of carbonates between organic materials and the groundwater almost always result in much *later* carbon-14 ages, as the carbonates usually present in ground water are of modern origin. This is the case for all samples tested from other limestone caves in China which have been dated by both carbonates and collagen; the dates on carbonates are invariably more recent, sometimes by as much as fifteen thousand years (CKKH shih-yen-shih and Ku-chi-chui 1976; Barnard 1977).

has postulated (1972) that these developments led eventually to a move-ment of Hoabinhian peoples out of the mountain habitat where they had thrived for millennia, into the lower river valleys, and eventually to and on the sea; he cites the absence of early sites in the lowlands to support his view. A hypothesis more in line with the continuity model will be developed here: that the population of the interior closely paralleled the coastal inhabitants in their development and that many of the innovations of this period may have originated in the coastal areas. But our focus will be on the possible internal mechanics of culture change.

The concept of a now submerged Sunda Land has been put forward on occasion in Southeast Asian archaeology but has not to my knowledge been elaborated with reference to the Neolithic in South China. Yet if one accepts the basic premise that the exposed continental shelves were in-habited at the end of the last glacial maximum, then such a concept is of considerable theoretical importance. And the premise seems highly prob-able: the attractions of the shoreline and coastal plain are obvious enough, and even early man with his limited technology must have found there a diversity and abundance of provisions which were seemingly inexhaustible. At low tides, a wide variety of shellfish, crabs, and other forms of life were there for the collecting, day after day. Turtles and their eggs would have been another easy prey, as would the marine mammals or fish stranded on occasion in small pools. The shallow sea held yet another assemblage of life to be exploited, as did the small streams, rivers, and plains near the coast. In the view of many geographers (e.g., Sauer 1948), subsistence must have been not only more reliable, but also supportive of a larger population than inland areas.

For the ten millennia beginning circa 16,000 B.P., as the sea underwent "the most rapid rise yet recorded in the geological record" (Fairbridge 1960), the inhabitants of coastal areas were being confined (perhaps con-centrated) on the remaining flat land near the sea. According to most estimates, at least a hundred-mile-wide strip of land off South China was submerged by circa 4000 B.C., when the present sea level was reached. A number of dated deposits from the seabed in the Hong Kong area give evidence of this rise of sea (Kendall 1975:29; Meacham 1975:35).

Among an increasingly concentrated coastal population, a greater ex-change of ideas and elaboration of techniques would be expected, perhaps coupled with an expanded role for previously unimportant facets of the economy. It cannot be said that population pressure would necessarily create a strain on the subsistence available by fishing and collecting, for the transgression of the sea did create a longer coastline, a greater number of bays, inlets, and peninsulas, and correspondingly more and varied food sources. However, in the adjustment required to exploit new grounds, or different types of animal or plant life, and in the larger numbers of people making the adjustment, there were undoubtedly more "accidental" discoveries, and improvements motivated by a search for efficiency. With a larger population applying its energies in a wider scope of activities (plant manipulation, pottery, polished tools, travel by boat), the stage would be set for a truly crystallitic period in the formation of local cultures. By 4000 B.C. in most areas bordering the South China Sea, clusters of ceramic and stone technological traits can be seen, often associated with a greatly increased incidence of sites.

The changing topography almost certainly would have contributed to the development of and reliance on boats—which would in turn have accelerated the flow of information. Though simple rafts and other flotation devices must have been in use long before, it is difficult to imagine their deployment on the open sea away from the sight of land, or even along the coastal waterways governed by strong winds and currents. The boats (if any) being used prior to circa 10,000 B.C. were probably simple bamboo rafts without directional control other than by poling in shallow water, or paddling, although their shape was likely to be too awkward for the latter to be very effective. But their utility in crossing bodies of still or slow-moving water can be envisioned, especially in the shallow delta areas or swamps and within small bays. Reliance on such rafts would have been minimal at first, since the shoreline was still predominately smooth and unbroken by the sharp twists or cliff faces which would appear as the sea moved inland. When the sea reached what is now the twenty-five-meter sub-marine contour, movement by boat would have become both more difficult and more necessary. Some groups would be stranded on islands or otherwise cut off from their traditional social or trade contacts; others may have had to travel greater distances to exploit the wide range of resources to which they were accustomed. Misfortune may have mothered inventions in the use of primitive sails, rudders, outriggers or other control devices as an occasional group would have been blown or carried out to sea.

The economic-cultural importance of the development of navigable boats and a thoroughgoing marine exploitation can hardly be overestimated. And yet, with such advances in technology and increase in food resources, life could have conceivably continued in its ancient pattern of food collecting for an indefinite period, as it did in many areas. The use of boats in fishing would have vastly increased the amount of food available from that source, and changes in the coast probably added enormously to the exploitable shell resources. But Sauer and many others have postulated that incipient agriculture originated in favorable conditions, where food was abundant, and that "most of the earliest cultivators of tropical and sub-tropical Southeast Asia inhabited estuarial plains and low terraces, and engaged for subsistence mainly in fishing" (Chang 1970:180). A stable and secure livelihood must have been assured, along with a close familiarity with plant resources for food (probably the yam, taro, and other edible tubers and fruits prior to the cereals), for containers (bottle gourd, bamboo), for fiber, cord, fish- and dart-poison, and for rudimentary medicinal purposes.

Sauer (1948) places great importance on the coastal areas as prime centers of experimentation with plant cultivation and reproduction. Given the important topographic-ecological changes associated with the rising sea level, his thesis seems more appropriate than others which point to climatological changes or population pressure as the main catalyst in the domestication of plants.

As the marine transgression reduced the width of the coastal plains and crowded back its inhabitants, it also improved the attractions of the seashores. The more the sea rose, the more sinuous and diversified the shore line became. Flooding of low valleys increased the vertical zone between high and low tide, which is most productive of food. There was a major growth of flood plains and alluvial valleys, parts of which were colonized by plants of high usefulness to man: grasses that yield canes and reeds and edible seeds; root plants and tubers; various water lilies and other marsh plants with succulent roots or stalks; possibly brackish water rice. The changes of topography provided an increasing number of sites optimal for plant growth and available for transplanting the favored "crops." Summarizing the events of the period 15,000 to 4000 B.C., Sauer concludes:

> With rising sea level were associated increased alluviation of river valleys and a continual burial of lowland living sites. Widely dispersed occupation was replaced by a few settlements along the margins of permanent or seasonal water. ... A new world took form, developing the physical geography into one of maximum opportunity for progressive and adventurous man. ... Given leisure and the intellectual curiosity to experiment, such communities needed only time to make the advance from fishing to farming.

The increasing population and improving communications were undoubtedly of great importance at this incipient stage, creating optimum conditions for the occurrence of ingenious or accidental discoveries of the transplanting and seeding of plants and the keeping and breeding of animals.

In summary, by the end of this period (6000–4000 B.C.) in the present coastal region, one should expect a wide variety of pottery styles, a polished stone industry of several distinct but overlapping traditions, extended sea travel by boat, an increase in or first appearance of sites where formerly there were few or none, and the cultivation of plants and keeping of animals in certain areas. This is, of course, largely the pattern of evidence which is emerging for the period to be designated as middle Neolithic and discussed below.

THE YÜEH AND OTHER REGIONAL HORIZONS IN THE NEOLITHIC OF COASTAL SOUTH CHINA

Recent discoveries have begun to throw light on the earliest coastal inhabitants from the Yangtze delta to the Hong river delta in North Vietnam. These new sites constitute firm evidence that a number of regional cultures had already taken shape by 6000–4000 B.C., and also that roughly the same area of the present coastline was inhabited by a population living near and probably often on the sea. Neither of these conditions can yet be said to have existed during the early Neolithic, although it is not unlikely that when more sites are reported of this period at least some regional traits or trends will be revealed. At present, it would seem best to follow the Vietnamese distinction of Hoabinhian-Bacsonian, as it is based on a large number of excavated sites, rather than to expand the Hoabinhian to the somewhat nebulous level of a "techno-complex," as Solheim (1972) and Gorman (1971) have done, or to employ a hypothetical "corded ware horizon," as Chang et al. (1969:221–25) suggest. Hsien-jen-tung and Tseng-p'i-yen (and probably many other cave-sites in the area) would thus be South China Bacsonian.

One of the most important sites on the South China coast is the shell-mound site of Fu-kuo-tun on Quemoy (Lin 1973). It is located on a fifteen-meter terrace behind a wide expanse of beach and sand dunes; the midden deposits were noted in four areas in recent terrace cuts, indicating that the deposits are extensive (Lin, personal communication, 1977). Although it has had only a brief survey, its importance lies in the fact that the three carbon-14 dates on shells from the midden fall within the range of 5200–4700 b.c. (NTU–63, NTU–64, NTU–65) and are associated with pottery of a rather impressive quality and decoration, considering its antiquity. The ware varies from coarse to medium in paste, and some pieces may have been fired as high as 600–700 degrees centigrade. A number of high rims (six centimeters) were noted, on vessels with rim diameters of twenty centimeters. The surface was well smoothed before decoration was applied. Five single types were noted: rows of fingernail impressions; a wavy line similar to the fingernail impressions; shell-edge impressions; wide, incised parallel lines; and short, deep-cut strokes. Almost all sherds have combinations of patterns, some involving as many as four steps in the decorating.

Even these very preliminary observations on the little material recovered indicate that a significant development of the ceramic industry had been achieved prior to 5000 B.C., probably within the Fukien-Taiwan area. On the basis of several features (notably, incised and pinprick band decoration) which occur again in later Yüeh pottery, the site can be classified as early Yüeh. Future investigation may show that the site had characteristics already distinguishing it from other Yüeh sites, and ancestral to some of the regional cultures of the Fukien-Taiwan area.

On Taiwan, no site can yet be dated to the period of Fu-kuo-tun. One carbon-14 date of 4320 b.c. (SI–1229) from a shell layer near Tainan is of dubious association with cultural material (W. H. Sung, personal communication, 1977). The Ta-p'en-k'eng, or "corded ware" culture, known from six to eight sites, is probably a little later and can be derived from a variant of the culture represented at Fu-kuo-tun.[3] The coast of Kwangtung similarly does not yet have any sites which can confidently be placed as early as 4000 B.C. The Hsi-chiao-shan sites near Canton have been estimated as somewhat earlier than the shellmounds (Kuang-tung-sheng 1961); the (stone) typological considerations motivating this estimate could equally well be explained by a functional variance of the former sites, which are located around the base of an old volcanic hill in the middle of an alluvial flood plain, some hundred miles inland. The pottery from Hsi-chiao-shan also bears close similarities to that of the coastal sites (Meacham 1978).

In Vietnam, along the coast of the Gulf of Tonkin, there are a number of early/middle Neolithic sites; here the problem is one of precise chronology. In the generally accepted sequence, Quynh-van, Da-but, and Dau-duong cultures all have open-air coastal sites dating between 8000 and 4000 B.C. It is not clear whether sites in the earlier phases were coastal at the time of

3. A date of 1750 B.C. (calibrated) is published for the lowest layer at Ta-p'en-k'eng (Chang et al. 1969: 161). Though Chang held the date to be "much too recent," it is in line with the two dates (1475 B.C., 450 B.C.) from the next, Yüan-shan stratum at the site. This date, along with that from Tainan, does fall within the probable time range for the "Ta-p'en-k'eng culture"; they may after all prove to be accurate dates for that culture.

occupation, but some do have marine shell middens. The absence of sedimentation in the lowlands at that time may have permitted the sea to move further inland than at present even with a lower sea level.

The pottery assemblages show some advance over the earlier Bacsonian, with a greater variety in cord- and basket-impressions, an infilled incised design juxtaposed with smoothed-out areas, and a wavy-line incision over cord marks. The size of the vessels is also larger; some have perforated foot-rims; and, by 4000 B.C. (Dau-duong), some are said to be wheel-made and kiln-baked. Stone tools are better and more completely polished, and a number of developments are suggested in the domestication of plants (tubers, fruit trees, hill-rice, tea, sugar cane, dye plants, etc.) and animals (water buffalo, pigs, cattle, fowl), in fishing (lines, nets, dugout canoes) and domestic arts (spinning, weaving). Many of these innovations have yet to be fully documented, but the cumulative evidence is of significant advances in many areas over the early Neolithic, and there is a clear indication of the incipient development of regional traditions (Quyhn-van and Bacsonian are now shown to have been contemporaries in coastal and upland regions, respectively). The coastal cultures can also be tentatively classified as early Yüeh, again on the basis of ceramic traits (use of the wheel, development of foot-rimmed vessels) which assume a larger importance in the third to second millennia B.C.

Another site which is probably in the Lungshanoid rather than the Yüeh sphere, but which must be mentioned here, is Ho-mu-tu, on the lowland south of Hangchow bay in Chekiang province. The culture there would almost certainly have been taken as late Neolithic were it not for the extraordinary dates 5008 and 4773 B.C. (BK–75057, ZK–263) on its lower layers (Ho-mu-tu culture) and 3718 B.C. (BK–75058) on its upper layer (Ch'ing-lien-kang culture). These dates will, I hope, lay to rest forever the residual doubts which hovered first over the antiquity of Ch'ing-lien-kang, then over the possibility of its derivation from preceding early/middle Neolithic cultures in the same area. Working with a model based on continuity and local evolution, I had written just weeks before the Ho-mu-tu data was published that

> the Ch'ing-lien-kang culture is now seen as a largely autonomous development in the 4th (and probably 5th) millennium B.C., with a firm economic basis in rice agriculture . . . [It and Yang-shao] had by ca. 4000 B.C. evolved into distinctive entities, *from antecedents as yet unknown* (Meacham 1977: 423).

Ho-mu-tu is about fifty kilometers from the sea, at an elevation of three to four meters above sea level. The deposits cover some forty thousand square meters and occur in a general area of dark clay thought to have been laid down in swampy conditions. There is striking evidence of agricultural activities, in the form of remains of rice in large quantity and in a distinctive type of *ssu* 耜 hoe made of the shoulder blade of a large mammal. The natural shape was selected for ease of hafting (traces were found) onto a pole, and two holes were made in the bone for that purpose.

> Thought previously to have been much later, this implement shows that already [by 5000 B.C.] these people had progressed beyond the use of slash-and-burn horticulture . . . and with such hoes could develop quite a large field . . . . Agriculture must have been the main economic activity (Che-chiang-sheng and Po-wu-kuan 1976).

Remains were found of possibly domesticated oxen, pigs, dogs, and water buffalo. A number of elaborately joined wooden structures (probably huts) were also found.[4] The pottery was almost all of organic (charcoal) temper, thick, handmade, and of simple shapes; from the lower layer only three painted sherds were found.

With the next cultural layer at Ho-mu-tu, and the succeeding phase in the southern coastal areas, the cultural patterns come into much clearer focus. In each major region a number of sites have been excavated, dated, and published in reasonable detail. In describing the cultures, a definition of the Yüeh horizon will be built up in material terms, although we will move away from the use of horizon markers in the direction of illuminating the wide areas of overlap in the assemblages. This occurs both horizontally, among the contemporaneous cultures, and vertically, among cultures that succeed one another in the same region. Such a description alone could be the subject of a lengthy study, and what follows below is simply the broadest, most superficial outline of a thesis which deserves much greater attention for each region. The vertical relations will be emphasized, in line with the stated intention to apply a continuity/local evolution model and investigate its theoretical implications. Less attention will be given to relating all the cultures described to a tightly defined "Yüeh horizon" than

---

4. A more detailed report on the Ho-mu-tu excavations (Che-chiang-sheng and Po-wu-kuan 1978) described these structures as *kan-lan* 干蘭, "pile-dwellings," which if correct demonstrates an amazing antiquity for this type of dwelling. An Chih-min (1963) has documented numerous instances of remains or representations of *kan-lan* which occur in the Neolithic and Bronze Age cultures south of the Yangtze, even down to Han times. Another important piece of information revealed in this report is the quite sophisticated development of the incised and painted decoration on lower-layer ceramics, the polished adzes of distinctive shapes and overall (if not thorough) polish, and the firm identification of rice, water chestnuts, pigs, and dogs as domesticated. Of particular note for our thesis is the attention given the continuity between the lower (Ho-mu-tu) and upper (Ch'ing-lien-kang culture) layers: "between them there is an internal consistency and developmental inheritance relationship."

to considering their ancestry and evolution as distinct entities. The diversity recognized by later Chinese writers in the phrase "hundred Yüeh" was foreshadowed in the great variety of local cultures which flourished in the third and second millennia B.C. in coastal areas.

Once again, North Vietnam offers the best-documented and dated sequence of the emergence and interaction of fully Neolithic cultures. The Dau-duong phase (ca. 4000–3000 B.C.) in the Hong river basin marks the beginning of an important developmental sequence in that area. It is now believed that by circa 3000 B.C. the formation of the delta was nearly complete, and Dau-duong represents the earliest colonization of this new landform. The major late Neolithic tradition of Phung-nguyen (ca. 3000–1500 B.C.) is derived from Dau-duong and grew from an intensification of the colonizing of that area. Phung-nguyen is now seen as the principal base on which the Vietnamese Bronze Age developed, through the Go-bong (ca. 2000 B.C.), Dong-dau, Go-mun, and finally the Dong-son stages (ca. 500 B.C.). Continuities between these stages are numerous and striking (Davidson 1975: figs. 6–8).

> The recognizable unity and coherent development of . . . a cultural and technical continuum from its origins in the Neolithic stage of Phung-nguyen down to the full florescence of late Bronze-Age Dong-son . . . is accepted by most North Vietnamese archaeologists (ibid. p. 90).

To the west, the Mai-pha culture of mountainous and upland river systems is distinguished from the Ha-long culture along the northern Tonkin coast. They are probably derived directly from preceding Bacsonian and Quynh-van early Neolithic in their respective areas.

That all these middle Neolithic regional cultures belong to the same broad system seems well established. There are virtually no important intrusive elements, there are no significant lags between areas, and a description of common traits reads like a catalog of excavated material: rectangular, stepped, and shouldered adzes; heavy chipped pebble tools; corded, incised, and painted pottery; footed bowls and pots, often with perforated foot-rims; slotted stone rings, perforated pendants, and bracelets; spindle whorls of a wide variety; multi-grooved sandstone polishers; and so on. Only minor variations in pottery and stone material allow regional cultures to be distinguished. Most of the Neolithic traits persist well into the Bronze Age, and bronze tools follow stone forms (most notably the shouldered ax). A stone *ko* of Phung-nguyen is identical to those of South China said to be stone copies of the Shang and Chou bronze weapon.

Along the Kwangsi and Kwangtung coasts, shellmound sites at Tung-hsing near Vietnam, Tung-yüan near Canton, and Ch'ao-an near Swatow have yielded material datable to 4000–2000 B.C. in their earliest phase. A carbon-14 date of 2494 B.C. (ZK–103) has been published for Tung-yüan (Hou-shan-kang). In addition, Sham Wan and four other sand-dune sites in Hong Kong have cultural deposits dated by a series of carbon-14 and thermoluminescence dates to 4000–2200 B.C.; S-O-N (Soa-kheng, abbreviated S-O-N by the excavator) in Hai-feng also belongs in this group. There is some diversity in pottery decoration, but the links between all these sites (compared in detail in Meacham 1978) are strong enough to assign them to the same cultural system. Like the Vietnamese sites, almost all middle Neolithic sites in Kwangtung have well-polished stone adzes (including stepped and shouldered forms) and ornaments, a multi-faceted ceramic industry, and a variety of topographic settings. All also have large numbers of pebble and heavy flake tools—but there can be no doubt about the separation of these middle Neolithic cultures from the Bacsonian of the upland caves (perhaps Weng-yüan and Ling-shan in Kwangtung, although the association of excavated materials is not clear). Further, the Tung-yüan, S-O-N, and Hong Kong sites have virtually indistinguishable ceramic and stone assemblages, and this distinctive Sham Wan culture may extend well beyond the central Kwangtung coast. The striking similarity in form, paste, and decoration of painted vessels from Hong Kong and Mai-pha was noted by Finn as early as 1933; and in 1975 I examined sherds from central Vietnam which were identical in paste (chalky, coarse) and decoration (corded, incised wavy lines, perforated low foot-rims) with sherds from the lower layer at Sham Wan. The three shellmounds plus Hsi-chiao-shan have been put in the same cultural system (Jao 1965) owing to their many similarities and equivalent technological stage. If Hsi-chiao-shan is earlier, it would be closely related to if not coterminous with the antecedent coastal cultures in shelf areas now submerged.

The late Neolithic (ca. 2200–1200) in Kwangtung, as well as in much of southeast China, witnessed the sudden appearance and spread of geometric pottery—the earliest stage of what has been termed the Geometric Horizon. However, evidence from most of the above-mentioned sites suggests that a continuity of development took place from middle to late Neolithic. Hsi-chiao-shan, Tung-yüan, the Hong Kong sites, and Ch'ao-an all continued to be occupied in the Geometric period and were used for similar functions as in previous occupations. Tung-yüan and Ch'ao-an again have shell middens; the Hsi-chiao-shan sites with geometric pottery again have many flake tools; and at Sham Wan, fish-bone middens were found in the same area of the site in both phases. Also, the relationship between material cultures is highly continuous: pebble tools and polished adzes of identical shapes, rock type, and use are found in both phases and, the clay used for the earliest geometric ware is of the same composition as the earlier chalky incised ware. A development of the geometric motifs out of the incised designs can be hypothesized (Meacham 1977:426), and a transitional site has recently been found in Macao. At Hsi-chiao-shan, the presence in both phases of the shouldered ax was taken as "a good indication that the sites belong to the same main culture group, though some predate others" (Kuang-tung-sheng 1959). The later Bronze Age phases of the Geometric Horizon in Kwangtung developed mainly out of the earlier phase, and again many Neolithic elements persisted well into the first millennium B.C. Clearly, this classification under the term "Yüeh" of middle Neolithic to middle Bronze Age cultures implies a greater vertical continuity than is apparent in a category such as the Geometric Horizon, which relies exclusively on the areal distribution of selected "marker traits." (It should be noted in passing that the "bronze drum culture" of southwest China-Vietnam is not included in the Geometric, although most of the decoration on the drums is of this type.)

Fukien and Taiwan present special difficulties in examining broad cultural affinities. There is little information on the Neolithic sequence in Fukien, with only two sites reported in detail and only T'an-shih-shan dated, to 1295 B.C. (ZK–98). At both sites painted pottery occurs alongside hard geometric ware and a fine eggshell black ware. These characteristics have not been seen together in Kwangtung. On the other hand, the stone tool industry is much the same, and the lower layer at Tung-chang has coarse corded and chalky incised ware not unlike that of Sham Wan.

Taiwan poses special problems, owing to the apparently conflicting affinities of several of its regional cultures. The non-Lungshanoid nature of especially the Yüan-shan (northwest Taiwan) was pointed out by Chang et al. (1969:233–234), who contrasted it with the Liang-chu (Chekiang) and Feng-pi-t'ou (south Taiwan) Lungshanoid: "As an articulated culture, the Yüan-shan apparently has a different major derivation." Chang concurs with Sung (1964:99), who puts Yüan-shan in a series of Neolithic cultures on the Kwangtung-Fukien coast. In brief, it was believed that Taiwan had been penetrated by elements or peoples from both Lungshanoid and more southerly cultures.

If one re-examines the prehistoric sequence in Taiwan with a view to local evolution, it seems quite possible that all of the later (after 2500 B.C.) Neolithic cultures developed principally on a corded ware (or "Ta-p'en-k'eng") culture base. A large number of shared traits can be documented horizontally, through Yüan-shan, Feng-pi-t'ou, and other contemporaneous cultures in every part of Taiwan. More important, the Ta-p'en-k'eng culture has a different possible vertical relation with each of the later regional cultures. Perhaps the most significant single piece of evidence in this regard is the rudimentary stepped adze found in the lower layer of Ta-p'en-k'eng, in that part of Taiwan (northwest) which alone would see a "stepped adze culture" in the next (Yüan-shan) phase.

The Ta-p'en-k'eng culture (ca. 4000–2500 B.C.) is fully Neolithic, with well-polished stone artifacts and a sophisticated ceramic industry. It is considerably separated in time and technology from the South China Bacsonian (or Chang's "corded ware horizon"), and may be contemporaneous with most of the earlier Kwangtung sites, but it is probably a little later than Fu-kuo-tun. It is clearly seen at six or eight sites in various parts of Taiwan, although recent data from the south (K. C. Li, personal communication, 1978) suggest that the cultural divide between the Ta-p'en-k'eng and Feng-pi-t'ou cultures there may not be so clear as previously believed. The number of traits present in Ta-p'en-k'eng which reappear (often with greater importance) in subsequent cultures again resembles an inventory: the stepped adze, rectangular adze, incised line patterns on the neck and rim, low perforated foot-rims, ceramic painting, perforated and stemmed arrowheads, waisted pebbles, pitted pebbles, chipped pebble tools, and so on. Site preferences are highly continuous, and at three major sites of this culture (Ta-p'en-k'eng, Yüan-shan, Feng-pi-t'ou), occupation continued directly into the next cultural phase—or at least, the later deposits lie directly on the earliest debris in some parts of the sites. On the east coast, Ta-p'en-k'eng "elements" persist in later cultures well after 1000 B.C., while in central Taiwan the Niu-ma-t'ou phase has a number of such elements but dates from 2500 B.C.

The question of the Lungshanoid status of Feng-pi-t'ou and Niu-ma-t'ou is not easily resolved, as there are unquestionably certain traits present there which are shared with Ch'ing-lien-kang, Liang-chu, and Liu-lin and not seen futher south. In fact, a distribution map of semi-lunar stone knives shows the southernmost extension of this artifact type on the mainland to be northern Chekiang, with southern Taiwan appearing as a rather isolated fragment well removed from the main area. My contention would be that, in view of the many horizontal and vertical links among all the material cultures on Taiwan in the period 4000–1000 B.C. (and much later as well), they should all be grouped within the same broad horizon, with the question of intrusive Lungshanoid elements still to be explained. This seems to be the consensus of field workers in Taiwan (Sung, Lien, personal communication, 1977); Feng-pi-t'ou would in any case be a highly localized variant of the Lungshanoid, were it so classified.

One should not, of course, expect a clear-cut boundary between Yüeh and Lungshanoid, and certainly both Feng-pi-t'ou and T'an-shih-shan are possible transitional cultures in the shifting mosaic of the prehistoric South China coast. Using horizon markers one would expect, and indeed one finds, a gradual attenuation of these traits as the distance from the center increases. When considering the overlapping of cultural traits, a gradual regional shift in culture content (ABCDE, BCDEF, CDEFG) will blur whatever boundaries one might wish to draw. Here we have laid greater stress on the time than on the space relations, and Taiwan offers an especially interesting opportunity to follow local evolution well into the present era, without significant intrusions. In the material from two areas which I have examined in some detail (Taipei, Taichung), a study of the many continuities from the earliest (Ta-p'en-k'eng, Niu-ma-t'ou) through to the latest, proto-historical (Shih-san-hang, Fan-tzu-yüan), would be well rewarded.

Taking Fukien-Chekiang as a very approximate boundary of the Yüeh-Lungshanoid systems, we note a decrease of stepped and shouldered adzes, pebble tools, shellmound sites, and low-footed pots or bowls north of this area and an increase in tripods, high-pedestaled *tou*, black pottery (later phases), and the other traits, especially vessel forms, designated as Lungshanoid. The sequence of development in the Hangchow bay-Yangtze delta area has been enormously clarified with the data and carbon-14 dates of recent years, from Ho-mu-tu (ca. 5000–4500 B.C.), Ch'ing-lien-kang (4500–3500 B.C.), Liang-chu (3500–2000 B.C.), and finally the Hu-shu geometric (2000–1000 B.C.) phases. This well-dated sequence of mainly (or entirely?) indigenous development in the lower Yangtze is the most important discovery of Chinese archaeology in the 1970s, although much of the material was excavated long ago. An assumption of local evolution, as opposed to nuclear area radiation, led to some remarkable perceptions on the part of a few fieldworkers. Su Ping-ch'i could write as early as the mid-1960s (1965:67) that "the earliest stage of Yang-shao culture was probably contemporaneous with the earliest stage of Ch'ing-lien-kang, and the two had contacts, although not very close." This assessment, so isolated and generally rejected just ten years ago, is now thoroughly demonstrated and is beginning to correct the former overemphasis on the Central Plains:

> In the past, we supposed that the Yangtze and Huai basin Neolithic cultures were later than those of the Central Plains. But now, we realize that our

ancestors were toiling hard in the Yangtze-Huai basin, as in the Huang Ho basin; so this area is also a cradle of development of ancient Chinese culture (Wu 1973:57).

But Hsia (1977:221), while affiirming that this area had reached an equivalent stage of evolution with the Huang Ho by 5000 B.C., seems to go too far in stating that "these two areas now certainly indicate the earliest Neolithic in China." Surely the upland areas of south and southwest China, and quite possibly the lowland river valleys along the southern coast, present equally early Neolithic cultures.

IMPLICATIONS FOR PROTOHISTORY

A largely local, in situ evolution of the Yüeh Coastal Neolithic must now be considered a strong possibility, along with a similar cultural process taking place in the Yangtze delta, the Central Plains, and probably a number of other regions. This reconstruction of the appearance of Neolithic cultures on the east Asia mainland has several implications for later culture change; the dating of early bronze cultures must be subjected to a much closer scrutiny than has previously been the case. Typological features associated with one phase of Shang or Chou in the Central Plains may appear earlier, contemporaneous, or later in other areas, and they may not be the clear chronological markers they were once thought to be. Obviously, the question of typology is closely bound up with the theoretical framework in which marginal cultures have been considered. Was there an appreciable impact of the rise of Shang on the peoples of its periphery? To what degree were they involved in this event, or isolated from it but experiencing simultaneous development along parallel lines?

The implications of local evolution must be reviewed in several examples. The most relevant to the Yüeh area is the appearance of geometric pottery, mainly in the second millennium B.C. Whereas this phenomenon was once almost universally attributed to the impact of Yin-Chou civilization, it is now unnecessary, even awkward, to make this link. The carbon-14 dating weighs heavily against such a derivation, with two protogeometric sites—P'ao-ma-ling in Kiangsi, Hou-shan-kang in Kwangtung—dated to 2807 and 2494 B.C. (ZK–51, ZK–103), respectively, and others dated firmly in the second millennium B.C. In addition, the evolution of geometric pottery on a local base can be reasonably hypothesized without recourse to an alien input or stimulus. The dating of geometric pottery by typology is thus thrown open until it can be fixed to well-dated sequences in each region. The fact that most estimates for the Hu-shu Geometric culture were off by a thousand years or more (e.g., Cheng 1963:146) should serve as a caution against the application elsewhere of a tight typological scheme worked out for the Bronze Age Central Plains, just as the antiquity of Ch'ing-lien-kang (with some estimates off by three thousand years!—e.g., Cheng 1966:10) is a lesson in the dangers of a similar application in Neolithic times.

Bronze is another trait the origin of which has often been linked directly with the rise of Shang. It is surely not unreasonable to suppose, however, that the same processes which brought the early Shang to the discovery or use of bronze were operating over a wide area. It can be argued that bronze was known as early as 2000–1500 B.C. in areas west of the Central Plains (predynastic Chou), the Yangtze delta (late Hu-shu), Hunan, Kansu (Ch'i-chia), Vietnam, Yunnan, northeastern Thailand, Liaoning, parts of Korea and the Soviet Maritime Province, and parts of central Asia. In most of these areas the earliest appearance of bronze is still much debated, but the distinct possibility that metallurgy had a wide distribution prior to and during the Early Shang should not be obscured by the supreme mastery and sophistication of the Shang bronze worker.

To consider a few examples, the controversial carbon-14 date of 1308 B.C. (ZK–10) from Hai-men-k'ou, Yunnan, now seems certainly associated with an activity layer yielding bronze artifacts. Hsia (1977:226) makes the point that, though the carbon-14 sample is from a wooden pile penetrating the layer, such would normally be the case for habitation debris accumulating around a stilt dwelling. With the perspective outlined above, the early dates for bronze in Thailand and Vietnam should have removed any element of surprise that metals were known in the southwest before 1000 B.C. Of much interest, though again not the least unexpected, is a new date of 664 B.C. (ZK–294) from a tomb at Li-chia-shan, Yunnan, which is assigned to the Shih-chai-shan or Tien culture. The full impact of this date will certainly be enormous (as discussed in detail in Barnard 1977:53–64), as the Shih-chai-shan culture has been almost universally dated to Ch'in-Han at the *earliest*. The dates from Yunnan form a bracket, mirroring that leading to the Dongson in Vietnam, with the appearance of the classical Heger I bronze drum (now virtually certain as of around 500–400 B.C.) as the aesthetic culmination of this tradition.

A number of sites now dated on typological grounds to Western Chou or Eastern Chou may well be several centuries earlier. Certain of the Bronze Age tombs in Kwangtung, for example, while generally given a late Spring and Autumn or Warring States date on the basis of a few purported Eastern Chou traits, could date as early as 1000 B.C. if compared with the Vietnamese materials. One tomb (Ssu-hui) dated to the Warring States period by the excavators (Kuang-tung-sheng 1975) has Dongson elements datable to as early as 600 B.C. and high-fired geometric pottery dated to 700 b.c. (I–9554) in Hong Kong, to 1260 b.c. (L–188C-1) in Hoi-fung, and to 1133 B.C. (ZK–204) in late Hu-shu of the lower Yangtze. Similar considerations would apply to most important Bronze Age sites of South China; a comparison with the bronze materials from Vietnam might suggest an earlier age than that indicated by typology tied to the chronology of the Central Plains. It now seems reasonable to suppose that bronze artifacts if not bronze metallurgy were known in both Kwangtung and Fukien in the second millennium B.C. Although there are as yet no absolute dates to support this contention, the fact that bronze is found in that period to the north (Hunan), northeast (Kiangsu-Chekiang), northwest (Yunnan), and west (Vietnam) would certainly lend much credence to the idea, as would the fact that late Neolithic kiln temperatures in Kwangtung had reached 1000–1100 degrees centigrade (Meacham 1978).

A similar approach based firmly on the possibility of local evolution rather than a strict typological scheme may open new horizons in the dating not only of bronze, but of proto-scripts, zoomorphic motifs, and other ostensibly Shang elements in areas outside the immediate Shang domain. I shall cite below three carbon-14 dates on Bronze Age sites, rejected by Hsia (1977) as too early and thus in error, which if correct would raise serious questions about the local development of bronze, and even about the recorded history in their respective areas. Of course, any one or all three may, as Hsia contends, be too early for the associated material; but it would seem equally possible that, in the light of the revelations in chronology described above, a pattern is beginning to reveal itself in these dates.

The first case is reportedly a Western Chou tomb at Pai-fu-ts'un, Ch'ang-p'ing-hsien, near Peking, with a carbon-14 date of 1272 B.C. (BK–75052) but "associated with documentary references dating from the beginning of Chou." Hsia rejects the date for this reason and because, if correct, "it would be earlier than the An-yang phase of Shang." The tomb has a number of bronze weapons, especially various types of *ko*, chariot fittings, axes, and two oracle bones with a single character inscription each. (Interestingly, Hsia accepts the date of 1360 B.C. for a bronze site on the Liaotung peninsula which also had several well-made bronze articles.) The second is a wooden boat found at Yen-ch'eng, Wu-chin-hsien, near Shanghai, associated with soft and hard geometric pottery, bronze implements, and "documentary references." The carbon-14 date was 1028 B.C. (ZK–27), in contrast to the original estimate of a late Spring and Autumn to Warring States period. Hsia agrees with this estimate, as the historical materials must be later than 1055 B.C. (It should be noted that the late Hu-shu level at Pei-yin-yang-ying had similar artifacts and was dated to the thirteenth to twelfth centuries B.C.)

Another case involves the dates from early Hsia-chia-tien culture levels in Liaoning province of 2406 B.C. (ZK–176) and 1879 B.C. (ZK–153). Bronze artifacts, pottery made on a fast wheel, and decorative styles similar to Erh-li-t'ou types were associated with the samples. Hsia believes that ZK–176 is too early and that 1890 B.C. is closer to the true age of the culture. Finally, an upper level at No-mu-hung, Tsinghai, which had bronze axes, knives, well-fashioned wooden carts, and generally quite an advanced material culture, gave a date of 2166 B.C. (ZK–61). Hsia holds that the date is much too early for the associated material, agreeing with the excavator's original estimate of a date in the Warring States to Han period, and remarks: "above all, it could never be earlier than Yin-Chou."

In each of these examples, there would not seem to be an absolute historical dating, as was the case at Ma-wang-tui tomb number 1, whose carbon-14 dates fell generally 40–150 years on either side of its known age (ca. 168 B.C.). The dates from the four sites in question are all on wood (a good dating material), are clearly associated with the artifacts described, and have a low ± range. The only possible source of error (other than laboratory error) is the age of the wood, but it is difficult to believe that in each case the wood used was five to fifteen hundred years old. The entire question deserves more attention, but it is certainly possible that one or more of the sites may be the first indicator, as was the rather early date from Ch'ing-lien-kang in 1972, of a local development not heretofore recognized.

From a perspective of local evolution, it would be expected not only that bronze metallurgy (like the cultivation of rice several millennia earlier) would spread rapidly into areas and cultures amenable to it, but also that it may have involved several, even dozens of "independent inventions" as late Neolithic technology reached the range of accidental or genius breakthrough to that combination of ceramic and stone industry represented by metal working. Bronze seems to appear simultaneously in a number of highly distinctive technical and decorative traditions on the east Asian mainland, and, to paraphrase Chang (1973 : 528) on rice, it is "futile as well as pointless to look further for the one spot within this vast area" where the invention(s) of bronze took place. We see as little evidence for a north-south as for a south-north movement of metallurgy in the China-Southeast Asia area. As Barnard (1975) has shown, the technology involved is not related; but even in cases where a similarity in techniques is established, a derivation from one single invention is not necessarily indicated, any more than it is in the many cases of similarity in pottery forms, decoration, and so on, in the Neolithic. It would seem that bronze, like many individual Neolithic traits, found its way at an early stage into a number of cultures and proceeded into various lines of development, most similar and parallel, others diverging.

This hypothesized early appearance and growth of bronze metallurgy is supported on several theoretical grounds. Multiple invention must now be considered probable, as a technological consequence of lengthy parallel development of the Neolithic cultures concerned out of a common early Neolithic (at least) substratum. The likelihood of rapid spread can be seen in the earlier widespread and virtually simultaneous appearances of pottery, polished stone, agriculture, travel by boat, and so on. And, most important, the knowledge and elaboration of bronze techniques, whether invented locally or acquired, would have been thoroughly adapted to local needs, traditions, social structures, and capabilities. As Renfrew (1971: 71–72) remarked in his masterful treatment of the diffusionist interpretation of European prehistory:

> we have completely undervalued the originality and the creativity of the inhabitants . . . . A greater reluctance [than in the past 40 years] to swallow "influences" or "contacts" as sufficient explanations in themselves, without a much more detailed analysis of the actual mechanisms involved, is to be expected.

A number of other "Shang" culture traits could and have been suggested as having originated either simultaneously with or earlier than the Shang in areas outside the Shang genesis area: burial and ritual traditions from the Huai-Yangtze area, art motifs from central Asia, oracle-taking traditions to the north and south, the chariot from West Asia, and so on. Far from tracing the origin of most major Shang elements to the nuclear area (as Ho 1975 attempts to do), we should be prepared to find them appearing throughout the vast cultural cauldron of East Asia. On the other hand, the elements probably unique to Early Shang—kingship, priesthood, an organized military, urban settlement, writing—mark the radically new epoch entered by the progenitors of Shang civilization.[5]

5. Efforts to find in the Yang-shao pottery marks a proto-Chinese script have thus far been unconvincing. It would seem that great caution is needed in distinguishing between the use of isolated marks or animal motifs as symbols, which occurs in Neolithic pottery in a number of cultures, and the combination of such symbols into a script (at however rudimentary a level) which would begin to have some structure and syntax. That the Shang system of writing was derived from the simple marks and representational art of its antecedent culture can hardly be questioned, but what has been and still is lacking is a "Lung-shan connection." If the Yang-shao marks represent, as is widely held, "the earliest stage of Chinese writing" and "a six-thousand-year history for the Chinese script," one should expect to see a much greater development of this "writing" in the Lung-shan. It would perhaps be wiser to establish first that Chinese script is forty-five hundred years old, before pushing it back to early Yang-shao!

There is little evidence at hand, however, to suggest that a convergence of innovations, ideas, and civilizational traits was taking place around 2000 B.C., with a vortex in Honan. Such a cultural implosion would not in any case satisfactorily explain the rise of Shang, and it would perhaps not be discernible in view of the difficulties mentioned above in pinpointing the place of origin and early spread of any given trait. In my view, based on the local continuity and evolution so apparent in the Neolithic in China, the stage was set for the rise of Shang by a widespread technological advance and cultural development among a number of tribal-ethnic-cultural groups. Though the Shang probably descended from the Honan Lung-shan, and obviously drew most heavily on this antecedent culture, the exchange and circulation of traits over a wide area during the course of the Neolithic insured that the essential bases of civilization were laid in the Central Plains, and probably in many other areas as well. It is still not clear to what extent, if at all, societies outside the Central Plains had moved toward "civilization" and state formation during the second millennium B.C. It does seem, however, that the Hu-shu and Vietnamese Bronze Age cultures were produced by societies beginning to move in that direction.

That the Shang dynasty arose when and where it did was certainly not made inevitable by such a widespread process of development, nor was it predetermined by the cultural and environmental setting. It is true that the fabric of Shang culture was closely interwoven with the physical setting, but it makes no more sense to speak of the Central Plains as having "produced" Shang civilization than it does to speak of the changing topography of the continental shelf "determining" the content of the emergent Neolithic cultures there. The stimuli once thought to have in-itiated cultural development exclusively in the Central Plains can now be perceived in many different environmental settings. While occasionally directly stimulating culture change, environmental factors must certainly have been secondary to the internal dynamics within each culture group. I have suggested elsewhere (1974) that these unique events/value changes/ combinations of ideas derived ultimately from the religio-ceremonial matrix, and this has been proposed in a somewhat different vein by Wheatley (1971). The ultimate causes of culture change may often prove to be intangible, and not adequately reflected in the archaeological record.

It can, however, be confidently said that we are nearer an accurate knowledge of the origins of Chinese civilization than has been the case at any time in the past. The data have ruled out certain phenomena (e.g., irrigation, migration) once suggested as the prime stimuli. We have seen the external diffusionist "western origins theory" discarded except for a few very isolated traits, and now the internal diffusionist "nuclear area hypothesis" no longer seems operable as an explanation of the cultural development which led to the Shang. It is suggested that the ultimate causes lie rather in the cultural dynamics themselves, and we must henceforth be cognizant of the unity and continuity of the broad cultural development on the one hand, and the uniqueness and creativity of each culture group at each point in time within this process on the other. As for the Shang, their uniqueness explodes on the scene and has often obscured the significance and creativity of their contemporaries. Here we have focused principally on the Neolithic ancestry of one of these groups, and some of the parallel cultural processes preceding the Shang. The fact that areas outside the genesis area were equally developed in Neolithic times, after all, heightens rather than lessens the sense of radical newness, and mystery, of the appearance of Shang civilization.

REFERENCES

Aigner, Jean
1979   "Pleistocene Ecology and Paleolithic Assemblages in South China." *Journal of the Hong Kong Archaeological Society* 8 : 52–73.

An Chih-min 安志敏
1963   " 'Kan-lan' shih chien-chu ti k'ao-ku yen-chiu '干蘭' 式建築的考古研究." *KKHP* 1963.2 : 65–86.

Barnard, Noel
1975   *The First Radiocarbon Dates from China*. Rev. and enl. Monographs on Far Eastern History 8. Canberra.
1977   "Radiocarbon Dates from China: Batch No. 4 and Some Others." Australian National University. Privately circulated paper.

Benedict, Paul
1967–1968 "Austro-Thai; Austro-Thai Studies." *Behavior Science Notes* 1.4 : 227–261.

Chang, K. C. [Kwang-chih]
1968   *The Archaeology of Ancient China*. New Haven.
1970   "The Beginnings of Agriculture in the Far East." *Antiquity* 44.2 : 175–185.

1973   "Radiocarbon Dates from China: Some Initial Interpre-
            tations." *Current Anthropology* 14:525–528.
1976   *Early Chinese Civilization: Anthropological Perspectives.*
            Cambridge, Mass.
1977   "Chinese Archaeology since 1949." *Journal of Asian
            Studies* 36.4:623–646.

Chang, K. C., et al.
1969   *Fengpitou, Tapenkeng, and the Prehistory of Taiwan.* New
            Haven.

Che-chiang-sheng and Po-wu-kuan   Che-chiang-sheng wen-kuan-hui
            浙江省文管會 and Che-chiang-sheng po-wu-kuan 浙江省
            博物舘
1976   "Ho-mu-tu fa-hsien yüan-shih she-hui chung-yao yi-chih
            河姆渡發現原始社會重要遺址." *WW* 1976.8:6–12.
1978   "Ho-mu-tu yi-chih ti-yi-ch'i fa-chüeh pao-kao 河姆渡遺址
            第一期發掘報告." *KKHP* 1978.1:39–94.

Cheng Te-k'un 鄭德坤
1963   *Archaeology in China*, vol. 3: *Chou China.* Cambridge,
            Eng.
1966   *Archaeology in China*, supp. to vol. 1: *New Light on Pre-
            historic China.* Cambridge, Eng.
1976   "Chung-kuo t'ien-yeh k'ao-ku yü shih-ch'ien-hsüeh
            中國田野考古與史前學." *Hsiang-kang chung-wen ta-hsüeh
            Chung-kuo wen-hua yen-chiu-so hsüeh-pao* 香港中文大學中國
            文化研究所學報 8.1:1–22.

CKKH shih-yen-shih and Ku-chi-ch'ui   CKKH shih-yen-shih 實驗室
            and Ku-chi-chui tung-wu yü ku-jen-lei yen-chiu-so shih-
            yen-shih 古脊椎動物與古人類研究所實驗室
1976   "Ku-chih piao-pen ti t'an-14 nien-tai ts'e-ting fang-fa
            骨質標本的碳-14年代測定方法." *KK* 1976.1:28–30, 58.

Creel, Herrlee Glessner
1970   *The Origins of Statecraft in China*, vol. 1: *The Western
            Chou Empire.* Chicago.

Davidson, J. C. S.
1975   "Recent Archaeological Activity in Vietnam." *Journal of
            the Hong Kong Archaeological Society* 6:80–99.

Eberhard, Wolfram
1968   *The Local Cultures of South China.* Leiden.

Fairbridge, R.
1960   "The Changing Level of the Sea." *Scientific American* 202.6:70–79.

Finn, D. J.
1933   "Archaeological Finds on Lamma Island." In *The Hong Kong Naturalist*, ed. G. A. Herklotts. (Reprinted in book form by Ricci Publications, Hong Kong, 1958.)

Gorman, C.
1971   "The Hoabinhian and After." *World Archaeology* 2.3: 300–320.

Ho, Ping-ti
1975   *The Cradle of the East: An Inquiry into the Indigenous Origins of Techniques and Ideas of Neolithic and Early Historic China, 5000–1000 B.C.* Hong Kong and Chicago.

Hsia Nai 夏鼐
1977   "T'an-14 ts'e-ting nien-tai ho Chung-kuo shih-ch'ien k'ao-ku-hsüeh 碳-14測定年代和中國史前考古學." *KK* 1977.4: 217–232. (Partially translated by Nancy Price in *Early China* 3 [Fall 1977]:87–93.)

Jao Hui-yüan 饒惠元
1965   "Lüeh-t'an tui-yü Yüeh-kan ti-ch'ü chih wai hsin-shih-ch'i yi-chih ti jen-shih 略談對於粵贛地區之外新石器遺址的認識." *KK* 1965.10:517–524.

Kendall, F. H.
1975   "High Island: A Study of Undersea Deposits." *Journal of the Hong Kong Archaeological Society* 6:26–32.

Khao Co Hoc
1976.2   "Reports on the "Cave of the Beasts' (Con Moong)": pp. 1–53.

Kuang-tung-sheng   Kuang-tung-sheng po-wu-kuan 廣東省博物館
1959   "Kuang-tung Nan-hai Hsi-chao-shan ch'u-t'u ti shih-ch'i 廣東南海西樵山出土的石器." *KKHP* 1959.4:1–15.
1961   "Kuang-tung Tung-hsing hsin-shih-ch'i shih-tai pei-ch'iu yi-chih 廣東東興新石器時代貝丘遺址." *KK* 1961.12:644–648, 688.
1975   "Kuang-tung Ssu-hui Niao-tan-shan Chan-kuo mu 廣東四會鳥蛋山戰國墓." *KK* 1975.2:102–108.

Lin Ch'ao-ch'i 林朝棨
　1973　　　"Chin-men Fu-kuo-tun pei-chung yi-chih 金門復國墩貝塚
　　　　　　遺址." *Kuo-li T'ai-wan ta-hsüeh k'ao-ku jen-lei hsüeh-k'an*
　　　　　　國立臺灣大學考古人類學刊: pp. 33–34, 36–37.

Long, Nguyen Phuc
　1975　　　"Les nouvelles recherches archéologiques au Vietnam."
　　　　　　Arts asiatiques 31 (special issue): 3–297.

Meacham, William
　1974　　　"Religion and the Rise of Shang Civilization." *Ching Feng*
　　　　　　17.2–3:63–74.
　1975　　　"Laichikok." *Journal of the Hong Kong Archaeological*
　　　　　　Society 6:33–36.
　1976　　　"New C-14 Dates from China." *Asian Perspectives*
　　　　　　18.2:204–213.
　1977　　　"Continuity and Local Evolution in the Neolithic of South
　　　　　　China." *Current Anthropology* 18.3:419–440.
　1978　　　"Sham Wan in the Prehistory and Early History of Hong
　　　　　　Kong and Kwangtung." In *Sham Wan, Lamma Island: An*
　　　　　　Archaeological Site Study, edited by William Meacham:
　　　　　　pp. 272–290. Hong Kong Archaeological Society Mono-
　　　　　　graph no. 3. Hong Kong.

Renfrew, Colin
　1971　　　"Carbon-14 and the Prehistory of Europe." *Scientific*
　　　　　　American 225.4:63–72.

Sauer, Carl
　1948　　　"Environment and Culture During the Last Deglacia-
　　　　　　tion." *Proceedings of the American Philosophical Society*
　　　　　　92.1:65–77.

Solheim, W. G.
　1972　　　"An Earlier Agricultural Revolution." *Scientific American*
　　　　　　226.4:34–41.

Su Ping-ch'i 蘇秉琦
　1965　　　"Kuan-yü Yang-shao wen-hua ti jo-kan wen-t'i 關於仰韶
　　　　　　文化的若干問題." *KKHP* 1965.1:51–82.

Sung, Wen-hsun
　1964　　　"The Stone, Bone, and Horn Industries of the Yüan-shan
　　　　　　Shell-mound." *Bulletin of the China Council for East Asian*
　　　　　　Studies 3:98–99.

Wheatley, Paul
  1971   *The Pivot of the Four Quarters: A Preliminary Enquiry into the Origins and Character of the Ancient Chinese City.* Chicago.

Wu Shan-ching 吳山菁
  1973   "Lüeh-lun Ch'ing-lien-kang wen-hua 略論青蓮崗文化." *WW* 1973.6:45–61.

7

The Relationship of
the Painted Pottery
and Lung-shan Cultures

LOUISA G. FITZGERALD HUBER

Just over fifty years ago, in 1928, the first specimens of Lung-shan pottery were brought to light at the site of Ch'eng-tzu-yai in northwestern Shantung province. The Lung-shan ware was recognized as a tradition independent of the so-called Yang-shao painted ware; the former was understood to be localized in the east, the latter in the Chung Yüan area of Central China (Li Chi 1934:1–2; Creel 1937:170ff). Since that time, numerous Lung-shan pottery sites have been discovered in the Chung Yüan, where invariably they have appeared stratigraphically above painted pottery finds and hence have come to be regarded as later in date. Most notable has been the excavation of Miao-ti-kou II, the Lung-shan level at that site which overlies the stratum containing painted wares.

As a consequence of such finds, the earlier two-culture theory was rapidly superseded by a second theory, which asserted not only that the Lung-shan tradition was chronologically later than the painted wares, but that it evolved directly from it. According to the new theory, the Chung Yüan area witnessed the genesis of both the Yang-shao and Lung-shan traditions. This evolutionary concept was an important corollary to the well-known "nuclear theory," whose chief and most eloquent proponent in

NOTE: This chapter is included with the kind permission of the *Bulletin of the Museum of Far Eastern Antiquities*, which has accepted my doctoral dissertation, "The Traditions of Chinese Neolithic Pottery," for publication in a forthcoming issue. The present paper draws upon material presented in parts of the dissertation; it is printed here primarily as a record of one of the contributions to the Conference on the Origins of Chinese Civilization.

the West has been Chang Kwang-chih.[1] The proposition rested primarily upon the observation that certain vessel types of the unpainted variety from Miao-ti-kou I bear some similarity to those in the Miao-ti-kou II stratum but seem, by contrast, somewhat simpler, or less advanced (CKKH 1959b:110–111; Chang 1968:135). This observation of itself never, of course, ruled out the possibility that the forms in question, namely, small *pei* 杯 (drinking cups) and certain tripods—both of which occur only rarely in painted pottery complexes—might have been the result of periodic contacts with outside cultures.

Although there was no question that in the Chung Yüan the Lung-shan tradition postdated the Yang-shao, there was never any compelling reason to suppose that the one developed out of the other. Even prior to the information afforded by the vast number of Lung-shan sites discovered in recent years throughout southeast China and the availability of carbon-14 dates for many Neolithic sites, a considerable body of evidence existed that ran strongly counter to this theory. It may be true that the Lung-shan pottery traditions in the Chung Yüan exhibit a certain degree of uniformity—the same basic types of unpainted, footed vessels occur throughout—but these very vessels signify an absolute distinction between the Lung-shan ware and that of the Yang-shao traditions. As a result, their occurrence has always strongly suggested the intrusive influence of a different and unrelated culture.

Although the evolutionary theory came to prevail, it was not to the mind of every scholar a foregone conclusion. Among others, both Li Chi and William Watson put severe questions to the theory, with the result that in the end both, apparently, would have favored in some form a revival of the two-culture theory. Li Chi in particular pointed out not only that there were significant discontinuities between Miao-ti-kou I and II, but that the chronological position of Miao-ti-kou II vis-à-vis other Chung Yüan Lung-shan sites was not unassailable, and hence that its role as a "transitional phase" was in doubt (Li 1963:12, 21–22). Watson, like Li Chi, was troubled by that aspect of the developmental theory which presupposes Miao-ti-kou II as the transitional phase (1971:17, 33–35).

What neither scholar could have foreseen was that the publication of

1. Chang 1968:84–87, 89, 129. Chang has tacitly withdrawn all mention of the nuclear theory from his 1977 revised edition of *The Archaeology of Ancient China*. Nevertheless, he does not seem to have relinquished this concept entirely, and he still adheres to the idea of Miao-ti-kou II as a transitional phase: "the interrelationship of the Yang-shao and Lung-shan cultures in the Chung Yüan remains as it was viewed in the 1960s—namely, that the Lung-shan culture in the Chung Yüan developed out of the Yang-shao culture through an intermediate transitional stage of the Miao-ti-kou II culture" (Chang 1977:154).

FIGURE 7.1. *Po.* Ta-ho-ts'un, Cheng-chou, Honan. (Ch'en 1973: pl. 1.2.)

certain carbon-14 dates would, in one swift blow, strike down the concept of Miao-ti-kou II as the transitional phase. Ash pit 558 belonging to the Lung-shan stratum at Miao-ti-kou has been carbon-dated (ZK–111) to 2776 B.C. $\pm$ 138, while dates ranging from (ZK–185) 3684 B.C. $\pm$ 124 to (BK–76004) 3071 B.C. $\pm$ 182 have been provided for the Cheng-chou site of Ta-ho-ts'un. Unlike Miao-ti-kou II, where there was hardly any painted ware, the finds at Ta-ho-ts'un represented an even mixture of late Yang-shao painted ware and unpainted Lung-shan vessels. Side by side within F 1, one of the town houses at Ta-ho, were found a superlative red ware *po* 缽 painted in black and red over a white slip (fig. 7.1) and several unpainted footed vessels, such as the *ting* 鼎 and the *tou* 豆 (fig. 7.2), whose specific forms strongly recall the kinds of wares typical of certain Lung-shan sites in Shantung and northern Kiangsu. It is suddenly Ta-ho-ts'un, then, that assumes the role of the much-sought-after transitional phase, and there the Lung-shan forms appear decidedly intrusive.

I have for some time been of the opinion that the Yang-shao and Lung-shan were in origin, and for the most part in their development, two

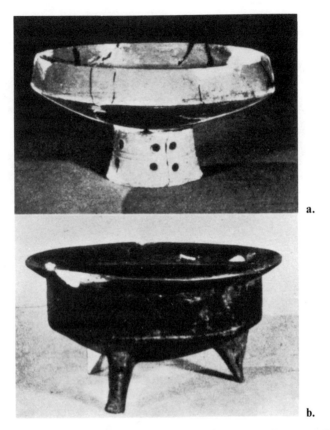

FIGURE 7.2. **Unpainted wares from Ta-ho-ts'un, Cheng-chou, Honan. a:** *Tou.* **b:** *Ting.* **(Ch'en 1973: pls. 3.2, 3.3, respectively.)**

separate cultures, the one localized in the Chung Yüan area along an east-west axis following the course of the Huang Ho, the other distributed over a vast area to the south and east (Huber 1974: chs. 7, 8). It would appear that the Lung-shan did not grow out of Yang-shao and move southward, as was believed; on the contrary, it was long established in the region south of the Huang Ho and came into contact with the Chung Yüan during the mature phase of the Miao-ti-kou tradition. Such a hypothesis is substantiated by the fact that painted wares of the Miao-ti-kou I type found in sites across the south and southeast always occur as an intrusive, that is, isolated element within the context of a highly developed Lung-shan culture. Beyond that, there are numerous instances of painted wares appearing in a southern or southeastern Lung-shan stratum that overlies yet another

Lung-shan stratum from which the Chung Yüan painted ware is conspicuously absent.[2]

But a correct assessment of the relation between the painted pottery and Lung-shan cultures requires first an understanding of the nature of the Chung Yüan painted pottery designs and a definition, or re-definition, of what is meant by the Lung-shan tradition.

THE CHUNG YÜAN PAINTED POTTERY

Despite the fact that our knowledge of Neolithic pottery traditions has greatly increased within the past few years, there is, amazingly, still no agreement as to how the designs on the most important painted Chung Yüan wares—namely, those of Miao-ti-kou—should be read. Until such designs are properly understood, the attempt to establish a relative chronology or dating of the painted pottery cultures is largely doomed to failure, carbon-14 dates notwithstanding.[3] As regards the Miao-ti-kou pottery, we face problems of a fairly severe sort, for to date no one seems to have established convincingly even what the subject matter of these designs is. Usually the patterns are interpreted as stylized renditions of birds or flowers, particularly the latter. Su Ping-ch'i has gone so far as to distinguish those which are more like roses and those which are more like chrysan-

2. Working on this problem four years ago, I detected a shadow of support for my version in a remarkable statement by Wu Shan-ching in his study of the chronological development of the southeastern cultures: "We used to consider that the Neolithic culture of the Chiang-Huai region generally had to be much later, or backward, in relation to the Chung Yüan territory. Nowadays we have come to see that, at least by the period corresponding to the Miao-ti-kou type of Chung Yüan Yang-shao culture, our forefathers were already engaged in productive labor in this area, [so, that] just like the Huang Ho drainage area, this region is equally the cradle that nurtured the ancient civilization of China" (1973:57). Wu stopped short of proposing a southern origin for the Lung-shan culture, but his statement implied a backing away from, or at least a qualification of, the developmental theory. In neither of the two recent articles treating extensively the periodization of the eastern seaboard cultures (Nan-ching 1978; Shan-tung-sheng 1978) does there appear a clear statement that the Lung-shan tradition originated in the south independent of influence from the Chung Yüan.

3. This pottery was the principal artistic form of the Neolithic period, and it more than anything else creates for us the character of the various cultures. It is the only medium in which a certain higher intellectual character of those times is reflected. Hence, in terms of the formation of Chinese civilization, an understanding of this pottery is a matter of some consequence. It is also, in terms of Chinese history per se, our most accurate key to the definition of cultural groups that existed during the Neolithic and the distribution of these groups; and it can provide the most precise record of contacts among these peoples. It affords more accurate clues to such matters than can any other aspect of cultures—tools, architecture, and the like—because the pottery, and its painted decoration in particular, is more distinctive than any of these, and it evolved at a more accelerated pace. It was, in short, permitted to change more rapidly because it was less tied to utilitarian or practical concerns, that is, less tied to matters of subsistence.

FIGURE 7.3. *P'en.* Miao-ti-kou, Shan-hsien, Honan. (CKKH 1959b: pl. 27.1.)

themums (Su 1965:57–59). This, of course, may strike us as entirely unconvincing; but Su's analysis is not quite to be ignored, because he has effectively distinguished two sub-groups within the Miao-ti-kou tradition, which, as it happens, follow one another chronologically. On the other hand, the tendency to read the designs as flowers has given rise to very misleading conceptions. In fact, no understanding has been reached as to whether these designs are to be read positively or negatively: that is, whether the painted areas or those in reserve constitute the main design.

It is my view, that the Miao-ti-kou patterns derive from certain types of designs that originated in the Wei river area of Kansu and that they presuppose a tradition of positive spiral configurations which have, through a slow process, been transformed into negative spirals (Huber 1974: chs. 2, 3, 5).

The negative spirals as they exist on various Miao-ti-kou vessels (fig. 7.3) were produced according to a highly complex and sophisticated formula, which can be explained as follows (see fig. 7.4): (1) a series of dots are placed equidistantly around the vessel; (2) pairs of crescentic arcs are drawn to encompass each dot; (3) diagonal curving lines are drawn from the lowest point of one crescentic arc to the uppermost point of the next crescentic arc

FIGURE 7.4. **The procedure for inscribing a Miao-ti-kou spiral design.**

to the right; (4) a partial segmental triangle is drawn, so that one side follows closely the curve of the upper crescentic arc, while the second follows the diagonal that leads to the next configuration on the right; this is repeated above and below the diagonal for each pair of crescentic arcs; (5) the segmental triangles are filled by various configurations; and (6) the crescentic arcs and those areas of the segmental triangles apart from the secondary configurations are painted in.

The very schematized method of producing these patterns, coupled with the fact that the spiral as such is not inscribed but appears almost mysteriously only as the last step of the formula is completed, caused the artists, we may assume, gradually to lose grasp of the fact that the purpose of the formula was the creation of a spiral. In time, only elements of the formula itself, crescentic arcs and the like, survived (fig. 7.5). This brings us precisely to the phase of Su Ping-ch'i's chrysanthemums (fig. 7.6), except that these patterns, mere outlines of discrete spiral designs, obviously possess no representational qualities.

FIGURE 7.5. **Degeneration of the Miao-ti-kou spiral design.**

The decline of the spiral might have had a singularly debilitating effect upon the Miao-ti-kou pottery had not the artists in the meantime built up a substantial repertory of secondary designs. Of these, two are most important: floral-like designs and those consisting of circles subdivided by segmental triangles (CKKH 1959b: pl. 25.3 and 5). These two patterns are based on the same type of structuring employed in the production of the spirals. In the case of the so-called floral patterns, a series of ovals are inscribed across the surface in alternating high and low positions; these are

FIGURE 7.6. *P'en*. Miao-ti-kou, Shan-hsien, Honan. (CKKH 1959b: pl. 26.1.)

embraced by segmental triangles whose tips reach to either the top or the bottom of the adjacent oval. When the segmental triangles are painted in, a design of ovals in reserve results, connected by more or less elliptical forms also in reserve. It seems evident that neither in technique nor in intent have even *these* designs anything to do with floral motifs, as has so often been maintained. The second pattern—that of adjacent circles in reserve subdivided by back-to-back segmental triangles—is constructed on the basis of similar principles applied in a more simplified manner.

From a geographical point of view, it was in the areas of Shensi, Shansi, and Honan that the Miao-ti-kou culture flourished. It is represented by terrace sites along the Wei river and its tributaries, along the lower Fen, and by sites along the Huang Ho continuing into eastern Honan. The Miao-ti-kou pottery within this area exhibits considerable variation, and the question must be posed whether these differences are attributable to local styles or whether they chiefly indicate distinctions of a chronological nature. I strongly incline toward the latter view. The information presently available suggests that an early stage of the culture is to be found farthest west, primarily in Shensi, while a middle stage is reflected predominantly in Shansi and the northwest corner of Honan. The latest phase, on the other hand, is in evidence along the Huang Ho in central and eastern Honan. Whereas, indeed, certain variations of a local, rather than chronological sort can occasionally be noted, the Miao-ti-kou culture can be categorized as follows:[4]

Early Stage
Shensi   Hsia-meng-ts'un, Pin-hsien
           K'o-hsing-chuang I, Sian
           Hsieh-tzu-ling, Sian
           Pan-p'o, Sian
           Liu-tzu-chen, Hua-hsien
Middle Stage
Shansi   Hsi-wang-ts'un, Jui-ch'eng-hsien
           Ching-ts'un, Wan-ch'üan-hsien
           Hsia-ma-ts'un, Yüan-ch'ü-hsien
           Hsi-yin-ts'un, Hsia-hsien   } traces of late stage
Honan   Miao-ti-kou I, Shan-hsien
           Yang-shao-ts'un, Mien-ch'ih-hsien   } mixture of middle and
           Chung-chou-lu, Lo-yang   } late stage
           Miao-wan, Yen-shih
Late Stage
Honan   Ch'in-wang-chai, Kuang-wu-hsien
           Ch'ih-kou-chai, Kuang-wu-hsien
           Ta-ho-ts'un, Cheng-chou

The painted pottery unearthed from sites east of Miao-ti-kou, such as Yang-shao-ts'un and Ch'in-wang-chai, can be divided into several types, one of which is a mere extension of the Miao-ti-kou designs, displaying degenerate spiriform configurations. New, however, is the application of more rectangularized designs to a surface covered with white slip (Arne 1925: pls. 4.11, 6.15). The more recently excavated site of Ta-ho-ts'un thus far marks the easternmost extension of the Miao-ti-kou/Yang-shao-ts'un phase, as exemplified by the striking, tall *po* (fig. 7.1) the shoulder of which is embellished with just such rectangularized patterns.

THE LUNG-SHAN TRADITION: A DEFINITION

If we have reached some clearer comprehension of the meaning of the painted pottery designs and of their historical development, we should, then, turn our attention briefly to a consideration of the term Lung-shan. A primary misconception about Lung-shan stems from its customary designation as the "black pottery culture." Black pottery is rare within that

4. Reference are in order of sites listed: *KK* 1960.1; Li Shih-kuei 1962; CKKH 1962: 17–19; Shih 1955: pl. 10.1; CKKH and Shensi 1963: pl. 161.2–22; *KK* 1959.11; Chang, Chang, and Ch'en 1962; G. D. Wu 1938: 80–83; Tai and Teng 1963; Andersson 1947: pls. 1–85; CKKH 1959a: pls. 2–5; Andersson 1947: pls. 127–149; Arne 1925: pls. 1–13; Ch'en 1973: pl. 1.1.

tradition and is primarily a late development. Lung-shan is more properly defined, on the other hand, as a tradition characterized by unpainted vessels whose chief formal attribute is that they are customarily elevated from the ground, either by a circular foot or by tripod legs. Understood in this manner, Lung-shan remains entirely distinct from Yang-shao and will be seen to encompass all the Neolithic pottery traditions of southern and southeastern China, within which local cultures and chronologically successive sub-cultures can be distinguished. If, in the face of the ever greater complexities that attend the continuing accumulation of new information regarding sub-cultures in Shantung and south of the Huang Ho, we are not to lose sight of larger cultural entities and cultural interactions, the term Lung-shan and the concept it implies must be retained.

The Lung-shan Tradition in Kiangsu

The relation between the painted pottery and Lung-shan traditions, and the evidence for an early phase in the interaction between the two, is most clearly revealed by sites in northern Kiangsu.

The first Kiangsu site that comes to our attention is Liu-lin, located about thirty kilometers northwest of P'i-hsien, near the Shantung border (map 7.1). The first Neolithic finds were made in 1958; subsequently there have been two extensive excavations, one in 1960 and another in 1964 (Yin and Chang 1962; Yin, Yüan, and Chi 1965). The most important discoveries made in 1960 were fifty-two graves, some belonging to an upper and some to a lower stratum. The authors of the report noted that the upper or later phase appears to be closely related to the Kiangsu site of Hua-t'ing and to the Shantung site near Ta-wen-k'ou; the finds from the lower level were claimed to resemble those of the Ch'ing-lien-kang culture as exemplified by the eponymic site in the Huai-an area of Anhwei (Yin and Chang 1962:98). The first season of excavations also revealed several significant features of the second phase of this Kiangsu culture. (1) Evidence of an advanced jade craft was afforded by skillfully worked beads, small disks, and axes, most of them perforated. (2) One meets at Liu-lin for the first time the curious burial habit of placing dogs at the feet of some of the dead. (3) Systematically drilled tortoise shells were found in certain graves.[5]

5. The Chinese archaeological reports do not specify whether the creatures in question are tortoises (*ti-kuei* 地龜) or turtles (*shui-kuei* 水龜). In the English language abstract (Yin, Chang, and Chi 1964:56) the term *kuei* is translated as "tortoise." This term is retained in my article for lack of any evidence that the designation "turtle" should instead be employed. David Keightley and James Berry have recently called attention to the fact during Shang, turtles, rather than tortoises, were used for divination, almost without exception (Keightley 1978:8–9, 157–158, 190–191).

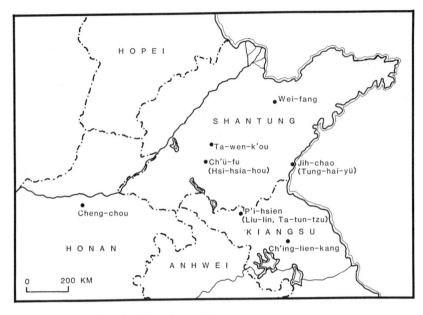

MAP 7.1. **Lung-shan sites in eastern China.**

During the 1964 excavation, nineteen additional trenches were opened. In the lowest of three strata were discovered no fewer than 145 burials. These graves were segregated into five clusters (Yin, Yüan, and Chi 1965:12):

1 T 403–405		24 graves
2 T 406–408		24 graves
3 T 412–413		28 graves
4 T 707, 708, 806, 807		21 graves
5 T 805, 905		47 graves

The authors proposed that the graves represent a common clan cemetery, whereas each of the five groups of burials belongs to a single family, or to several closely related families within the clan. The contents of each cluster of graves, however, are sufficiently unlike to disabuse us of any notion that they might form convenient chronologically discrete units; on the other hand, the stratigraphic level containing the graves is differentiated into three additional substrata, and the graves are chronologically distinguishable in a ready manner according to whether they are positioned in the upper, middle, or lower level. The artifacts they contain have been roughly classified as belonging to an "early" or a "late" period (ibid.: charts following p. 47).

Although a few painted sherds were found scattered throughout the trenches, only those from the graves were possessed of a significant strati-graphic context. Two of the four painted vessels from the graves are classi-fied as Miao-ti-kou types; the painted bowl from M 72 is illustrated (ibid., p. 37, fig. 26) and leaves no doubt that it is in the Miao-ti-kou style; the same, presumably, is true for the other painted bowl, from M 102. As noted in the report, what distinguishes these two vessels from the typical Miao-ti-kou painted pottery is the softer paste and easily peeling decoration, which suggests that they were probably products of local kilns under the influence of the Chung Yüan (ibid., p. 47). The entirely coherent but rather re-gimented pattern on the *po* from M 72 and the introduction of red pigment support the hypothesis of local manufacture.[6]

The stratigraphic position of the graves containing the two Chung Yüan style *po* is obviously crucial. Burial M 72 is located in the upper of the three levels; M 102 is recorded as being in the second level but is situated precisely 0.2 meters lower than M 72 (ibid.: chart p. 14, line 5). It is noteworthy that neither of these graves was found in the lowest, or earliest, level. On the basis of their contents, M 72 was classified as belonging to the late phase at Liu-lin; M 102, however, was classified as early. It should be pointed out, nevertheless, that M 102 contained no vessels of the most primitive Liu-lin type, although the vessels it did contain are clearly somewhat earlier than those of M 72.

The classification of these two tombs as early and late, as well as the relationship of the painted ware to the rest of the Liu-lin pottery, can be clarified through the characterization given in the report (ibid., pp. 32–43) of the two stages represented by the excavated finds from this site. The authors believe with good reason that the pottery remains that were unearthed during the second season at Liu-lin mark two distinct stages of a continuously evolving culture. These stages are represented by the major types of vessels found in the lower and upper levels, respectively; it may be helpful to examine these levels in some detail.

The most startling of all Liu-lin vessels and the unquestionable master-pieces of their potters are the *pei*, or drinking vessels. The *pei* can be assigned to seven distinct types (ibid., p. 38, fig. 28): (1) the simple, flat-bottomed *pei* with flaring mouth; (2) the "soda glass" type with contracted stem; (3) the trumpet-mouth version with three small feet; (4–5) the trumpet-mouth *pei* with cylindrical stem and small feet; (6) the most superb

---

6. Red pigment apparently does not come into use in the Chung Yüan until the somewhat later Miao-ti-kou/Yang-shao-ts'un period.

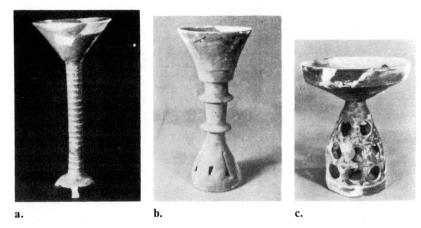

a.   b.   c.

FIGURE 7.7. **Vessels from Ta-tun-tzu, P'i-hsien, Kiangsu. a: *Pei* (Liu-lin phase). b: *Pei* (Hua-t'ing phase). c: *Tou* (Hua-t'ing phase). (Yin, Chang, and Chi 1964: pls. 16.2, 16.1, 11.4, respectively.)**

type, characterized by a much attenuated and less flaring mouth, a slender, horizontally grooved stem, and higher feet (see fig. 7.7a); and (7) the tallest version, with broad mouth and long stem, girt in the middle by a thicker band of clay. Of these, types 1–5 are considered early and 6–7 late.

Another vessel, the *tou* (ibid., p. 33, fig. 23; p. 34, fig. 24; p. 40, fig. 30) is classified into three types: the earliest is rounded in form, whereas the two types linked to the late period exhibit a more sharply delineated silhouette, with the more advanced example showing a perforated foot. The *ting* are divided into two groups, the *p'en-ting* 盆鼎 and the *kuan-ting* 罐鼎, depending on the depth of the bowl. The earlier *p'en-ting* (ibid., p. 34, fig. 24) have softly rounded bowls and rounded feet; those of the later period are approximately triangular in profile, and the legs are beveled at the bottom, reducing the feeling of roundness and lending them poise. The early *kuan-ting* (ibid., p. 40, fig. 30) are characterized primarily by their tall, rounded legs that jut out from the bowl; they are either beveled at the foot or thin and wedge-shaped, set in radial order and serrated at the edges.

At Liu-lin, then, one witnesses the evolution of basic vessel types spanning a considerable period of time, during which the forms consistently become more clearly articulated and the formal attributes of each type of vessel are variously explored. The *pei* stems grow ever taller; the *tou* feet are structured by perforations; *ting* feet are serrated. In general, the vessels grow increasingly ornate, and the alternations in form are of aesthetic rather than functional significance. Such is particularly the case with the *pei*—a vessel restricted no doubt to ceremonial drinking—which, growing ever more elegant, also comes to be precarious on its feet and inconvenient to handle.

Of the graves at Liu-lin that held painted pottery of the Miao-ti-kou variety, the "late" M 72 yielded four *kuan-ting* of the late Liu-lin type, four late *p'en-ting*, and advanced Stage 6 tripod *pei*. There were *kuan-ting* and *p'en-ting* of the early type in M 102, but also a mature Stage 3 *pei* (ibid.: chart following p. 47). Since it is established that the Miao-ti-kou style painted ware in neither instance is associated with any rudimentary form of the Liu-lin culture, and since no graves in the lowest stratum contained any painted ware, there is no evidence at Liu-lin that a painted pottery culture inspired by the Chung Yüan gradually gave way, or evolved into, a Lung-shan culture. Rather, pottery of the Miao-ti-kou variety occurs in each instance within an advanced Lung-shan assemblage, and it is manifestly intrusive.

An investigation of the second P'i-hsien site, that of Ta-tun-tzu, lends additional weight to this interpretation. The cultural deposits are located on an elevated oval plateau with a maximum diameter of 250 meters. The finds from the third level are considered to belong to the Liu-lin culture, while those from the ashpits underneath are again typical of the Ch'ing-lien-kang culture (Yin, Chang, and Chi 1964:9, 47–49). The third level is sub-divided into five strata, and the forty-two Neolithic graves are categorized according to the substratum in which they are located (ibid., p. 20):

	T 1	*T 3*	*T 5*	*T 7*
level 1	M1, 42	M 16, 36	M 38–40	M 5
2	M 2–4, 20	M 17, 18, 25	M 41	M 9, 12
3	M 6–8, 19, 33	M 30, 31, 44		M 10, 11, 14, 15, 43
4	M 21–23	M 26–29, 32		
5	M 34–35, 37			

Because the tombs are distributed in so many stratigraphical levels, it would seem tempting to regard them as representing five different chronological phases, as happened with the graves at Liu-lin. It soon becomes evident, though, that such an attempt is entirely futile, for the graves in any one level yield entirely disparate finds. But the graves can be separated into two groups on the basis of their contents: those which the authors of the site report claim exhibit a closer resemblance to the finds from Liu-lin and those they would link to the Kiangsu site of Hua-t'ing. The distribution of these two types of graves within the four trenches is significant (as it was not at Liu-lin): of the fifteen Hua-t'ing type graves, no less than twelve are located in T 5 and T 7; in neither of these two trenches were there graves of the Liu-lin type. Of the other three "Hua-t'ing" graves, two, M 36 (located in T 3) and M 42 (located in T 1) are separate from the "Liu-lin" graves in these trenches (ibid., p. 20–22). Moreover, M 16 in T 3, one of the Hua-t'ing graves, overlies the Liu-lin grave M 30; on the basis of this overlap, the Hua-t'ing graves are considered later than those of the Liu-lin type (ibid., p. 20).

Unfortunately, at the time the Ta-tun-tzu report was prepared, the second report on the Liu-lin site, which showed that the Liu-lin culture comprised two consecutive stages (apart from the lowest Ch'ing-lien-kang level), had not yet been published; as a result, the Ta-tun-tzu report makes no distinction between the relative earliness or lateness of the Liu-lin type of finds at Ta-tun-tzu. But it now seems certain that these materials belong exclusively to the late Liu-lin phase.[7]

The "Hua-t'ing" pottery (ibid., p. 37, fig. 30; p. 40, fig. 35; p. 43, fig. 36) by contrast has an individuality all its own. Nevertheless, the classes of vessels are entirely familiar and are closely affiliated with the later Liu-lin phase, whose slightly more advanced descendants they surely are. The Hua-t'ing vessels display the same clearly articulated profiles, yet they are altogether more massive in appearance. The *p'en-ting* have deeper bowls than before, while the legs, thin, wedge-shaped, and radially arranged, are now indented on top so they jut out slightly before tapering almost to a point. Some legs are notched along their outer edges, others are decorated with triangular perforations. The *tou* normally resemble the late Liu-lin type with a perforated foot, but the unusually high foot of one even more ornate example presents a complex structure of large circular perforations set between pairs of smaller triangles (see fig. 7.7c above). The single example of the Hua-t'ing tripod *pei* resembles closely that of Liu-lin Stage 7. But more revealing of the Hua-t'ing style is a new type of *pei* with a sturdier circular foot (fig. 7.7b). This particular *pei* recalls the older variety in the shape of its bowl and the hollow stem, which here is encircled by thick, protruding bands of triangular cross-section. On the whole, the vessels are less graceful; but at the same time they are more practical and more imposing in character.

Of the ten pieces of painted pottery found at Ta-tun-tzu, eight came from the "Liu-lin" graves and two from the "Hua-t'ing" graves. From M 30, a rich grave containing twelve objects, came two painted bowls. Both

7. The slender tall-stem *pei* found in M 30 and M 33 are identical to the late Stage V *pei* from Liu-lin; that from M 44 is most closely matched by the late Stage VII variety. The *tou* have sharply articulated profiles and perforated stems and the *ting* display bevelled feet—all features particular to the late Liu-lin period.

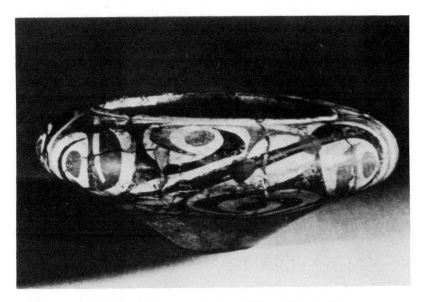

FIGURE 7.8. *Po.* **P'i-hsien, Kiangsu.** (*Genius of China* **1973, no. 38.**)

are in the Miao-ti-kou style but, like those from the Liu-lin site, differ from
the Chung Yüan examples primarily in the use of a white slipped ground
and the application of red, as well as black, paint. The fragment of one
(ibid.: pl. 31.1) exhibits a complex reserve spiral similar to that from M 72
at Liu-lin. The design is executed according to the standard Miao-ti-kou
formula and was, assuredly, similar to the complete *po* from P'i-hsien (see
fig. 7.8; no site is given) included in the Chinese Exhibition of 1973–1975.

   The technically less demanding secondary "floral" pattern of Miao-ti-
kou, constructed on the basis of subdividing the surface with segmental
triangles, was used on the second painted vessel from M 30 (ibid.: pl. 1,
upper). The *p'en* (pl. 2, lower), in turn, presents a variation on the floral
pattern, incorporating the oval divided by segmental triangles. Apart from
a tripod *pei* of a more advanced type than that found in M 33, M 44
contained a bowl with star-like motifs painted in white on a pink ground
(ibid.: pl. 1, lower). Coloring and motif would make this bowl appear as a
purely local invention, were it not for a similar vessel excavated recently at
Tung-chuang-ts'un, Jui-ch'eng-hsien, Shensi (*KKHP* 1973:16, fig. 15.4).
The comparatively simple design painted on the surface of a *ting* from M 22
(Yin, Chang, and Chi 1964: pl. 9.2), however, is a local variant.

   The two examples of painted ware found in the Hua-t'ing phase M 38 are not illustrated, but they are said to resemble sherds from the Honan site of Ch'in-wang-chai (ibid., p. 49). If the authors' analysis of the two pieces is correct, as we are left to assume it is, then we can relate the "Liu-lin" graves chronologically to the Miao-ti-kou period in the Chung Yüan and the "Hua-t'ing" graves to the slightly later Miao-ti-kou/Yang-shao-ts'un phase.

Let us summarize the results of the two excavations at Liu-lin and the one at Ta-tun-tzu. From the first Liu-lin report it can be concluded that the Liu-lin finds postdate those of the Ch'ing-lien-kang culture. The second report enables us to divide the Liu-lin pottery into two chronologically successive phases. The Ta-tun-tzu excavation revealed a lower stratum of Ch'ing-lien-kang material, above which lay graves of the Liu-lin phase, which in turn were overlaid by those of the Hua-t'ing period. Thus we arrive at the following chronological seuqence:

Kiangsu	*Chung Yüan*
	Pan-p'o
	(ZK–38) 4773 ± 141 B.C.—(ZK–127)
	4294 ± 165 B.C.
Ch'ing-lien-kang	
(ZK–90) 4497 ± 208 B.C.	
	Hou-kang
	(ZK–134) 4392 ± 221 B.C.—(ZK–76)
	4189 ± 165 B.C.
Liu-lin I	
	Miao-ti-kou I
	(ZK–110) 3915 ± 115 B.C.
Liu-lin II	
Hua-t'ing	Miao-ti-kou/Yang-shao-ts'un phase Ta-ho-ts'un
	(ZK–185) 3684 ± 124 B.C.—(BK–76004)
	3071 ± 182 B.C.

Notwithstanding the high antiquity of the Ch'ing-lien-kang phase of the Lung-shan culture indicated by the carbon-14 date for the Ch'ing-lien-kang level at Ta-tun-tzu, Pan-p'o retains the distinction of being even older. Because of the pronounced differences between the pottery and other artifacts characteristic of these two cultures, we are led to the ineluctable conclusion that even during this very early period there were two independent Neolithic cultures of major importance flourishing in separate parts of China. Moreover, contemporary with the Miao-ti-kou period in the Chung Yüan, there existed in Kiangsu a highly developed branch of the Lung-shan culture, defined in particular by its tradition of unpainted pottery, whose featured vessels were the *pei*, *tou*, and *ting*. This culture had at its disposal an advanced jade craft; and it made use of tortoise shells, presumably for ritualistic purposes. It should be noted as well that the ornate and highly stylized *pei* strongly suggests customs of ritualistic or ceremonial drinking for which there is no verifiable precedent in the Chung Yüan area.

Added to certain of the Kiangsu graves containing these sophisticated unpainted vessels are the gaudier—and livelier—Miao-ti-kou style *po*, together forming a decidedly unhomogenous but nonetheless impressive array; the owners were, so to speak, the fortunate recipients of the best of two worlds. Without exception, the painted wares were found only in the most opulent graves distinguished by a large number of grave goods, all of exceptionally high quality. It may be assumed that such painted wares were rare and treasured items, restricted to the graves of select members of the elite. The Miao-ti-kou style vessels, however, remained exotic items which did not alter the course of the local Kiangsu pottery style. Possibly, cultural transmission during this period was primarily a one-sided affair, for evidence of importation into the Miao-ti-kou sphere is negligible. It is apparently not until the somewhat later Miao-ti-kou/Yang-shao-ts'un phase, typified by Ta-ho-ts'un, where there suddenly appear Lung-shan vessels of the Hua-t'ing or Ta-wen-k'ou phase, that we are presented with any strong indications of influence upon the Chung Yüan area stemming from the southeast.

The Lung-shan Tradition in Shantung

To demonstrate the continued independence of the Lung-shan culture and to evaluate the importance of its contributions, relative to those of the Chung Yüan tradition, to the formation of the early Bronze Age civilization in China, the course of the eastern Lung-shan development must be followed somewhat further in time.

An analysis of the Shantung Lung-shan pottery and other cultural properties suggests that this branch of the Lung-shan tradition evolved directly out of the later phases of the Kiangsu cultures and that it is, for the most part, subsequent in date. The earlier stages of Ch'ing-lien-kang and Liú-lin do not appear to have extended into the Shantung area. On the other hand, the phase represented by the upper level at Ta-tun-tzu can be recognized further to the north, in central Shantung, at a fair number of sites. At such locations as Yeh-tien in Tsou-hsien (Shan-tung-sheng 1972), the T'eng-hsien site of Kang-shang (Shan-tung-sheng 1963), and in the lowest of the three strata at Ta-wen-k'ou (Shan-tung-sheng and Chi-nan-shih 1974:14, fig. 6), we find pottery almost identical to that of the Kiangsu

Hua-t'ing culture, including the *tou* with conical foot fashioned in open-work, the *pei* with protruding bands around the stem, and the *ting* with wedge-shaped legs in radial position. And at this point it becomes import-ant to begin to take note of another type of vessel, namely the *kuei* 鬶 tripod, a pouring vessel or ewer, which plays an increasingly prominent role in the subsequent history of Lung-shan ceramics. During the Hua-t'ing/Ta-wen-k'ou period, the *kuei* is found to occur only in a form supported by three solid legs (Shan-tung-sheng 1978:62–63).

Especially worthy of attention is the site of Hsi-hsia-hou, which is stratified into two distinct levels representing two further stages in the evolution of this east coast culture (Kao and Jen 1964). Added to the full assemblage of the typical eastern cultural paraphernalia—jade bracelets and axes, tortoise shells, hafted deer teeth, and the like—is a large array of ceramics. The tripod *kuei* in the lower level are of two types; one, with solid feet and the handle joined to the base of the neck (fig. 7.9a), remains almost identical to the lower Ta-wen-k'ou examples save for the extended pouring channel, but we also meet with a second and more novel type characterized by an extended pouring channel and by hollow legs of the *li* 鬲 type.[8] In the upper level at Hsi-hsia-hou (fig. 7.9b) the version with solid legs is rarely seen; moreover, the *kuei* with hollow legs has been altered so that the vessel gains a rounder and more even body, and shorter, less bulbous legs. The corners of the pouring channel are bent in over the mouth, and an appliqué band around the body of the vessel has become a more or less standard feature.

But it is the large *tou* and the *pei* that have undergone the most dramatic transformations. The *tou* from the lower level (fig. 7.10a) exhibits a broad, shallow bowl; the stem, whether tall or short, is almost straight-walled and flares only slightly toward the foot. The stems are perforated with circles and slim triangles with one curved side—a looser and less coherent arrange-ment of the same elements that composed the openwork patterns on the *tou* stems from Hua-t'ing and Ta-wen-k'ou. The *tou* from the upper level (fig. 7.10b) have changed radically; their bowls, although deeper than those in the lower level, are essentially the same, but here the similarity ends. No short, broad-stemmed *tou* appear, nor do any with particularly high stems. Instead, a compromise is achieved: the stem is short but narrow, concave in profile, and it flares toward an entirely innovative step-like molded base. This new *tou* is reassuringly stable by comparison to either of the previous

8. It seems at the moment that the hollow *li*-type legs owe their invention to the east coast Lung-shan potters.

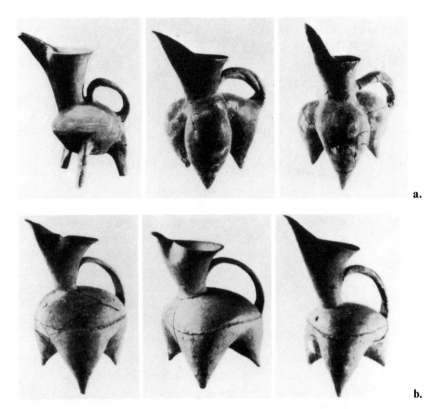

FIGURE 7.9. *Kuei*. Hsi-hsia-hou, Ch'ü-fu-hsien, Shantung. a: *Kuei* from lower stratum. b: *Kuei* from upper stratum. (Kao and Jen 1964: pl. 4.1–6.)

types. Furthermore, on the stems the openwork decor of circles and triangles, characteristic of the examples from the lower level, has been replaced by yet more simplified designs consisting merely of circles in vertical rows alternating with rows of rhombic perforations.

The wide variety of *pei* found on the lower level have been similarly amalgamated into one type and transformed much in the same manner as the *tou*. In the upper level, the bowl of the *pei* (fig. 7.11) becomes much deeper, and its sides curve to create a concave silhouette. The stem is contracted, bulging somewhat in the middle, and the foot, like that on the *tou* of the same period, ends in a pronounced molded base. The stems are similarly perforated with circles and diamonds. With these alterations the *pei* is transformed into a veritable goblet.

The evolution of the vessel forms from one level to the other at Hsi-hsia-

FIGURE 7.10. *Tou*. Hsi-hsia-hou, Ch'ü-fu-hsien, Shantung. a: *Tou* from lower stratum. b: *Tou* from upper stratum. (Kao and Jen 1964: pls. 6.1–6, 7.1–3, respectively.)

FIGURE 7.11. *Pei.* **Hsi-hsia-hou (upper stratum), Ch'ü-fu-hsien, Shantung. (Kao and Jen 1964: pl. 9.4–7.)**

hou is entirely obvious. The pottery from the lower level corresponds fairly closely to the Hua-t'ing phase in northern Kiangsu and to the early period at Ta-wen-k'ou and other related Shantung sites, whereas none of the distinguishing stylistic features of the upper-level appear in any of the aforementioned pottery complexes.

Apart from that, certain characteristics observable at the upper level of Hsi-hsia-hou form a link to another set of Shantung sites farther to the northeast, including localities in Jih-chao-hsien and Wei-fang (Liu 1958; Feng 1960; Cheng 1963; Wu Ju-tso 1977). It is now certain that a fourth and fifth chronologically successive phase of the Shantung Lung-shan culture can be recognized at the important stratified site of Tung-hai-yü in Jih-chao. The report of the excavations at this site was published late in 1976 (Shan-tung-sheng, Tung-hai-yü, and Jih-chao 1976); but prior to the availability of stratigraphical evidence, it seemed fully apparent that the pottery associated with the Jih-chao and Wei-fang areas—where we meet for the first time a high percentage of black wares turned on a fast wheel—represented a phase subsequent to that at Hsi-hsia-hou.

To understand the significance of what was discovered in each of the three levels at Tung-hai-yü we can for the sake of simplicity limit our attention to one or two of the most revealing vessel forms. From the lower level came *pei* and *kuei* identical to those from the upper level at Hsi-hsia-hou. In the middle level was discovered a somewhat different type of *pei,* with a broader foot and a bowl less convex in profile than before which flares strongly to the rim (ibid.: chart p. 379). The *pei* from the upper level at

a.   b.

FIGURE 7.12. **Vessels from Tung-hai-yü, Jih-chao-hsien, Shantung. a: *Pei*. b: *Kuei*. (Shan-tung-sheng, Tung-hai-yü, and Jih-chao 1976: pls. 6.3, 6.5, respectively.)**

Tung-hai-yü are not greatly different from those in the lower; but the one feature new in the period represented by the middle level—the flaring rim—is now given considerably more emphasis (fig. 7.12a). Moreover, it is by the period of the upper level that the tripod-*kuei* reaches the ultimate stage in its evolution: it stands now straight and tall, its body and neck extending upward, centered directly above the *li*-legs (fig. 7.12b) instead of being set off to one side.

It is to that late stage in the evolution of the eastern Lung-shan culture that we must also assign the masterful vessels from the Wei-fang area such as the *kuei* and *pei* (fig. 7.13) familiar from the Chinese Exhibition of 1973–1975. To this phase too belongs the invention of the classical *tou* with

a.   b.

FIGURE 7.13. **Vessels from Wei-fang-hsien, Shantung. a: *Pei*. b: *Kuei*. (*Chinese Exhibition* 1975, nos. 56, 54, respectively.)**

shallow bowl and relatively broad stem; a magnificent censer-like vessel with perforated bowl and molded foot; the *ting* with legs of V-shaped section, often with a median appliqué flange; and the as yet unnamed tripod with a ring foot cut away in three sections to form three broad legs whose walls are parallel to the curvature of the body (Cheng 1963: pl. 2.5; pl. 2.1; pl. 3.3). It is also at this stage that the *hsien* 甗 tripod makes its first appearance (ibid.: pl. 3.7).

The general stylistic evolution of the Shantung Lung-shan pottery can be summarized as follows: the Ta-wen-k'ou phase is characterized by vessels usually betraying slight irregularities in shape, but of a delicate and sometimes almost fragile aspect, which results primarily from the excessively tall legs or stems that support many of them and from the elaborate openwork designs that embellish the stems of the *tou*. Buff or light red are the dominant colors of the ware; gray occurs; black is hardly in evidence.

The same variety of buff and some light gray ware is also typical of the pottery from the lower level of Hsi-hsia-hou, but by contrast to those of Ta-wen-k'ou the vessels are more standardized and more perfectly symmet-

rical in shape, and the surfaces are more even. The amount of openwork on
the stems of the *tou* is greatly reduced and the patterns are simplified or
abbreviated. With the second Hsi-hsia-hou phase, the vessels take on a
decidedly mannered appearance. There is a particular insistence on dis-
sociating the various parts of the vessel from one another; in the case of the
tou and *pei*, the stem is contracted in width and thus explicitly set off from
the bowl and the foot. The bowl of the *pei* becomes almost perversely
concave in profile. Far greater stress upon the silhouette results from the
emergence of dark gray and black as the dominant color of the ware.
Openwork is retained, but it no longer counts as a feature of special
emphasis.

The latest of the Lung-shan vessels, represented by the Tung-hai-yü and
related sites—by contrast to the preceding styles—whether of egg-shell
ware or heavily potted are far more assertively substantial and at the same
time more refined and regal, owing in part to the effects produced by the
increased use of the fast wheel. The vessels look, many of them, like so
many pieces from some fantastic chess set. Moreover, during the late Lung-
shan period, decoration came to consist primarily of raised horizontal ribs
and appliqué bands, with great attention to such features as lugs and
handles: in other words, the decoration has become additive in nature
rather than subtractive as in the earlier styles, where openwork was the
preferred form of embellishment.

From the foregoing analysis it can be concluded that the sites in northern Kiangsu and Shantung belong to one and the same cultural complex
and that the pottery found in the two areas exhibits an internally consistent
and uninterrupted evolution, climaxing with the predominantly wheel-
made black ware of the late Lung-shan stage. The periodization of this
eastern culture is as follows: the Ch'ing-lien-kang phase preceded Liu-lin I
and II, which in turn are succeeded by the Hua-t'ing phase; the Hua-t'ing
phase is closely contemporary with the Ta-wen-k'ou stage in Shantung,
which is followed by Hsi-hsia-hou I and II; the upper level at Hsi-hsia-hou
is approximately contemporary with the earliest of the three sequential
phases at Tung-hai-yü.

Northern Kiangsu	Western Shantung	Eastern Shantung
Ch'ing-lien-kang		
Liu-lin I		
Liu-lin II		
Hua-t'ing		
	Ta-wen-k'ou	
	Hsi-hsia-hou I	
	Hsi-hsia-hou II	Tung-hai-yü I
		Tung-hai-yü II
		Tung-hai yü III

THE CORRELATION BETWEEN THE EASTERN
LUNG-SHAN TRADITION AND THE CHUNG-YÜAN

We are now in a position to relate the various stages of the independent eastcoast Lung-shan culture to the developments in the Chung Yüan area. We have already arrived at the following assessment: the Ch'ing-lien-kang culture, carbon-dated (ZK–90) to 4497 ± 208 B.C., is close in time to the Pan-p'o culture in the Chung Yüan (ZK–38:4773 ± 141 B.C.; ZK–127:4294 ± 165 B.C.). The succeeding Liu-lin phase, due to the intrusive painted ware bowls in many of the burials, is to be equated chronologically with the florescence of the Miao-ti-kou culture. The Kiangsu Hua-t'ing phase, merely on the basis of unpublished sherds from the Hua-t'ing level at Ta-tun-tzu which are said to be similar to those from Ch'in-wang-chai, is loosely correlated with the late Miao-ti-kou/Yang-shao-ts'un phase.

But since it is also known that Yeh-tien, Kang-shang, and the lower level at Ta-wen-k'ou are the Shantung equivalents of the Kiangsu Hua-t'ing phase and are strictly contemporary with it, additional evidence can be provided for the contemporaneity of the Hua-t'ing phase in these two provinces with the last phase of the painted ware in Honan. First, at Ta-wen-k'ou we find one vessel painted with a design not found on any other vessels from this site: a trellis pattern (Shan-tung-sheng and Chi-nan-shih 1974: pl. 43.5), precisely one of the main traits of certain vessels belonging to the late Miao-ti-kou/Yang-shao-ts'un period (e.g. Arne 1925: pl. 7.18, 20). Second, at the late painted ware site of Ta-ho-ts'un in Honan there is a small, oval-bodied, round-bottom *hu* 壺 with a prominent cylindrical neck (Ch'en 1973: pl. 3.1)—a simple enough form, but one apparently unprecedented in the Chung Yüan. An exact counterpart of this *hu* is known from Yeh-tien and several close approximations of it from Ta-wen-k'ou (Shan-tung-sheng 1972, p. 30, fig. 20); one of the Ta-wen-k'ou examples (Shang-tung-sheng and Chi-nan-shih 1974: pl. 41) incorporates in its painted decor a circular motif with a central dot similar to that found on the Ta-ho *hu*. We can feel more assured, then, of the correspondence of the Miao-ti-kou/Yang-shao-ts'un phase with the Hua-t'ing/Ta-wen-k'ou phase. On the basis of the carbon-14 dates for Ta-ho, it can be assumed that the Hua-t'ing stage likewise dates to around 3500–3000 B.C.

How, then, can we account for the unpainted *tou* and *ting* at Ta-ho (fig. 7.2), forms again unprecedented in the Chung Yüan? The analogies that can be provided are not exact, but it is worth noting that the feet on the Ta-ho *ting* are radially oriented and wedge-shaped, a typical feature of the Hua-t'ing stage *ting*. The Ta-ho version of the *ting* with relatively straight wall and gently rounded underside is also found at Yeh-tien, whereas the round-bodied *kuan-ting* at Ta-ho seems, again, to be an adaptation of a Yeh-tien type (Shan-tung-sheng 1972:29, figs. 11–13). The *tou* with shallow bowl from Ta-ho is similar in form to those from the upper level at Ta-tun-tzu (Yin, Chang, and Chi 1964: pl. 9.1–2), but the almost straight-sided ring foot with small circular perforations is both shorter and simpler than those from Hua-t'ing sites. The large gray ware amphora from Ta-ho, unparalleled in the Chung Yüan, has similarities to those from the Hua-t'ing phase at Ta-tun-tzu (Ch'en 1973:335, fig. 6, left; Yin, Chang, and Chi 1964: pl. 15.2).

Additional weight to support the argument for the equivalence of Ta-ho-ts'un and the Hua-t'ing phases is brought to bear by excavations at the site near Ku-shui-ho, Yü-hsien, southwest of Cheng-chou (*KK* 1978.1:25–30). This site, which will doubtless assume considerable importance in future discussions, was found to contain a mixture of Yang-shao and Lung-shan material, certainly coeval with Ta-ho, but including a far more extensive range of Lung-shan forms. Among the most significant is the *pei* with angular bowl and large triangular perforations on the stem, for which the exact counterpart exists at Kang-shang (Shan-tung-sheng 1963: pl. 5.7). This particular vessel does not seem to occur at any site that can be distinguished as later than the Hua-t'ing phase.

Thus it can be said that those forms at Ta-ho that seem like deviants in the context of the Chung Yüan painted pottery tradition are to be explained as ideas emanating from the Hua-t'ing age culture in Kiangsu and Shantung; they are not inventions of the Honan potters but intrusions from the southeastern cultures, where the history of such forms reaches back a millennium in time. That the presence of the unpainted elevated vessels in Honan does not signify any massive migration or invasion from the east, but a less overpowering form of contact, is verified by the fact that these new vessel forms at Ta-ho stand side by side with the old Chung Yüan forms, the painted ware *po* and the cord-impressed *p'ing* 缾.

We can be certain that Ta-ho-ts'un is the transitional phase signaling the introduction of the Lung-shan pottery tradition into Honan. Soon thereafter, the Chung Yüan altogether relinquished its painting tradition, which to judge from the evidence at Ta-ho-ts'un had already fallen into decadence at least as early as 3000 B.C. Gradually a new style of unpainted vessels evolved, based upon a combination of ancient Chung Yüan forms (including corded ware largely alien to the southeast Lung-shan tradition) with new forms derived from the Lung-shan complex in the east.

To date, in the Chung Yüan area and westward into Kansu, the long period from approximately 3000 B.C. to 1500 B.C., or the beginnings of dynastic Shang, is known to us primarily by way of the following major sites.[9]

> K'o-la-wang-ts'un, Cheng-chou
> Erh-li-t'ou I, Yen-shih
> Wang-wan III, Lo-yang
> Hsia-wang-kang late II, Hsi-ch'uan
> Pu-chao-chai, Mien-ch'ih
> San-li-ch'iao, Shan-hsien
> K'o-hsing-chuang II, Sian
> the Ch'i-chia sites in Kansu

The carbon-14 dates available for Wang-wan III (ZK−126:2388 B.C. ± 134) and for the Ch'i-chia site of Ta-ho-chuang (ZK−15:2038 B.C. ± 161 and ZK−23:2001 B.C. ± 161) indicate that the Chung Yüan Lung-shan pottery represented at these widespread but otherwise quite closely related sites is a late manifestation of a style that had been initiated as much as a thousand years previously. The date of (ZK−111) 2776 B.C. ± 138 for Miao-ti-kou II would of course take us farther back in time. However, it seems quite likely that the Miao-ti-kou II pottery is the result of a localized intrusion of the Hupei branch of the southern Lung-shan culture, namely Ch'ü-chia-ling, and hence may not be fully representative of the earlier Honan Lung-shan as a whole.

Insofar as we still lack the archaeological evidence that would enable us to visualize the Lung-shan pottery styles that followed upon Ta-ho-ts'un, it is not possible to present substantial correlations between the Shantung and Honan Lung-shan traditions immediately subsequent to that period. And whereas we are able to observe by way of stratified sites a powerful surge northward as the Shantung culture develops through time, we are hampered by the lack of radiocarbon dates for the later Lung-shan phases. Nevertheless, there are some useful clues, notably one or two vessel types, that may assist our understanding.

First, it should be noted that the *kuei*-tripod characteristic of the Honan Lung-shan culture of approximately 2000 B.C. is of a specific type: the tall, upright variety with the upper body positioned directly above the conjunction of the *li*-legs (Ho-nan-sheng and Ch'ang-pan 1972:10, figs. 40, 42; Lo-yang 1978: pls. 5.2–3; also Shensi K'o-hsing-chuang II in CKKH 1962: pl.

9. Chao and Liu 1958 (K'o-la-wang-ts'un); Fang 1965 (Erh-li-t'ou); Ch'eng, P'eng, and Li 1964:174–178, pls. 2–4 (Wang-wan III); Ho-nan-sheng and Ch'ang-pan 1972 (Hsia-wang-kang); Andersson 1947:78–108, pls. 86–126 (Pu-chao-chai); CKKH 1959b:92–102, pls. 80–92 (San-li-ch'iao II); CKKH 1962:43–69, pls. 25, 26 (K'o-hsing-chuang II); Bylin-Althin 1946:382–429; Cheng and Hsieh 1960; Hsieh 1964; Kuo 1960 (Ch'i-chia sites).

29.1, 2). Since, as pointed out before, this particular type of *kuei* does not make its appearance in Shantung until the upper, or third, of the Lung-shan levels at Tung-hai-yü, it would seem that the late Shantung Lung-shan culture should be placed within close range of 2000 B.C.

The second important vessel is that so far unnamed tripod with broad legs in parallel curvature to the vessel wall. Again, this vessel is not found in Shantung prior to the late Lung-shan phase, and one specimen of it was discovered in the company of an upright *kuei* in the upper level at Shang-chuang (Wang et al. 1978:41, figs. 3, 4). The same type of tripod appears at the Lo-yang site of Tung-ma-kou, a site which on account of its ceramic repertory has been correlated with Erh-li-t'ou II (Lo-yang 1978: pl. 4.4, 5). The tripod also figures at Erh-li-t'ou II itself (Fang 1965: pl. 3.8).

For Erh-li-t'ou I, we have the following carbon-14 dates: 1906 ± 104 B.C. (ZK–212) and 1885 ± 91 B.C. (ZK–285); for the Erh-li-t'ou I level at the Lo-yang site of Ts'o-li (Ts'o-li level 4) we have the date 2001 ± 184 B.C. (Sui and Fang 1978.1:17; ZK–353). Hence there would be every reason to place the late phase of the Honan Lung-shan roughly contemporary with the early levels at Erh-li-t'ou, and in turn to equate the late Lung-shan period in Shantung with this Honan phase.

In summary, I propose the following chronological correlations between the east coast Lung-shan tradition and the developments in the Chung Yüan region:

East coast Lung-shan	*Chung-yüan*	
	Pan-p'o	
Ch'ing-lien-kang		
Liu-lin I		
	Miao-ti-kou	florescence of painted
Liu-lin II		ware
Hua-t'ing/Ta-wen-k'ou	Miao-ti-kou/	termination of painted
	Yang-shao-ts'un	ware
Hsi-hsia-hou I		
	Honan Lung-shan	
Hsi-hsia-hou II		
Tung-hai-yü II		
Tung-hai-yü III	Erh-li-t'ou I	
	Erh-li-t'ou II	
	Erh-li-t'ou III	dynastic Shang starts?

What further conclusions can, then, be drawn from this equation? (1) It is immediately apparent that the late Lung-shan wares in Shantung mark the apex of a long, uninterrupted, self-sufficient tradition in that area which moved northward as it matured. Clearly, not until that period do the vessels of the Shantung Lung-shan truly attain to the level of what can be called works of art. (2) Although the Chung Yüan potters of the same period are to be credited with considerable achievements, they were no match for the Shantung craftsmen. During the late Lung-shan, beyond any doubt, the superlative tradition of pottery in China belonged to Shantung. (3) Although there is plentiful evidence at this period of significant intrusions into the Chung-Yüan tradition of pottery forms originating from Shantung, there is no evidence of any elements from Honan affecting the Shantung tradition, which remains entirely internally consistent.

(4) There are marked differences between the Chung Yüan and Shantung pottery traditions in the late Lung-shan period. The major difference would appear to be this: the most distinctive of the Chung Yüan Lung-shan vessels do not belong strictly within *any ceramic* tradition. I speak of certain small ewers and the larger pouring vessels, namely the *ho* 盉 and *li-ho* 鬲盉 (fig. 7.14 b–d). These vessels, as has long been realized, are clearly metallic in character. Such features as the imitation rivets on the apron of the handles, the broad, thin handles, the fact that certain of these vessels when not raised from the ground by *li* legs have flat bottoms, and the tendency for them to be relatively thin-walled, all mark them as copies of wrought metal vessels—the same wrought metal vessels that also served as the direct models for the earliest cast bronze vessels.[10] Although we have in hand no single example of such wrought metal vessels, their existence within the late Chung Yüan Lung-shan culture cannot be doubted. The tradition of sheet metal vessels, as indicated by their ceramic copies, also extended west as far as the Ch'i-chia sites in Kansu (fig. 7.14a) and Shensi (for example, K'o-hsing-chuang II; CKKH 1962: pl. 29.1); and evidence of this tradition has appeared recently at the Ma-ch'iao site at Shanghai in vessels from the fifth stratum, believed to be representative of the Liang-chu culture and assigned to the period of circa 2000 B.C. (see map 7.2) (Huang 1978:136, pls. 1.3; 2.1, 2).

On the other hand, while bits of metal have been found amid the remains of the late Lung-shan culture in Shantung, there is still no shred of evidence that in Shantung vessels were ever fashioned of metal during this period;

10. I presently incline toward the view that the earliest evidence for the wrought metal tradition in China is to be found in Kansu. As noted by Robert Bagley (1977:196–198), the *li-ho* characteristic of the Chung Yüan (see fig. 7.14d) is a vessel whose spout and dome correspond to possible sheet metal forms, whereas the legs are distinctly ceramic in type. The *ho*, as found in Kansu (fig. 7.14a) and at some sites further east (fig. 7.14c), is, on the other hand, wholly a sheet metal form. Since it now seems likely that the convention of the *li* legs was a creation of the eastern Lung-shan people (see n. 8), later adopted by the Chung Yüan, it is possible that the Chung Yüan *li-ho* should be interpreted as an adaptation of the Kansu pouring vessel to Chung Yüan taste, rather than vice versa.

b.   c.   d.

FIGURE 7.14. Ceramic vessels based on sheet metal prototypes. a: *Ho*; formerly in the Museum of Far Eastern Antiquities, now in the People's Republic of China; acquired in the Lan-chou area. b: Pouring vessel; Ch'ih-kou-chai, Kuang-wu-hsien, Honan. c: *Ho*; Hsia-wang-kang, Hsi-ch'uan-hsien, Honan. d: *Li-ho*; Tung-ma-kou, Lo-yang, Honan. (Respectively, Andersson 1943: pls. 38, 35.1; Ho-nan-sheng and Ch'ang-pan 1972: 18, fig. 42; Lo-yang 1978: pl. 5.4.)

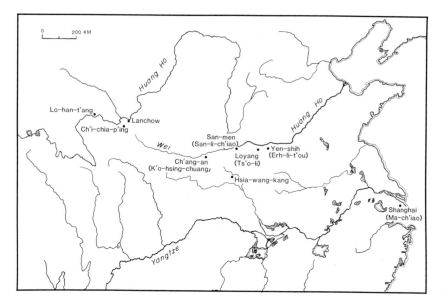

MAP 7.2. **The distribution of ceramic copies of wrought metal vessels in China, ca. 2000 B.C.**

there are no signs among the pottery vessels in Shantung of any metallic features—the vessels remain firmly and wholly ceramic in character. So that, while the magnificent Lung-shan ceramics flourished in Shantung, a whole new tradition, that of vessels made of metal, was developing in the Chung Yüan.

(5) Because the late Chung Yüan Lung-shan, including the early phase (or phases) at Erh-li-t'ou, can be placed around 2000 B.C., no alternative remains at present but to assign this phase to the period of the Hsia dynasty or its immediate predecessors. In due course it will be the tradition of the wrought metal vessel that will be recognized as the outstanding cultural characteristic of the Hsia period—that by which it will be defined.

(6) Moreover, though it is by now perfectly evident that many distinctive traits of the Shang civilization—plastromancy, ritual drinking, and, not least in importance, the fact that all bronze vessels were to be elevated from the ground either by a circular foot or by tripod legs—owe their origins to the Shantung branch of the Lung-shan culture, it is also fully apparent that these traits did not enter the Chung Yüan area on the heels of the Shang but were the result of an entire millennium or more of interaction

between the two regions.[11] The origins of that group of people who called themselves Shang pose no mean question in terms of the Chinese dynastic record. Some scholars would propose Shantung as their homeland (e.g., Chang, "'Early Shang' in Shang Archaeology," in ch. 16 below). But we are without concrete evidence one way or the other on this issue. In terms of Chinese civilization or culture, the advent of the Shang dynasty may be a matter of less import than one might expect. Nothing would incline us at present to see any significant influence from Shantung in the later phases at Erh-li-t'ou or, certainly, Cheng-chou. Moreover, it should be pointed out that when the bronze casters whom we take to be at the service of the early Shang finally began—in the wake of a long tradition of undecorated pottery vessels, followed by some centuries (?) of undecorated wrought metal vessels—to embellish the surface of their vessels, we find, particularly by way of certain vessels found at Cheng-chou and P'an-lung-ch'eng, that one of the specific designs called into service was a complex spiral, remarkably like that of the old Chung Yüan, or specifically Miao-ti-kou, painted pottery tradition (Hu-pei-sheng 1976:31, figs. 9–12; 32, fig. 11). Designs of a spiral nature and the underlying abstract mentality they reveal, in evidence nowhere but in the Chung Yüan, were to be one of the significant elements in Shang bronze design. How these spiral designs, which had long disappeared from pottery, may have been preserved is an open question. But whatever the answer, we conclude that despite the considerable influence exerted on the Chung Yüan region by that powerful cultural entity in Shantung, there can be no question but that the primary artistic tradition of the Shang developed essentially from the cultural tradition of the Chung Yüan area.

REFERENCES

Andersson, J. G.
1943   "Researches into the Prehistory of the Chinese." *BMFEA* 15:1–304.
1947   "Prehistoric Sites in Honan." *BMFEA* 19:1–124

---

11. The question whether in China scapulimancy or plastromancy came into use first is unresolved. The Kansu site of Ta-ho-chuang, belonging to the Ch'i-chia culture, so far provides the earliest evidence of scapulimancy (Cheng and Hsieh 1960:9–11, pl. 1.5). The two carbon-14 dates available for this site (ZK–15:2038 ± 161 B.C. and ZK–23:2001 ± 161 B.C.) would seem to indicate that priority must at present be accorded to plastromancy, in evidence at such east coast sites as Ta-tun-tzu (Yin, Chang, and Chi 1964:29–30), which in all likelihood date well into the fourth millennium. For further discussion of the issue see Keightley 1978:3–9.

Arne, T. J.
1925   *Stone Age Pottery from the Province of Honan, China.*
        Peking.

Bagley, Robert W.
1977   "P'an-lung-ch'eng: A Shang City in Hupei." *Artibus Asiae*
        39.3–4:165–219.

Bylin-Althin, Margit
1946   "The Sites of Ch'i Chia P'ing and Lo Han T'ang in
        Kansu." *BMFEA* 18:383–489.

Chang Kwang-chih
1968   *The Archaeology of Ancient China.* Rev. and enl. ed. New
        Haven.
1977   *The Archaeology of Ancient China.* 3d ed., rev. and enl.
        New Haven.

Chang Yen-huang 張彥煌, **Chang Tzu-ming** 張子明, **and Ch'en Ts'un-hsi**
陳存洗
1962   "Hsi-chin nan ti-ch'ü hsin-shih-ch'i shih-tai ho Shang-tai
        yi-chih ti tiao-ch'a yü fa-chüeh 西晉南地區新石器時代
        和商代遺址的調查與發掘." *KK* 1962.9:459–464.

Chao Ch'ing-yün 趙青雲 **and Liu Tung-ya** 劉東亞
1958   "Cheng-chou K'o-la-wang-ts'un yi-chih fa-chüeh pao-kao
        鄭州㐌㕓王村遺址發掘報告." *KKHP* 1958.3:41–62.

Ch'en Li-hsin 陳立信
1973   "Cheng-chou Ta-ho-ts'un Yang-shao wen-hua ti fang-chi
        yi-chih 鄭州大河村仰韶文化的房基遺址." *KK* 1973.6:
        330–336.

Cheng Hsiao-mei 鄭笑梅
1963   "Shan-tung Wei-fang Yao-kuan-chuang yi-chih fa-chüeh
        chien-pao 山東濰坊姚官莊遺址發掘簡報." *KK* 1963.7:
        347–350.

Cheng Nai-wu 鄭乃武 **and Hsieh Tuan-chü** 謝端琚
1960   "Lin-hsia Ta-ho-chuang Ch'in-wei-chia liang-ch'u Ch'i-
        chia wen-hua yi-chih fa-chüeh chien-pao 臨夏大何莊秦
        魏家兩處齊家文化遺址發掘簡報." *KK* 1960.3:9–12.

Ch'eng Ying-lin 程應林, **P'eng Shih-fan** 彭適凡, **and Li Chia-ho** 李家和
1964   "Chiang-hsi Lin-ch'uan hsin-shih-ch'i shih-tai yi-chih tiao-
        ch'a chien-pao 江西臨川新石器時代遺址調查簡報." *KK*
        1964.4:169–175.

Chinese Exhibition
>   1975   *The Chinese Exhibition: A Pictorial Record of the*
>   *Exhibition of Archaeological Finds of the People's Republic*
>   *of China.* Kansas City.

CKKH
>   1959a   *Lo-yang Chung-chou-lu (hsi-kung-tuan)* 洛陽中州路
>   (西工段) Chung-kuo t'ien-yeh k'ao-ku pao-kao-chi k'ao-
>   ku-hsüeh chuan-k'an ting chung ti-ssu-hao 中國田野考古
>   報告集考古學專刊丁種第四號. Peking.
>   1959b   *Miao-ti-kou yü San-li-ch'iao* 廟底溝與三里橋. Chung-kuo
>   t'ien-yeh k'ao-ku pao-kao-chi k'ao-ku-hsüeh chuan-k'an
>   ting chung ti-chiu hao 中國田野考古報告集考古學專刊
>   丁種第九號. Peking.
>   1962   *Feng-hsi fa-chüeh pao-kao* 灃西發掘報告. Chung-kuo
>   t'ien-yeh k'ao-ku pao-kao-chi k'ao-ku-hsüeh chuan-k'an
>   ting chung ti-shih-erh-hao 中國田野考古報告集考古學
>   專刊丁種第十二號. Peking.

CKKH and Shensi   CKKH and Shen-hsi-sheng Hsi-an Pan-p'o po-wu-
>   kuan 陝西省西安半坡博物館
>   1963   *Hsi-an Pan-p'o* 西安半坡. *Chung-kuo t'ien-yeh k'ao-ku*
>   *pao-kao-chi k'ao-ku-hsüeh chuan-k'an ting chung ti-shih-ssu*
>   *hao* 中國田野考古報告集考古學專刊丁種第十四號.
>   *Peking.*

Creel, Herrlee Glessner
>   1937   *Studies in Early Chinese Culture, 1st ser.* American
>   Council of Learned Societies Studies in Chinese and
>   Related Civilizations, no. 3. Baltimore.

Fang Yu-sheng 方酉生
>   1965   "Ho-nan Yen-shih Erh-li-t'ou yi-chih fa-chüeh chien-pao
>   河南偃師二里頭遺址發掘簡報." *KK* 1965.5:215–224.

Feng Ch'eng-tse 馮承澤
>   1960   "Lo-yang chien-pin Yang-shao Yin wen-hua yi-chih ho
>   Sung mu ch'ing-lüeh 洛陽澗濱仰韶殷文化遺址和
>   宋墓清略." *KK* 1960.9:10–14.

Genius of China
>   1973   *The Genius of China: An Exhibition of Archaeological*
>   *Finds from the People's Republic of China.* London.

Ho-nan-sheng and Ch'ang-pan   Ho-nan-sheng po-wu-kuan 河南省
>   博物舘 and Ch'ang-pan k'ao-ku-tui Ho-nan fen-tui
>   長辦考古隊河南分隊

1972   Ho-nan Hsi-ch'uan Hsia-wang-kang yi-chih ti shih-chüeh
            河南浙川下王崗遺址的試掘 ." *WW* 1972.10:6–19, 28.

Hsieh Tuan-chü 謝端琚
1964   "Kan-su Lin-hsia Ch'in-wei-chia yi-chih ti-erh-tzu fa-
            chüeh ti chu-yao shou-huo 甘肅臨夏秦魏家遺址第二次
            發掘的主要收獲." *KK* 1964.6:267–269.

Huang Hsüan-p'ei 黃宣佩
1978   "Shang-hai Ma-ch'iao yi-chih ti-yi, erh-tz'u fa-chüeh
            上海馬橋遺址第一、二次發掘 ." *KKHP* 1978.1:109–137.

Huber, Louisa G. Fitzgerald
1974   "The Traditions of Chinese Neolithic Pottery." Ph.D.
            dissertation, Harvard University.

Hu-nan-sheng   Hu-nan-sheng po-wu-kuan 湖南省博物舘
1972   "Li-hsien Meng-hsi hsin-shih-ch'i shih-tai yi-chih shih-
            chüeh chien-pao 澧縣夢溪新石器時代遺址試掘簡報 ."
            WW 1972.2:31–38.

Hu-pei-sheng   Hu-pei-sheng po-wu-kuan 湖北省博物舘
1976   "P'an-lung-ch'eng Shang-tai Erh-li-kang ch'i ti ch'ing-
            t'ung ch'i 盤龍城商代二里岡期的青銅器 ." *WW* 1976.2:
            26–41.

Kao Kuang-jen 高廣仁 and Jen Shih-nan 任式楠
1964   "Shan-tung Ch'ü-fu Hsi-hsia-hou yi-chih ti-yi-tz'u fa-
            chüeh pao-kao 山東曲阜西夏侯遺址第一次發掘報告 ."
            KKHP 1964.2:57–106.

Keightley, David N.
1978   *Sources of Shang History: The Oracle-Bone Inscriptions of
            Bronze Age China.* Berkeley.

KK
1959.11   "Shen-hsi Hua-hsien Liu-tzu-chen ti-erh-tz'u fa-chüeh ti
            chu-yao shou-huo 陝西華縣柳子鎮第二次發掘的
            主要收獲": pp. 585–587, 591.
1960.1   "Shen-hsi Pin-hsien Hsia-meng-ts'un yi-chih fa-chüeh
            chien-pao 陝西邠縣下孟村遺址發掘簡報 ": pp. 1–4.
1978.1   "1975 nien Yü-hsi k'ao-ku tiao-ch'a 1975年豫西考古
            調查 ": pp. 23–34.

KKHP
1973.1   "Shan-hsi Jui-ch'eng Tung-chuang-ts'un ho Hsi-wang-
            ts'un yi-chih ti fa-chüeh 山西芮城東莊村和西王村遺址
            的發掘 ": pp. 1–63.

Kuo Te-yung 郭德勇
1960   "Kan-su Wu-wei Huang-niang-niang-t'ai yi-chih fa-chüeh
            pao-kao 甘肅武威皇娘娘臺遺址發掘報告." *KKHP*
            1960.2 : 53–71.

Li Chi 李濟
1934   *Ch'eng-tzu-yai* 城子崖. Nanking.
1963   "Hei-t'ao wen-hua 黑陶文化." *Kuo-li T'ai-wan ta-hsüeh
            k'ao-ku jen-lei hsüeh-k'an* 國立臺灣大學考古人類學刊
            21–22 : 1–12.

Li Shih-kuei 李詩桂
1962   "Shen-hsi Pin-hsien Hsia-meng-ts'un Yang-shao wen-hua
            yi-chih hsü-chüeh chien-pao 陝西邠縣下孟村仰韶文化
            遺址續掘簡報." *KK* 1962.6 : 292–295.

Liu Tun-yüan 劉敦愿
1958   "Jih-chao Liang-ch'eng-chen Lung-shan wen-hua yi-chih
            tiao-ch'a 日照兩城鎮龍山文化遺址調查." *KKHP* 1958.1 :
            25–42.

Lo-yang   Lo-yang po-wu-kuan 洛陽博物舘
1978   "Lo-yang Tung-ma-kou Erh-li-t'ou lei-hsing mu-tsang
            洛陽東馬溝二里頭類型墓葬." *KK* 1978.1 : 18–22.

Nan-ching   Nan-ching po-wu-yüan 南京博物院
1978   "Ch'ang-chiang hsia-yu hsin-shih-ch'i shih-tai wen-hua jo-
            kan wen-t'i ti t'an-hsi 長江下游新石器時代文化若干
            問題的探析." *WW* 1978.4 : 46–57.

Shan-tung-sheng   Shan-tung-sheng po-wu-kuan 山東省博物舘
1963   "Shan-tung T'eng-hsien Kang-shang-ts'un hsin-shih-ch'i
            shih-tai mu-tsang shih-chüeh pao-kao 山東滕縣崗上村
            新石器時代墓葬試掘報告." *KK* 1963.7 : 351–361.
1972   "Shan-tung Yeh-tien hsin-shih-ch'i shih-tai mu-tsang yi-
            chih shih-chüeh chien-pao 山東野店新石器時代墓葬遺址
            試掘簡報." *WW* 1972.2 : 25–30.
1978   "T'an-t'an Ta-wen-k'ou wen-hua 談談大汶口文化." *WW*
            1978.4 : 58–66.

Shan-tung-sheng and Chi-nan-shih   Shan-tung-sheng wen-wu kuan-li-
            ch'u 山東省文物管理處 and Chi-nan-shih po-wu-kuan
            濟南市博物舘
1974   *Ta-wen-k'ou* 大汶口. Peking.

Shan-tung-sheng, Tung-hai-yü, and Jih-chao   Shan-tung-sheng po-wu-
            kuan 山東省博物舘, Tung-hai-yü fa-chüeh hsiao-tsu

東海峪發掘小組, and Jih-chao-hsien wen-hua kuan
日照縣文化舘

1976 "Yi-chiu-ch'i-wu nien Tung-hai-yü yi-chih ti fa-chüeh
一九七五年東海峪遺址的發掘." *KK* 1976.6:377–382.

Shih Hsing-pang 石興邦
1955 "Feng Hao yi-tai k'ao-ku tiao-ch'a chien-pao 豐鎬一帶
考古調查簡報." *KK* 1955.1:28–31.

Su Ping-ch'i 蘇秉琦
1965 "Kuan-yü Yang-shao wen-hua ti jo-kan wen-t'i 關於仰韶
文化的若干問題." *KKHP* 1965.1:51–82.

Sui Yü-jen 隋裕仁 and Fang Hsiao-lin 方孝廉
1978 "Lo-yang Ts'o-li yi-chih shih-chüeh chien-pao 洛陽矬李
遺址試掘簡報." *KK* 1978.1:5–17.

Tai Tsun-te 代尊德 and Teng Lin-chi 鄧林季
1963 "Shan-hsi Yüan-ch'ü Hsia-ma-ts'un fa-hsien hsin-shih-ch'i
shih-tai t'ao-ch'i 山西垣曲下馬村發現新石器時代陶器."
KK 1963.5:278–279.

Wang et al. Wang En-t'ien 王恩田, Li Sheng-kuei 李盛奎, Wu Wen-
ch'i 吳文棋, and Wu Shih-ch'ih 吳詩池
1978 "Shan-tung Ch'ih-p'ing-hsien Shang-chuang yi-chih ti-yi-
tz'u fa-chüeh chien-pao 山東荏平縣尚莊遺址第一次
發掘簡報." *WW* 1978.4:35–45.

Watson, William
1971 *Cultural Frontiers in Ancient East Asia.* Edinburgh.

Wu, G. D.
1938 *Prehistoric Pottery in China.* London.

Wu Ju-tso 吳汝祚
1977 "Shan-tung Chiao-hsien San-li-ho yi-chih fa-chüeh chien-
pao 山東膠縣三里河遺址發掘簡報." *KK* 1977.4:262–267.

Wu Shan-ching 吳山菁
1973 "Lüeh-lun Ch'ing-lien-kang wen-hua 略論青蓮崗文化."
WW 1973.6:45–61.

Yin Huan-chang 尹煥章 and Chang Cheng-hsiang 張正祥
1962 "Chiang-su P'i-hsien Liu-lin hsin-shih-ch'i shih-tai yi-chih
ti-yi-tz'u fa-chüeh 江蘇邳縣劉林新石器時代遺址
第一次發掘." *KKHP* 1962.1:81–102.

Yin Huan-chang 尹煥章, **Chang Cheng-hsiang** 張正祥, **and Chi Chung-ch'ing** 紀仲慶

1964   "Chiang-su P'i-hsien Ssu-hu-chen Ta-tun-tzu yi-chih ti-yi-tz'u fa-chüeh pao-kao 江蘇邳縣四戶鎮大墩子遺址第一次發掘報告." *KKHP* 1964.2: 9–56.

Yin Huan-chang 尹煥章, **Yüan Ying** 袁穎, **and Chi Chung-ch'ing** 紀仲慶

1965   "Chiang-su P'i-hsien Liu-lin hsin-shih-ch'i shih-tai yi-chih ti-erh-tz'u fa-chüeh 江蘇邳縣劉林新石器時代遺址第二次發掘." *KKHP* 1965.2: 9–47.

8

The Origins of Chinese Civilization: Soviet Views

KARL JETTMAR

The views of Soviet scholars working on the origins of Chinese civilization have varied markedly in recent decades. The materials they present and the interpretations they offer are frequently new and challenging, but they need to be considered in the widest possible context. I can best accomplish this in a single chapter by analyzing a recent Soviet publication that bears on the issues and by showing how its authors' views differ from those of earlier writers. The book is that of M. V. Kriukov, M. V. Sofronov, and N. N. Cheboksarov, *Drevnie Kitaitsy: problemy etnogeneza* (The ancient Chinese: problems of ethnogenesis) (Moscow, 1978). It has been published on behalf of two institutions of the Soviet Academy of Sciences, the Institute for the Far East and the Ethnographical Institute.

Two of the authors are sinologists. Kriukov, for example, has worked on kinship systems in modern and ancient China (1972). Sofronov has studied ancient Chinese inscriptions (1977). The third author, Cheboksarov, is a physical anthropologist. But neither the Archaeological Institute nor any archaeologist has contributed to this book. There is no contribution, for example, by Stanislav Kuchera, a Polish research fellow and member of the Soviet Academy Institute of Oriental Studies, who worked on a survey of the results of Chinese archaeology during the years 1965–1974; the first volume of his survey appeared in 1977.[1]

---

1. As his earlier work indicates, Kuchera too is mainly a sinologist. Presumably he was given the task of filling the gap created since 1962 by the sudden death of the foremost expert, S. V. Kiselev. Kiselev, initially a specialist for southern Siberia, had been serving as an advisor in China (see Kiselev 1960; also his two lectures reported in *KK* 1960.2).

The term "ethnogenesis" was originally interpreted to mean the isolation of basic ethnic elements and their subjection to a process of fission and fusion, after which a community of a higher order would develop. This line of research originated at a time when the social mechanisms of the formation of states were regarded as wholly explainable through the writings of Marx and Engels; all that remained unresolved was the question about the carriers, or vehicles, of the social processes involved. Even this question was believed to have been adequately covered conceptually in the writings of Nikolai Marr.

The approach nowadays is much more differentiated. The introduction of the Soviet collective volume clearly indicates that the authors base themselves on numerous Soviet works in which a theory of ethnos as a dynamic system has been developed. Julian Bromlej's book (published in German in 1977), for example, conveys certain conclusions drawn from these efforts. I cannot do justice here to the theories elaborated in his book; suffice it to say for our purposes that communal spiritual solidarity plays an important though not decisive role in the Soviet theory of ethnos. In this way, various naïvetés linked with the term "nation building" are avoided. It becomes clear that one individual can identify himself with various communities, especially if they are in a hierarchical relationship. Certain identifications can be either emphasized or repressed, depending on the situation. Furthermore, one must carefully distinguish between the physical, linguistic, and ethnic ancestors of a people. The "ethnic" ancestry comes from a community that itself merges into a higher unit, giving this higher unit its specific traits in material culture, custom and ideology.

After considering how Chinese scholars have handled this problem, the three Soviet authors turn to the writings of L. S. Vasil'ev, one of which is on the topic of the Berkeley conference: *Problemy genezisa kitaiskoi tsivilizatsii: Formirovanie osnov material'noi kul'tury i etnosa* (Problems of the genesis of Chinese civilization: Formation of the foundations of material culture and of the ethnos; Moscow, 1976). The authors vehemently reject Vasil'ev's work, claiming that single civilizing achievements have nothing to do with the topic and that the explanations offered by H. Ecsedy, a Hungarian research scholar, are more important. Ecsedy (1974) asked for criteria that would permit differentiation between the creators and bearers of Chinese civilization on the one hand and the other peoples of Asia, particularly of East Asia, on the other.

What range of source material is gone into, what set of disciplines applied? The authors mention paleoanthropology, archaeology, epigraphy, the historical analysis of source literature, and even linguistics and ethnography; they then take up the question of periodization. We hear that

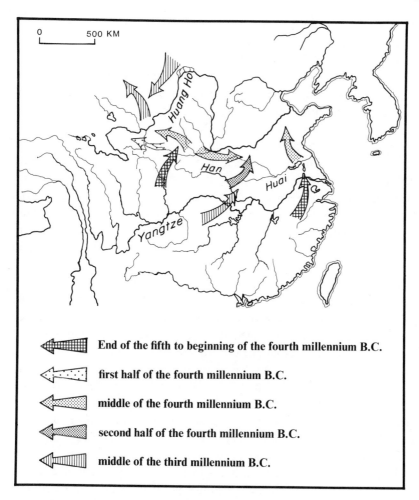

MAP 8.1. **Neolithic migrations in China between the fifth and third millennia B.C. (Redrawn from Kriukov et al. 1978:148.)**

Primitive Society lasts till the end of the Neolithic period, and Slave-Owning Society is said to have begun during the period of the Warring States. Between these two periods exists an early class society which has not been described in any detail.

PALEOANTHROPOLOGY (CHEBOKSAROV)

Paleoanthropology is given considerable weight in the Soviet collective volume. This emphasis is not ideological; it reflects rather the reputation the discipline has won through systematic work. It has never been possible to accuse Soviet anthropologists of serving the cause of racism. Their spokesmen, G. F. Debets and M. G. Levin, were excellent cultural historians who knew how to utilize intelligently the opportunities afforded them by their research area. The Soviet part of Asia lies in the area of contact between human races of the first order (the so-called great races): the Europoids and the Mongoloids. Excavations over a vast area have permitted the documentation of regional types and hybrids at different time levels. On comparing the perspectives of different periods, Cheboksarov develops important circumstantial evidence about the history of migration, evidence that is independent of the cultural perspective (see map 8.1). Cheboksarov still belongs to the first generation of research scholars who have depicted the racial history of North Asia in this manner. Compared to his study, Howells' contribution to the present volume (ch. 11, below) seems guarded.

Cheboksarov takes forty pages (18–59) to discuss the oldest finds of skulls, including those of the Mesolithic period. He claims to identify in the Neolithic residents of the Wei valley during the Yang-shao culture phase (pp. 120–122) a stage intermediate between the eastern and southern branches of the Mongoloid Great Race. He also comments (pp. 122–130) on the observations made by Davidson Black in his work on the Kansu skulls. He is of the opinion that the skulls could be called proto-Chinese, but a comparison of these proto-Chinese skulls with those from the Wei valley indicates that the Wei skulls possess more distinct Mongoloid features. This fact was taken by Debets as evidence that a hybridization with a Europoid population had taken place in Kansu, but Cheboksarov prefers another explanation: the Kansu skulls do not have a very highly specialized form, and they preserve certain features peculiar to the late Paleolithic emigrants to the New World, for which reason this less differentiated form of the Mongoloid race could even be designated Americanoid. Skulls obtained from excavations of graves dating back to the fourth and the beginning of the third millennia B.C. in Shantung and Kiangsu evince characteristics of the southern branch of the Mongoloid Great Race more distinct than those observed in the Wei valley. Cheboksarov explains this as the result of an immigration to the coastal area from the south. The immigrants were probably bearers of Austronesian languages.

Cheboksarov moves further south to Indochina and east to Japan, making use of modern Vietnamese contributions, presumably those of his students. The expanse that constitutes modern China clearly emerges as greatly affected by the diffusion of the southern Mongoloids. But in their southern periphery these people mixed with Australoids. The Tai peoples, the Austro-Asiatics, and the Austronesians could have developed in such bordering zones. Northern Mongoloids, as represented today by the Tungus and other Siberian tribes, have been encountered only in Hsi-t'uan-shan, southwest of Kirin and consequently far removed from Chinese agricultural centers. The position of the proto-Chinese can be satisfactorily explained by placing them within the contact area of second-order Mongoloid races. The presence of Western (Europoid) immigrants, either unmixed or as hybrids with local Mongoloids, has not been proven.

Some of the skulls excavated in An-yang and its immediate vicinity have been brought to Taiwan and some (from later excavations) are in Peking. Although Cheboksarov was unable to measure the latter (pp. 193–204), he studied them carefully. The Taiwan series is heterogeneous. Five subgroups were discerned, the largest consisting of fifty-one skulls, the smallest of only two. Cheboksarov is of the opinion that northern Mongoloid characteristics are observable, as well as southern Mongoloid and even Australoid-Mongoloid hybrid forms; of course there is also a strong local element.

The appearance of the Peking series is totally different. The skulls with raised cranial structure, flat and high faces that are rather broad with tendencies to alveolar prognathism and relatively small nasal orifices, all correspond to a type that had been predominant in the same area since the Neolithic period. Cheboksarov explains this discrepancy. The homogeneous Peking series originates from graves of the dominant ethnic group. There are richer and poorer graves, but the rite of burial in each case is the same: inhumations in which the face is turned upward and there are grave goods made of bronze, or at least ceramic vessels. The heterogeneous Taiwan series, on the other hand, originates from sacrificial pits and consists mostly of skulls from decapitated victims. It is important to note that each of the sacrificial pits were relatively homogeneous, indicating that the skulls of members of a certain ethnic group all ended up in one pit.

According to Cheboksarov, relatively homogeneous anthropological communities existed not far from the capital (he suggests distances of two or three hundred kilometers) that were nevertheless different from the Shang population. These communities were either potential slaves or enemies. He believes that such outsiders were depicted on certain bronzes. The Sumitomo Collection in Kyoto includes a famous bronze vessel in the shape of an ogre holding a small human figure, and Cheboksarov claims to recognize non-Chinese facial features in this figure. The presence of Europoids among the sacrifices, however, has not been established.

Furthermore, no brachycephalic skulls exist that could be ascribed to immigrants from the West, thus removing any basis for Vasil'ev's contentions. At the same time a population existed in Kansu that was the bearer of the Ch'i-chia culture. Cheboksarov claims that this population preserved Americanoid attributes in spite of the brachycephalization, which could be imputed to local evolution. These people were possibly the ancestors of the present Tibetans.

In the provinces of Kirin and Liaoning, as well as in neighboring Korea, skulls dating to the late second and the first millennia B.C. have been found in graves. Cheboksarov classifies them as belonging partly to the continental branch of the Mongoloid Great Race (pp. 204–214) and suggests that they could belong to the ancestors of the Altaians and the Paleo-Siberians. Some others of the skulls belong to the eastern Mongoloids of the Pacific area. Some of the skulls are dolichocephalic, much like the proto-Chinese; others are more brachycephalic, like the Tunguso-Manchurians and Koreans. There are all conceivable transitional forms between the types described, as would be expected.

So far, little is known about South China, says the author. The southern branch of the far eastern Mongoloids was dominant, even during the second millennium B.C. Australoid features appear. The term "Indonesian race" has been coined for a cross-breed of Mongoloids and Australoids, and it should be clear that this term possibly encompasses the ancestors of many ethnic groups.

Europoids have lived in southern Siberia since the Neolithic period, but it is not known when they appeared in the Tarim basin. Their hybridization with the continental Mongoloids has been observed; but there is no evidence of hybridization with the proto-Chinese. For a time it was believed that the expansion of the Karasuk culture into the Minusinsk basin had gone hand in hand with the invasion of the far eastern Mongoloids. This assertion has now been abandoned.

Up to the Han period, no change in the above constellation has been noted, according to Cheboksarov.

ARCHAEOLOGY (KRIUKOV)

The section in the collective volume devoted to archaeological studies is more modest in size. The introductory survey of climatic zones and the more important cultivated plants is brief (pp. 80–85). Kriukov limits himself to the observation that between the fourth and second millennia B.C. in the southern and eastern zones of the Neolithic cultures, the most important food plant by far was rice (*Oryza sativa* L.). "Italian" millet (*Setaria italica*) prevailed in the western and central zones. Considering the similarity of the general environment, this difference should be explained by different agricultural traditions. The expansion of rice cultivation northward took place much later, at about the end of the second millennium B.C.

Kriukov then describes the research history of the Huang Ho basin at unnecessary length (pp. 85–110). We first learn of the chronological classification by J. G. Andersson, then about the research of Liang Ssu-yung; thereafter, the excavations of the fifties (before the Cultural Revolution) are described, and finally we are told about the absolute datings provided by the Radiocarbon Laboratory in Peking since 1972. And Vasil'ev's interpretation, which attempted to preserve a Western element in the composition of the Chinese Neolithic, once again undergoes destructive criticism.

Kriukov develops his own hypothesis with great caution. He stresses that he not only depends on an analysis of ceramics, house-building, and grave forms, but that he also takes into account the conclusions drawn by his co-authors (pp. 110–120). His hypothesis can be taken as the central statement concerning ethnogenetics in the book, therefore it will be quoted here, with minor editorial changes, from the English summary (pp. 337–338):

> An analysis of archaeological, linguistic, and anthropological material makes it possible to formulate a hypothesis that the sources of the North Chinese Neolithic should be sought in regions to the south. It can be presumed that one of the groups of the early Neolithic population in South China, which had occupied a marginal position in the center of cultures of the later Hoabinhian type, migrated in the fifth millennium B.C. along the Chia-ling Chiang (in the present province of Szechwan) and, having found passes through the Ch'in Ling range, reached the basin of the Wei river. The population the migrants had come across here was very sparse (those few settlements with microlithic implements which are known in the middle reaches of the Huang Ho apparently belonged to it).
>
> The favorable natural conditions of the Wei valley contributed to the formation and swift progress of agriculture on floodlands in the area. At the end of the fifth and the beginning of the fourth millennia B.C., a developed middle Neolithic, painted pottery, Yang-shao culture (local variant: Pan-p'o) came into being in the Wei basin. The settlers of Pan-p'o, Pao-chi, Hua-hsien and other sites belonged in physical type to an eastern group of the Pacific Mongoloids, with pronounced distinctive features pointing to their southern origin (alveolar prognathism, wide noses). This Neolithic population can probably be regarded as a branch of the tribes speaking Sino-Tibetan languages.
>
> In the fourth millennium B.C., the area of Neolithic culture that had emerged in the Wei valley expanded considerably. On the basis of a chronologically later variant of Miao-ti-kou, two groups of the population appeared; one was shifting to the east, the other to the west. The first while moving along the Huang Ho

came into contact, in the western part of the present Honan province, with the inhabitants of settlements of the Ch'in-wang-chai type, who had originated in the Han basin. The interconnection of these tribes, different as they were in cultural patterns and, it can be presumed, language, laid the foundation for the shaping of the Shang (Yin) community. The language of the Yin, so far as we can judge on the basis of extant inscriptions of the late second millennium B.C., was Ancient Chinese; basically Sino-Tibetan, it nevertheless revealed some features which were unusual for other languages of this family.

The group of Yang-shao tribes that had spread west in the fourth millennium underwent further differentiation. One of its branches, which had come to the upper reaches of the Huang Ho (the present province of Kansu), later became known as Ch'iang (or Jung), whereas another branch became the backbone of the Chou. At the end of the second millennium B.C., the Chou defeated an alliance of tribes formed by the Yin in the Central China Plain.

On the basis of early state forms created as a result of the Chou invasion, and because of intensive inter-action with neighboring tribes speaking Tibetan-Burmese, proto-Tungus, Austronesian, and Thai languages, an ethnic Hua-Hsia 華夏 entity took shape in the sixth to fourth centuries B.C. in the Central China Plain; this can be called "Ancient Chinese."

This thesis, which is illustrated by sketch maps (Kriukov et al. 1978:148; and see map 8.1 above), proposes that in the Wei valley, before the invasion of the southern culture bearers, there was no intermediate stage—not to mention an indigenous development—between the phases of microlithic implements and the Yang-shao culture. Thus the earlier criticized thesis of cultural transfer from the West is replaced instead by one that posits a transfer from the south. It would be difficult to reconcile the latter thesis with the observations of the paleobotanists who spoke at the conference in Berkeley and who imply the existence of more than one focus.

Two further chapters of the book, unsigned, present more specific archaeological material. They begin with the acceptance of the thesis developed by Kuo Mo-jo (Go Mo-zho 1956; 1959; both in Russian) which states that the Ti, who influenced the fate of China between the seventh and fourth centuries B.C., owed part of their origin to the Scythians (Kriukov et al. 1978:179–184). This could account for the appearance in North China of the Scythian Triad—the combination, also known in the West, of specific equestrian armaments, horse trappings and the Animal Style (Grakov and Meliukova 1954:93). Objects with Animal Style motifs have been identified over a wide area that stretched along the margin of the Chin state during the Spring and Autumn period. This corresponds to evidence indicating the adoption of barbaric customs, taken presumably from the Scythians, in the Chung-shan state. The bronzes of the Dagger Grave culture are then ascribed to the northern or mountain Jung (Shan Jung) tribe (pp. 185–187). This tribe had connections with the principalities known as Yen, Ch'i and Lu.

The attentive reader will notice that the cultures north of the Chinese empire which now form part of the Soviet Union (or the People's Republic of Mongolia) are ignored in the writings of Kriukov and his colleagues. In assessing the importance of this area for the political and ethnic history of China, Soviet scholars changed their minds in accordance with the general feelings of their fellow countrymen.

In 1947, Cheboksarov appeared as a spokesman not only in his own field of physical anthropology. He wrote that "there does not remain the slightest doubt of the extreme ethnocultural resemblance of the ancient settlers of the 'loess country' to the descendants of their northern neighbours, who probably belonged to the Manchurian linguistic group" (Okladnikov 1959/1965:131). In 1959, in the days of Soviet-Chinese friendship and cooperation, the inter-dependence of North China and eastern Siberia (particulary the Amur basin) was developed and interpreted in more detail. Okladnikov, for example, (1959/1965:132) stated:

> in the earlier phases of the Maritime region and Tung-pei [Manchuria] there existed a Neolithic culture which was sharply distinguished from that of the agriculturists of China proper. But later, when the basically new culture of the shell mounds appeared in the Maritime region and in the coastal regions of Korea and Liaotung adjacent to it, the situation essentially changed. In these districts north of the Huang Ho basin are suddenly found a multitude of elements of material culture and way of life that previously were known only in the south, in the regions of the Yang-shao and Lung-shan cultures. Thus we may draw the conclusion that the source of all these innovations for the population of ancient China and the northern regions adjacent to it was precisely China and not the north.

Agriculture was considered by Okladnikov to be one of the innovations of southern origin. Agricultural implements (grinders—boat-shaped querns) were observed in several sites of the Coastal Region (the strip north of Vladivostok, i.e., the Gladkaia river and Tetiukhe). The account of a Shang prince, Ch'i Tzu, who fled in the direction of Liaotung, was also discussed. Such escape movements could have caused a rise in the cultural standards of Manchuria and the Coastal Region and could also explain the early appearance of iron in the Amur country (ibid., p. 133).

In 1969, the situation looked totally different: Okladnikov and Brodianskii (1969:13) proposed that there had been an indigenous agricultural center in the central Amur area, the Ussuri country and the southern part of the Coastal Region. Millet seeds had been found in Kirovskoe (southern Coastal Region) giving a radiocarbon date of 2197 ± 60 b.c. (p. 4). Stone agricultural implements—querns and grinding stones, as well as harvesting knives of the Chinese type—had been found in the same time-layer. Later layers even revealed stone plowshares, as in Korea. Different strains of millet appeared next to one another. Soviet botanists believed they could trace these strains to the many wild forms of millet identified in the luxuriant and varied vegetation of the Amur country. Even the soybean had perhaps been derived from one of the wild progenitors in the Ussuri region; possibly it was later crossed with a southern variety.

It was opined further that rice cultivation had its source in South China and millet cultivation in North China and the Amur region. Possibly—although this was still considered an open question—the Amur center could be ranked as the primary one compared to North China! The stone plowshare might have spread to China from there. If this center had been stimulated externally, it could only have been along the Pacific coast from Southeast Asia. Later research, mostly by students or co-workers of Okladnikov (Andreeva 1977; Derevianko 1973; 1976), has shown that millet cultivation was dominant in this Amur and Coastal Region during the first millennium B.C., with barley appearing as well. Meanwhile, a late Neolithic culture with permanent settlements and typical agricultural tools has been discovered in eastern Mongolia (the Tamsag-Bulag culture, Dorzh 1971 : 79–89); and even there, it is speculated, millet cultivation had resulted from indigenous wild varieties.

As proof for the existence of a primary cultural center in this area, Okladnikov and his co-workers rely upon some early hints of iron winning and casting in the central Amur area believed to date to the second millennium B.C. This raises the question whether the transition to iron that occurred there (where no copper mining is to the found) could have developed independently, leading to a later transfer of the knowledge to China (Derevianko 1973:243–245). The fact that Kriukov and his colleagues do not give importance to this subject in their book may mean that they doubt the accuracy of the datings attributed to the appearance of iron and that they consider the hypothesis of dissemination from the south made by Okladnikov in 1959 as more probable.

The influence from the south on areas north of the Gobi is indicated by *li* tripod vessels discovered in the so-called slab tombs, which belong to the first half of the first millennium B.C. (Okladnikov 1959:128). *Pi* rings have been found in the graves of the Glazkovo culture (second century B.C.) west of Lake Baikal. Good quality white nephrite in large quantity is found in the Saian at two tributaries of the Angara (Kitoi and Belaia). Rings and discs were fashioned from it in the immediate surroundings of the settlements there, but rarely pieces of jewelry of a more complicated sort. The technique employed, however, was different from that in China, where hollow drills made from bamboo were used. Rings of the Siberian technique, as far as I know, have not yet been observed in China (but this must be re-examined), although they appear as export products in the Ural and on the banks of the Kama river. This points to a system of trade by which raw material was imported into China. In return, the "idea" of such jewels (or symbols) was transmitted, which was then laboriously emulated in Baikalia using compasses with stone points (Okladnikov 1955:174–189).

EPIGRAPHY AND LINGUISTICS (SOFRONOV)

Although one of the authors had earlier tackled the problem of the proto-Chou script (Kriukov 1965), I was unable to find any relevant new statement about epigraphy in Sofronov's treatment, which merely summarizes old information (Kriukov et al. 1978:214–230). On the other hand, importance is given an older attempt to define the structure of Ancient Chinese, in the frame of a typology that uses as its starting point the sequence of semantic elements (pp. 231–251).

This section of the book starts in the following manner. There are two basic language types in East Asia, the first comprised of languages with the sequence subject-object-verb. This sequence characterizes the northern group of languages, to which belong the Ural-Altaic, the Paleo-Asiatic and the Sino-Tibetan languages, including Chinese and Karen. The southern language group, on the other hand, has the sequence subject-verb-object and encompasses Thai and the Austro-Asiatic languages. The syntactic positions of the numerals, adjectives, prefixes, and affixes are then arranged, using the above sequential classification as a basis. The exposition concludes with the remark that Chinese was originally a language of the southern Asian type (as proved by the oldest known oracle inscriptions) and that it later acquired qualities of the northern type (to which the Sino-Tibetan group belongs) as it became rooted in a new milieu.

I am in no way qualified to judge competently the above system, the foundations of which were laid by Terrien de Lacouperie and W. Schmidt (for a detailed account, see Sofronov 1977:192–204). I shall, however, suggest in my concluding remarks where the tendency to adopt such a concept originates.

At a later point, in the joint volume, Sofronov describes the classification of Chinese dialects during the Han period, rather literally following Serruys and his interpretation of the *Fang yen* dictionary. He considers the problem of where a substratum of non-Chinese origin could be inferred, attributing paralled development in certain areas to political linkages over a wider region. A close look at this material shows that the former view of the oppositional nature of the northern and southern elements is no longer decisive. A western and an eastern dialect group are clearly delineated.

PALEOETHNOLOGY (KRIUKOV)

Soviet scientists, unlike some Western authors, do not overestimate the role of the subjective element, that is, the role of individual consciousness in evaluating the sense of national belonging. The consciousness of belonging is, to be sure, learned with all the possibilities of choice and manipulation that such a learning process implies, but Soviet scholars are only too aware that the heritage of past generations has an inescapable influence. They do not deny that peculiarities of material culture can bring people together or separate them. For this reason, clothing and hair-styles, food and shelter, and even means of transport are handled in more detail than would be expected from an ethnogenetic work (1978:251–266). Kriukov emphasizes that the regulation of living habits, including the compulsory clothing regulations during the long rule of the Chou dynasty, would have contributed much to the creation of national unity. He depends heavily on Kozhin (1977) for his treatment of the chariot, which he correctly says could serve as a means of transport only conditionally: right from the start it was a symbol of honor, and it remained so even when it was used later in warfare. Kriukov fails to mention the essential point made by Kozhin that the chariots of the Shang period represent the further development of forms that went out of use in the Middle East after the fifteenth century B.C. Kozhin concludes from this point that, since the centrally located axle was more practical for mountainous regions, there must have been a high-level protonomadic culture (in fact, a "civilization") in central Asia that obtained and preserved the elsewhere outdated variant of the two-wheeled war-chariot. According to Kozhin, this culture used rope snaffles with toggles stuck through them for their draft horses, thus explaining the early appearance of such trappings, along with cheek-plates, in China. In any case, horse and chariot are an indication—almost the only one—of influence from the West during the formative period of statehood in China.

THE ETHNOGENETIC INTERPRETATION OF HISTORICAL TEXTS (KRIUKOV)

Kriukov, who presents in his section of the volume a survey of historical events (1978:150–174), perceives a set of transformations in the concept of the Chinese state as seen by its own people, in terms of its specific character and its function in providing a framework for the we-group. In the Shang period, the city of Yin was thought to be the center of the universe (1978: 267–272). It was bordered by land that belonged to it and that was sub-divided according to the four cardinal points of the compass. More than fifty tribes, recorded in the oracle inscriptions, were grouped around this core area; their names were either totemistic, that is, taken from plants or animals, or indicated certain characteristics of clothing or hair-style. There was no clear and lasting boundary between the periphery of the tribes and the outer limits of city-owned land, perhaps because the opposition be-tween the Shang and the tribes was of a political and not an ethnic nature. (This contradicts the view of Cheboksarov, cited above, that most of the skulls of decapitated sacrifices could be clearly distinguished from those of the indigenous population.)

The situation seems to have remained unchanged during the early part of the Chou dynasty. In the seventh and sixth centuries B.C., however, designations appear that imply the assertion of a common origin and could therefore be considered to be ethnonyms. The term Hsia established a connection to the name of the oldest dynasty, as does the name Hua (1978:272–274). In Kriukov's view, the Hua-Hsia considered themselves superior to their neighbors, approximately in the same way the Hellenes compared themselves to the barbarians. Nevertheless, only about half the states that formed the federation of the Chou empire belonged to the inner circle of the non-barbarians during the Spring and Autumn period. Kin-ship feeling was used as a political element at that time, and the losers in conflicts claimed to belong to the Hua-Hsia—whose name can be trans-lated as "Chinese"—to save themselves from being sacrificed en masse or enslaved. The outsiders, on the other hand, were called wild beasts, jackals, and wolves, and brutality was allowed against them.

Evidently, the barbarian tribes at first had individual names, but during about the middle of the first millennium B.C., they were classified schemati-cally according to the four cardinal points of the compass (1978:272–282). This would, in the final analysis, mean that once again territory had become the primary criterion of the we-group, whereas the consciousness of common origin remained secondary. What continued to be important were the factors of language, the acceptance of certain forms of material culture, the adherence to certain rituals, and, above all, the economy and the way of life. Agriculture was the only appropriate way of life for the Hua-Hsia.

Kriukov thus believes he can observe a dialectic sequence involving several decisive criteria. Initially, a genealogical consciousness existed that was limited only to the aristocracy. The kinship system of the Shang and the early Chou depended on a matrimonial alliance based on exogamous lineages with partrilineal cross-cousin marriages as the normal match. Such a system leads necessarily to the emergence of paired intermarrying lineages. It has been proved that the Chou also took marriage partners from the ruling groups of certain tribes. The subjects of the aristocracy, by contrast, were organized according to a system of territorial distinctions. In a second phase, the kinship principle and the classification into exogamous units (which were no longer sub-classified into pairs) was transferred to populations over large areas. Among the upper classes of the time, seniority began to be emphasized. In the fifth century B.C., a reinforcement of the territorial principle is once more recognizable. This reinforcement became necessary as knowledge about the absorption of immigrants with "Scythian culture" from the steppes could no longer be repressed.

Many variations on the model described here were present throughout the Chou period. Indeed, barbarian ancestry was even a matter for pride in some states. The territory of the central tribes expanded only gradually to form a "celestial empire."

CONCLUSION

The assertions made in the collective volume require further interpretation, which I shall attempt here.

The disclosure of the Chinese excavations after the Cultural Revolution, especially publication of the radiocarbon datings from the Peking Laboratory, came as a shock to Soviet cultural historians. We can understand this only if we consider that their concern with their own history is greater and deeper than ours, and that they were thereby threatened with a painful re-evaluation. Okladnikov (1972), who rejected the new datings and the consequences drawn from them as exaggerated, was rewarded (according to Sladkovski 1977:8) by acrimonious polemic from Chinese archaeologists.

The scientific apparatus of the Soviet Union reacted in turn to the Chinese outburst. Symposia were held, one in 1973 and two in 1974 (Gokhman and Reshetov 1974; Kriukov 1975). It was *expressis verbis* stated that the last session was to prepare a collective volume of contributions in order to reject the falsifications by the Chinese. Only some of the symposium lectures were published (Cheboksarov, Kriukov, and Sofronov eds., 1977). A summary of the others was made available, but the discussions which followed were not reported at all. Nevertheless, the course of the argument is clear: it became obvious that contesting the validity of the dating would not win the dispute.

Western and particularly American research on the continental and maritime regions of Southeast Asia had produced some very early (if not always reliable) datings. These might indicate regional sequences of development that led early to a producing economy and to metallurgy (see, e.g., the bibliography in Hutterer 1976). Supported by this material, the concept of a Chinese cultural primacy could be undermined. In the Soviet view, the nucleus of the Chinese state in Honan appears when seen in this manner as located at the periphery, and the obsolete west/east gradient is replaced by a south/north gradient. Such a conceptual solution would find sympathetic resonance with Vietnamese allies as well as Soviet researchers responsible for the region concerned (Its 1972; Chesnov 1976).

It should be noted that the authors of the collective volume do not adopt these provocative arguments, although such arguments were available in clear formulations and were supported by Soviet research results in the paleobotanist tradition of Vavilov (Chesnov 1977). Nevertheless, this background underlies their detailed statements in the fields of paleoanthropology and linguistics, as well as their neglect of botany.

The underlying assumption of the material presented at the symposium can be paraphrased as follows: it is desirable to consider the ethnogenesis and the formation of the state in southern and southeastern Asia strictly as an internal problem of that region. A consequence of this attitude is the refusal to take into consideration the interaction between the agricultural centers of west and central Asia on the one hand and those of east Asia on the other. This reticence is all the more bewildering because a connecting link, the Bactriano-Margianic Complex, had been made known through the research of Soviet authors in Afghanistan and south central Asia (Askarov 1973; 1977; Mandel'shtam 1968; Piankova 1974; Sarianidi 1976; 1977a; 1977b). Amiet's research (1977; 1978) has shown that this complex dates back to the third millennium B.C. The Tokharian appearance in east Turkestan, which has been dealt with by V. V. Ivanova following Pulleyblank (see Gokhman and Reshetov 1974:143), could be explained in the light of these linkages. The Kurgan culture that has preoccupied western linguists does not on the other hand explain these linkages, and it does not extend as far into the east as Gimbutas (1978:331, fig. 23) implies.

The Bactriano-Margianic Complex is important as a center of diffusion for the horse and chariot in much of the steppes. The use of the horse and chariot is reflected in the numerous rock paintings which have since been studied in Tajikistan, the Pamirs, Kirgizia, Kazakhstan, Tuva, the Altai, and Mongolia (Novgorodova 1978). The densest group of rock paintings has been studied by Kadyrbaev and Mar'iashev (1977) in the Karatau mountains in southern Kazakhstan.

I think it possible that China adopted the use of the horse and chariot as a symbol of nobility from the same complex. (The Soviet colleagues do not speak of a culture, but of a complex, because they are aware of the possibility that assemblages and pertinent, stray finds may merely represent the close interaction of nomadic as well as sedentary tribes. This complex could also have transmitted to East Asia "Western" cultivated plants (barley and wheat), along with certain domestic animals, particularly the horse.

It could justifiably be asked here whether a Western stimulus assisted in the formation of the state in China. Chesnov (1977:133), as we have seen, proposes that the development of China took place under the patronage of the south up to the Shang period but thereafter under Western patronage. None of this, however, is mentioned in the collective volume; perhaps its authors were only too conscious of the counterclaims that would follow. The millet strains and the rice that appear in Assyria as early as the ninth century B.C. could have reached the west through an inner Asian center. Whether knowledge of true (tin) bronze in Caucasia was transmitted from the east—from, in the last analysis, Southeast Asia—still remains an open question (Selimkhanov 1970:71). An argument in favor of this thesis is the otherwise inexplicable appearance in the Bactriano-Margianic Complex of celts with an oval cross-section (Sarianidi 1977a: pl. II/3, lower right). They distantly resemble the ones found in northeastern Thailand (Solheim 1968; 1972).

The Soviet research scholars did not, at least in this collective volume, exhaust the material available to them. They tended throughout to be cautious and very conscious of their responsibility. It should be possible to fill some of the gaps. The structure of the Late Shang "state," for example, as presented by Keightley (ch. 17, below), is so reminiscent of the organization of the earliest chiefdoms of the steppe nomads that one could suppose a similar ideology. This ideology could be rooted in the Bactriano-Margianic Complex, which had no real urban centers, but villages, and nomads grouped around elaborate ceremonial centers. But to deal with this further would take us beyond the scope of this essay.

REFERENCES

Amiet, Pierre
1977   "Bactriane proto-historique." *Syria* 44:89–112
1978   "Antiquités de Bactriane." *La revue du Louvre et des musées de France* 28:153–164.

Andreeva, Zh. V.
1977   *Primor'e v epokhu pervobytnoobshchinnogo stroia: zheleznyi vek.* Moscow.

Askarov, A.
1973   *Sapallitepa.* Tashkent.
1977   *Drevnezemledel'cheskaia kul'tura epokhi bronzy iuga Uzbekistana.* Tashkent.

Bromlej, Julian V.
1977   *Ethnos und Ethnographie.* Übersetzt von W. König. Veröffentlichungen des Museums für Völkerkunde in Leipzig, Heft 28. Berlin.

Cheboksarov, N. N.
1947   "K voprosu o proiskhozhdenii kitaitsev." *Sovetskaia Etnografiia* 1:30–70.
1978   Various contributions in Kriukov et al. 1978.

Cheboksarov, N. N., Kriukov, M. V., and Sofronov, M. V., eds.
1977   *Ranniaia etnicheskaia istoriia narodov Vostochnoi Azii.* Moscow.

Chesnov, Ia. V.
1976   *Istoricheskaia etnografiia stran Indokitaia.* Moscow.
1977   "Zemledel'cheskie kul'tury kak etnogeneticheskii istochnik." *Ranniaia etnicheskaia istoriia narodov Vostochnoi Azii*: 109–136. Moscow.

Derevianko, A. P.
1973   *Rannii zheleznyi vek Priamur'ia.* Novosibirsk.
1976   *Priamur'e (I tysiacheletie do nashei ery).* Novosibirsk.

Dorzh, D.
1971   *Neolit Vostochnoi Mongolii.* Ulan Bator.

Ecsedy, H.
1974   "Cultivators and Barbarians in Ancient China." *Acta Orientalia* (Budapest) 28.3:327–349.

Gimbutas, Marija
1978   "The First Wave of Eurasian Steppe Pastoralists into
            Copper Age Europe." *The Journal of Indo-European
            Studies* 5.4:277–338.

Go Mo-zho (Kuo Mo-jo)
1956   *Epokha rabovladel'cheskogo stroia.* Moscow.
1959   *Bronzovyi vek.* Moscow.

Gokhman, V. I., and Reshetov, A. M.
1974   "Dva simposiuma po problemam rannikh etapov etniches-
            koi istorii narodov Vostochnoi Azii." *Sovetskaia
            Etnografiia* 6:139–145.

Grakov, B. N., and Meliukova, A. I.
1954   "Ob etnicheskikh i kul'turnykh razlichiiakh v stepnykh i
            lesostepnykh oblastiakh Evropeiskoi chasti SSSR v skifs-
            koe vremia." *Voprosy skifo-sarmatskoi arkheologii*: 39–93.
            Moscow.

Hutterer, Karl L.
1976   "An Evolutionary Approach to the Southeast Asian
            Cultural Sequence, with CA comment." *Current
            Anthropology* 17.2:221–242.

Its, R. F.
1972   *Etnicheskaia istoriia iuga Vostochnoi Azii.* Moscow.

Kadyrbaev, M. K., and Mar'iashev, A. N.
1977   *Naskal'nye izobrazheniia khrebta Karatau.* Alma-Ata.

Kiselev, S. V.
1960   "Neolit i bronzovyi vek Kitaia (Po materialam nauchnoi
            kommandirovki v KNR)." *Sovetskaia Archeologiia*
            4:244–266.

KK
1960.2   C. B. Chi-hsieh-lieh-fu t'ung-hsün yüan-shih tsai Pei-ching
            so tso ti hsüeh-shu pao-kao: C. B. 吉謝列夫通訊院士在北京所
            作的學術報告: "(yi) Nan-Hsi-po-li-ya ho wai Pei-chia-erh-
            hu ti-ch'ü ku-tai ch'eng-shih sheng-huo ti hsin tzu-liao
            (一)南西伯利亞和外貝加爾湖地區古代城市生活的新資料":
            pp. 45–50. "(erh) Su-lien ching-nei ch'ing-t'ung wen-hua
            yü Chung-kuo Shang wen-hua ti kuan-hsi (二)蘇聯境內
            青銅文化與中國商文化的關係": pp. 51–53.

Kozhin, P. M.
1977   "In'skie kolesnitsy" *Ranniaia etnicheskaia istoriia narodov Vostochnoi Azii*: pp. 278–287. Moscow.

Kriukov, M. V.
1964   "U istokov drevnikh kul'tur Vostochnoi Azii." *Vestnik drevnii istorii* 6:85–99.
1965   "Problema protochzhouskoi pis'mennosti." *Narody Azii i Afriki* 6:122–127.
1972   *Sistema rodstva kitaitsev*. Moscow.
1975   "Simposium po etnicheskoi istorii kitaitsev." *Sovetskaia Etnografiia* 4:148–150.

Kriukov, M. V., Sofronov, M. V., and Cheboksarov, N. N.
1978   *Drevnie kitaitsy: problemy etnogeneza*. Moscow.

Kuchera, Stanislav
1977   *Kitaiskaia archeologiia 1965–1974gg.: paleolit-epokha In'*. Moscow.

Mandel'shtam, A. M.
1968   *Pamiatniki epokhi bronzy v Iuzhnom Tadzhikistane.* Materialy i issledovaniia po arkheologii SSSR, no. 145. Leningrad.

Marr, Nikolei Iakovlevich
1933–37   *Izbrannye raboty*. 5 vols. Leningrad.

Novgorodova, E. A.
1978   "Drevneishie izobrazheniia kolesnits v gorakh Mongolii." *Sovetskaia Arkheologiia* 4:192–206.

Okladnikov, A. P.
1955   *Neolit i bronzovyi vek Pribaikal'ia*, vol. 3. Materialy i issledovaniia po arkheologii SSSR, 43. Moscow and Leningrad.
1959   "Tripody za Baikalom." *Sovetskaia Arkheologiia* 3:114–132.
1965   *The Soviet Far East in Antiquity: An Archaeological Study of the Maritime Region of the U.S.S.R.* Arctic Institute of North America. Anthropology of the North: Translations from Russian Sources, no. 6. Toronto.
1972   "Novoe v arkheologii Dal'nego Vostoka." *Problemy Dal'nego Vostoka*, 3:97–117.

Okladnikov, A. P., and Brodianskii, D. L.
1969   "Dal'nevostochnyi ochag drevnego zemledeliia." *Sovetskaia Etnografiia* 2:3–14.

Piankova, L. T.
1974   "Mogil'nik epokhi bronzy tigrovaia Balka." *Sovetskaia Arkheologiia* 3:165–180.

Sarianidi, V. I.
1976   "Issledovanie pamiatnikov Dashlinskogo oazisa." *Drevniaia Baktriia*: pp. 21–86. Moscow.
1977a   *Drevnie zemledel'ts Afganistana*. Moscow.
1977b   "Ancient Bactria: New Aspects of an Old Problem." In *International Symposium on Ethnic Problems of the Ancient History of Central Asia, Dushanbe Oct. 17–22, 1977. Abstract of Papers Presented by Soviet Scholars*: pp. 43–46. Moscow.

Selimkhanov, I. R.
1970   *Razgadannye sekrety drevnei bronzy*. Moscow.

Sladkovskii, M. I.
1977   "Etnicheskaia istoriia Vostochnoi Azii i sovremennye problemy Kitaia." *Ranniaia etnicheskaia istoriia narodov Vostochnoi Azii*. Moscow.

Sofronov, M. V.
1973   "I tsennoe nasledie, i tiazhnoe bremia (o zviazakh kitais-koi pis'mennosti i kul'tury)." *Problemy Dal'nego Vostoka* 3:153–161.
1977   "K tipologicheskoi kharakteristike iazyk in'skikh nad-pisei." *Ranniaia etnicheskaia istoriia narodov Vostochnoi Azii*: pp. 189–208. Moscow.
1978   Various contributions in Kriukov et al. 1978.

Solheim, Wilhelm G.
1968   "Early Bronze in Northeastern Thailand." *Current Anthropology* 9.1:59–62.
1972   "An Earlier Agricultural Revolution." *Scientific American* 226.4:34–41.

Vasil'ev, L. S.
1976   *Problemy genezisa kitaiskoi tsivilizatsii. Formirovanie osnov material'noi kul'tury i etnosa*. Moscow.

9

Further Evidence to Support the Hypothesis of Indigenous Origins of Metallurgy in Ancient China

NOEL BARNARD

In some respects the title above may appear to be a misnomer. Evidence that has come to light over the past six years of happily uninterrupted archaeological exploration in Mainland China does little more than confirm the general picture of metallurgical development in ancient China in practically the same centrifugal terms as demonstrated throughout the distribution maps in *Metallurgical Remains of Ancient China* (Barnard and Satō 1975). There is, of course, a marked increase of data, to be noted in the greater number of site-areas and the large amount of new information from

NOTE: A companion study on other aspects of the origins of metallurgy in China will appear in the proceedings of the Moesgård conference (Barnard in press [a]). The Moesgård paper is designed to follow up certain issues raised in the course of the Berkeley conference. Among them, the subject of mining in ancient China is explored extensively for the first time and in considerable detail; arguments advanced in support of organizational determinism as against technological determinism in the formative stages of metallurgy in China (see Franklin, ch. 10 below) are critically reviewed with appropriate intercomparison of mining conditions throughout the ancient Western world, on which there is a large body of published research. Although relevant data from Chinese excavations is presently limited and the radiocarbon-dated Ta-ching mining complex of Lin-hsi-hsien, Liaoning/Nei Meng-ku has not, at the time of writing, been reported (mid-point dates range from 1147 ± 119 B.C. to 840 ± 103 B.C.) there nevertheless exists an appreciable corpus of evidence which, when viewed carefully, appears to throw important light on metal-winning aspects of the beginnings of metallurgy in China. And because of the highly advanced nature of mining technology and the machinery employed in the Spring and Autumn period mines of T'ung-lü-shan, Ta-yeh-hsien, Hupei (cf., for instance, the well-known Laurion mines of Greece), the hypothesis of the independent discovery of metallurgy gains further support.

many of those surveyed earlier.[1] Radiocarbon dating of some sites has clarified further the antiquity of the metal-producing cultures of the Nuclear Area. See table 9.1 and figure 9.1. The earliest of these, viewed in relation to radiocarbon dated Ch'i-chia remains, would seem now to be validly datable appreciably before 2000 B.C.[2] Even so, there remains a dearth of evidence which might be taken to suggest that the Chinese Metal Age could have claims for an antiquity approximating that of the Mesopotamian and other such distant Western cultures. In its earliest manifestations, Chinese metallurgy will, it seems certain enough, be seen always as one of several latecomers in the world history of metal-using cultures.

Because of the belated appearance of metallurgy on the Chinese scene and the apparent brevity of certain of its presently earliest known developmental stages, those of the diffusionist persuasion (and followers of "stimulus diffusion") continue to interpret such evidence as they are able to cull from translated sources solely in tune with their essentially Garden of Eden bias.[3] A recent review of *Metallurgical Remains* contains such sentiments as:

> This reviewer, while granting that technical elaboration occurs differently in different locations, finds it impossible to believe that the basic ideas of metallurgy were so easy to come by *ad nuovo*. It is incredibly difficult to invent

1. A follow-up table of sites and remains is in preparation and will appear in a companion volume projected for publication in four or five years. Distribution maps along the lines of those in *Metallurgical Remains* will be presented. Our work on the new table is not yet sufficiently advanced to use as the basis for the present chapter.

2. In two informally published papers (Barnard 1977; 1979) dealing with C-14 dates additional to those incorporated in my earlier survey (1975), attention is drawn to several instances of what appear to be primitive metallurgy in an otherwise ceramic cultural context. Interesting as these apparent precursors of Chinese metallurgy seem, it is still premature to elaborate upon this kind of evidence—which, no doubt, will ultimately become a major basis for theorizing in one direction or the other. But tabulation of the C-14 data presently covering Yang-shao, Lungshanoid, and Lung-shan ceramic sites (table 9.1), and the diagrammatic arrangement of this data together with those of the earliest C-14-dated metal-bearing sites (fig. 9.1) indicate the direction in which the evidence currently available (February 1979) is heading. It seems reasonable now to think in terms of 2500–2000 B.C. as the period in which metallurgy in China commenced.

3. See Kroeber 1940 for an introduction to the concept of idea-diffusion or "stimulus diffusion." Although the examples cited are very much open to question in several cases, a number of recent writers seem to have become enamored of the idea of "a stimulus toward an *original but induced local invention* in China"—in respect to the invention of writing (Kroeber 1940:6; my italics); but they seem oblivious to the curious contradiction which pervades the arguments in question. Either the invention or discovery is *original* (i.e., it has occurred for the first time) or it is a re-discovery of a different time and in a different place, *without any contact* with the culture which earlier made the same discovery. The idea of local originality can hardly be maintained when an outside stimulus is suggested in the same breath. The discovery, or invention, must be either original (if this word is to be used) or *not* original.

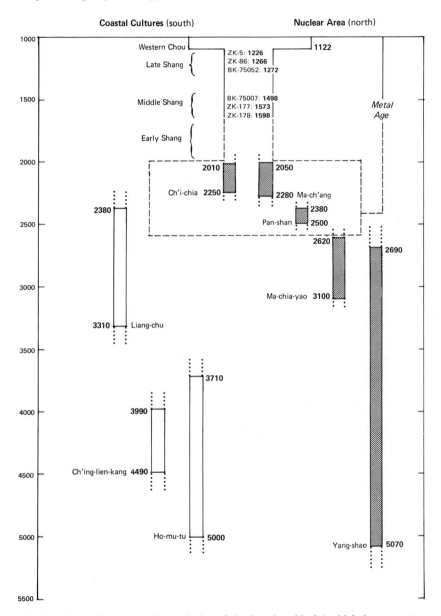

FIGURE 9.1. **A diagrammatic rendering of the data in table 9.1 which demonstrates the present situation of the various pre-Metal Age ceramic cultures in calibrated radiocarbon-date ranges. The available radiocarbon-dated metal-bearing sites, which now extend well into Middle Shang, are also plotted in this diagram. The gap between Ch'i-chia and Middle Shang will, no doubt, continue to be filled in.**

TABLE 9.1 **Radiocarbon-Dated Sites of Yang-shao, Lung-shan, and Lungshanoid Types**

Sample Number	Cultural Character and Place of Origin	Bristlecone-Pine Dates in Calendar Years (DFLW)	Chang Kwang-chih's Assessments (1977)
BK-76019	Early Yang-shao (Shuang-miao-kou)	5075 ± 174 B.C.	
BK-75054/55	Early Yang-shao (Shuang-miao-kou)	5047 ± 219 B.C.	
ZK-38	Yang-shao (Pan-p'o)	4773 ± 141 B.C.	
ZK-121	Yang-shao (Pan-p'o)	4617 ± 137 B.C.	
BK-76020	Early Yang-shao (Shuang-miao-kou)	4562 ± 210 B.C.	
ZK-122	Yang-shao (Pan-p'o)	4552 ± 208 B.C.	
ZK-134	Yang-shao (An-yang)	4392 ± 221 B.C.	Yang-shao
ZK-127	Yang-shao (Pan-p'o)	4294 ± 165 B.C.	6000–3000 B.C.
ZK-76	Yang-shao (An-yang)	4189 ± 165 B.C.	
ZK-110	Yang-shao (Miao-ti-kou)	3915 ± 115 B.C.	
ZK-185	Yang-shao (Cheng-chou)	3684 ± 124 B.C.	
BK-76003	Late Yang-shao (Ta-ho-ts'un)	3424 ± 129 B.C.	
BK-76001	Late Yang-shao (Ta-ho-ts'un)	3132 ± 154 B.C.	
BK-76004	Late Yang-shao (Ta-ho-ts'un)	3071 ± 182 B.C.	
ZK-169	Late Yang-shao (Li-chia-ts'un)	2689 ± 139 B.C.	
ZK-49	Liang-chu (Ch'ien-shan-yang)	3311 ± 136 B.C.	
ZK-108	Ma-chia-yao (Ts'ao-chia-tsui)	3101 ± 154 B.C.	
BK-75020	Ma-chia-yao (Chiang-chia-p'ing)	3071 ± 154 B.C.	
BK-?	Pan-shan (Ch'ing-kang-ch'a)	2863 ± 136 B.C.	
ZK-51	Lung-shan type (P'ao-ma-ling)	2807 ± 139 B.C.	
ZK-111	Lung-shan (Miao-ti-kou)	2776 ± 138 B.C.	
ZK-91	Lung-shan (Huang-lien-shu)	2722 ± 139 B.C.	
ZK-125	Lung-shan (Ch'ü-chia-ling)	2696 ± 190 B.C.	
ZK-124	Lung-shan (Ch'ü-chia-ling)	2634 ± 143 B.C.	
ZK-21	Ma-chia-yao (Yung-ching)	2620 ± 143 B.C.	
ZK-200	Lung-shan (Shang-p'an-wang)	2514 ± 134 B.C.	
BK-75033	Pan-shan (Lo-tu-hsien)	2501 ± 136 B.C.	Lung-shan
ZK-25	Pan-shan (Ch'ing-kang-ch'a)	2470 ± 137 B.C.	3000–2400 B.C.
ZK-78	Lung-shan (Shuang-t'o-tzu)	2463 ± 134 B.C.	

ZK-176	2406 ± 130 B.C.	Hsia-chia-tien (Chih-chu-shan)	Lungshanoid
ZK-126	2388 ± 134 B.C.	Lung-shan (Wang-wan)	2400–ca. 200? B.C.
ZK-242	2374 ± 134 B.C.	Liang-chu (Ch'üeh-mu-ch'iao)	
ZK-133	2336 ± 130 B.C.	Lung-shan (An-yang)	
BK-75009	2273 ± 130 B.C.	Ma-ch'ang (Tung-tu-hsien)	
BK-75010	2238 ± 164 B.C.	Ch'i-chia (Tung-tu-hsien)	
BK-75028	2171 ± 158 B.C.	Ma-ch'ang (Chiang-chia-p'ing)	
BK-75012	2134 ± 156 B.C.	Ma-ch'ang (Tung-tu-hsien)	
BK-75017	2044 ± 156 B.C.	Ma-ch'ang (Chiang-chia-p'ing)	
ZK-15	2038 ± 161 B.C.	Ch'i-chia (Yung-ching)	
ZK-23	2001 ± 161 B.C.	Ch'i-chia (Yung-ching)	
ZK-79	1334 ± 105 B.C.	Lung-shan (Shuang-t'o-tzu)	
ZK-10	1308 ± 105 B.C.	Lung-shan (Hai-men-k'ou)	

SOURCE: Barnard 1977: table 2.

anything really new, while information albeit garbled and incomplete, is easily carried by travellers (Smith 1977:81).[4]

Looking toward China from the vantage point of several decades of published studies, archaeological reports, and laboratory investigations dealing with Western metal artifacts of high antiquity, the Western scholar can hardly avoid some degree of concurrence with the "History begins at Sumer" concept. So little information is readily available to him from faraway Chinese sources that any judgment about ultimate origins strongly tends to favor the cultural areas with which he is more familiar.

My view (or working hypothesis, as I prefer to describe it) has developed gradually and with increasing conviction as I have come to know the Chinese archaeological scene and have become as familiar with the technical aspects of the subject as a layman might attempt; it is also one which results from extensive reading in the history of metallurgy generally. Data from Chinese sources simply will not allow a painstaking and systematic researcher to view the beginnings of metallurgy in China as anything but the probable result of indigenous discovery. I first published this view in 1961, elaborated it considerably in 1975, and now, with seven years of post-Nixon-visit archaeological reports to consult, I believe it is a working hypothesis (at least) that is even better supported than before.

In my continued acceptance of the general significance of the Chinese archaeological data, I have often sought to test a resultant hypothesis from the viewpoint of the "discoverer" as well as that of the "discovery." The latter is the avenue of research most generally pursued because it is concerned mainly with material data, but it does sometimes result in interpretations of rather artificial character, and the investigator tends to lose sight of the fact that we must all seek to understand something of the discoverer if we are to appreciate more fully the motivating factors leading to the discovery. To obtain an understanding of the discoverer and his environment, we still must consult the same source material. But a variation in approach and interpretative aim is introduced into our research, and we add to the available data such understanding as one human being can have of another, albeit separated by such factors as time, geography, race, and culture.

4. Diffusion versus independent invention of metallurgy in China has been a subject of argument between Cyril Smith and me for some years, and we have had many enjoyable and profitable sessions discussing this and more technical aspects of metallurgy. In *Metallurgical Remains* I took Cyril to task on some points (pp. 83–88) and arranged with our publisher to have a review copy forwarded to him; his response was generous and stimulating. The present chapter is in effect a continuation of our arguments.

The simplest explanation of the origins of a technique with regard to its later appearance in a remote cultural area is that offered by the diffusionist: men travel and trade, so ideas will accompany them and take root elsewhere. Stimulus diffusion is nowadays regarded as a less naïve and accordingly more acceptable version of the process, and the concept would seem to have some merit in that it allows the recipient of an idea to *re*-invent or *re*-discover the idea or technique with an appreciable degree of innate inventiveness, and then develop it along lines that accord with the requirements of his immediate environment. The two explanations, nevertheless, are both based on the assumption that the invention, or discovery, was made once only; its appearance elsewhere was due to direct instruction or to the mere arrival of what is called "the germ of an idea." The receiver had to be intelligent enough, naturally, to be able to carry out his part thereafter. But the stimulus diffusionist is really juggling with a compromise concept which is aimed to appease both the classical diffusionist and the reactionary advocate of independent discovery.[5]

Independent invention, or discovery, on the other hand, is a concept which allows for the possibility that the innate intelligence of any human being is such that he will often respond in much the same way to a given situation in different places and at different times. It does not, of course, presuppose that *all* human beings will respond identically—or that they will necessarily respond at all. But it does maintain the premise that the potential act of "discovery" or "invention" is a universal potential which at one time or another will come to the notice of one or more intelligent beings; and the potential will not only be noted and gradually developed by the discoverer or inventor, but other members of his family or of the community will follow suit, and knowledge will be passed on to succeeding generations. That only one man will initiate a new technique or find a new

5. Kroeber remarks: "Obviously this process is one which will ordinarily leave a minimum of historical evidence . . . Positive proofs of the operation of idea-diffusion are therefore, in the nature of the case, difficult to secure long after the act, or wherever the historical record is not quite full. Theoretically, they would be best observed in contemporary culture, were it not that the culture historian necessarily lacks perspective in interpreting the contemporary." From this point, such exemplary caution is, however, thrown to the winds, and the case for stimulus diffusion commences with almost contemporary examples: "Fortunately, however, we possess a few cases that are at least near-contemporary and supported by a fair degree of factual evidence" (1940:1–2). It would be outside the limits of this chapter to contest Kroeber's handling of data (for either near-contemporary or early cases), such as those concerning the "invention of porcelain in Europe," "Sequoya's syllabary of the Cherokee language," etc., but the ease with which his hypothesis—or rather, its terminology—has appealed to various scholars, and has been seized in preference to classical diffusion, becomes in itself an interesting topic of study.

material that can be processed by some slight or major variation of existing techniques, and that this inventor will be born in only the one community (and there can be no "reincarnation" in any other) is a concept which this school of thought finds difficult to accept, especially in respect of man in the ancient world. Can one wholeheartedly agree with the following premise? "Where originality is needed, one man of keen mind is required. If he fails, the job may well stay undone forever" (Chandler 1960:497).

Accordingly, I believe it essential that we give a great deal of thought to the inventive capacity of ancient man in general—as reflected in his works—and not seek to view him largely as a mere copyist or plagiarist. If an idea or technique has been transmitted from one cultural area to another in the past, we should conduct our relevant investigations upon the assumption that artisans in the receiving culture will, unwittingly at least, record some evidence of the matter. To theorize that there will be a minimum of historical evidence, and positive proofs will be difficult to secure, is simply an admission of one's inability to find such evidence—it is surely not proof that the evidence does not exist!

It is necessary not only to consider the viewpoint of the discoverer or inventor and the environment at the time of the discovery, but also the nature of the potential principle, material, technique, or functional device awaiting discovery. Take, for instance, a simple invention such as a ceramic vessel with legs: a round-bottom vessel has obvious disadvantages, and the need for some kind of stabilizing device can be appreciated. We can easily visualize situations leading to the ancient potter's creation of amphora-type vessels whose pointed extension ("one-leg" vessels) functioned well enough within certain limits. Where the hemispherical-shaped vessels were placed on rocks, three or more in number, in a fireplace, the imaginative step toward the affixing of clay appendages to them is one we can easily appreciate. That three equidistant legs of equal length form the ideal device both to stabilize and to raise the vessel to the required height above the flames would soon be discovered. Similarly, the addition of legs to a square or rectangular-shaped vessel would result in a total neither more nor less than four. Discoveries or inventions of functional devices of such kinds must have been made in one ceramic manufacturing community after another without the slightest need for instruction or stimulus from some far-distant community whose potters had earlier invented legged vessels for themselves. Communities in close proximity no doubt mutually profited by one another's discoveries, and diffusion would be a key element in the overall pattern of their development. But it must always be kept in mind that many inventions awaiting discovery were pre-ordained,[6] in that, for example, the inventors of wheeled vehicles would be limited to two wheels for chariots or gigs; if they aimed to make a larger vehicle, then four wheels would become necessary; if a wheel-barrow, then one only. If the vehicle were to be drawn by horses and the need for shafts had been realized, then the placement and number of shafts would be set by simple technical considerations: two shafts for a single-horse vehicle and one shaft for a vehicle drawn by a team of two or four horses. As I have observed elsewhere,

> scores, and probably hundreds, of such rigid principles governing the ultimate design, size, shape, functional limitations, etc., of numerous artifacts exist. Because of our familiarity with them, we do not consciously appreciate always either their presence or their significance, and armed as we are with hindsight, it is not so simple a matter as it may appear, for us to envisage just how ancient man gradually came to the stage of making a specific discovery. Even to visualize a man in the past who had no conception of metal, let alone its potential value as a material for manufacture, and to attempt to assess his thoughts, reactions, etc., (i.e., to get into his mind, as it were) becomes a very difficult but necessary undertaking if we are to understand what happened, and how it happened. (Barnard and Satō 1975:85; cf. Barnard 1974: xlvii ff)

In our attempts to ascertain the nature of the origin and early development of a particular technique in a given community, we should use as a basis in our theorizing the information available on the level of civilization in that community at the time the technique seems earliest to have appeared. It would be essential, too, that the growth and development of the civilization should be reasonably well understood (generally this would be from archaeological evidence) over an appreciably long period prior to the apparent time of the discovery. If it were, indeed, an indigenous invention, evidence of an appropriate kind can be expected; it would be demonstrable in terms of relevant materials, industrial applications, artifact designs, and functions, having progressed toward the stage at which the technique and

6. Well after the writing of these lines, my colleague Dr Helmut Loofs brought to my attention two works of H. G. Barnett (1942; 1953). For convenience, I refer only to the former here. What is termed a pre-ordained invention above is in many respects reminiscent of Barnett's Class B inventions. These "are striking because they appear to spring up from nowhere; that is, they do not draw upon an existing prototype for a principle, and for this reason they are more uncommon, call for more experimentation and insight, and in their consequences are more startling. Each such discovery of a principle with its totally new form then follows the familiar pattern of a functional substitution for an old trait" (p. 18). In citing this passage out of context I do not wish to create the impression that I take Barnett as a supporter of independent discovery, but rather that I see in his arguments stimulating ideas that might well be adopted by those of us who do support the hypothesis.

its underlying principles became ripe for discovery, or should we say realization. On the other hand, if the technique had been introduced from an alien culture far away, its passage, if indirect, should be found marked at one stage or another somewhere among the archaeological remains of intervening cultures. Whether direct or indirect, its adoption by the receiving culture would be adequately recorded in the archaeological remains of that culture by the relatively sudden appearance of a variety of innovations associated with it. And, no doubt, there would be found also in that archaeological context (as well as those of the intervening cultures) numbers of other (and unrelated) innovations adopted, or adapted, by the receiving culture at the same time (and evident in the intervening cultures at earlier stages).[7]

In the case of China, we are in the happy position of having as a basis of study a culture so far removed from the source-springs of Western civilization that alien materials, techniques, and ideas, can be expected to show themselves rather markedly. So far as the advent of metallurgy is concerned, its early appearance and subsequent development in the highly advanced ceramic civilization of late Lung-shan China has been surveyed in some detail in *Metallurgical Remains*, and the conclusions drawn from the extensive corpus of data assembled by Satō Tamotsu and myself are inescapably in support of independent invention. There should be little need to reiterate here, for instance, the long list of metallurgical techniques practiced widely throughout the ancient West (pp. 72–75), among which one only, direct casting in piece-mould assemblies, could be claimed by the rather too imaginative diffusionist, or stimulus diffusionist, to be the result of alien introduction.[8] I propose instead to discuss the significance of a

---

7. It is of course appreciated that, lacking as we do sufficient understanding of the areas extending north, west, and south of the modern boundaries of China, we have little choice but to confine the more reliable of our observations to data deriving from the past five or six decades of archaeological discovery within China. As Karl Jettmar demonstrated in his two papers delivered at the Berkeley conference, there is a tremendous amount of new material reported in Russian sources which will have an interesting impact upon earlier and current theories relating to communication between China and the West.

8. This is one of the main arguments, of course, for independent discovery. Introduction of metallurgy from any of the earlier metal-using cultures in the West could hardly have succeeded in avoiding instruction in the art of annealing; i.e., at least some of the smithy techniques universally employed in Western cultures should have entered the Chinese scene. Few of our more technical reviewers have commented on this point, but those who would advocate alien introduction of metallurgy should give special attention to the matter. It has been somewhat a matter of disappointment not to receive critical response here; if the principle of annealing could be demonstrated to have been known in the earliest stages of Chinese metallurgy, we would have to carefully re-examine the hypothesis of independent discovery. If good reasons for its lack of transmission can be advanced, I would welcome notice of them as valuable bases for further research into the validity of the hypothesis.

number of aspects of metallurgy in ancient China which have not been covered, or elaborated sufficiently, in *Metallurgical Remains* and which seem to me to throw further light on the problems of origin.

METEORIC IRON

Let us first consider the case of meteoric iron, and in particular the recent finds of wrought meteoric iron blades with bronze handles in archaeological contexts of Late Shang-early Western Chou. One reviewer has remarked: "How in the midst of a text, ultra 'anti-diffusionist' in its tone, can a find of a wrought meteoric iron axe blade at T'ai-Hsi-ts'un [T'ai-hsi-ts'un] (ca. 1000 B.C.?) be casually attributed to 'the result of occasional contacts with the nomadic peoples far to the West' and relegated to a foot note?" (Fleming 1976:91).[9] Here this query will be answered in some detail; but my response is more especially concerned with Cyril Smith's general and very thought-provoking plea: "I cannot help but feel that it is now more useful to study why a society will not absorb things with which it is brought into contact than to insist that contact has not occurred" (Smith 1977:84).

Two iron-blade *yüeh* 鉞 axes with bronze handles have been excavated to date; and we have the two earlier-known examples from the "early Chou dynasty, plundered before liberation from Hsün-hsien Honan province and now in the collection of the Freer Gallery of Art" (Li 1976:34), which have been thoroughly examined in the laboratory and reported in considerable detail.[10] These four artifacts provide the earliest evidence of iron in worked form in China, and they pre-date the beginnings of casting in iron (ca. 700–600 B.C.) by some four or five centuries.

Examinations of the highly corroded iron blades in each case seem to indicate fairly conclusively that the iron is of meteoric origin. In general, those who have written about these bi-metallic artifacts have assumed that

9. Cyril Smith comments, in respect to the meteoric iron blades: "Does transmission have to leave a record? Even the authors of these books accept the diffusion of iron casting and crossbows *from* China, while dismissing the appearance of hammered meteoric iron dagger blades in Honan as a mere intrusion!" (1977:81). As responses to the hypotheses advanced in *Metallurgical Remains* appear in reviews, I have little recourse but to cite them and do so at risk of occasionally appearing disputatious or even querulous. However, I believe most authors, like myself, welcome critical appraisals of their work as a constructive step toward the clarification of details that for various reasons could not be more fully dealt with in the body of the work.

10. See Gettens, Clarke, and Chase 1971. The influence of this excellent report on recent articles in Mainland Chinese archaeological journals is noteworthy (cf. Hsia 1973; Ho-pei-sheng po-wu-kuan, T'ai-hsi, and Ho-pei-sheng wen-kuan-ch'u 1974 [but source not cited]; Li 1976, etc.).

both the blades and the handles were manufactured in China. The latter
certainly were, but there are good reasons to question the assumption
about the fashioning of the blades. I believe it sufficient to cite my previously published remarks about the alien origin of iron blades:

> Until the opportunity occurs to write at greater length on the subject I would
> simply observe here that the presence of meteoric iron in shaped form—
> particularly the FGA items (34.11) with dove-tail cutting of the iron blade—
> must indicate an alien source of origin. Such articles would have entered the
> Middle States' area as the result of occasional contacts with nomadic peoples far
> to the west and beyond the present boundaries of China. *There is no evidence at
> all which would allow us to assume that these meteoric iron blades could have been
> worked by Chinese artisans in Shang and Western Chou times.* On the contrary,
> one might now point to this early evidence of the metal iron in China and
> comment upon the fact that its introduction (a) made absolutely no impact on
> current and later metallurgical technology (i.e. smithy work did not develop),
> and (b) had nothing to do with the Chinese discovery of cast-iron some five or six
> centuries later. The unusual articles were simply treated as a curiosity (Barnard
> and Satō 1975:85, n. 5; italics added).

The significance of these bi-metallic artifacts—even with the addition of
the most recent find at Liu-chia-ho, P'ing-ku-hsien, Peking (Yüan and
Chang 1977)—has not altered since the above observation was written.[11]
The italicized sentence above is the key point, and the continued lack of
evidence of metal-working in any form (other than gold leaf), so strikingly
characteristic of the ancient Chinese metallurgical scene, shows beyond a
reasonable doubt that the four meteoric iron blades could not have been
fabricated by Chinese artisans with the knowledge and technical facilities at
their command.[12] One could expand this observation at length and write
an apparently impressive essay repeating much of what is discussed in
Metallurgical Remains on the theme of "no smithy work" in China at the
time, as well as duplicate data relating to the nature of meteoric iron
already authoritatively reported in Gettens, Clarke, and Chase (1971), then
elaborate on the working of meteoric iron, a subject likewise dealt with

11. The earlier of the two meteoric iron blades is a *yüeh* ax recovered from the T'ai-hsi-
ts'un site, Kao-ch'eng-hsien, Hopei (Ho-pei-sheng po-wu-kuan, T'ai-hsi, and Ho-pei-sheng
wen-kuan-ch'u 1974:45). The site is reliably radiocarbon-dated to 1498 ± 114 B.C. by
samples taken from small-wood timber structures in well bottoms (BK–75007; see my roneod
survey, Barnard 1977:23–25). It is, indeed, interesting that the presence of meteoric iron
should appear in China well before 1300 B.C. The second item excavated from the Liu-chia-ho
site also derives from a Middle Shang context.

12. The term "metal-working" is employed throughout in the generally accepted sense of
smithy applications, wrought metal work, etc. (i.e., methods of artifact production other than
direct casting in sectional moulds, or by *cire-perdue*). The metal is in the solid state throughout
the metal-working processes. Some confusion of technical terms of this kind occurred during
the conference, and I should like to note that there is a list of terms and definitions in Barnard
1976:80–83 (addendum in Barnard in press [b]).

more than adequately by eminent metallurgical historians.[13] The conclusions would still be the same.

Let us now consider Cyril Smith's plea in light of these four meteoric iron blades. We know from the general archaeological milieu that they had no impact on the ancient artisan's knowledge of iron (a) as a metal which derives from ores, (b) as a metal which exists in the native state, and (c) as a metal which can be worked. In other words, these meteoric iron blades at different times and in different places came to their attention in the foundry (as proven by their addition of typical cast bronze handles), and no resultant effect on Chinese metallurgical techniques is anywhere evidenced among the vast numbers of metal artifacts excavated to date from sites datable up to, say, 700 B.C. Obviously, it would appear that the already worked blades not only came into the Middle States' area from far afield, but also that their entry was unaccompanied by relevant technical data. Many generations later, the casting of iron in China commenced independent of any other metallurgical culture. And there is no connection between these meteoric iron artifacts and the later discovery of iron casting.[14] If we can accept the appearance of *worked* meteoric iron in China as an intrusion, then it must seem evident that the germ of an idea—in this case an unknown material already worked into a functionally familiar form—may have no impact unless it is fully enough understood by the receiver.

13. Problems attending the working of meteoric iron are well covered by Coghlan (1956:29–37) and Tylecote (1962:9–13; 1976:2–3, 42–43). In his highly technical study of the T'ai-hsi-ts'un meteoric iron blade, Li Chung (1976:31) concludes that it has been formed by smithy methods but does not elaborate further. The writers of the several Chinese reports seek to interpret the meteoric iron blades as evidence of knowledge of iron (and its properties) and of smithy work as early as Shang times. But their appraisals are largely influenced by a knowledge of Western developmental patterns; thus wrought iron working should, they believe, appear in China, too, at an earlier stage than does cast iron. As so little research is being done in China on the history of metallurgy and the laboratory work is often so limited in scope, it is not surprising that the reporters do not recognize an anomolous situation when it arises.

14. In the northern sector of the F4 cultural layer at T'ai-hsi-ts'un, the find of ten or so fragments of iron "slag" which have been subjected to analysis by X-ray diffraction (Fe_3O_4, $Fe\ PO_4.2H_2O$) and by chemical (wet method) analyses (Fe: 3.2 percent, P: 4.32 percent) is taken as possible evidence, along with the meteoric iron blade, of the use [i.e., manufacture] of iron as early as Shang times (Ho-pei-sheng po-wu-kuan, T'ai-hsi, and Ho-pei-sheng wen-kuan-ch'u 1974:47). The reporters correctly observe that the high phosphorous content is doubtless due to chemical changes during burial and thus not originally present in the slag. also that there is no way to determine if the slag derives from wrought iron or from cast iron. On comparison, however, with the data relating to iron slags from Roman sites in England (Tylecote 1962:246–255), it seems obvious that we would want a great deal more information on site details here, as well as an exhaustive series of tests on the iron slag, to determine whether the material is indeed slag.

PSEUDOGRANULATION

Similarly, we can consider the case of "pseudogranulation," the Chinese founders' attempt to reproduce the decorative filling known as granulation or colloid hard-soldering—a technique which in its original form involved the fusing of small, equal-size granules of gold to a plain surface of the same metal.[15] Artifacts containing this decorative feature came to their notice but again without even the germ of an idea as to how it was done. The decorative motif appealed to the designer; he employed the materials and methods of manufacture with which he was familiar to create a similar motif. It seems reasonable enough to regard this as a case of stimulus diffusion, not of a technique, but of the decorative results of a technical application. Although the original granulation decor would have been executed in gold, it is not a surprise to see the Eastern Chou founders restricting their efforts to bronze; casting of gold seems to have been rare.[16] The lesson of this example and the one preceding is that a receptive culture may not have fully absorbed innovations simply because the technical background remained unknown to the artisans best able to emulate them, and there was nothing in their knowledge of metals and methods of processing metals that would have allowed them to re-invent true granulation.[17] The decorative feature appealed to their designers, and foundry-

15. Before returning from the Moesgård conference entitled "Origins of Agriculture and Technology: West Asia or East Asia?" I had the good fortune to be able to view firsthand many ancient Scandinavian metal artifacts, molds, crucibles, etc., including scores of examples of granulated ornaments. A valuable morning was spent at the Arkeologiska Forskuings Laboratoriet, Stockholm University, with Dr. Birgit Arrhenius, whose detailed studies of the granulation technique and excellent electronic microscopic photographs were impressive and informative. However, the overall impression resulting from a "sudden switch" from the familiar field of Chinese Bronze Age technology to that of the "Far" West accentuated my impression of how remarkably alien ancient Western technology must appear to anyone steeped in that of ancient China; direct study and handling of the artifacts was instrumental in this impression.

16. Interestingly, cast gold artifacts (a hairpin, bangles, and earrings) of appreciable size (see illustrations in Yüan and Chang 1977:6) were excavated at the Liu-chia-ho site near Peking, where the fourth of our meteoric iron blade *yüeh* axes was unearthed. Analysis shows that the gold content is 85 percent, with "a comparatively large proportion of silver" and a "minute amount of copper." The significance of these details—also of the design of the bangles and earrings—requires further research. Similar earrings in bronze have come to light in other Hopei sites, and I suspect a northern route of entry may be demonstrable for this style of jewelry. Up to recently, the main form of cast gold of any size excavated in pre-Han sites has been the well-known gold "biscuit" currency of Ch'u. A further relevant point, noted also by Franklin (ch. 10 below) is the lack of jewelry for personal ornament of gold or other metals among the earliest metal-bearing sites up to Shang times at least.

17. The making of granules, or grain, would in itself have required knowledge of shotting: pouring molten metal from a height into a tank of water. The pellets or grain so formed freeze into irregular round shapes before hitting the water at the end of the fall. For very fine grains, the use of wire cut into snips of regular length, or filings of metal for ultra-fine grains, which

men endeavored to simulate the motif in metal in the only ways the techniques with which they were familiar would allow.

SPLAY-BLADE AXES

Splay-blade axes, notably the *yüeh* 鉞 ax and the *ch'i* 戚 ax, which date back to Middle Shang, provide a further example of the Chinese response to an alien theme in artifact design. As Hayashi Minao has pointed out (1971 : 133), the lunate blade ax is much rarer in the archaeological context than are such weapons as the *ko* 戈 dagger ax and *mou* 矛 spearhead, which are usually highly ornamented. This latter characteristic is possibly rather significant. But most important is the fact that all splay-blade weapons in the Middle States, Ch'u, Yüeh, and so on, are cast fully in this peculiar shape. They do not result from the hammering of the cutting edge of an originally rectangular shaped casting. There is, therefore, no known indigenous antecedent that could have led to the shaping of the lunate blade in China; only if the principle of annealing were known, and smithy work were actually practiced, would blades of this form have originated, or have developed after due adoption of alien metal-working techniques.[18]

Here, it can be claimed, we have the obvious adoption of an alien shape whose smithy antecedents in the original cultural areas concerned is well known to us; but nothing of the alien technology which led to its develop-

---

are then placed in layers of charcoal powder in a crucible and heated, is conveniently described by Untracht (1968 : 202–211). The use of a paste of cupric hydroxide ($Cu[OH]_2$) and an organic glue to bond the grains to the base metal upon carefully controlled heating is an elaborate combination of materials and techniques which probably could not be reconstructed easily by metal-workers unfamiliar with certain materials used for bonding the grains. It would not be facetious, I believe, to claim that the discovery of metallurgy would be an easier undertaking than the task of re-inventing the method of granulation. Attention should be drawn to the Shih-chai-shan metal-workers' obvious acquaintance with true granulation ornament as demonstrated in attempted reproductions (Yün-nan-sheng 1959: pls. 105.5, 106.1–2), which probably are *cire-perdue* castings. Highly skilled in the modeling of wax, these workers sought to simulate the decorative feature in this medium. True granulation appears earliest north of the Great Wall in Han times (Mizuno 1946: pl. 59).

18. Working of an originally rectangular shaped cast to form the splayed cutting edge requires, of course, a knowledge of annealing. In the final stages cold-working is applied to form a hard, durable cutting edge. To minimize the labor in producing the flaring edge on the anvil, Aegean bronze implements were later cast as close as possible to the required shape; thereafter only minimal hammering was needed to complete the sharpening and hardening of the edge (see general discussion in Branigan 1974: 83–85). I shall cover elsewhere (Barnard in press [b] the supposed existence of metal-working in Early Shang proposed by Robert Bagley, Tom Chase, and Louisa Huber during the Berkeley conference. Here, I would merely reiterate that there is not the slightest archaeological evidence of metal-working in China prior to, say, the Spring and Autumn period. The alleged record of presumed metal-working practices preserved in ceramic ware of Lung-shan and Early Shang date does not stand up to careful examination of the evidence.

ment came with it to China. The introduced shapes as seen by Late Shang-early Western Chou founders were probably cast entirely (in bronze) in the splayed form, and there was only a comparatively small amount of cold-work hardening applied around the cutting edges. Not unexpectedly, the Chinese founders imitated the lunate blade almost in terms of a two-dimensional silhouette in the earliest versions. There is little to show in cross-section that the prototype was a full-bodied, naturally tapering, smithied blade. The Chinese blade is generally, merely a "cut-out in sheet metal." Because of such aspects of the shape, we can assume that this particular germ of an idea was introduced, but only superficially; even hardening of the blade edge by cold-working—a further important aspect of smithy work—long remained unknown in ancient China.[19]

THE "GERM OF AN IDEA" AND ITS RECEPTION

The examples selected for discussion thus far would seem to represent various possible results that could attend the introduction through contacts from alien cultures of various materials, artifacts, and decorative elements into the Chinese metallurgical scene. In considering the significance of developments, or of lack of development, following such contacts, we must keep in mind that we are surveying introductions—from long-established metallurgical cultures situated far distant from China—into a cultural area which already had a highly advanced metallurgical industry, although its origins were not so distant in time. Despite this situation, these germs of ideas either failed to take root or gave rise merely to a rather insipid adaption, or to a technically uncomprehending adoption, of the ideas which were fundamentally beyond the Chinese craftsmen's appreciation simply because the technical background was not known to them. Thus, when confronted with already worked meteoric iron blades, the mysterious magical metal was naturally prized, and decorative handles of bronze were cast on to the blades. But the Chinese artisans still knew nothing of the art of annealing and its technical ramifications, in respect of either iron or bronze.

When we examine situations such as the preceding, which can be discussed with a reasonable degree of authority (because most of the essential

19. It is interesting to observe that bronze axes cast in rectangular form and hammered to a splayed edge appear in early radiocarbon-dated contexts at Ban Chiang (and Non Nok Tha) in Thailand; preliminary discussion on the significance of this feature is in Barnard 1977:58–61. As the relevant Ban Chiang materials have been dated as early as mid-third millennium B.C., obvious inferences regarding the beginnings of Chinese metallurgy arise.

factual background is fairly readily available), and observe how ineffectual mere introduction of the germ of an idea can be from one metallurgical culture to another, distant metallurgical culture, we may well ponder the validity of diffusionist theorizing, which assumes the introduction of metallurgy per se. Some metal artifact—let it be copper so as to give the diffusionist hypothesis every possible scope—comes into the Lungshanoid ceramic scene, presumably from the Middle East, either directly or indirectly. If it arrives in the same manner as meteoric iron blades, splayed blades, and granulation (i.e., without technical instruction), the copper artifact could hardly stimulate the Lungshanoid ceramists, or the lithic craftsmen of the time, to discover either native copper or copper ores and thence learn for themselves how to work copper or cast bronze. The latter technique would have been no more likely to arise from the chance introduction of the metal copper in artifact form than the discovery of cast iron was likely to have resulted from the sporadic entry of meteoric iron blades, unless sufficient background knowledge of ores and the properties of metals and alloys accompanied the already processed materials.[20] Thus must we be prepared to theorize not only in terms of an introduction of the material (and the artifact made from it); but also, the hypothesis must account for introduction of the technique along with instruction on how to obtain the material to be processed, if it is something completely unknown to the receiving culture.

Let us now look at the inventive capability of the ancient Chinese artisan along the same lines as above, basing our research upon the known and extending our interpretations backward in time to the unknown. It is not necessary to engage in an extensive appraisal of the subject, as this characteristic of Chinese craftsmen is seldom disputed; but merely to accept that the ancient Chinese craftsman was inventive, and not to investigate just what his inventiveness really amounts to, results in a loss of valuable understanding that could cast light upon such a fundamental problem as

20. To theorize in terms of a Lungshanoid potter accidentally melting a copper artifact as the prelude to the stimulated discovery of metal and its casting properties still leaves open the question of how the process of selecting and smelting ore would come about. It could be claimed, however, that the search for native copper and gold would be stimulated by the arrival of artifacts or ornaments made from these metals: lithic craftsmen would probably discover how to work the new material, and even the art of annealing and cold-working, within a short space of time. Such hypotheses may sound good, but the complete absence of smithy work in the Chinese archaeological scene offers substantial evidence (albeit negative) that the situation was such that (a) there was no instruction coming from alien cultures in metal-working techniques, and (b) knowledge of metal properties would thenceforth be limited to those associated with casting (i.e., the discovery and development of metallurgy was essentially one effected in a ceramic environment).

the human element in the process of discovery and subsequent research and development applications. The following exercise will not necessarily prove the validity of the hypothesis of independent discovery of metallurgy in China, but it should have the desirable effect of encouraging those of the diffusionist persuasion to view the relevant data more carefully in terms of the human element.

THE HINGE

I propose to survey briefly just one example: the hinge. The hinge is selected for consideration here because it represents several principles in design, functional approaches, and constructional methods which are demonstrably peculiarly Chinese in origin. Further, the development of the functional artifact itself can be traced to humble beginnings in the Chinese cultural area without any need to postulate theoretical assumptions of alien introduction.

So far as hinges in the West are concerned, a few general observations are sufficient. In ancient Egypt the earliest archaeological evidence of the hinge appears to date from circa 1350 B.C.; in imperial Roman times hinges with three, five, and nine knuckles are common. Manufacture was by metal-working, and the mechanical principle involved was the to and fro movement of one leaf and its terminal cylindrical shaped sockets—knuckles—in relation to another similar unit (with a greater or lesser number of knuckles) around a pin with rivet caps at both ends. In principle, the design has persisted in the West for three millennia with practically no fundamental change, even in manufacturing methods, except for the development of more sophisticated machinery to produce hinges.

The Western version of the hinge was prepared from sheet metal cut to the required shape and size for each leaf, with protruding flaps to be fashioned into cylindrical knuckles, as demonstrated in figure 9.2. Nail-holes were perforated by drill or punch, and the knuckles were formed by bending and hammering. A rod of suitable diameter and length, with one end hammered to form a rivet-like cap, was inserted through the knuckle-cylinders, and the other end was likewise hammered to form a second rivet cap so as to lock the assembly together. The rivet-like caps of the pin, together with the inter-lock of the inner and outer knuckles and the comparatively large surface area of contact between knuckles and pin, all add up to an effective, strong mechanism. Greater strength could be attained by increasing the number of knuckles, rather than by using heavier plate and rod, with the attendant difficulties in smithy work. The leaf plus

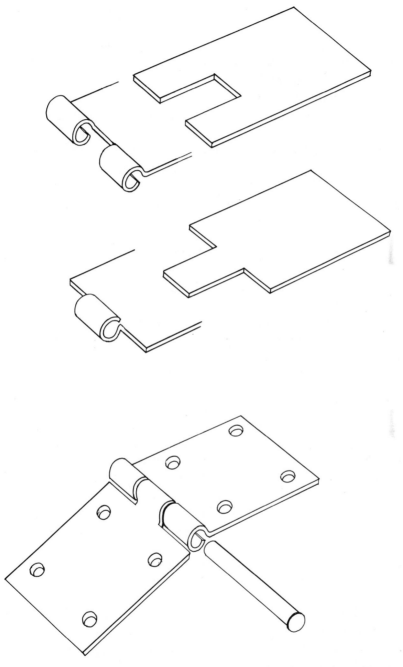

FIGURE 9.2. **Construction of a leaf hinge from a metal sheet by smithy methods, a characteristic Western method which dates back to the mid-second millennium B.C.**

knuckle units were never cast to their ultimate form in molds, nor were the rods cast as such.

The mechanical principle of the pre-Han Chinese hinge is, prima facie, not unlike that of the Western hinge; but upon careful observation and analysis of the mechanism in terms of its basic design and construction it exhibits quite different approaches. First, there is no metal-working in any stage of its manufacture except for varying degrees of post-cast abrasive polishing and the eradication of casting fins. All details, even to the fashioning of nail holes, were executed during the ceramic preparation of model, molds, and cores. With few exceptions (the significance of which will be discussed later) the pin, in its role as an axle, does not form a specific element of the hinge mechanism in the earliest Chinese examples. Interlock of the two component parts, the stability of one in relation to the other during articulation, and the very means and effectiveness of articulation all owed their origin to the general fund of age-old knowledge and experience among Chinese founders in the designing and casting of "mechanical" appliances—mainly in the form of connecting links, bosses around which second-pour units were cast, revolving units on a stationary axle, and so on. Probably of most importance among these was the second-pour casting of appurtenances onto bosses, or trunnions. However, with slight modification in design these could be made into articulating members: the *t'i-liang* 提梁 swing-handles of *yu* 卣 flasks offer a particularly instructive example of this (i.e., those that were cast onto trunnions incorporated on the vessel body for this purpose).

When it came to designing hinge-like mechanisms, the ancient craftsmen would naturally plan the new structure on the basis of either links or trunnions. Where the Western inventor, many centuries earlier, had opted for a rod or pin as the means of connecting separately made hinge plates together and as the axle around which each would move, the Chinese inventor chose the trunnion. In other words, the function of the pin was effected by trunnions cast as one with the solid-cast central knuckle, and they extended into recesses within the adjacent knuckles. The latter (together with the remainder of the structure of which they are part) were accordingly cast directly onto the pre-cast unit (with its trunnions protruding from the central knuckle). As a result, the sockets enclosing the trunnions within the knuckles of the second-pour unit were formed upon solidification of the second-pour molten bronze directly upon its contact with the solid surfaces of the pre-cast unit. All this should become clear through study of figure 9.3.

Superficially, the knuckles of the Chinese hinge and their apparent

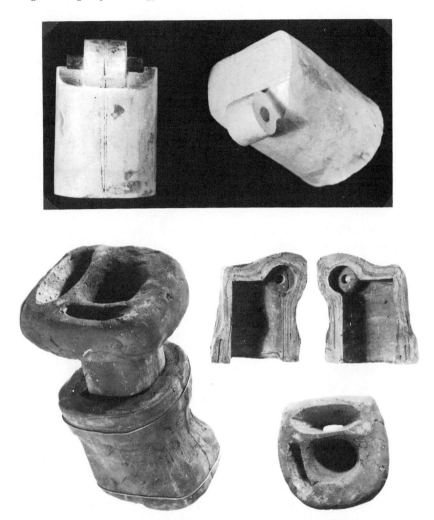

FIGURE 9.3. Above, the model for one unit of hinge; below, the two-piece mold assembly and core, with sprue inlet, prepared from the clay model. When cast, the second unit is molded on the basis of this cast unit and then cast onto it, thus completing the hinge mechanism. (Photos of hinge-casting experiments in association with Wan Chia-pao and Ho Shih-k'un, Academia Sinica, Taiwan.)

internal mechanism do not appear to differ from their Western counterparts, but in fact the movement is that of pivots turning in sockets (or
sockets turning around pivots), whereas in the Western hinge the movement takes place along the entire length of the pin (which, as we have noted,
essentially functions as an axle), which may or may not join in the movement of one or the other of the two leaves. Both mechanisms effect the same
to and fro movement, but the constructional means to achieve this movement (and hence the mechanical principles used) are quite different. The
variant principles followed derive from (a) the general background and
approach to the mechanics of movable joinery in each general cultural
sphere and (b) the materials and methods of processing them as known to,
or favored by, artisans in each sphere. Possibly other considerations should
also be taken into account, not the least of which would be the nature of the
over-all structure in which the articulated joinery functioned, and the
function of this main structure in the environment in which it was used.

Plate hinges are rare in the early Chinese archaeological scene. One, of
early Han date, is associated with a lacquered box(?) (Hu-nan-sheng
1959:651; see fig. 9.4 below); *pu shou* 鋪首 ring handles were also found
close by. So far as I can discover, there is no evidence for plate hinges
among archaeological finds earlier than Warring States times; and even for
the Warring States period there are no definite instances reported and none
illustrated. Confusion on this point has arisen, however, because of the
Chinese term *ho-yeh* 合葉 (叶, or 頁). Needham writes: "For doors or
windows the pin tended to be long and the 'leaves' (the Chinese used the
same term *ho yeh* [合頁]) broad and flat," and in his note *g* he refers to
"ornamented flat bronze plate hinges of early Chou time" (1971:69). The
piece he refers to is from the well-known Marquis of Ts'ai tomb, and not
only is it incorrectly dated by him as early Chou, but it is also mistaken for a
plate hinge (of Western style). The exact nature of this hinge is assessible
from the rubbings in the original report (An-hui-sheng po-wu kuan and
An-hui-sheng wei-yüan-hui 1956: pl. 100; see fig. 9.5), where, fortunately,
the ends of the hinge are presented as rubbings and show the normal
vertical join line, thus indicating that there is no pin in the mechanism. The
hinge is the characteristic pivot-and-socket type.

When the Chinese term *ho-yeh* is applied to hinges in several of the
archaeological reports, it is important to realize that in the devices in
question the "leaves" usually comprise *two* parallel plates cast as one to
form a U-shaped structure; they do not move in relation to one another, as
do Western hinges (see fig. 9.6) but simply function as a holding device for a

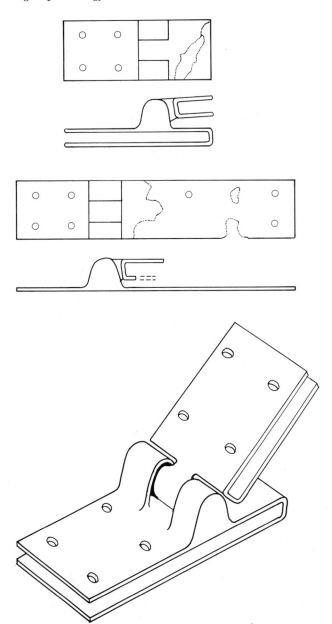

FIGURE 9.4. **The transition from the *huo-chia* articulated terminal grip to the hinge is demonstrable on the basis of intermediate forms of the kind above. M2717:186 (and 175) datable to late Spring and Autumn-early Warring States. (After CKKH 1959:111.)**

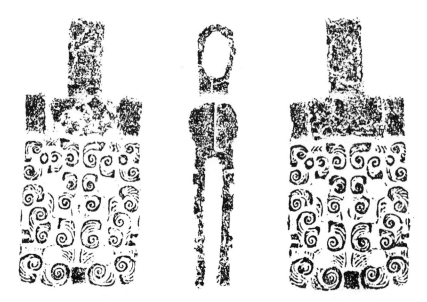

FIGURE 9.5. **Rubbings of the Ts'ai-hou-mu hinge which demonstrate that the U-shaped parallel plate unit was cast in a two-piece mold assembly in the traditional Chinese manner.**

leather strap(?) or something similar.[21] Whatever was gripped between the parallel plates of the hinge was intended to swing on the center perforated knuckle, which in turn was affixed to (and presumably held firmly by) a further device. Thus the function of this particular mechanism is quite clear, but the full context in which it operated is not. Furthermore, we might wonder if the device should be called a "hinge" in the generally accepted sense of the English term. As it obviously had nothing to do with

21. This was also noted by Kuo Pao-chün in his report on the Shan-piao-chen finds (1959:36). He recorded the presence of leather remnants and lacquered leather remnants—black with red designs—between the "leaves." He uses the more appropriate term *huo-chia* 活夾, "articulated (terminal) grips," and divides them into two classes: those hammered into shape with rivet-like caps on the center knuckle and those with the "perforated knuckle" (see fig. 9.5 above). I have examined the pieces now in Nankang and can dispute Kuo's statement inferring smithy methods of manufacture of his first class of *huo-chia*. They are definitely cast in piece-molds and exhibit clear evidence of their method of manufacture, as will be described shortly. But a cursory examination could result in the impression that the U-shape was effected by smithy techniques. Kuo's record of the presence of leather and lacquered leather remnants is, however, important. So far as I recall, these traces are not now visible; certainly no record appears in my notes. Possibly the remnants have been lost, but further and closer examination should result in recognition of faint vestiges still adhering to the inner surfaces of the leaves.

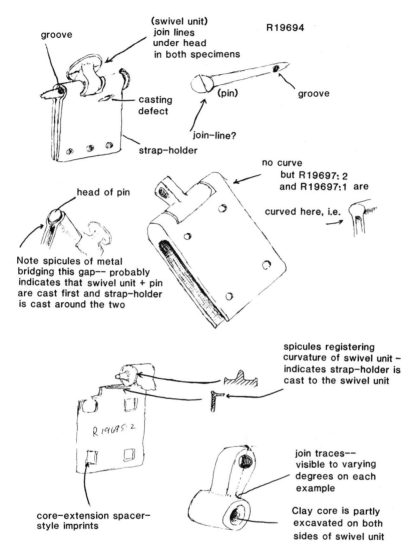

FIGURE 9.6. **The structure of the *ho-yeh* (or *huo-chia*) strap terminal with articulated connecting link. (Selected sketches and notes from author's field records made at Nankang, May 1974.)**

doors, lids, and so on, its function is not really that of a hinge as we usually use the term.

The preceding discussion is important: the devices in question are among the earliest articulated joinery that might appear to have something in common with relevant aspects of Western hinges. But so far as I know, there are no really comparable devices like the *huo-chia* (see n. 21) among the remains of Western cultures of about the seventh century B.C. or earlier.[22] The *huo-chia* articulated terminal grip seems to have been used in some kind of leather accoutrement having to do with human beings and not horses—the devices are, for the most part, not associated with chariot burials—and from Kuo Pao-chün's report (1959) we know that the leather trappings with which they were associated in the Shan-piao-chen site were decorated with red on black lacquer designs. Unfortunately, other sites, such as Shang-ts'un-ling, Shou-hsien, and Lo-yang (the Royal Ontario Museum examples) are not as fully reported as one would wish in respect to necessary background details that might assist our understanding of the *huo-chia*. However, the seven tombs in the Shang-ts'un-ling site-area containing *huo-chia* would seem to indicate that the device was not necessarily a piece of chariot equipment, as some have thought, but that it had to do with military trappings.[23] The site-area is also important in allowing us to date the artifact with a reasonable degree of certainty to circa 700 B.C.; the process of invention and development, no doubt, would permit an appreciably earlier date for its first appearance.

To regard the *huo-chia* as a Chinese invention would seem reasonable, particularly as those of earliest date are made on the pivot-and-socket principle. This feature, too, would preclude theorizing along "stimulus diffusion" lines as, indeed, would the results of a comprehensive investigation into directly related mechanisms of even earlier date in China.

True hinges (those functionally comparable to the Western hinge) come upon the scene within a century or so (ca. 600 B.C.). But these mechanisms, too, are designed on the pivot-and-socket principle and differ from the

22. Just how far back in time Roman buckles such as those illustrated in Flinders Petrie (1974: pls. 18.6–7, 15–16, etc.) may be dated is yet to be fully investigated. I mention these in case it is felt that they are relevant, though there is abundant evidence that this form of buckle did not enter the Chinese scene earlier than late Warring States/Han.

23. Further investigation is to be conducted on this point, as there are specific instances of *huo-chia* in chariot burials, e.g., in the Ch'in tombs of Sung-ts'un, Hu-hsien, Shansi (Wu and Shang 1975:58); in this case a single one was located well to the rear of one horse but closely associated with lacquered shields (ibid., fig. 6). The Sung-ts'un site is dated to the early Spring and Autumn period, a point of interest regarding the beginnings of this artifact in China. Photographs are sufficiently clear to demonstrate the high standard of casting and sophisticated level of design.

Western version in a complexity of structure characteristic of direct casting technology. Whereas the Western hinge is a simple plate hinge, the Chinese version has, instead of plate-like leaves, sturdy box-like sockets into which were inserted wooden poles or beams, often of an appreciable thickness. The knuckles, as already observed, are solid and pivot around trunnions of considerable strength cast as one with the center knuckle. Nowhere in the contemporary (or earlier) ancient world was hinged joinery designed and cast with such a variety of functional applications, shapes, and sizes. Many examples can be studied in the Royal Ontario Museum, Toronto, and at Academia Sinica, Nankang. I have worked on almost all the relevant items in these two collections, and throughout the several periods of direct study of the mechanical pieces I have felt intense admiration for the ancient founders who produced such ingenious devices.

Between the earlier (late Western Chou) period of *huo-chia* manufacture and that of the sophisticated hinges of the Warring States and Han, some indications of experiment and developmental change are to be observed. The evolution of the *huo-chia* into the hinge proper is interestingly suggested (if not attested) by the two examples from the diggings near Lo-yang (CKKH 1959:111, pl. 68.1:9). As reconstructed in figure 9.4 above, this hinged mechanism is clearly an intermediate form, with its substantial gripping functions in both leaves; it is definable as a hinging device rather than a simple swinging articulated terminal grip. The step from the *huo-chia* terminal grip to the present hinged grip terminals thence to the sophisticated hinged joinery of the middle Warring States period and later times is a perfectly natural progression involving human ingenuity and endeavor prompted, no doubt, by purely local requirements. This evolution did not need the stimulus of ideas from an alien culture, at its inception or at any other stage—except, perhaps, for the somewhat later plate hinge (fig. 9.7) and possibly the associated use of a pin therein, as in the Western hinge.

Articulation in cast metal artifacts is a well-known phenomenon which dates from as early as Shang times and can be seen in such examples as the construction of *t'i-liang* swing-handles in *yu* flasks, the link connections between lid and body of *ho* 盉 kettles, horses' bits, and the revolving four-headed dragon in *kuei* 毁 tureens from Hsiao-t'un.

During the developmental period (the early and middle Warring States period) of the hinge and related mechanisms, experiments with links as hinging devices in joinery were apparently made. Because of the founders' considerable accumulation of experience with links and similar mechanisms, it is not surprising to discover among the finds of recent decades

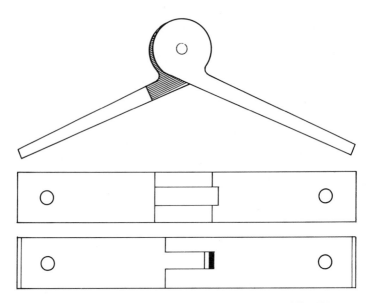

FIGURE 9.7. **An early Han plate hinge (after Hu-nan-sheng 1959:651) apparently with an axle-pin, as in Western-style hinges. Both the plate and knuckle units, however, appear cast rather than worked.**

joinery of this kind from Fen-shui-ling, Ch'ang-chih, Shansi, as illustrated in figure 9.8. Unfortunately, the photographs reproduced in the report (*Wu-sheng* 1958: pl. 64.4) are the only illustrations of these hinges available, thus my reconstruction must be verified when foreign scholars in our field are allowed to enter China to conduct research directly upon such materials—which in the meantime must apparently continue to lie idly unstudied in storage or in exhibition cases. I have also taken into account a brief published description of the pieces (Shan-hsi-sheng 1957: 116; see also the caption to fig. 9.8).

It would not be my aim to assert that articulated joinery of such unique design provides a definite missing link, as it were, in the evolution of the Chinese hinge from the earlier link mechanisms of Shang and Western Chou; but the possibility that such avenues of step-by-step trial and error were in progress in the design and manufacture of articulated artifacts is amply illustrated among the general corpus of mechanical bronzes available for study. Once the need for stable articulated mechanisms arose—links that would allow the adjacent bronze terminals of wooden structures to swivel in one plane and not wobble erratically in relation to one another—it would soon be realized that at least two links would be

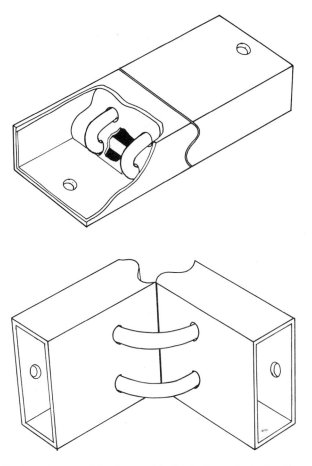

FIGURE 9.8. **A most unusual development in the design and construction of hinges; apparently associated with cabinetry (*WW* 1955.10:118). From the Warring States period tomb (no. 14), Fen-shui-ling, Ch'ang-chih, Shansi. (After *Wu-sheng* 1958: pl. 64.4.)**

needed, and that they would have to be kept parallel. Accordingly, the two bronze terminals would have to be designed so as to allow only parallel movement of the links passing through them. Further, the end surfaces of the bronze terminals would need to maintain as large an area as possible of mutual contact, and such contact should be as close as possible at all times throughout the angle of turn. Once the two linked terminals attained their ultimate linear, or angular, position (as required in the structural complex for which they were designed), the surface contact of the terminal ends would necessarily attain its greatest area of mutual contact, and no further movement in that direction would take place. This result is due partly to the shape and geometry which the hinge must naturally assume, partly to intentional aspects of the design, and partly to the exigencies of the structural complex in which it functions. As will be noted among the several hinges illustrated in this chapter, the mechanisms are by no means simple in design or crude in manufacture; the planning of joinery of this high standard and its casting solely by sectional mold techniques would be a major challenge to any present-day foundry.

Sufficient detail is visible from the photographs of the Fen-shui-ling hinges in *Wu-sheng* (1958) to allow a reasonably reliable reconstruction of the casting procedure. Two pins, one just visible thanks to the breakage of the lower leaf unit of the right-hand hinge (see fig. 9.8), and the two links were cast first. A clay model of the upper leaf unit was then prepared with channels incised to accommodate two pre-cast links. These were inserted, together with one of the pins. Insterstices in the channels and links which were *not* to be filled with metal from the pouring for the lower leaf unit were filled with clay. Thence the outer mould assembly and core for the lower leaf unit was prepared around this model, which incorporated the two pre-cast links and one pin. The two ends of the pin were positioned so that the molten bronze forming the lower leaf unit would envelop them and lock them firmly in place. After the cast was released from the mold assembly, the assembly for the remaining leaf unit was similarly prepared and the second pin inserted through the other ends of the two links so that it, too, would be locked in place when the pouring was effected. *The already cast surface of the terminal end-face of the first casting* (the lower leaf unit) *acted as the mold surface for the terminal end-face of the second casting* (the upper leaf unit). This practice of employing the contact surface of a pre-cast unit as the casting face in the mold assembly of the second unit in two-unit devices is characteristically Chinese and, so far as I can ascertain, is unique to this cultural area. From the point of view of precision engineering— especially for achieving "completeness of the constraint of motion" (so far as this is applicable to hinge mechanisms with their maximum to-and-fro movement of, say, 170 degrees)—the importance of this aspect of early Chinese casting practice cannot be over-stressed.

If we reflect a little further upon the Fen-shui-ling hinges, allowing the assumption that the use of links in this manner may have preceded a development from the *huo-chia* into the three-knuckle and four-knuckle pivot-and-socket hinges, hypotheses of the evolution of connecting links into a pivot-and-socket mechanism could be entertained. Direct evidence is not available, although inferences from known articulated devices and foundry techniques could well be brought to bear upon the subject. The general line of reasoning would be that (a) instead of two links, a wider unit (the center knuckle) would develop, and (b) instead of locking the pin in place by second-pour casting, it would be designed as an integral part of the cast, that is, as a trunnion. But these thoughts are speculative, and it may well be that the Fen-shui-ling hinges are merely another of the manifold examples of inventive ingenuity so characteristic of the early Chinese founder.

Some insight into the development of hinge mechanisms with pins is obtained by studying several available examples. Two from the Shan-piao-chen find are especially informative (referred to briefly in note 21). The method of manufacture is quite clear: the pin and swivel unit were each cast separately. The pin was cast first in a two-piece mold assembly, and the two-piece mold assembly to form the swivel unit was later prepared and placed around the pre-cast pin so it would act as core. With the casting of the swivel unit completed and the pin in place, the "threaded" pin was then placed within the mold assembly for the U-shaped grip, and the latter was cast around it. Again the pin temporarily served the dual purpose of core. In the construction of the mold assembly for the U-shaped grip, attention should be drawn also to the dual function of the "nail" holes. They functioned as a means of holding a leather strap—probably tied in place by cord? Clay protrusions extending from the core surface which formed the perforations acted also as core-extension spacers. In the many relevant castings I have examined, I have observed that all such perforations in the castings, not only in joinery but in most other bronze artifacts, result from the founders' fashioning of dual-purpose core-extension spacers.

Pins made of iron began increasingly to be employed in middle to late Warring States joinery (see fig. 9.9). In Han they are quite often found. I assume they would originally have been hammered at both ends to form rivet caps, but those I have examined are far too corroded for assessments by visual examination. Hinges with bronze pins date from about the same time. Whether these artifacts indicate some aspect or other of stimulus diffusion or are simply re-inventions is a subject deserving further investigation. As they appear comparatively late in the Chinese scene, however, they have no bearing upon the origins of the *huo-chia* and the pivot-and-socket hinges.

I have dwelt in some detail on the origins and development of *huo-chia* and hinges in China mainly to demonstrate the significance of many minor features in design or casting practice in respect to the versatility of the ancient founders. When examining these minutiae, one may feel oneself in

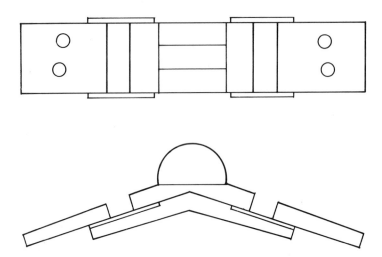

FIGURE 9.9. **A Han period hinge with iron pin from Sha-hu-ch'iao, Ch'ang-sha. The reporters' description is not much clearer than their diagram. (After Li and P'eng 1957:54–55.)**

closer rapport with craftsmen of the time, and sense with them the nature of the technical problems as they arose and how they were approached and solved. A certain amount of subjectiveness necessarily comes into this form of historical appraisal; but after all, it is a case of technically minded men of the present seeking to appreciate fundamental aspects of technical thinking among craftsmen of several millennia ago. The evidence, for the greater part, comprises data of archaeological origin which is sometimes supplemented by the results of scientific investigations of the artifacts themselves, site data, and comparable data from the remains of other cultures. Just as the historian builds his general understanding of the past on the basis of normal documentary evidence, seeking to understand more thoroughly the inner working of the minds of historical personages he studies by "reading between the lines," so too must the historian of technology look deeply into the products of men of the past in his attempts to assess their knowledge, their capabilities, and the degree of their inventiveness. Being in direct contact with artifacts manufactured by the very people he is studying, the historian working on such evidence has a far more direct avenue of communication with men of the past than has the historian proper whose "primary" sources were, at the time of compilation, more often than not essentially "secondary" in scope. The bronze inscription, for instance, records only what the compiler, or the compiler's patron, desired to have recorded for posterity. When endeavoring to build up a picture of Chinese society on the basis of the inscription content, the historian is well enough aware of the limitations attending such sources. He may find all kinds of supplementary evidence resulting from the archaeological activities upon which he draws. But in his quest to understand the upper strata of the society of the time, he will seldom succeed in getting as close to an individual of antiquity as may the historian of technology who is concerned with the products of foundry personnel, potters, lithic craftsmen, or carpenters.

CONCLUSION

Having made these points (which, of course, could be further elaborated), let us cast our attention back to a more remote period, when the progenitors of these craftsmen were in the process of creating what was later to become one of the most advanced metallurgical cultures of the ancient world and, indeed, the most prolific of all in terms of sheer quantity of manufacture and variety in artifact design. The embryo Chinese metallurgist made his appearance in a ceramic milieu that was at least equal to, if not appreciably in advance of, the leading pottery cultures elsewhere, distant from the Chinese scene. Study of kilns, the pottery produced from them, and the long period of development through Yang-shao results in a marked impression of particularly skillful and gifted artisans whose expertise was sufficient to take full advantage of any chance discovery of metal as a product of the smelting of particular ores.[24]

Little thought seems to have been given by those of us who have written

24. I have purposely avoided discussion here of the problem of mining, ore selection, smelting, etc., which Franklin (ch. 10 below) speaks of as Act I in the story of man's mastery of metal, and classes as a highly significant element in the so-called flowering of bronze technology in Shang China; she raises the relevant question whether metallurgy should be "seen as a trigger and an instrument of social advancement" or as "a consequence and indication of a new social order, rather than its cause." Franklin has quite rightly drawn attention to the failure of the authorities she has cited to investigate more fully, in their appraisals of the beginnings of metallurgy, the "metal-winning phase." There are, however, many other scholars who have published valuable surveys and informative articles on ancient mining as practiced in both the Old World and New World cultures; in the case of the latter, some particularly important surveys are available with valuable laboratory-derived data. Study of these researches is especially useful to the historian of Chinese metallurgy, and with due care, extrapolation of some of the data can be made to supplement aspects of our knowledge of Chinese metal-winning activities. Researching the question of mining, both in its pre-Metal Age and Metal Age manifestations, naturally brings to the fore the "question of imported vs. indigenous knowledge of metallurgy," and little if anything of its "sting" is lost. On the contrary, we soon begin to realize that, as Franklin observes, "the all-important knowledge of the transformation by heat of a specific mineral into a metal" is not really such "a major intellectual quantum jump" as some have supposed. As to such "societal requirements" as "a large pool of forced labor," etc., Meacham's timely appraisal (1978) brings us closer to reality and away from the dangers of such pre-conceptional frameworks as "organizational" or "technological determinism" (see Carneiro 1974 for these concepts).

about the beginnings of metallurgy to the time element in the "big bang" stage.[25] Usually, it would appear, the latter-day historian visualizes the pre-historic inventor or discoverer as a rather unimaginative being of limited intellect who will eventually learn only after many generations of forebears have stumbled by accident toward knowledge of a technique, the potential of which can only be slowly perceived and equally slowly applied and developed. I believe some degree of revision of these ideas is required, and that we should consider more realistically (a) the innate ability of man both to invent and to preserve knowledge of his discoveries and (b) the fact that the process of invention and its immediate and effective application is fast rather than slow. Once the discovery is made, its potential realized, and its practicability demonstrated—all of which may occupy the space of mere minutes, or an hour or two—the further understanding of the materials employed, the development of the techniques applied to them, and the appreciation of the full functional value of the resulting artifact, as well as the future extension of the discovery toward the manufacture of other artifacts, and so on, are to be seen as the actual processes that require time and effort (even by modern man).

The hypothetical first true bronze founder in the pre-historic Chinese scene would, as I visualize the situation, have understood and seen the potential of metal as a material that could be molded in a matter of seconds. The right person at the right time would have needed merely to observe a trickle of molten metal issuing from a smelt, filling a natural depression in the ground, and solidifying and taking the form of the depression. Immediately the idea of open mold casting of an artifact would arise and almost certainly be put into practice while it was still possible to retrace the procedure which gave rise to the trickle of molten metal. Similar, and presumably accidental, smelting may well have occurred and caught the notice of other members of the same community, but the phenomenon was treated by them merely as a curiosity. Nevertheless, the discoverer might upon due enquiry be led to the ore site. In the days that follow, we can imagine trial and error attempts at smelting and simple mold production, the adaptation of the kiln for melting, the adaptation of ceramic containers into crucibles, and the search for ways and means to obviate the unsightly

25. The diffusionist will, no doubt, seize upon my use here of this astronomical term as more appropriate to the concept of diffusion than to independent invention or discovery; i.e., there would only have been one "big bang". Whether there is room for multi-bang theorizing in respect to the origins of the universe is well outside my field, but one cannot help but wonder if Judeo-Christian concepts might not have some degree of influence on the interpretation of astronomical data, much as they have on the study of mere human beings.

oxidized exposed surface of the first primitive uni-valve castings. All this, it seems reasonable to assume, would necessarily take place within a short period of time and, to be really successful, under the aegis of the discoverer himself.

Such a hypothesis may raise doubts in the reader's mind; yet further reflection should result in some measure of concurrence in this view. After all, the Chinese invention of roast pork passed fairly rapidly from the initial technique of house-burning to that of kitchen-cooking—and within the lifetime of Bo-bo himself! We can seek a close analogy in the case of a discovery such as the art of metal casting: it would likewise be found wasteful of time and effort to cast metal artifacts directly from the smelter, and re-melting of the smelted "ingots" in the controlled conditions of a kiln (functioning as a furnace) would have come into operation promptly. With so advanced a ceramic industry in Lung-shan/Ch'i-chia China, our hypothetical first founder would have had little difficulty, in the early research and development stages, in having his newly discovered material exploited successfully. He may even have been a potter himself; but we, unlike Charles Lamb, shall never be able to name him. With the centuries-long accumulated experience of many generations of ceramists available to the first founder, the casting of comparatively unsophisticated artifacts would have rapidly passed through the stages of smelting (plus, probably, primitive attempts to directly mold the smelt), melting (involving making crucibles in suitable clay and adapting the kiln for metal melting), and casting (involving the preparation of molds and the prompt discovery that bi-valve moulds would obviate the problems of shaping the exposed metal surface that resulted from primitive uni-valve moulds).

The hypothesis proposed here would appear to offer a possible solution to at least one of the conundrums that have long plagued those who have attempted to explain the alleged "sudden appearance of a highly developed metallurgical art" in ancient China. As I have pointed out in various writings, the least *archaeologically* acceptable theory is that of alien introduction, yet it is this view that has gained so many adherents. Diffusion, or the almost identical concept, stimulus diffusion, has been applied, mainly by those unfamiliar with the basic data within the boundaries of modern China, to "explain" the beginnings of metallurgy there. Together with this lack of fundamental information from the crucial source area, there is often a more serious lack of understanding of the technique in question and the characteristics of the materials to which it is applied, as well as of the standard of technical attainments in the highly relevant ceramic industry in which it made its debut.

It would be fruitless to attempt an assessment of the circumstances attending the first Chinese recognition of metal in both its liquid and solid states. I have loosely referred above to the "smelter" and to "a trickle of molten metal" issuing from it; such looseness is intentional. Many avenues of speculation are possible; but before we can formulate a hypothesis relevant to the discovery of the technique of melting and molding metal, we must allow for the recognition of metal as a material and the awareness of its solid and liquid states. Unless these three fundamental matters had come to the attention of the discoverer-to-be, he would probably have been unable to conceive the idea of casting artifacts in metal. It is at this point (Act II; see n. 24), therefore, that we can utilize known technical data and available archaeological information to reconstruct a model of what essentially took place. And these are the only two types of data we can employ with confidence to establish a working hypothesis.

First, we know from archaeological sources that the stage was set for the casting of metal artifacts as soon as knowledge of the material and its properties in liquid and solid forms had come to the attention of the right person. The relevant details of the highly advanced ceramic industry are conveniently available in *Metallurgical Remains* and need not be repeated here. Second, we know from studying the metal artifacts unearthed from the earliest manifestations of metallurgy reported to date that the principle of annealing was unknown and that there was no metal-working in ancient China. Accordingly, arguments for diffusion or stimulus diffusion cannot be sustained without recourse to highly speculative interpretations (see *Metallurgical Remains* for a comprehensive appraisal). Third, we must consider the practical aspects of the discovery process of the technique under review; metals behaved identically in antiquity as they do now under comparable conditions. So, we can take into account the essential characteristics of metals as a means of establishing how the discovery of casting progressed (once the materials and their characteristics were recognized) and, most important for purposes of interpretation, the speed with which the embryo founder progressed from uni-valve to multi-valve casting.

Only while writing about the transition from uni-valve to bi-valve molds some months ago did the significance of the time involved in the Chinese case suddenly strike me.[26] Obviously, the discoverer had to become aware

---

26. It seems useful to recall here that ideas often come to light suddenly during the course of daily research and writing; and once their significance in a wider context is appreciated, actually writing them up may take only an hour or two—or a long period of further research and careful presentation. Analogies with the discoveries of metals and their casting properties and, of course, with almost everything else man has discovered or invented may be valid here.

of metal as a (presumably) new material in his experience. But he still would not have discovered casting until he had learned that the new material could be melted and would assume the inside shape of the container in which it solidified. How he discovered these properties of metals is a problem of minor importance; that the discovery was made is all we need be concerned with now.

The hypothetical first founder would have progressed rapidly toward bi-valve casting and, during the course of his research and development of the new technique, would have overcome most of the problems with the crucible, furnace, and molds. The use of cores may well have developed within a short period; and it would not be surprising if even the successful casting of containers took place in the lifetime of the first founder! I put forth this hypothesis of speed quite seriously, but not with any claims to long and mature thought: the idea was barely twenty-four hours old as I originally wrote these lines.

REFERENCES

An-hui-sheng po-wu-kuan and An-hui-sheng wei-yüan-hui An-hui-sheng po-wu-kuan 安徽省博物舘 and An-hui-sheng wen-wu kuan-li wei-yüan-hui 安徽省文物管理委員會.

1956   *Shou-hsien Ts'ai-hou-mu ch'u-t'u yi-wu* 壽縣蔡侯墓出土遺物. Peking.

Barnard, Noel

1961   *Bronze Casting and Bronze Alloys in Ancient China.* Monumenta Serica Monograph No. 14. Canberra and Tokyo.

1975   *The First Radiocarbon Dates from China.* Monographs on Far Eastern History No. 8. Rev. and enl. ed. Canberra.

1976   "Notes on Selected Bronze Artifacts in the National Palace Museum, the Historical Museum, and Academia Sinica." In *Ancient Chinese Bronzes and Southeast Asian Metal and Other Archaeological Artifacts*, edited by Noel Barnard: pp. 47–82. Melbourne.

1977   "Radiocarbon Dates from China: Batch No. 4 and Some Others." Mimeographed. Canberra.

1979   *Radiocarbon Dates and Their Significance in the Chinese Archaeological Scene: A List of 280 Entries Compiled from*

Chinese Sources Published up to Close of 1978. Canberra.

in press (a)   "Some Observations on Metal-Winning and the
'Societal Requirements' of Early Metal Production in
China." In the Proceedings of the Conference "The Origin
of Agriculture and Technology: West or East Asia?" held
in Moesgard, 21–25 November 1978.

in press (b)   "Wrought Metal-Working Prior to Middle Shang(?): A
Problem in Archaeological and Art-Historical Research
Approaches." *Early China* 6 (1980–81).

Barnard, Noel, editor

1974   *Early Chinese Art and its Possible Influence in the Pacific*
Basin, Authorized Taiwan ed. pp. xvii–lvii.

Barnard, Noel, and Satō, Tamotsu

1975   *Metallurgical Remains of Ancient China.* Tokyo.

Barnett, H. G.

1942   "Invention and Cultural Change." *American Anthro-*
pologist, n.s. 44:14–30.

1953   *Innovation: The Basis of Cultural Change.* New York.

Branigan, Keith

1974   *Aegean Metalwork of the Early and Middle Bronze Age.*
Oxford.

Carneiro, Robert L.

1974   "A Reappraisal of the Roles of Technology and Organization in the Origins of Civilization." *American Antiquity*
39.2:179–186.

Chandler, Tertius

1960   "Duplicate Inventions." *American Anthropologist,* n.s.
62.3:495–498.

Chang, Kwang-chih

1977   *The Archaeology of Ancient China.* 3d ed., rev. and enl.
New Haven.

CKKH

1959   *Lo-yang Chung-chou-lu (Hsi-kung tuan)* 洛陽中州路
（西工段）. Chung-kuo t'ien-yeh k'ao-ku pao-kao-chi k'ao-
ku-hsüeh chuan-k'an ting chung ti-ssu-hao 中國田野考古
報告集考古學專刊種第四號. Peking.

Coghlan, H. H.

1956   *Notes on Prehistoric and Early Iron in the Old World.*
Oxford.

Fleming, Stuart
1976   [Book Review of] "Noel Barnard, *Metallurgical Remains of Ancient China.*" *New Scientist*, July 1976:90–91.

Flinders Petrie, W. M.
1974   *Objects of Daily Use.* 1927. Reprinted London.

Gettens, R. J., Clarke, R. S., Jr., and Chase, W. T.
1971   *Two Early Chinese Bronze Age Weapons with Meteoric Iron Blades.* Freer Gallery of Art, Occasional Papers No. 4.1. Washington, D.C.

Hayashi Minao 林巳奈夫
1971   *Chūgoku In Shū jidai no buki* 中国殷周時代の武器. Kyoto.

Ho-pei-sheng po-wu-kuan, T'ai-hsi, and Ho-pei-sheng wen-kuan-ch'u
Ho-pei-sheng po-wu-kuan 河北省博物舘, T'ai-hsi fa-chüeh hsiao-tsu 台西發掘小組, and Ho-pei-sheng wen-kuan-ch'u 河北省文管處.
1974   "Ho-pei Kao-ch'eng-hsien T'ai-hsi-ts'un Shang-tai yi-chih 1973 nien ti chung-yao fa-hsien 河北藁城縣臺西村商代遺址1973年的重要發現." *WW* 1974.8:42–49.

Hsia Nai 夏鼐
1973   "Fu-lu: Yeh-chin kung-yeh-pu kang-t'ieh yen-chiu-yüan shih-yen pao-kao 附錄: 冶金工業部鋼鐵研究院試驗報告." *KK* 1973.5:270–271.

Hu-nan-sheng   Hu-nan-sheng po-wu-kuan 湖南省博物舘
1959   Ch'ang-sha-shih tung-pei-chiao ku-mu fa-chüeh chien-pao 長沙市東北郊古墓發掘簡報." *KK* 1959.12:649–654.

Kroeber, A. L.
1940   "Stimulus Diffusion." *American Anthropologist*, n.s. 42.1: 1–20.

Kuo Pao-chün 郭寶鈞
1959   *Shan-piao-chen yü Liu-li-ko* 山彪鎮與琉璃閣. K'ao-ku-hsüeh chuan-k'an yi chung ti shih-yi hao 考古學專刊乙種第十一號. Peking.

Li Cheng-kuang 李正光 and P'eng Ch'ing-yeh 彭青野
1957   "Ch'ang-sha Sha-hu-ch'iao yi-tai ku-mu fa-chüeh pao-kao 長沙沙湖橋一帶古墓發掘報告." *KKHP* 1957.4:33–69.

Li Chung 李衆
1976   "Kuan-yü Kao-ch'eng Shang-tai t'ung-yüeh t'ieh-jen ti

fen-hsi 關於藁城商代銅鉞鐵刃的分析." *KKHP* 1976.2:
17–34.

Meacham, William
1978   "Stratification, Exploitation, Slavery, and the Origins of
            Chinese Civilization." *Ching-feng* 20.3:152–161.

Mizuno Seiichi 水野清一
1946   *Wan-an Pei-sha-ch'eng* 萬安北沙城. Tōhō Kōkogaku
            sōkan itsushu dai-gosatsu 東方考古學叢刊乙種第五册.
            Tokyo.

Needham, Joseph
1971   *Science and Civilization in China*, vol. 4: *Physics and
            Physical Technology*. Part 2: "Mechanical Engineering,"
            with the collaboration of Wang Ling. Cambridge,
            England.

Shan-hsi-sheng   Shan-hsi-sheng wen-wu kuan-li wei-yüan-hui
                          山西省文物管理委員會
1957   "Shan-hsi Ch'ang-chih-shih Fen-shui-ling ku-mu ti
            ch'ing-li 山西長治市分水嶺古墓的清理." *KKHP* 1957.1:
            103–118.

Smith, Cyril Stanley
1977   [Book Reviews of] "Noel Barnard and Tamotsu Satō,
            Metallurgical Remains of Ancient China; and Ping-ti Ho,
            *The Cradle of the East: An Enquiry into the Indigenous
            Origins of Techniques and Ideas of Neolithic and Early
            Historical China, 5000–1000 B.C.*" *Technology and Culture*
            18.1:80–86.

Tylecote, R. F.
1962   *Metallurgy in Archaeology*. London.
1976   *A History of Metallurgy*. London.

Untracht, Oppi
1968   *Metal Techniques for Craftsmen*. London.

Wu Chen-feng 吳鎮烽 and Shang Chih-ju 尚志儒
1975   "Shen-hsi Hu-hsien Sung-ts'un Ch'un-ch'iu Ch'in mu fa-
            chüeh chien-pao 陝西戶縣宋村春秋秦墓發掘簡報."
            WW 1975.10:55–67.

Wu-sheng
1958   *Shen-hsi Chiang-su Je-ho An-hui Shan-hsi wu-sheng ch'u-t'u
            chung-yao wen-wu chan-lan* 陝西江蘇熱河安徽山西五省
            出土重要文物展覽. Peking.

WW

1955.10   "Shan-hsi-sheng Wen-kuan-hui tsai Ch'ang-chih-shih pei-chiao ch'ing-li le yi-p'i ku-mu 山西省文管會在長治市北郊清理了一批古墓 ": pp. 117–118.

Yüan Chin-ching 袁進京 and Chang Hsien-te 張先得

1977   "Pei-ching-shih P'ing-ku-hsien fa-hsien Shang-tai mu-tsang 北京市平谷縣發現商代墓葬." *WW* 1977.11:1–8.

Yün-nan-sheng   Yün-nan-sheng po-wu-kuan 雲南省博物館

1959   *Yün-nan Chin-ning Shih-chai-shan ku-mu ch'ün fa-chüeh pao-kao* 雲南晉寧石寨山古墓羣發掘報告. 2 vols. Peking.

NOTE: I wish to express my gratitude to Miss Winifred Mumford for undertaking the task of preparing the artwork in this paper.

10

On Bronze and Other Metals
in Early China

URSULA   MARTIUS   FRANKLIN

PERSPECTIVES

The past three decades have given those who are interested in the development of Chinese bronze technology a rich harvest of new finds. The amount of material and its diversity is almost overwhelming. It might therefore be useful to step back from the abundance of detailed evidence to address the more general question: What can the appearance of metal—in small or large quantities—tell us about an ancient society, particularly Chinese society? After all, interest in an artifact is not directed solely to the object per se, as a product, but to the information conveyed by the object about the processes by which it was created, both in technological and societal terms.

To discuss the archaeological significance of bronze and other metals in a contemporary context, one must acknowledge the profound re-examination of the scholarly base and the interpretive assumptions of anthropology and archaeology that has occurred throughout the world. The very meaning of artifacts and their weight and role in the reconstruc-tion of prehistorical societies is being questioned and reassessed. The effectiveness of various levers of social change, from population pressure and ecological changes to migration and war, are now studied, modeled, and debated by archaeologists such as Renfrew (1973) and Klejn (1977).

NOTE: The work reported here is part of a larger study supported by Canada Council and the National Research Council of Canada.

The increased use of scientific tools in the study and evaluation of artifacts, in the characterization and dating of archaeological finds, and in the correlation of evidence and model-building has had considerable impact on archaeological theory and practice (Brothwell and Higgs 1969; Franklin 1977). Increased archaeological activities have yielded new and different forms of evidence, obtained under more controled and better described conditions. Probably the most spectacular increase in archaeological material has come from the People's Republic of China.

In light of these major developments one might find it surprising that, although much has been written about metal in early China, surprisingly little has changed in the perspectives of the discussions over the years. To understand why so much of the new evidence relating to bronze in ancient China is used to answer old questions, it may be helpful to recall the intellectual framework in which the discussions began.

When ritual Chinese bronzes of considerable antiquity first became part of the global inventory of ancient artifacts, their appearance, type, and style had to be explained both in terms of their being Chinese and in terms of their being bronze. The Chinese historical records provided adequate guidance for placing the artifacts in their social context within China; but attempts to place them also into the accepted archaeological framework revealed a mis-match that was immediately noted. Chinese bronzes did not seem to fit well into the essentially evolutionary ideas of the development of all civilizations along analogous patterns.

Even objects that were considered chronologically early seemed to be technologically and artistically mature. The expected path of learning, the slow progression from the simple to the sophisticated, could not be traced on these bronzes to art historians' satisfaction.

Because ideas of the growth of civilizations had been so strongly influenced by the successful grouping of European antiquities into Stone, Bronze, and Iron "ages," and by the useful extension of this scheme to the Mediterranean and the Near East, the appearance of metal objects took on pronounced evolutionary connotations. Bronze objects especially were endowed with an almost mythical significance. In some way they were seen as signaling the transition into adulthood of a civilization, thus becoming an essential element in the definition of civilization itself. It is well to remember the value-laden persuasiveness of this somewhat axiomatic assumption in the archaeological theory of the time when one tries to understand the debates about the origin of Chinese metallurgy.

After World War II, the United Nations Scientific and Cultural Organization (UNESCO) asked Sir Leonard Woolley to compile a chapter on the Bronze Age for its *History of Mankind: Cultural and Scientific Development* (see Woolley 1963). Wooley stressed in many ways the central role of the Bronze Age in the development of all mankind. For instance, in summarizing his chapter he stated, "Our account began at the point at which man was emerging from his primitive savagery, and, with the invention of metal, embarked upon the adventure of progress" (p. 545). Woolley drew the evolutionary dividing line in human history between the Stone Age and the Bronze Age, stating:

> The distinction is a real one, but the vast gulf that separates the cultural state of the neolithic men from that of the developing bronze ages was not due only to the use of metal as such, but to the many other arts and activities, such as sculpture and carpentry which accompanied and were encouraged by metallurgical knowledge (p. 548).

Although Woolley acknowledged that bronze was not necessarily the earliest metal used, he emphasized strongly the significance of bronze. "The chalcolithic age, in spite of the fact that metal was used, is but a late phase of the neolithic and has nothing in common with the bronze age, because the basis of distinction is not the existence of metal, but man's knowledge of metallurgy" (ibid.) It is not surprising, then, that the debates about the origin of Chinese metallurgy, which began within this conceptual framework, were carried out with so much vigor and righteousness in the search for the way China attained the knowledge of metallurgy, that is, civilization.

What seems surprising is that the discussion largely remains within such unaltered perceptual confines (Barnard 1975; Ho 1975). Are we still trying to rehabilitate the Chinese from the blow that bronze objects of the Near East are chronologically much older than those found in China? In order to take a different look at the place of Chinese metallurgy in the scheme of things, we must first consider metal itself.

METAL AS A CLASS OF MATERIALS

It is important to realize that metal as a category of materials is a retrospect concept. What is unique about metals? They are ductile rather than brittle and are therefore resistant to mechanical and thermal shock. Many metals can be dissolved one in another, over considerable ranges of composition, to form alloys with properties different from those of the parent metals. Metals melt congruently, and the shape of the melt is retained on solidification. Metals are good conductors of heat, and they become soft as temperature increases. Because of their ductility they can be mechanically shaped and joined. They can be hardened by mechanical working and take a hard edge. Their very characteristic surface properties include high reflectivity of visible light.

The presence of several of these characteristic properties in different substances leads to recognition of the larger category we call metals. Since the classification is based on behavior and properties, rather than on color, weight, taste, or smell, it can be recognized and applied only *after* these properties have been sufficiently well explored and reproduced. In other words, it is easy to recognize a metal, once it is known what metals are; but it is neither easy nor obvious to speak of metals without enough common experience to recognize the general category. The difficulty of identifying clear and unambiguous terms for specific metals in the early phases of most written languages may well be explained along these lines.

METAL AS A DERIVED MATERIAL

For ancient users of metals, the unique properties of these materials must have been their prime attraction. For the archaeologist and the historian of metallurgy, another of their characteristics is even more important: metals and alloys are *derived* materials. Only gold, and to a very limited extent copper, occurs in nature as metal. All other metals must be produced from suitable ore by a smelting process (Tylecote 1976; Tylecote, et al., 1977).

Figure 10.1 shows a general schematic classification of materials selection and processing from an archaeological perspective. The Group I materials in the first row are substances in which human intervention consists of careful choice of naturally available materials. Flint, granite, obsidian, or jade were carefully chosen, separated from unwanted rock, and prepared into objects by early artisans. Nature provided the raw material; the object was generally fashioned by removing excess material in the shaping process.

In the Group II materials, preparation of the raw material for making an object is more elaborate. In the case of pottery, the naturally occurring constituents—clay, water, and temper—must be selected, prepared, and mixed in proper proportions. From this new composite raw material the object is shaped, usually by addition rather than removal of material. The object is heated to more or less elevated temperatures, producing a new material which does not exist in nature, as well as a new object.

Metals are the prototype of Group III materials, and the necessary steps for raw materials selection and processing are more complex and sophisti-

MATERIALS SELECTION AND PROCESSING

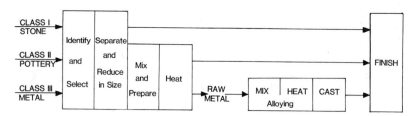

FIGURE 10.1. **Schematic classification of materials selection and processing.**

cated. Figure 10.1 shows schematically that here one is dealing with a two-part operation. Before it is possible to fashion a metal object, the raw material has to be derived by a distinct and separate production process. It is not sufficient to select and mix the component of the starting material. No longer are the details of the raw material preparations directly related to the object to be made, as was the case in the choice of proper clay and temper for ware of a particular type. With metals, preparation of the essential raw material becomes a separate and separable production activity because the raw materials must be derived in a complex manner from naturally occurring minerals.

The mining/smelting phase yields the raw metal ingots or the cakes of matte; they are then purified, alloyed, and made into objects by a variety of techniques.

METAL-WINNING PLUS METAL-FABRICATION EQUALS METALLURGY

One must, therefore, recognize that two areas of knowledge are combined in what is commonly called metallurgy. Since we wish to trace factors that may have influenced the beginning of metallurgy in China, it may be helpful to delineate these areas of knowledge and experience and to specify what each entails.

Metal-winning includes, approximately, the modern field of mining and extractive metallurgy. In this area belongs the all-important knowledge of the transformation by heat of a specific mineral into a metal. The achievement of this knowledge has always been regarded as a major intellectual quantum jump. Here a new and not obvious consideration has entered man's emerging experience with materials. It is for this reason that such experienced historians of metallurgy as Cyril Smith believe humanity may have made this discovery only once (Smith 1973).

But there is more to metal-winning than knowledge of the relation between metal and ore. Suitable minerals must be found, removed from the rock, gathered and separated from gangue, and concentrated and prepared for smelting. Smelting itself requires knowledge of the appropriate conditions of temperature and air supply, of fuel, and of fluxes, as well as avoidance of all substances that would have a detrimental effect on the resulting raw metal. Smelting produces slags which often contain residual metal. In antiquity, slags were often broken up and the metal-rich parts reprocessed (Rothenberg 1972).

The second area of metallurgical knowledge and experience, metal-fabrication, begins when raw metal is available to the artisan. Knowledge of metal purification, refining, and alloying is now needed. The temperature regime for alloying and casting must be known, and fuel, furnaces, crucibles, and tools must be on hand. The expertise of fashioning an object, shaping, decorating, and repairing it falls into the area of metal-fabrication.

Metal artifacts are reasonably stable with respect to time and influence of the environment. Furthermore, it is not too difficult to reconstruct metal fabrication techniques from external examination or technical studies of ancient metal objects (Smith ca. 1968). The micro-structure of a metal retains, as a permanent imprint, evidence of the making and shaping of an artifact. The very certainty and the reproducible details of this information tend to convey the impression that one knows *all* about an object from such studies, when in fact the information pertains to nothing more than Act II in the life of the artifact.

It is far more difficult to discover direct evidence of Act I, the winning of metal, through technical examinations of artifacts. The matching of trace impurity patterns from the analysis of ore sources and artifacts has so far been successful only in limited situations in Europe, for example, in the Austrian Alps (Pittioni 1951), and in some parts of the Soviet Union, where major work in this area is being carried out (Cernych 1977).

Because metal artifacts reveal so much more about metal-fabrication than about metal-winning, the latter is rarely considered in sufficient depth by archaeologists. The presence of suitable ore has often been regarded as sufficient evidence that the necessary raw materials could be obtained. Conversely, the absence of discernible ore bodies or other known sources of raw material has frequently lead to speculations about war, trade, barter, and so on. But even when sources are listed, how and by whom the available raw material was recovered has been given too little thought. With all his interest in bronze, V. Gordon Childe gave Act I barely a passing acknowledgment when remarking, "the exploitation of copper on a large scale implied the solution of delicate problems of mining engineering" (Childe 1930).

There is, nevertheless, an important question here that goes beyond the delicate problems of mining engineering. This is especially so in the case of China because, in my opinion, study of the metal-winning phase of Chinese metallurgy can provide fresh insight into the role of metallurgy in the evolution of Chinese civilization.

METAL TECHNOLOGY: A QUESTION OF SCALE

I have analyzed in such detail the two constituent elements of metallurgy because I wanted to stress that they can be functionally separated. But the advance of metal technology is in fact determined by their interplay.

Whether metal-winning or metal-fabrication determines the rate of progress of metallurgical activities depends on the *scale* of those activities. Considerations of scale are important in reconstructing the technical and societal processes that the occurrence of certain artifacts can indicate. I therefore introduce a distinction between small-scale metallurgical activities, which I call *metal-working*, and large-scale activities, which I call *metal-production*.

In the context of this chapter, the mastery of metal-working signifies the accumulation of experience that leads to the ability to produce metal artifacts, including those made from smelted ore. One would consider as metal-working all those activities that result in a limited number of hand-made objects, such as one might find in late Neolithic settings. Such metal-working activities indicate that craftsmen within a culture can find and process minerals and fashion individual metal objects (most of them small). The size of the objects, as well as the frequency of their occurrence, may provide an indication of time and resource that could be brought to metallurgical activities. Nevertheless, metal-working testifies to the presence of the basic knowledge of metallurgy.

When metal objects are made for a large variety of particular uses, when they make up a sizable fraction of the archaeological inventory and appear in definable and predictable shapes and contexts, it is justifiable to speak of metal-production. Evidence of metal-production is usually interpreted as an indication of social stratification, professional specialization, and permanent production centers. The increase in the scale of metallurgical activities that the transition from metal-working to metal-production indicates certainly signals a growth in technical competence. The increase in technical knowledge is a necessary condition for this transition, but not a sufficient one. It is here worthwhile to inquire into the factors, other than technical knowledge, that made bronze production possible in Shang China. We know in today's world that adequate know-how is not enough to transfer a technology successfully from the laboratory to the factory.

BRONZE PRODUCTION IN EARLY CHINA

It is indeed a picture of bronze production that emerges from the accumulating archaeological evidence. On the basis of new finds, workshops and living quarters of bronze-workers can be reconstructed. The reasonably prestigious placement of the artisans' living and working quarters within the Shang city has been stressed by several commentators (Wheatley 1971; Chang 1977). It is worth noting that in none of the foundries excavated so far were there indications of smelting operations. Raw materials found in the workshops were either copper-carbonates or raw metal ingots; the slags appeared to be melting and refining slags rather than products of smelting.

Literary and archaeological sources reveal much about the status and activities of those who "used" the bronzes. Recent excavations have greatly extended the bronze inventory, providing us with more examples of the utilitarian use of bronze, as well as an abundance of ceremonial and military objects. Referring to all Shang materials technologies, Wheatley has stated: "In short, the overwhelming impression left by a survey of Shang technology is that its progress was a response to, not a determinant of, the emergence of a social class whose primary concerns were with ritual and ceremony" (p. 74). In the reconstructed picture, the bronze foundries appear; so does the class that demands the foundries' products. But what about metal-winning? What do we know about the supply of raw material or mineral concentrate? Very little, indeed, particularly about the politcal or social aspects of this phase of metallurgy.

Shih Chang-ju (1955) has listed and documented the copper and tin deposits located around the Shang capitals, which were mentioned in historical records and were possibly exploited at that time. But ore in the ground cannot be equated with raw material in the workshops. Even in the richest deposits, the useful mineral content is less than 5 percent of the total rock (Toguri 1978). In order to increase the scale of bronze production, a correspondingly large increase in metal-winning activities is needed. The absence of smelting slags in the bronze foundries of Shang cities indicates that smelting must have been carried out at or near the mines. Who were the miners and smelters who provided the large quantities of raw materials? This is no trivial question: such mining, concentrating, and smelting is a major production that requires knowledge, organization, and labor.

MINING IN EARLY CHINA

Evidence of early mining operations is notoriously difficult to obtain because most deposits were exploited more than once; even ancient slags have been reprocessed (*WW* 1975.2:19–25). The archaeological and literary evidence of Chinese mining available to date applies to periods later than the one considered here. The Hupei copper mines, tentatively assigned to the Spring and Autumn period, are sophisticated, large-scale enterprises which show the technical competence with which the Chinese mined in this locality and at that date.

But some characteristics of mining operations apply to the process per se—whenever and wherever it took place. Ancient mining was always highly labor intensive, and very unpleasant and dangerous for the worker. Thus it was usually carried out by forced labor, captives, slaves, or criminals. The description that Diodorus of Sicily gave of the conditions in the Nubian gold mines (see Appendix II) may well apply, in most respects, to all ancient mining. Commenting on this and other classical texts, Rostovtzeff observed for the Hellenistic world:

> Free labour could hardly be used extensively in the ancient mines, for no free man, if he could help it, would commit slow suicide in this way. It is not surprising therefore that whenever we hear of exploitations of mines and quarries we find slaves and criminals, or sometimes the forced labour of free men employed at work . . . . Mass production of metals could not be organized in any other way (1941:1219).

In the context of early China, the sheer scale of bronze production is as impressive as the quality of the craft. Such a level of bronze production demands, as a prerequisite, a well-organized large-scale mining and smelting industry. It seems to me that this could not have been in effect without a large pool of forced labor, a pool much larger in number than the workers required to produce the objects.

Mining may have been only one component in a network of organized labor activity that existed in Shang China. Keightley (1969) has documented the extent of the permanent and temporary work forces at the disposal of the Shang ruler. He shows the major role they played in agriculture, construction, and warfare. Mining could well have been part of such activities.

If one accepts this analysis, the beginnings of bronze production in China indicate the presence of a social order with sufficient organization and force to generate and replenish the required reservoir of forced labor. Whereas the metallurgical competence of the bronze founders may explain the technical quality of the objects, only the social order, in terms of supply of forced labor, can account for the quantity produced. In this framework, arguments about the beginning of metal production focus much more on social organization; and the question of imported versus indigenous knowledge of metallurgy loses much of its sting. One can now see that in the early phase of metal-working a society will develop the experience with and understanding of metals as part of the exploration of their material world. Where and how this understanding is utilized, developed, and expanded is far more a question of supply and demand, that is, societal factors, than of technical competence.

Returning to the original archaeological paradigm in which metallurgy is seen as a trigger and an instrument of social advancement, it should be emphasized again that from the perspective developed here, the "flowering of bronze technology" in Shang China was more a consequence and indication of a new social order than its cause. A feedback process was involved in which this newly emerging social order made the application of a particular technology interesting and feasible. This development resulted in the strengthening of that particular social order which in turn would have led to a further advancement of the technology.

One might assume that historians and archaeologists would be kept occupied by the question of whether a certain type and scale of production—such as the winning of metal—needed the establishment of a certain social order before it could be carried out. Most of them, even those of Marxist training, have been interested instead largely in trade, redistribution, and the development of property. The arguments of Wittfogel (1957) and his commentators appear to me to bear only marginally on early metal-production. Wittfogel is basically concerned with the impact of certain public works on the mode of governance. Wilbur (1943), Pulleyblank (1958), and others (e.g., Jones 1956), who have discussed slavery, have focused mainly on human beings as private or state property. Even discussions within China on the periodization of Chinese history have centered heavily on the development of private property (Dirlik 1974).

They do not seem to have addressed in detail the question of the origin of bronze, in terms of societal requirements for its production.

For the specific case of early China, however, it may be possible to test the reasoning developed here by calling on other sources of evidence. Foremost among them are oracle bone records. Keightley ("Conclusions: The Incipient Dynastic State," in ch. 17 below) points to the changing content of these inscriptions. He comments that "the reduced scope and routine nature of the late divination record may reflect precisely the increasing secularization of the king's activities, his increasing ability to command rather than cajole." The tribal wars, the military campaigns, and the "hunting expeditions" recorded in these inscriptions have been examined (Keightley 1969; ch. 17 below). Ho (1975:187) has suggested that the interest of the later Shang kings in southern Shansi was related to safeguarding the major region of copper supply. Do the expeditions relate to sources of raw materials or to the supply routes? A re-examination of the archaeological and inscriptional evidence with such hypotheses in mind may well throw more light on the links between state formation and technology.

In terms of the question posed at the beginning of this chapter regarding what the appearance of metal can convey about an ancient society, the central argument I put forward here is one of scale. A distinction between metal-working and metal-production has been introduced. Metal-working—demonstrated in the archaeological inventory by a limited number of artifact types, many of them small—shows the presence of the basic knowledge of metals technology. The transition to metal-production, on the other hand, is seen to signify more than just greater knowledge. To cast the large and sophisticated bronze vessels of Shang China required labor resources, particularly for the metal-winning, that were different in scale from the resources needed for metal-working.

Thus a social order in which a large pool of forced labor could be mobilized and maintained was necessary for bronze production. Seen in this light, the Shang bronzes testify that this type of social order was present when they were made.

APPENDIX I: A METALLURGICAL PUZZLE

Having focused in the body of this chapter on what Chinese metal-workers did, it may be instructive to examine what they chose not to do. It is perhaps normal to assume that whatever could be done technically would be done; but, surveying the world-wide inventory of early metal-work,

TABLE 10.1 **Finds of Gold Foil in Shang China**

Location	Reference	Number of Items
Shantung		
Yi-tu	Shan-tung-sheng 1972	14
Hopei		
P'ing-ku	Pei-ching-shih 1977	unknown
Honan		
Cheng-chou	*KKHP* 1957.1	unknown
An-yang	Shih 1970	7
An-yang	Shih 1974	24
An-yang	Ma, Chou, and Chang 1955	unknown
An-yang	*KK* 1958.8	unknown

some striking examples exist of what Chinese craftsmen chose not to fashion from metal. A few remarks about the use of gold and the nature of personal ornaments in early China are appropriate here.

Gold is of interest because more gold objects exist in early China than is commonly assumed. The samples are mostly foil, often thinly and carefully hammered. Table 10.1 presents several of the more important Shang examples. (The dating is that of the excavators.) Since gold is a favorite target of tomb robbers, the actual inventory may have been much larger.

There is little question that gold was available; what is surprising is the almost trivial use to which it was put. For instance, gold sheets were wrapped around wooden objects and apparently were used mainly for their contrasting color. One such object, a standard from Hsiao-t'un, has been described in detail by Shih (1970). Apparently the gold foil was wrapped around the tip of the standard. Twenty-four pieces of foil cataloged by the excavators range in thickness from 0.05 to 2 mm. Similar dimensions have been reported from other sites. At somewhat later sites gold foil is used in inlays of bronze vessels. One excavator noted, in commenting on the fine, even quality of the gold foils he had found, that "at this time gold and turquoise inlays were well-known" (Shan-tung-sheng 1972). Thus gold appears to have been valued because with it decorative effects could be achieved that no other material could provide: gold conveyed beauty, but not necessarily status.

The deployment of gold is indicative of a peculiar Chinese preference that becomes apparent in comparing the inventory of early metal objects from a variety of civilizations. In many cultures one observes a characteristic pattern of incorporation of any new metal: it is first used in an ornamental fashion that does not require good mechanical properties. At this stage one finds pendants, rings, and tubular beads, as well as needles, awls, or pins. (As the metal-working knowledge and supplies develop, ritual, ceremonial, and military uses of the metal occur before purely utilitarian applications.) It is common in many cultures that personal ornaments of copper, bronze, or gold are indications of status and accompany the owner into the after-life.

It is therefore striking that personal ornaments in early China are *not* made of metal. There are ornaments of shells, bone, and jade, or ceramic and stone beads, but not of metal. I know of nothing in early China that corresponds to the metal bracelets and ankle bands found in Thailand or the tubular beads, rings, and pendants so abundant in southern Siberia. These are well represented by the head decorations found in situ during a recent excavation of a Karasuk cemetery site in the Minusinsk basin (Zurba 1977). A leather band was placed around the head of the deceased. The band was decorated with two spirals of arsenical copper, one at each temple; and a piece of antler, a small metal "button," and several tubular beads seem to have been sewn onto the band. A necklace of tubular beads was also on the skeleton. The excavators consider this a standard Karasuk burial. It is to be hoped that C–14 dates will be available soon for this site.

Although there is an abundance of simple personal metal ornaments in southern Siberia, and metal objects are used as personal decoration, the situation in China is quite different. Cheng Te-k'un (1960) lists in detail the Shang industries and the types of objects they produced; personal decorations in metal are not among them. Horses and chariots are lavishly decorated with bronze ornaments, but people are adorned with "natural" materials. (Belt hooks, which are of course later than the period discussed here, are more an item of clothing than of personal ornamentation.) There must be profound cultural reasons for not using metals, precious or ordinary, as they could have been used at any time.[1]

---

1. Investigators have reported a few gold items identified as personal ornaments, such as rings, hairpins, and earrings. The most notable earring sets are reported from a Shang tomb at Yung-ho, Shansi (Kuo Yung 1962), and from Shih-lou, Shansi (Shih-lou-hsien 1977). Earrings, armlets, and hairpins were recently reported from a Shang dynasty tomb in P'ing-ku-hsien, Peking (Yüan and Chang 1977). This site has drawn considerable interest because it also contained a *yüeh* ax with an iron blade (see "Splay-Blade Axes," in Barnard, ch. 9 above). The gold objects were analyzed and found to be 85 percent gold and 15 percent silver and were thought to be cast. The bronze of the *yüeh* ax is high in tin. The excavators have dated the site as not later than An-yang. Although such finds do exist and more may come to light, they represent but a small fraction of personal ornaments, considering the large number of shell, bone, and jade objects of personal decoration that have been found.

APPENDIX II: DIODORUS OF SICILY ON GOLD
MINING IN NUBIA

. . . here the overseers of the labour in the mines recover the gold with the aid of a multitude of workers. For the kings of Egypt gather together and condemn to the mining of the gold such as have been found guilty of some crime and captives of war, as well as those who have been accused unjustly and thrown into prison because of their anger, and not only such persons but occasionally all their relatives as well, by this means not only inflicting punishment upon those found guilty but also securing at the same time great revenues from their labours. And those who have been condemned in this way—and they are a great multitude and are all bound in chains—work at their task unceasingly both by day and throughout the entire night, enjoying no respite and being carefully cut off from any means of escape; since guards of foreign soldiers who speak a language different from theirs stand watch over them, so that not a man, either by conversation or by some contact of a friendly nature, is able to corrupt one of his keepers. The gold-bearing earth which is hardest they first burn with a hot fire, and when they have crumbled it in this way they continue the working of it by hand; and the soft rock which can yield to moderate effort is crushed with a sledge by myriads of unfortunate wretches. And the entire operations are in charge of a skilled worker who distinguishes the stone and points it out to the labourers; and of those who are assigned to this unfortunate task the physically strongest break the quartz-rock with iron hammers, applying no skill to the task, but only force, and cutting tunnels through the stone, not in a straight line but wherever the seam of gleaming rock may lead. Now these men, working in darkness as they do because of the bending and winding of the passages, carry lamps bound on their foreheads; and since much of the time they change the position of their bodies to follow the particular character of the stone they throw the blocks, as they cut them out, on the ground; and at this task they labour without ceasing beneath the sternness and blows of an overseer.

The boys there who have not yet come to maturity, entering through the tunnels into the galleries formed by the removal of the rock, laboriously gather up the rock as it is cast down piece by piece and carry it out into the open to the place outside the entrance. Then those who are above thirty years of age take this quarried stone from them and with iron pestles pound a specified amount of it in stone mortars, until they have worked it down to the size of a vetch. Thereupon the women and older men receive from them the rock of this size and cast it into mills of which a number stand there in a row, and taking their places in groups of two or three at the spoke or handle of each mill they grind it until they have worked down the amount given them to the consistency of the finest flour. And since no opportunity is afforded any of them to care for his body and they have no garment to cover their shame, no man can look upon the unfortunate wretches without feeling pity for them because of the exceeding hardships they suffer. For no leniency or respite of any kind is given to any man who is sick, or maimed, or aged, or in the case of a woman for her weakness, but all without exception are compelled by blows to persevere in their labours, until through ill-treatment they die in the midst of their tortures. Consequently the poor unfortunates believe, because their punishment is so excessively severe, that the future will always be more terrible than the present and therefore look forward to death as more to be desired than life (Oldfather 1933).

REFERENCES

Barnard, Noel
1961   *Bronze Casting and Bronze Alloys in Ancient China.*
        Monumenta Serica Monograph No. 14. Canberra and
        Tokyo.

Brothwell, D., and Higgs, E.
1969   *Science in Archaeology: A Survey of Progress and
        Research.* London.

Cernych, E. N.
1977   "Metallurgische Bereiche des 4.–2. Jahrtausand v. Chr. in
        der USSR." In *International Congress of Prehistoric and
        Protohistoric Sciences*: pp. 177–196. Nice.

Chang, K. C.
1977   *The Archaeology of Ancient China.* 3d ed., rev. and enl.
        New Haven.

Cheng, Te-k'un
1960   *Archaeology in China,* vol. 2: *Shang China.* Cambridge,
        Eng.

Childe, V. Gordon
1930   *The Bronze Age.* Cambridge, Eng.

Dirlik, Arif
1974   "Mirror to Revolution: Early Marxist Images of Chinese
        History." *Journal of Asian Studies* 33.2:193–223.

Franklin, U. M.
1977   "The Science of Ancient Materials—A New Scholarly
        Field." *Canadian Mining and Metallurgy Bulletin*
        70.3:1–4.

Ho, Ping-ti
1975   *The Cradle of the East: An Inquiry into the Indigenous
        Origins of Techniques and Ideas of Neolithic and Early
        Historic China, 5000–1000 B.C.* Hong Kong and Chicago.

Jones, A. H. M.
1956   "Slavery in the Ancient World." *Economic History Review*
        2d ser. 60.2:185–199.

Keightley, David N.
1969   "Public Work in Ancient China: A Study of Forced Labor

in the Shang and Western Chou." Ph.D. dissertation, Columbia University.

KK
1958.8   "Ho-nan An-yang Hsüeh-chia-chuang Yin-tai yi-chih, mu-tsang ho t'ang-mu fa-chüeh chien-pao 河南安陽薛家莊殷代遺址, 墓葬和唐墓發掘簡報 ": pp. 23–26.

KKHP
1957.1   "Cheng-chou Shang-tai yi-chih ti fa-chüeh 鄭州商代遺址的發掘 ": pp. 53–73.

Klejn, Leo S.
1977   "A Panorama of Theoretical Archaeology." *Current Anthropology* 18.1:1–41.

Kuo Yung 郭勇
1962   "Shih-lou Hou-lan-chia-kou fa-hsien Shang-tai ch'ing-t'ung chien-pao 石樓後蘭家溝發現商代青銅簡報." *WW* 1962.4/5:33–34.

Liang Ssu-yung 梁思永 and Kao Ch'ü-hsün 高去尋
1974   *Hou-chia-chuang 1500-hao ta mu* 侯家莊1500號大墓. Taipei.

Ma Te-chih 馬得志, Chou Yung-chen 周永珍, and Chang Yün-p'eng 張雲鵬
1955   "Yi-chiu wu-san nien An-yang Ta-ssu-k'ung-ts'un fa-chüeh pao-kao 一九五三年安陽大司空村發掘報告." *KKHP* 1955.9:25–90.

Oldfather, C. H., trans.
1933   *Diodorus of Sicily*. Book 3, vol. 2:115–118. Cambridge, Mass., and London.

Pei-ching-shih   Pei-ching-shih wen-wu kuan-li-ch'u 北京市文物管理處
1977   "Pei-ching-shih P'ing-ku-hsien fa-hsien Shang-tai mu-tsang 北京市平谷縣發現商代墓葬." *WW* 1977.11:1–9.

Pittioni, R.
1951   *Prehistoric Copper Mining in Austria: Problems and Facts*. Institute of Archaeology, University of London, Report no. 7:16–43.

Pulleyblank, E. G.
1958   "The Origins and Nature of Chattel Slavery in China." *Journal of Economic and Social History of the Orient* 1:185–220.

Renfrew, C., ed.
1973   *The Explanation of Culture Change: Models in Prehistory.*
            Proceedings of a meeting of the Research Seminar in
            Archaeology and Related Subjects held at the University
            of Sheffield. London.

Rostovtzeff, M.
1941   *The Social and Economic History of the Hellenistic World.*
            Oxford.

Rothenberg, B.
1972   *Timna: Valley of the Biblical Copper Mines.* London.

Shan-tung-sheng   Shan-tung-sheng po-wu-kuan 山東省博物舘
1972   "Shan-tung Yi-tu Su-fu-t'un ti-yi-hao nu-li-hsün tsang-mu
            山東益都蘇埠屯第一號奴隸殉葬墓 ." *WW* 1972.8:17–29.

Shih Chang-ju 石璋如
1955   "Yin-tai ti chu-t'ung kung-yi 殷代的鑄銅工藝," *BIHP*
            26:95–129.
1970   *Hsiao-t'un ti-yi-pen: yi-chih ti fa-hsien yü fa-chüeh, ping-*
            pien: Yin-hsü mu-tsang 小屯第一本: 遺址的發現與發掘,
            丙編: 殷虛墓葬. Nanking.

Shih-lou-hsien   Shih-lou-hsien wen-wu-kuan 石樓縣文物舘
1977   "Shan-hsi Yung-ho fa-hsien Yin-tai t'ung-ch'i 山西永和
            發現殷代銅器." *KK* 1977.5:355–356.

Smith, C. S.
circa 1968   "The Interpretation of Microstructures of Metallic
            Artifacts." In *Applications of Science in Examination of*
            Works of Art: pp. 20–52. Boston.
1973   "Bronze Technology in The East." In *Changing*
            Perspectives in the History of Science: Essays in Honour of
            Joseph Needham, edited by M. Teich and R. Young:
            pp. 21–32. London.

Toguri, J. M.
1978   Personal communication.

Tylecote, R. F.
1976   *A History of Metallurgy.* London.

Tylecote, R. F., Ghaznavi, H. A., and Boydell, P. J.
1977   "Partitioning of Trace Elements Between the Ores, Fluxes,
            Slags and Metal During the Smelting of Copper." *Journal*
            of Archaeological Science 4:305–333.

Wheatley, P.
1971   *The Pivot of the Four Quarters: A Preliminary Enquiry into the Origins and Character of the Ancient Chinese City.* Chicago.

Wilbur, C. M.
1943   "Industrial Slavery in China." *Journal of Economic History* 3:56–69.

Wittfogel, K.
1957   *Oriental Despotism: A Comparative Study of Total Power.* New Haven.

Woolley, Leonard
1963   *History of Mankind: Cultural and Scientific Development,* vol. 1. Part 2 of *The Beginnings of Civilization,* UNESCO. London.

WW
1975.2   "Hu-pei T'ung-lü-shan Ch'un-ch'iu Chan-kuo ku k'uang-ching yi-chih fa-chüeh chien-pao 湖北銅綠山春秋戰國古礦井遺址發掘簡報": pp. 1–12.
            "Hu-pei T'ung-lü-shan Ch'un-ch'iu Chan-kuo ku k'uang-ching yi-chih shih nu-li ch'uang-tsao li-shih ti kuang-hui chien-cheng 湖北銅綠山春秋戰國古礦井遺址是奴隸創造歷史的光輝見証": pp. 13–18.
            "T'ung-lü-shan ku k'uang-ching yi-chih ch'u-t'u t'ieh-chih chi t'ung-chih kung-chü ti ch'u-pu chien-ting 銅綠山古礦井遺址出土鐵製及銅製工具的初步鑒定": pp. 19–25.

Yüan Chin-ching 袁進京 and Chang Hsien-te 張先得
1977   "Pei-ching-shih P'ing-ku-hsien fa-hsien Shang-tai mu-tsang 北京平谷縣發現商代墓葬." *WW* 1977.11:1–8.

Zurba, Roman
1977   Personal communication

11

Origins of the Chinese People:
Interpretations of the Recent Evidence

W. W. HOWELLS

The physical origin of the Chinese people is rendered obscure by the paucity of evidence—evidence which is remarkably poor for so great and important an area. I shall here consider ways of looking at this problem (which involves conflicts of view past and present), then proceed to methods of evaluating such data as do exist and of extracting legitimate information from them. The central questions are: (1) how the whole Mongoloid branch of living man arose and, more important here, (2) how and when further differentiation took place within it, leading in this case to what we recognize as the Chinese.

For ultimate origins, we must not ignore the Peking man population of Chou-k'ou-tien, the group of fossil specimens which largely serves to define *Homo erectus* of the Middle Pleistocene. Weidenreich (1943), and Coon (1962) after him, argued for genetic continuity from Peking man to modern Mongoloids on the basis of common cranial and dental features (for

NOTE: The main data reported in this chapter were gathered in work supported by National Science Foundation grants GS–2645. I am greatly obliged to my colleague Kwang-chih Chang for guiding me through Chinese literature. I am also indebted for help in the gathering of material and for hospitality to Professors Li Chi and Yang Hsi-mei of Academia Sinica and Yü Chin-ch'üan of National Taiwan University. I am grateful, too, to the hosts of the Paleoanthropolgical Delegation which visited the People's Republic of China in 1975, and to the sponsors of the delegation via the Committee for Scholarly Communication with the People's Republic of China: the American Council of Learned Societies, the National Academy of Sciences, and the Social Science Research Council. Funding was provided by the National Science Foundation.

example, special bony growths like mandibular tori or exostoses in the ear canal and shovel-shaped incisors, which are varyingly common in present-day Mongoloid populations). This argument is not unpersuasive, but it is not especially helpful without fuller concrete knowledge of the actual pattern of intervening hominid evolution. Nor is it helpful regarding the specific origins of the Chinese, except to make East Asiatic continuity a logical hypothesis. Both Weidenreich and Coon believed that Peking man was ancestral exclusively to the Mongoloids, and that separate contemporaneous early hominids led to the other races of present-day man. Other writers, myself included, think it more likely that, because of their basic cranial similarities, all modern men have a common ancestor who was later than Peking man. In this case Peking man, or the general *Homo erectus* matrix of which he formed a part, might well be the direct source of that common ancestor. Such a possibility would be enhanced by excluding Europe and western Asia from consideration on the grounds that they are the homeland of a different line of ascent culminating in the Neanderthals. Even so, the slowly gathering evidence has yet to point unequivocally to the hearth of modern populations.

Nor is the age of recognizably modern man, and thus the maximum age of a definably Mongoloid branch, any clearer at the moment. Present estimates are mostly guesses, sometimes poor. A definitely modern skeleton, though racially unassignable, from the Omo valley in East Africa is likely to be at least one hundred thousand years old (Day 1972.) A minimum for the existence of fully developed racial forms like those of today is forty thousand years, set by the establishment of the aboriginals in Australia, followed by the datable Caucasoid invasions of Europe a few thousand years later. Shakier evidence admits the American Indians to the Americas not long after (Stewart 1974).

Datable Mongoloids, however, other than the American branch, hardly exist. The Liu-chiang skeleton found in Kwangsi is, I fully agree with Woo Ju-kang (Woo 1959), definitely of a generalized Mongoloid character, though the date is indefinite. It has a somewhat un-Chinese appearance, particularly in the short face and low orbital openings. At the least, it seems to place Mongoloid occupation of South China as far back as the late Pleistocene. We may remark that Mongoloid populations, in history and prehistory, seem to have moved outward rather than to have suffered important incursions of non-Mongoloids; this is reflected in the original populating of the Americas, of course, as well as in later pressures of movement into Indonesia and the Pacific—all before the historic invasions of the West. This makes it all the harder to discern some well-localized area for an origin but it is not necessary to assume such a localization rather than a region of common development characterized by an internal balance of gene flow with local micro-evolution and diversification.

In this context we come to a major point of anthropological theorizing. About two generations ago, intermixture or hybridizing of diverse racial strains or types was assumed to be the explanation of any detectable local physical diversity, as well as of any appearance of variety, or seemingly different "types," within a given population. A single American Indian cranial series has been analyzed as representing an amalgam of Negroids, Australoids, Mediterranean Caucasoids, and of course Mongoloids. Polynesians have been viewed as a mixture of migrant Melanesians, Indonesians, Caucasoids, and others (including, in a more recent evangel, American Indians of both continents). This kind of scenario puts the matter of origins back a whole stage—races are mixtures of previous races—and creates a picture of energetic migrations of quite distinct peoples around and through northeast Asia, for example, something not supported by archaeological evidence. (It is true that proponents of these ideas have softened them somewhat by assuming that alleged Negroids were not fully developed like the Africans but were in an incipient stage; but this does not affect the basic hypothesis.)

This theory is also unsupported by the actual cranial evidence. Polynesians and American Indians, though their local tribes or groups are varied in this respect, each have unifying and distinctive cranial conformations which seem to establish them as major regional varieties (of Mongoloid) in their own right. For example, from work which is still preliminary, I find that Indians in general have a Mongoloid flatness across the upper face which, in their case, *excepts* the nasal saddle; they also have unusually receding frontal bones. Polynesians share the latter but have a prominence of the middle part of the lower frontal margin, overhanging a rather recessed face, a special Polynesian cranial trait.

How should the Mongoloids be viewed in general? I suggest that they are a complex of populations, of considerable antiquity and with considerable local and regional diversity, including Polynesians, American Indians, and others, of which few such populations or divisions can be regarded as possibly resulting from mixture with other major racial groupings of man. This does not coincide with traditional ideas. As a result of early efforts to classify mankind, we have tended to typify Mongoloids as people having straight, coarse black hair but meager beards or body hair; well-marked folds of skin over the upper eyelid, especially at the inner canthus; flattish faces with low noses and wide and prominent cheekbones; a yellowish or darker skin lacking the pink blood tinge of Europeans; and "shoveling" of the incisors, resulting from raised enamel ridges on the edges of the inner surfaces (Bowles 1977:343). But American Indians, for example, are not consistent in these traits, though they have shoveled incisors to a high degree. Other peoples are also less than "typical." This does not mean they are un-Mongoloid; rather, there seems to be a range in physical appearance from American Indians, Burmese, and others to peoples with excessively developed Mongoloid traits, found especially in northeast Asia. Are these last "purer," as was once argued?

It is the hypothesis of Coon et al. (1950) that these extreme traits—the facial flatness, the eyes protected by fatty lids—arose in the late Pleistocene of northern Asia as a protective adaptation to extreme cold. To test the idea experimentally, Steegmann (1972), using as subjects young men with heads and faces of varying shapes, measured the fall in skin temperature at various sites when the subjects' heads were exposed to controlled chilling drafts. Results did not conform convincingly to Coon's predictions, though the experiment may not have been crucial. On the other hand, it has been shown (Koertvelyessy 1972; Shea 1975) that reduction of frontal and maxillary sinuses in Eskimo skulls (within their generally reduced bony brows) was most marked in samples from the most severely cold habitats in North America. The explanation offered was that such reduction results from selection by disease resulting from exposure to cold. Coon's hypothesis should certainly serve until it is clearly disproved.

I have in the past called these extreme Mongoloid peoples "specialized" rather than "pure" as a way of conveying a difference in viewpoint. At any rate, there is a sort of gradient, beginning with Eskimos and northeast Siberians (all very flat in the face and having the facial skeleton actually set more forward from the skull relative to other peoples) and sloping off in these and other ways into American Indians, Polynesians, Southeast Asians, and Indonesians. About mid-way on the scale are, by general appearance, Japanese, Koreans, and Chinese, all of whom in historical times have swelled into major populations.

The latter three are actually much alike cranially—more so, it might be said, than in outward appearance. Gordon Bowles, the foremost student of general Asian physical anthropology, has in a recent book (1977) subjected a large number of measured series to a uniform objective treatment by cluster analysis. I shall return to this later, noting here only that he finds what amounts to a set of north-south zones in East Asia, which explicitly places the North Chinese, Koreans, and Japanese in a position intermediate to further northern and southern peoples in their measurable features of head and face.

THE LATE PALEOLITHIC: UPPER CAVE, CHOU-K'OU-TIEN

This important deposit has only recently yielded a radiocarbon date of 16,922 b.c. (ZK–136–0; Barnard 1980:27). It is important because of its skeletal remains, including three restorable skulls. These have been taken to represent a single contemporaneous group, even a family, which Wu Hsin-chih (1961; also conversation, 1975) shows from excavation records to be quite wrong, since the human remains did not come from a single level in the cave. The three crania have also been assessed as representing distinct types—as by Weidenreich (1939), who viewed them as primitive Mongoloid (or possibly Cromagnonoid), Eskmoid, and Melanesoid respectively, types which have also been perceived by others in American Indians. These, said Weidenreich, were not necessarily of the outright racial forms the names suggest, but at least they represented "on the soil of Asia different racial types even in the earliest appearance of modern mankind," types which were at the time "not at all sharply isolated from each other." This interpretation, not confined to Weidenreich, well exemplifies the earlier disposition to see types in a population. We now know that modern races had taken definitive form well before the Upper Cave date. And Wu (1961), re-examining the material from surviving casts of the skulls, regards them as sharing early Mongoloid traits, in common with other marginal Mongoloids and differing from recent Chinese, for example (as do American Indians), in a less flat nasal region. Wu does not, however, find these crania to fall significantly outside the range of a number of modern Chinese skulls in their measurements, although this is not proof of identity.

Georg Neumann, highly experienced with American Indian crania, judged the Upper Cave skulls to approximate Indians more closely than present Asiatics. My own discriminant analysis also places skull number 101 in the vicinity of Plains Indians (and next closest to northern Europeans!).

Such an assessment, essentially making the Upper Cave individuals pre-Chinese, "unspecialized" Mongoloids resembling American Indians, is logical and satisfying. If they are typical of the population of the region of Chou-k'ou-tien in the late Pleistocene—and the non-contemporaneity of the several individuals suggests some duration of time and thus a real occupation of the area—then it must be asked where, at the time, were Mongoloids as specialized as the Chinese, or more so? The cold-stress hypothesis supposes them to have evolved earlier, at least during the cold extreme of the Würm, twenty thousand years or more ago; and the whole panoply of such people can hardly have appeared since the time of the

Upper Cave. There are actually no serious dilemmas here, only lack of data.

The Tzu-yang skull from Szechwan, once thought to be of Pleistocene age, has been radiocarbon-dated at only 5535 b.c. (ZK–19; Barnard 1980:81). Unfortunately, it is too incomplete to judge its relations, although it is generally Mongoloid. On its morphological appearance, it would be difficult to exclude the skull definitely from modern Chinese populations, although the degree of ruggedness in brow ridges and mastoid processes would be unusual among them. But the state of the specimen precludes relating it one way or the other to the somewhat later Neolithic people.

THE NEOLITHIC

For this period the potential, from village cemeteries, is considerable but the actual collections, and the work done, are still very limited. Apart from some older material excavated by Andersson and studied by Black (1928), the data consist of a few very small samples of crania—usually a few usable cases, about five to twelve, out of much larger groups of badly damaged specimens. This makes it impractical to do more than generalize; but at least we can ask what we might hypothetically expect, in the way of intervillage variation, within a limited area of North China and a fairly limited time span. As models we could use some region of pre-Columbian Indians practicing simple agriculture, such as the southeast, or the Pueblos or, closer to our problem, the aboriginal tribes of Taiwan.

The more recently published material is the work of Yen Yen, covering villages of North China more or less strung along the thirty-fifth parallel: three Yang-shao settlements in Shensi and two of the slightly later Hua-t'ing (earlier Lungshanoid) culture in northern Kiangsu and southern Shantung (see Chang 1977:98, 135). From measurements and published photographs, these skull samples all seem to be physically Chinese; that is, there is no evidence that they could be excluded as samples of the modern populations. This was also Davidson Black's conclusion in 1928. The only material I have seen myself is skeletons at the village of Ta-ho near Cheng-chou, in a small cemetery section exposed for eventual in situ preservation but not yet reported upon. I was courteously allowed to inspect them and make personal notes on their appearance, though not to measure them before Chinese scholars have been able to do so. The skulls struck me as of uniformly Mongoloid cranial and facial conformation, and specifically as resembling modern Chinese in the character of the orbits and of the midfacial and subnasal regions.

TABLE 11.1 **Mean measurements of Chinese cranial series**

	North China[a]	An-Yang[b]	Hainan[b]	South China[c]	Hsi-Hsia-Hou[d]	Ta-Wen-K'ou[e]	Hua-Hsien[f]	Pan-P'o[g]	Pao-Chi[h]
GOL	178	181	176	180	180	(181)	179	181	180
XCB	138	139	138	141	141	(146)	141	139	143
BBH	137	140	137	137	148	(143)	145	139	142
BNL	99	101	100	98	106	99	106	–	103
BPL	95	98	97	99	102	98	103	–	102
ZYB	133	136	133	133	139	141	134	–	137
NPH	75	69	70	74	72	75	75	76	73
NLH	55	53	52	53	57	55	54	56	52
NLB	25	28	27	25	28	27	28	27	27
OBH	36	33	34	35	34	35	33	34	34
OBB	41	39	39	38	41	40	40	–	41

SOURCES:
[a] Black 1928.   [c] Harrower 1926.   [e] Yen 1972.   [g] Yen 1963.
[b] This chapter.   [d] Yen 1973.   [f] Yen 1962.   [h] Yen et al., 1960.
NOTE: Measurements in lefthand column are, in order, cranial vault length, breadth, height; basion-nasion length; basion-prosthion length; breadth and height of face; height and breadth of nose, orbit.

The measurement means for Yen's five Neolithic villages, all represented by small samples, are shown in table 11.1, together with similar figures for some other groupings. This table is not very informative and is in fact an example of what anthropologists have long struggled with: trying to see a pattern in columns of figures of this sort. I have cut the means down to round numbers, which are well within the limits of error, considering the sample sizes. The four groups on the left are larger samples: two general ones from North and South China, respectively, and two well localized ones I have myself studied, the An-yang Bronze Age skulls and a modern series from Hainan Island. Certain apparent differences result from different measuring techniques; other differences are not remarkable.

The five Neolithic village samples on the right seem to diverge remarkably little in spite of small size and some cultural differences. Yen Yen (1973) ran t-tests among the first three, two Lungshanoid and one Yangshao. In all the measurements he found no significant differences, except for one involving the transverse ear-to-ear arc, which I suspect was due to the marked cranial deformation in the Ta-wen-k'ou series, although Yen doubted this. Thus the differences could be random fluctuation from sampling. In the future, with opportunities for larger samples, wider coverage, and more intensive statistical work, a more informative pattern might be seen.

For comparison, we can turn to a study of living Taiwan aboriginals by C. K. Chai (1967). Among eight tribes, analysis of variance demonstrated

highly significant variation in almost all measurements; and other multivariate computations, especially generalized distance, provided significant
distances among tribes, in a coherent pattern which is sustained by the
congruence of the two sexes. These findings can be compared with the
meager evidence for the Chinese Neolithic, remembering that we are
comparing skeletons with living people, as well as samples which are far less
reliable because of small numbers and less specific in ethnic identity. The
comparison suggests nonetheless that the Chinese Neolithic local populations exhibited no such degree of differentiation as is seen in the
Taiwanese tribes (a differentiation admittedly rather great for an area of
that size). Yet the aboriginal Taiwanese might well be expected to represent
the kind of ethnic diversity which existed in South China at the time Taiwan
was colonized by food-producers, although the diversity might conceivably
have become somewhat augmented on Taiwan (judging from the linguistic
diversity among the Austronesian speakers there) by local isolation and
further differentiation since then. The only indications of any kind for the
Neolithic of South China consist of a few fragmentary crania recently
examined by Wu (1978), from the Chin-lan-hsi site, Tseng-ch'eng-hsien,
Kwangtung. In Wu's opinion these belonged to a population of modern
Mongoloid morphology. The same can be said of the Tzu-yang skull, and it
tells us little about variance from contemporary North Chinese.

It would be sheer speculation, though not necessarily unwarranted, to
suggest from this that ethnic diversity among the farmers of North China
was somewhat less during the Neolithic than further south and was in fact
small: that the people of the north had a more definite community of origin
and also were closer to that origin. As another, possibly more gratuitous
observation, I would venture that the contemporary Jomon populations of
Japan, from what I know of their crania, were a good deal more varied
physically than the Neolithic North Chinese.

THE BRONZE AGE

Here the evidence is of quite another nature. It consists essentially of the
crania from the Shang tombs at An-yang. In these excavations several
thousand human skulls were recovered, mostly decorporated and placed in
sacrificial pits in groups of ten to over thirty (Li Chi 1978). The collection
traveled extensively, in the vicissitudes of war, suffering depletion all the
way, until 398 skulls came to rest at Academia Sinica in Taiwan. They were
the subject of limited measurement by Li Chi, and later were completely
measured and examined by Yang Hsi-mei (1966). Unfortunately, Professor

Yang has not been able to publish the results fully, especially the measurement means. By the great courtesy of both scholars I have been permitted to remeasure the skulls using my own methods, which are somewhat different from traditional ones. My series was limited to forty-five male skulls—all that were sufficiently complete for my purposes (except four "type" skulls, to be mentioned later). I have also a series, of similar size, of recent Chinese skulls collected on Hainan Island by the energetic Takeo Kanaseki; these are at National Taiwan University, where I studied them through the kindness and hospitality of Professor Yü Chin-ch'üan. Thus there are two series, one from Shang times and one recent, from a far southern settlement of Chinese, for intensive comparison.

I have noted that, in such mean measurements as can be compared, the An-yang series does not appear to differ from the Neolithic samples discernibly; and Davidson Black long ago reached the opinion, from evidence then available, that there was no essential difference between Neolithic and modern Chinese. A new question arises, however. Were the An-yang people (largely sacrificial victims) of composite or mixed origin? Many might be expected to be captives from non-Chinese peoples. More important, does the population represent an amalgam of diverse strains? Li Chi found some measurements unusually variable. Coon (1954:322; 1958) gave it as his opinion that a mixture of North European and one or more Mongoloid types might be involved. And Yang became impressed with the variation in appearance of the specimens. Many were classically Mongoloid, but others strongly recalled other recognized racial forms: skulls selected from the series were "almost duplicates" (1966:3) of Chukchi (or Buriat), Melanesian, Eskimo, or Caucasoid (or perhaps Plains Indian). Have such strains entered into the Bronze Age Chinese, and by extension into the quite similar Neolithic people?

In fact, photographs and specimens selected by Yang do suggest these other populations forcibly to the eye. In the above interpretation, two ideas are entangled: on one hand, a potpourri of lower-class sacrificial victims and war captives, that is, a fresh mingling of physically quite diverse human specimens; on the other hand, a long-established mixture of several physically distinct populations, perhaps antedating the Neolithic. A mixture of groups and a mixed group are different things, and the measurable variation is always higher in the first: a hybridized people quickly settles down to the kind of variation normal to any population (Howells 1974). Whether ancestral strains continue to manifest themselves in individuals remains a question. I believe they do not.

Yang showed that the standard deviations of the An-yang series, over a

TABLE 11.2 **Standard deviations of Hainan and An-yang series compared to generalized world mean standard deviations**

	Generalized standard deviations, male crania[a] SD	Hainan males[b] (n = 45)		An-yang males[b] (n = 42)		An-yang males[c] (n = 175–319)	
		SD	Percent	SD	Percent	SD	Percent
GOL	5.82	6.14	105	4.27	73	6.20	107
XCB	4.95	4.26	86	5.43	110	5.90	119
BBH	4.96	4.47	90	5.33	107	5.38	108
BNL	3.88	4.00	103	4.07	105	5.16	133
BPL	4.83	5.72	118	4.28	89	6.00	124
ZYB	4.42	4.63	105	5.07	115	5.68	129
NPH	3.98	3.76	94	3.09	78	3.74	94
OBH	1.93	2.13	110	1.60	83	1.90	98
OBB	1.61	1.64	102	1.34	83	1.90	118
NLH	2.70	2.53	94	2.26	84	3.12	116
NLB	1.83	1.87	102	2.10	115	1.96	107
MAB	3.15	3.33	106	3.55	113	2.94	93
Mean percent			101		96		112

SOURCES:
[a] Howells 1973:215–217.
[b] This chapter.
[c] Yang 1966.
NOTES: Measurements in lefthand column are, in order, cranial vault length, breadth, height; basion-nasion length; basion-prosthion length; breadth and height of face, nose, orbit; palate breadth.
A figure of 100 percent in this table indicates a standard deviation equivalent to average.

number of measurements, were high relative to average figures for this measure of variation. I therefore began the present investigation with this high variability in mind, as bearing on the nature of the An-yang sacrificial population. I happened to test the standard deviations of my own An-yang and Hainan series in the same way, but using a set of basic estimates for a generalized standard deviation in each measurement derived from the pooled within-group variance of a number of populations (Howells 1973). I consider these the best estimates available (although the estimates used by Yang were also earlier ones of my own; Howells 1941.) In the results (see table 11.2), Yang's standard deviations, as re-tested by me, were indeed relatively high; but to my surprise the same figures for my own An-yang sample were *lower* than the average for populations generally. I do not understand this difference. I can think of no sampling bias (which might occur, for example, by selecting a subgroup of the An-yang skulls which happened to be in a better state of preservation than the whole) which would produce the smaller variation; and my sample is of the same order of size as those used as a base, so sample size would not produce low average

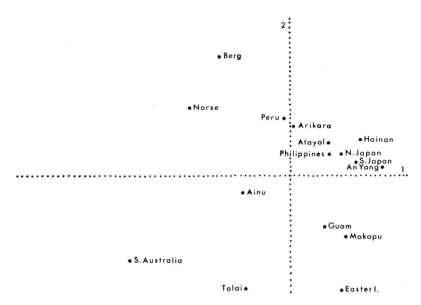

FIGURE 11.1. **Discriminant analysis using sixty measurements made on sixteen series of male crania. This plots the mean position, or centroid, of each series from its scores on the first two, most important, discriminant functions. Note that major regions are each represented by pairs of series: Europe (Norse; Berg); Americas (Arikara; Peru); Japan (Hokkaido; North Kyūshū); China (An-yang, Shang Dynasty; Hainan Island); Polynesia (Hawaii, Mokapu Peninsula; Easter Island); ethnic Indonesia (Philippines; Atayals of Taiwan); Southwest Pacific (South Australia; Tolais of New Britain).**

standard deviations. Nevertheless I have confidence in my figures, which I feel leave the supposed high variability of the An-yang sacrificial skulls in doubt.

For further exploration of the internal variation in the An-yang crania (including the existence of distinct ethnic elements, pure or mixed), as well as of their external resemblances, I must digress into a discriminant analysis. This method has, of course, been applied so widely, from the Pauline epistles to the Houses of Parliament, as hardly to need explanation. As a simple reminder it transforms direct measurements into discriminant functions (or canonical variates); these maximize group differences relative to the general internal variation; the functions are hierarchical, so that a few will carry the preponderance of the information; they are independent, so that they can be used to place the populations and individuals in a Euclidean space. Also, such methods are blind, not depending on what the eye thinks it sees, or judges from columns of figures. (The work was done

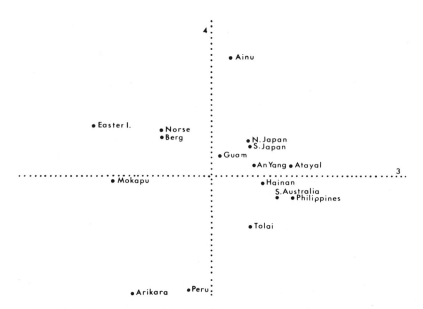

FIGURE 11.2. **Plot of discriminant functions 3 and 4, from the same analysis and material as figure 11.1. These functions are mutually orthogonal (as shown, being independent and uncorrelated), and both are also orthogonal to functions 1 and 2.**

using the SPSS programs available at the Harvard-MIT computing center.)

In one analysis I have used cranial series, taken in pairs corresponding to general ethnicity. Figures 11.1 and 11.2 show that, in a space of four dimensions (necessarily plotted two at a time), the mean positions of the various populations pair off fairly well according to expectations. The two Chinese groups, An-yang and Hainan Island, cluster closely with recent Japanese of Hokkaido and Kyushu, apparently slightly more closely than do the pairs of Europeans, American Indians, or Polynesians. All are well distinguished in the total space: if Polynesians and Americans seem relatively near the Chinese in the first two functions, they are separated from them by the next two. All this is strong evidence of Chinese continuity in cranial form from the Bronze Age to the present, as well as of likeness of Chinese and Japanese in cranial form.

The remaining analyses are of the same kind, done on eight groups relating to problems raised herein. With the two Chinese populations are included various others partly suggested by such types as have been perceived in the An-yang crania: North Europeans, Melanesians (New Britain Tolais), Hawaiians, Buriats, Eskimos, Plains Arikara. All are closely defined in locale and origin; they are not generalized groupings.

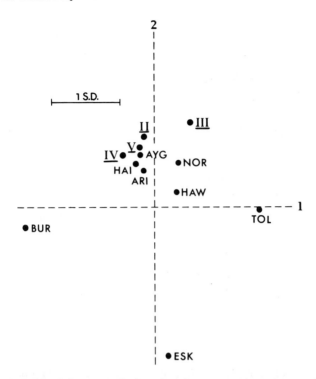

FIGURE 11.3. **Discriminant analysis using forty measurements on eight male cranial series selected with reference to "types" perceived in the An-yang crania. NOR = Norse; TOL = Tolais of Melanesia; HAW = Hawaiians of Mokapu Peninsula, Oahu; BUR = Buriats of Siberia; ESK = Greenland Eskimos, Inugsuk culture, Greenland; ARI = Arikara Plains Indians; AYG = total An-yang series; HAI = Hainan, recent Chinese.**

The figure plots the centroids, or mean positions, of each group on discriminant functions 1 and 2. Roman numerals show the plotted positions of individual type specimens in the An-yang series: II = Melanesoid; III = northern European; IV = Eskimoid; V = Hawaiian-like? The bar measures one standard deviation in the scores of groups, on either function, and suggests that none of the four single specimens deviates by more than this limited distance from the An-yang centroid.

Different runs, based on differing special criteria in producing discrimination, all produced very similar results. Figures 11.3 and 11.4 show plots of four functions from a run in which the special criterion was to maximize the distance between the two closest populations, here the two Chinese groups. The four functions account for 84 percent of total possible discrimination. Closeness between the Chinese groups persists nonetheless, and the two are clearly set off, as populations, from the others. In figure 11.3, plotting the first two functions, the Chinese seem close to the Norse,

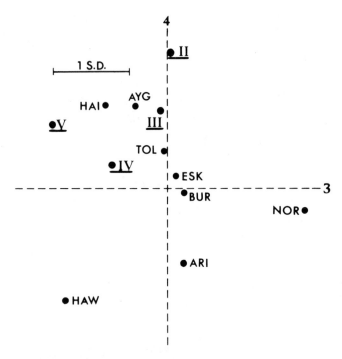

FIGURE 11.4. **Same as figure 11.3, but plotting mean positions of the same series and individual specimens on functions 3 and 4 of the analysis.**

the Arikara, and the Hawaiians. But figure 11.4, for functions 3 and 4, shows that these three are not really in the same part of the space: for example, on the third dimension, if plotted with the first two, the Norse would be far above the plane of the paper with the Chinese somewhat below it. Once again the closeness of the An-yang and Hainan peoples is emphasized in spite of the fact that the computer was asked to make their mutual differences as great as possible within the whole context.

Discriminant functions can be powerful. With informative measurements useful in describing shape (a large number was available here), and enough functions, it is possible to achieve a high degree of discrimination, that is, to assign almost all the individuals to their correct original group. (This is, however, partly spurious, for reasons I will not elaborate here.) In the particular analysis on which the results below are based, I somewhat relaxed the conditions set as to number of functions used to discriminate and number of measurements entered, in order to see what "mistakes" of this kind would appear. That is, the clouds of individuals will overlap in the

TABLE 11.3 **"Hits-and-misses" table of classification by discriminants**

	NOR	TOL	HAW	BUR	ESK	ARI	AYG	HAI
NOR	54					1		
TOL		55						
HAW		1	48			2		
BUR				52		2		
ESK					54			
ARI	2		1			39		
AYG						1	30	14
HAI						1	9	32

NOTE:
NOR: Norse, medieval Oslo
TOL: Tolais of New Britain, Melanesia
HAW: Hawaiians of Mokapu Peninsula, Oahu
BUR: Buriats of Siberia
ESK: Greenland Eskimos, Inugsuk culture
ARI: Arikara Plains Indians
AYG: Total An-yang, Shang
HAI: Hainan, recent Chinese

discriminant space, with some falling closer to the mean position of another population than to that of their own, leading them to be classified statistically with that wrong population.

The result of the classification is seen in table 11.3. Altogether, over 91 percent of individuals are correctly placed. But—and this is what I wished to see—most of the "errors" were mutual misclassings between the two Chinese series, twenty-three out of thirty-three such errors. This befell about a third of each of the two series; without them, the total correct classification would be about 97.5 percent. This is simply another sign of mutual closeness of the two populations.

The constitution of the An-yang series can be inspected in greater detail. If there were actual "foreign elements" included, specimens of these would be expected to align themselves not with the An-yang series but with others more appropriate to their actual ethnic origin, such as European or Eskimo. (The original purpose of discriminant analysis was to classify specimens of uncertain or unknown affiliation to known groups.) Here, one skull among the forty-five from An-yang does classify itself as (most probably) Arikara, as does one from Hainan Island. Altogether, these are not persuasive deviations: no Norse, Hawaiian, Buriat, or Eskimo affiliations appear. By the same logic, if the makeup of the An-yang population (as represented by the crania) were heterogeneous in morphology because of variety in ethnic origins, the distribution of the individual skulls in the multivariate space (that is, when plotted on functions) might be expected to show clumps representing the hypothetical strains brought together by whatever social or historical factors had introduced them to the sacrificial pits. But there is no sign of a non-normal multivariate distribution, or of unusually high variation, on the functions, of the An-yang crania.

Finally, again through the kindness of Professor Yang, I have my own measurements of four "type" specimens, selected by him from among the An-yang male crania. They are types II, Melanesoid; III, north European; IV, Eskimoid; and V, an undefined small type, conceivably Hawaiian-like. (The specimens are illustrated in Yang 1966, beginning at plates 16, 22, 29, and 34, respectively.) In classification by the discriminants, two of the four type specimens were placed with the An-yang series and two with the Hainan; in each case, the second most likely classification was the other of these series. Actual positions on the four functions of each specimen are likewise shown in figures 11.3 and 11.4: these suggest possible deviations in the direction of their supposed racial types on one or another function, and the function scores agree. Therefore some aspect of shape, also visible to the eye, can be registered in this way. (I have not been able to pursue the analysis to the point where such aspects can be defined.) Nevertheless, the analysis finds that in each case the basic conformation, as conveyed by relations among a large number of critical dimensions, is characteristically Chinese.

I am aware from experience that such seemingly foreign types may strongly strike the eye in many series of skulls which are in fact drawn from a single normal population; I would attest this independently of numerous older cranial studies which made use of such types. And, of course, if within a known population one assembles a subgroup of skulls which seem to resemble a different ethnic form because they are, for example, short-faced, then this subgroup will deviate significantly from the total group in average face height. But when multivariate methods are used, which take account of total conformation, it is evident that the "types" do not stand the objective test of their apparent discreteness. They are, I would say, superficial deviations in appearance which do not actually depart as far as they seem to in basic features from the range of characteristic variation of the actual population.

I have gone into this at length because the issue is central to interpretation of the one present body of Bronze Age evidence, that from An-yang. In sum, I can see no indication that the people buried in the sacrificial pits were other than ordinary members of the Shang Chinese population. I would not deny that the actual victims might have been drawn from a wide area and might have included members of peripheral populations. And I would not deny that the Chinese population itself may have had some kind of mixed origin, as other scholars have believed, because as I have said the achievement of normal population variation following hybridization can be rapid. However, the process would be less rapid the broader the area involved, and the An-yang sample does not seem to have variation above the normal. At the moment, the safest hypothesis seems that the population of China in this northern region has been constant in physique, or at least in cranial form, and also surprisingly homogeneous, since the Neolithic.

RECENT VARIATION AND RELATIONSHIPS

The conclusion offered above rests partly on the lack of distinction between the An-yang and Hainan cranial series, widely separated in time and space, which have been compared by using many measurements on samples of reliable size and by using advanced statistical analysis. With the same methods we can obtain a little minor information by classifying, singly or in twos and threes, available skulls of other ethnic groups. (The data were gathered incidentally by me, in the same institutions which lodged the principal cranial series.) This is not very good evidence because it requires assuming that the specimens belong to one of the groups in the main analysis, which of course they do not: they are obliged to classify themselves, but they may not actually be within a reasonable "distance" of the chosen group at all.

Some legitimacy is evident: a Norwegian skull is properly classed as such, and two Siberian Eskimos go with the original Eskimo group (which is actually of the Inugsuk culture in Greenland). Two Chukchi also go with the Eskimos.

Ten Fukienese (of which two are Taiwan Hoklo) are almost evenly divided between An-yang and Hainan, which once again suggests lack of great differentiation between them. Two South Korean skulls are also "Hainan" in slight preference to "An-yang."

Fringe people otherwise do not associate themselves with Chinese except rarely (a Borneo Dyak, one Tungus). A Tungus and two Yakuts are "Buriats"; another Yakut is "Arikara." South Asiatics and Indonesians— a few specimens only—approach Arikara, Hawaiians, Melanesians. In conclusion, Mongoloids north and south of China do not readily approach Chinese, just as major groups in the main analysis (Buriats, Hawaiians, Eskimos, Indians) also keep their distance. Rather, this slim evidence seems to unify all Chinese, with their nearest kin Koreans and Japanese (see figs. 11.1 and 11.2.)

A point mentioned earlier: measurements made on a cast of Chou-k'ou-

tien Upper Cave 101 (the only one of the three skulls sufficiently un-
distorted to use) result in classing the skull as "Arikara," that is, as
American Indian, of the large-faced Plains variety.

For further information, taken from the living, the work of Bowles
(1977) may be relied on. Bowles has assembled a large number of male
samples for all of Asia, for which mean measurements of stature and eight
measures of the head and face were available, and has subjected them to a
multivariate analysis akin to those already described: computing generalized distances and applying clustering techniques to them. This constitutes
a united framework for interpretation; and a number of different runs of
the data for different areas indicates a satisfactory reliability and stability.

In the results, here simplified, the peoples of eastern Asia fall into a series
of rough north-south zones:

   1. Siberia and the eastern woodlands (e.g., Ainu; Ostyak, Yakut, Tungus, and
so on; Koryak, Chukchi, Eskimo)
   2. Caspian Sea to Manchuria (e.g., Kalmuks, Uyghurs, Kazakhs, Mongols,
Buriats)
   3. North China, Korea, Japan. Denoted "Intermediate Populations"
   4. Eastern, western, southern China (the boundary with the peoples in number 3
is between the Huang Ho and Yangtze basins)
   5. Yunnan, Kweichow, Vietnam (including Taiwan aboriginals in three different subclusters)
   6. Indochina (except Vietnam), Thailand, Malaya

No such broad analysis and organization have ever before been
attempted on living peoples. Because a full display and detailed discussion
of this kind of analysis would constitute a monograph in itself and could
not be included in a general book, Bowles's presentation does not provide
either the actual distinctions in measurements or the degree of distance
within and between clusters; thus it is not possible to see how abrupt the
differences may be between these major groupings, or to judge whether
North Chinese are actually closer to those southward than to Mongols,
Manchurians, Tungus, and so on, to the north. The work does organize
vast amounts of data as a first step. And Bowles does recognize North
Chinese as "intermediate": they are lighter-skinned than the southerners,
with lighter eyes; in measurements he finds that their closest approximation
is Uyghurs and Tibetans. Koreans, he finds, are intermediate between
North Chinese and Tungusic populations. South Chinese, on the other
hand, approximate their non-Chinese neighbors (Miao and Thai-Shan)
more than they do the northerners.

Bowles's opinions are evidently based on inspection of records of individual series, rather than on the clustering analysis. Actually, in the latter,

China as a whole is vastly under-represented: there are only two North Chinese samples, and six mainland samples for the east, west, and south (plus one each for the Ta-ch'en Islands and the Pescadores).

There is somewhat of a disagreement between Bowles's evidence from the living and mine from crania. The latter, of course, is highly restricted as to number of populations—two—but provides a much greater depth of information. According to Bowles, all China is uniform below the north, which is distinct and is allied with Korea and Japan. The crania, on the other hand, provide no significant differentiation of north and south, both of which are close to Japan. The resolution of the discrepancy may be historical: after the time of the An-yang burials, during the Han and later, the older North Chinese moved south in force, while barbarians of Tungus or Manchu derivation affected the surviving northern population—something which would not show up in our An-yang evidence.

But this does not seem a likely explanation. Japan was not affected by any barbarian gene flow; and the discriminant analysis first described, and shown in figures 11.1 and 11.2, places the recent South Chinese of Hainan close to the Japanese samples. It is unfortunate that no sizable and well-documented series of North Chinese later than the Shang is available. From the small evidence, I believe the modern Chinese are more uniform than much of the above discussion might indicate. In any case, our problem is with the origins of the Chinese, and if the more recent northerners have been significantly affected by gene flow from beyond the borders (which I doubt), at least a known element would be accounted for.

CONCLUSION

The simplest reconstruction would be something like this. In the late Paleolithic there were physically varied Mongoloid populations, of a generally unspecialized kind, throughout China proper. The only one known skeletally, the Upper Cave people of North China, was one of them, resembling North American Indians as much as any group. Inference about others further south can only be drawn from surviving aboriginals, including those of Taiwan.

But by the Neolithic, that is, by 5000 B.C. or earlier, the villagers of North China show us a population apparently indistinguishable from modern Chinese, already in place. They can be considered the first "Chinese" we know of. These people exhibited little internal variety. In origin, there is no sign that they were a blend of other identifiable northern peoples. On the contrary, they are more likely to have been one branch growing out of a common stem with Koreans and Japanese, the latter of whom did not leave the mainland until much later. We must leave to linguists and archaeologists estimates of the time of separation of these three divisions.

Two general views about place of origin are possible. These northern Chinese might have developed by direct descent from the Upper Cave people between nineteen thousand and seven thousand years ago. If this is the case, then either we are mistaken in seeing the Upper Cave skulls as similar to American Indians or else this population underwent a moderately rapid and special evolution which occurred in no American Indians in similar environments. If it is not the case, then the Neolithic Chinese replaced the Upper Cave population in the Peking region—arriving from somewhere else, which could have been at any distance or any point of the compass. The place is not likely to have been the south, for reasons stated above: the aboriginals of Taiwan, physically different from the Chinese and more varied, probably descend from farmers of southeast China who were generally contemporaneous with the northerners. (Bowles finds the *present* people of South China to be nearest physically to Tibetans and others in the headwaters of the Yangtze; but this tells us little about *how* different they may actually be from the northerners of either the present or the Neolithic.)

It is reasonable to suppose that our "first Chinese" of the Neolithic in the north did not migrate from far away, if they migrated at all. Given the Korean connection in physique, we could look for a common source in a northeasterly direction. But we have no real clues about either time or place. We could in the future learn more about the sources if (1) a broader matrix of well-fixed cranial series could be developed, as a background for multivariate analyses, by which to judge (2) well-documented crania provided by archaeologists from relevant areas and from the millennia of early Neolithic and pre-Neolithic times. This is a good deal to hope.

Similarly, expanded and refined work might help with later history, making more explicit the possible physical divergences between north and south. The analyses performed for this chapter are limited. Also, little-understood matters of process are involved. Small, semi-isolated segments of a primitive population may diverge in physical features over time, while large, cosmopolitan populations do so much less. Also, although it is often assumed that admixed populations will faithfully reflect the physical features of parental strains in due proportion, this has not been shown to be so. On the contrary, it appears from some instances that a numerically dominant gene pool may be able to digest a good deal of admixture while showing little effect of it. In their expansion as a cosmopolitan population the Chinese do appear to have kept a considerable physical homogeneity; and it would be difficult to estimate the actual effect of influx of non-Chinese in the north, or of physical absorption of non-Chinese in the south, from evidence we have. This chapter should show how limited and disarticulated that evidence is.

REFERENCES

Barnard, Noel
1980   *Radiocarbon Dates and Their Significance in the Chinese Archaeological Scene: A List of 420 Entries From Chinese Sources Published up to Close of 1979.* Canberra.

Black, Davidson
1928   "A Study of Kansu and Honan Aeneolithic Skulls and Specimens from Later Kansu Prehistoric Sites in Comparison with North China and Other Recent Crania," pt. 1: "On Measurement and Identification." *PS* ser. D, 6.1.

Bowles, G. T.
1977   *The People of Asia.* New York.

Chai, C. K.
1967   *Taiwan Aborigines: A Genetic Study of Tribal Variations.* Cambridge, Mass.

Chang, Kwang-chih
1977   *The Archaeology of Ancient China.* 3d ed., rev. and enl. New Haven.

Coon, Carleton S.
1954   *The Story of Man: From the First Human to Primitive Culture and Beyond.* New York.
1958   "An Anthropogeographic Excursion Around the World." *Human Biology* 30:29–42.
1962   *The Origin of Races.* New York.

Coon, Carleton S., Garn, S. M., and Birdsell, J. B.
1950   *Races: A Study of the Problems of Race Formation in Man.* Springfield, Ill.

Day, M. H.
1972   "The Omo Human Skeletal Remains." In *The Origin of*

Homo Sapiens, edited by F. Bordes. Proceedings of a symposium organized by UNESCO with INQUA, September 2–5, 1969: pp. 31–35. Paris.

Harrower, Gordon
1926   "A Study of the Hokien and the Tamil Skull." *Transactions of the Royal Society of Edinburgh* 54.3:573–599.

Howells, W. W.
1941   "The Early Christian Irish: The Skeletons at Gallen Priory." *Proceedings of the Royal Irish Academy* 44.C.3:103–220.
1973   *Cranial Variation in Man: A Study by Multivariate Analysis.* Peabody Museum Papers, 67. Cambridge, Mass.
1974   'The Population of Zalavár: A Problem in Cranial Variation." *Anthropologiai Közlemenyek* (Budapest) 18:91–96.

Koertvelyessy, T.
1972   "Relationships Between the Frontal Sinus and Climatic Conditions: A Skeletal Approach to Cold Adaptation." *American Journal of Physical Anthropology* 37:161–172.

Li Chi
1978   *Anyang.* Seattle.

Shea, Brian
1975   "Cranial Adaptation to Cold in Eskimos: An Investigation of the Effect of Climate on the Capacity of the Maxillary Sinus." Senior honors thesis, Harvard University.

Steegmann, A. T., Jr.
1972   "Cold Response, Body Form, and Craniofacial Shape in Two Racial Groups of Hawaii." *American Journal of Physical Anthropology* 37:193–221.

Stewart, T. D.
1974   "Recent Developments in Understanding the Relationship Between the Neanderthals and Modern Man." In *Grafton Elliot Smith: The Man and His Work*, edited by A. Elkin and N. W. G. Macintosh: pp. 67–82. Sydney.

Weidenreich, F.
1939   "On the Earliest Representatives of Modern Mankind Recovered on the Soil of East Asia." *Peking Natural History Bulletin* 13:161–180. (Reprinted in *The Shorter*

Anthropological Papers of Franz Weidenreich, edited by S. L. Washburn and D. Wolffson. New York, 1949.)

1943   "The Skull of *Sinanthropus pekinensis.*" *PS* ser. D, 10:127.

Woo, Ju-kang
1959   "Human Fossils Found in Liukiang, Kwangsi, China." *Vertebrata PalAsiatica* 3.2:109–118.

Wu, Hsin-chih
1961   "Study on the Upper Cave Man of Choukoutien." *Vertebrata PalAsiatica* 5.3:181–210. (In Chinese; English abstract).
1978   "Neolithic Human Crania from Jinlansi Site, Kwangtung Province." *Vertebrata PalAsiatica* 16.3:201–204. (In Chinese; English abstract).

Yang, Hsi-mei
1966   "A Preliminary Report of Human Crania Excavated from Hou-chia-chuang and Other Shang Dynasty Sites at An-yang, Honan, North China." *Annual Bulletin of the China Council for East Asian Studies* 5:1–13.

Yen Yen 顏誾
1962   "Hua-hsien hsin-shih-ch'i shih-tai jen-ku yen-chiu 化縣新石器時代人骨研究." *KKHP* 1962.2:85–104.
1963   "Study of Skeletal Remains at Pan-p'o." In CKKH and Shen-hsi-sheng Hsi-an Pan-p'o pu-wu-kuan 陝西省西安半坡博物館, *Hsi-an Pan-p'o* 西安半坡. Chung-kuo t'ien-yeh k'ao-ku pao-kao-chi k'ao-ku-hsüeh chuan-k'an ting chung ti-shih-ssu-hao 中國田野考古報告集考古學專刊丁種第十四號: pp. 234–251. Peking. (In Chinese; English abstract.)
1972   "Ta-wen-k'ou hsin-shih-ch'i shih-tai jen-ku ti yen-chiu pao-kao 大汶口新石器時代人骨的研究報告." *KKHP* 1972.1:91–122.
1973   "Hsi-hsia-hou hsin-shih-ch'i shih-tai jen-ku ti yen-chiu pao-kao 西夏侯新石器時代人骨的研究報告." *KKHP* 1973.2:91–125.

Yen, Yen, Liu, Ch'ang-chih, and Ku, Yü-min
1960   "Report on the Skeletal Remains from the Neolithic Site at Bao Ji, Shensi." *Vertebrata PalAsiatica* 4:103–111.

III

LANGUAGE
AND WRITING

12

Recent Archaeological Evidence Relating to the Origin of Chinese Characters

CHEUNG KWONG-YUE
(Translated by Noel Barnard)

As a result of continuing archaeological activities over the past fifty years ceramic vessels and sherds bearing what are termed marks, symbols, or characters have come to light from many sites representative of prehistoric and early historic cultures. I shall simply call them inscriptions, graphs, or marks, without seeking, in this preliminary survey of the materials, to bring into the picture modern conceptions of what constitutes a pictogram, an ideograph, a glyph, a logograph, a symbol, and other such terms.[1] Where radiocarbon dates are available, I date the materials according to the revised (DFLW) calibrations of carbon-14 assessments. I offer tentative assessments of sites not yet dated by carbon-14 tests with reference to the generally accepted datings of comparable cultures; such chronologies are necessarily relative.

EARLY POTTERY MARKS: FIELD SURVEYS, 1928–1977

1. Pottery inscriptions from Pan-p'o-ts'un, Hsi-an-hsien (Sian), Shensi: Unearthed between 1954–1957 (CKKH and Shen-hsi 1963).

---

1. It is appreciated that readers would like to see greater precision than this. My view is that the time is not yet ripe to systematize our understanding of the marks until there is a large enough "vocabulary" resulting from further excavations which may help clarify the role of the marks in the development of Chinese characters. Without more examples of two or more graphs in one inscription (we have only the Liang-chu and the few Wu-ch'eng examples to draw upon) scholars can do little more than speculate.

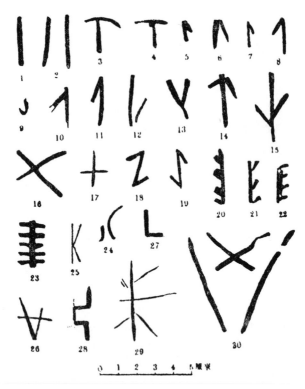

FIGURE 12.1. **Examples of incised marks on pottery from the Pan-p'o site, Sian, Shensi. (CKKH and Shen-hsi 1963: fig. 141.) Yang-shao culture, 4800–4200 B.C.**

Pan-p'o is one of the most important Yang-shao culture sites of the Wei Shui valley. Inscribed pottery and sherds have revealed marks executed in the broad black decor bands or in the black triangular units of decor, painted just below the rims on the outsides of the vessels. Altogether, 113 examples have been excavated, the majority of which are from the settlement cultural levels and were found mainly in the form of sherds; only two round-bottomed *po* 鉢 jars used as burial urns were complete. The marks are made with simple strokes and are of regular shapes; there are 22 varieties of graphs executed by means of horizontal, vertical, slanting, and forked strokes. There are also some comparatively complex marks, but of these there are presently no more than a dozen examples (see fig. 12.1:20–30).

Five radiocarbon dates have been published from Pan-p'o samples:

ZK–38   4773 ± 141 B.C.
ZK–121   4617 ± 137 B.C.

ZK–122   4552 ± 208 B.C.
ZK–127   4294 ± 165 B.C.
ZK–148   4194 ± 204 B.C.

If there is no major variation in future relevant C-14 (and possibly thermo-luminescence) dates with regard to the above assessments, the upper and lower levels can be taken as the approximate limits of the Pan-p'o Yang-shao culture; there would be (in terms of the mid-point dates) a range of nearly six hundred years: 4800–4200 B.C.[2]

2. Inscribed sherd from Hsin-yeh-ts'un, Ho-yang-hsien, Shensi: Excavated 1953 (*KK* 1956.5).

The one inscription from this Yang-shao site is the graph 𝄃 (cf. the Pan-p'o examples, fig. 12.1 : 20–22). It is likewise incised in the painted decor band on the outside surface (pl. 1.2 of the original report).

3. Inscribed sherd from Wu-lou, Ch'in-tu-chen, Hsi-an-hsien, Shensi: Excavated 1953 (Shih Hsing-pang 1955).

One inscribed fragment only was found during trial excavations. The inscription, the graph 𝄃 neatly cut into the painted decor band, can perhaps be compared with the Pan-p'o graph 𝄃 (see fig. 12.1 : 23), although the mode of "writing" differs slightly (Shih Hsing-pang 1955: 29; pl. 10.2). Pottery from both the Hsin-yeh-ts'un and the Wu-lou sites is similar to the Pan-p'o Yang-shao type; they are probably of comparable age.

4. Four pottery inscriptions from Chiang-chai, Lin-t'ung-hsien, Shensi: Excavated 1972–1974 (*WW* 1975.8).

These particularly interesting inscriptions (see fig. 12.2) derive from the relatively undisturbed Yang-shao layer in the Neolithic remains at Chiang-chai (*WW* 1975.8 : 82). Although the report does not state clearly on which artifacts the inscriptions appear, it is nevertheless evident from the original caption, "*Po* jar with incised symbol," that they are probably all executed

---

2. Hsia Nai (1977) has been consulted for guidance in cultural period ranges; but his use of the DLW calibration, and the appearance of new radiocarbon assessments, has necessitated some appropriate adjustments. Because of the need to check carefully the background of each C-14 date in order to obtain the best possible appreciation of the sample/site context associations, and the often incomplete reporting of such crucial details, I have listed (as above) comprehensive groupings of C-14 dates from specific cultural areas, and on the basis of mid-point dates have proposed *possible* period ranges in calendar date terms. Later adjustments are to be expected as increasing numbers of relevant dates become available and associated reports are published. Space is insufficient to allow necessary discussion on the validity of individual C-14 assessments, not only of sample/site associations, but also of sample materials submitted for testing, problems relating to isotopic fractionation, etc. (See general notes in Barnard 1980 on this; and Polach 1976 for a detailed survey on the subject.)

FIGURE 12.2. Graphs inscribed on pottery from Chiang-chai, Lin-t'ung-hsien, Shensi. (*WW* 1975.8:82, fig. 1.) Yang-shao culture, 4800–4200 B.C.

on pottery vessels. Furthermore, in his study of the origins of Chinese characters, Ch'en Wei-chan (1978:73) states: "It is said that since totaling up the Chiang-chai inscriptions [on pottery] it was noted that they amounted to more than twice the number recovered from Pan-p'o." It is hoped that in the near future it will be possible to see the full array of the Chiang-chai pottery inscriptions.

The Chiang-chai site can be divided into three cultural layers: Pan-p'o type (Pan-p'o Early Period), Miao-ti-kou type, and Pan-p'o Late Period type. But the report does not indicate the stratigraphic association(s) of the inscribed pottery. If one were to be overly cautious and assume that the inscriptions come from the Late Period layer, they would be datable to circa 4000 B.C. A radiocarbon date has recently been made available:

BK–77041   4682 ± 141 B.C.

The sample is a section of charred wooden rafter from 73LGZF29. However, as the inscribed pottery associations are not clear, it is impossible to take advantage of this C-14 assessment, which would almost certainly be from the Yang-shao Early Period layer.

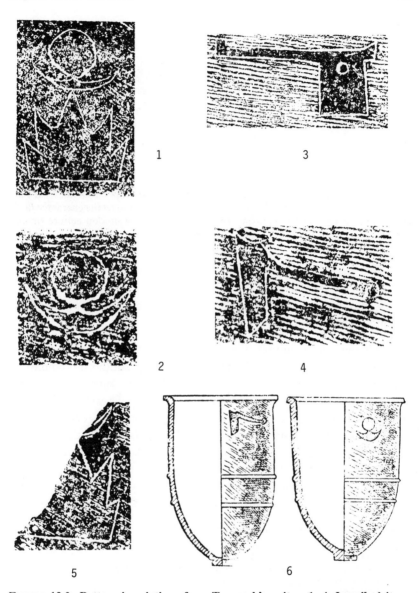

FIGURE 12.3. **Pottery inscriptions from Ta-wen-k'ou sites. 1–4: Inscribed items from Ling-yang-ho, Chü-hsien, Shantung. 5: The Ch'ien-chai graph which, though incomplete, is probably identical to the combination of elements in number 1. 6: Two examples of the parent vessels, showing the location of inscriptions 2 and 3. Ta-wen-k'ou culture, 4300–1900 B.C. (Shan-tung-sheng and Chi-nan-shih 1974: fig. 94.)**

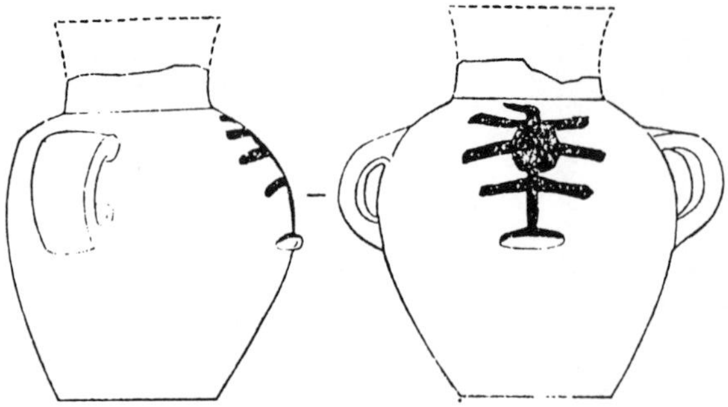

FIGURE 12.4. **A painted symbol on a flat-backed *hu* vase from burial no. 75 at Pao-t'ou-ts'un, Ning-yang, Shantung, considered by T'ang Lan to be the character *fu* 桒. (Shan-tung-sheng and Chi-nan-shih 1974: fig. 59.8). Ta-wen-k'ou culture (middle period), ca. 3500–2500 B.C.**

5. Inscribed pottery from Ta-wen-k'ou culture sites (Shan-tung-sheng and Chi-nan-shih 1974).

The Ta-wen-k'ou culture sites cover an area stretching north to south from the southern banks of the Huang Ho to the southern boundary of Shantung and west to east from the Wen and Ssu river valleys to the shores of the Yellow Sea. This culture embraces not only Ta-wen-k'ou, Ching-chih-chen, and Kang-shang in T'eng-hsien, the earliest reported manifestations of the culture, but also such sites as Hsi-hsia-hou in Ch'ü-fu, Ling-yang-ho in Chü-hsien, Yeh-tien in Tsou-hsien, Ta-fan-chuang in Lin-yi, Tung-hai-yü in Jih-chao, and others. In the sites of Ling-yang-ho and Ch'ien-chai in Chu-ch'eng, Pao-t'ou in Ning-yang, and Kang-shang, inscribed pottery has been unearthed from time to time, as follows:

a. From Ling-yang-ho, four grey pottery *kung* 缸 jars, each incised with glyphs (*t'u-hsiang wen-tzu* 圖象文字), were excavated ca. 1959 (see Shan-tung-sheng and Chi-nan-shih 1974: 117; and fig. 12.3: 1–4).
b. An incomplete version of the Ling-yang-ho graph (see fig. 12.3: 1) incised on a sherd from a large pottery *kung* jar was excavated at the Ch'ien-chai site in 1973 (fig. 12.3: 5). It is clearly identical in structure. According to the original report (Jen 1974: 75) the inscribed fragment belongs to the Ta-wen-k'ou Late Period.
c. A graph painted in red on a type III grey pottery flat-backed *hu* 壺 vase exists from burial number 75 at Pao-t'ou-ts'un (see fig. 12.4). In the original report (Shan-tung-sheng and Chi-nan-shih 1974: 72) it is taken to be merely a picture; but both T'ang Lan (1977b: 21) and Kao Kuang-jen (1978: 27) regard it as a character. T'ang (1978: fig. 5) has gone further and interprets it

as the character *fu* 枹 [root of grass?].[3] Chang Chih-min (1978:72) follows T'ang's rendering. Burial number 75 is dated as Middle Period.

d. In the pottery from Kang-shang were several vessels with inscribed marks (*chi-hao* 記號) on the bases. Among these, three type III sand-tempered red ware *kuan* 罐 vases are reported with incised markings "like the character *hsiao* 小 'small'," but no reproduction is given in the report (Shan-tung-sheng 1963:353, 355). Type III *tou* 豆 pedestal-bowls of fine black ware from burial number 5 occasionally had imprints of vegetable fibers, or incised marks like 冋 on the bases. The reporters, in discussing the period of the site (p. 361), consider that it covers both early and late Lung-shan and that Kang-shang and Pao-t'ou are earlier than Liang-ch'eng, Ch'eng-tzu-yai, and Yao-kuan-chuang. More recent finds suggest that the Kang-shang type sites may belong to the Ta-wen-k'ou culture. On the basis of C-14 dates we can tentatively suggest for the Ta-wen-k'ou culture a range of 4300–1900 B.C. in terms of mid-point dates:

*ZK–468	4262 ± 159 B.C.
*ZK–469	4210 ± 165 B.C.
*ZK–461	3993 ± 146 B.C.
*ZK–464	3960 ± 139 B.C.
*ZK–460	3549 ± 175 B.C.
*ZK–463	3276 ± 129 B.C.
*ZK–470	2863 ± 150 B.C.
*ZK–479	2689 ± 181 B.C.
ZK–317	2336 ± 134 B.C.
ZK–391–0	2024 ± 191 B.C.
ZK–361–0	1891 ± 113 B.C.

The first two assessments are from the Ta-wen-k'ou site itself and, together with those following (all are marked with asterisks) comprise the most recently published C-14 data from Ta-wen-k'ou sites. Hsia Nai's suggested range, based on the two following dates (1977:225; see also his fig. 1, p. 220), would be 4500–2300 B.C. in terms of mid-point dates:

ZK–90	4497 ± 208 B.C.
ZK–317	2336 ± 134 B.C.

The first of these is from the Ta-tun-tzu site at Ssu-hu, P'i-hsien (T105:40, layer 3 lower section, associated with Ch'ing-lien-kang culture) and the second from the Lu-chia-k'ou site in Wei-hsien (74SWLIT1, layer 5).

6. Pottery with inscribed marks from Wang-yu-fang, Yung-ch'eng, Honan: Excavated spring 1977 (Shang-ch'iu and Chung-kuo 1978).

Reference is made in the report (p. 36) to incised marks on pottery found in fireplaces, but no description or reproduction appears. Mention is made of C-14 dating in progress. Since then four dates relevant to the fireplaces and three others from the excavations have been published:

---

3. See Lung (1963) for a detailed investigation into the meaning of this character. T'ang does not give it a meaning.

*ZK–539	2950 ± 198 B.C.
ZK–457	2501 ± 137 B.C.
*ZK–538	2451 ± 177 B.C.
*ZK–459	2446 ± 152 B.C.
ZK–541	2425 ± 144 B.C.
ZK–456	2407 ± 145 B.C.
*ZK–458	2388 ± 130 B.C.

The asterisks indicate the charcoal samples from fireplaces numbers 46, 40, 2, and 16, respectively. According to the original report, fireplaces numbers H13 and H16 belong to the lower settlement level and the remainder to the upper. As ZK–458 derives from charcoal in H16 there may be a slight anomaly here. However, since ZK–538 and ZK–539 are located in square 4, and since we have no clear indication of the site context of the other two fireplaces, we can do little else than assess the site age at circa 2900/2500–2400 B.C.[4]

7. Inscribed pottery from Ch'eng-tzu-yai (lower layers), Shantung: Excavated 1930–1931 (Li Chi 1934).

Pottery from the upper layers was the grey ware of Western and Eastern Chou; that from the lower layers was Lung-shan black pottery ware. Among some 20,000 sherds, 88 contained inscriptions (see fig. 12.5). The following tabulation in the report is of interest:

Type of symbol:	1	2	3	4	5	6	7	8	9	10	11	12	13	14	15	16	17	18	Other	Total
Number of sherds:	25	2	5	1	13	4	3	1	1	1	2	2	1	1	1	2	4	1	18	88

Note the reporters' observations:

> Among 88 sherds 9 pieces showed evidence that the scoring had first been made on the unbaked pottery, after which it was then fired. The remaining 79 pieces were those which were scored after being fired . . . Among these 88 pieces only numbers 12, 1a, and 1b [of fig. 12.5] were of the earlier period (i.e., the lower cultural stratum). The others all were of the later period and so it can be seen that the custom of marking symbols on the pottery began to flourish in the later period. At An-yang in Honan and Lin-tzu in Shantung, and at the ancient city of P'ing-ling-ch'eng, there have also been found fragments of pottery *tou* pedestal bowls with similar kinds of symbols" (Li Chi 1934:100; 1956:53–54).

A tentative range for the Lung-shan culture at Ch'eng-tzu-yai can perhaps be proposed with reference to the somewhat similar sites at

---

4. It would seem useful to illustrate thus the presence of apparent anomalies in groups of dates such as these. To assume a range of 2900–2400 is risky. [Translator's note.]

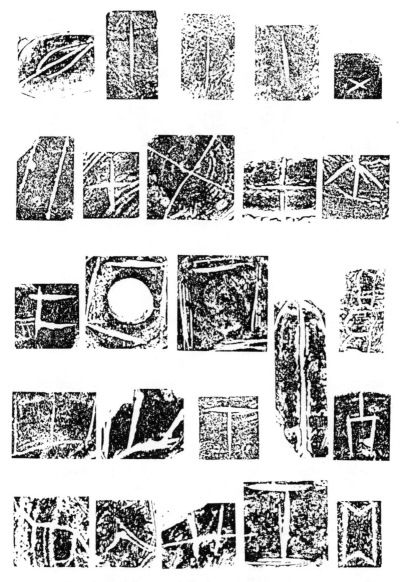

FIGURE 12.5. **Inscriptions on potsherds from Ch'eng-tzu-yai. (Li Chi 1934: pl. 16.) 1a, 1b, and 12 derive from pottery of the lower (Lung-shan black pottery) levels, ca. 2500–2000 B.C. The remainder are inscribed grey pottery fragments of Western and Eastern Chou date.**

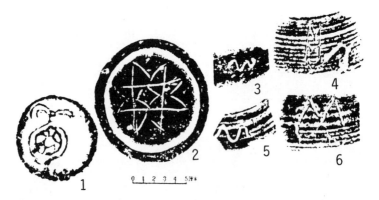

FIGURE 12.6. **Marks incised on pots from Sung-tse-ts'un, Ch'ing-p'u-hsien. (Shang-hai-shih 1962: fig. 6.) 1–3, from the middle layer, are dated by the reporters as late Neolithic.**

Shuang-t'o-tzu (Lü-ta-shih, Liaoning: 64L22F16) and Lu-chia-k'ou (Wei-hsien, Shantung: 74SWLIT1, layer number 5), which have been radio-carbon-dated (Hsia Nai 1977: 224–225) as, respectively:

ZK–78	2463 ± 134 B.C.
ZK–321	2012 ± 161 B.C.

8. Inscribed sherd from Chao-ts'un, Ch'ing-tao-shih: Excavated 1964 (Sun Shan-te 1965).

This involves mainly surface finds which the reporter considers of Lung-shan date; one pottery fragment had an X-shaped incised mark (p. 481).

9. Inscribed pottery from Sung-tse-ts'un, Ch'ing-p'u-hsien, Shanghai: Excavated 1960 and 1961 (Shang-hai-shih 1962).

Among the numerous varieties of pottery unearthed from the middle layer culture, individual vessels had incised marks, some shaped like animals (see fig. 12.6). This middle layer is considered by the reporters late Neolithic in date (p. 27). Carbon-14 dating of human bone from square 3, burials 12 (Sung 76T3M12) and 15 (Sung 76T3M15), and also of wood from the nearby Feng-hsi site can be tentatively taken to indicate a range for the culture. Until full reports are published, however, a firm basis for assessment is not possible. The C-14 dates are, respectively:

ZK–438–0	3915 ± 226 B.C.
ZK–437–0	3233 ± 140 B.C.
ZK–292	2551 ± 137 B.C.

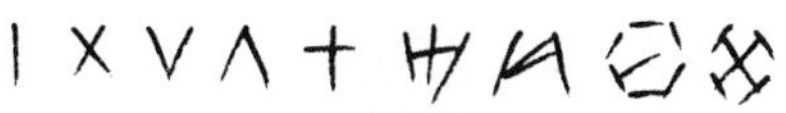

I X V Λ + Ϧ Ⴊ ◠ ⅏

FIGURE 12.7. **Hand-copies of marks incised on pots of Liang-chu culture date discovered at Liang-chu, Hang-chou-shih. (Ch'iu 1978:163.)**

This appears to suggest a range of 3900–3200/2500 B.C. in terms of mid-point dates.

10. Inscribed Liang-chu culture pottery of Hang-chou-shih. Three groups known to date are:

    (a) A black pottery *p'an* basin with seven graphs around the lip. None of the characters can be deciphered (Chang Kwang-chih 1977a, citing Ho T'ien-hsing 1937 and Shih Hsin-keng 1938).

    (b) Simple incised markings noted by Ch'iu Hsi-kuei (1978) (see fig. 12.7).

    (c) A red pottery fragment of a large bowl (diameter of the mouth 19.8 cm.) with three dotted markings on the lip (⫴⫴ ∥ ⫽⩘) from Liang-chu-chen, Hang-chou-hsien, excavated in a find of black pottery vessels in 1955 (Che-chiang-sheng 1956:27). Although the possibility that the markings are decor must be considered, they have something in common with the late Neolithic pottery marks from Hong Kong which also use dotted lines (cf. fig. 12.27: 29–31).

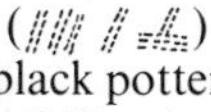

11. Pottery inscriptions from Ma-ch'iao-chen (layer 5), Shanghai: Excavations 1959, 1960, 1961 (*KKHP* 1978.1).

Among the fine grey and black ware which formed the major portion of the pottery unearthed from layer 5 at the Ma-ch'iao site, characters and marks were found incised on the bases of individual items (p. 115 of the report; see fig. 12.8 below). Below this layer, in sandy natural soil, were found shells of various bi-valves together with other debris accumulated by wave action in the past. Radiocarbon-dated shell from this stratum has some value in indicating a possible lower-limit age for layer 5:

        ZK–344–1   4391 ± 254 B.C.

However, we can tentatively propose a range of 3800–2400 B.C. in terms of C-14 mid-point dates from the following Liang-chu culture sites:

ZK–433	3838 ± 253 B.C.
ZK–49	3311 ± 136 B.C.
ZK–97	3306 ± 129 B.C.
ZK–47	2764 ± 133 B.C.
ZK–50	2627 ± 133 B.C.
ZK–292	2551 ± 137 B.C.
ZK–242	2374 ± 134 B.C.
ZK–254	2247 ± 161 B.C.

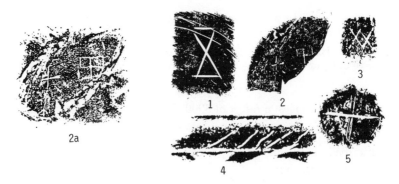

FIGURE 12.8. **Marks incised on pots from Ma-ch'iao, layer 5. (1–5: *KKHP* 1978.1:115, fig. 10 [original reduced 3/5]. 2a [a clearer rubbing of 2]: Kuo 1976:107, fig. 16.)**

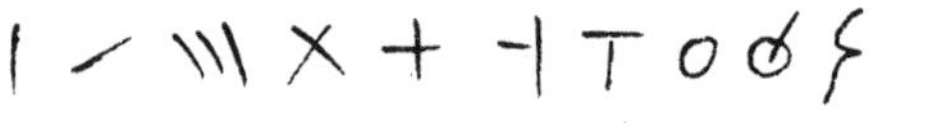

$$ \text{I} \quad \diagup \quad \text{\\\\\\} \quad \text{X} \quad + \quad \text{⌐} \quad \text{T} \quad o \quad \emptyset \quad \text{\textipa{f}} $$

FIGURE 12.9. **Hand-copies of incised pottery graphs, Pan-shan/Ma-ch'ang cultures (Ma-chia-yao). (Ch'iu 1978:162.)**

12. Pottery inscriptions from Hsia-wang-kang, Hsi-ch'uan, Honan (Chiang-hsi-sheng, Pei-ching ta-hsüeh, and Ch'ing-chiang-hsien 1975).

A *tou* pedestal-bowl from H34 had the graph X incised on the stem (p. 60, n. 16). The radiocarbon-dated Huang-lien-shu site nearby can perhaps be tentatively taken as an indication of the age of the Hsia-wang-kang remains:

$$ \text{ZK–91} \qquad 2722 \pm 139 \text{ B.C.} $$

13. Inscribed pottery from Pan-shan and Ma-ch'ang in Kansu (Shih Hsing-pang 1955).

In reference to a report by Nils Palmgren in *Palaeontologia Sinica* (1934:174–179), Shih Hsing-pang (p. 29) cites the statement: "Many marks (*fu-hao* 符號) were found painted on pottery amongst the Ma-ch'ang and Pan-shan burials in Kansu." Ch'iu Hsi-kuei (1978) reproduces some examples (see fig. 12.9).

On the basis of C-14 mid-point dates, the range of the Pan-shan/Ma-ch'ang cultures of Kansu could be determined from the relevant radiocarbon assessments published to date:

FIGURE 12.10. **Hand-copies of graphs painted on Ma-ch'ang style pottery from Liu-wan, Lo-tu-hsien, datable within the range 2400–2000 B.C. (*KK* 1976.6: 376, fig. 17.)**

Pan-shan (Kansu):

ZK–407	2676 ± 143 B.C.
ZK–25	2470 ± 137 B.C.
BK–75029	2375 ± 137 B.C.
ZK–406	2348 ± 169 B.C.
ZK–405	2344 ± 141 B.C.

Ma-ch'ang (Kansu):

ZK–21	2620 ± 143 B.C.
BK–75028	2171 ± 158 B.C.
BK–75017	2044 ± 156 B.C.

A range of six to seven centuries, from approximately 2700 to 2000 B.C., seems acceptable.

14. Pottery with inscriptions from Liu-wan, Lo-tu-hsien, Tsinghai: Excavated 1974 (*KK* 1976.6).

Burials classified as Ma-chia-yao culture (Pan-shan and Ma-ch'ang types) and Ch'i-chia culture were found in the Liu-wan ancient cemetery area. On the painted pottery of Ma-ch'ang type, some fifty varieties of marks and characters(?) were found. These were painted on the lower waist area and on the bases (p. 376 of the reports; see fig. 12.10). Radiocarbon dates from the Ma-ch'ang remains in this area do not, unfortunately, include burials 197, 211, and 564, from which the greater proportion of inscribed vessels were obtained. However, an impression of the antiquity of the inscribed ware can be gauged from the following:

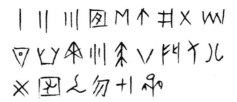

FIGURE 12.11. **Hand-copies of pottery inscriptions from Erh-li-t'ou sites (late period), datable toward the close of the range 2000–1400 B.C. (*KK* 1965.5: 222.)**

ZK–348	2414 ± 258 B.C.
ZK–345	2281 ± 152 B.C.
BK–75009	2273 ± 130 B.C.
BK–75012	2134 ± 164 B.C.
ZK–346	2025 ± 153 B.C.

A range of four hundred years in terms of mid-point dates can be proposed here, from 2400 to 2000 B.C. We should keep in mind, too, the fact that the samples derive mainly from coffin wood. Details of the nature of the wood have yet to be published.

15. Inscribed pottery from Erh-li-t'ou, Yen-shih, Honan: 1960–1964 (*KK* 1965.5).

    Among inscribed pottery from the Erh-li-t'ou sites, a variety of twenty-four graphs appear; all belong to the Late Period, and the bulk of them are incised on the inside surface of the lips of wide-mouthed *tsun* 尊 beakers (p. 222 of the report; see fig. 12.11). In this report the Erh-li-t'ou sites are considered to be later than the Honan Lung-shan culture, but earlier than the Cheng-chou Erh-li-kang phase of Shang culture. Radiocarbon dates include one (ZK–257) from approximately the same cultural stratum:

ZK–31–1	2393 ± 149 B.C.
ZK–212	1906 ± 104 B.C.
ZK–285	1885 ± 91 B.C.
ZK–286	1604 ± 101 B.C.
ZK–257	1429 ± 105 B.C.

As the samples for ZK–31–1 and ZK–212 derive from shell material, one must keep in mind the associated problems. However, a range for the Erh-li-t'ou culture of about six hundred years (2000–1400 B.C.) could be tentatively proposed on the basis of mid-point dates (cf. "The Question of Hsia in Chinese Archaeology," in ch. 16 below), whereas the inscribed sherds could be placed in the last century or so of the range-period.

FIGURE 12.12. **Tracing of a painted graph on a sherd from the Miao-wan site, Yen-shih. (*KK* 1964.11:548, fig. 5.6.)**

FIGURE 12.13. **Marks incised on potsherds from the Early Shang level (layer 3), Hsia-ch'i-yüan, Tz'u-hsien. (Ho-pei-sheng 1979:196, fig. 14.)**

16. Inscribed pottery from Miao-wan, Yi Ho, Yen-shih, Honan: Discovered 1960 (*KK* 1964.11).

On a pottery sherd from this site is a painted graph (see fig. 12.12) very close in structure to that from the Hsia-wang-kang site, Hsi-ch'uan (item 12 above). Thus I regard it as probably a character. The reporters consider the Miao-wan pottery comparable in age to that of Lo-yang Wang-wan Period II (p. 548). At that site a C-14 date for the earlier Period III (Honan Lung-shan culture) is available and useful for chronological guidance here:

$$ZK-126 \qquad 2388 \pm 134 \text{ B.C.}$$

17. Inscribed pottery from layer 3, Hsia-ch'i-yüan, Tz'u-hsien, Hopei: Excavated 1974–1975 (Ho-pei-sheng 1979).

Four cultural layers have been defined here: Erh-li-t'ou (number 4), Early Shang (3), Middle Shang (2), and Late Shang (1). Inscribed pottery appears in each of the Shang layers. The Early Shang examples are reproduced in figure 12.13. The report refers to the nearby Lung-shan culture site

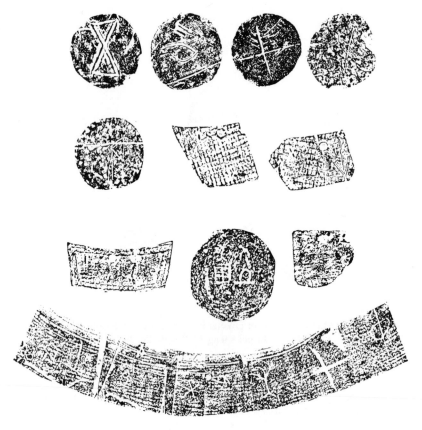

FIGURE 12.14. **Rubbings and photographs of the inscriptions from Wu-ch'eng, Ch'ing-chiang, Kiangsi, dated to Period I (Middle Shang). (T'ang 1975 [inscriptions renumbered].)**

Shang-p'an-wang, which, it may be noted, has been radiocarbon-dated:

ZK–200   2514 ± 134 B.C.

18. Pottery inscriptions from Wu-ch'eng, Ch'ing-chiang, Kiangsi: Excavated 1973–1974 (Chiang-hsi-sheng, Pei-ching ta-hsüeh, and Ch'ing-chiang-hsien 1975; Li K'o-yu and P'eng Shih-fan 1975).

A total of 66 incised graphs among 38 Shang period ceramics and stone casting molds was unearthed at this site. The inscriptions were single graphs, as well as groupings of 2 to as many as 12 graphs. Such groupings are rarely found in ceramics of comparable or earlier age elsewhere. The graphs had been incised in the clay surface prior to baking. Those in the stone casting molds were incorporated after manufacture; the presence of inscriptions in such molds is unusual.

The Shang remains at Wu-ch'eng have been divided into three periods: Period I, equivalent to Cheng-chou Upper Erh-li-kang (Middle Shang); Period II, equivalent to Early and Middle An-yang; and Period III, equivalent to Late An-yang and early Western Chou (p. 77 of the report). The inscribed ceramics derive from each period: 15 items (plus 1 surface find) from Period I, with inscriptions on the bases, shoulders, surface (undefined) totaling some 39 graphs and symbols, among which were groupings of 12, 7, 5, and 4 graphs, as well as individual graphs. The reporters regard these as "earlier than the oracle-bone graphs of the An-yang site and of a type of Shang script from an earlier period" (p. 56). Period II had less: 16 items with a total of 19 graphs (2 only with groupings of 2 each). Period III had even less: 8 items (incised or stamp-impressed), all single graphs (see table 12.1; figs. 12.14, 12.15).

Two C-14 assessments of the Wu-ch'eng site have recently appeared:

ZK–446	1789 ± 156 B.C.
ZK–447	1651 ± 105 B.C.

The first is described as deriving from a Shang period level; both appear to confirm the remains and its pottery script as datable earlier than An-yang.

19. Inscribed pottery from Erh-li-kang, Cheng-chou, Honan: Excavated 1953 (An Chih-min 1954; *KKHP* 1957.1; CKKH 1959a).

Of the inscribed pottery unearthed at the Erh-li-kang site, by far the greater proportion had been incised on the inner surfaces of the lips of wide-mouth *tsun* vases after firing; inscriptions appear on only a few other vessel types. They compare closely to some of the pottery inscriptions from An-yang, Ch'eng-tzu-yai, Liang-chu Neolithic sites, etc., but also have their own characteristics (see fig. 12.16). Two radiocarbon dates from relevant Cheng-chou sites allow a tentative assessment of the lower limits of the age of the culture:

ZK–178	1598 ± 110 B.C.
ZK–177	1573 ± 140 B.C.

20. Inscribed pottery from Nan-kuan-wai, Cheng-chou: Excavated 1955 (Ho-nan-sheng 1973).

On the inner walls and below the lips of some of the wide-mouth *tsun* beakers many varieties of marks were incised (see fig. 12.17). These pottery

TABLE 12.1 **Complete List of Pottery Inscriptions from Wu-ch'eng**

Site details	Type of vessel	Location of inscription	Inscription (hand-copy)	Dating
出土层位、编号	器 物 名 称	刻划部位	辛 文	分 期
74 秋 T7⑤:51	泥质灰陶鉢	器 底	𐩐𐩑𐩒	—
74 秋 T7⑤:58	泥质黄陶盂	器 底		—
74 秋 T7⑤:46	泥质黄釉陶罐	肩部一周		—
74 秋 T7⑤:79 74 秋 T7⑤:57	陶 鉢	器 底	𐋡 、𐋡	—
74 秋 T7⑤:42	长方形陶刀	背 面		—
74 秋 T7⑤:44	马鞍形原始瓷刀	背 面	↓	—
74 秋 T7⑤:40、41 等三件	马鞍形陶刀	背面两侧		—
74 秋 T7⑤:41	马鞍形陶刀	背面中央	匝 (或半)	—
74 秋 T7⑤:60	陶 盂	器 底		—
74 秋 T7⑤:80 74 秋 T7⑤:18	陶 鉢	器 底	半 、𐌓	—
74 垣 基西区取土采集	泥质灰陶鉢	器 底		—
15 件			39 字 (符号)	—
74ET10③:19	泥质红陶碗	器 底		二
74ET13H6:25	泥质软陶片	正反两面		二
74ET13H6:33 74ET6II2:17	红色粉砂岩石范	背 面	坐 业 、业	二
74ET13H6	灰色粉砂岩石范 (或砺石)	器 表	≪	二
74ET9③、④等三件	陶 鉢	器 底	× 、十	二
74ET10:56	陶 鉢	器 底	川	二
73T6③ 73 正 M1	泥质黄陶罐 泥质红陶罐	器表肩部	十 、十	二
73T4③:370 73T4⑤:67	釉陶豆 石 范	圈 足 器 表 浇铸口上方	↓ 、↓	二
73 杨 H2:3	马鞍形陶刀	器表正面		二
73T4⑤	泥质灰陶鉢	器 底	卜 、Ⅲ	二
74WT4②	陶 罐	器表肩部	≪ (锥形、残半)	二
16 件 (片)			19 字 (符号)	二
74秋ET9H11:10	泥质黄陶鬲	颈腹部器表		三
74 秋 ET2③ 74 秋 ET1③:3	印纹陶片 泥质红陶罐	器 表 器表肩部	十 、十	三
73 竹 T1②	马鞍形陶刀	器表背面	∠	三
73 杨 H1 74 秋 ET2③	陶 罐 陶 片	器表肩部 器 表	小 、𐤄	三
74 秋 ET2④ 73 正 T1:7	陶 罐 原始瓷豆	器表肩部 (均压印)		三
8 件 (片)			8 字 (符号)	三
总计 38 件			66 字 (符号)	

SOURCE: Chiang-hsi-sheng, Pei-ching ta-hsüeh, and Ch'ing-chiang-hsien 1975:56–57.

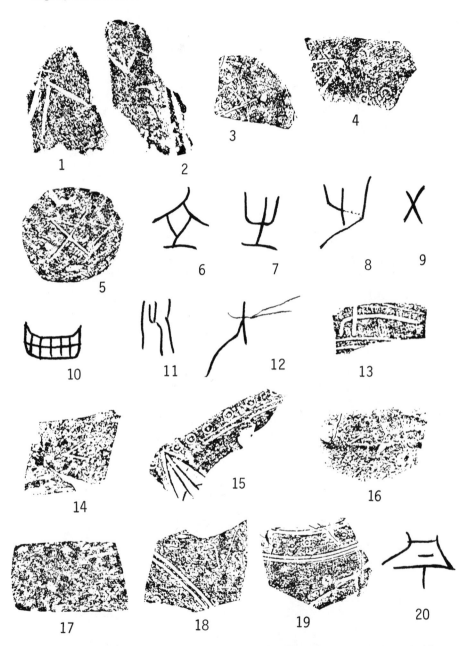

FIGURE 12.15. **Rubbings and photographs of the Wu-ch'eng inscriptions. 1–12: Period II (early-middle An-yang). 13–20: Period III (late An-yang–early Western Chou). (T'ang 1975 [inscriptions renumbered].)**

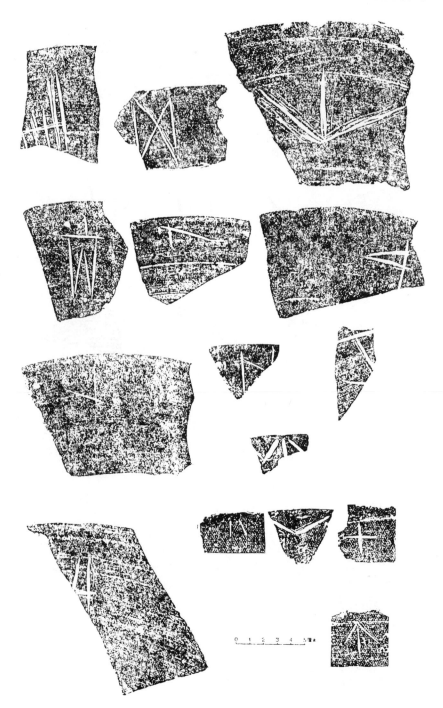

FIGURE 12.16. **Inscriptions on potsherds from Erh-li-kang (An 1954:105, fig. 12; *KKHP* 1957.1:68, fig. 14; CKKH 1959a; fig. 31.) Datable ca. 1600 B.C. or later.**

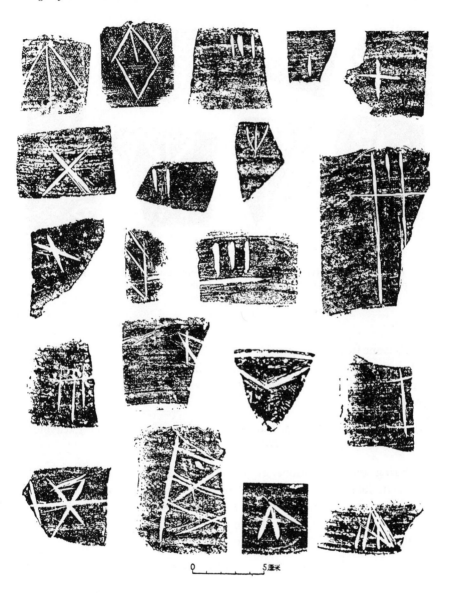

FIGURE 12.17. **Inscriptions on potsherds from Nan-kuan-wai, Cheng-chou, Honan. (Ho-nan-sheng 1973:84, fig. 5.) Datable ca. 1600 B.C. or later.**

vessels came from the upper layer of the Shang culture remains (pp. 83–84 of the report). Generally the pottery is similar to Erh-li-kang types; the upper layer of Shang culture is also considered comparable in age to Upper Erh-li-kang (p. 91).

21. Inscribed pottery from T'ai-hsi-ts'un, Kao-ch'eng, Hopei: Excavated 1973 (Chi 1974; *WW* 1979.6).

During the excavations at T'ai-hsi-ts'un, 77 incised sherds were obtained; items 1–7 (fig. 12.18) are of comparatively early date, the remainder later, but not later than Early An-yang. All were incised in the clay before firing (Chi: 1974:51). Only one C-14 assessment has been made for the site (Middle Shang, wood from a well basin):

BK–75007   1498 ± 114 B.C.

22. Inscribed pottery from layer 2, Hsia-ch'i-yüan, Tz'u-hsien, Hopei: Excavated 1974–1975 (Ho-pei-sheng 1979).

This level, which is of Middle Shang date, had a comparatively large number of incised sherds (see fig. 12.19).

23. Inscribed pottery from the upper cultural layer at Ch'eng-tzu-yai (Li Chi 1934).

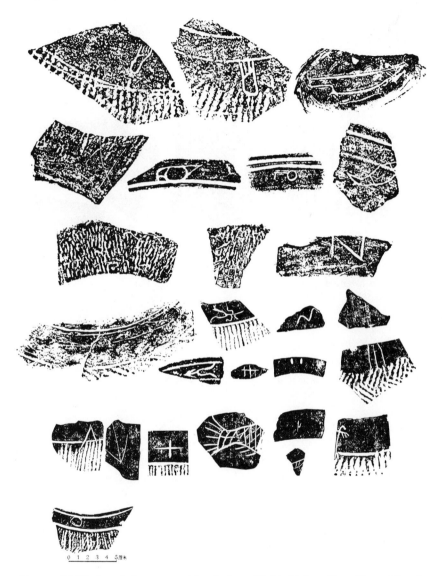

Figure 12.18. **Inscriptions on potsherds from T'ai-hsi-ts'un, Kao-ch'eng, Hopei. (1–12: Chi 1974:50, fig. 1. 13–26: *WW* 1979.6:37, fig. 3.) Datable ca. 1500 B.C. or earlier.**

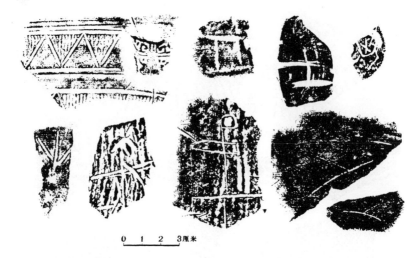

FIGURE 12.19. Pottery graphs from the Middle Shang level (layer 2), Hsia-ch'i-yüan, Tz'u-hsien, Hopei. (Ho-pei-sheng 1979:205, fig. 22.)

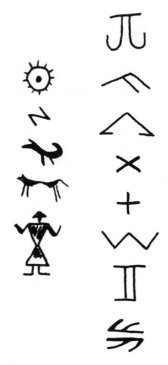

FIGURE 12.20. Right: A selection of eight signs from Hsin-tien, Kansu, pottery urns, which Andersson took to be characters. Left: Five further instances of painted elements located in much the same position as Andersson's examples. (Andersson 1943: pls. 122–123, 127–128, 130–140.)

This level is considered by Hsia Nai (1977:217–232) as comparable to the upper Shuang-t'o-tzu level at Lü-ta-shih, which has been radiocarbon-dated:

ZK–79   1334 ± 105 B.C.

24. Inscribed pottery of "Hsin-tien Age."

Among the painted pottery from the Hsin-tien area in Kansu obtained by Andersson (1943:173–179) in 1923–24 are several painted signs which seemed to him to resemble ancient character-like marks. Comparison of Andersson's painted signs with other decorative elements located in the same positions on similar vessels (cf. fig. 12.20) would seem to demonstrate far more definitely than the ambiguities and insufficiency of negative evidence that these signs simply have a decorative function. Andersson suggested a range of 1300–1000 B.C. for the culture; but note Chang Kwang-chih's more realistic placement of it in a Chou period setting (1977b:397–409; 474, table 18). For our purposes, the "Hsin-tien Age" marks are accordingly of limited interest, notwithstanding T'ang Lan's acceptance of some of the pictographs as belonging to the same evolutionary stem as that of oracle-bone and bronze inscription graphs (1965.1:26–27). Among those who have doubted that the marks are forerunners of characters is Chou Fa-kao, who, in his comparative study of archaeological and traditional text evidence, remarks that "there being no context there can be no clear evidence that they functioned as characters" (1970–71:10). However, an argument along such lines would have to be applied to almost all pottery graphs such as are assembled in the present survey! Comparison with actual decorative elements among Pan-p'o examples (e.g., CKKH and Shen-hsi 1963: figs. 120–123) would clarify the matter.

25. Inscribed pottery from layer 4, Ma-ch'iao, Shanghai: Excavated 1959, 1960, 1966 (*KKHP* 1978.1).

Many varieties of pottery marks were recovered from this level (see fig. 12.21), and they are mainly incised on the inner lip surface. Other than those illustrated in the rubbings, two inscribed items are referred to in the text of the report but not illustrated; one, TIII: 8 (a *fu* 釜 basin) is stated as having the graph 卅 incised on the inner lip surface (p. 128). The reporters assess the date of the layer 4 culture as from Middle to Late Shang to early Western Chou. Thermoluminescence dates for the middle layers have been published recently: 3030 B.P. and 3470 B.P. (averaging 3250 B.P.: 1272 B.C.; see Wang Wei-ta 1979:86).

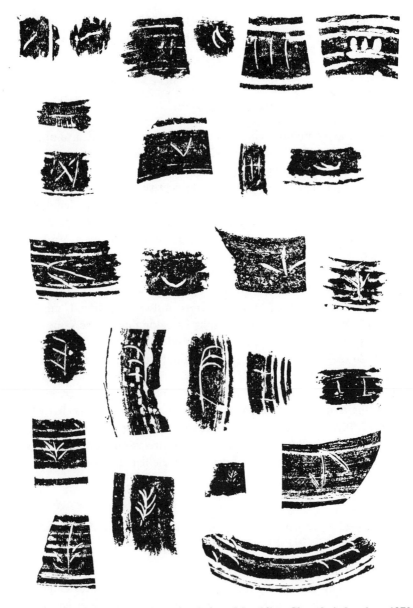

FIGURE 12.21. **Inscriptions on potsherds from Ma-ch'iao, Shanghai, dated ca. 1270
B.C. by thermoluminescence. (*KKHP* 1978.1:127–128, figs. 19, 20.)**

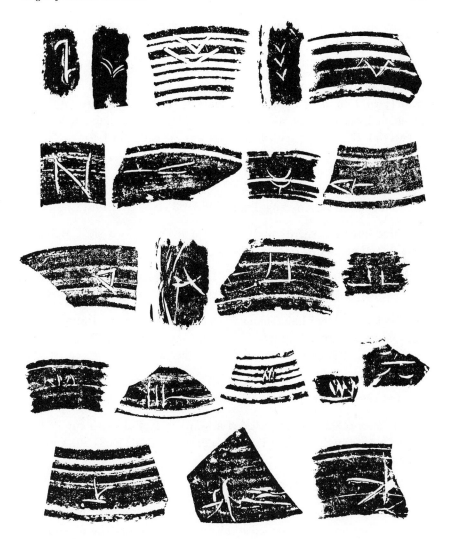

26. Inscribed pottery from Hsiao-t'un, An-yang: Excavated 1928–1936 (Li Chi et al. 1956).

Some 82 inscribed sherds were recovered from the 25,000 pieces excavated. With the exception of one sherd from Ta-ssu-k'ung-ts'un, all came from Hsiao-t'un sites (see fig. 12.22). Only two radiocarbon tests have been conducted, one of which was for a charcoal layer containing oracle bones (71ASTT1: ⑦, west of the village) that was excavated in 1971:

ZK–86   1266 ± 95 B.C.

27. Inscribed pottery from Mei-yüan-chuang Period II and Ta-ssu-k'ung-ts'un Period II, An-yang: Excavated 1958–1959 (*KK* 1961.2).

Three inscribed sherds were recovered from the two sites. Both are datable to Late Shang (see fig. 12.23).

28. Inscribed pottery from layer 1, Hsia-ch'i-yüan, Tz'u-hsien, Hopei: Excavated 1974–1975 (Ho-pei-sheng 1979).

This level is dated Late Shang. A *hu* 壺 vase with an inscription on the rim base and three ╋ graphs incised on the bottom (T29 ①:1216) is reported (p. 207) and rubbings of other sherds are reproduced (see fig. 12.24).

29. Inscribed pottery *pei* 杯 cup (unattested).

The inscription in figure 12.25:1 appears in a pottery *pei* cup of Late Shang type from the Russell Tyson Collection (1964.933, 684.39), Chicago Fine Arts Museum.

30. Inscribed pottery *ku* 瓶 beaker (unattested).

A graph depicting a decapitated man is painted in red on the inside surface of the lip, and an incised graph appears on the inside wall of the rim base (see fig. 12.25:2). This and the preceding item are noted here as a matter of interest only. Possibly other examples exist in public and private collections.

31. Inscribed pottery from Feng-pi-t'ou, Kao-hsiung, Taiwan: Excavated 1956.

There is a total of 11 incised marks, 8 on the interior and 3 on the exterior surfaces of vessel lips (Chang et al. 1969:100, fig. 57; pl. 54); rubbings of 6 of these, made by the author, appear in figure 12.26. Seven of the incised sherds were excavated from pit K-3; the others were from K-1, K-2, N-A,

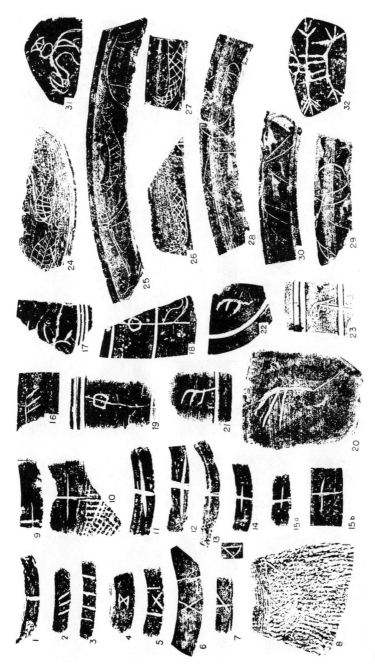

FIGURE 12.22. Inscriptions on potsherds from Hsiao-t'un, An-yang, Honan. (Li et al. 1956: pls. 61–63.)

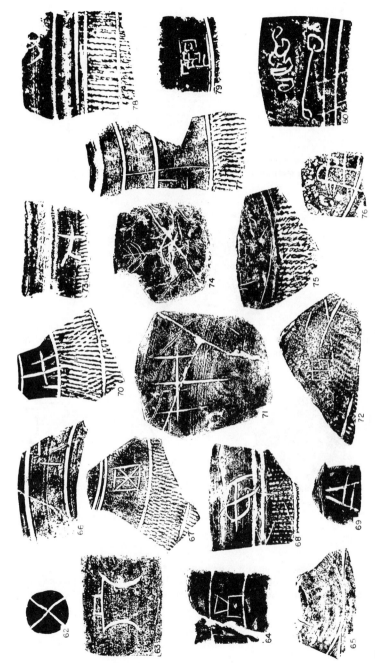

FIGURE 12.22. (continued)

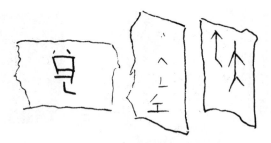

FIGURE 12.23. **Late Shang inscribed potsherds from Mei-yüan-chuang Period II and Ta-ssu-k'ung-ts'un Period II, An-yang, Honan.** (*KK* 1961.2:74, fig. 12.)

FIGURE 12.24. **Inscriptions on potsherds from the Late Shang level, Hsia-ch'i-yüan, Tz'u-hsien, Hopei.** (Ho-pei-sheng 1979:207, fig. 25.)

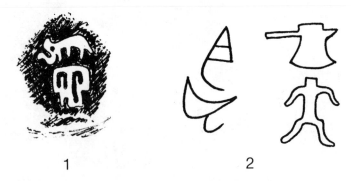

FIGURE 12.25. **Inscriptions on unprovenanced ceramics in public and private collections. 1: An inscribed pottery *pei* cup of Late Shang type, Russell Tyson Collection. 2: Two inscriptions in a pottery *ku* beaker, Avery Brundage Collection, San Francisco.**

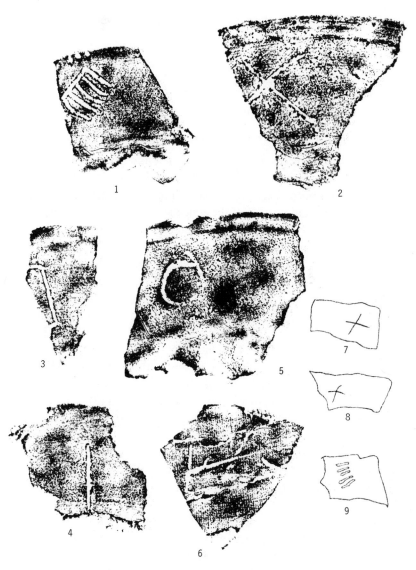

FIGURE 12.26. **Inscribed potsherds from Feng-pi-t'ou, Taiwan. (7–9: Chang et al. 1969; the remainder are rubbings made by the author, courtesy of the Department of Anthropology, National Taiwan University.)**

and E-sec. Radiocarbon dates associated with these layers follow:

Y–1649 (N-A)	1171 ± 124 B.C.
Y–1584 (K-1)	876 ± 94 B.C.
Y–1648 (K-3)	876 ± 78 B.C.
Y–1577 (K-1)	586 ± 145 B.C.

The calibrated dates give a mid-point range of 1170–590 B.C.

32. Incised pottery from Hoi-fung (Hai-feng) and Hong Kong.

These inscribed pieces number more than a hundred and are presently stored in the Museum of History (Archaeological Division), Hong Kong, with a small number of pieces in the Feng P'ing-shan Museum, Hong Kong University. The main portion of the collection, which once comprised the separate collections of Fathers D. J. Finn and Rafael Maglioni, resulted from excavations, surface finds, and local purchases in such places as Hoi-fung, Po-lao (Pao-lou), and Sam-kok-mei (San-chiao-wei), in Kwangtung, as well as Wu-p'ing, in Fukien.

The inscriptions fall into two general categories: (1) straightforward single-line incisions (see fig. 12.27:1–24) and (2) comb-like (multi-pronged) stylus incisions (fig. 12.27:25–36). They are dealt with in more detail in Cheung (1976–1978). Finn (1958) has assessed the age of the artifacts recovered from around Hong Kong at about 500 B.C.; that date is tentatively followed here for the inscribed pottery. Radiocarbon dates from two geometric horizon sites in the Hoi-fung area (3125 ± 150 b.p.; for SOS [Soa-khe (Sha-k'eng), South] and 2950 ± 400 b.p. for TAS [Tang-khe (Tung-k'eng), South] [Beyer 1956:86]—as cited by Chang 1974:451) would, as Chang observes, "place the painted pottery horizon in this same region (Maglioni's SOW [Soa-khe (Sha-k'eng), West]) before 1000 B.C." Carbon-14-dated shells from the Sha-heng-nam (Sha-k'eng-nan) settlement site are reported at 1050 ± 100 b.c.; Maglioni (1975:11) assessed this site as earlier than the Tung-k'eng (Pat-tsai-yün culture) and Sam-kok-mei culture. Thus the inscribed pottery ware from Hoi-fung can be regarded as dating from 800 to 500 B.C.; although this is a little earlier than the Hong Kong inscribed pottery, the two sites can be conveniently treated as one in this general discussion.

RECENTLY EXCAVATED POTTERY INSCRIPTIONS: CHRONOLOGICAL RELATIONSHIPS

Such then is the present record of pre-historic and early historic in-scribed pottery in China. Finds later than Shang and Chou in well-

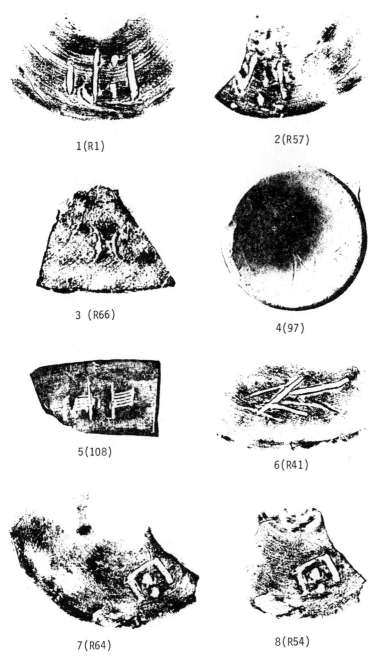

FIGURE 12.27. **Pottery inscriptions from Hoi-fung and Hong Kong. (Courtesy of the Hong Kong Archaeological Society and the Hong Kong Museum.)**

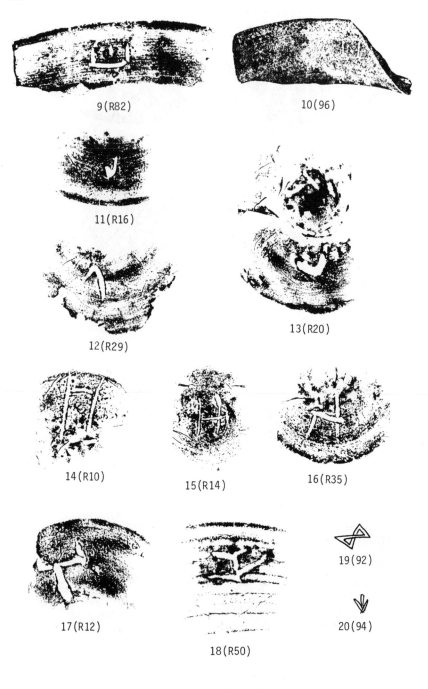

9(R82)

10(96)

11(R16)

13(R20)

12(R29)

14(R10)

15(R14)

16(R35)

19(92)

20(94)

17(R12)

18(R50)

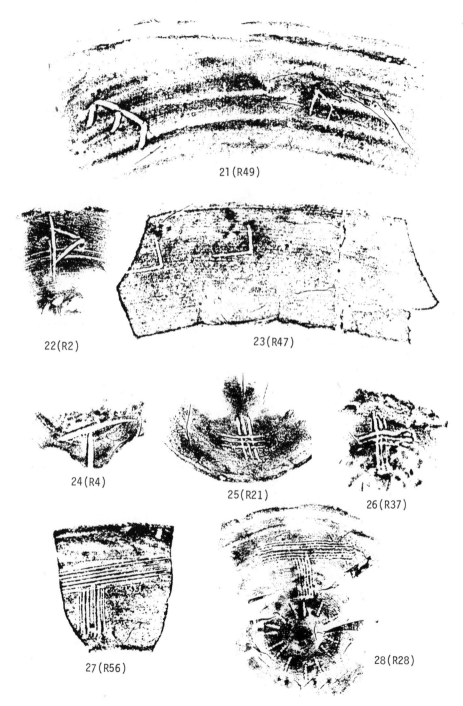

21(R49)

22(R2)

23(R47)

24(R4)

25(R21)

26(R37)

27(R56)

28(R28)

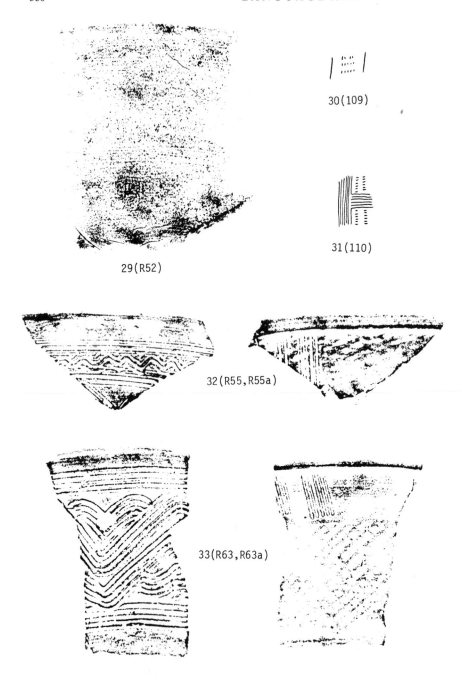

30(109)

31(110)

29(R52)

32(R55,R55a)

33(R63,R63a)

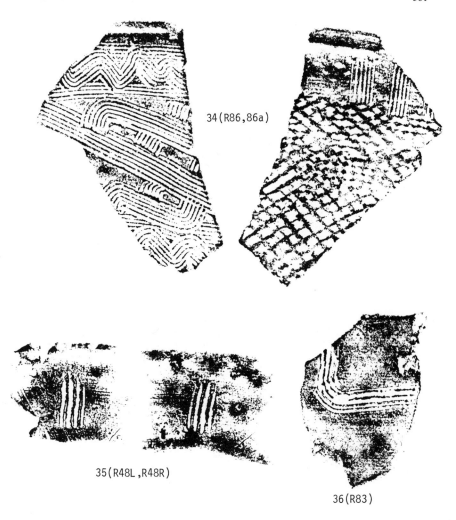

34 (R86, 86a)

35 (R48L, R48R)

36 (R83)

established historical areas are of limited significance for this survey. The materials assembled here comprise all available data in publication up to July 1979, together with hitherto unpublished inscribed sherds from Taiwan, Hong Kong, and Hoi-fung. The problem which now confronts us concerns the role and significance of the pottery inscriptions in the evolution of Chinese characters. This I propose to approach, first by examining the interrelation of the pottery graphs found in the various pottery cultures viewed chronologically; second by considering the relation of these graphs

TABLE 12.2 **Chronological list of sites with inscribed pottery**

Sites	Approximate Datings	Number of Characters
1. Pan-p'o, Sian 半坡西安	4773 ± 141 B.C. to 4194 ± 204 B.C.	113
2. Hsin-yeh-ts'un, Ho-yang 莘野村郃陽		1
3. Wu-lou, Ch'in-tu-chen 五樓秦渡鎮		1
4. Chiang-chai, Lin-t'ung-hsien 姜寨臨潼縣	4682 ± 141 B.C.	4
	(Yang-shao culture 4800–4200 B.C.)	
5. Ling-yang-ho, Chü-hsien 陵陽河莒縣	4262 ± 159 B.C. to 1891 ± 113 B.C.	5
5. Ch'ien-chai, Chu-ch'eng 前寨諸城		1
5. Pao-t'ou-ts'un, Ning-yang 堡頭村寧陽		1
5. Kang-shang-ts'un, T'eng-hsien 崗上村滕縣		4 (?)
	(Ta-wen-k'ou culture 4300–1900 B.C.)	
6. Wang-yu-fang, Yung-ch'eng 王油坊永城	2900/2500 B.C. to 2400 B.C.	?
7. Ch'eng-tzu-yai (lower layers) 城子崖（下文化層）	2463 ± 134 B.C. to 2012 ± 161 B.C.	3
8. Chao-ts'un, Ch'ing-tao-shih 趙村青島市		1
	(Lung-shan culture—lower levels 2500–2000 B.C.)	
9. Sung-tse-ts'un, Ch'ing-p'u-hsien 崧澤村青浦縣	3915 ± 226 B.C. to 2551 ± 137 B.C.	4
10. Liang-chu, Hang-chou-shih 良渚杭州市	3838 ± 253 B.C. to 2247 ± 161 B.C.	9 (?)
11. Ma-ch'iao-chen (layer 5), Shanghai 馬橋（五層）上海		5
	(Liang-Chu culture 3800–2400 B.C.)	
12. Hsia-wang-kang, Hsi-ch'uan 下王岡淅川	2722 ± 139 B.C.	1
13. Pan-shan, Kansu 半山甘肅	2676 ± 143 B.C. to 2344 ± 141 B.C.⎱	10 (?)
13. Ma-ch'ang, Kansu 馬廠甘肅	2620 ± 143 B.C. to 2044 ± 156 B.C.⎰	
14. Liu-wan, Lo-tu-hsien 柳灣樂都縣	2414 ± 258 B.C. to 2025 ± 153 B.C.	52
15. Erh-li-t'ou, Yen-shih 二里頭偃師	2393 ± 149 B.C. to 1429 ± 105 B.C.	24
16. Miao-wan, Yi-Ho, Yen-shih 苗灣伊河偃師	2388 ± 134 B.C.	1

TABLE 12.2 (cont.)

Sites	Approximate Datings	Number of Characters
17. Hsia-ch'i-yüan (Layer 3), Tz'u-hsien 下七垣 (三層) 磁縣	Early Shang period	2
18. Wu-ch'eng, Ch'ing-chiang 吳城清江	1789 ± 156 B.C. to 1651 ± 105 B.C.	66
19. Erh-li-kang, Cheng-chou 二里岡外鄭州	1598 ± 110 B.C. to 1573 ± 140 B.C.	35
20. Nan-kuan-wai, Cheng-chou 南關外鄭州	1573 ± 140 B.C.	9
21. T'ai-hsi-ts'un, Kao-ch'eng 臺西村藁城	1498 ± 114 B.C.	26
22. Hsia-ch'i-yüan (layer 2), Tz'u-hsien 下七垣 (二層) 磁縣	Middle Shang period	8
23. Ch'eng-tzu-yai (upper layer) 城子崖 (上文化層)	1334 ± 105 B.C.	85
24. Hsin-tien, Kansu 辛店甘肅	1300–1000 B.C.	8 (?)
25. Ma-ch'iao (layer 4), Shanghai 馬橋 (四層) 上海	1272 B.C. (thermoluminescent dating)	38
26. Hsiao-t'un, An-yang 小屯安陽	1266 ± 95 B.C.	82
27. Mei-yüan-chuang II 梅園莊二期	Late Shang period }	3
28. Ta-ssu-k'ung-ts'un II 大司空村二期	Late Shang period }	5
28. Hsia-ch'i-yüan (layer 1) 下七垣 (一層)	Late Shang period	9
31. Feng-pi-t'ou, Kao-hsiung, Taiwan 鳳鼻頭高雄臺灣	1171 ± 124 B.C. to 586 ± 145 B.C.	
32. Hoi-fung, Kwangtung 海豐廣東	800–500 B.C. }	68
32. Hong Kong 香港	500 B.C.	

to the later oracle-bone and bronze characters of Shang and Western Chou; and third by exploring the significance of the geographical distribution of the practice of inscribing pottery in China, again taking chronological considerations into account. For the reader's convenience, the relevant sites are tabulated and arranged chronologically in table 12.2.

As demonstrated earlier, the use of character-like markings incised on pottery commenced sometime during the period 4800–4300 B.C. Comparison of the date for items (1) to (4) indicates that the practice of inscribing pottery was widespread in Yang-shao culture area. Whether or not it is valid to class the Pan-p'o pottery marks among the earliest forms of characters, we must face the fact that

> these marks were purposefully and knowingly incised by human beings to represent definite concepts. Although we have not yet been able to determine fully their meanings we may nonetheless appreciate the fact that, lacking at the time characters (as we now know them) to record events, these men when expressing their plain and simple ideas were able to do so objectively and within the realities of their situation and employed all kinds of avenues of expression. These marks accordingly reflect the conceptions of men of that time about certain events or objects . . . and thus have a close affinity with our characters. It is, furthermore, possible that they comprise primitive versions of our ancient characters (CKKH and Shen-hsi 1963: 198).

That the Pan-p'o pottery marks in item 1, above, may be early versions of characters has also been recognized by Yü Hsing-wu (1973), who defines the marks × as 五, "five"; ┤ as 七, "seven"; 十 as 十, "ten"; ‖ as 二十, "twenty"; 丅 as 示, "altar stand"; 丰 as 玉, "jade"; ∀ as 矛, "*mou* spear"; ↑ as 艸, "grass"; ㇏ as 阜, "mound"; and so on. Similarly, Ch'en Wei-chan (1978) follows some of Yü's identifications but interprets ∀ as 竹, "bamboo," and adds the identifications of ⟩(as 八, "eight"; 米 as 釆, "footprint"; and 𗀻 as 網(?), "net." However, leaving aside "numerals" and graphs common to pottery marks of other periods, other graphs give rise to problems. Identifications of the graphs 丅, 丰, 人, ∀ as 示, 玉, 竹, 艸 are based only on shape similarities; such graphs as 米 and 𗀻 are more complex in structure, but there is no basis for accepting their identification as 釆 and 網. Certainly we could seek comparisons between other early script, as in the bronze inscriptions, and the Pan-p'o marks of similar appearance, for example, ↑ and ⌐; but this leads us nowhere, as the bronze graphs have not yet been identified. Ho Ping-ti (1975: 394) seeks to identify the Pan-p'o graphs ⌐ or ⌐ as 人, "man," but supporting evidence is lacking.

Although we can propose a general time range on the basis of C-14 assessments for the Pan-p'o Yang-shao culture, and the site is divided into successive levels, the relation of the inscribed pottery to these levels is not clearly stated in the reports. But careful reading elicits the information that at least two inscribed sherds have a definite place in the archaeological context: figure 12.1:22, which derives from H122, a storage pit in the northern sector of Early Period sequence; and P4107 (fig. 12.1:3), from H21, a pit of Later Period sequence. Only these two "datable" pottery marks are available, but they indicate the range of time attending the practice of inscribing pottery at this site.

The discovery of inscribed pottery at Chiang-chai, Lin-t'ung-hsien (item 4), following immediately upon that of Pan-p'o was stimulating news to those concerned with the origin of Chinese characters. The graph 峯 (see fig. 12.2) was structurally more complex than the various Pan-p'o marks; and, moreover, it was seen as being exceptionally close to the oracle-bone form for the character *yüeh* 岳 "mountain" (峯[*Kikkō* 2.20.16]; 峯 [*Shih-yi* 2.10]; 峯 [*T'ieh-yün* 224.2]; etc.). The lower part of the Chiang-chai graph is identical to the upper part of almost all the oracle-bone examples of the graph *yüeh*. The oracle-bone versions are considered to depict ranges of mountains piled one upon the other, and in the case of the version 峯, there are trees on the lower range (Ch'ü 1960:62–67; Sun Yi-jang 1905: *ch.* 1, 20); the Chiang-chai graph contains elements vaguely reminiscent of these features in the graph *yüeh* and so might be its primitive progenitor.[5] However, this is simply theorizing on structural similarities; more substantial proofs would be required to confirm the apparent identity. What we can conclude is that among the Chiang-chai pottery marks graphs appear which have broken away from the simple single element structures and which are sufficiently advanced in structural form to be regarded as primitive characters. It is to be hoped that the remaining inscribed sherds from this site will soon be published.

As noted earlier, a sample from the Chiang-chai site has been radio-carbon-dated to 4682 ± 141 B.C., but the sample/site association is not clear. Furthermore, the stratification of the inscribed sherds is not re-

---

5. Akatsuka (1977:75–176) has discussed at some length the problematic graph 峯. He takes the upper element to be *yang* 羊, "sheep," and the lower to be *shan* 山, "hill." But the upper element in oracle-bone texts is in the greater proportion of cases written as 峯, and in only a few cases is it executed as 峯 (which form could naturally be transcribed as *yang*, "sheep"). *Yang*, "sheep," on the other hand is nowhere written in the form 峯 in the oracle bones; accordingly, Akatsuka's interpretation is open to doubt. For a full discussion on a comprehensive assembly of the 峯 graphs see Li Hsiao-ting (1965:2915–2941), in which they are listed under the entry *yüeh* 嶽, and Chang Ping-ch'üan's study (1949).

ported, and as a matter of caution a 4000 B.C. date was proposed. It is nevertheless evident that a close relationship exists between the Pan-p'o and Chiang-chai cultures. Those who may question the significance of the pottery marks of the former must, in respect of the evidence attending the latter incised ware, conclude that the beginnings of Chinese characters go back in history at least six thousand years.

Besides this close affinity of Pan-p'o and Chiang-chai regarding the origins of Chinese characters, the inscribed pottery from Ta-wen-k'ou culture sites (item 5) appears also to have received influences from the nuclear area and continued its own development thereafter. There are, of course, points of similarity between the Yang-shao and Ta-wen-k'ou cultures; for example, the painted pottery *ting* 鼎, *tou* 豆, and *kuan* 罐 from Ta-wen-k'ou sites show much the same developmental stages as their Yang-shao counterparts. The Ta-wen-k'ou report pursues the subject in some detail and concludes that the two cultures commenced their development very early, that later they were closely related, and that the ages of the two cultures are close, Ta-wen-k'ou coinciding with Middle and Late Yang-shao (Shan-tung-sheng and Chi-nan-shih 1974:121). Thus the possibility that the inscribing of pottery in the Ta-wen-k'ou sphere was directly or indirectly the result of Yang-shao influences is strong.[6]

The Ling-yang-ho pottery graph 炅 is clearly one that has proceeded beyond primitive marks or pictorial representation of objects (i.e., *hsiang-hsing* 象形, "simple ideographs"); it can be classed as a *hui-yi* 會意, "composite ideograph." Yü (1973:32) analyzes it as "sun," "clouds," and "hills" and takes it to be the character *tan* 旦, "morning." T'ang Lan (1977a; 1977b; 1978) transcribes it as *je* 熱, "hot," and analyses it as "sun," "fire," and "hills," that is, "the light of the sun shining down on the hills causes them to be bathed in flame." The graph 炅 : 炅 occurs three times in the pottery inscriptions. One is actually the simplified or more primitive(?) version: 炅:炅. The fact that the two versions of the graph derive from the two different sites, Ling-yang-ho and Ch'ien-chai, suggests that the meaning of the graph was widely understood by people of that time and that it had attained a standard structure accepted over a wide area.

Inscriptions 3 and 4 in figure 12.3 are representations of respectively, an ax and an adze. Tools of this kind were widely in use at the time. Com-

---

6. It is appreciated, of course, that there are some marked differences between the two general areas of pottery production; and the view that we may have to think in terms of coastal cultural influences proceeding to the Chung Yüan area rather than the reverse is advanced by Huber (ch. 7, above). A directional change of emphasis would not necessarily mean that nothing was received in return.

parison can be made with an Eastern Chou *tou* 豆 pedestal-bowl from Chung-chou-lu, Lo-yang—with a representation of a socketed *pu* coin (*k'ung-shou-pu* 空首布) incised on it (CKKH 1959b:26, fig. 12; 28). The pictographic intent is clear to anyone familiar with the original objects.

With the Ta-wen-k'ou culture apparently covering the rather lengthy period 4300–1900 B.C. (Hsia 1977:225), one might well wonder about the ages of the Ling-yang-ho and Ch'ien-chai sites with their examples of composite ideographs. As a general rule, the more advanced the stage of writing in a particular culture, the later the date. Accordingly, we might regard the Ta-wen-k'ou inscribed pottery as falling somewhere between 3000 and 2500 B.C. Jen Jih-hsin (1974:75) in his report on the Ch'ien-chai site considers the inscribed pottery fragments as Late Ta-wen-k'ou and bases his premise on the advanced stage of the characters. Shao Wang-p'ing (1978:76) proposes a date circa 2500 B.C., which is in line with my assessment. Until the relevant sites have been radiocarbon-dated there is little more we can do to establish an acceptable chronology.

Regarding the assessments made by T'ang Lan (1977a; 1977b; 1978;40), giving variously 5,500 years, 6,000 years, and 6,000 to 7,000 years ago for the commencement of writing in China, it would appear that he has relied on the radiocarbon-dated Ta-tun-tzu site

ZK–90   4497 ± 208 B.C.

to indicate the upper limit of Ta-wen-k'ou culture, but has not realized that the incised pottery is generally regarded as from the later period. In advancing these assessments, however, T'ang Lan also lent the stamp of authority to them, and even to his proposal that the Chiang-chai pottery graphs had been influenced by Ta-wen-k'ou culture. Thus Ch'en Shao-t'ang, in his study of recently excavated pottery inscriptions, follows T'ang Lan:

> Six thousand years ago, Chinese characters had become quite complex; they had left behind the period of simple ideographs and indicators, and had entered the stage of composite ideographs, some comprising as many as three elements. The construction of these 6,000-year-old graphs is identical to that of the *liu-shu* 六書, "the six types of scripts," of later times (1976:42–43).

So Ch'en, and others too, have accepted T'ang's assessment. But more realistic appraisals of the matter have recently been published, for example, the editorial note in *K'ao-ku* (1979.1), which considers various problems relating to Ta-wen-k'ou culture; in summarizing views on the pottery graphs it concludes that because the number of inscribed pieces and the variety of the graphs are so limited, they give no indication of being applicable to literary expression. And because they are datable to so late in the period, it can hardly be maintained that the writing, such as it may have developed, was a feature of the whole period.

Although only three pottery graphs deriving from the lower cultural layer at Ch'eng-tzu-yai (item 7) have appeared, it can be stated that they are closely connected with the development of pottery characters of the Ta-wen-k'ou cultural sites. This is because, as Hsia Nai has observed, "the Shantung Lung-shan culture, aside from mutual influences between it and the typical Honan Lung-shan culture, appears to have had its own local origins. Archaeological discoveries of the last year or two prove that it is the Ta-wen-k'ou culture from which it derives" (1977:224). This situation strongly supports speculations about the Ta-wen-k'ou origins of the pottery inscriptions of the lower levels of Ch'eng-tzu-yai; the inscribed pottery of Wang-yu-fang, Yung-ch'eng (item 6), and Chao-ts'un, Ch'ing-tao-shih (item 8), may partly compensate for the insufficiency of the lower level Ch'eng-tzu-yai material.

At first glance there seems to be an appreciable variety of graphs among the inscribed sherds from around Liang-chu (item 10). If we leave aside "numerals" and those graphs of a different tradition, however, the remainder appear to be practically identical in type to those of the inscribed pottery from the nuclear area. Significant among the Ma-ch'iao layer 5 pottery graphs (item 11) are the 弋 and 卪 on the one sherd, B10:11 (see fig. 12.8:22a). The former graph is like the character *ko* 戈, but the latter is too unclear to be precisely defined. But compared to other graphs in pottery of the same level, these appear somewhat more complex in structure. This holds too for the pottery marks recovered from level 4 (item 25), which may be as much as a thousand years later, thus exhibiting an apparent anomaly in the development of writing as seen in this area. No doubt as further excavation is undertaken and more examples are unearthed the matter will be clarified.

Is there a relation in traditions between the pottery graphs of Liang-chu, Shanghai, and so on, and those of Lung-shan? The range of the Liang-chu culture in terms of C-14 mid-points is approximately 3800–2400 B.C. The commencement is slightly earlier than that of the Shantung Lung-shan but coincides closely with Late Period Ta-wen-k'ou in the lower limits, as well as the Shantung Lung-shan Middle and Later Periods. Notwithstanding their location in the middle and lower reaches of the Yangtze, the Liang-chu sites fall within the area of influence of the formative Lung-shan culture (K. C. Chang 1977b:180–184). Accordingly, Ch'eng-tzu-yai and Liang-chu might conceivably have experienced some degree of inter-cultural diffusion, but, given the virtual absence of inscribed sherds from the lower layer of Ch'eng-tzu-yai, effective evidence of this is still lacking; however, the upper layer inscribed sherds (item 23) have many features in common with pottery graphs from the various Liang-chu sites and from Ma-ch'iao layer 4. Contacts at one time or another must be allowed for, at least in the later phases.

The construction of the Pan-shan and Ma-ch'ang pottery graphs (item 13) resembles that of the Liu-wan graphs (item 14). As the two cultural areas are close in geographical and chronological identity, it is not surprising to find a pronounced degree of calligraphic similarity. The Liu-wan pottery graphs are considerably more advanced than those of Pan-p'o, but they reveal some calligraphic features which differ from those of the pottery graphs of the nuclear area. Certainly, if we set aside those graphs which comprise just one or two simple strokes and those which seem certain to be defined as numerals, the remainder offer difficulties in identification. As to Ch'en Wei-chan's transcriptions of ○ as 日, *jih* "sun"; ＃ as 井, *ching* "well"; 口 as 口, *k'ou* "mouth"; ### as 册, *ts'e* "bamboo tablets"; 兀 as 其, *ch'i* "his"; ⅄ as 午, *wu* "seventh cyclical graph (earth)"; ∧ as 入, *ju* "enter"; 目 as 目, *mu* "eye"; 巾 as 巾, *chin* "kerchief"; and so on, and his assertion that "they can be recognised at a glance" (1978:73), careful scrutiny of the graphs, as well as comparisons with oracle-bone script (the earliest extant examples dating nearly a millennium later), cannot but lead one to doubt the reliability of his transcriptions. For instance, the Liu-wan pottery graphs ＃, ＃, 淼, ###, and ### can only be accepted as belonging to the same type of written form; their variations are simply due to elaboration or simplification of one form. The square graph 口 surely cannot be read as *k'ou* 廿:口 ! The graph 兀 appears in Eastern Chou inscriptions as an abbreviated form of the character 其, whereas the form 箕 is mainly Western Chou. In Shang the lower element 兀 does not appear at all; how then can a pre-Shang form be taken as equivalent to an Eastern Chou form? Similarly, to read the pottery graph 目 as modern 日, bypassing the Shang/Chou form 𓂆 in its evolution during Eastern Chou to the form 目, from which modern 日 derives, is unacceptable. Transcriptions of 巾, ○, ⅄, and ∧ as modern 巾, 日, 午, and 入 are possible, but no proof can be brought to bear. If we were to follow Ch'en's approach, the graph 禾 would be *t'ien* 天, "heaven," the graph 4 would be arabic 4, and so on. Fortuitous similarities in shape can be of little significance unless there is contextual support.

Inscribed pottery from Erh-li-t'ou (item 15) derives only from Late Period layers, but these are earlier than the Shang Erh-li-kang level of Cheng-chou. Many of the pottery graphs are written on much the same principles as the Middle/Late Shang oracle-bone characters of Hsiao-t'un—for example, 囟 (死?) and 囟 (俎?)—demonstrating instances of possible filiation.

Pottery inscriptions from Erh-li-kang (item 19) seem not to have proceeded far beyond the Pan-p'o style of simple incisions; possibly they are really nothing but marks. However, it would be expected that by that time some signs of development toward characters would be evident; the evidence perhaps is yet to be unearthed. Unfortunately, the latest relevant material (comprising two inscriptions of Early Shang date only, from layer 3, Hsia-ch'i-yüan, Tz'u-hsien) is insufficient to help resolve the matter.

Inscribed pottery from the T'ai-hsi site, Kao-ch'eng (item 21), contains several instances of characters approximating Shang oracle-bone forms: 屮: 止, chih "foot"; ⊘: ⊘: 目, mu "eye"; ▽: ∂: 刀, tao "knife"; and so on. These, like the Hsia-ch'i-yüan layer 2 examples (item 22), are datable to the Middle Shang, and among them are some quite complex structures (e.g., fig. 12.19:4, 6; the former is, in some respects, close in structure to the oracle-bone graph 屮: cheng 爭, the name of a diviner). As in the case of Hsiao-t'un incised pottery, the T'ai-hsi graphs are, for the most part, incorporated in much the same locations on the vessels, even among variant vessel types. A common practice of this kind may indicate some degree of cultural inter-communication.

Inscribed pottery from Wu-ch'eng (item 18) includes graphs which are entirely different from those of Shang and Chou. As T'ang Lan observes:

> This is specially so in Period I (Middle Shang) remains: the seven character grey pottery po 鉢 vase and the five character yellow pottery yü 盂 basin are conspicuous in this regard. It is quite possible that these yet again provide an instance of another written language long lost to us. In Periods II (Middle to Late Shang) and III (Late Shang to early Western Chou), the graphs show evidence of influences from the Shang culture area and these non-Shang types of characters are less often found (1975:75).

Chao Feng (1976) has made a comparative study of the graphs among the Wu-ch'eng pottery examples which have much in common with oracle-bone graphs. Some of his identifications can be noted in table 12.3 below, reproduced from his essay. In general, he concludes (p. 60) that the Wu-ch'eng pottery graphs preserve primitive elements more than do the Shang oracle-bone characters, and that there can be noted among them "graphs" and "marks" which show clearly the close relationship between the Wu-ch'eng Shang culture and that of the nuclear area. Thus the Wu-ch'eng graphs can be regarded with considerable interest, as they appear to exhibit an independent development in their earliest stages, and only later (Shang

TABLE 12.3 **Pottery Graphs from Wu-ch'eng Compared with Graphs from Oracle Bones and bronze Inscriptions**

The first horizontal column has the modern character forms; in the second appear the pottery graphs. Oracle bone graphs (together with source references) of "early," "middle," and "late" Shang are presented in the next three columns. Bronze inscription characters (together with source references) of "early," "middle," and "late" Western Chou date appear in the last three columns.

		材	上串	寮	田	土	于		之	祀	在
陶文		𝌽		早	田	𝤀	于		止	𝖰	┼
甲	早	粹1108 金13.2	乙3411 林1.22.19	屑上23.14	人281 佚323	乙3409 庫1549	后上7.11 后下42.9	粹1043	粹1115 乙2587	天81	
骨	中	佚184.3 人615 粹148 外57		甲903 粹433 粹10	人2363	粹18 戰1.1	乙1474 外50	人3169 甲668 京津3645 甲889			
文	晚	前3.28.5			前3.28.5	粹907	甲3659	金728 前3.28.5 前2.9.7 前1.42.1			
西	早				盂鼎	大丰殷 沈子殷	保卣 大盂鼎 矢方彝 小臣謎殷				
周	中				卯殷		縣改殷 君夫殷 曶鼎	鄭殷			
金	晚				揚殷	散盤	大克鼎 毛公鼎	卯蔞殷 休盤			

SOURCE: Chao 1976:224–225.

to Western Chou) do they reveal signs of nuclear area influence. Much later still (Western Chou to Spring and Autumn), these developments resulted in a common written language, as in the case of the states of Hsü 徐, Ch'u 楚, Wu 吳, and Yüeh 越 (Kuo 1972:10).

T'ang Lan's observation that the development toward a single written Chinese language in the area of the Han peoples was necessarily gradual is most relevant in respect to the Wu-ch'eng graphs. There was not, as he points out, just a single [written] language existing from most ancient times to the present.

Pottery graphs from the upper layer of Ch'eng-tzu-yai (item 23) and those from the various An-yang sites of Hsiao-t'un, Mei-yüan-chuang, and Ta-ssu-k'ung-ts'un (items 26 and 27) are essentially of a common cultural lineage, and their calligraphic execution is close to that of the oracle-bone characters.

Although the materials from Feng-pi-t'ou, Hoi-fung, and Hong Kong are of comparatively late date, they nevertheless derive from Neolithic contexts and preserve features of a potential written script in its primitive stages.

Only a few inscribed pottery sherds from Feng-pi-t'ou (item 31) have appeared to date (fig. 12.26). With the exception of four pieces with the mark × (*wu* 五, "five"?) and one with a vertical mark which could be

TABLE 12.4 **Comparison of Identical and Nearly Identical Pottery Graphs from Various Sites in Chronological Order**

Relevant characters from Shang and Chou are presented in the lower columns, with modern transcriptions in the lowermost column.

	Site with Inscribed Pottery / Pottery graphs	1	2	3	4	5	6	7	8	9	10	11	12
1	Pan-p'o, Hsi-an 西安半坡	I	II			X					七	X	E
2	Hsin-yeh Ts'un, Ho-yang 郃陽莘野村												E
3	Wu-lou, Ch'in-tu Chen 秦渡鎮五樓												
4	Chiang-chai, Lin-t'ung Hsien 臨潼姜寨	I				X							
5	Ling-yang Ho, Chü Hsien 莒縣陵陽河												
6	Ch'ien-chai, Chu-ch'eng 諸城前寨												
7	Pao-t'ou Ts'un, Ning-yang 寧陽堡頭村												
8	Kang-shang Ts'un, T'eng Hsien 滕縣崗上村												
9	Wang-yu-fang, Yung-ch'eng 永城王油坊												
10	Ch'eng-tzu-yai (Lower level) 城子崖(下文化層)	I											
11	Chao Ts'un, Ch'ing-tou Shih 青島趙村					X							
12	Sung-tse Ts'un, Ch'ing-p'u Hsien 青浦崧澤												
13	Liang-chu, Hang-chou Shih 杭州良渚	I				X		∧	V	+			
14	Ma-ch'iao Chen (Layer 5), Shanghai 上海馬橋(五層)					XX	X						
15	Hsia-wang-kang, Hsi-ch'uan 淅川下王岡						X						
16	Pan-shan, Kan-su 甘肅半山												
17	Ma-ch'ang, Kan-su 甘肅馬廠	I		III		X				+			
18	Liu-wan, Lo-tu Hsien 樂都柳灣	I	II				X	∧	V	+			
19	Erh-li-t'ou, Yen Shih 偃師二里頭	I	II	III	IIII	X			V	+|	)(		
20	Miao-wan, Yi Ho, Yen Shih 伊河苗灣						X						
21	Hsia-ch'i-yüan (Layer 3),Tz'u Hsien 磁縣下七垣(三層)					X(1)							
22	Wu-ch'eng, Ch'ing-chiang 清江吳城					X	X			+			
23	Erh-li-kang, Cheng-chou 鄭州二里岡	I	II	III		X		IX		+			
24	Nan-kuan-wai, Cheng-chou 鄭州南關外			III		X / IX		✳					
25	T'ai-hsi Ts'un, Kao-ch'eng 藁城台西					X		∧		+			
26	Hsia-ch'i-yüan (Layer 2) 下七垣(二層)	-				X(1)							
27	Ch'eng-tzu-yai (Upper level) 城子崖(上文化層)					X							
28	Hsin-tien, Kan-su 甘肅辛店					X							
29	Ma-ch'iao (Layer 4), Shanghai 上海馬橋(四層)			III		X / XI		✳					
30	Hsiao-t'un, An-yang 安陽小屯	I		III	IIII		X			+			
31	Mei-yuan-chuang II 梅園莊 二期												
32	Ta-ssu-kung Ts'un II 大司空村二期												
33	Hsia-ch'i-yüan (Layer 1) 下七垣(一層)					X(1)							
34	Feng-pi-t'ou, Kao-hsiung, Taiwan 高雄鳳鼻頭	I				X							
35	Hoi-fung, Canton 廣東海豐						IX	X				)(	
36	Hong Kong 香港												
37	Oracle bone inscriptions 甲骨文	一(十)	二	三			X	∧		+	)(		
38	Bronze inscriptions 金文	一(中)	二	三			X	介		+	)(		
39	Pi-sha-kang, Cheng-chou 鄭州碧沙崗										)(		
40	Lo-yang, Chung-chou-lu 洛陽中州路										)(		
41	Ch'ing-yüan, Kwang-tung 廣東清遠												
42	Pai-chia-chuang, Cheng-chou 鄭州白家莊					X							
43	Modern character transcriptions 譯文	一(十)	二	三	四	五(畫五)	?	六	!	七(西)	八	?	

13	14	15	16	17	18	19	20	21	22	23	24	25	26	27	28	29	30	31	32	33	34	35	36	37	38	39	40	41

Chart of ancient Chinese character forms (columns 13–41).

Bottom row of characters:

示(1)　草(1)竹(1)丘(1)　壘　癸　戈(1)　世(1)　目　止　有　左/右　矢　夫　戍　井　九(1)

regarded as "ten," the others cannot be recognized, nor can they be acceptably paralleled with other mainland pottery graphs.

Hoi-fung and Hong Kong pottery graphs (item 32) fall into two main categories: in the first, numbers 1 and 2 (fig. 12.27) are clearly duplicatons of the same complex graph ⺀, a structure which has proceeded beyond the more simple types and which, by virtue of its duplication in different pots, must have had specific implications to those who wrote and read it. Numbers 3 and 4 can be read as 〉((pa 八, "eight") and |X (shih-wu 十五, "fifteen"), respectively. Number 5 ⺀ appears as a further case of an advanced character structure strongly reminiscent of oracle-bone and bronze inscription structures. Numbers 7 and 8 each resolve into the same structure 冂 and differ from numbers 9 and 10 ⺌ by only a single stroke; since one group is reversed in relation to the other, they are probably two entirely different graphs. Duplications of these two, as well as the graph ✓ in numbers 12–13 and the graph ⼁ in numbers 14–16, illustrate the extensive and repeated use of identical marks, or graphs, and the tendency toward identity of calligraphic structures when repeated. This is evident also in the second category, the "comb"-written graphs—for example, numbers 25 and 26 (fig. 12.27): ⽥ —while the large array of "T"-shaped marks ⾦ ·(numbers 27–28) offers especially good evidence of the wide use made of this graph alone.

Let us now compare some of the Hoi-fung/Hong Kong graphs with those in pottery elsewhere; this can be done conveniently with reference to rows 35 and 36 in table 12.4. Although these southern structures are simple, it would nonetheless seem evident that they were all involved in the general process of development of Chinese characters and were representative of the earliest primitive forms. Apart from basic features that may have been directly influenced by the pottery graphs of other spheres, the more important consideration concerns those that were nurtured within the local cultures and independently developed. The characteristic double F motif found as a decoration on pots from this region provides good supporting evidence of such aspects of local initiative. Taking all such factors into account, the cases of identity with particular graphs from Pan-p'o, Erh-li-kang, Ch'eng-tzu-yai, and so on, would allow us to propose that the first category graphs (fig. 12.27:1–24) followed the same evolutionary path toward writing. Of special interest is the graph ⺀ (fig. 12.27:5), which structurally appears to be a combination of two five-finger hand elements each holding an object, reminiscent of the oracle-bone/bronze inscription graph ⺀ (shou 受, "receive"); as such it could be regarded as an instance of the hui-yi composite graph developing in this southern cultural complex.

In the second category (fig. 12.27:25–36), the "comb"-written graphs are distinctive and the writing of the marks orderly; in no other early pottery culture in China have such comb-written marks as yet appeared. However, the use of dots in numbers 29, 30, and 31 is close to the technique noted in certain Liang-chu inscribed red pottery sherds (item 10c above). This feature on its own might suggest a common origin, but further archaeological evidence will be required to resolve the issue.

It may be asked if the comb-marks should be viewed as graphs at all, since they were executed by the same comb instrument employed in effecting the decor elsewhere on the vessels (cf. fig. 12.27:32–34). Each sherd has decor on the inside of the lips, and occasionally comb-written graphs appear in the midst of decor on the outside surface; obviously the basic nature of the marks is close to that of the decor, but the latter is to be distinguished from the former, as evidenced in number 35. In the case of number 36, the pattern in the inside lip area is in the same class as the decorative patterns on the outside surfaces of other sherds, showing that it was intended to be a piece of decoration and nothing else; the patterns on both surfaces of numbers 33 and 34 are likewise decor only. Thus it can be concluded that the comb markings started off, and continued, as decorative features, but that at some later stage the instrument used to execute them was also employed to make specific marks on either the inside or the outside surfaces of the vessels. These marks had some particular significance. They were not decor and can be compared to those in the first category.

Let us now turn our attention to the pottery inscriptions in table 12.4. Although it is possible to find an appreciable number of examples for comparison among the various sites, by far the greater number of graphs occur once only, thus limiting this aspect of the survey. The sites in table 12.4 are arranged in chronological order (i.e., they follow the assessments discussed in the preceding pages) and identical or nearly identical graphs from each are listed in the same columns. In the lower section of the table, comparable characters from Shang oracle bones, bronze inscriptions, and Warring States period pottery graphs are noted for comparative purposes only; there is no intention to indicate absolute relationships between the two, although one need not be so cautious in the case of some of the graphs, particularly the numerals. In his study referred to earlier, Ch'iu Hsi-kuei (1978:163) remarked about the evidence when viewed along such lines: "This cannot be mere coincidence; the numerals [in later Chinese writing] must have derived from such marks on pottery." However, Ch'iu emphasizes the point:

If Chinese writing [the characters] has in part derived from some of these pottery marks this does not necessarily mean that the marks themselves were originally characters; the examples cited above [Pan-p'o, Ma-ch'ang, Liu-wan, Ta-wen-k'ou] clearly were not able to constitute a full system of written characters, and at the same time they do not even appear to be primitive characters (p. 164).

Generally we can agree with these sentiments, except that notwithstanding the apparent lack of a full character system among the pre-historic pottery graphs, such examples as we have studied from Chiang-chai (item 4), Ta-wen-k'ou (item 5), and Ma-ch'iao, layer 5 (item 11), do in fact exhibit the features of primitive characters (i.e., the establishment of composite ideographs); thus we cannot dismiss the possibility that at that time a character system was already being established.

Looking at it from another aspect, pottery graphs as such are not especially suited to writing (to the composition of sentences); we cannot take these limited materials as sole evidence of the number of graphs in active use. As characters proper developed in later times, for instance, we find them co-existent with pottery marks—for example, in the Warring States period layer of the Pai-chia-chuang, Cheng-chou, site from which was excavated both incised and stamped pottery (*WW* 1956.4). The stamped graphs had developed into a very mature kind of character, but the incised graphs still remained in a simple and primitive form (see fig. 12.28). Thus no matter how many more inscribed pottery marks come to light from future excavations, they cannot be regarded as representative of the entire corpus of writing at any particular stage, even in much earlier times. Nevertheless, as demonstrated in table 12.4, the frequency with which identical graphs recur among the pottery marks in different periods provides particularly persuasive evidence of their connection to the true characters of later times and supports the view that some of the marks incised on the Pan-p'o pots were graphs denoting numerals, and that some may practically be classifiable as characters.

As a result of geographical and cultural differences, the development of pottery inscriptions in various places often exhibits local characteristics. For instance, the pottery graphs of Ma-ch'ang (item 12) and Liu-wan (item 14) and those of the nuclear area of the same period can be grouped into two distinct kinds, and the Wu-ch'eng pottery graphs (item 18) have their special characteristics. Nevertheless, upon examination it becomes evident that the variant features as such are due only to the influences of local cultural traits; so far as origins are concerned, these graphs and those of the nuclear area derive from a common ancestral stem.

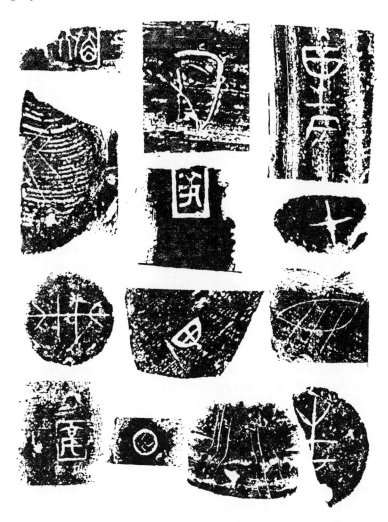

FIGURE 12.28. Examples of the concurrent appearance of both "primitive" and "advanced" graphs in pottery inscriptions. It will be noted that some of the latter are stamped, as well as incised, in the clay. From the Warring States level, Pai-chia-chuang, Cheng-chou. (*WW* 1956.4:8, fig. 28.)

Among the pottery graphs, those we take to be numerals recur in practically every period, and their influence extends down to Shang, Chou, and later times. This aspect of the story has been well dealt with by Cheng Te-k'un (1973:41–58) and Ho Ping-ti (1975:231–236). But there is another feature associated with the primitive form of numerals which deserves attention, for it may serve to indicate a long-lost tradition concerning the use of numerals in the development of Chinese writing. Figure 12.29 presents hand-copies of curious combinations of numerals found on a Shang oracle bone from Ssu-p'an-mo, An-yang, and on two oracle bones of Shang date from the Feng-Hao region near Sian. Various bronze inscriptions contain comparable graphs. Among Western Chou settlement sites at Chang-chia-p'o, Feng-hsi, a number of bone arrows were incised with similar individual elements and in some cases had less complex combinations. In pottery there are a few examples, but the dating is uncertain.

T'ang Lan (1957) believes that in these combinations the numerals functioned as an alphabet and that the structures, based as they are on simple pottery marks, exhibit a development in writing. He suggests that the Shang numerals 1 to 8 may have derived from these complex combinations; or, because of the near identity with Shang and Chou *ku-wen* characters, it is possible that the combinations originated from the Shang numerals. But with the wealth of data we now have from pottery, bone, and bronze inscriptions relating to numerals, it would appear evident that these unusual combinations would have been based on numerals already in use, whereas the combinations as such reflect some peculiar line of development in written expression whose significance is not presently ascertainable. Kuo Mo-jo (1972) also expressed the view that they belonged to the same line of development as the pottery graphs and that the numerals 1 to 8 in Shang derived from the same source. As to their functioning as a kind of alphabet, however, Kuo, Cheng Te-k'un (1973), Li Hsiao-ting (1969), and others show no sign of agreement. Li points out the impracticability of the idea and then suggests that the combinations of numerals could have been a kind of clan lineage sign depicting the generation of the person recording it. Thus, whatever interpretation may be proposed, it remains evident that these numeral combinations represent a particular use of numerals whose original significance, when thus combined, has long been lost.

THE GEOGRAPHICAL DISTRIBUTION OF RECENTLY EXCAVATED INSCRIBED POTTERY

In the foregoing sections we have been largely concerned with the chronological considerations in appraising the inter-relationships of the

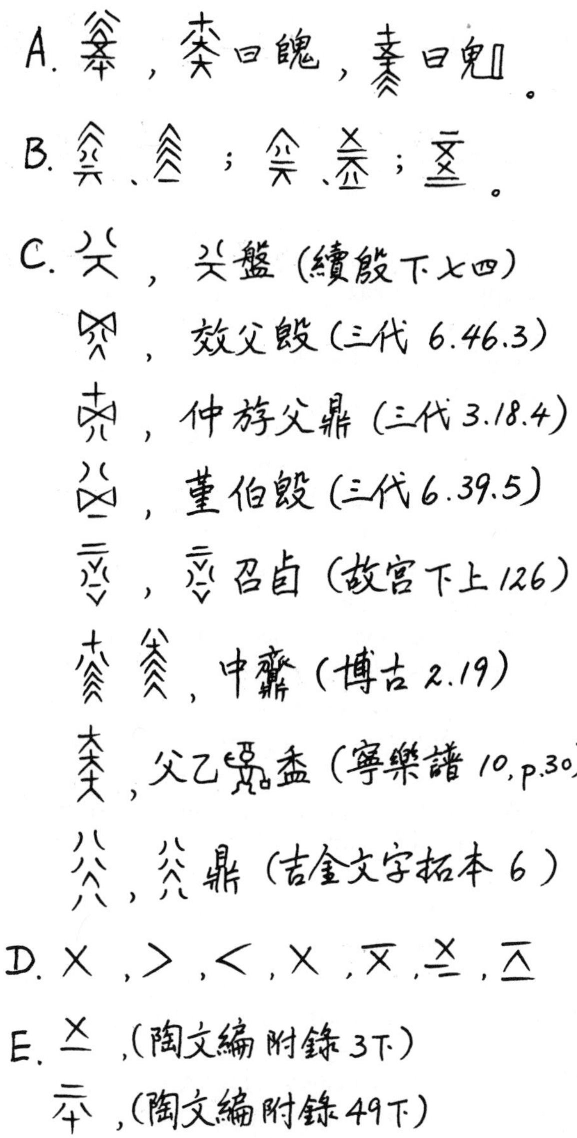

A. 夒 , 夒曰魄 , 夒曰鬼刂 。

B. (symbols) 、 (symbols) ; (symbols) 、 (symbols) ; (symbol) 。

C. (symbol) , 尖盤 (續殷下七四)

   (symbol) , 效父殷 (三代 6.46.3)

   (symbol) , 仲斿父鼎 (三代 3.18.4)

   (symbol) , 堇伯殷 (三代 6.39.5)

   (symbol) , (symbol)召卣 (故宮下上 126)

   (symbol) , 中齋 (博古 2.19)

   (symbol) , 父乙(symbol)盉 (寧樂譜 10, p.30)

   (symbol) , (symbol)鼎 (吉金文字拓本 6)

D. X , > , < , X , X̅ , X̲ , △

E. (symbol) , (陶文編 附錄 3下)

   (symbol) , (陶文編 附錄 49下)

FIGURE 12.29. Examples of unusual combinations of numerals which may indicate the genealogical situations of the persons using them. A: Ssu-p'an-mo, An-yang, Honan. (Redrawn from Hsiang 1951: pl. 41.) B: The Feng-Hao area, Sian, Shensi. (Redrawn from T'ang 1957: 34–36, fig. 1.) C: Examples redrawn from various bronze catalogs. D: Inscribed arrowheads. (Redrawn from CKKH 1962: 91.) E: Examples from pottery. (Redrawn from Chin 1964.)

inscribed pottery. If we now examine the geography of the finds, further appreciation of the inter-relationships results. It is important to keep in mind, however, that in any particular area inscribed pottery has not necessarily been recovered from all cultural levels, and not all corners of the country have been archaeologically explored. Thus obvious difficulties in interpretation arise. This situation notwithstanding, I have plotted the various sites in map 12.1 and for general convenience in discussion have grouped them on the basis of inscription types and chronological assessments into fifteen general areas (numbers are provided for identification purposes only).

From both the geographical and the chronological viewpoint, the Yang-shao culture cluster around Pan-p'o—comprising Hsin-yeh-ts'un, Wu-lou, and Chiang-chai (items 1–4)—forms the center of the early nuclear area development of the practice of inscribing pottery. The presence of a number of common traits among the pottery characters has already been demonstrated. This group will be denoted Area 1. Area 2 comprises the affiliated inscribed pottery sites of Ling-yang-ho, Ch'ien-chai, and Pao-t'ou-ts'un of the Ta-wen-k'ou culture, to which Area 3 (Kang-shang-ts'un) could be added because of the presence therein of Ta-wen-k'ou culture characteristics (these sites are all grouped under item 5). But we have already observed that although there was an appreciable influence on the Ta-wen-k'ou culture from the Yang-shao of the nuclear area, all the inscribed materials of Areas 2 and 3 are datable only to the Late Period and thus are far removed from the Yang-shao in time; the two cultural areas are also geographically distant. Some kind of intermediate or transitional cultural stage between the two areas would be expected, but none has as yet appeared. The recently discovered Hsia period sites at Hsia-hsien, Shansi, and Teng-feng-hsien, Honan, where pottery inscriptions of a type reminiscent of Erh-li-t'ou are said to have been found may demonstrate such a connecting link.[7] Area 4, the lower layers of Ch'eng-tzu-yai (item 7), contains incised sherds which suggest a strong influence from the Late Ta-wen-k'ou. The Liang-chu sites (items 9–11) of Area 5 with inscribed sherds most likely received influences from the Late Ta-wen-k'ou and the Lower Ch'eng-tzu-yai Lung-shan.

At about the same time these developments were occurring in the Late Ta-wen-k'ou, Lower Ch'eng-tzu-yai, and Liang-chu levels, the Pan-shan and Ma-ch'ang sites (item 13) of Kansu and the Liu-wan site (item 14) of

---

7. Li Hsüeh-ch'in 李學勤, personal communication (15 March 1979) during the visit of the Chinese Academy of Social Sciences to Canberra.

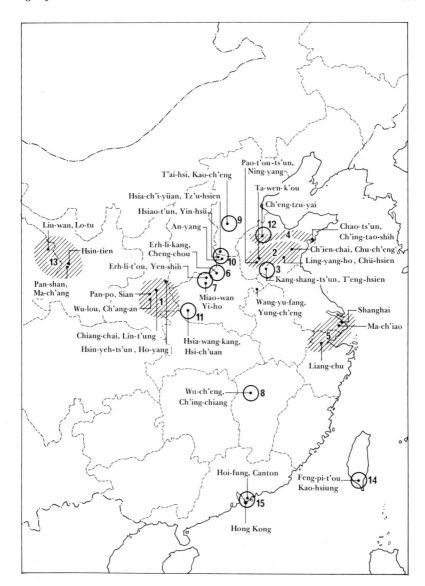

MAP 12.1. Sites with inscribed pottery surveyed in this chapter. The area numbers allocated to each site are for reference only. The shading indicates sites earlier than ca. 2400 B.C.

Tsinghai (Area 13) were being influenced by the westward extension of the Yang-shao of the nuclear area, and inscribed pottery appears in their remains. Due no doubt to geographical reasons, the pottery graphs of Liu-wan differ in some respects from those of the nuclear area sites and from those to the east, much as do the remarkable variations attending the Wu-ch'eng pottery graphs (item 18) well to the south.

The pottery inscriptions of Hsia-wang-kang (item 12; Area 11) are similar to those of Erh-li-t'ou (item 15) and Miao-wan (item 16). Although we cannot be really sure that the pottery graphs from the latter are indeed inscriptions rather than decor, the features may, nevertheless, reflect influences from the Hsia-wang-kang area, which is earlier than Erh-li-t'ou.

Leaving aside the probability of influences from Areas 2, 3, and 4 traveling west, and of influences from Area 1 proceeding east, the pottery inscriptions from Areas 6 and 7—Erh-li-kang (item 19) and Erh-li-t'ou (item 15)—manifest local cultural developments whose origins probably derive from the early Lungshan of Honan. The pottery graphs excavated in 1977 from Wang-yu-fang (item 6) which belong to the eastern Honan Lung-shan culture (Shang-ch'iu and Chung-kuo 1978) may, when published, throw light on this question.

The Wu-ch'eng inscribed pottery (item 18; Area 8) manifests a mature stage of development; it originated at an earlier date than the preceding examples. The later development of this pottery script would probably have been influenced by a variety of sources, including Areas 2 to 7 above. Further developments in the general area south of the Yangtze, taken together with those in Area 5, may have had some basic influence on the later Ch'u and Yüeh script. The inscribed pottery from T'ai-hsi (item 21; Area 9) probably resulted from influences from Areas 2–7 and, furthermore, manifests a definite relation to early Yin-hsü period pottery graphs. Inscribed pottery from the upper layers of Ch'eng-tzu-yai (item 23; Area 12) and from Hsiao-t'un (item 26; Area 10) has clearly passed through a long period of development resulting in the appearance of primitive graphs of a late type. In Area 10 attention may also be drawn to the Hsia-ch'i-yüan site (item 22), which has inscribed pottery from all three periods (Early, Middle, and Late Shang) and is very close to the inscribed pottery sites of T'ai-hsi and Hsiao-t'un, thus exhibiting close geographical and temporal relationships.

Although it is evident that the pottery inscriptions of Feng-pi-t'ou (item 31; Area 14) would have received influences from the nearby coastal mainland area and the Liang-chu culture, we cannot dismiss the possibility that the nuclear area culture may have influenced this southern area. Though the comparatively late appearance of the practice of incising pottery in Area 15, Hoi-fung and Hong Kong (item 32), might well have resulted from a variety of inspirations, until further archaeological data is forthcoming the picture here will remain somewhat out of focus.

In conclusion, despite doubts that may be held regarding the status of Pan-p'o pottery graphs (item 1) as primitive characters, the Chiang-chai graphs (item 4) of only a few centuries later allow us to propose a date of circa 4000 B.C. for the commencement of a viable, albeit primitive form of Chinese character. And the influence from this area reaching west to Tsinghai, east to Shantung, north to Hopei, and possibly south to Kwangtung and even Taiwan would have resulted in a prolific and active period of experimentation with forms of written expression, the manifestation of which we presently know only through the practice of inscribing pottery.

This survey does not seek to press the view that the case for the independent origins of writing in China can be proved upon the basis of currently available materials. The evidence is obviously still insufficient, although it would appear certain enough that there is almost nothing unearthed as yet which suggests diffusion from the West, or anything that might indicate the arrival of that elusive "germ of an idea" so ardently espoused by the stimulus diffusionist. On the positive side, however, the evidence does point toward a primitive system (or possibly several embryo systems) of elements combining to form single graphs. So far as Chinese characters are concerned, it is precisely this step which marks the difference between *hsiang-hsing* simple ideographs—the universal form of "writing" invented time after time, in place after place, during the millennia-long progression of mankind toward culture and civilization—and the *hui-yi* composite ideograph (better still, let us use the term multi-element graph) which is the essence of the Chinese writing system. It would not be incautious, in the present state of our knowledge, to propose that archaeological discovery over the next few years, if the current rate of progress continues, may well confirm the independent development of characters and composition in the nuclear area and a centrifugal diffusion of writing throughout the Chinese sphere.

REFERENCES

Akatsuka Kiyoshi
1977   *Chūgoku kodai no shūkyō to bunka—In ōchō no saishi*
           中国古代の宗教と文化ー殷王朝の祭祀. Tokyo.

An Chih-min 安志敏
1954   "Yi-chiu wu-erh nien ch'iu-chi Cheng-chou Erh-li-kang fa-
           chüeh chi 一九五二年秋季鄭州二里岡發掘記." *KKHP*
           1954.8:65–109.

Andersson, J. G.
1943   "Researches into the Prehistory of the Chinese." *BMFEA*
           15:1–304.

Barnard, Noel
1980   *Radiocarbon Dates and Their Significance in the Chinese
           Archaeological Scene: A List of 420 Entries Compiled from
           Chinese Sources Published up to Close of 1979.* Canberra.

Barnard, Noel, editor
1974   *Early Chinese Art and Its Possible Influence in the Pacific
           Basin.* Authorized Taiwan edition, pp. xvii–lvii.

Beyer, H. O.
1956   "Preliminary Notes [to Eight Papers on Chinese Archae-
           ology and Early History]." *Proceedings of the 4th Far-
           Eastern Prehistory and the Anthropology Division of the 8th
           Pacific Science Congresses Combined*, pt. 1, fasc. 1: pp.
           83–88.

Chang Chih-min 章知敏
1978   *Yang-shao wen-hua* 仰韶文化. Hong Kong.

Chang, K. C. [Kwang-chih]
1974   "Neolithic Cultures in Southeast Asia." In *Early Chinese
           Art and Its Possible Influence in the Pacific Basin*, edited
           by Noel Barnard. Authorized Taiwan edition, pp. 431–
           457.
1977a   "Prehistoric and Shang Pottery Inscriptions: An Aspect of
           the Early History of Chinese Writing and Calligraphy."
           Paper prepared for the Conference on Chinese Calli-
           graphy, Yale University, Spring 1977.
1977b   *The Archaeology of Ancient China.* 3d ed., rev. and enl.
           New Haven.

Chang, K. C., et al.
1969   *Fengpitou, Tapenkeng and the Prehistory of Taiwan.* New
            Haven.

Chang Ping-ch'üan 張秉權
1949   "Chia-ku wen-tzu lei-pi yen-chiu li (X tzu ti cheng-li)
            甲骨文字類比研究例(𤔫字的整理)." *BIHP* 20.2:175–221.

Chao Feng 趙峯
1976   "Ch'ing-chiang t'ao-wen chi ch'i so fan-ying ti Yin-tai
            nung-yeh ho chi-ssu 清江陶文及其所反映的殷代農業和
            祭祀." *KK* 1976.4:221–228.

Che-chiang-sheng   Che-chiang-sheng wen-wu kuan-li wei-yuan-hui
            浙江省文物管理委員會
1956   "Liang-chu hei-t'ao yu yi-tz'u chung-yao fa-hsien
            良渚黑陶又一次重要發現." *WW* 1956.2:25–28.

Ch'en Shao-t'ang 陳紹棠
1976   "Ts'ung chin-nien ch'u-t'u wen-tzu shih-liao k'an Ch'in-tai
            shu t'ung-wen ti chi-ch'u chi ch'i kung-hsien 從近年出土
            文字史料看秦代書同文的基礎及其貢獻." *Hsin-ya shu-
            yüan hsüeh-shu nien-k'an* 新亞書院學術年刊 18:29–72.

Ch'en Wei-chan 陳煒湛
1978   "Han-tzu ch'i-yüan shih-lun 漢字起源試論." *Chung-shan
            ta-hsüeh hsüeh-pao: Che-hsüeh she-hui k'o-hsüeh pan*
            中山大學學報: 哲學社會科學版 1978.1:69–76.

Cheng Te-k'un 鄭德坤
1973   "Chung-kuo shang-ku shu-ming ti yen-pien chi ch'i ying-
            yung 中國上古數名的演變及其應用." *Hsiang-kang chung-
            wen ta-hsüeh hsüeh-pao* 香港中文大學學報 1:37–58.
1976   "Chung-kuo t'ien-yeh k'ao-ku yü shih-ch'ien-hsüeh
            中國田野考古與史前學." *Hsiang-kang chung-wen ta-hsüeh
            Chung-kuo wen-hua yen-chiu-so hsüeh-pao* 香港中文大學
            中國文化研究所學報 8.1:1–22.

Cheung Kwong-yue 張光裕
1976–1978   "Hsiang-kang po-wu-kuan so ts'ang t'ao-wen ti ch'u-pu
            k'ao-ch'a 香港博物館所藏陶文的初步考察." *Journal of the
            Hong Kong Archaeological Society* 7:68–76.

Chi Yün 季云
1974   "Kao-ch'eng T'ai-hsi Shang-tai yi-chih fa-hsien ti t'ao-chi
            wen-tzu 藁城臺西商代遺址發現的陶器文字." *WW* 1974.8:
            50–53.

Chiang-hsi-sheng, Pei-ching ta-hsüeh, and Ch'ing-chiang-hsien   Chiang-hsi-sheng po-wu-kuan 江西省博物館, Pei-ching ta-hsüeh li-shih-hsi k'ao-ku chuan-yeh 北京大學歷史系考古專業, and Ch'ing-chiang-hsien po-wu-kuan 清江縣博物館
1975   "Chiang-hsi Ch'ing-chiang Wu-ch'eng Shang-tai yi-chih fa-chüeh chien-pao 江西清江吳城商代遺址發掘簡報." *WW* 1975.7:51–76.

Chin Hsiang-heng 金祥恆
1964   *T'ao-wen-pien* 陶文編. Taipei.

Ch'iu Hsi-kuei 裘錫圭
1978   "Han-tzu hsing-ch'eng wen-t'i ti ch'u-pu t'an-so 漢字形成問題的初步探索." *Chung-kuo yü-wen* 中國語文 (Peking) 1978.3:162–171.

Chou Fa-kao 周法高
1970–71   "Ti-hsia tzu-liao yü shu-pen tzu-liao ti ts'an-hu yen-chiu 地下資料與書本資料的參互研究." *Lien-ho shu-yüan hsüeh-pao* 聯合書院學報 1970–71.8:1–13.

Ch'ü Wan-li 屈萬里
1960   "Yüeh yi chi-ku 岳義稽古." *Ch'ing-hua hsüeh-pao* 清華學報 2.1:53–68.

CKKH
1959a   *Cheng-chou Erh-li-kang* 鄭州二里岡. Chung-kuo t'ien-yeh k'ao-ku pao-kao-chi k'ao-ku-hsüeh chuan-k'an ting chung ti-ch'i-hao 中國田野考古報告集考古學專刊丁種第七號. Peking.
1959b   *Lo-yang Chung-chou-lu (Hsi-kung tuan)* 洛陽中州路 (西工段). Chung-kuo t'ien-yeh k'ao-ku pao-kao-chi k'ao-ku-hsüeh chuan-k'an ting chung ti-ssu-hao 中國田野考古報告集考古學專刊丁種第四號. Peking.
1962   *Feng-hsi fa-chüeh pao-kao* 灃西發掘報告. Chung-kuo t'ien-yeh k'ao-ku pao-kao-chi k'ao-ku-hsüeh chuan-k'an ting chung ti-shih-erh-hao 中國田野考古報告集考古學專刊丁種第十二號. Peking.

CKKH and Shen-hsi   CKKH and Shen-hsi-sheng Hsi-an Pan-p'o po-wu-kuan 陝西省西安半坡博物館
1963   *Hsi-an Pan-p'o* 西安半坡. Chung-kuo t'ien-yeh k'ao-ku pao-kao-chi k'ao-ku-hsüeh chuan-k'an ting chung ti-shih-ssu-hao 中國田野考古報告集考古學專刊丁種第十四號. Peking.

Damon, P. E., Ferguson, C. W., Long, A., and Wallick, E. I.
1974   "Dendrochronologic Calibration of the Radiocarbon Time Scale." *American Antiquity* 39.2:350–366.

Finn, Daniel J.
1958   *Archaeological Finds on Lamma Island near Hong Kong.* Hong Kong.

Ho, Ping-ti
1975   *The Cradle of the East: An Inquiry into the Indigenous Origins of Techniques and Ideas of Neolithic and Early Historic China, 5000–1000 B.C.* Hong Kong and Chicago.

Ho T'ien-hsing 何天行
1937   *Hang-hsien Liang-chu-chen chih shih-ch'i yü hei-t'ao* 杭縣良渚鎮之石器與黑陶. Shanghai.

Ho-nan-sheng   Ho-nan-sheng po-wu-kuan 河南省博物舘
1973   "Cheng-chou Nan-kuan-wai Shang-tai yi-chih ti fa-chüeh 鄭州南關外商代遺址的發掘." *KKHP* 1973.1:65–91.

Ho-pei-sheng   Ho-pei-sheng wen-wu kuan-li-ch'u 河北省文物管理處
1979   "Tz'u-hsien Hsia-ch'i-yüan yi-chih fa-chüeh pao-kao 磁縣下七垣遺址發掘報告." *KKHP* 1979.2:185–214.

Hsia Nai 夏鼐
1977   "T'an-14 ts'e-ting nien-tai ho Chung-kuo shih-ch'ien k'ao-ku-hsüeh 碳-14測定年代和中國史前考古學." *KK* 1977.4:217–232. (Partially translated by Nancy Price in *Early China* 3 [Fall 1977]:87–93.)

Jen Jih-hsin 任日新
1974   "Shan-tung Chu-ch'eng-hsien Ch'ien-chai yi-chih tiao-ch'a 山東諸城縣前寨遺址調查." *WW* 1974.1:75.

Kao Kuang-jen 高廣仁
1978   "Ta-wen-k'ou wen-hua ti she-hui hsing-chih yü nien-tai 大汶口文化的社會性質與年代." *Kuang-ming jih-pao* 光明日報 27 April 1978.

KK
1956.5   "Huang-ho San-men-hsia shui-k'u k'ao-ku tiao-ch'a chien-pao 黃河三門峽水庫考古調查簡報": pp. 1–11.
1961.2   "1958–1959 nien Yin-hsü fa-chüeh chien-pao 1958—1959年殷墟發掘簡報": pp. 63–76.
1964.11   "Ho-nan Yen-shih Yi-ho nan-an k'ao-ku tiao-ch'a shih-

chüeh pao-kao 河南偃師伊河南岸考古調查試掘報告 "
pp. 543–549, 590.

1965.5   "Ho-nan Yen-shih Erh-li-t'ou yi-chih fa-chüeh chien-pao
          河南偃師二里頭遺址發掘簡報 ": pp. 215–224.

1976.6   "Ch'ing-hai Lo-tu Liu-wan yüan-shih she-hui mu-ti fan-
          ying ti chu-yao wen-t'i 青海樂都柳灣原始社會墓地
          反映的主要問題 ": pp. 365–377.

1979.1   "Ta-wen-k'ou wen-hua ti she-hui hsing-chih chi yu-kuan
          wen-t'i ti t'ao-lun tsung-shu 大汶口文化的社會性質及
          有關問題的討論綜述 ": pp. 33–36.

KKHP

1957.1   "Cheng-chou Shang-tai yi-chih ti fa-chüeh 鄭州商代
          遺址的發掘 ": pp. 53–74.

1978.1   "Shang-hai yü Ma-ch'iao yi-chih ti yi, erh tz'u fa-chüeh
          上海與馬橋遺址第一、二次發掘 ": pp. 109–136.

Kuo Mo-jo 郭沫若

1972   "Ku-tai wen-tzu chih pien-cheng ti fa-chan 古代文字之
          辨証的發展." *KK* 1972.3: pp. 2–13.

Kuo Mo-jo, ed.

1976   *Chung-kuo shih-kao, ti-yi-ts'e: yüan-shih she-hui, nu-li she-
          hui* 中國史稿, 第一冊: 原始社會, 奴隸社會. Peking.

Kuo Pao-chün 郭寶鈞

1951   "Yi-chiu wu-ling nien ch'un Yin-hsü fa-chüeh pao-kao
          一九五〇年春殷墟發掘報告." *KKHP* 1951.5: 1–61.

Li Chi 李濟

1934   *Ch'eng-tzu-yai* 城子崖. Nanking.

1956   *Ch'eng-tzu-yai: The Black Pottery Culture Site at Lung-
          shan-chen in Li-ch'eng-hsien, Shantung Province*, edited
          with Liang Ssu-yang and Tung Tso-pin. Translated by
          Kenneth Starr. Yale University Publications in
          Anthropology no. 52. New Haven.

Li Chi, et al.   Li Chi, Tung Tso-pin 董作賓, Shih Chang-ju 石璋如, and
          Kao Ch'u-hsün 高去尋

1956   *Hsiao-t'un ti-san-pen: Yin-hsü ch'i-wu, chia-pien: t'ao-ch'i*
          小屯第三本: 殷虛器物, 甲編: 陶器. Nankang.

Li Hsiao-ting 李孝定

1965   *Chia-ku wen-tzu chi-shih* 甲骨文字集釋. Chung-yang yen-
          chiu-yüan li-shih yü-yen yen-chiu-so chuan-k'an chih wu-
          shih 中央研究院歷史語言研究所專刊之五十 8 vols.
          Nankang.

1969 "Ts'ung chi-chung shih-ch'ien ho yu-shih tsao-ch'i t'ao-wen ti kuan-ch'a li-ts'e Chung-kuo wen-tzu ti ch'i-yüan 從幾種史前和有史早期陶文的觀察蠡測中國文字的起源 ." *Nan-yang ta-hsüeh hsüeh-pao* 南洋大學學報 3:1–28.

1972 "Han-tzu shih hua 漢字史話." *Wen-wu hui-k'an* 文物彙刊 1:49–77.

1974 "Chung-kuo wen-tzu ti yüan-shih yü yen-pien 中國文字的原始與演變," *BIHP* 45.2:343–396; 45.3:529–560.

Li K'o-yu 李科友 and P'eng Shih-fan 彭適凡
1975 "Lüeh-lun Chiang-hsi Wu-ch'eng Shang-tai yüan-shih tz'u-ch'i 略論江西吳城商代原始瓷器." *WW* 1975.6:77–83.

Lung Yü-ch'un 龍宇純
1963 "Chia-ku-wen chin-wen mou tzu chi ch'i hsiang-kuan wen-t'i 甲骨文金文某字及其相關問題." *BIHP* 34.2:405–433.

Maglioni, Rafael
1975 *Archaeological Discovery in Eastern Kuangtung.* Hong Kong Archaeological Society Journal Monograph no. 2. Hong Kong.

Palmgren, Nils
1934 "Kansu Mortuary Urns of the Pan Shan and Ma Chang Groups." *PS*, ser. D, vol. 3, fasc. 1: pp. 1–204.

Polach, Henry
1976 "Radiocarbon Dating as a Research Tool in Archaeology—Hopes and Limitations." In *Ancient Chinese Bronzes and Southeast Asian Metal and Other Archaeological Artifacts*, edited by Noel Barnard: pp. 255–298. Melbourne.

Shan-tung-sheng Shan-tung-sheng po-wu-kuan 山東省博物舘
1963 "Shan-tung T'eng-hsien Kang-shang-ts'un hsin-shih-ch'i shih-tai mu-tsang shih-chüeh pao-kao 山東滕縣崗上村新石器時代墓葬試掘報告." *KK* 1963.7:351–361.

Shan-tung-sheng and Chi-nan-shih Shan-tung-sheng wen-wu kuan-li-ch'u 山東省文物管理處 and Chi-nan-shih po-wu-kuan 濟南市博物舘
1974 *Ta-wen-k'ou* 大汶口. Peking.

Shang-ch'iu and Chung-kuo Shang-ch'iu ti-ch'ü wen-wu kuan-li wei-yüan-hui 商邱地區文物管理委員會 and Chung-kuo she-

　　　　　　hui k'o-hsüeh-yüan k'ao-ku yen-chiu-so Lo-yang kung-
　　　　　　tso-tui 中國社會科學院考古研究所洛陽工作隊
1978　　　 "1977 nien Ho-nan Yung-ch'eng Wang-yu-fang yi-chih fa-
　　　　　　chüeh kai-k'uang 1977年河南永城王油坊遺址發掘概況."
　　　　　　KK 1978.1：35–40, 64.

Shang-hai-shih　　Shang-hai-shih wen-wu pao-kuan wei-yuan-hui
　　　　　　上海市文物保管委員會
1962　　　 "Shang-hai-shih Ch'ing-p'u-hsien Sung-tse yi-chih ti shih-
　　　　　　chüeh 上海市青浦縣崧澤遺址的試掘." *KKHP* 1962.2：
　　　　　　1–30.

Shao Wang-p'ing 邵望平
1978　　　 "Yüan-ku wen-ming ti huo-hua—t'ao tsun shang ti wen-
　　　　　　tzu 遠古文明的火花—陶尊上的文字." *WW* 1978.9：
　　　　　　74–76.

Shih Hsin-keng　施昕更
1938　　　 *Liang-chu—Hang-hsien ti-erh ch'ü hei-t'ao wen-hua yi-chih
　　　　　　ch'u-pu pao-kao* 良渚—杭縣第二區黑陶文化遺址初步
　　　　　　報告. Hangchow.

Shih Hsing-pang　石興邦
1955　　　 "Feng-Hao yi-tai k'ao-ku tiao-ch'a chien-pao 豐鎬一帶考
　　　　　　古調查簡報." *KK* 1955.1：28–31.

Sun Shan-te 孫善德
1965　　　 "Ch'ing-tao-shih chiao ch'ü fa-hsien hsin-shih-ch'i shih-tai
　　　　　　ho Yin-Chou yi-chih 青島市郊區發現新石器時代和殷周
　　　　　　遺址." *KK* 1965.9：480–481.

Sun Yi-jang 孫詒讓
1905　　　 *Ming yüan* 名原. N.p.

T'ang Lan　唐蘭
1957　　　 "Tsai chia-ku chin-wen chung so-chien ti yi-chung yi-ching
　　　　　　yi-shih ti Chung-kuo ku-tai wen-tzu 在甲骨金文中所見的
　　　　　　一種已經遺失的中國古代文字." *KKHP* 1957.2：33–36.
1965　　　 *Ku-wen-tzu-hsüeh tao-lun* 古文字學導論. Hong Kong. 2
　　　　　　vols.
1975　　　 "Kuan-yü Chiang-hsi Wu-ch'eng wen-hua yi-chih yü wen-
　　　　　　tzu ti ch'u-pu t'an-so 關於江西吳城文化遺址與文字的
　　　　　　初步探索." *WW* 1975.7：72–76.
1977a　　 "Ts'ung Ta-wen-k'ou wen-hua ti t'ao-ch'i wen-tzu k'an wo
　　　　　　kuo tsui-tsao wen-hua ti nien-tai 從大汶口文化陶器文字
　　　　　　看我國最早文化的年代." *Kuang-ming jih-pao* 光明日報
　　　　　　14 July 1977.

1977b   "Chung-kuo wen-ming shih ying wei liu-ch'ien nien
         中國文明史應爲六千年." *Ta-kung pao* 大公報 (Hong
         Kong) 21 July 1977.
1978   "Chung-kuo yu liu-ch'ien to nien ti wen-ming shih
         中國有六千多年的文明史." In *Ta-kung pao tsai Kang fu-
         k'an san-shih chou nien chi-nien wen-chi* 大公報在港
         復刊卅周年紀念文集. Part 1: pp. 23–58.

Wang Wei-ta 王維達
1979   "Ku-tai t'ao-ch'i ti je-shih-kuang nien-tai 古代陶器的
         熱釋光年代." *KK* 1979.1:82–88.

WW
1956.4   "Cheng-chou Pai-chia-chuang yi-chih fa-chüeh chien-pao
         鄭州白家庄遺址發掘簡報": pp. 3–8.

1975.8   "Lin-t'ung Chiang-chai hsin-shih-ch'i shih-tai yi-chih ti
         hsin fa-hsien, wen-po chien-hsün 臨潼姜寨新石器時代
         遺址的新發現, 文博簡訊": pp. 82–86.
1979.6   "Ho-pei Kao-ch'eng T'ai-hsi-ts'un Shang-tai yi-chih fa-
         chüeh chien-pao 河北藁城臺西村商代遺址發掘簡報":
         pp. 33–43.

Yü Hsing-wu 于省吾
1973   "Kuan-yü ku wen-tzu yen-chiu ti jo-kan wen-t'i
         關於古文字研究的若干問題." *WW* 1973.2:32–35.

NOTE: I wish to express my gratitude to Miss Winifred Mumford for undertaking the task of preparing the artwork in this paper.

13

Archaic Chinese

FANG KUEI LI

This chapter is not intended as a technical report about Archaic Chinese, the language of roughly the first millennium B.C. It attempts to present in non-technical language what Archaic Chinese looks like and in a general way how we reconstruct the phonological system of Archaic Chinese. The reason for such reconstructions has been given in detail in various published writings (see References at the end of this chapter). Nor is it assumed that the reconstruction presented here will necessarily be accepted by all. It is chiefly my own, with all my personal biases and prejudices. I am of course indebted to many scholars, such as Walter Simon, Bernhard Karlgren, Tung T'ung-ho, Wang Li, S. E. Iakhontov, and E. G. Pulleyblank, for their ideas, which I either accept or reject with reasons of my own. If this chapter gives rise to different opinions and interpretations, that is its purpose. There are many points about which we entertain doubts and many problems which we are not yet ready to solve.

The name Archaic Chinese was probably first given by Karlgren (1923:16–33) from his study of *hsieh-sheng* 諧聲 characters (phonetic compounds) and has been used by him to designate particularly the language of the *Shih-ching* and also the language of the early Chou period. It is, however, difficult to determine the exact dates of a language or exactly how long it lasted, particularly from such heterogeneous material as the *hsieh-sheng* characters and the rhymes of poetry, which probably originate from different localities. I have pointed out that the *hsieh-sheng* characters represent in part a slightly earlier stage of the language than the rhymes (Li

1971:27). Nevertheless, in spite of the heterogeneity the rhymes and the *hsieh-sheng* characters show, with rare exceptions, a remarkable uniformity, from which the archaic language can be reconstructed (cf. Karlgren 1936:157–178).

No doubt dialects existed in Chou times as they exist now in modern China. Some differences in dialect can be observed (Chang and Chang 1972), but there is little evidence that enables us to make a systematic reconstruction of the Archaic dialects. A few words can be suspected to be of southern origin or even to be loans from other languages, such as *chiang* 江 (< *krung*); the northern dialects prefer *ho* 河 (< *gar*) or *shui* 水 (< *hwrjidx*). For the time being the problem of dialects will have to be neglected, not because they are not important, but because we have nothing systematic to say about them. It may be possible, for instance, to reconstruct a proto-Min dialect from modern dialect material, but the lack of early documentary evidence renders this a hazardous task. The Archaic Chinese we reconstruct can be assumed to represent only the standard language of the northern China plains.

The study of Archaic Chinese has been going on for the past three hundred years or more, chiefly by Chinese philologists interested in the phonological system largely as a means to elucidate old Chinese texts, as Karlgren did in his *Shih-ching* and *Shu-ching* glosses (1964 and 1970, respectively), which are also partly based on his phonological researches. But the Chinese phonologists did not use any phonetic alphabet or symbols. They used a set of technical classificatory terminologies such as *yin* 陰, *yang* 陽, *ju* 入, *yün-pu* 韻部, *tui-chuan* 對轉, and *p'ang-chuan* 旁轉, which would be difficult to understand without putting them into phonetic terms. It is not my purpose to introduce such terminologies, but scholars such as Tuan Yü-t'sai (1735–1815) (Tuan 1966), Wang Nien-sun (1744–1832) (Wang 1966), and Chiang Yu-kao (?–1851) (Chiang 1966) have gathered a tremendous amount of material which is indispensable to any study of Archaic Chinese.

In recent years, the study of early stages of the Chinese language has engaged the attention of many scholars. For several decades since Karlgren (1923) and Simon (1927–28), attention has focused on the reconstruction of Archaic Chinese and on interpretation of the material collected by earlier Chinese scholars. This is the first level of reconstruction. There are attempts to examine Archaic dialects, and to reconstruct a protolanguage, from which both the northern standard language (here called Archaic Chinese) and some southern dialects can be derived (Chang and Chang 1972). This is the second level. There is also a third level of reconstruction, which consists of comparing Chinese with other Sino-Tibetan languages (chiefly Tibetan) and of adjusting Archaic Chinese reconstructions to conform to the Tibetan models (Schuessler 1974). This can be called pre-Chinese, approaching proto-Sino-Tibetan. It is difficult to reconcile the levels of reconstruction. There is no doubt that all these researches have a bearing on the phonological system of Archaic Chinese. I shall confine myself here to the system of Archaic Chinese, for which we have much material from Chinese sources alone.

THE PHONOLOGICAL SYSTEM OF ARCHAIC CHINESE

Our knowledge of Archaic Chinese phonology is chiefly derived from three sources: (1) the rhyming system in Archaic Chinese literature, (2) the system of *hsieh-sheng* characters (phonetic compounds), and (3) the system of Ancient Chinese (from about A.D. 600) as reconstructed by Karlgren from a study of both documentary evidence, such as the *Ch'ieh-yün* 切韻 and rhyme tables, and modern dialects (Chao, Lo, and Li 1948). It is understood that Karlgren's system of Ancient Chinese is not necessarily accepted by all, but it is a convenient reference. I have made some emendations, chiefly typological, to better reflect the system of the *Ch'ieh-yün*. Some emendations are based on a T'ang manuscript of the *Ch'ieh-yün* referred to as "Wang Jen-hsü's recension", which was unavailable to earlier authors and became available only in 1947 (Wang Jen-hsü 1964).

The *Ch'ieh-yün* system is considered by some to be an artificial system which was intended by the original authors to establish some kind of standard language by incorporating many dialectal distinctions which could not be found in any one language (Chou Tsu-mo 1966). From practical experience, we know that few literary documents and standard languages are free from dialect mixtures. The incorporation of certain dialectal features may even have some informational value, not only for dialects of that period, but also for the reconstruction of older stages of the language. It may indicate that certain distinctions can be traced back to the Archaic period; they have merged in some dialects but are kept distinct in others. The Han literature (206 B.C.–A.D. 220) presents a slightly different system from Archaic Chinese and also from Ancient Chinese (Lo and Chou 1958). It seems that the Ancient system cannot be derived directly from the Han standard language; but I think both the Han system and the *Ch'ieh-yün* system can be derived from Archaic Chinese with certain dialectal variations.

THE VOCALIC SYSTEM OF ARCHAIC CHINESE

The vocalic system is chiefly reconstructed on the basis of the rhyme words, the *hsieh-sheng* characters, and their reflexes in the *Ch'ieh-yün* system. One important assumption I shall make is that the same vowel, together with other features, is required in order for the words to rhyme and the characters to form a phonetic series. It is also necessary that the vocalic system we reconstruct be able to account for most, if not all, the distinctions in the *Ch'ieh-yün* system. It is necessary to reconstruct four vowels for this purpose: two high, one central, and one low:

High	i		u
Central		ə	
Low	a		

The exact phonetic nature of these vowels is difficult to determine; there is insufficient evidence to go into detail about them here.

Because of the proliferation of vowels in Ancient Chinese, due to the influence of the initial consonant, the medial element, and the final consonant, scholars began to make distinctions in quality and quantity of the vowels in Archaic Chinese to account for its large number of vowels. Karlgren (1954:281–367) distinguishes fourteen vowels and Tung (1967:67–118) twenty. Some phonologists would like to postulate the distinction of long and short vowels (Wang Li 1957–1958); Tung (1944:67–118) seems to prefer the distinction of tense and lax vowels in Archaic Chinese. There is, however, little evidence to show that there were distinctions of length and/or intensity in Archaic Chinese. As tense and lax vowels are not the same vowels, we can hardly expect them to rhyme in the same rhyme group. Nor can we expect long and short vowels to rhyme, against our general principle of rhyming.

There are attempts to reduce the inventory of Archaic vowels to two or three (Chou Fa-kao 1969; 1970; Pulleyblank, as summarized by Ting 1975:30–33). This is done by proliferating the medial elements and/or the final consonants. They do not seem to simplify the Archaic phonological system.

Although the four Archaic vowels seem to account for most of the later developments in Ancient Chinese, there are cases for which we have to assume diphthongs. We assume three diphthongs, *−ia−, *−iə−, and *−ua−; they are rather defective in distribution and may need further research. Recently Bodman (1977:12) has assumed a six-vowel system without the diphthongs, but he recognizes that his reconstructions are for an earlier stage than the *Shih-ching* rhymes.

Gong Hwang-cherng (1978) made a comparative study of the Chinese, Tibetan, and Burmese vowel systems in which he concluded that Sino-Tibetan also had a four-vowel system. The etymologies on which he based his conclusions seem sound and his conclusions worthy of notice.

The Medials (*Chieh-yin* 介音)

In Ancient Chinese of the sixth century, it is known that there are three elements, called medials, which can occur between the initial consonant and the main vowel. They are −j−, −i−, and −w− (or −u−). The −i− medial is considered part of the diphthong * −ia−, and * −iə− in Archaic Chinese, and is eliminated from the class of medials. The vowel −i−, whether standing alone or in the diphthong, has no palatalizing influence on the preceding consonant; compare the Old English *ascian*, "to ask," where the −i− vowel does not cause umlaut or the palatalization of −k− (written c). The medial −w− (or −u−) is considered either as part of the diphthong * −ua−, or as secondarily developed according to definite rules, or as due to the initial labio-velar consonant, such as *kw−, *khw−, or *gw−. I should like to eliminate it from our class of medials, although some scholars would retain the medial −w− in Archaic Chinese. The medial −j− is retained in our system chiefly because of its influence on the preceding consonant; the palatalization of *t−, *th−, *d−, and *n− to tś−, tśh−, dź− or ź−, and ńź−. Thus, out of the three medial elements in Ancient Chinese, only one is retained for Archaic Chinese.

There is another medial element to be reconstructed for Archaic Chinese which has disappeared in most cases from Ancient Chinese. It is the retroflex element, reconstructed as * −r−. It causes the preceding dental stops and sibilants to become retroflexes, namely, *t−, *th−, *d−, *n−, *ts−, *tsh−, *dz−, and *s− > ṭ−, ṭh−, ḍ−, ṇ−, tṣ−, tṣh−, dẓ−, and ṣ−. It is also reconstructed after labials, velars, and labio-velars due to their influence on the main vowel, although it has disappeared in such cases in Ancient Chinese.

The two medial elements * −j− and * −r− in Archaic Chinese have an influence not only on the preceding consonant—namely palatalization and retroflexion, respectively—but also on the following vowel. The medial * −j− tends to raise the following low vowel * −a− to a front higher vowel −ä−, and the retroflex element * −r− tends to lower the high and the central vowels and to raise the low vowel and to shift them to the central area. The shifts are roughly indicated in the accompanying diagram. The five vowels newly generated in Ancient Chinese show many splits and mergers, chiefly due to the influence of the final consonants.

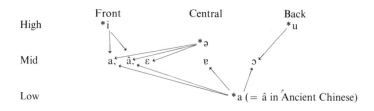

The reconstruction of a palatalizing medial *−j− and a non-palatalizing vowel *−i− in Archaic Chinese seems to cause uneasiness on the part of some phonologists. Pulleyblank says "the supposed effects of the various medials −i−, −j−, −ji−, etc. seem to me to have little plausibility in terms of general phonetic theory" (1977:130). I am not aware which phonetic theory he has in mind. I shall give examples from living languages where such distinctions can be observed. In Siamese (Thai) there are words such as ʔim "to be satisfied, full," jim "to smile," jam "to blend," jiam "to visit," and ʔiam "an intensive particle." There is also in English some slight difference between −j− and −i− and their effects on the preceding consonant. As I am not a native speaker of English, I am indebted to colleagues who are for some of the following examples: compare the difference between year and ear, yeast and east, bad year and bad ear, last year and last ear (of corn), did you and did he, dew (jew to some speakers), and deed. There seems to be a strong tendency to palatalize the dental before −j−, occasionally even to an affricate, but not before −i−. Perhaps there are languages in which −j− and −i− both palatalize, but j and i still have different kinds of palatalization.

THE CONSONANT SYSTEM

The Archaic consonants will be discussed in three sections: (1) the simple initial consonants, which can be determined by the *hsieh-sheng* characters and their reflexes in Ancient Chinese, (2) the initial consonant clusters, which can be determined the same way, and (3) the final consonants, which can be determined by both the *hsieh-sheng* characters and the rhyme words, as well as by their reflexes in Ancient Chinese. Here the principles governing the formation of *hsieh-sheng* characters play an important role, more than do the rhyme words.

The simple initial consonants

The principles governing the formation of *hsieh-sheng* characters were first formulated by Karlgren (1923:16–33). They can be briefly summarized and slightly modified in application to the initial consonants. Characters are permitted to form one *hsieh-sheng* series when they had, in Archaic Chinese, initial consonants of the same place of articulation: namely, labials, dentals, sibilants, velars, labio-velars, and others, such as *tan* 且 < **tan : t'an* 坦 < **than : tan* 但 < *dan : tai* 待 < **dəg : t'e* 特 < **dək : ch'ih* 持 < **drjəg : shih* 恃 < **djəg*. As long as the initial consonants belong to the same series of consonants, different tones and different medials do not prevent them from forming one *hsieh-sheng* series, as can be observed from these examples. Similarly, whether the consonants are voiced or voiceless, aspirated or not, does not prevent them from forming one series of *hsieh-sheng* characters. What can be gathered from the principle of *hsieh-sheng* characters is that the consonants must be from the same place of articulation. This does not seem like much, but as the consonants have been influenced by the medial elements and have shifted their place of articulation in the later language, the principle is important in guiding reconstructions. Whether a word has an aspirated or unaspirated, voiced or voiceless initial, a medial *−r−* or *−j−*, and so forth, has to be determined by reflexes in the later language, the *Ch'ieh-yün* language, or the modern dialects.

Some special phenomena should also be observed. The glottal stop *ʔ−* and the rounded glottal stop *ʔw−* often go together with the velars and labio-velars. On the other hand, the nasals do not normally form *hsieh-sheng* series with stops or fricatives of the same place of articulation. Tung (1967:12–13) was able to reconstruct a voiceless nasal *hm− for words having x− or xw− in Ancient Chinese because their *hsieh-sheng* characters have m−; for example, he reconstructs **hmək* for *hei* 黑, which is the phonetic in *mo* 墨 < **mək*; and he reconstructs **hməg* for *hui* 悔, which has the phonetic *mei* 每 < **məg*. (I have slightly modified his reconstructions according to our system here.) A number of voiceless nasals and *hl− have been thus reconstructed.

We assume, then, the following sets of simple initial consonants:

	Stops and Affricates			Nasals		Continuants
	Unaspirated	Aspirated	Voiced	Voiced	Voiceless	
Labials	p−	ph−	b−	m−	hm−	
Dentals	t−	th−	d−	n−	hn−	l− hl− r−
Sibilants	ts−	tsh−	dz−			s−
Velars	k−	kh−	g−	ng−	hng−	h−
Labio-velars	kw−	khw−	gw−	ngw−	hngw−	
Laryngeals	ʔ−					h−
Labio-laryngeals	ʔw−					hw−

In this list of Archaic Chinese consonants I have simplified the Ancient system but also added a few consonants. The following Ancient Chinese initials are given for comparison:

	Stops and Affricates			Nasals	Continuants
Labials	p	ph—	g	m	
Dentals	t—	th—	d—	n—	i—
Retroflexes	ṭ—	ṭh—	ḍ—	ṇ—	
Dental sibilants	ts—	tsh—	dz—		s— z—
Retroflex sibilants	ṭs—	ṭsh—	ḍẓ—		ṣ—
Palatal sibilants	tś—	tśh—	dź—	ńż—	j, ji— ś— ż—
Velars	k—	kh—	g—	ng—	h— γ—
Laryngeal	ʔ—				

We have eliminated the retroflex and the palatal series because they can be demonstrated to be derived from dentals through the influence of the medial *—r— and *—j—. The voiced fricatives, z— and ż— have also been eliminated because they can also be derived from stops and *r—; but a labio-velar series is added because of the close relation between rounding and the velars. We have similarly added a voiceless series of nasals.

Tung (1967: 15–17, 28–33) assumes there is a set of palato-velars because of certain peculiar *hsieh-sheng* characters which mix the velars and the palatals in one series, such as *ch'ü* 區 < Ancient Chinese *khju* and *shu* 樞 < Ancient Chinese *tśhju*; *chih* 支 < Ancient Chinese *tśje* and *chi* 技 < Ancient Chinese *gje*. I consider this set of palato-velars to be derived from velars through the combined influence of the medial *—rj— (Li 1976: 1143–1150); for example, *chih* 支 < *krjig*, *ch'ih* 赤 < *khrjak*, *yi* 臣 < *grjig*.

The initial consonant clusters

A phenomenon which has engaged the attention of many Sinologists is pairs of *hsieh-sheng* characters such as *ko* 各 : *lo* 洛; *chien* 監 (< *kam*): *lan* 藍; *pien* 變 : *lien* 戀. It has been suggested that such words go back to clusters like *kl— and *pl—. Karlgren (1934: 57–58) uses the following formula to reconstruct the initials of such words:

$$*kl— > k— \quad : \quad *khl— > kh— \quad : \quad *gl— > l—$$
$$*pl— > p— \quad : \quad *phl— > ph— \quad : \quad *bl— > l—$$

This formula is not necessarily accepted by all; but if we do accept it, we can see that the second element l — is an integral part of the initial system, and therefore we treat such words as having an initial cluster. This is different from the medial —r—, which does not play any significant role in the formation of *hsieh-sheng* characters.

Another phenomenon which requires some explanation is the consonant s—, which normally forms a *hsieh-sheng* series with words having the sibilant initial s—. It is found, however, to form *hsieh-sheng* series with words having all sorts of initial consonants—nasals, dental stops, velar stops, and so on. We assume that such an s— goes back to consonant clusters such as *sn—, *st—, and *sk—. For example:

hsieh 楔	< siet	< *skiat,	cf.	ch'i 契	< khiej	< *khiad
sui 歲	< sjwäi	< *skwjad,	cf.	kuei 劌	< kjwäi	< *kwjiad
hsiu 修	< sjəu	< *stjəgw,	cf.	t'iao 條	< dieu	< *diəgw
hsi 犀	< siei	< *smid,	cf.	wei 尾	< mjwei	< *mjəd
sang 喪	< sâng	< *smang,	cf.	wang 亡	< mjwang	< *mjang
hsiang 襄	< sjang	< *snjang,	cf.	nang 囊	< nâng	< *nang

The following type of word is also reconstructed with an s-cluster:

sui 穗	< zjwi	< *sgwjid,	cf.	hui 惠	< γiwei	< *gwid
tsao 造	< dzâau	< *sgəgw,	cf.	kao 告	< kâu	< *kəgw

The s-cluster thus reconstructed can be considered as having an s-prefix whose function is not always clear in Chinese. There is an s-prefix in Tibetan, with which the Chinese s-clusters can be compared. The s-prefix in Tibetan is both a noun prefix and a verb prefix, forming chiefly causative and denominative verbs (Conrady 1896).

There are also special *hsieh-sheng* series which I suspect are derived from clusters of some sort but which I have not been able to reconstruct successfully. Since we depend on the *hsieh-sheng* characters to reconstruct clusters, it is possible that clusters may have existed where the characters would not show them. These will have to be reconstructed by a comparative study of Chinese and other Sino-Tibetan languages on the basis of dependable etymologies. Such reconstructions need not be pre-Chinese, but should supplement our Archaic reconstructions, which are based on Chinese material alone.

The final consonants

The final consonants in Archaic Chinese can be reconstructed from information in the rhyme words, from information in the *hsieh-sheng* characters, and from their reflexes in the Ancient Chinese. The final consonants consist chiefly of two types, stops and nasals. There is no distinction of aspirated and unaspirated stops in the final position, and the distinction of voiced and voiceless is also in doubt. I have used the final *—b, *—d, *—g, and so on, merely as an orthographical device without going into their phonetic details. There is no Chinese dialect or Sino-

Tibetan dialect, so far as I know, in which there are two series of stops. The following final consonants are therefore assumed:

Labials	− p	− b	− m	
Dentals	− t	− d	− n	− r
Velars	− k	− g	− ng	
Labio-velars	− kw	− gw	− ngw	

Final * − r, as first reconstructed by Karlgren, is meant to explain certain special *hsieh-sheng* characters such as *no* 儺 < *nâ* < **nar*, whose phonetic element is *nan* 難 < *nân* < **nan*; and *po* 播 < *puâ* < **par*, whose phonetic element is *fan* 番 < *phjwɒn* < **phjan*. It has also been reconstructed by others as * − l. We shall simply use it to denote some sort of dental which has disappeared without leaving a trace in Ancient Chinese.

The final stops * − p, * − t, and * − k are preserved in Ancient Chinese and, to this date, in some southern dialects such as Cantonese. The final * − kw merged with − k even before the Ancient Chinese period. Similarly, the finals * − m, * − n, and * − ng are preserved in Ancient Chinese and in some modern dialects, but * − ngw merged with * − ng before the Ancient Chinese period.

The series of finals * − b, * − d, * − g, and * − gw is reconstructed differently by different authors, for example, as * − ɣ, * − wɣ, * − r (Chou Fa-kao 1969; 1970; he later [1973] considers * − ɣ in * − wɣ as redundant) or as * − i, * − w, * − j, * − l, * − h, * − ts, and so forth (Pulleyblank, according to Ting 1975: 30–33; a revised system has not yet been published). The reason for such diversity of opinion is that it is the series which is later either lost or vocalized to − i or − u (as in diphthongs − ai, − au, etc.). In interpreting the data, scholars tend to go into phonetic details based on their own theories; but we cannot treat thoroughly all those theories here. The final * − b is reconstructed only on the basis of *hsieh-sheng* characters such as *nei* 內 < *nuâi* < **nəb*, compare *na* 納 < *nâp* < **nəp*, and *ju* 入 < *ńźjəp* < **njəp*. In the *Shih-ching* rhymes, such words already rhyme with words in * − d, showing an early change of * − b to * − d. This indicates also that the *hsieh-sheng* system is slightly earlier than the rhyme system.

I have also attached the letters − x and − h after the final consonant to indicate the tones in Archaic Chinese (see below). They do not indicate consonant clusters.

All previous attempts to reconstruct the final system are based on the rhyme groups established by earlier Chinese scholars, which are supposed to have the same main vowel and preferably the same final consonant. The reconstruction of consonant clusters according to tone, such as * − ts and

* — ns, as suggested by some scholars, seems to present certain difficulties in the explanation of some frequent rhymes such as *hai* 害 < γai < *gad (*gats?) rhyming with *lieh* 烈 < *ljät* < *ljat, fa 發 < *pjwɐt* < *pjat, chieh 揭 < *kjɐt, po* 撥 < *puât* < *pat—or *chien* 澗 < *kan* < *kran (*krans?) rhyming with *k'uan* 寬 < *khuân* < *khwan and *yen* 言 < *ngjen* < *ngjan. As some scholars believe that the Chinese tones came into being through the loss of some final consonants, there is the attempt to reconstruct * — s or * — h to indicate the *ch'ü-sheng* and — ʔ to indicate *shang-sheng*.

THE ARCHAIC CHINESE TONES

Shen Yüeh (441–513) was the first to talk about the four tones, though this does not mean they did not exist before his time. He gave them the names *p'ing, shang, ch'ü,* and *ju.* For some time Chinese scholars were skeptical about tones in Archaic Chinese. Chiang Yu-kao (1966) finally determined that there were four tones, just as in Ancient Chinese, because of the persistent tendency to rhyme words of the same tone in the *Shih-ching* (Mattos 1971). There are exceptional *tonal* rhymes, and there are shifts of tones from the Archaic to the Ancient period; but, on the whole, the four tones can be shown to have existed in Archaic Chinese.

The tones of Ancient Chinese and Archaic Chinese have not been systematically reconstructed. We do not know exactly how the four developed into the great variety of tones in the modern dialects. We know only the tone classes, indicated here simply by an orthographic device. I use the letter —x to indicate *shang-sheng* and the letter —h, *ch'ü-sheng* in Archaic Chinese: no special letters are required to indicate *p'ing-sheng* and *ju-sheng.* Thus:

P'ing sheng:	*tu* 都 < *tag	*t'ang* 湯 < *thang
Shang-sheng:	*tu* 睹 < *tagx	*tang* 黨 < *tangx
Ch'ü-sheng:	*tu* 度 < *dagh	*tang* 宕 < *tangh
Ju-sheng:	*t'o* 託 < *thak	

Assuming there were tones in Archaic Chinese, we can see also that the final consonant * — g need not be interpreted as a voiced velar, but can be considered a variety of * — k according to distributional principles. It can be rationalized, nevertheless, that the final * — k (orthographically written * — g) may have been voiced before it became vocalized later (often into — i or — u) in Ancient Chinese. Such a process may have occurred after the Archaic period.

There is, of course, the problem of how tones came into being in Chinese. This seems to me to belong to pre-Archaic Chinese. There is the interesting theory that tones arise through the loss of certain types of final consonant. Haudricourt (1954) first suggested this for the Vietnamese language, and other scholars soon adopted it for the Sino-Tibetan languages, including Chinese. I do not wish to deny the possibility that such a theory is appropriate in Sino-Tibetan or proto-Chinese, but a theory remains a theory and must be established by comparative evidence based on good etymologies. There is not sufficient evidence in Archaic Chinese to show that such final consonants existed, even though they can be assumed for proto-Chinese or pre-Chinese. Rhymes in Archaic Chinese such as *−ks : *−k, *−ts : *−t, *−ngs : *−ng, and *−ns : *−n do not seem good rhymes.

THE ARCHAIC SYLLABIC STRUCTURE

From the preceding discussion of the various elements of the Chinese syllable, a general structural scheme for Archaic Chinese can be formulated, namely, $C_1(M)VC_2 + T$, where

C_1 = any initial consonant or consonant cluster
(M) = an optional medial element, *−j−, *−r−, or *−rj−
V = any of the vowels or diphthongs
C_2 = any of the permitted stops or nasals, or *−r
T = tone

As this is a general formula, there are restrictions among the occurrences of the different elements in a syllable. The details of this problem cannot be pursued here, but a problem in the distribution of vowels and final consonants can be pointed out. The vowels *−a− and *−ə− may occur before any of the following consonants: *−p, *−b, *−m, *−t, *−d, *−n, *−k, *−g, *−ng, *−kw, *−gw, *−ngw, and *−r (but not *−angw). On the other hand, the vowel −i− occurs only before *−t, *−d, *−n, *−k, *−g, and *−ng. It does not occur before any final consonant with lip closure or lip rounding: *−p, *−b, *−m, *−kw, *−gw, or *−ngw. It can be supposed that −i− did exist in such environments, in proto-Chinese or pre-Chinese, but that there was a shift to some other syllabic type in Archaic Chinese. Further restrictions can be observed in the occurrence of the vowel *−u−, which only appears before *−k, *−g, and *−ng. It requires no great stretch of imagination to consider the final velars here as rounded on account of the preceding rounded vowel, therefore the final consonants could be reconstructed as labio-velars. The vowels *−i− and

−u− would then be in complete complementary distribution—−ik, *−ig, *−ing : *−ukw, *−ugw, *−ungw—and we could, then, re-construct *−ikw, *−igw, and *−ingw instead of *−uk, *−ug, and *−ung. I have rejected this solution because there is no contact in the *Shih-ching* rhymes between *−ik, *−ig, *−ing and *−ikw, *−igw, *−ingw (i.e., *−uk, *−ug, and *−ung), while contacts are common between *−ək, *−əg and *−əkw, *−əgw, and even between *−əngw and *−əm.

In the formula presented above, there is no provision for open syllables, syllables ending in a vowel. For those who have reconstructed final −ʔ, −h, −w, −j, and others, syllables with such finals will be considered closed syllables. Tung (1967) and Chou Fa-kao (1969) have only one open type: syllables with the vowel *−a. Karlgren has a few more: *−a, *−o, and *−u (he has fourteen vowels in Archaic Chinese). Apparently there are great differences in the interpretation of Chinese rhymes and *hsieh-sheng* series, also of the comparative data from the Sino-Tibetan. Bodman has recently reconstructed a whole series of open syllables (1977: 12–13). The reason for such differences of opinion is not often explicitly stated.

PROTO-CHINESE AND SINO-TIBETAN

The interest in Chinese phonology in recent years is due to the desire to know better the early stages of the language and to extend its history a little further than the Archaic period. This can be done by thoroughly investigating dialects such as the Min which are suspected not to be of the northern variety. Theories can also be developed about the morphology of Chinese, such as prefixes, suffixes, and infixes, but there is little evidence for this purpose from the Chinese material alone. There is in Chinese the alternation of initial consonants, voiceless versus voiced, with semantic distinctions. It may eventually go back to different prefixes, but what prefixes there were is not evident. Similarly, there is the alternation of tones with semantic distinctions. This situation may derive from different suffixes, but those suffixes that would have to be assumed are equally uncertain. Perhaps when reasonable correspondences can be made between Tibetan prefixes and suffixes with similar functions and the alternation of initials and tones in Chinese, then something more definite can be said about Old Chinese morphology. In short, we will have to resort to the comparative study of Sino-Tibetan languages to which Chinese is supposed to be genetically related. All this is beyond the intent of this chapter. Whatever we can get from such future studies will eventually affect our understanding of Archaic Chinese, modify our reconstructions, and solve many problems

which cannot be solved at present. Nevertheless, Archaic Chinese remains
the basis from which further advances will be made.

REFERENCES

Bodman, Nicholas C.
  1977   "Proto-Chinese and Sino-Tibetan." Manuscript, privately
                circulated. Part 1.

Chang, Kun, and Chang, Betty Shefts
  1972   *Proto-Chinese Final System and the "Ch'ieh-yün."* Institute
                of History and Philology, Academia Sinica monograph
                series A, no. 26. Taipei.

Chao Yüan-jen 趙元任, Lo Ch'ang-p'ei 羅常培, and Li Fang-kuei 李方桂
  1948   *Chung-kuo yin-yün-hsüeh yen-chiu* 中國音韻學研究.
                Translation into the Chinese, with emendations, of
                B. Karlgren's *Études sur la phonologie chinoise.*

Chiang Yu-kao 江有誥
  1966   *Yin-hsüeh shih-shu* 音學十書. Reprint, Taipei.

Chou Fa-kao 周法高
  1969   "Lun shang-ku yin 論上古音" *Hsiang-kang chung-wen
                ta-hsüeh Chung-kuo wen-hua yen-chiu-so hsüeh-pao*
                香港中文大學中國文化研究所學報 2.1:109–178.
  1970   "Lun shang-ku ho Ch'ieh-yün yin 論上古和切韻音."
                *Hsiang-kang chung-wen ta-hsüeh Chung-kuo wen-hua yen-
                chiu-so hsüeh-pao* 香港中文大學中國文化研究所學報
                3.2:321–457.
  1973   Preface to Chang Jih-sheng 張日昇 and Lin Chieh-ming
                林潔明, *Chou Fa-kao shang-ku yin-yün piao* 周法高上
                古音韻表. Taipei.

Chou Tsu-mo 周祖謨
  1966   "Ch'ieh-yün ti hsing-chih ho t'a ti yin-hsi chi-ch'u 切韻的
                性質和它的音系基礎." In Chou, *Wen-hsüeh chi* 問學集:
                vol. 1:434–473. Peking.

Conrady, A.
  1896   *Eine indochinesische Causativ-Denominativ-Bildung und ihr
                Zusammenhang mit dem Tonaccenten.* Leipzig.

Gong Hwang-cherng 龔煌城

1978   "Han-Tsang-mien-yü yuan-yin ti pi-chiao yen-chiu 漢藏緬語元音的比較研究." Paper presented at the Eleventh International Conference on Sino-Tibetan Language and Linguistics. Tucson.

Haudricourt, André-G.

1954   "De l'origine des tons en vietnamien." *Journal asiatique* 242:69–82.

Iakhontov, S. E.

1959–60   "Fonetika kitaiskogo iazyka I-ogo tysiacheletiia do n.e." *Problemy Vostokovedeniia* 2:137–147; 6:102–115.

1960   *Consonant Combinations in Archaic Chinese.* Twenty-Fifth Congress of Orientalists. Moscow.

Karlgren, Bernhard

1923   *Analytic Dictionary of Chinese and Sino-Japanese.* Paris.

1934   "Word Families in Chinese." *BMFEA* 5:9–120.

1936   "On the Script of the Chou Dynasty." *BMFEA* 8:157–178.

1954   "Compendium of Phonetics in Ancient and Archaic Chinese." *BMFEA* 26:211–367.

1957   "Grammata Serica Recensa." *BMFEA* 29:1–332.

1960   "Tones in Archaic Chinese." *BMFEA* 32:113–142.

1964   *Glosses on the Book of Odes.* Stockholm.

1970   *Glosses on the Book of Documents.* Stockholm.

Li Fang-Kuei 李方桂

1971   "Shang-ku-yin yen-chiu 上古音研究." *Ch'ing-hua hsüeh-pao* 清華學報 9.1–2:1–61.

1976   "Chi-ke shang-ku sheng-mu wen-ti 幾個上古聲母問題." *Tsung-t'ung Chiang-kung shih-shih chou-nien chi-nien lun-wen chi* 總統蔣公逝世週年紀念論文集: pp. 1143–1150. Taipei.

Li Jung 李榮

1952   *Ch'ieh-yün yin-hsi* 切韻音系. Peking.

Lo Ch'ang-p'ei 羅常培 and Chou Tsu-mo 周祖謨

1958   *Han Wei Chin Nan-pei ch'ao yün-pu yen-pien yen-chiu* 漢魏晉南北朝韵部演變研究. Peking.

Mattos, Gilbert L.

1971   "Tonal Anomalies in the Kuo-feng Odes." *Ch'ing-hua hsüeh-pao* 清華學報 9.1–2:306–325.

Pulleyblank, E. G.

1962   "The Consonantal System of Old Chinese." Part 1: *Asia Major* n.s. 9.1:58–144. Part 2: *Asia Major* n.s. 9.2:206–265.

1963   "An Interpretation of the Vowel System of Old Chinese and Written Burmese." *Asia Major* n.s. 10.2:200–221.

1977   "[Book Review of] Ting Pang-hsin, *Chinese Phonology of the Wei-chin Period: Reconstruction of The Finals as Reflected in Poetry.*" *Journal of Chinese Linguistics* 5.1:125–133.

Schuessler, Axel

1974   "R and L in Archaic Chinese." *Journal of Chinese Linguistics* 2.2:180–199.

Simon, Walter

1927–28   "Zur Reconstruktion der altchinesischen Endconsonanten." *Mitteilungen des Seminars für Orientalische Sprachen* 30:147–167; 31:157–204.

1930   "Tibetische Chinesische Wortgleichungen: Ein Versuch." *Mitteilungen des Seminars fur Orientalische Sprachen* 32, offprint. Berlin.

Ting Pang-hsin 丁邦新

1975   *Chinese Phonology of the Wei-chin Period: Reconstruction of the Finals as Reflected in Poetry*. Institute of History and Philology, Academia Sinica special publication, no. 65. Taipei.

Tuan Yü-ts'ai 段玉裁

1966   *Liu-shu yin-yün piao.* 六書音韻表. Reprint, Taipei.

Tung T'ung-ho 董同龢

1944   *Shang-ku yin-yün piao kao* 上古音韻表稿 Li-chuang, Szechwan. Reprinted as Institute of History and Philology, Academia Sinica monograph series A, no. 21, 1967. Taipei.

Wang Jen-hsü 王仁昫

1964   *T'ang hsieh-pen k'an-miu pu-ch'üeh Ch'ieh-yün* 唐寫本 刊謬補缺切韻. 1947. Reprint, Taipei.

Wang Li 王力

1963   *Han-yü yin-yün* 漢語音韻. Peking.

1957–1958 *Han-yü-shih kao* 漢語史稿. 3 vols. Peking.

Wang Nien-sun 王念孫

1966   *Ku-yün p'u* 古韻譜. Reprint, Taipei.

IV

TRIBE AND STATE

14

The Chinese and Their Neighbors in Prehistoric and Early Historic Times

E. G. PULLEYBLANK

Though the history of Chinese civilization and the history of the Chinese-speaking people are intimately bound up with one another, they are by no means synonymous. On the one hand, through the medium of the Chinese written language, Chinese culture has extended beyond China to other East Asian countries—Korea, Japan, Vietnam—and has deeply influenced them, particularly but not exclusively at the level of high culture. On the other hand, within China, especially at the level of illiterate peasant culture but no doubt not exclusively so, there may well be hidden continuities with non-Chinese substrata that have been swallowed up and assimilated in the advance of the dominant language.

As we go back in time, the easy assumption that the culture of the territories now embraced by the Chinese state can be treated as a unity defined by the Chinese language becomes less and less tenable even within what used to be called China proper, that is, excluding the territories attached to China by conquest under the Manchu dynasty: Tibet, Sinkiang, Mongolia, and Manchuria. At the dawn of history we find the Chinese, self-identified by such terms as Hsia and Hua, surrounded and interspersed by other peoples with whom they were frequently in conflict and whom they typically looked down upon as inferior beings in the same way the Hellenes looked down on the *barbaroi* and, indeed, as human we-groups have always looked down on their neighbors. Since we have very little contemporary evidence of the languages of the non-Hsia peoples of China in the second and first millennia B.C., it is, strictly speaking, open to question whether they were all linguistically non-Chinese; and it has indeed often been argued that many of them may have been linguistically closely related to the Chinese, perhaps differing only in the way that modern Chinese dialects such as Cantonese differ from Mandarin. Against this comfortable assumption—comfortable for those who are anxious to project Chinese-ness as far as possible into the past and make it as comprehensive as possible—is the fact that even today there are sizable remnants of non-Chinese-speaking populations in the upland regions of southern, south-western and western China. The advance of Chinese at the expense of the non-Chinese languages in the south and southwest is well documented in recent times, and it is hardly engaging in wild speculation to project this kind of development into the past and to see in peoples such as the Yi, Ti, Jung, and Man—with whom, according to historical records, the Chinese contended for mastery of the valleys of the Huang Ho and Yangtze in the first millennium B.C.—peoples as different from the Chinese as the modern Ch'iang, Yi (Lo-lo), Miao, Yao, or Chuang.

These peoples have been largely illiterate, and our knowledge of their history must come mostly from what is found in Chinese sources. There is a considerable amount of such information, but it is highly inadequate in quantity and quality. The Chinese were seldom interested in their "barbarian" subjects or neighbors except from a narrow, military intelligence point of view. Records of foreign words recorded phonetically in Chinese script are very difficult to interpret. Yet all this material needs to be studied in conjunction with the results of modern linguistic and ethnographic investigation. Some work of this kind has been done both inside and outside China but not nearly enough. Pending the results of such researches, the preliminary survey offered in this chapter can only be very tentative in many of its conclusions, and no doubt there will always be large areas of obscurity. Nevertheless, it seems important in discussing such a momentous question as the origin of Chinese civilization to take this aspect of the problem into account as fully as possible.

I shall discuss in turn, in summary fashion, each of the language families which are now represented within China and try to project back possible connections with peoples known to the Chinese in the early historical period. I shall also discuss certain ancient peoples that may not be linguistically related to any of the present language families represented within Chinese territory, for example, the Ti, about whose language I cannot offer even a plausible speculation, and the Hsiung-nu, who may have been related to the Kets of Siberia.

THE CHINESE

Hsia 夏 and Hua 華

Our first indisputable evidence for the presence of the Chinese language comes from written records on the Shang oracle bones. It is clear not only that the Shang script represents an ancestral form of the later Chinese writing system, but also that the underlying spoken language must have been a form of Chinese. This has to be explicitly mentioned, since we know that in later times Chinese script was adapted ideographically to write languages as different from Chinese as Japanese and Korean. The phonetic elements that are found in the Shang script which are continuous with phonetic elements in the later script, however, guarantee that the transition from Shang to Chou involved no such drastic replacement of the underlying linguistic base.

We still cannot flatly assert, however, that the spoken languages of the Shang and Chou peoples were the same or even that they were both forms of Chinese. What we know is that the chancellery languages of Shang and Chou were both forms of Chinese. We do not know in either case what portion of the population as a whole spoke Chinese. There may have been small Chinese-speaking aristocracies ruling over non-Chinese subject populations; or, given the tradition of an earlier Hsia dynasty, which may have been the originator of the writing system, the Shang rulers could have been originally non-Chinese speakers who had adopted the language of their Hsia subjects. The same applies to the Chou, who were evidently already using the (Chinese) written language of the Shang before the conquest, and whose descendants later identified themselves as Hsia but who came out of Jung territory and seem to have had other connections with the Jung. Such hypotheses, though impossible to verify in the light of present knowledge, are not inherently far-fetched, as can be seen through parallels from other times and places.

A positive identification of Hsia in the archaeological record, with written documents to prove it, might clarify the situation—or it might further complicate it. Kwang-Chih Chang's proposal to identify certain "early Shang" archaeological sites as Hsia (see "The Question of Hsia in Chinese Archaeology," in ch. 16 below), though of the greatest interest in itself, does not contribute to this question, since there are as yet no written remains.

The Chinese monopoly of literacy in East Asia

Recently, much has been made of the possibility that marks on Neolithic pottery dated to as early as the fifth millennium B.C., which has been found from Kansu to Taiwan, may be early forms of Chinese writing. Interesting as this material is, it has not yet been shown that it is in any sense an approach to true writing. If the signs in question were intended to convey meanings—which is plausible but has not been demonstrated so far as I know—they were probably conventional marks of a much more limited character than true writing. The very fact that they have such a wide geographical distribution makes it unlikely that they stood for words in a particular language, as they would have to do if they were true writing.

It is, of course, true that there are pictographic and other iconic elements in the Chinese script as there were in other early scripts in Egypt and Mesopotamia; but in its fully developed form the association of graph and spoken word is virtually as complete in Chinese as in a fully phonetic script. Graphs can be borrowed for their sound for words completely unrelated in meaning. The opposite principle, to borrow a graph for its meaning and disregard the sound, is rare. Such a case is *shih* 石, "stone," read *tan* as a measure of weight, but there are few parallels.

Whatever gropings there may have been in Neolithic times toward graphic semiotic systems, it is highly probable that the actual invention of writing in China took place rapidly and that it was close in time to the other major innovations which we associate with the emergence of civilization. Without such an assumption, it is hard to understand the monopoly of the Chinese writing system in East Asia for so many centuries.

This monopoly is in striking contrast to the profusion of writing systems that emerged among the competing civilizations of the Near East. According to present evidence, the first fully developed system appeared in Sumeria by 3100 B.C. It did not remain unique for long, however, but was followed in short order by Proto-Elamite, Egyptian, Indus Valley, and Minoan. Moreover, only a few centuries after its creation, Sumerian cuneiform was adapted to the unrelated Akkadian language, then to Hittite and other neighboring languages. By the second half of the second millennium, when writing is first attested in China, many languages were being written in a wide variety of scripts including the first alphabets.

In East Asia, on the other hand, there is no evidence for the presence of any script but the Chinese until the intrusion of Kharoshti from India into Sinkiang in the second century of the present era. There is not even evidence of the use of Chinese script to write another language (apart from occasional phonetic transcriptions of foreign words included in Chinese texts) until the Japanese and Koreans began to do this in T'ang times. In general, the borrowing of the Chinese script meant the borrowing of the Chinese language. This was true even in Korea, Japan, and Vietnam, where the local languages continued to be spoken alongside Chinese and where the pronunciation of Chinese was adapted to local phonological systems. Inside China the spread of the Chinese literary language accompanied the ultimate disappearance of the pre-existing local languages, such as those of Ch'u and Wu. Eventually scripts imitative of rather than borrowed from Chinese were invented for Khitan, Tangut, and Jürchen and for some of the tribal languages of the south like Mo-so and Lo-lo, but this was long after the formative period of Chinese civilization.

The Chinese monopoly of literacy must have been one of the most powerful factors in the spread of Chinese, and with it Chinese culture, at the expense of other languages of the region. Of course it can be argued that it was the strength of the culture rather than the political organization that backed it up that gave the Chinese written language its prestige and ensured its monopoly; but that is simply the other side of the coin. Literacy was not only the vehicle for Chinese political organization and high culture, but also the groundwork on which it rested.

The origins of the Chinese script are obviously a matter of the utmost importance for the question central to this book. If it could be shown that Chinese writing developed upon a basis that had been gradually laid over many centuries among the Neolithic peoples of China, this would go far toward proving that it was a wholly indigenous invention; but then it would be strange that only the Chinese made this step, and not other Neolithic competitors like the Yi and Man. The lateness of the invention in China as compared with the Near East and India also suggests that one should keep one's mind open to the possibility of some stimulus from outside.

What such a stimulus could have been is, of course, a serious difficulty in that, as far as we know from evidence, there were no literate peoples closer to China than the Indus valley from whom the idea of writing could have been transmitted. At the time of the Berkeley conference in 1978 I still held to the view, announced in an unpublished paper presented to the West Coast Branch of the American Oriental Society at Stanford University in March 1975, that the twenty-two calendrical signs known as *kan-chih* were phonograms representing the consonants of the proto-Chinese language, and that they were directly related to the twenty-two consonantal signs of the early Semitic alphabet. I further suggested that both sets of signs might be derived from an unknown Indo-European system of writing that had traveled both east and west with the expansion of the Indo-Europeans in the third and second millennia B.C. I have since concluded that, though a phonogrammatic interpretation of the *kan-chih* signs seems to offer the best explanation for them within the Chinese writing system (Pulleyblank

1979), a comparison with the Semitic alphabet is probably untenable in spite of a number of striking coincidences in form and sound. Several of the most striking formal comparisons are with late forms of the Semitic letters, and the resemblances are not as good when the earliest attested forms are taken into account. A further important point is that, though the number twenty-two is of the essence as far as the system of *kan-chih* signs is concerned (ten "heavenly stems" and twelve "earthly branches"), it is probably accidental as far as the Semitic alphabet is concerned. The standard Semitic alphabet of twenty-two letters seems to have come into existence in Phoenicia and to be based on the number of consonantal phonemes in Phoenician around the end of the second millennium. There is good evidence, however, especially from the Ugaritic cuneiform alphabet, that the Phoenician alphabet was preceded by other related Semitic alphabets with more letters.

If the formal similarities between the alphabet and the *kan-chih* signs turn out to be illusory, the hypothesis of an unknown Indo-European writing system as an intermediary between east and west Asia becomes even more vacuous. One must obviously take seriously the possibility that Chinese writing (like Mayan writing in the New World) was an indigenous invention. Such an assumption does not by itself solve the problem, however. We still have to account for its unique appearance in one, and only one, of the Neolithic cultures of China and (apparently) its association with a complex of other major cultural innovations that occurred in the same culture over a comparatively short period. One can only hope that in the rapidly advancing state of archaeological discovery in China, new evidence will appear that will give more substance to speculation on the topic.

TIBETO-BURMAN

By common consent, the language family to which Chinese is most likely to be genetically related is Tibeto-Burman. Indeed, such a connection is regarded as well established by most scholars, even if there is still much disagreement about details. The primary evidence for such a genetic relation is provided by shared items of basic vocabulary. One can readily list a few dozen obvious cognates between Chinese, Burmese, and Tibetan that involve numerals, names of body parts and of common animals, and words for elementary notions such as: sun, day, night, year, die, kill, loose, bitter, I, you. Moreover, the phonetic correspondences, though they show regularity, are in many cases not so simple and transparent as to lead to a suspicion of borrowing.

The list could be extended, but not indefinitely. In spite of the pioneering work of scholars like Conrady, Simon, Wolfenden, Shafer, and Benedict, and the more recent efforts of younger linguists, the number of generally agreed-upon cognates between Chinese and the other languages of the family remains fairly modest. Individual scholars have much more extensive lists, but they usually depend on admitting ad hoc semantic shifts and phonetic developments that, though they have varying degrees of plausibility, cannot yet be tested by objective criteria and therefore do not command universal acceptance. Much more work needs to be done on reconstructing the internal phonological history of the major languages for which we have historical documentation—Chinese, Tibetan, and Burmese —based on more complete and exact descriptions, as well as on comparison of the numerous modern languages and dialects.

In these circumstances, we are far from able to use historical linguistics in any detailed and exact way to assist in the reconstruction of the interrelationships and movements of the various peoples involved. Shafer and Benedict have both offered classification schemes of the Tibeto-Burman languages, but they rarely give explicit criteria, and their conclusions seem essentially impressionistic.

Tibetan, like Chinese, has a classical written language with many divergent spoken dialects. Though these have been inadequately described and compared, it seems that the standard literary language has had a unifying effect throughout the country and that, for a large part of the vocabulary, the dialects use forms relatable by regular rules to written forms. On the periphery of the country, both east and west, there are more divergent languages of Tibetan type, such as Rgyarong in western Szechwan. The original unification of Tibet in the seventh century apparently came from south to north, and tradition associates the origins of Tibetan royalty with an area somewhat east and north of Lhasa. There seems to be no way at present to tell how long Tibetan-speaking people had been in that region or if they were, as has often been assumed, related to the Jo Ch'iang 婼羌, nomads whom the Chinese place south and west of Tun-huang, that is, on the western borders of Tsinghai and Sinkiang, in the Han period. A document in the Zhang-zhung language, which seems to have preceded Tibetan in central and western Tibet, is known from Tun-huang and is said to show affinities with Tibeto-Burman languages of the western Himalayas such as Kanauri (Thomas 1933).

Zhang-zhung is traditionally associated with the pre-Buddhist Bon religion of Tibet. A Tibetan/Zhang-zhung dictionary has recently been published in Delhi by the Bon-po Association, so it would appear that the language is not lost after all. According to Haarh (1968:26), the new evidence supports Thomas's general conclusions about the affinities of the language.

The Burmese came into Burma from the north, apparently in the wake of the Nan-chao invasion of the Pyu kingdom in A.D. 832. They established their kingdom at Pagan in upper Burma and later went on to conquer the Mon kingdom in lower Burma also. The Burmese language spread throughout the country and has diverged dialectally, but numerous other languages survive in Burma as well, many of them Tibeto-Burman languages that had preceded Burmese into the country. Burmese is most closely related to the Lo-lo (Yi) languages of southern Szechwan and Yunnan. These in turn are thought to be related to the surviving Ch'iang languages of Szechwan and the extinct Tangut language of the Hsi-hsia kingdom, which ruled Kansu and neighboring parts of Mongolia and Shensi in the tenth to thirteenth centuries. Great progress has been made in deciphering the Tangut script, but uncertainties remain about the phonology, and there has been only limited success so far in using this potentially rich material for comparative purposes.

Historical evidence to trace the movements of other Tibeto-Burman peoples now found in southwest China, northern Burma, Assam, Nepal, and northern India seems almost wholly lacking. Certainly the arrival of Tibeto-Burmans in those regions must have occurred many centuries ago (if we are right in assuming that they came in from the north). There are some inscriptional remains of the language of the Pyu kingdom which preceded the Burmese, but they are too fragmentary to permit precise conclusions about the language, except that it was certainly Tibeto-Burman. Shafer (1943) compared the language with Karen, which is not implausible on geographical grounds, since the Karens are farther south than the other Tibeto-Burman peoples of Burma and are the only ones found in the plains, but proof seems impossible at present. The evidence he presents could as well be used to show a relation to Kuki-Chin, a group of tribal languages in the western borderlands between Burma and India. Benedict (1972:10) suggests rather a connection with Nung, which in turn is said to stand between Burmese/Lo-lo and Kachin.

Turning back to early historical sources, what peoples known to the Chinese in the second and first millennia B.C. can we identify as Tibeto-Burman? First there are the Ch'iang 羌, who figure prominently in Han records as trouble-makers on the northwest frontier and whose name and presence in the same general area can be continuously attested down to the present. As already noted, the Tanguts of the T'ang, Sung, and Yüan periods were of Ch'iang origin. Ch'iang also appears as an ethnic name a thousand years earlier on the Shang oracle bones, as well as in the *Shih-ching* and the genuine parts of the *Shu-ching*. There are two difficulties with straightforward identification of the earlier and later uses: (1) the fact that Ch'iang is so seldom found as an ethnonym in other texts of the Chou period, and (2) the wide geographic separation between the home of the Ch'iang in the Han period and any place within range of Shang military power.

Nevertheless, it seems likely that the word is the same in both usages and that it gives evidence of the presence of Tibeto-Burmans of the Ch'iang type among the foes of Shang. This conclusion is not contradicted by the geographical analysis of Shima Kunio (1958:404, 423), who places the Ch'iang of Shang times in the northwest. It is also supported by the fact that in the *Shih-ching* the names Ch'iang and Ti 氐 occur in association. The Ti (EMC **tej**,* not to be confused with Ti 狄 [EMC **dejk**]) are associated with the Ch'iang in Han times but are seldom mentioned in earlier texts. They have not been identified on the oracle bones. The combination Ti Ch'iang also occurs in a passage in *Hsün-tzu*, evidently referring to a type of barbarians but without any geographical indications.

According to the *Shuo-wen*, the Ch'iang belonged to the Western Jung 西戎. Though such a statement in a second-century A.D. source is weak evidence in itself, it makes good sense on a number of grounds to identify Jung as the general name for non-Chinese Tibeto-Burmans, including the Ch'iang and Ti, of Chou times. Though the Jung are associated primarily with the west, that is, with the upland regions of Shensi, it should be noted that there were also Jung groups interspersed among the Central States of the Huang Ho plain in the Spring and Autumn period.

The Jung differed from the Chinese not only in customs and material culture but also in language. For this we have explicit testimony in the speech of a Jung chieftain: "We Jung are not the same as the Chinese (Hua) in drink or food or clothing. We do not carry on gift exchanges with them or communicate with them through language (*yen yü pu ta* 言語不達)" (*Tso-chuan* 278/Hsiang 14/1). A certain Yu Yü, a refugee among the Jung from the state of Chin, was consequently bilingual and was used by the Jung as an envoy to Ch'in (*Shih-chi* 5:192). In spite of their ethnic dif-

---

*EMC refers to Early Middle Chinese, LMC to Late Middle Chinese. These are reconstructions of the standard languages of the sixth and eighth/ninth centuries, respectively. For LMC see Pulleyblank 1970–71. A monograph on EMC is in preparation. Phonetic values are expressed in terms of the International Phonetic Alphabet. Reconstructions for periods earlier than EMC are preceded by an asterisk.

ferences there was sometimes diplomacy and inter-marriage, as well as war, between Chinese states and various groups of Jung. There is also intriguing evidence of rather close ties between the royal house of Chou and the Jung people. The two most prestigious clan names of the Chou, Chi 姬 and Chiang 姜, were found also among the Jung. The Chiang Jung are mentioned in the *Ch'un-ch'iu* and *Tso-chuan* under the thirty-third year of Duke Hsi as allies of Chin against Ch'in, and again in the passage from which the quotation above about the Jung language is taken. Evidence for the presence of the surname Chi among the Jung comes from the fact that wives whom Duke Hsien of Chin took from two different groups of Jung had this surname. One of them was the mother of the famous Ch'ung-erh, who became Duke Wen of Chin and achieved hegemony over all the feudal states (*Tso-chuan* 74/Chuang 28/fu).

Chi was the surname of the royal house of Chou. Chiang was the surname of a number of important feudal houses including Ch'i 齊, Lü 呂, Shen 申, and Hsü 許, but, more important, it was the clan from which the principal wives of the Chou kings were regularly chosen. The mother of Hou-chi, the ancestor of Chou, was Chiang Yüan 姜嫄, "Chiang Source," and later queens seem always to have that surname. A passage in the *Kuo-yü* (10:8) gives a mythological account of the origin of the two clans from the Yellow Emperor and the Flame Emperor (Yen Ti 炎帝, equated with Shen Nung, the Divine Husbandman), respectively. According to this account the Yellow Emperor and the Flame Emperor were brothers. They grew up beside different streams, called Chi and Chiang, respectively, in consequence of which they acquired different but complementary "virtue" (*te*). The passage goes on to give a rationale for the practice of clan exogamy, which has been a prominent feature of Chinese social structure at least since Chou times.

The phonetic and graphic similarities between the surname Chiang and the ethnic name Ch'iang are obvious and have been noted since ancient times. The *Hou-Han shu*, history of the later Han dynasty (117) says that the Ch'iang are a separate branch of the Chiang clan. But the word Chi is also phonetically similar to both Chiang and Ch'iang. Chi, EMC **kɨ**, has another reading of Yi, EMC **jɨ**. Chiang, EMC **kɨaŋ**, has 羊 EMC **jɨaŋ** as phonetic. It is not certain how we should explain this alternation between Middle Chinese **k–** or **k'–** and **j–** in the same *hsieh-sheng* series; but whatever the explanation, it shows that the two series were phonologically parallel in initial consonants. The finals were also related. Chi came from the Old Chinese **–əɣ** rhyme category, whereas Chiang came from the **–aŋ** category. Both the alternation between the vowels **ə** and **a** and that between final −ɤ and −ŋ are common in morphologically related sets; compare EMC *zɨ*ʔ 似, "resemble," and EMC *zɨaŋ*ʔ 象, "imitate, image."

Ch'iang is not analyzed in the *Shuo-wen* as having "sheep" as phonetic, but is considered a *hui-yi* compound, "sheep" plus "man," referring to the pastoral way of life of the Ch'iang. It seems obvious, however, that this is incorrect and that "sheep" has the same phonetic role here as in Chiang. The association with pastoralism is accidental and secondary. Chi and Chiang are thus apparently derived from the same semantic root as the name of the Ch'iang people. They may originally have been the names of exogamic moieties into which the Jung as a whole were divided.

In light of this it would appear that Mencius may have been accurate in referring to King Wen as a Western Barbarian (Hsi Yi 西夷) (*Meng-tzu* 30/4B/1). If the Chou were originally Jung people, they must have undergone a process of sinicization before the conquest. The recent discoveries of oracle bones from preconquest Chou indicate that the Shang written language was already in use (unless, as seems possible, the writing was done by Shang scribes during a visit to the area by the Shang king; private communication, David Keightley 1978). Whether this process of acculturation had been imposed by Shang conquest or was a spontaneous reaction to the example and threat of Shang power is not clear, but in the end it was successful in creating the necessary basis for the Chou to supplant the Shang as overlords of the merging civilization of China. Due to this acculturation the Chou lost their identity with those Jung who retained their own customs and language, and turned against them—though probably never with the savagery to which the Jung had been subject under the Shang. As we shall see, much the same process must have taken place in Ch'u, which emerged from among the Man people of the middle Yangtze, acquired literacy and Chinese-style statehood, gave up its Man language in preference for Chinese, and began to treat the remaining independent Man as barbarians. A similar process took place later in Wu and Yüeh.

At the time of the conquest, however, it would seem that Chou had not yet become alienated from its ethnic brethren. In the "Mu shih" section of the *Shu-ching* (quoted also in *Shih chi* 4), King Wu addresses among his followers "the men of Yung 庸, Shu 蜀, Ch'iang 羌, Mou 髳, Wei 微, Lu 盧, P'eng 彭 and P'u 濮." The presence of Ch'iang in the list needs no further comment. Shu is well known as the later name for Szechwan. It occurs on the oracle bones as a place name which Shima (1958:378–379, 382–383) locates around the T'ung-kuan at the great eastward bend of the Huang Ho. A cache of inscribed bronzes associated with the Wei family, which held a hereditary office in Western Chou, has recently been reported (*WW*

1978.3). Yung appears as a small state in the *Ch'un-ch'iu* under the sixteenth year of Duke Wen (610 B.C.), identified with the later Chu-shan in Hupei, which was extinguished jointly by Ch'u, Ch'in, and Pa after it had led various barbarians, including the Hundred P'u (another name that occurs in the list of King Wu's allies) in an attack on Ch'u, then beset by famine.

The genuineness of the "Mu shih" as an original document of the time of King Wu may be open to dispute, but it may in any case embody a genuine tradition. The tradition that King Wu was accompanied against Shang by Western barbarians does not seem likely to be a later invention. The same tradition is no doubt behind a statement in the genuine *Chu-shu chi-nien* that King Wu led Western Barbarians (Hsi Yi 西夷) against Shang (*Ku-pen chu-shu chi-nien chi-chiao* 6b).

If we assume that Chou's non-Chinese allies were all from the same Tibeto-Burman "Jung" stock as Chou itself, an inference that seems reasonable though it cannot be definitely proved in the light of present evidence, we must next ask how far south the Tibeto-Burmans extended at that period. The displacement of the name Shu from the region of the T'ung-kuan to Szechwan between the Shang and the Warring States periods suggests that there had been a southward movement of Tibeto-Burmans during that millennium. It is, unfortunately, by no means certain that the two uses of the name are directly connected. Even if the same word is involved in both cases, the two applications of it as a proper name could be independent. Shu also occurs as a place name in Shantung in the Spring and Autumn period. But the southwesterly location of Yung and especially of the still tribal P'u in the Spring and Autumn period does suggest a southward movement. The other main ethnic name associated with Szechwan before the Chinese penetration from Ch'in in the fourth century B.C. is Pa 巴. This name occurs in the Spring and Autumn period but has not been identified with certainty on the oracle bones. The Pa still existed as a non-Chinese tribal people in southeastern Szechwan in Han times. The *Hou-Han shu* classified them as Man 蠻, which ought to mean that they were Miao-Yao speakers rather than Tibeto-Burmans.

By the Later Han, there were certainly Tibeto-Burman peoples stretching all along the western side of what is now Szechwan province. The *Hou-Han shu* classifies them as separate branches of the Ch'iang which descended from the same ancestor as the primary group of Ch'iang in the upper reaches of the Huang Ho. A song in the native language of one of these groups, the White Wolf people, is transcribed in Chinese characters together with a Chinese translation. Though there are many uncertainties about the interpretation of this material, enough words can be identified to leave no doubt that the language was Tibeto-Burman (Wang Ching-ju 1932; Coblin 1979).

If, as Chinese historians suggest, these southern "Ch'iang" tribes of the Han period were comparatively recent immigrants from farther north, one might conjecture that during Shang times Tibeto-Burmans had not penetrated much south of the watershed of the Huang Ho. Archaeological evidence may also be consistent with such a conclusion. According to K. C. Chang (1977:442–453), before the Chinese penetration into Szechwan in the Warring States period, the eastern part of the province, (the territory of the Pa) showed close cultural affinities with Ch'u, while farther west in the Ch'eng-tu area there are features in common with contemporary civilizations in Yunnan (Dongson and Tien). In the northwest of the province, on the other hand, the Li-fan and Kan-tzu sites show northern cultural connections, as well as influences from contemporary China.

If this is the correct picture, it further suggests that, looking back to still earlier times, we could find the heartland of the Sino-Tibetan peoples as a whole in the Yang-shao Neolithic, the Chinese being an easterly branch that evolved in the Central Plain, absorbing influences from the Austro-Asiatic Yi culture of Shantung and the Huai region. It is to be hoped that further studies based on archaeology and on such linguistic evidence as that of place names will throw more light on the matter.

THE MIAO-YAO 苗傜

In the southern half of China and stretching into Indochina there are numerous languages which resemble Chinese typologically, particularly in their monosyllabism and their tonal systems. These include the Miao-Yao and Tai and related languages and also Vietnamese, which is now classified as Mon-Khmer (Austro-Asiatic). All these languages also contain a large amount of Chinese vocabulary, but this is considered the result of borrowing rather than common inheritance. Most of the basic vocabulary remains quite distinct. The present situation seems to be the result of centuries of contact, with Chinese playing the role of a politically dominant and culturally prestigious superstratum. The similarities in the tonal systems of all these languages provide a particularly good illustration of how the process must have worked.

There is by now an accumulation of evidence to show that the Chinese tones have developed within the last two thousand years through the replacement of initial and final segmental features by features of pitch and contour. The first stage was reached in Early Middle Chinese (before A.D. 600), in which syllables other than those ending in a stop consonant, which were classified as the "entering" tone, were divided into three tonal categories: "level", "rising" and "departing." Syllables in the rising tone had earlier ended in a glottal stop, while those in the departing tone had ended in −**h**, from earlier −**s**. These two tones were probably still characterized to some extent by glottalization and aspiration at that period. Next a further split occurred by which the existing tones were divided into upper and lower registers, depending on the voicing of the initial consonants. Subsequently obstruent initials were devoiced in most dialects. Miao-Yao, Tai, and Vietnamese all show the same basic pattern in their tonal systems, modified, as in the case of Chinese dialects, by various later mergers and splits. On the other hand, genetically related languages that have not had the same degree of intimate contact with Chinese either lack tones altogether or show only parts of the pattern. One cannot test this for Miao-Yao and Tai, since all the present-day languages of these groups show the pattern. Mon-Khmer languages other than Vietnamese and the closely related Mườ ng languages, however, lack developed tone systems, though some of them, like Cambodian and Mon, may be moving in that direction. In Tibeto-Burman there is also a widespread development of tonal systems in the modern languages; but classical Tibetan evidently did not have tones, and the tonal systems of Burmese and modern Tibetan dialects only partly correspond to the Chinese pattern, reflecting the fact that Chinese influence has been less intense.

The Miao-Yao languages are among the lesser known of the non-Chinese languages of China, though the appearance quite recently of a number of studies including dictionaries has improved the situation somewhat. Unlike the Vietnamese, who, after centuries of Chinese rule, have been independent for nearly a thousand years—or the Tai, who, while continuing to live in large numbers within China, have established independent nations in Thailand and Laos with their own literate traditions—the Miaos and Yaos have survived only as oppressed minorities in the upland areas of central and south China; or, when in comparatively recent times they have moved south into Indo-China, they have not created independent states, but have continued as mountain-dwelling minorities in Vietnam, Laos, and Thailand. Though there is a considerable amount of material in Chinese sources from which to reconstruct their history, it has not yet been adequately studied.

The modern representatives of this language family are divided into three groups, called in Chinese Miao, Yao, and She 畬. No information is available about the original language of the She, who are found in small pockets in Kiangsi, Chekiang, and Fukien, and it seems possible that their language is already extinct; but they are classified as Miao-Yao on ethnographic grounds, in particular because of the myth of the dog-ancestor P'an-hu which they share with the Yao (Lebar et al. 1964:85; Stübel and Li 1932:32).

Both Miao and Yao are divided into a number of quite widely divergent dialects. Enough work has now been done in comparing the dialects and in comparing Miao with Yao to prove that they are branches of a common linguistic stock and to make a start on reconstructing the proto-language. The two linguistic stocks provide complementary information to this end, in that the Miao has greatly simplified its system of finals but retains complex initials, whereas Yao has simplified the initials but retains more distinctions in the finals.

The wider connections of Miao-Yao are still undetermined. Modern publications from China classify them as Sino-Tibetan, but, if this is so the connection must be very distant. Other scholars, such as Forrest (1965:92–101), have listed word resemblances to Mon-Khmer. Benedict (1975b) now treats Miao-Yao as distantly related to his Austro-Thai family (Tai and Austronesian). Much work remains to be done, not the least of it to sort out the various layers of Chinese loanwords and, conversely, to identify Miao-Yao substratum words in Chinese, particularly in southern dialects.

The first problem which arises when one tries to trace back the Miao-Yao in Chinese historical records is that of their names. The name Miao, written with the identical Chinese character, is found in legends about the time of Yao and Shun, apparently referring to a non-Chinese people. It does not reappear, however, until the Yüan period; so it is doubtful, to say the least, whether one can identify the two usages of the word. As it is now applied, Miao appears to be a Chinese term not used by the native people themselves, who call themselves Hmong or Hmu. The terms Mnong and Mlao are reported from among the Miao of Vietnam (Lebar et al. 1964: 72). The latter, if a genuine native name, looks as if it could underlie the Chinese term. Vietnamese Mèo differs from the regular Sino-Vietnamese reading of Miêu for the character Miao and also requires explanation.

Although the greatest numbers of Miao now live in Kweichow and other parts of South China and Indochina, the area of greatest concentration is still northwest Hunan, and it is likely that their settlement in that region has been continuous since the Han.

The name Yao occurs earlier than Miao, possibly as early as the *Sui shu*

(history of the Sui dynasty) and certainly since the Five Dynasties and
Sung, when it had wide currency, referring apparently to Miaos as well as
Yaos. The modern Yaos refer to themselves as Mien or Mun. In Vietnam
they are called Màn, a word that differs in tone from Sino-Vietnamese
Man. Just to complicate the picture still more, the so-called Miao of
Hainan are in fact linguistically Yaos.

The Yaos, like the Miaos, are widely scattered at present, but the
greatest concentrations seem to be in southern Hunan and adjacent regions
of Kwangtung and Kwangsi.

In spite of the discontinuity in nomenclature, one can confidently connect the later Miao-Yao with the various Man 蠻 peoples who lived in the
Yangtze watershed in Chou and Han times and who are first described in
some detail in the *Hou-Han shu*. One of the clearest proofs of this identity is
the P'an-hu dog-ancestor myth, which is related in the *Hou-Han shu*
account of the Man of Ch'ang-sha and Wu-ling.

To the north and west of the Man of Ch'ang-sha and Wu-ling were the
Man of the Pa 巴 and Nan 南 commanderies (eastern Szechwan and northwestern Hupei), who had a different origin myth. The ancestors of their five
clans were said to have been born in two caves in a certain mountain. The
ancestor of the Pa clan, who achieved pre-eminence and was later known as
Lord Lin (Lin chün 廩君), was born in a red cave. The other four ancestors
were born in a black cave. After his death, Lord Lin was said to have turned
into a white tiger, to which the Pa people offered human sacrifice. The
prevalence of tiger motifs in archaeological finds from the Pa region has
been plausibly connected with this tiger mythology (Chang 1977: 447, 453).

A white tiger plays a different role in another legend told of a branch of
the Pa people, the Pan-tun 板楯 or Board Shield Man, from whom came Li
T'e, founder of the Ch'eng 成 state in Szechwan in the fourth century A.D.
It is said that in the time of King Chao-Hsiang of Ch'in (306–251 B.C.) a
white tiger was terrorizing the land, and the king offered a large reward to
anyone who could kill it. A man from this tribe shot it with a crossbow
made of white bamboo, in return for which his people were given exemp-
tions from land tax and other privileges in perpetuity.

De Beauclair (1960) describes a belief, among present-day Miao, in the
possibility of the continuance of human souls after death in the form of
blood-sucking, vampire-like tigers. Graham's collection of Miao stories
(1954) also contains tales of the transformation of men into tigers, and
similar beliefs have been reported for the Yao in Kwangsi (de Beauclair
1960). There seems an obvious connection between such material and the
Pa cult of the tiger as described in the *Hou-Han shu*, providing circumstan-

tial evidence that the Pa people belonged to the Miao language family. It must be noted that according to the *Hou-Han shu*, the ancestor of the Ch'iang was protected from his Ch'in pursuers by the apparition of a tiger, which saved him from being burned after he had taken refuge in a cave. The mere occurrence of tiger legends is not sufficient, therefore, to distinguish ethnic affiliations. But the fact that the archaeological remains from Pa territory show close affinities with Ch'u does strengthen the case for connecting them with the Miao rather than the Ch'iang.

The civilization of Ch'u, which later made its own distinctive contribution to the syncretic Chinese civilization of Ch'in and Han, arose during the first millennium B.C. in the middle Yangtze region in the midst of the Man tribes. Though Ch'u became Chinese in language and eventually took its place among the contending Chinese states, there is abundant evidence that originally it was considered and considered itself to be of Man origin. Possibly it was founded as a state from the north, as some traditions have it, or it may have been a spontaneous local reaction to expanding Chinese pressure. In either case, the formation of a state and the acquisition of literacy meant adopting the Chinese written language and eventually the spoken language also. This in turn meant that Ch'u dropped its Man identity and began to treat the unsinicized Man around it as "barbarians"—the same process that separated the Chou people from the Jung.

There are a few transcriptions in early sources of allegedly Ch'u words. In *Tso-chuan* (184/Hsüan 4/fu) we find: "The people of Ch'u call 'to suckle' *ku* 穀 and call 'tiger' *yü-t'u* 於菟." In the *Hou-Han shu* (100A) the same words are cited, but "tiger" is written *yü-shih* 於檡. According to the commentator Yen Shih-ku, the first character, meaning "suckle," is to be read either according to its normal reading of EMC **kowk** or as EMC **now²**. The latter reading is very strange in that *hsieh-sheng* series. The *Shuo-wen* does, however, contain a character 㲋, meaning "milk, breast," which the *Kuang-yün* reads as EMC **kow²**, **now²**, and **nowʰ** (the last for the variant form 㸋). The readings with initial **n** look like variants of the Chinese word *ju* 乳 (EMC **nua²**). I can offer no further suggestions to elucidate this puzzle.

Yü-t'u, the word for "tiger," offers more promising possibilities. It can be reconstructed as EMC ʔia – t'ɔʰ < *ʔà – lʰáx or EMC ʔia – ciajk < *ʔà – lʰàk. The *Fang-yen* (8.1a) also quotes this word in the form *yü-t'u* 於檡. Kuo P'u's commentary adds: "The barbarians of the mountains of Chiang-nan of today call 'tiger' [*yü*–] *t'u*, pronounced 苟賚 (EMC **kow²dowʰ** < *kɔʔ-lówx)." This is interesting not only for the variant form but because it seems to confirm the existence of the word among the putative ancestors of the present Miao-Yao.

Mei and Norman compare this word with Austo-Asiatic forms like Old Mon *kla*, Old Khmer *klā*, Khmer *khlā*, "felines," and others. This is quite persuasive. The same word is also found in Burmese-Lolo: Burmese *kya:* (inscriptional *klya*), Lahu *lâ*, and so on. As Mei and Norman suggest, it probably also underlies the standard Chinese word *hu* 虎 (EMC xɔ⁷), for which I would conjecture a reconstruction **xʷláʔ*.

If Chinese **xʷláʔ*, "tiger," is indeed the same word as the Austro-Asiatic forms cited above, which seems probable, it must be an early loanword. In view of the centrality of tiger mythology among the Miao, it seems less likely to be a borrowing in the Man language. If Miao-Yao is ultimately related to Austro-Asiatic, the Ch'u form could be part of the original Miao-Yao vocabulary. Whether it could be connected to forms like *cyo* and *tšo* found in present-day Miao dialects is not clear.

How far east did the Miao-Yaos extend in early historical times? The present-day eastern branch, the She mentioned above, about whom so little is known, are now found in Chekiang, Kiangsi, and Fukien. The word *she*, also read *yü*, means "slash-and-burn cultivation," and it may be that the people became known as She *min* 畲民 or She *man* 畲蠻 because of their use of this agricultural method. On the other hand, the word is strikingly similar to Shu 舒 (EMC ɕɨz), the name of a people mentioned several times in the *Tso-chuan* as living between Ch'u and Hsü 徐. They are referred to as *ch'ün* 群 Shu or *chung* 衆 Shu, "the many Shu," as if they were an unorganized tribal people rather than a Chinese-style city-state. According to the commentary of Tu Yü they were in the neighborhood of Lü-chiang in Anhwei, that is, along the Yangtze between Ch'u and Wu. It seems quite possible, though difficult to verify, that they were the ancestors of the modern She.

The old name of Fukien, Min 閩 (EMC **min** < **mrə̀n*), is phonologically similar to Man 蠻 (EMC **maṛn** < **mrán*) and may represent a variant of the same word. Though the Yüeh people who extended along the coast from Chekiang to Vietnam were probably Austro-Asiatic, related to the modern Vietnamese, the original inhabitants, who preceded the Austro-Asiatics and presumably still lived in the interior, may have been an eastward extension of the Man (Miao-Yao) people.

The Tan 蜑, now found in the coastal regions of Fukien and Kwangtung as houseboat-dwellers, have been known under that name since before the T'ang. There is evidence that they formerly had settlements on land and were not, as now, confined to a life on the water. Nothing is known of their original language, and they are not among the recognized minorities of present-day China. Some modern Chinese writers (e.g., Liu 1969:780) classify them as Miao-Yao but without giving strong evidence.

TAI AND RELATED LANGUAGES (KADAI)

The Tai languages are now best known as the national languages of Thailand and Laos. They also include the Shan languages of Burma and the extinct Ahom language of the Shan rulers of Assam. The southward movements which have brought these various groups of Tai speakers out of China into Southeast Asia have all taken place within approximately the last thousand years. Although it is no longer generally thought that the Nan-chao kingdom of Yunnan was ruled by Tai speakers, it no doubt included Tai speakers among its subjects, and it seems likely that the southward and westward spread of the Tais was associated with the fortunes of that kingdom. Large numbers of Tai speakers still remain in China, particularly in Kwangsi but also in Kweichow and Yunnan. Other Tai groups constitute minorities in northern Vietnam.

The Tai languages proper are all quite closely related, no doubt reflecting their recent dispersion. Fang-kuei Li (1977:xii) distinguishes three main dialectal divisions: (1) a southwestern group, including Thai or Siamese, Lao, Shan, and various lesser languages in Vietnam, Thailand, Burma, and Yunnan, (2) a central group, including the Tho dialects of northern Vietnam and various dialects spoken in Kwangsi, (3) a northern group, including the Chung-chia or Pu-yi dialects in Kweichow and the Chuang dialects in Kwangsi. More remotely related are the Bê language on Hainan Island and the Kam (called Tung by the Chinese) and Sui languages to the north of the Chuang in Kwangsi and Kweichow, extending into southern Hunan.

Outside this group of languages, whose relations to one another are well established, lie a number of lesser known languages which have been claimed to be related. Benedict (1942) grouped together four such—the Li of Hainan, the Kelao of Kweichow, and the Lati and Laqua of northern Vietnam—as the Kadai languages, which, according to him, formed a link between Tai and Austronesian. To these must now be added the recently discovered Lakkia language, which seems definitely to be related to Tai, spoken by a small group of people included within a Yao-speaking minority in Kwangsi (Haudricourt 1967). Recent additions to our knowledge about the Li language also strengthen the probability that it is related to Tai. Haudricourt suggests that, rather than constituting a distinct group related to but separate from Tai and Kam-Sui, the so-called Kadai languages are as remote from each other as from Tai and should be compared separately. This seems to make better sense geographically.

The early history of the Tais proper is not easy to trace in Chinese sources. The largest group of Tai speakers now in China, the Chuang of Kwangsi, appear under that name only from the Ming dynasty on. Ruey Yih-fu (1969) thinks, no doubt correctly, that they are referred to in Sung dynasty sources under the term Tung 洞 (also written as 峒 and 崬), which appears to be the name of a territorial unit rather than an ethnic term. It is presumably the same as Tung 侗, the name by which the Tai-related people who call themselves Kam are now referred to by the Chinese.

Tung 洞 (EMC **dowŋ**ʰ) seems to represent a native word meaning "mountain valley" or "level ground between cliffs and beside a stream." *Lung* 弄, which according to the Aichi *Chūnichi daijiten* (1968) is a Chuang word with this meaning, is presumably a form of the same word. The shift to the meaning "village" or "settlement" implied by some of the usages no doubt reflects the settlement patterns of the Tai people. By further extension it could be used as a proper name for the people who lived in such settlements. A complication is the fact that the word *tung* is also used in Chinese to mean "cave, grotto." Though the usage is post-classical, quotations can be found from as early as the third century A.D. (see Morohashi, *Daikanwa jiten*). Presumably this is unrelated to the Tai word.

Tung, written 洞 or 崬, is frequent in place names in Kwangsi and is also found in various parts of Kweichow. It presumably indicates the presence or former presence of Tais. The possible significance of the term as a means of showing a connection between the Kelao and the Tais will be discussed below.

Ruey attempts to push the history of the Chuang 獞 (now written 僮 or 壯) back into pre-T'ang times by identifying them as Hsi 溪, a term used as an ethnic designation in some texts of the Southern Dynasties. Hsi, which simply means "mountain stream," is primarily a geographical term, referring to the Five Hsi of western Hunan, a mountainous region still occupied by Miao and Tibeto-Burman T'u-chia. It is likely that there were also Tai-related people in the southern part of the region in earlier times. Even today the Kam extend into southern Hunan. Ruey's arguments for identifying the Hsi of the Nan-pei ch'ao specifically with Chuang and for thinking that what he calls "northern Chuang" have migrated south from Hunan into Kwangsi seem tenuous, however. He finds evidence of the use of the term *tung* to refer to local territorial units of people described as Hsi, but this merely links them with Tais in the broad sense rather than with the Chuang.

So does the evidence of the importance of fishing in their culture. The surname Huang 黃 occurs both among the Hsi and among the Chuang in Kwangsi but is hardly enough to prove a migration.

One of Ruey's arguments seems particularly specious. Having argued on linguistic grounds that the Chuang could not have come to Kwangsi from the Yüeh territory to the south and east or from the Kelao territory to the west, he infers that they could only have come from the north. This leaves out the possibility that, at least within the time span under consideration, they may have been indigenous to the Kwangsi area. In fact, he ends by saying just that about what he calls the "southern Chuang."

The present distribution of the Tais, with more remotely related Kam-Sui speakers forming a band to their north, strongly suggests that they did not migrate into their present locations from more northerly regions in historic times. Probably the Hsi of the Nan-pei ch'ao were, like the Kam-Sui of today, culturally and linguistically of the same origin as the Tais but not Tai in the narrower sense.

This brings us to the question of the relations between the Tais and the Kelao or Lao. Unfortunately, though they played an important part in Chinese history from the third century A.D. onward, the Kelao have been on the point of extinction for some time and little is known about their language. There are only a few short vocabularies, collected by Chinese officials under the empire or by missionaries. From this material one can make a number of word comparisons with Tai that seem to involve basic vocabulary and systematic sound correspondence. In the following list, based on Benedict (1942), Northern Kelao (N.Kl.) stands for the material from Kweichow gathered by Clarke (1911). Southern Kelao (S.Kl.) refers to the list from northern Vietnam given by Lunet de Lajonquière (1906). Proto-Tai and Siamese are from Li (1977); Sui is from Li (1965).

	N.Kl.	*S.Kl.*	*Proto-Tai*	*Siamese*	*Sui*
dog	*mu*	*mă*	**hma*	*maa*	*ṃu*
pig	*ma*	*miă*	**hmu*	*muu*	*ṃu*
fire	*bai*	*p'i*	**vɛi*	*fai*	*wi*
fowl	*k'ai*		**kai*	*kăi*	*qai*
eye	*dau*		**tra*	*taa*	*da*
ear	*rau*		**xr—*	*huu*	*qha*
tooth	*baŋ*		**v—*	*fan*	*wjan*
foot	*k'au*		**kha*	*khaa*	*pa, qa*
hand	*mau*		**mwī*	*mīī*	*mja*

A Tai connection thus seems quite likely, though it can hardly be considered proven without more material.

The modern form of the name Kelao in Chinese is 仡佬, pronounced *ko-*

lao or *ch'i-lao*. This was formerly written 仡狫 and is found as early as the Sung. Other disyllabic forms encountered from T'ang onward include 葛獠, 獦獠, 狤獠, and 犵獠. In Yüan times we also find the forms T'u-lao-man 土老蠻 and T'u-la-man 禿剌蠻. Marco Polo refers to the Toloman or Coloman, who must be the same people.

In pre-T'ang texts one generally finds only the single character Lao, but as Ruey Yih-fu (1948) has demonstrated, there can be little doubt that it refers to the same people. It first appears in texts referring to the third century A.D. at a time when initial clusters probably still existed in Chinese. It was presumably pronounced something like **klaw***²* or **glaw***²*. De Beauclair (1946) gives the self-designation of the Kelao as *glao*, and Ruey gives a form *klao*—which must both be the same word. The *Kuang-yün* gives an alternate reading for 獠 as EMC **tarw***²*, pointing back to an earlier ***tráw***²* (possibly more like ***tlaw***²* at the relevant period). (A third reading of LMC **liaw** and EMC **lew** is irrelevant; it belongs to an old word meaning "to hunt at night" and has nothing to do with the name of the Kelao. But it is sometimes erroneously found in Western language references to the Lao.)

The earliest historical references to the Lao are in the *San-kuo chih* and in works cited in its commentary. In the biography of Chang Yi (*Shu chih* 13), the *Yi-pu ch'i-chiu chuan* 益部耆舊傳 of Ch'en Shou (233–297) is quoted to the effect that after Ma Chung had pacified the south in 233, the Lao in Tsang-ko and Hsing-ku commanderies again revolted. This places them in present Kweichow and western Yunnan.[1] A later reference in the *San-kuo chih* (*Shu chih* 11) refers to a campaign against the Barbarian (Yi 夷) Lao in Yung-ch'ang commandery, which lay farther west in what is now Yunnan.

The Lao are also mentioned several times in the *Hua-yang kuo-chih*, the local gazetteer of Szechwan from the Chin period. In some cases a disyllabic form Chiu-lao 鳩獠 (EMC **kuw-law***²*) is given (*ch.* 4:62), anticipating the disyllabic forms which became normal from the T'ang and Sung onward.

In the next century, Lao tribes invaded Szechwan and caused much

---

1. Tsang-ko commandery was established in the Han and corresponded roughly to present Kweichow. According to the *Ku-chin ti-ming ta-tz'u-tien*, Hsing-ku commandery, with its seat one hundred *li* west of present P'u-an-hsien in Kweichow, was not established until Chin. This is incorrect. It was established by Shu of the Three Kingdoms in 225 (*Hua-yang kuo-chih* 4:62). Ruey Yih-fu mispunctuates the *Hua-yang kuo-chih* line牂牁興古獠種復反as *Tsang-ko hsing. Ku Lao-chung fu-fan*—"Tsang-ko arose. The old Lao race again revolted"—and argues that this must mean that the Lao had been known previously. *Hua-yang kuo-chih* 4:62 goes on to say that in Hsing-ku "there are many Chiu-Lao 鳩獠."

difficulty for the local Ch'eng Han state which was ruling at that time. Several texts inform us explicitly that the Lao had not been in Szechwan previously and had only recently emerged from the mountainous country to the south. They continue to be mentioned in texts of the Northern and Southern dynasties with reference both to Szechwan and to their home-lands in the south. It is interesting to note that the Lao are mentioned in works of the Southern dynasties far to the southeast in northern Vietnam. In 537 a local rebel (presumably Vietnamese) named Li Fen, when defeated and pressed by the Chinese governor of Chiao-chou (Hanoi), tried to take refuge in the "valleys (*tung* 洞) of the Ch'ü-lao 屈獠" but was killed and handed over to his pursuers (*Ch'en shu* 1 : 2–3). The unusual disyllabic form Ch'ü-lao ensures that this is not merely a generalized use of Lao to refer to any kind of southern barbarian. The term *tung* is also of interest, since it seems to link the Lao with this Tai cultural feature. It leads one to suspect that Lao was used in a broad sense to refer to the Tai-related populations of South China and that there was some basis for this in native usage.

In the Kwangtung region the terms Li 俚 and Lao are linked to refer to the local non-Chinese inhabitants (see *Nan shih* 66 : 1599 and *Sui shu* 80 : 1803). Li and Lao of Nan-hai (Kwangtung) and Chiao-chih (northern Vietnam) are discussed together in the "Ti-li chih" of the *Sui shu* (31 : 888) with no clear distinction.

As a separate term, Li occurs already at the beginning of the Later Han and is frequent thereafter with reference to the natives of Kwangtung and northern Vietnam (Ruey 1956). Ruey is at pains to distinguish the Li and Lao as separate peoples, though he thinks they were related and shows that they had important cultural traits in common. It may not be going too far to suggest that there was a continuum of Tai-related peoples from the coast of Kwangtung, Kwangsi, and northern Vietnam stretching inland through Kweichow into Yunnan and north into Hunan and southern Szechwan. No doubt they were already somewhat differentiated in culture and lan-guage before the coming of the Chinese, having adapted to the different environments in which they had lived.

It is not impossible that the names Li and Lao are etymologically connected. The native name of the Li is variously reported as Dli, Bli, Le, K'lai, and B'lay (Forrest 1965 : 102; Lebar et al. 1964 : 240). This variety of prefixed consonants could make sense if the original word was something like *k^w'laj, with a labio-velar which sometimes developed as a labial and sometimes lost its rounding and became a plain velar or assimilated to a dental before l, depending on the dialect. The Chinese character originally used to write Li also implies an Old Chinese cluster initial of some kind, and the assumption of labio-velar plus — r — would account best for the various initials found in the *hsieh-sheng* series: *li* 里, 貍 (EMC li² < *wrɔ́ɤ²), *mai* 埋 (EMC merj < *wrɔ́ɤ), *k'uei* 悝 (EMC k'wəj < *xʷrɔ́ɤ [?] [one would expect the EMC Grade II rhyme of xwerj or k'werj to reflect an Old Chinese *xʷraɤ, but examples of such words derived from the Old Chinese —ə category are not numerous; perhaps retroflexion was lost in some cases, or perhaps one should reconstruct *xʷlɔ́ɤ]), and 萑 (EMC xuwk, tr'ɨk, tr'uwk < *xʷrɔ̀k). I propose an initial *wr— for the words which give modern *li*, but there may have been some velar friction [ɤw]. Note also that the original Chinese transcription implies a final with a central off-glide [əɯ], a kind of diphthong found in modern Tai dialects, rather than a diphthong in —j. The possibility of an original labio-velar in the name of the Kelao is suggested by the earliest disyllabic transcriptions 鳩獠, EMC kuw-law², and 屈獠, EMC k'ut-law². From this it is apparent that the names of the Li and Lao were similar phonetically and may have been related to one another. It is tempting to try to connect Kelao/Lao also with the Lao of Laos, but this is probably unjustified. At any rate, the tones do not show the expected correspondence.

In his discussion of the origin of the Chuang, Ruey Yih-fu (1969) excludes the possibility of connecting them with the Lao on linguistic grounds. But the evidence we have suggests the opposite conclusion. If we assume that the Tais are included in the general cover terms Li and Lao before the T'ang period, we no longer have to ask where they came from when they appear in a more differentiated way later. The Lao are described as savage cannibals in Chinese accounts. Possibly the tribesmen who descended on Szechwan from the fastnesses of Kweichow were fiercer and less civilized than the peasant cultivators of Kwangtung. They had some traits in common, however, that seem to link them with what we know of the Tais. One was the use of pile dwellings with space for domestic animals beneath the family living quarters. This is typical of Tai villagers in many parts of Southeast Asia. The Lao word for this type of dwelling is transcribed in Chinese as *kan-lan* 干蘭 or *ko-lan* 閣蘭 (EMC kɑk-lan), the latter suggesting a form like *kălan or *kăran, with an unaccented first syllable. This can perhaps be compared to the common Tai word for "house," which Li reconstructs as proto-Tai *rïan. In the Kam-Sui languages we have Sui ₎yan, and Mak ₎žaan, with tonal irregularities in some dialects.

Other Lao practices include drinking through the nose and knocking out teeth as a form of personal adornment. Like the Tais and Mon-Khmers, the Lao are said to have no clans, which makes them notably different from the Chinese, with their pattern of surnames and patrilineages. Both the Lao and the Li are reported to have engaged in selling their own people, and even their own relatives, as slaves. There was in fact an active slave trade in "southerners" (*nan-k'ou* 南口) from the Han at least until the late T'ang and possibly later. It should be studied in much more depth than it has been so far. The Tai-related peoples were no doubt one of the main sources of such slaves, but one suspects that, as in seventeenth- and eighteenth-century Africa, the corruption in social mores was a response to Chinese demand, not a simple result of natural depravity in the people.

One aspect of Lao and Li culture that is particularly noteworthy is the importance occupied by bronze drums. This is mentioned in several texts and immediately makes one think of the Dongson culture and the recently unearthed bronze culture of Tien in Yunnan. We have seen that the Lao first emerged from Tsang-ko commandery, east of Tien in Kweichow in the territory that had belonged to the kingdom of Yeh-lang 夜郎, but other passages place them farther west.

It is tempting, but no doubt premature, to identify the Tien bronze culture of Yunnan as Tai. The local non-Chinese language of Tali and K'un-ming, formerly known as Min-chia, is now referred to in Chinese as Pai 白, equivalent to the native word transcribed as Ber or Pe. This name has been plausibly identified by Ruey Yih-fu (1951) with Po 僰 (EMC **pǝk**), a term used in the Han to designate inhabitants of that region, especially in the expression Po *t'ung* 僰童, "Po slaves," implying a continuity from the Han to the present. Unfortunately the affinities of the Pai (Min-chia) language are still uncertain. Much of the vocabulary is Chinese, consisting partly of recent borrowings from Mandarin and partly of a much earlier layer of borrowings. There is still an underlying non-Chinese layer of basic vocabulary, however, and the syntax is non-Chinese in a number of ways. This underlying layer has been variously identified as Mon-Khmer or Tai, but apparently on insufficient grounds. The best current opinion seems to be that it is Tibeto-Burman, related to Lo-Lo (Yi) (Wen 1940). It should be noted, however, that Tali was the center of the Nan-chao kingdom (eighth to thirteenth centuries), whose rulers were most likely Lo-Los. It is therefore possible that the Lo-Lo elements were acquired at that period and that the name Pai comes from the subject population, which had a different linguistic background. Whether there is a still deeper substratum in the Pai language still surviving from this pre-Nan-chao population must await further study.

AUSTRONESIAN (MALAYO-POLYNESIAN)

This far-flung language family, stretching from Hawaii to Madagascar, is not now represented on the Chinese mainland. The diverse native lan-

guages of Taiwan, however, belong to it. Opinions differ on their classification within the Austronesian family. Some scholars make them a separate branch, Northern Austronesian, coordinate with two other major
divisions, Western Austronesian or Indonesian and Eastern Austronesian
or Oceanic. Others see relatively close relationships with Philippine languages and make them a subgroup of Western Austronesian. A variant
theory distinguishes the northern, Atayalic, group of Taiwan languages
from the rest as a separate, primary branch of Austronesian. What does
seem clear is that Austronesian speakers have inhabited Taiwan for a long
time. It has even been suggested on lexicostatistical grounds that Taiwan
may be the primary point of Austronesian dispersal (Dyen 1965). Unfortunately, lexicostatistics have been rather thoroughly discredited as a
method of solving such questions in the absence of other evidence.

From our present point of view, the most important question is not the
prehistoric relations of Taiwan with the islands to the south, but cultural
contacts with the mainland. According to K. C. Chang (1977:87), the cord-
marked pottery of the Ta-p'en-k'eng culture from northern Taiwan, dated
by carbon-14 to the mid-fourth millennium B.C., relates it to mainland
Neolithic cultures in Fukien and Kiangsi for which we now have dates going
back into the seventh millennium. The Feng-pi-t'ou culture from the
southwest coast of the island, with dates in the second and first millennia, is
classified by Chang as Lungshanoid with close connections to coastal
mainland cultures (1977:169). (See also Meacham, ch. 6 above, for another
interpretation of these relations.)

Such archaeological ties between South China and proto-Austronesian
(?) peoples on Taiwan have been correlated with Paul Benedict's (1942;
1975) theory of a genetic relationship between Tai, including the Kadai
languages, and Austronesian. Unfortunately, the linguistic relationship
must be regarded as far from proved. There are some striking correspondences, as, for instance, between: Indonesian *mata*, "eye," and Siamese
taa < *tra*, earlier *pra*, and Saek *praa*; and between Indonesian *mataj*,
"die," and Siamese *taai* < *traj*, earlier *praaj*. But Benedict's efforts to
extend the comparisons and reconstruct protoforms for a hypothetical
proto-Austro-Thai have not yet been widely accepted. His further hypothesis that the speakers of proto-Austro-Thai were once the cultural leaders
in Southeast Asia and South China and that their language was the source
of many early culture words in Chinese is still less convincing. It is more
likely that the major cultural influences from the south upon the formation
of Chinese civilization came through the medium of Austro-Asiatic (Mon-
Khmer) rather than either Tai or Austronesian.

There seems little that early Chinese written records can contribute to the solution of the problem of Taiwan's early settlement or ties with the mainland. Taiwan is not mentioned until medieval times, far too late to be of help.

AUSTRO-ASIATIC (MON-KHMER)

The presence in prehistoric times of Tibeto-Burmans in Shensi and northern Szechwan, Miao-Yaos in the Yangtze valley, and Tais farther south from eastern Yunnan to Kwangtung and stretching down into northern Vietnam is more or less what one might expect from the modern distribution of these peoples. The presence of Austro-Asiatics stretching up the coast, perhaps as far as the Huai valley and the Shantung peninsula, is more surprising and, if it can be demonstrated, obviously has an important bearing on the question of prehistoric cultural relations between Southeast Asia and China and the possible contributions from that direction to the nascent civilization of the Huang Ho valley.

The Austro-Asiatic language family contains, in the first place, two major languages, Mon and Khmer, that have played an important role in Southeast Asia for many centuries; hence the name Mon-Khmer that is sometimes used as a designation for the family as a whole. The Mons, who once ruled lower Burma, gave their alphabet and other elements of civilization to the Burmese; they survive as a dwindling minority in that country and adjacent parts of Thailand. Though the Khmers or Cambodians still maintain a separate country, it too is much reduced from its former state.

The Austro-Asiatic language family also contains numerous tribal languages of Southeast Asia, of which Palaung and Wa are found in small enclaves in Chinese territory in Yunnan. The Munda languages of India and Nicobarese are also considered distant relatives of Mon-Khmer. More important for our inquiry is the fact that Vietnamese is also an Austro-Asiatic language. Because it has a tonal system similar to that of Chinese, Miao-Yao, and Tai, Maspero (1912:116; see also 1952) assumed it could not be related to the non-tonal Mon-Khmer languages. Haudricourt (1954) has shown, however, that there is a regular correspondence between Vietnamese tones and segmental features in other Austro-Asiatic languages and that, in spite of the large admixture of Chinese vocabulary it shares with Tai, the basic vocabulary of Vietnamese remains predominantly Austro-Asiatic. Closely related to Vietnamese are the tribal Mu'o'ng languages of Vietnam.

Vietnam, with its primary center in the Red River/Hanoi-Tonkin region, has been independent of China since the end of the T'ang dynasty but was under Chinese rule for most of the preceding thousand years, after it had first been conquered by Ch'in in 208 B.C. In Han times it was part of what was known as Southern Yüeh, whence the modern name of the country. The name Yüeh 越, sometimes Pai Yüeh, Hundred Yüeh, was also applied in a general way to the coastal non-Chinese peoples of Kwangsi, Kwangtung, and Fukien. Earlier, Yüeh was the name of a state in Chekiang which played an important part in Chinese affairs at the end of the Spring and Autumn period.

The extension of the name Yüeh down the coast from its first location in Chekiang as geographical horizons expanded is prima facie evidence that there was an ethnic and linguistic identity among the inhabitants of the whole region, but of course it does not prove that this was so. It could be a misapplication by the Chinese of a familiar name to quite unrelated peoples. One may feel that the continuity in the use of the name makes such a possibility unlikely, but it cannot be ruled out a priori.

Fortunately, there is some direct linguistic evidence to support the hypothesis that a language of Austro-Asiatic type, like Vietnamese, was spoken in the Yüeh regions of coastal China. This has been pointed out by Mei and Norman (1976) and I cite the following examples from their work.

In Cheng Hsüan's commentary to the *Chou-li* (15:543) we find that "the people of Yüeh say *cha* 札 (EMC tṣ̌ert) for 'die'." The same word occurs again in the *Chou-li* (22:817) in the expression *ta cha* 大札, glossed as *yi li* 疫癘, "pestilence," in the commentary but without a reference to Yüeh. It is also found in two passages in the *Tso-chuan* (352/Chao 4/1 and 397/Chao 19/*fu* 5) and in the *Shih-ming*, enlarged in some versions of the text by radical 104 to 疕. From this we can see that *cha*, "die, death," was a word known in pre-Han and Han China. Cheng Hsüan said it came from Yüeh; we can assume he meant the Yüeh region of China—Chekiang—not Southern Yüeh. The fact that it was known so early in China would in itself almost preclude a direct borrowing from such a distant region as Kwangtung or Tonkin. As Mei and Norman point out, this must be cognate to Vietnamese *chêt*, "die," and to the general Austro-Asiatic word; compare Mon *chot*, Chrau *chu't*, Bahnar *kycit*, and other forms cited by Mei and Norman. Shorto (1971:60) reconstructs a proto-Mon-Khmer form *$kcat$. As Mei and Norman point out, this word for "die" is quite different from the Sino-Tibetan, Miao-Yao, and Tai words and points unmistakably to Austro-Asiatic.

Another Austro-Asiatic word borrowed into general Chinese that has remained in common use is *chiang* 江, "river," referring especially to the

Yangtze. This is EMC **kɔrŋ** < ***kráŋ**ʷ. It is undoubtedly the Austro-Asiatic word found in Old Mon *kruŋ*, Bahnar and Sedang *kroŋ*, Vietnamese *sông*, and so on. Siamese *kloŋ*, "canal," is not found in common Tai and, if related, is presumably a separate borrowing from a Mon-Khmer language. This is probably also true of Tibetan *kluŋ*, *c'u-kluŋ*, "river," and Burmese *khyauŋ:*, "large brook, rivulet, tributary, stream." The same word has been borrowed into mainland Austronesian languages: Cham *krauŋ* and Malay *kroŋ*. Maspero (1933) pointed out these connections; I have also noted the probability that the Chinese word was borrowed from Austro-Asiatic (Pulleyblank 1966). Mei and Norman (1976) suggest that the word came into Chinese from the state of Ch'u on the middle Yangtze. This would imply an extension of Austro-Asiatic up the river from the coast. The borrowing could, however, have come from the state of Wu at the lower end of the Yangtze, which was probably related to Yüeh in language and culture, or from the Yi of the Huai marshes and Shantung. It seems to be chiefly in the Wu region that rivers other than the Yangtze are referred to as *chiang*. Note the use of *Chiang* in two places in *Kuo Yü* (19) to refer to the Wu-sung Chiang, also known as the Wu Chiang or Sung Chiang and in English as Soochow Creek, which flows from the T'ai Hu past Soochow to Shanghai and the sea (*Kuo yü* 19:87, 94, with commentary).

The Austro-Asiatic connections of the Chinese word for "tiger" have already been discussed, with the suggestion that the word was also borrowed into the Ch'u language and thence into the Man dialects of the central Yangtze, or that the word was common to Austro-Asiatic and Miao-Yao.

Mei and Norman also want to derive Chinese *ya* 牙 (LMC ŋja: EMC ŋarʲ/ŋɛ), "tooth," from Austro-Asiatic, citing Vietnamese *ngà*, "ivory," proto-Mnong (Bahnar) **ngoʲla*, "tusk," and Tai *ŋaa*, "tusk, ivory." This is less convincing. Not only is the word less widely distributed within Austro-Asiatic, but the more specialized meaning in those languages and in Tai suggests that the borrowing has been from Chinese rather than the other way around.

The word *nu* 弩 (EMC **nɔʲ** < *** − naʔ**), "crossbow," is found in Austro-Asiatic and Tai as well as Chinese and may have been borrowed into Chinese from the south; but since it is not attested before the Warring States period, it is too late to be of significance in proving the presence of Austro-Asiatic influence at the dawn of Chinese civilization.

The evidence adduced by Mei and Norman to show that a number of colloquial words in Min dialects are of Austro-Asiatic origin, implying an

Austro-Asiatic substratum in the pre-Chinese population of Fukien, is very significant.

The Chinese dialects of Fukien are probably descended from the colloquial language that was general in southern China in the pre-T'ang period as opposed to the upper-class literary language which was brought from the north at the fall of Western Chin in A.D. 314, and they probably preserve words which were once current farther north in Chekiang and Kiangsu and not merely in Fukien.

This kind of linguistic evidence supports the conclusion that the people of ancient Yüeh were linguistically related to the people of modern Vietnam and that the extension of the name from one to the other was based on the recognition of a genuine identity. Most likely Wu was also Austro-Asiatic.

Still farther north lay the territory of the Yi 夷 in the Huai marshes and Shantung. This is the region of the classic Lung-shan culture, which has been regarded as a direct antecedent of Shang civilization. The Yi, like the other ancient peoples we have been discussing, must certainly have been non-Chinese in language. Their name furnished the primary Chinese term for "barbarian" and is sometimes used in such a generalized sense as early as the Spring and Autumn period. At the same time it continued to have a specific reference, denoting especially the Yi of the Huai river region, who constituted a recognized political entity.

Paradoxically the Yi were considered the most civilized of the non-Chinese peoples. There is, for example, the curious legend of King Yen 偃 of Hsü 徐 (a state of Yi origin), who, according to Han Fei-tzu, achieved hegemony in Honan, stretching as far as the Han River, through cultivating the Confucian virtues of humanity and righteousness (*jen* and *yi*), but who was overthrown by the military power of Ch'u when he could not bear to risk the lives of his people in battle. Han Fei places these events in the time of King Wen of Ch'u (689–677 B.C.), but they are not mentioned in the *Ch'un-ch'iu* or *Tso-chuan* and could hardly be fitted into the history of that period. The *Shih-chi* twice refers to a "rebellion" by King Yen of Hsü but puts it much earlier, in the time of King Mu, the fifth Chou ruler (*Shih-chi* 5; 43). If there is any historical reality behind the tale, the date in the *Shih-chi* is more likely. King Yen, whose presumption in assuming the title *wang* would have been a direct challenge to Chou sovereignty, may have been the leader of an attempt by the Yi to replace the Chou. The legend that in doing so he sought to rule by virtue and eschewed the resort to military force remains interesting even if we do not know exactly what it may have meant in fact.

From later sources it is apparent that King Yen was the object of a local cult in Hsü. A passage in the *Po-wu chih* of Chang Hua, quoted with some variants in the *Shui-ching chu* (8), tells a story of his miraculous birth and relates that after his death a temple was erected in his honor. It places the events of his life in the time of King Mu but attributes his overthrow to an unnamed king of Ch'u acting under King Mu's orders. This is apparently the source of the briefer version which appears in the chapter on the Eastern Yi in the *Hou-Han shu*. As quoted in the *Shui-ching chu*, the *Po-wu chih* cites as its source the *Hsü-chou ti-li chih* of Liu Ch'eng-kuo (Liu Hsi, a scholar of the Later Han best known as the author of the *Shih ming*). Liu Hsi, like the Han imperial house, came from the Hsü region, which was no doubt why he recorded its antiquities.

There was also a temple to King Yen of Hsü at Lung-Ch'iu, present Lung-yu in Chekiang. The T'ang dynasty writer Han Yü wrote the text of a commemorative inscription recording the renovation of this temple in 814 by a prefect with the surname Hsü (*Han Ch'ang-li wen-chi* 6:237). He records that there were many people of that surname in the district and that they regarded King Yen as their ancestor. There was a local tradition that after his defeat he had actually fled south to Yüeh. There is no way of telling how old the tradition was when Han Yü recorded it but it is interesting as possibly indicating a connection between the ancient Yi and Yüeh peoples.

It is also worth noting that from Han to Sui, Lung-ch'iu had the name T'ai-mo 太末 and that before that the name was Ku-mo 姑末 (EMC **kɔ-mat** < *kɑ-mat) or Ku-mieh 姑蔑 (EMC **kɔ-met** < *kɑ-ʲmat [I assume that the palatal element was from a prefix, not a medial]). The variations in the name and the change to T'ai-mo in the Han period suggest that it was originally a Yüeh word. In the form Ku-mieh it occurs both in the *Tso-chuan* and in the *Kuo-yü*. In the latter it is named as marking the western extremity of Yüeh territory, and the commentator locates it at T'ai Hu. In the *Wu Yüeh ch'un-ch'iu* it is replaced by Ku-mo, which is called the *southern* extremity of Yüeh and is identified in the commentary with T'ai-mo (Lung-ch'iu). Whether there were actually two places in Yüeh called Ku-mieh or Ku-mo is hard to determine. There was, however, another Ku-mieh far to the north in the territory of Lu, said to be east of present Ssu-shui in Shantung (*Tso-chuan* 459 Ting 12/10). It is also called simply Mieh (*Tso-chuan* 1/Yin 1/2) with the variant Mo 眜 or Mei 眛 in the text of the *Ch'un-ch'iu* and in the *Ku-liang* and *Kung-yang* commentaries. (眜, EMC **mat**, seems correct, 眛 being a simple graphic corruption.) Thus we have in Shantung and Chekiang the same disyllabic place name, presumably transcribing a non-Chinese word in both cases. In both cases there is also some reason to think that the first syllable may have been a separable element, perhaps equivalent to Chinese *t'ai*, "great." One might also recognize the same first element in Ku-su 姑蘇 — the name of the hill on which the capital of Wu was built, from which the modern name Su-chou is derived. All this suggests, though it is hardly sufficient to prove, that the language of the Yi in Shantung and the Huai river region was related to that of Wu and Yüeh and, by extension, that it was Austro-Asiatic. In that case the Yi language would have been the probable source for the earliest contacts between Austro-Asiatic and Chinese.

It is, of course, highly relevant in this connection that K. C. Chang (1977:174) classifies together the Lung-shan culture of Hangchow Bay (Liang-chu culture) and the classical Lung-shan culture of Shantung and northern Kiangsu as coastal Lung-shan in contrast to the Chung Yüan Lung-shan cultures farther inland. Archaeological and linguistic evidence thus seem to point in the same direction. Also of interest is the recent discovery of the Shih-hsia culture in Kwangtung, said to have connections with Neolithic Kiangsi, southern Kiangsu, and northern Chekiang (Su 1978:17).

BARBARIANS OF THE NORTHEAST: MO 貊, WEI 穢, AND OTHERS

The earliest term for northeastern barbarians is Mo 貊 (EMC **marjk** < ***mrák**). A curious problem about their name is that it is often written with the character 貉. This character also has a reading *ho* (EMC **ɣak**), as the name of an animal variously identified as a raccoon-dog or badger. In the sense of an ethnic name, however, the *Kuang-yün* gives it the same reading as 貊. This is surprising for a word with 各, EMC **kak**, as phonetic, but it is not unparalleled. The *Kuang-yün* also contains a character 貊, EMC **p'ak**, **pak**, "fly away." Such alternations between velar and labial initials can sometimes be accounted for by positing labio-velars, but the velar initials in this series are not labialized. I cannot offer any solution at present.

The Mo are mentioned twice in the *Shih-ching*. The first reference is an ode (Mao 261) which celebrates the enfeoffment of the Marquis of Han 韓, who is given charge of the Chui 追 (otherwise unknown) and the Mo. There is a difference of opinion among commentators on the location of the fief. Some would like to identify it with the present Han-ch'eng in Shensi province. But a Han-ch'eng in northern Hopei is mentioned in *Shui-ching chu* 12 and identified with the "city of Marquis Han." This must be correct.

The ode mentions that the "hosts of Yen" (*yen shih* 燕師) were employed to wall the new city. The existence of an early Chou fief in Yen—the neighborhood of Peking—has been doubted by some modern scholars but, as Creel (1970:357ff) points out, Western Chou remains have been unearthed in that region (see also *KK* 1974.6:370). It is likely that the local population remained non-Chinese in language for some considerable time, but that does not mean there could not have been Chou overlords established in walled cities with Chinese garrisons.

The second *Shih-ching* reference to the Mo occurs in the "Lu Sung" section (Mao 300), in which the Prince of Lu is praised in hyperbolic terms as commanding the allegiance not only of the Huai Yi, who were relatively close to Lu, but also of the Man and Mo and the Southern Yi. As far as we know from other sources Lu never extended its boundaries to this extent, but at least the ode provides additional testimony for the existence of the Mo as a "barbarian" entity in early Chou times. The Mo are not mentioned in the *Tso-chuan*. Possibly the Mo south of the Great Wall (which, of course, did not yet exist) were becoming sinicized by the Spring and Autumn period.

An interesting passage in the *Meng-tzu* (6B/10) refers to the poverty and backwardness of the Mo, who allegedly had only *shu* (glutinous millet) of the five cereal crops and who lacked cities, houses, temples, sacrificial rites, diplomatic exchanges of gifts, and government officials. Where these Mo lived is not stated. Passages in *Mo-tzu* place them in the northeast near the countries of Yen and Tai (northern Shansi) and the nomadic Hu. Presumably the reference is by then to people living beyond Yen in southern Manchuria.

This is the region in which the Mo reappear in Han times. By this time Mo is most often coupled with another name, Wei, variously written as 濊, 穢, and 獩 (EMC ʔuaj[h] < *ʔwàts) (濊 has a number of other readings in other senses.) It is not clear whether the Wei were originally ethnically distinct and had, perhaps, been conquered by the Mo or vice versa, or whether they were simply a different group of the same people. During Han we also hear for the first time of two states said to be of Wei-mo origin, Fu-yü 夫餘 (Korean Puyŏ) and Kao-kou-li 高句麗 (Korean Koguryŏ). Interesting accounts of both states are found in the *Hou-Han shu* and *San-kuo chih*, based chiefly on the third century *Wei chih*. As described there, Fu-yü was in eastern Manchuria, around modern Ch'ang-ch'un; Kao-kou-li was farther east and south. A separate group of Wei-mo were said to be part way down the east coast of the Korean peninsula.

Apart from the question of ethnic relation, the picture we have of Fu-yü from the accounts in the *Hou-Han shu* and *San-kuo chih* is fascinating as an example of a state forming itself on the borders of China and evidently in imitation of China. As described, it was an agricultural country in which cattle raising and hunting were also important. It had a strongly marked division between an upper class who were the officials and warriors and a servile lower class who were presumably tillers of the soil and who did not engage in battle but brought supplies of food and drink for the soldiers. From a Chinese point of view, the men of Fu-yü (presumably the upper classes) were quite civilized in their use of dishes and goblets for food and drink, in their dress, and in their ceremonious behavior. Criminal law was strict. Murderers were executed and their families were enslaved—a practice reminiscent of Ch'in law in China. As in early China, though not in the contemporary Han dynasty, when important men died large numbers of followers were killed to accompany them to the grave. Unlike the Chinese but like the Hsiung-nu, they practiced levirate, that is, younger brothers married the wives of a dead older brother. They worshipped Heaven and took oracles, but by the examination of ox hooves rather than by scapulimancy. The ruler was blamed in case of crop failure due to drought or excessive rains and could be changed or killed.

Not the least interesting report about Fu-yü is the son of heaven myth related about the founder, Eastern Light (*tung ming* 東明). This is found not only in the sources already mentioned, but also in the *Lun-heng* of Wang Ch'ung, which was completed circa A.D. 100, so it must have been current in China early in the Later Han, if not before. According to the story, Eastern Light came from a country still farther north called variously T'o-li 橐離, So-li 索離, or Kao-li 高離. While the king of the country was away from home one of his servant girls became pregnant. The girl, when the king had returned and was about to kill her, said a vapor like a hen's egg had come down from the sky, as a result of which she became pregnant. Once the child was born the king had him placed in a pig pen, but the pigs warmed the baby with their breath and he did not die. The same thing happened when the king had him put in the horse stables. Suspecting that this might be a son of heaven, the king allowed the boy to live but made him a groom to the horses. Later, fearing that the boy would rob him of his kingdom, he tried once more to kill him. Eastern Light fled south to the Shih-yen 施掩 river. To cross and escape his pursuers he struck the water with his bow, at which the fish and turtles rose to form a bridge which dispersed after he had crossed. He then founded his kingdom, in Fu-yü.

Reminiscences of the Hou-chi legend in the *Shih-ching* spring to mind, reinforcing the impression that Fu-yü's statehood was modeled on that of

Chou China. If so, the tale of Eastern Light may be important for our understanding of the son of heaven concept in China, since it is much more explicit than the Hou-chi legend in connecting the miraculous birth of the dynastic founder with heaven and giving son of heaven a literal rather than merely a metaphorical meaning. Unfortunately, we do not know the chronology of Fu-yü's statehood. The kind of sociopolitical organization described for Fu-yü seems very archaic in terms of Han China. Was Fu-yü so old that it could have found a direct model in China? Or should we look for a still more ancient common, pre-state, source for the concepts of social stratification and of the mythological basis for sovereignty that are shared by Chou and Fu-yü? It may be significant that the explicit son of heaven mythology—which has obvious analogies in the far West, not only in Greek and Roman mythology but also in the Christian birth story— though common among peoples to the north and northwest of China, does not seem to be found among those to the south. The miraculous birth stories in the origin myths of the Man and other southern peoples, so far as I can tell, lack this feature.

Kao-kou-li later pushed down into the Korean peninsula and became the northernmost of the Three Kingdoms among which Korea was divided in Sui and T'ang times. Paekche, the southwestern kingdom, was said to have been founded by invaders from Fu-yü, so that the Wei-mo are intimately involved in early Korean history in several ways. They probably moved further still. According to the "horse rider" theory of the origin of the Japanese ruling house advanced by Egami (1967) and developed further by Ledyard (1975), Japan was invaded from Paekche, and hence ultimately from Fu-yü, in the fourth century A.D. There is no way to tell, of course, whether these invaders were directly descended from the Mo who had lived near Peking around 1000 B.C., or to what extent they had been diluted by other ethnic and linguistic elements in their various way stations.

I have not found evidence from which one could directly infer anything about the language of the Mo when they were known to the Chinese in Chou times. There is a phonetic resemblance between their name and that of the Man. Both words have the type of Middle Chinese syllable which would lead us to reconstruct *mr – clusters in Old Chinese, as do the names Min and Miao. This alliterative similarity was perhaps responsible for the coupling of Man and Mo in the *Shih-ching*. Such a contact is suggestive, but without any other evidence it would provide frail support for hypothesizing that the Mo were related to the Miao-Yaos. There is more reason to look for connections to the north.

Some evidence about the Koguryŏ language is found in the *Samguk sagi*, a retrospective account of early Korean history compiled during the Koryŏ dynasty. This material is of great interest and has excited much controversy because of obvious similarities of some of the words, including several numerals, to Japanese. Whether it has a bearing on the question of the Mo language is a separate problem. Other ethnic elements could have entered the picture before the Koguryŏ state established itself in northern Korea.

Other peoples in the northeast known to the Chinese in Han and earlier times include:

> (1) the Eastern Hu—Hsien-pei (*Särbi) and Wu-huan (*Avar)—probably proto-Mongols.
> (2) the Yi-lou 挹婁, (EMC ʔjip-low), who lived to the east of Fu-yü reaching as far as the seacoast. Described as rude and hardy pig keepers who lived with their animals in caves, these people were probably Tungusic.
> (3) the Han 韓 (EMC ɣan), who lived in the lower part of the Korean peninsula and fell into three main divisions: Ma Han to the east, Ch'en Han to the west, and P'ien Han at the south end of the peninsula closest to Japan. Each was subdivided into many small "countries" (*kuo*). These were presumably the ancestors of the Koreans.

Mongolian and Tungusic are separate branches of the Altaic language family. Korean and Japanese are typologically similar, both to each other and to the Altaic languages. Some scholars regard them as genetically related to Altaic, but their efforts to demonstrate such connections have not been fully convincing so far. The situation is judiciously summed up by Lewin (1976), who suggests that in both cases a substratum which he identifies as probably Austronesian has been overlaid by an Altaic language brought in by conquerors. From our present point of view the interesting question is whether the source of this Altaic overlay can be identified with the Mo, in which case we have Altaic speakers in contact with China from protohistoric times.

THE NORTHERN TI 狄

The people whose name became synonymous with northern barbarians in general in the same way the Man were associated with the south, the Yi with the east, and the Jung with the west were the Ti 狄, EMC **dejk** (to be distinguished from the Tibeto-Burman Ti 氐, EMC **tej**, who were associated with the Ch'iang). These Ti, divided into two principal groups known as the White and the Red, were found in the Spring and Autumn Period mainly in present Shansi province, spreading across the Huang Ho into eastern Shensi and eastward across the T'ai-hang mountains into western Hopei.

The Ti are frequently mentioned in the *Ch'un-ch'iu* and *Tso-chuan*, particularly in connection with the state of Chin. Typically their relations with the Chinese were hostile, but not invariably so. Ch'ung-erh, the hero who later bacame Duke Wen of Chin, found refuge among the Ti during his exile before coming to the throne. By the end of the Spring and Autumn period the Ti territories had been largely brought under Chin control and their sinicization must have been well advanced. In the early part of the Warring States period the state of Chung-shan, with its capital at Han-tan in Hopei, had a ruling house of Ti origin named Hsien-yü 鮮虞, but there is little else to distinguish it from the Chinese states of the period. It was annexed by Chao in 295.

To judge by the published scholarship on the subject, one might easily suppose it had been well established that the Ti were related to the later steppe peoples such as the Hsiung-nu and that they spoke an Altaic language. Looking more closely at the evidence used to justify these assumptions, however, it becomes clear that this evidence amounts to scarcely more than the fact that the Ti and the later nomad enemies of the Chinese lay in the same compass direction. The territory of the Ti was not the steppe, however. There is no evidence that they were horse riders. On the contrary, there is explicit evidence that they fought on foot, unlike the Chinese nobility who went to war in horse-drawn chariots (*Tso-chuan* 343/Chao 1/6). Nor is there any particular reason to think that stock rearing played a larger part in their economy than in that of their Chinese neighbors.[2]

The steppe lands of the north were unknown territory to the Chinese of the Spring and Autumn period, at least insofar as their textual records tell us. Whether there were yet horse-riding nomads at all in East Asia at that period is a moot point.

2. Ma Ch'ang-shou (1962) cites a passage from the *Kuan-tzu* (20:126) which implies that the Ti were "mounted marauders" (*ch'i-k'ou* 騎寇), but in view of the uncertainties about the date of this work it can have little value as evidence. It is probably an anachronism coming from the time when the northern enemies of the Chinese were well known to be horse riders. The commentaries to the *Ch'un-ch'iu* and *Tso-chuan* by Tu Yü (Chin dynasty) and Liu Hsüan (Sui dynasty) which Ma cites as evidence that the Ti were nomadic tent dwellers are even more suspect. The texts do not say anything of the sort. As Ma admits, other passages in the *Ch'un-ch'iu* and *Tso-chuan* make it clear that at least some of the Ti had cities like the Chinese.

Another point made by Ma to connect the Ti with the later steppe nomads is that the color names by which different groups of them were designated are like the directional color terminology used by the steppe nomads from the Hsiung-nu onward: red for south, white for west, black for north, blue for east, yellow for center. He suggests that only the southern (Red) and western (White) Ti were known to the Chinese because they had moved in off the steppe and partly adapted their way of life to the new environment. This sounds plausible, but there is really no evidence to back it up. In any case, it is altogether likely that this directional symbolism, which corresponds to the Five Elements theory, is of Chinese origin and was borrowed from China by the Hsiung-nu, who passed it on to such other peoples as the Turks.

Unfortunately, a later confusion about the name Ti has reinforced the idea that they were somehow connected with Hsiung-nu or Turks. By coincidence, the same character that was used to write Ti was also used in Ti-li 狄歷, one of several transcriptions of the name of a Turkish confederacy out of which the Uyghurs eventually emerged. The earliest form of this name was Ting-ling. It appears for the first time in the second century B.C. as the name of a far northern people conquered by Mao-tun, founder of the Hsiung-nu empire. Even if the names were identical, the possibility that there could have been any connection between these Ting-ling and the Ti who had lived in China in Chou times would be quite remote, and in fact the connection between them was not made until much later. By that time the Ting-ling had come much closer to China. After the overthrow of the Hsiung-nu empire they moved south into the Altai and adjacent steppe lands, where they became known by the name High Carts, *kao ch'e* 高車, as well as by various alternative transcriptions of their native name such as 狄歷, EMC **dejk-lejk**, 直勒, EMC **drɨk-lək**, 特勒, EMC **dək-lək**, and 鐵勒, EMC **t'et-lək**. These, as well as Ting-ling 丁靈 (EMC **tejŋ-lejŋ**), have been interpreted by Hamilton (1962) as based on Turkish *tägräg* "circle, hoop," making the same allusion as the Chinese name High Carts to the special type of wagon, with very large wheels, which they were noted for using. The old monosyllabic name Ti (EMC **dejk** < ***lákʲ**) can have had nothing to do with this Turkish disyllable. (Old Chinese *l— is indicated, among other things, by the alternation of Ti with Yi 易 [EMC **jiajk** < ***làkʲ**] in the name of the cook of Duke Huan of Ch'i, Yi-ya 易牙 or Ti-ya 狄牙. See Morohashi, *Dai kanwa jiten*.)

A further coincidence that has added to the confusion is that there were Ting-ling elements, along with other subject peoples, among the Hsiung-nu who settled in Shansi in the Later Han dynasty. They are mentioned on a number of occasions in the fourth and fifth centuries. Ma Ch'ang-shou notes that the surname Hsien-yü 鮮于, which looks like the old Ti name Hsien-yü, occurs among the Ting-ling who were in the neighborhood of ancient Chung-shan 中山 and who revolted against the T'o-pa Wei in 428. Possibly there were actually descendants of the ancient Ti living in the Chung-shan region who were drawn into the Ting-ling uprising, but this does not make the Ting-ling descendants of the Ti. This surname is not mentioned among the T'ieh-le or High Carts who remained outside China.

The ancient Ti, who are often coupled with the Jung and seem to share some of the latter's characteristics, may have been Tibeto-Burmans; they may have been connected with the Eastern Hu and been Altaic; or they may have had quite different ethnic and linguistic affinities. I know of no way to solve this question at present.

THE HSIUNG-NU 匈奴

Ssu-ma Ch'ien begins his chapter on the Hsiung-nu with a summary of the northern enemies of the Chinese in earlier times. There is really nothing but the compass direction to connect any of them with the Hsiung-nu. Two peoples are mentioned whose names vaguely resemble Hsiung-nu and who have often in the past been assumed to be their ancestors. These are the Hsün-yü 葷粥 (EMC **xun-juwk**), and the Hsien-yün 獫狁 (EMC **xiam-jwin**). The former are mentioned in the *Meng-tzu* as barbarian enemies of pre-dynastic Chou in the upper Wei valley. Since so little is known about them, it is not profitable to try to connect them with later peoples, though phonetically there is a degree of correspondence with Hun-yü 渾庾 (EMC **ɣwən-jua**), the name of a tribe lying west of China in early Han times who were conquered by the Hsiung-nu.

The Hsien-yün present a more intriguing problem. They are mentioned on a number of bronze inscriptions and in four poems in the *Shih-ching* as having made sharp attacks on the Western Chou empire in the Wei valley around 780 B.C. Their incursions were followed by the attacks of other barbarians, which eventually led to the downfall of Western Chou and the transfer of the capital to Lo-yi in the east. Thereafter, the Hsien-yün disappear finally. Their name certainly has nothing to do with Hsiung-nu, but the suddenness of their appearance and disappearance suggests that they may have been invaders from the steppe. They come on the scene not long after the first appearance of mounted warriors in the west, and it has been suggested that they were an eastern reflex of the revolutionary introduction of horse-riding nomadism that appeared around the beginning of the first millennium B.C. and dominated the history of central Asia until modern times. Haloun (1937) even suggested a connection between their name and that of the Cimmerians. Průšek (1971), rejecting this linguistic identification, nevertheless wants to see them as the first horse riders in the Far East. The difficulty remains that there is no explicit evidence in Chinese sources that the Hsien-yün were horse riders, and Průšek's ingenious efforts to find indirect support for such a conclusion remain unconvincing. What is clear is that, if the Hsien-yün raids were the first experience by the Chinese of mounted warfare, they had no immediate sequel and did not lead to any of the changes in military technology that came about from the end of the fourth century onward, when horse riding begins to be explicitly mentioned.

The first unmistakable horse-riding nomads with whom the Chinese came into contact were called Hu 胡 (EMC ɣɔ < *gá), a name that comes into use for the first time in the Warring States period in texts relating to the northern states of Chao and Yen, on whose territory they impinged. In 457

B.C. Chao incorporated the kingdom of Tai 代, located in the region of present Ta-t'ung in northern Shansi, into its territory. Though the sources are less explicit than could be wished, it seems clear that the inhabitants of Tai were non-Chinese, possibly Ti 狄. But there is no reason to think that they were horse-riding nomads—rather the contrary, since after the conquest, but before the adoption of cavalry by Chao, they were ruled as a feudal appanage by princes of Chao. The occupation of Tai did, however, bring Chao into contact with the steppes and was a prelude to the famous debate in 307 B.C. on the adoption of "Hu clothing" (*Hu fu* 胡服), the riding gear of the nomads, as a necessary step in acquiring the military technique of mounted archery. The accounts of this debate in *Chan-kuo ts'e* (19) and *Shih-chi* (43) may, as has been suggested (Creel 1965), have undergone literary retouching; but there seems no reason to doubt the main point, that the introduction of mounted archery into Chinese military technology dates from around the end of the fourth century. Thereafter we find references to cavalry not only in Chao but also in the other leading states of the time.

It is interesting to note that the Chao ruler's motive in adopting the nomads' method of warfare was not, apparently, so much to defend himself against nomad incursions as to increase his own aggressive potential. A few years after the famous debate, this same ruler, "wearing Hu clothing," led an expedition to the northwest into nomad territory with a view to outflanking Ch'in and invading it from the north (*Shih-chi* 43:1812). The nomads with whom Chao had had to deal up to this time do not, in fact, seem to have been either powerful or aggressive. Three groups of Hu are distinguished. From west to east, they were the Woods Hu (Lin Hu 林胡), the Lou-fan 樓煩, and the Eastern Hu (Tung Hu 東胡). With its new cavalry, Chao was able to establish its dominance over the Woods Hu and the Lou-fan. A boundary wall was built which was a precursor of the Great Wall of Ch'in. One Han dynasty text uses the name Hsiung-nu instead of Woods Hu in connection with the events of this time, but this is probably an anachronism.

The situation changed during the third century. We now find the Chao general Li Mu having to defend the northern frontier against nomad raiders, establishing a pattern for the northern frontier of China which was to last for most of the next two thousand years. The enemies of Li Mu are also now identified as Hsiung-nu, but whether the new name means they were new arrivals on the scene or merely a new political grouping cannot easily be determined. The subsequent history of the Hsiung-nu—how they were driven out of the Ordos by the Ch'in general Meng T'ien, after which they first fought for living space among their steppe neighbors and then embarked on a successful wave of conquest and created the first empire of the eastern steppes, mirroring and rivaling the Han empire to the south—and the story of their conflicts with Han until their final break-up and disappearance in the second century A.D. are well known.

I have shown elsewhere (1962) that, contrary to what has often been believed, there is no evidence that the Hsiung-nu were either Turkish or Mongolian in their linguistic and ethnic affinities. Indeed, there are cogent linguistic arguments against their having spoken an Altaic language of any kind. On the other hand, as Ligeti (1950) was the first to point out, there is a good possibility that they may have spoken a language belonging to the Palaeo-Siberian family, the only surviving member of which is Kettish, also known as Yenissei-Ostyak. Several languages related to Kettish were still spoken in Siberia, some of them by horse-riding nomads, when the Russians first arrived there in the seventeenth and eighteenth centuries. The few Hsiung-nu words transcribed in Chinese characters for which semantic glosses are supplied show a number of striking contacts with Kettish or with recorded items of vocabulary from the extinct Palaeo-Siberian languages. Though little is known about the earlier history of the Palaeo-Siberians, the possibility that they are a remnant of a linguistic family which included the Hsiung-nu and once played an important role in East Asian history deserves to be seriously studied.

The identification of the Hsiung-nu with the European Huns was first proposed by de Guignes in the eighteenth century and has been much debated ever since. As far as the names are concerned, one can now assert confidently that they must be the same. It is unnecessary to discuss this issue here or the more complicated question of the transmission of the name from east to west and what it may mean in terms of ethnic, linguistic, and political continuites.

Of greater bearing on this discussion is the clear evidence of specific cultural affinities between the Hsiung-nu and the Scythians (Egami 1948; 1951; Pulleyblank 1962 and in press [a]). These extend beyond what can be accounted for by the exigencies of nomadic life and into specific religious customs. Horse-riding nomadism evidently originated as a specific creative adaptation to the steppe environment and spread from a center by conquest or imitation.

The coming of full-blown horse-rider nomadism in the first millennium B.C. was an event of great moment in both western and eastern Asia. Though it was too late to have a direct bearing on the origins of Chinese civilization, it may have indirect relevance to our discussion. Horse-rider nomadism as perfected by the Scythians and the Hsiung-nu was merely the final stage in the process of adapting the horse to warfare that had begun over a thousand years earlier, when the horse was harnessed to the light two-wheeled chariot. Though we have little documentation yet of the spread of the horse-drawn chariot into the eastern steppe and thence to China, it is certain that this event did occur, and it is entirely likely that it brought with it consequences of the same order of magnitude as the advent of horse riding.

THE PROTO-MONGOLS: EASTERN HU — HSIEN-PEI 鮮卑 (*SÄRBI) AND WU-HUAN 烏恒 (AVAR)

The Eastern Hu, mentioned in the *Shih-chi* along with the Woods Hu and the Lou-fan as barbarians to the north of Chao in the fourth century B.C., appear again as one of the first peoples whom the Hsiung-nu conquered in establishing their empire. Toward the end of the Former Han, as the Hsiung-nu empire was weakening through internal dissension, the Eastern Hu became rebellious. From then on they played an increasingly prominent role in Chinese frontier strategy as a force to play off against the Hsiung-nu. Two major divisions are distinguished, the Hsien-pei to the north and the Wu-huan to the south. By the end of the first century B.C. these more specific names had supplanted the older generic term.

In the middle of the second century A.D. a great Hsien-pei war leader, T'an-shih-hui 檀石槐, appeared; he established a short-lived steppe empire, replacing the Northern Hsiung-nu, who thereafter disappear from the historical record. The Hsien-pei empire did not survive after T'an-shih-hui's death, but within a few generations tribal states of Hsien-pei origin appeared all along the Chinese frontier, from the T'u-yü-hun 土谷渾 in Tsinghai and the Ch'i-fu 乞伏 in Kansu to the Mu-jung 慕容 in Liao-hsi. The T'o-pa 拓跋 in northern Shansi eventually succeeded in conquering North China and establishing the Northern Wei dynasty.

The chance similarity in modern pronunciation of Tung Hu, "Eastern Hu," and Tungus led to the once widely held assumption that the Eastern Hu were Tungusic in language. This is a vulgar error with no real foundation. Evidence that, on the contrary, they were proto-Mongols has been provided by Paul Pelliot in various notes scattered through his voluminous publications, and the question has recently been argued afresh, particularly with regard to the T'o-pa, by Ligeti (1970, with references to earlier literature). The hypothesis arises in the first place from the fact that, according to Chinese records, the historical Mongols first emerged as a tribe of the Shih-wei 室韋, who lived in northern Manchuria in the sixth century A.D. Shih-wei, EMC **cit-wɨj**, is quite likely a later transcription of the same name that underlies Hsien-pei, EMC **sian-pjia**, both transcriptions representing something like *särbi* or *širvi*. This connection would be somewhat fragile by itself, but it can be supplemented by direct linguistic evidence indicating that various tribes which emerged from the Hsien-pei in post-Han times spoke forms of Mongolian. Thus Pelliot found Mongolian words in the Chinese accounts of the T'u-yü-hun and among the names of the rulers of the Juan-juan, the leading power on the Mongolian steppe in the fifth and first half of the sixth centuries. Ligeti concludes that the language of the T'o-pa was also basically Mongolian, and this was certainly also true of the Yü-wen (Pulleyblank, in press [b]), who founded the Western Wei and Northern Chou, successor states to the T'o-pa Wei. There were probably also Turkish as well as other non-Mongolian elements among the tribes incorporated into the T'o-pa confederacy, but Ligeti's conclusion seems sound concerning the ruling group.

During the Eastern Han the more southerly branch of the Eastern Hu, the Wu-huan, were as prominent in Chinese records as the Hsien-pei; but thereafter they largely disappear. There is reason to think, however, that they too were involved in the expansive movement that took elements of the Hsien-pei west in the second century A.D. The name Wu-huan 烏桓, (EMC **ʔɔ-ɣwan** < *ʔá-ɣʷán*) is a good transcription of *Awar according to the principles that apply in the Han period. What is evidently the same name recurs in both Chinese and Western accounts of the Hephthalite kingdom in Afghanistan in the fourth and fifth centuries, out of which the Avars of Europe came as refugees when the Hephthalite kingdom was overthrown by the Turks (Pulleyblank 1962:258–259). The matter is complicated by a statement in Byzantine sources that Avars who came from the Hephthalite kingdom were pseudo-Avars, and that the real Avars were another people, also defeated by the Turks, who must be identified with the Juan-juan. Though the Juan-juan are not connected with the Wu-huan in Chinese sources, they were undoubtedly proto-Mongol in language, and their ruling group may well have come from the Wu-huan fraction of the Eastern Hu. In this case both the "true Avars" and the "pseudo-Avars" may have been entitled to the name.

A specific point that connects the Wu-huan both with the Hephthalites and with the historical Mongols concerns their head-dress. In the account of the Wu-huan in the *San-kuo chih* and *Hou-Han shu*, based on the third century *Wei shu*, reference is made to a head-dress called *chü-chüeh* 句決 (EMC *kua-kwet*), decorated with gold and precious stones, worn by married women. This must transcribe Mongolian *kökül*. The same characteristic Mongolian woman's head-dress, a tall horned cap, is also described (without the name) in a Chinese account of the Hephthalites. It was later spread throughout Eurasia by the conquests of Genghis Khan, creating a vogue both in Europe, where it was known as the hennin, and in China, where it was known as *ku-ku*, with 姑姑 (among other transcriptions) representing the original Mongol word (Schlegel 1893; Egami 1951; Pulleyblank 1962:259).

The accounts of the Hsien-pei and Wu-huan based on the third-century *Wei-shu* contain other interesting ethnographic details. It is evident that though the proto-Mongols of the Han period used mounted archery as their method of warfare, their economy was not based on full-blown nomadism like that of the Hsiung-nu. Agriculture played an important role. Their political organization was also less advanced They had no hereditary chiefs, but only temporary war leaders as the occasion demanded. This is no doubt the reason why the second-century Hsien-pei empire dissolved immediately after the death of T'an-shih-hui. It was not until several generations later that local Hsien-pei dynasties with succession in the male line began to found states.

If the Eastern Hu were Mongolian, one would be inclined to argue that the other Hu tribes (the Woods Hu and the Lou-fan), who appear in Chinese records at the same time, were probably also Mongolian. This may be correct, in spite of the fact that Hu very soon became a generic term for steppe nomads and was applied in Han times especially to the Hsiung-nu, whom we do not regard as proto-Mongols. If the more westerly Hu, like the Eastern Hu, were not yet fully nomadic, and had formerly been a kind of buffer between the Chinese and the full-blown steppe nomads, this would help account for the absence of a serious nomad threat on the Chinese northern frontier before the Hsiung-nu appeared in the middle of the third century A.D.

THE PROTO-TURKS: TING-LING (*TÄGRÄG), CHIEN-K'UN (QYRQYZ), HSIN-LI (SYR), WU-CHIEH (OYUZ)

The immediate antecedents of the Turks (Chinese T'u-chüeh 突厥 = Türk, Pulleyblank 1965c), who appear suddenly in the middle of the sixth century A.D., are obscure. One early source calls them "mixed barbarians" (*tsa-hu* 雜胡) from P'ing-liang 平涼 (Kansu), which suggests that their ruling clan may have been from among the debris of the Southern Hsiung-nu who settled along the northern Chinese frontier in Han times and who included diverse subject peoples as well as true Hsiung-nu. However this may be, there are several other Turkish peoples, well known from the T'ang period and later, whose origins can be traced back to the period of Hsiung-nu domination in the second century B.C. At that time they lay to the north and west of the Hsiung-nu in southern Siberia, and it is likely that this region was their original homeland.

After defeating the proto-Mongol Eastern Hu and the Indo-European Yüeh-chih on his two flanks, Mao-tun, the founder of the Hsiung-nu empire, moved north and west, conquering five peoples: the Hun-yü, Ch'ü-shih 屈射, Ko-k'un 鬲昆, Ting-ling 丁靈, and Hsin-li 薪犁. The first two names are not found again in the historical record and cannot be identified with certainty; Ch'ü-shih, EMC **k'ut-ziajk**, suggests Skujaka, Scythians. The possibility of finding this ancient and celebrated Iranian name in the eastern steppe in the second century B.C. is intriguing but tells us little, since the Ch'ü-shih are not mentioned again. The other three names are those of Turkish peoples.

The Ting-ling reappear from time to time in Han sources as a people to the north of the Hsiung-nu, apparently in the region of Lake Baikal. As we have already noted, Ting-ling elements entered north China in the Later Han as part of the Southern Hsiung-nu and preserved some degree of separate identity there under this name as late as the fifth century. The main body of the Ting-ling, however, moved into western Mongolia and the Altai region after the collapse of the Hsiung-nu empire, and they reappear from the fourth century on as the High Carts. As we have seen, their original non-Chinese name also reappears in a number of new transcriptions, the best known of which is T'ieh-le 鐵勒. That the T'ieh-le were Turkish is certain, since the Turkish speaking Uyghurs emerged from them during the T'ang period. There are also some clearly Turkish words recorded in Chinese accounts of the High Carts of the fifth century (Pulleyblank, in press [b]).

Ko-k'un (EMC **kerjk-kwən**) is the earliest transcription of the name Qyrqyz (probably originally Qyrqyř). In other sources of the Han period these people are called Chien-k'un 堅昆 (EMC **ken-kwən**). Unlike the Ting-ling, the Qyrqyz remained in the far north in post-Han times and were still in approximately the same region in the ninth century when they participated in the overthrow of the Uyghur empire.

The Hsin-li were a less prominent people, not referred to again in Han sources. Their name, EMC **sin-li**, can, however, be confidently interpreted as a transcription of Syr—the name of a Turkish tribe known from the

Orkhon inscriptions in the T'ang and transcribed in Chinese sources of that period as Hsüeh 薛 (EMC **siat**).

Another name which is not mentioned in connection with the conquests of Mao-tun but occurs in later Han dynasty references to peoples lying beyond the Hsiung-nu is Hu-chieh 呼揭 (EMC **xɔ-giat**) or Wu-chieh 烏揭 (EMC **ʔɔ-giat**). These forms probably stood for something like *Hagaŕ, perhaps an early form of Turkish Oɣur ~ Oɣuz. They appear to have been the most westerly of the Turkish-speaking peoples of that time.

This brief summary passes over many philological problems that should be discussed at much greater length. But the general conclusion must be that—contrary to what has often been assumed—of all the Altaic speakers, the Turkish-speaking peoples were the farthest removed from China in pre-historic times.

THE INDO-EUROPEANS

Before the archaeological explorations of Sinkiang that took place in the last decade of the nineteenth century and the first decade of the twentieth, it was assumed that the Indo-Iranians were the easternmost branch of the Indo-Europeans. Then it was discovered that during the first millennium A.D. a literate Buddhist culture flourished on the north side of the Tarim basin from Kucha to Turfan, using languages which belonged to a hitherto unknown branch of the Indo-European family. The states in question were already known from Chinese historical records beginning with the first Chinese penetration into the region, namely, the journey of Chang Ch'ien to try to find the Yüeh-chih around 130 B.C. How much earlier they had been there cannot be told from any historical record, and archaeology has so far not provided an answer.

Naturally there has been no lack of speculation. When the Tocharian languages, as they have come to be called, were first studied, it soon became apparent that they belonged to the *centum*, not the *satem*, branch of Indo-European. This primary division is based on the treatment of the Indo-European palatal stops, which are represented as velars in languages like Latin, Greek, Celtic, and Germanic but become sibilants in Indo-Iranian, Balto-Slavic, and Armenian. The word for "hundred" is the shibboleth: it appears as Latin *centum*, Greek *hekaton*, English *hundred* (with $h < x < k$), Old Irish *cēt*, but as Sanskrit *śata*, Avestan *satem*, Lithuanian *szimtas*, and Russian *sto*. The Tocharian word is *känt* in the eastern A dialect and *kante*, *känte* in the western B dialect.

Until the discovery of Tocharian, the classification of Indo-European languages into the *centum* and *satem* divisions corresponded to a west-east geographical division. It was therefore natural to assume that the Tocharians had originated somewhere in the west, presumably in northern Europe, passed through the long stretch of intervening *satem* country from Baltic to Iranian, and finally settled in Sinkiang. No independent evidence, archaeological or otherwise, has ever been found for this remarkable migration. It is much more likely that resemblances to the Western Indo-European languages are the result of the shared retention of archaic features from proto-Indo-European. In the example given above one can assume that Indo-European $\hat{k}$ changed first to an affricate and then a fricative in a certain contiguous group of dialects, but remained a stop in other dialects to the east as well as to the west.

In many other respects, Tocharian is quite unlike all the other Indo-European languages. Though the verbal inflection shows many inherited features, the declension of nouns is different, probably as the result of long contacts with languages of non-Indo-European type.

All this suggests strongly that the Tocharians always lay to the east of the Indo-Iranians and that they had a long period of development in which there was little close contact with the Indo-Iranians before the penetration of Buddhism into the region in the second century A.D. Unfortunately, this still does not give us a date for their arrival in Sinkiang. One can assume it was before the time of the Achaemenid ruler Darius (522–486 B.C.), who campaigned against Iranian Sakas east of the Caspian, but it may have been long before that. Only archaeological investigation directed toward answering this problem can further enlightenment.

Besides the people of the city-states who wrote their documents in the Tocharian languages, it is highly probable that other peoples of the region who left no such remains also spoke related languages. Lou-lan (Krorayina) in the Lop-nor region, which was also known as Shan-shan, used a northwest Indian Prakrit as its administrative language in the third century A.D. but probably had a Tocharian dialect as its native speech (Burrow 1935). Most important of all from the point of view of our present enquiry, certain nomadic peoples, including the Yüeh-chih and the Wu-sun, also probably spoke languages related to Tocharian.

The Yüeh-chih 月氏, whose homeland was said to be in the Ch'i-lien mountains south of the Kansu corridor, were a major nomadic power at the beginning of the second century B.C. As a result of their defeat by the Hsiung-nu, part of their tribe, thenceforth known as the Great Yüeh-chih, moved west, eventually occupying first Sogdiana (present Uzbekistan) and then crossing the Oxus into Bactria (northern Afghanistan) and putting an end to the Greek kingdom there. Another part of the tribe, the Little Yüeh-chih, remained in Kansu and continues to be mentioned in that region for some centuries.

I will not recapitulate here all the linguistic arguments that led me to conclude that the Yüeh-chih and Wu-sun were probably Tocharian speakers (Pulleyblank 1966). Although the evidence is inevitably not abundant, a network of inter-related facts makes such an assumption probable, certainly much more so than any alternative theory that has been suggested.

Again, we are badly in need of aid from archaeologists to help identify the Yüeh-chih in Kansu and to enable us to come to some conclusion about when they arrived there. More is known about the archaeology of Kansu than about Sinkiang. According to Chang (1977), the Yang-shao culture spread from the central plain into eastern Kansu around the middle of the fifth millennium, followed about a thousand years later by the local Ma-chia-yao phase and, after 3000 B.C., by the Ma-ch'ang and Pan-shan phases. The Lungshanoid and Lung-shan cultures that followed Yang-shao farther east did not penetrate this region. Instead we find, in Chang's words, "several new cultures whose origins remain unclear but which seem to have some sort of connection with the sub-Neolithic and possibly Neolithic peoples to the north and west in the steppe regions" (pp. 194–195). The first of these, the Ch'i-chia culture, now dated from around the end of the third millennium, is important from the point of view of the origins of Chinese civilization because its copper artifacts are "one of the earliest dated metal finds in China." It is followed by a number of other cultures which have common features but also individual differences. What such differences may imply in terms of ethnic origins is, as Chang remarks, an open question. Speculation that the Ssu-wa culture of the T'ao Ho valley might be connected with the Ch'iang who are associated with the region in Han times is not unreasonable, but there were also Little Yüeh-chih in the same general area. Perhaps more complete knowledge both of the internal developmental sequence in Kansu and of the connections with neighboring cultures to the west, north, and east will resolve such issues.

The presence of Indo-Europeans in Sinkiang and Kansu in the second century B.C. and the probability that they had been there for some considerable time is obviously of great importance if one is looking for a route by which influences from the West could have come to China when literate civilization was developing there for the first time, in the second millennium B.C. One such item that no one seems prepared to gainsay is the horse-drawn chariot, though the tendency has often been to minimize its significance and date it as late as possible. The role of the horse and chariot in Chinese culture for the following thousand years, however, is so obvious that it can hardly be dismissed so lightly. The coming of the chariot presumably also meant the coming of wheeled vehicles as such, even if we as yet lack archaeological evidence for other kinds of wagons in Shang times. And if one technological advance as important as this came from the West it is unlikely that there were not other things as well. If, as I have suggested in other publications (Pulleyblank 1965a; 1965b; 1975), Indo-European and Sino-Tibetan are genetically related, this will push the contacts between these two linguistic families into a much more remote antiquity. But this must remain a subject for future investigation.

CONCLUSION

To attempt such a comprehensive survey of the linguistic situation in China and around its periphery during the period when a literate civilization was emerging is no doubt a somewhat foolhardy undertaking, and it is possible that many details will have to be altered as new knowledge emerges. It is presented, nevertheless, in the hope of providing a framework, however tentative, for realistic hypotheses about the relation between the rapidly emerging archaeological data and the societies they reflect.

The hypotheses that arise from this survey can be summarized as follows:

(1) The Sino-Tibetans probably had their common homeland in the Yang-shao Neolithic culture in northwest China. The Chinese (linguistically defined) appear with the (still at least semi-legendary) Hsia dynasty, from which they took their first self-designation.

(2) Hsia was already strongly under eastern cultural influences which we can associate, as did Fu Ssu-nien (1935), with the "barbarian" Yi of proto-historical times. The Yi were probably Austro-Asiatic (Mon-Khmer) in linguistic affiliation, part of a cultural complex stretching up the coast through Wu and Yüeh (Kiangsu and Chekiang) from Southeast Asia. Yi influence was apparently even stronger in the Shang than in the Hsia, though the Shang inherited the Chinese written, and presumably also spoken, language from the Hsia.

(3) Out of the more westerly Sino-Tibetans, who became differentiated from their more culturally advanced Chinese neighbors, came other "bar-

barian" peoples such as the Ch'iang and Jung. These were the ancestors of
the later Tibeto-Burman tribes of the western Chinese borderlands. It is
suggested that the ancestors of the Chou dynasty came from such "barbarians" rather than from the direct "Chinese" line of the original Hsia
people.

(4) The prehistoric civilizations of the Yangtze valley and eastern
Szechwan belonged to the Man "barbarians," whom we can identify as
probably Miao-Yao speakers, possibly distantly related in language to the
Austro-Asiatics of the coast. Ch'u emerged as a sinicized state out of the
Man in the Spring and Autumn period.

(5) Farther south lay the Tai family of languages (including the more
distantly related Li and Lao or K'o-lao), whose speakers may have been
responsible for the Tien bronze culture in Yunnan.

(6) Austronesian (Malayo-Polynesian) speakers on Taiwan were subject
to cultural influences from the adjacent mainland. Whether there were also
linguistic connections between Austronesian and Austro-Asiatic and/or
Austronesian and Tai, as has been alleged, and what such connections
might mean for the prehistoric movements of people remain open
questions.

(7) To the north we can identify peoples with Altaic affinities in (a) the
proto-Mongol Eastern Hu, and possibly other Hu groups farther west,
known to the Chinese only from the fourth century B.C.; (b) the proto-
Turkish tribes—Ting-ling, Chien-k'un, and so on—of southern Siberia,
known only from Han times; (c) the proto-Tungusic (?) Yi-lou in eastern
Manchuria, also known only from Han. The Mo, who had later connections with Fu-yü, Koguryŏ, Paekche, and Japan, were in northern Hopei in
early Chou and may also have been Altaic. If so, this may push the contacts
between the Chinese and Altaic speakers into proto-historic times. The Ti
of Shansi could also have been Altaic or Tibeto-Burman, but evidence is
lacking.

(8) The Palaeo-Siberian (?) Hsiung-nu come into contact with the
Chinese only in the third century B.C.

(9) By the beginning of the second century B.C., the oases of northern
and eastern Sinkiang were occupied by Tocharian-speaking city-states, and
nomads related to them in language (Yüeh-chih and Wu-sun) were in
Kansu and the T'ien Shan. The time of their arrival cannot yet be determined, but it is suggested as early in the second millennium B.C. at the
latest; also that they were the intermediaries in the transmission of cultural
influences from the West to the nascent civilization of China.

REFERENCES

A. Chinese Sources

Dynastic histories and the *Shih-chi* are cited in the new punctuated edition of the Erh-shih-ssu shih, published by the Chung-hua shu-chü, Peking, 1959–1977.

The following works are cited in the editions of the Harvard-Yenching Index Series: *Ch'un-ch'iu* and *Tso-chuan*, *Hsün-tzu*, *Meng-tzu*, *Mo-tzu*, *Shih-ching*, *Shu-ching*.

Chan-kuo ts'e 戰國策. Wan-yu wen-k'u 萬有文庫 reprint, Shanghai, 1931.

Chou li 周禮. Shih-san ching chu-shu 十三經注疏 reprint, Peking, n.d.

Fang yen 方言. *Fang-yen chiao-chien chi t'ung-chien* 方言校箋及通檢, edited by Chou Tsu-mo 周祖謨 and Wu Hsiao-ling 吳曉鈴. Peking, 1956.

Han Ch'ang-li wen-chi chiao-chu 韓昌黎文集校注 by Han Yü 韓愈 (768–824), with commentary by Ma Ch'i-ch'ang 馬其昶. Reprint, Taipei, 1967.

Han Fei-tzu 韓非子. Chu tzu chi-ch'eng 諸子集成 reprint, Peking, 1954.

Hua-yang kuo-chih 華陽國志. Kuo-hsüeh chi-pen ts'ung-shu 國學基本叢書 reprint, Peking, 1958.

Kuan-tzu 管子. Chu tzu chi-ch'eng 諸子集成 reprint, Peking, 1954.

Kuo-yü 國語. Wan-yu wen-k'u 萬有文庫 reprint, Shanghai, 1931.

Ku-pen chu-shu chi-nien chi-chiao 古本竹書紀年輯校. In *Hai-ning Wang Chung-ch'üeh Kung yi-shu* 海寧王忠愨公遺書, edited by Wang Kuo-wei 王國維. N.p., 1927–1928.

Lun-heng 論衡. Chu tzu chi-ch'eng 諸子集成 reprint, Peking, 1954.

Miao-fang pei-lan 苗防備覽, by Yen Ju-yü 嚴如煜, preface 1820. Reprint, Taipei, 1969.

Po-wu chih 博物志. Ts'ung-shu chi-ch'eng 叢書集成 reprint, Shanghai, 1939.

Samguk sagi 三國史記, by Kim Pu-sik 金富軾 (1075–1151). In *Gembun wayaku taishō Sangoku shiki* 原文和譯對照三國史記, edited by Aoyagi Tsunatarō 青柳綱太郎. Reprint, Tokyo, 1975.

Shih-ming 釋名. Ssu-pu ts'ung-k'an 四部叢刊 reprint, Shanghai, 1929.

Shui-ching chu 水經注. Kuo-hsüeh chi-pen ts'ung-shu 國學基本叢書 reprint, Shanghai, 1936.

Shuo-wen chieh-tzu ku-lin 說文解字詁林, compiled by Ting Fu-pao 丁福保, 1928. Reprint, Taipei, 1970.

Wu Yüeh ch'un-ch'iu 吳越春秋. Wan-yu wen-k'u 萬有文庫 reprint, Shanghai, 1937.

B. Secondary Works

Aichi Daigaku Chūnichi daijiten hensan sho 愛知大学中日大辞典編纂処
1968   *Chūnichi daijiten* 中日大辞典. Tokyo.

Benedict, Paul K.
1942   "Thai, Kadai, and Indonesian: A New Alignment in Southern Asia." *American Anthropologist*, n.s. 44:576–601.
1975a   *Sino-Tibetan: A Conspectus.* Cambridge, Eng.
1975b   *Austro-Thai Language and Culture.* New Haven.

Burrow, Thomas
1935   "Tokharian Elements in the Kharosthi Documents from Chinese Turkestan." *Journal of the Royal Asiatic Society* 1935:667–675.

Chang, Kwang-chih
1977   *The Archaeology of Ancient China.* 3d ed., rev. and enl. New Haven.

Clarke, Samuel R.
1911   *Among the Tribes in Southeast China.* London.

Coblin, W. South
1979   "A New Study of the Pai-lang Songs." *Ch'ing-hua hsüeh-pao* 清華學報 12:179–216.

Creel, Herrlee G.
1965   "The Role of the Horse in Chinese History." *American Historical Review* 70:647–742.
1970   *The Origins of Statecraft in China*, vol. 1: *The Western Chou Empire.* Chicago.

de Beauclair, Inez
1946   "The Keh Lao of Kweichow and Their History According to the Chinese Records." *Studia Serica* 5:1–44.
1960   "A Miao Tribe of Southeast Kweichow and Its Cultural Configuration." *Chung-yang yen-chiu-yüan min-tsu-hsüeh yen-chiu-so chi-k'an* 中央研究院民族學研究所集刊 10:125–205.

Dyen, Isidore
1965   "Formosan Evidence for Some New Proto-Austronesian Phonemes." In *Indo-Pacific Linguistic Studies*, edited by G. B. Milner and E. J. A. Henderson: vol. 1: 285–305. Amsterdam.

Egami Namio 江上波夫
1948   *Yūrashiya kodai hoppō bunka.* ユーランヤ古代北方文化.
          Tokyo.
1951   *Yūrashiya hoppō bunka no kenkyū.* ユーランヤ北方
          文化の研究. Tokyo.
1967   *Kiba minzoku kokka: Nihon kodaishi e no apurōchi.*
          騎馬民族国家: 日本古代史へのマプローチ. Tokyo.

Forrest, R. A. D.
1965   *The Chinese Language.* 2d ed. London.

Fu Ssu-nien 傅斯年
1935   "Yi Hsia tung-hsi shuo 夷夏東西說." In *Ch'ing-chu Ts'ai
          Yüan-p'ei hsien-sheng liu-shih-wu sui lun-wen chi* 慶祝
          蔡元培先生六十五歲論文集, vol. 2: 1093–1134.

Gimbutas, Marija
1970   "Proto-Indo-European Culture: The Kurgan Culture
          During the Fifth, Fourth and Third Millennia B.C." In
          Indo-European and Indo-Europeans, edited by G. Cardona
          et al.: pp. 155–197. Philadelphia.

Graham, D. C.
1954   *Songs and Stories of the Ch'uan Miao.* Washington, D.C.

Haarh, Erik
1968   *The Zhang-Zhung Language: A Grammar and Dictionary
          of the Unexplored Language of the Tibetan Bonpos.*
          Copenhagen.

Haloun, Gustav
1937   "Zur Üe-tsï-Frage." *Zeitschrift der Deutschen
          Morgenländischen Gesellschaft*: pp. 243–318.

Hamilton, James
1962   "Toquz-Oγuz et On-Uyγur." *Journal Asiatique*
          250: 23–63.

Haudricourt, A. G.
1954   "L'origine des tons vietnamiens." *Journal Asiatique*
          242:69–82.
1967   "La langue lakkia." *Bulletin de la Société Linguistique de
          Paris* 62:165–182.

K'ai-feng and Chung-kuo   K'ai-feng shih-fan hsüeh-yüan ti-li-hsi
          開封師範學院地理系 and Chung-kuo k'o-hsüeh-yüan Ho-
          nan-sheng fen-yüan ti-li yen-chiu-so 中國科學院河南省
          分院地理研究所

1959   *Chung-kuo min-tsu ti-li tzu-liao hsüan-chi* 中國民族
            地理資料選集. Peking.

KK
1974.6   "Liao-ning K'o-tso-hsien Pei-tung-ts'un ch'u-t'u ti Yin-
            Chou ch'ing-t'ung ch'i 遼寧喀左縣北洞村出土的殷
            周青銅器 ": pp. 364–372.

Lebar, Frank M., Hickey, Gerald C., and Musgrave, John K.
1964   *Ethnic Groups of Mainland Southeast Asia.* New Haven.

Ledyard, Gari
1975   "Galloping Along with the Horseriders: Looking for the
            Founders of Japan." *Journal of Japanese Studies*
            1:217–254.

Lewin, Bruno
1976   "Japanese and Korean: The Problem and History of a
            Linguistic Comparison." *Journal of Japanese Studies*
            2:389–412.

Li, Fang-kuei
1965   "The Tai and Kam-Sui Languages." In *Indo-Pacific
            Linguistic Studies*, vol. 2, edited by G. B. Milner and
            E. J. A. Henderson: pp. 389–412. Amsterdam.
1977   *A Handbook of Comparative Tai.* Honolulu.

Ligeti, Louis
1950   "Mots de civilisation de Haute Asie en transcription
            chinoise." *Acta Orientalia Hungarica* 1:141–188.
1970   "Le Tabghatch: Un dialecte de la langue sien-pi." In
            Mongolian Studies, edited by L. Ligeti: pp. 265–308.
            Amsterdam.

Liu Yi-t'ang 劉義棠
1969   *Chung-kuo pien-chiang min-tsu shih* 中國邊疆民族史. 2
            vols. Taipei.

Lunet de Lajonquière, E.
1906   *Ethnographie du Tonkin septentrional.* Paris.

Ma Ch'ang-shou 馬長壽
1962   *Pei Ti yü Hsiung-nu* 北狄與匈奴. Peking.

Maspero, Henri
1912   "Etudes sur la phonétique historique de la langue
            annamite: Les initiales." *BEFEO* 12:1–127.
1933   "La langue chinoise." *Conférences de l'Institut de
            Linguistique de l'Université de Paris* 1:33–70.

1952 "Les langues thai." In *Les langues du monde*, rev. ed., 2 vols., edited by A. Meillet and M. Cohen: pp. 571–608.

Mei, Tsu-lin, and Norman, Jerry
1976 "The Austroasiatics in Ancient South China: Some Lexical Evidence." *Monumenta Serica*. 32:274–301.

Morohashi Tetsuji 諸橋轍次
1959 *Dai kanwa jiten* 大漢和辞典, 12 vols. Tokyo.

Piggott, Stuart
1974 "Chariots in the Caucasus and China." *Antiquity* 48:16–24.
1975 "Bronze Age Chariot Burials in the Urals." *Antiquity* 49:289–290.

Průšek, Jaroslav
1971 *Chinese Statelets and the Northern Barbarians in the Period 1400–300 B.C.* Dordrecht.

Pulleyblank, Edwin G.
1962 "The Consonantal System of Old Chinese." *Asia Major* 9:58–144, 206–265.
1965a "Close/Open Ablaut in Sino-Tibetan." In *Indo-Pacific Linguistic Studies*, vol. 1, edited by G. B. Milner and E. J. A. Henderson: pp. 230–242. Amsterdam.
1965b "The Indo-European Vowel System and the Qualitative Ablaut." *Word* 21:86–101.
1965c "The Chinese Name for the Turks." *Journal of the American Oriental Society* 85:121–125.
1966 "Chinese and Indo-Europeans." *Journal of the Royal Asiatic Society* 1966:9–39.
1970–71 "Late Middle Chinese." *Asia Major* 15:197–239 and 16:121–168.
1975 "Prehistoric East-West Contacts Across Eurasia." *Pacific Affairs* 47:500–508.
1979 "The Chinese Cyclical Signs as Phonograms." *Journal of the American Oriental Society* 99:24–38.
in press (a) "The Hsiung-nu." To appear in *Philologiae Turcicae Fundamenta* 3.
in press (b) "The Nomads in China and Central Asia in the Post-Han Period." To appear in *Philologiae Turcicae Fundamenta* 3.

Ruey Yih-fu 芮逸夫
1948 "Lao wei Ch'i-lao shih-cheng 僚爲仡佬試證 ." *BIHP* 20.1:343–357.

1951   "Po jen k'ao 僰人考." *BIHP* 23.1:245–278.
1956   "Lao jen k'ao 僚人考." *BIHP* 28:727–769.
1969   "Chuang jen lai-yüan ch'u-t'an 僮人來原初談." *BIHP* 39.2:125–154.

Schlegel, Gustav
1893   "Hennins or Conical Ladies' Hats in Asia, China and Europe." *T'oung Pao* 3:422–429.

Shafer, Robert
1943   "Further Analysis of the Pyu Inscriptions." *Harvard Journal of Asiatic Studies* 7:313–366.
1955   "Classification of the Sino-Tibetan Languages." *Word* 11:94–111.

Shima Kunio 島邦男
1958   *Inkyo bokuji kenkyū* 殷墟卜辞研究. Hirosaki.

Shorto, Harry L.
1971   *A Dictionary of Mon Inscriptions from the Sixth to the Sixteenth Centuries.* London.

Stübel, H., and Li, Hua-min
1932   *Die Hsia-min vom Tse-mu-schan.* Nanking.

Su Ping-ch'i 蘇秉琦
1978   "Shih-hsia wen-hua ch'u-lun 石峽文化初論." *WW* 1978.7:16–22.

Thomas, F. W.
1933   "The Żaṅ-żuṅ Language." *Journal of the Royal Asiatic Society* 1933:405–410.

Wang Ching-ju 王靜如
1932   *Hsi-hsia yen-chiu* 西夏研究, pt. 1. Kuo-li chung-yang yen-chiu-yüan li-shih yü-yen yen-chiu-so tan-k'an chia chung chih pa 國立中央研究院歷史語言研究所單刊甲種之八. Peking.

Wen Yu 聞宥
1940   "Min-chia yü chung t'ung-yi tzu chih yen-chiu 民家語中同義字之研究." *Studia Serica* 1:67–84. (English abstract.)

WW
1978.3   "Shan-hsi Fu-feng Chuang-po yi-hao Hsi-Chou ch'ing-t'ung-ch'i chiao-ts'ang fa-chüeh chien-pao 陝西扶風庄白一號西周青銅器窖藏發掘簡報": pp. 1–18.

15

Tribe to State or
State to Tribe in Ancient China?

MORTON H. FRIED

Since the middle of the nineteenth century, theories about the origin of
the state have involved a concept of the tribe as an essential preparatory
sociopolitical form and level of organization. This chapter challenges such
views and attempts a preliminary counter-case in the context of present
understandings of the rise of the state in North China.

The theories of Marx and Engels about the origins of the state are very
important in current studies of Chinese state origins, if only because the
present regime sets its own declared view of their theory as the basemark
against which work on the topic will proceed. Actually, in their understanding of "tribe" Marx and Engels were typical of scholars of their time, for
they totally accepted the necessity of a tribal stage en route to the formation
of the state. In *Die Deutsche Ideologie* (1845–1846), Marx declared that the
first form of ownership in human society was tribal, *Stammeigentum*. There
is a certain ambiguity about that term, however, since the relevant root,
Stamm, at the time of Marx's writing could have meant either "clan" or
"tribe." It was not until Marx read Lewis Henry Morgan's *Ancient Society*
that the two concepts were divided in his and Engels' work. As Marx died
before he could produce the work he intended on this subject, it remained
for Engels to use, in his writing of *Der Ursprung der Familie: Privateigentums und die Staat*, both Morgan's work and the extensive notes on it left
by Marx. *Der Ursprung der Familie* and Engels' *Anti-Dühring* are the
most quoted in the archaeological literature of the People's Republic of
China, especially in the context of the synthetic reconstruction of socio-

political evolution. In the immediate instance, the former work is worth citing because it demonstrates a relatively clear appreciation of the distinction between clan and tribe in the later works of Marx and Engels. The ambiguity was overcome when the term *Gens*, borrowed from Morgan, came to distinguish "clan" from *Stamm*, now intelligible only as "tribe." This is illustrated by the sentence: "Greischen und Pelasger und andre stammverwandte wolker schon seit forgeschichtlicher Zeit geordnet nach derselben organischen Reihe wie die Amerikaner: Gens, Phratie, Stamm, Bund von Stämmen" (Engels 1892:93).

That the "formation of a larger society results only from the joining of such smaller societies," where the latter were tribes and the former were nations or states, seemed obvious in the nineteenth century. Herbert Spencer, whose remark this is, quotes in turn Gaston Maspero (1878:18) to the effect that the Egyptian state formed from "a great number of tribes" that coalesced (Spencer 1896:456; cf. 1967:11). Half a century later, when V. Gordon Childe translated a well-known French work on the origins of the Egyptian state into the English, he entitled it *From Tribe to Empire* (Moret and Davy 1926).

Against this background, it may seem quixotic to query such widely accepted usage. Let me say only that this criticism of the easy use of the concept of tribe in both general theoretical discussions of sociopolitical evolution and specific cases, such as the Chinese, is not intended to be merely semantic, but more deeply revisionist. It is an attempt to get scholars to re-examine some of the structures and processes taken for granted in the study of state formation—things that are part of the problem, hence call out for analysis. This attitude must be encouraged specifically in the case of China because of the unusually pivotal nature of the Chinese example. Though not the earliest of known state-level societies, China's case is one of the best documented, in both archaeological and literary materials. Unfortunately, this does not necessarily mean that questions about the evolution of the state can be answered definitively by using available Chinese data. It is not even clear, as yet, whether the questions that remain can ever be answered, anywhere, since the critical archaeological evidence, even when recovered, is subject to contradictory interpretation. Yet this essay is offered in question of certain basic assumptions long taken for granted by theorists. In particular, the agnostic thrust is directed at the pivotal notion that states arose from tribes. Since such a suggestion may seem at best disingenuous, let me first indicate what it means, beginning with some consideration of what is usually understood by the concept of tribe.

THE NOTION OF TRIBE

"Fried could not do with the 'tribe'," says Richard N. Adams, "I cannot do without it. Indeed, if there were no word *tribe*, I would have to invent one" (Adams 1975:225). Adams goes on to indicate that he considers the word tribe excellent for designating the simplest level of coordination above that of the single contiguous community. He is aware of some of the difficulties arising from use of the notion of tribe. For example, he understands that coordination among the component communities comprising the tribe need not always be peaceful. Such concessions, however, are not enough to validate the concept of tribe. Let us see what is involved, because these arguments may affect our understanding of political development in China several millennia ago.

Adams' work represents an enlightened effort to hold on to the concept of tribe, and I note that the word performs simultaneously in two areas for him. In the first place, it enables him to deal with a level of societal organization so vaguely articulated in vivo that one who wishes to see its forms must use a technique analogous to staining in microscopic biology. The comparison is not really a good one: where staining reveals real structures, the use of the term tribe may be creating the illusion that they exist. But that applies only to the first use to which Adams puts his concept of tribe. A second use is heuristically more suited to social evolution theory: the tribe is a society in the process of becoming a state. It is not necessary that all tribes evolve into states; it is usually considered necessary, however, that populations somehow develop into tribes before they take the additional steps necessary to become states. Again to take advantage of the convenient counter-argument advanced by Adams:

> To [Fried], "most so-called tribes" seemed "at close range to be curious melanges rather than homogeneous units." And, in this, I can only agree; that is exactly the way they are, and that is precisely why they so aptly fill the structural necessity that relates bands, lineages, clans, and/or villages. Without them, there could have been no further evolution to chiefdoms (Adams 1975:227).

Adams then asks what motivates the formation of centralized inter-unit aggregates of tribal type, and answers his own question: first, there is safety in numbers, and extended organization provides better defense. "While there are advantages in extending the area of peace, there are also advantages in being able to go to war" (p. 228). Interestingly, he illustrates the point by referring to Lucy Mair's analysis of East African societies, specifically Gusii and Mandari, where the ability of individuals to inherit ritual power and the correlated ability to attract and keep a following "through the attachment of clients, supporters who, in these cases, usually came from neighboring societies or other, less successful components of the same tribe" (ibid.), led to "kingship." Adams deftly interprets Mair's "kingship" as synonymous with his own "chiefdom," thereby providing the desired evolutionary sequence.

The argument is so logically satisfying, so deeply rooted in conventional Western political theory (see Fried 1976), as to render completely understandable the irritation provoked by challenging it. Why then continue to be perverse? My motivation is patent: despite a comforting appearance, the tribal argument does not conform to what has been learned in a century of hard work. It is supported neither by ethnography nor by comparative ethnological analysis, nor by archaeology carried out in the ruins of what can be called the pristine state societies.

Briefly, pristine states are those that form as the result of a process that is not influenced by the presence or activities of other pre-existing states. All other states are secondary—formed by processes which included or stemmed from the presence or activities of already existing states. The reason for insisting on this distinction is fundamental: the processes by which a state-level society emerges sui generis are necessarily quite different from those by which states emerge when other states have preceded them and provided models of state-building, or when state organization is not merely exported but imposed. Further, consider the possibility that the formation of tribes was probably a reaction to the pushing of state organization into regions of more simply organized populations. If this is so, it is clear that the attempt to identify the emergence of the pristine state with a prior tribal form of organization may well create a very misleading anachronism.

Contemporary Chinese archaeological interpretation is dominated by formulations traceable to Lewis Henry Morgan. It is of considerable consequence that Morgan based his conception of the evolution of the state on Aztec, Greek, and Roman polities. To the first he denied state organization, treating its society as an example of "upper barbarism" that he equated with an advanced form of unilineal descent group structure but saw as falling short of the territorial political state. When he came to choose Greece and Rome for his models of the transition from pre-state to state society it was an unfortunate choice. Both Greece and Rome were secondary states, built upon the stimuli and directly exported institutional complexes of a series of preceding states, some of which had flourished two thousand years earlier. Because Greece and Rome were secondary states, it should not surprise us to find them in an environment populated by tribes.

Applied to China, the Morgan theory reinforces the expectation that the Chinese state will also emerge in a context of pre-existing tribes. If we find references to other populations in the early records, populations such as Jung 戎, Ti 狄, or Man 蠻, the expectation seems confirmed. Yet if China is a case of pristine state development, and if my theory is correct, the achievement of tribal status by the Jung or the Ti would have followed upon, rather than preceded, the emergence of the state in China. How can this problem be solved?

Let us begin with an attempt to specify more closely what is usually meant by tribe. A tribe, as ordinarily denoted in scholarly literature and in popular usage, is a reasonably well-defined social, economic, and political unit, often comprised of several bands or settlements but united by a distinct language and culture and often distinguished by a common name. In fact, how tribes are seen can be expressed by a three-dimensional chess board, or a stack of typewriter paper. The point is that the general conception of tribe provides a reticulation or stacking of systems: of territories, of biological entities, and of a variety of cultural articulations—common language and shared patterns of economic production and exchange, of kinship, residential and other social patterns, of political ties, of religious belief and ritual. This is represented in figure 15.1 by the separate stacks of "papers." Each sheet, so to speak, represents a level of institutional interaction. The bottom sheet in each pile might represent a territory inhabited by (now moving to the next higher sheet) a population invariably conceived of as relatively homogeneous in genetic constitution, especially since the tribe is often imagined as an endogamous unit. The third sheet, still moving upward, can be identified as the linguistic level. Here the tribe is sometimes seen as the bearer of a particular language, more often as speaking a dialect or even a particular idiom or, minimally, as having a somewhat distinct code, particularly if language is broadly construed to include everything that goes into a human communications system. The next level might comprise the material culture or at least the productive technology, and above that would be the relations of production and then the relations of distribution. It is usually assumed that a sociometric analysis of these relations will show that the boundaries of tribes furnish the limits of the largest productive groupings, but even more often, the limits of the system of exchanges whereby goods and services circulate through the society.

It should be evident by now that the number of "sheets" or institutional subsystems that can be discerned is both great and variable. An eight-layered three-dimensional chess board will not begin to suffice. However, although analytical systems vary, one institutional subsystem is of particular importance and should be mentioned: the political. Even where the tribe is not assumed to have a central decision-maker like a chief or cacique, it is believed to have coordinating political functions displayed acephalously; at a minimum, it is assumed to exist as a unit within which peace is maintained, or one that ultimately reacts to war by providing the necessary personnel.

Tribes, then, are usually regarded as networks of networks, where the lower level networks relate to specific properties or activities (territory, population, language, economy, politics, religion, art styles) and the network of networks is the tribe itself. This simple image is represented in figure 15.1.

In figure 15.2 I illustrate my conception of sociocultural reality in pre-state society. Instead of neatly bounded subsystems (e.g., "1," "2," "3"), these subsystems are quite protean. More important, they do not stack congruently, as they so evidently do in figure 15.1. This represents the relative absence of isolating factors in the real world. Under these conditions, defining "tribe" is somewhat like taking an earth core. But whereas geologists realize that their cores are an artifact of their drilling machinery, social scientists and others tend to regard "tribes" defined by a comparable method of their own to be of a higher reality.

What complicates this analysis is the realization that a condition approximating the one represented in figure 15.1 is likely to be precipitated by the encroachment of one or more previously existing states. In the Chinese case, this would mean that non-articulated and shifting differences among the pre-state populations of the Chinese area could have been more or less quickly catalyzed into articulation once the state appeared in the area. Actually, I believe the process would have produced more or less simultaneously two rather different kinds of units plus a third kind a bit later on.

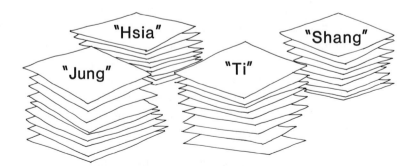

FIGURE 15.1. **The "tribe" as a neatly bounded system.**

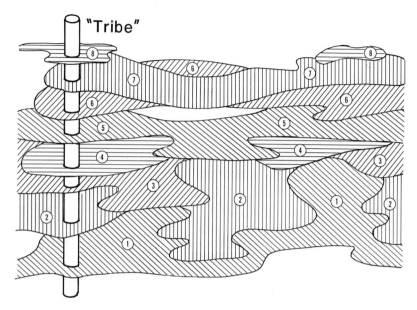

FIGURE 15.2. **The "tribe" as a test core.**

One possibility is that, once precipitated, the state would have triggered the formation of its own counterparts more or less in its own form: other states. This would be likeliest to occur where ecological conditions were similar to those in the original state and where the existing means of production, especially the local technology, were also similar. Where these conditions did not apply, tribes rather than states were likely to be generated.

Circumstances could vary greatly. One course might see tribes emerging as defensive military counters to the probing state. Another might see the state itself taking the lead in providing more organization for the simple societies encountered in its expansion. The state would do this in its own interest, supplying a means for easier manipulation and exploitation of such populations. But such action brings its own dialectical twist: the enhanced ability of the simpler society, now effectively organized in tribal form, with chiefs and possibly other officers, to contest the hegemony of the state. It also furnishes powerful motivations for tribal onslaughts on the state, partly because of new tastes for goods, partly because the newer forms of organization place fiscal demands on the populations that would enjoy these new forms.

As the system continued to grow, it is likely that the swallowing of some of these (newly formed) tribes would lead to the undigested presence in the state population of elements distinct both by self- and other-identification from the general citizenry. Thus would have been generated what we today call ethnic groups or minorities.

The view being suggested is quite different from that which has long been accepted. The conventional view requires that tribes precede the state in the evolution of political organization. What is now suggested, to the contrary, is that all tribes are of secondary nature, formed by the prior activity of state-organized societies. This includes not only tribes in North and South America and Africa, but also in Europe (Alani, Belgae, Scythians, etc.) and in Asia (e.g., Jung, Man, Ti).

Now let us look again at what a tribe is supposed to be in conventional understanding—or even in the most technical anthropological vocabulary. A tribe is a loosely organized set of people comprising a number of villages or migratory camps, depending on the mode of subsistence. Tribal organization is supposed to coordinate a wide range of activities under some kind of centralized leadership that has little or no coercive power. The tribe consists of a network of networks. A network is simply a field of interaction marked by a relatively high frequency of inter-relations. Network boundaries appear where there is a marked decline in the frequency of inter-relations. If we investigate ethnographically known simple human societies and trace the ties that bind individuals, we note that even in the simplest societies the clumping of relations takes place along what can be designated as institutional lines. For example, there are usually two sets of economic ties, those involved in the production of use-values and those involved in their distribution. Another set of interactions characterizes a population identified by bonds of kinship; at a minimum this involves a further dichotomy, the circle of "consanguinei" and the category of affinals. There are other networks: the one within which peace is to be kept at almost any cost, another said to mark the limits of easy security. Still others can be described, such as those characterized by an identity of language, slipping off to the point of unintelligibility, or the network of shared and exchanged ritual and religious belief. There are even diffuse cultural networks involving not the interactions between people but the proportion of shared cultural items. Methodologically, the last should probably be carefully set apart from the others, but in fact people who talk of tribes often have this last meaning in mind.

To return to the key element in the conventional conception of the tribe: the critical criterion is supposed to be the reticulation of networks providing the multilocal polity that breaks the bounds of the single community and provides a basis for the expansion that, it is believed, will culminate in a state. Unfortunately, the scenario just rendered is legendary. When we actually look at ethnographically known simple societies, we do not find any marked tendency to congruence of the several institutional networks sketched above. Economic networks are not particularly coordinated with religious ones. Such networks fail in many instances to fully occupy a particular linguistic space or idiolect, while in others, networks cross-cut rather drastic linguistic differences. Units designated as tribal may see the greater proportion of hostile encounters occurring internally. Conversely, tribal military organization is not merely a rarity; it is either entirely absent or it can be shown to be an artifact of the encroachment on the populations in question of an already functioning state. One of the most interesting things about the state, to use a biological metaphor, is that it is born with a ravenous appetite and will "consume" less developed societies within its range. As asserted earlier, this process of consumption may end with the less complexly organized society swallowed whole by the state and reappearing as an ethnic minority. If this groups remains outside the body of the state, it usually assumes the appearance of a tribe. Pressures from the impinging state or states force congruence on the subsumed institutional systems so that these populations and their societies indeed become organized, bounded, reticulated networks. What is more, they quickly take on or develop centralized positions of command and coercive power. It is by encouraging this higher level of organization that states introduce a modicum of efficiency into their exploitation of simpler societies.

If a pristine state arose in the area now designated as China, and if my theory is correct, it would have been in an area of hamlets and occasional migratory bands with little or no intersettlement cohesion and certainly no tribes in the sense of the reticulated networks discussed above. On the other hand, if the first Chinese state(s) emerged in a setting already occupied by recognizable tribes, and if my thesis applies, it would indicate that the state appeared in North China as a secondary phenomenon. This was a popular theory not long ago, but the archaeological discoveries of recent times have weakened adherence to it except perhaps among certain Soviet scholars. However, if the possibilities have dimmed that the Chinese state and civilization were catalyzed by diffusions from the West, it is still possible that events in North China might have been stimulated by earlier developments in southeastern China (see Meacham, ch. 6 above) or in adjacent Indochina. It should be stressed that, on the basis of available evidence, neither of the possibilities seems as likely as that North China was the site of an indigenous, pristine state.

If China does represent a pristine state development, its earliest state(s)

—Hsia(?), Shang, or Hsia/Shang/Chou (see Chang, ch. 16 below)—would have immediately initiated the process of conversion of the amorphous populations of the hinterland into the neater groupings we now identify as tribes. But how, in a tribeless landscape, can the pristine state emerge?

THE EVOLUTION OF THE STATE: A TRIBELESS SCENARIO

One of the first things we must do in imagining a world without tribes is to try to realize that the seemingly solid evidence of tribes in historical accounts is largely illusory. Particularly in Europe and America, the influence of early travelers' records of voyages to the New World is great. Yet, if the accounts of Columbus (as preserved by Bartolomeo de Las Casas), Verrazano, Cabot, Pigafetta, Cartier, and others are scrutinized, it is seen that the word "tribe" is completely absent, although words for people, country, or kingdom abound. It is also clear that the Europeans, while transferring their images of political structure to the populations who greeted them, were well aware that their experiences related to individual settlements.

Not to pursue the matter too deeply here, European political science was deeply affected by such explorers' accounts but took liberties with them. Whether the vision of primitive society was one of perpetual ferocity and danger, as in Hobbes, or of benign innocence and harmony, as in Rousseau, the image provided usually included an aggregate of settlements under a political leader. By the late sixteenth century, these imaginary formations were called "nations," and a hundred years later they were referred to as "nations or tribes." Only in the eighteenth century did the word tribe begin to stand by itself in such a context (Fried, 1980). Still, this is not the forum in which to quibble about words in the political lexicon; our intent is to provide a plausible model of state formation that can function in the absence of tribes.

It does not help to leap to the time of the Romans or even earlier to the Greeks, for, as already indicated, these examples of state formation are clearly of "secondary" type, and the same forces that generated these states would certainly have called tribes into existence. The central question is: What occurred in the areas of pristine state formation?

Before attempting to discuss that question in terms of data from ancient China, let me offer a hypothetical model of state formation in the absence of pre-existing tribes.

In its earliest forms, which persisted for most of its duration, human society was egalitarian. As argued elsewhere, this does not mean a society of absolute equality, but one that placed no barriers to the rights of access of human begins to the basic resources required to subsist. Such societies were also characterized by the presence of a number of preferred statuses equal to the number of locally available persons capable of filling them. If the local group at one time was blessed with three or four "mighty hunters," that would be their number. If there were none, that, alas, would be the number. A key element is the variability of that number. I happen to believe that under usual circumstances of life, such societies could and readily did absorb additional individuals, particularly persons of productive age. Group structure was open, providing a model of the larger society that is clearly in opposition to that generated by Hobbes. I also believe that economic sharing was a fundamental characteristic of such groups, and this activity may indeed provide the radical discontinuity between non-human and human primate societies; but this is not the place for such a discussion.

For reasons that are not yet entirely clear but probably have to do with massive changes in floral and faunal distributions stemming from prior climatic changes—with these followed in turn by major shifts in human demography and in the technological inventories of local cultural traditions—a new form of society grew up, appearing at first in certain late Palaeolithic situations and later becoming much more widespread in Neolithic economies. I call this new form "ranking society." It shares a fundamental feature of egalitarian society, namely, the absence of restrictions on the access of group members (members of the residential community whether relatively sedentary or mobile) to basic resources. The critical difference, however, was the imposition of a strict limit on the number of positions of valued status. But, in the absence of differential access to basic resources, the degree to which the occupant of a valued status could use it to coerce the behavior of others would remain minimal if not nil. Comparative ethnographic data from New Guinea, Polynesia, and aboriginal North and South America provide a picture in which the main potential economic power of a simple redistributor, a "big man," is difficult and dangerous to activate. In parallel fashion, the evident potential for power of a high-status ritualist or shaman is hemmed in by the same difficulties and dangers. These are perhaps greatest for the person who would activate such power, leading either to the withdrawal of clientele, or to witchcraft or the charge of witchcraft. Even highly ranked but still unstratified communities have powerful egalitarian currents and leveling devices.

It is with the emergence of the stratified society that the approach of finite, coercive political power is signaled; although it may not make its entrance in every case where stratified society has emerged, it is present in the wings.

Stratification is based upon one criterion. A society is said to be stratified when its members have different rights of access to the basic resources required for subsistence. In order to obtain access to the means of subsistence, some people in the community accept statuses of formal dependence, yielding rents, corvées, tithes, and other services to those who have unimpeded access rights. If the definition of exploitation depends upon the extraction of surplus value, the return to the producer of only a portion of the value created by labor, then it is in the stratified society that the threshhold of exploitation is traversed. In a pristine situation, exploitation emerges in a single community and divides a society comprised of relatives into haves and have-nots. Such a society is obviously caught in deep contradictions. The ideology of kinship is basically one of inclusion supported by systems of prescribed economic exchanges. The reality of simple stratified society is exclusion, people being pushed first into "distant" categories of relationship and ultimately out of relationship entirely. At the same time, whatever may remain of reciprocal exchange within the bonds of kinship is being attenuated by the growth of unequal exchanges. Such a society cannot long endure unless it manages to invent a new set of institutions which can maintain the order of stratification by means other than kinship. These means comprise the state (see Fried 1960). Briefly put, a state has two basic tasks: (1) maintenance of the order of stratification and (2) the maintenance of general order in a situation in which kinship can no longer function to do so except on a partial, hence inadequate basis. There are corollaries of the interaction of (1) and (2), such as the priority of attention given to breaches of social order that are particularly menacing to the order of stratification (see Fried 1968).

More useful is the enumeration of some common specific mechanisms whereby emergent states deal with the two tasks. Perhaps the first of these is the definition and bounding of the population comprising the state. In the particular Chinese case we have later historical evidence for this, and it involves precisely a new and extensive use of terms such as "Jung," and "Ti," and "Man." In a sense, what we see here may well be an artifact of the state's creation of tribes and ethnic groups. But there are other functions to be served in defining the state: bounding it geographically, making clear the distinctions between members and non-members and among different categories of members, and finally, particularly in the Chinese case, estimating the size of the population by census. Another set of functions relates to the maintenance of the unit in an environment of similar units, the means of summoning and maintaining a military force. Let me say here that I find no reason why states must emerge from military backgrounds. (This puts me at substantial odds with current interpretations in the People's Republic of China which make intertribal warfare a main cause of the state formation process.) I do not think it a non sequitur that the emergence of a state quickly catalyzes its hinterland so that a military necessity of defense is precipitated at the moment a state is born. I also believe that under usual circumstances the leap to state occurs in a field of such leaps, and that newly born state A finds itself not too far from newly born state B. Even were that not the case, the state at birth is, as previously asserted, an extraordinarily predatory formation and will impose its form on less complexly structured societies that can bear it. Less complexly organized societies that cannot sustain the state form will become tribes.

Next, the requirement of maintenance of general order and of a specific order of stratification requires the development of mechanisms operating toward that end: an apparatus that supports norms by coercing norm-breakers. This function and all of the foregoing require logistical support and financial management, thereby calling into existence a treasury and some means of filling it, usually by tax, at first in kind.

Although I cannot prove it, I think such a development is likely to take place within a fairly tight area, perhaps an area nucleated about a single village. One problem with the tribe, as I see it, is that it lacks internal organization and has less compulsion to form such organization than does the simple developing community. For many social philosophers, the incentive to create inter-community organization is found in extension of the peace unit or enlargement of the war unit. Whether these are regarded as two entities or as facets of one, the difficulty lies in the ethnographic record, where there is ample indication that, on one hand, in some cultures there is no better or more frequent adversary than one's "tribesmates" (the Yanamamo are a splendid example [Chagnon 1968]; so too are various Newguineans, e.g., Tsembaga and Enga [Rappaport 1968; Berndt 1962]), whereas alliances are often forged without reference to any units usually identified as tribes. (Although clearly representative of secondary formations, much of the alliance phenomena in late eighteenth- and nineteenth-century American Indian plains warfare is illustrative here.)

A major difficulty of warfare-based models of state formation, which have retained considerable favor even since the time of Spencer, Gumplowicz, and Oppenheimer, is the difficulty of deriving stratification

from them, as each of these authors tried to do. In fact, most studies of
primitive warfare emphasize its sporadic nature and the invariable lack of
followup (Turney-High 1949). Even where alliances may be formed, as in
providing men for war parties, coordination is minimal and entirely ad
hoc; it is not merely that no permanent leadership structure is created
capable of spanning two or more communities. In fact it hardly appears
even for the duration of the current engagement, and no basis is laid for
continuing it.

In my reading of the evidence, the same conclusion can be derived from
so-called primitive slavery, where slaves are identified as war captives kept
for drudge labor. It is my belief that such a functional incorporation of
aliens into a simple society can only occur after a prior differentiation has
taken place within the social fabric of the community that would hold
slaves. Otherwise, it seems to me that the status of slave is difficult, if not
impossible, to differentiate from low-ranked statuses within the context of
rank society. (I believe that egalitarian societies are incapable of assimilat-
ing persons in any statuses other than those that apply to the other
members of the society of the same sex and age categories.) Thus, it is my
view that the loci of emergent ranking and emergent stratification in both
instances is to be sought first in the internal development of particular
communities. Those that have evolved more complex structure, that is,
have developed ranking or especially those that have developed stratification (as previously defined), are in an excellent position to develop a
genuine class (caste in some instances) of slaves. Particularly where stratification already exists, there is a pre-existing basis for exploitation, with
slavery providing an extreme case of exploitative relations. Slavery can also
play an additional role in speeding up the precipitation of state institutions.
It does this by providing a number of people within the framework of the
community who lack any shred of claim upon the kinship ties that still link
the emergent elite with the part of the local population that lacks direct
access to the basic means of subsistence. Indeed, one can readily see a
critical role for a population of alien clients or slaves. These people are
completely dependent on their masters and can be used as a violent force
against restive expropriated locals. Simultaneously, it can be expected that
such persons provide perhaps the first target against which the expropriated will strike, given the chance. From early state formation times it is
this group that plays lightening rod and scapegoat. Conversely, these
several functions are a likely stimulus to the marked tendency to expansion
which every pristine state displays. The stratified local community that has
gone into formal state organization looks like a city-state and utilizes its

less well-organized surroundings as a source of manpower and raw materials. In its expansion it creates tribes in the hinterland and ethnic groups within its own polity.

Now that the theoretical background has been sketched out, we can take a brief look at some of the concrete data, beginning by considering the status of the concept of tribe in Chinese usage.

"TRIBE" IN CHINESE USAGE

In modern Chinese the primary equivalent of the word *tribe* is rendered *pu-lo* 部落 which is preferable to *tsung-tsu* 宗族 often given as a synonym. The latter is more traditional but quite ambiguous, since it more usually denotes a clan or lineage. It is interesting that older Chinese literature makes no distinction between clan and lineage, nor any distinction between either of those and tribe. At present and since late Ch'ing times some distinctions are made, at least between clan or lineage on one side and tribe on the other. This is done by using *shih-tsu* 氏族 for clan (or "clan society") and *pu-lo* for tribe. It is not unusual, however, to find that current literature often makes use of the compound morpheme *shih-tsu pu-lo* 氏族部落 "clan tribe." Chinese lapses into ambiguity reflect those already pointed out in the early work of Marx and Engels. We will return to this matter in the final section of this chapter; here it is worth noting that recent writings in the People's Republic of China concerning the evolution of the Chinese state from its Neolithic roots leave no doubt that current theory posits a tribal stage as antecedent to and necessary for the subsequent turn to state organization.

If writers in Chinese or German seem at times to take advantage of the ambiguity of certain critical words, this cannot be said of those who write in English, for in this language the distinction between unilineal kinship groups (lineages, clans) and those social groups designated as tribes has usually been clear, at least since "tribe" took on its approximate modern sense in the mid-eighteenth century. For our purposes here, let me cite two recent works that will illustrate the usage to which I object while providing examples of direct relevance to the arguments that follow. It is interesting to pursue the arguments of H. G. Creel (1970:60) as he attempts to understand the rise of the Chou: "Our evidence is hardly adequate to enable us to decide whether, in fact, the Chou did in so short a period develop from a relatively simple tribe to a people able not only to conquer the Shang territories but able to organize and administer them." The indicated usage of "tribe" is not casual, but represents a view to which

Creel, in his work, is clearly committed. Thus, he refers a bit earlier to the situation which, according to Mencius, produced the move which brought Chou into the territory of Shang. The migration was "a response to the pressure of surrounding tribes" in the former locale (ibid., p. 59). The word that Creel renders "tribe" appears in the *Meng-tzu* as *yi* 夷, more often translated as "Northern barbarians," a point that Creel himself makes elsewhere: "Who, in fact, were the barbarians? The Chinese have no single term for them. But they were all the non-Chinese, just as for the Greeks the barbarians were all the non-Greeks" (p. 196). He goes on:

> There seems to be no single Chinese character that may be properly translated as "barbarian." While various names were used for groups regarded as barbarian, four came to predominate: Jung 戎, Ti 狄, Man 蠻, and I 夷. These were probably the names of ethnic groups originally; there were specific peoples called the Huai I . . . the White Ti, etc. . . . . The Chinese gradually came to use these terms in a conventional manner (pp. 197–198).

As might be expected from someone focusing on the development of Chinese civilization, Creel is more concerned with the content of the epithet "barbarian" than he is with "tribe," but I think that with few exceptions he makes no meaningful distinction between the two: "The populations over which they [the Chou] ruled were in part Chinese, but undoubtedly large numbers of the people theoretically within many states were non-Chinese tribesmen" (p. 205).

It is interesting to compare Creel's usage with the earlier but very similar treatment of comparable ideas by Owen Lattimore. Here I shall highlight only Lattimore's easy use of the concept of tribe. Indeed, it was he who refined it to the point of providing a concept of "tribal reservoir" that he used to animate another of his conceptions, that of "the 'Frontier Style' of Chinese history." Beyond the "reservoir of tribal invasions," said Lattimore, "lay the 'lands of the unregenerate,' the tribes that had not participated in the conquest" (Lattimore 1940:248). It is fitting for me to note that Lattimore, who draws in his 1940 work on the earlier archaeological contributions and syntheses of Creel, proposed a theory that ultimately stimulated my own. Lattimore states in several ways his notion that the tribal formations of steppe pastoralism constituted a development partly parallel to the rise of the Chinese state and partly stimulated and driven by it. Nonetheless, he projects at times another, simpler view of tribalism as a characteristic of earlier horizons:

> The question of the ethnic identity of the early Chinese and the barbarian tribes with which they were in contact need not yet be discussed. It would be interesting to know whether two or more races, or a mixture of peoples, took part in the

founding of China; but the matter is not of decisive importance, because the major interest at this level of history is not the blood that ran in people's veins but rather the question of the way of life—its capacity for elaboration within the original landscape and its adaptation to a wider range of territory (ibid., p. 32).

It is curious that one of the more recent works published on the origins of Chinese civilization should represent a step backward from the understanding achieved at least forty years earlier, separating factors of biology or race from those involved in cultural evolution; I refer to the work of Ho Ping-ti, who begins by noting that "prehistoric and early historic China was always a cultural mosaic and . . . the birth of China was the outcome of the coalescence of various cultures created by the men of genius of many peoples" (Ho 1975: 351). Ho goes on to distinguish three major elements in the mosaic. The main one is identified as "proto-Chinese," of "the 'Southern Mongoloid' racial family," Sinitic speakers separated only by dialectical differences. The two minor elements in the mix are "the proto-Turcic Jung and Ti and the proto-Tungusic Mountain Jung" (ibid.). Not only does Ho attach racial labels, he also ascribes tribal status to the various populations concerned: "By Chou times, the Ch'iang people were relatively quiet and had probably been driven west by various tribes belonging to two ethnic groups generically referred to as the Jung and the Ti . . . Some of the Jung and Ti tribes formed enclaves within the Chou domain" (p. 345).

The tribal unit is generally ascribed by Ho to Neolithic social organization in the Chinese area: "We know [nothing] specific about units of social and territorial organizations larger than kinship groups and village communities. We can only infer from the following that larger tribal and territorial organizations probably did exist in Yang-shao times" (p. 279). Ho speaks of "interlocal and intertribal 'trade' and barter, which in turn would imply limited agreements among the chiefdoms" (ibid.). Such a remark reflects the easy equation of tribe and chiefdom but also includes some sweeping assumptions about the nature of economic exchanges in pre-state society. Is there any reason why such circulation of goods as can be deduced from archaeological evidence pertaining to the pre-state period cannot be attributed to the activity of kinship networks, both consanguineal and affinal, intermittently linking villages not otherwise affiliated in tribal terms? At any rate, Ho is among those who see the Chinese state emerging from a tribal past. He does not hesitate, therefore, to speak of "the Shang, the Chou and the Ch'in tribes" (p. 275).

Against this background of the use of the concept of tribe, let us now come to grips with Chinese interpretations of the emergence of the state in what is presently China.

TRIBE TO STATE OR STATE TO TRIBE IN
ANCIENT CHINA?

Introducing his own solution to the riddle of the genesis of inequality, Rousseau comments, "what is still more cruel, as every advance made by the human species serves only to remove it still further from its primitive condition, the more we accumulate new knowledge, the more we deprive ourselves of the means of acquiring the most important of all" (1967:168). Hyperbole, perhaps, but the point is relevant to this chapter. The search for the nature of societies existing totally in the absence of encroaching states has often provided chimerical images, curious institutional collages that may bear little resemblance to the originals they are supposed to portray, "like the statue of Glaucus which time and sea and storms had so much disfigured that it resembled a wild beast more than a god" (ibid., p. 167), to return to Rousseauian metaphor.

In fact, it is impossible to adjudicate the present dispute by the evidence at hand, or by methods currently in use, including those associated with the "new archaeology." Although this flat statement may be distressing it is not pessimistic. Books like the present volume are predicated more upon the lacunae in our command of our subject matter than upon our achievements. We seek to reduce the gaps by critically pooling our knowledge and ideas; were the gaps all filled, we would lose our purpose. We need have no fear—the gaps we contemplate are far from filled. On the other hand, consider, as did Chang Kwang-chih in his third edition of *The Archaeology of Ancient China*, the truly remarkable strides accomplished in just half a century: "It is already clear that archaeology since 1920 has given us a new version of ancient China that was surely beyond imagination a mere fifty-six years ago" (1977:478). One facet of change emphasized by Chang relates to the areal nature of indigenous Chinese cultural origins. On one side, although he favors the likelihood that Chinese culture was essentially an East Asian product in roots and development (as opposed to theories placing weight upon diffusion from outside the greater Chinese area), he admits that he sees few specific continuities between Paleolithic and Neolithic horizons in the region. I am less interested in that than in his subsequent assertion, that he has been forced by accumulating evidence to change his mind. Where he formerly thought "Chinese culture began only in the nuclear area of North China, whence it gradually radiated outward to absorb the non-Chinese cultures on its peripheries," he now sees it differently:

> we are compelled to see that cultural continuities extend into more than the
> nuclear area of North China. The Ch'ing-lien-kang and related cultures of the

Pacific seaboard may have been derived, at least in part, from the nuclear-area tradition, but even if they were not, they were obviously ancestral to the historical Chinese civilization, and they were as much Chinese as the Yang Shao (ibid., p. 480).

Let us reflect for a moment on this specific utterance. What was Yang-shao in its own time: a particular simple Neolithic village, a "tribe" aggregated of more or less comparable villages, a culture area? It is quite evident that the time is long past, if it ever existed, when Yang-shao was considered a particular village; from its discovery it has always stood for a large territorial expanse, many different communities, and even a certain variation in culture. Again taking Chang's lead, let it be noted that

the temporal and historical relationship between the Pan-p'o and Miao-ti-kou phases of the Yang-shao culture has been a focus of archaeological debate. Some believe Pan-p'o is the earlier of the two; others insist it is the later. Shih Hsing-pang and Su Ping-ch'i are both convinced, however, that these phases represent two parallel and contemporaneous "tribal groups" (pp. 122, 125).

My attention is drawn, of course, to the reference to "tribal groups." Indeed, the originals cited by Chang (Shih 1962; Su 1965) speak of *pu-lo*, but they do not use quotation marks to indicate less than full acceptance of the concept of the tribe; furthermore, they use the term *pu-lo* sparingly. From my limited reading on the subject it seems that Chinese usage of the tribal concept expanded after 1975. The usage in question, however, is limited to discussions of ancient sociopolitical organization and is not applied to modern units; variations on "minority" are used for those purposes.

References to tribe or tribal society are specifically couched in terms of the evolution of social stratification and the state. The usage is linked to passages from Marxist classics, particularly Engels' *Der Ursprung der Familie: Privateigentums und die Staat* and *Anti-Dühring*. Both these works are cited, for example, by T'ung Chu-ch'en (1975). A critical passage quotes from *The Origin of the Family*: " . . . slavery, at first only of prisoners of war but already preparing the way for the enslavement of fellow members of the tribe and even of the gens" (Engels 1972:169). In Chinese, the translation is *shih-tsu* for gens and *pu-lo* for tribe (T'ung 1975:219), as expected from our previous remarks. The Engels quotation comes hard on the heels of one of the most Hobbesian utterances in the Marxist literature: "Outside the tribe was outside the law. Wherever there was not an explicit treaty of peace, tribe was at war with tribe, and war was waged with the cruelty which distinguishes man from other animals" (Engels 1972:160). This does not appear in the Chinese work, but the emphasis on intertribal warfare as an agent in the rise of the state is made explicit in more recent Chinese publications.

In one of these—the pamphlet *Chung-kuo yüan-shih she-hui*, issued by the Pan-p'o Museum—tribalism as a phenomenon of primitive Chinese society is taken back to at least upper Paleolithic times (Shen-hsi-sheng 1977:29). This is not surprising, since the rudiments of the clan system are located in the lower Paleolithic (ibid., p. 3), with matriliny and mother right dating to about forty thousand or fifty thousand years ago (p. 22). The genesis of the tribe is said to lie in the expansion and development of the matri-clan, which becomes either a *pao-tsu* 胞族 (a "womb-clan," that is, matri-clan, but probably better rendered as a predatory segmentary clan) or a *pu-lo*, "tribe" (p. 29). In any case, the tribal village (*pu-lo ts'un-chuang* 部落村庄) is believed to be the product of the development of clans (p. 43). The tribe is a common interest group that shares a settlement area, has its own chief (*shou-ling* 首領) and council (*min-chu yi-shih hui* 民主議事會), common activities and festivals, and is the unit of peaceful cooperation (*ho-p'ing hsiang-ch'u* 和平相處) (p. 55). But the tribe, in turn, largely as a result of the rapacity of its chieftain and elite (*hsien-kuei* 顯貴), is constantly fighting wars and raiding for booty: this brings into being the tribal confederacy (*pu-lo lien-meng* 部落聯盟) (p. 102).

In another pamphlet, Hsia is identified as a tribe comprising more than ten segments, with each subunit identified as a "clan-tribe" (*shih-tsu pu-lo* 氏族部落) (Ku 1975:4). All are described as "closely related" and as forming a tribal confederation. The original leader of the Hsia confederacy, Yü, was chosen by the tribes but instituted the system of succession by sons. According to Ku, Shang and Chou also had tribal beginnings.

To a considerable extent, the remarks of Ku parallel those of Creel, cited earlier. The acceptance of the idea of a tribal past from which state organization emerges is nearly universal, and it cross-cuts one of the major boundaries of current intellectual life, that between Marxists and non-Marxists. What is more, the past decade of Chinese work has seen extensive interdigitation of the archaeological record with the theory. Does this mean that the querying of the commonly held belief that tribe is a stage en route to state is quixotic at best?

Obviously I think not. There are substantial reasons for holding the opposite view and even better ones for agnosticism. To begin with, despite my reference to the attempts of the Chinese to weave archaeological data into the argument, this is done with varying degrees of success. Even in the area in which their arguments are most impressive there are difficulties arising from the unquestioning acceptance of early pronouncements of

Marx and Engels. There are frequent assertions of the critical importance of the emergence of private property in which varieties of burial in different Neolithic sites are offered to express evolutionary differences in the formation of private property. Not faced are the problems of the differences between rank and stratification and, following this, the very real problem for archaeologists of differentiating between grave goods that express ceremonial rank as contrasted with indications of wealth associated with differential access to strategic resources, that is, stratification—using these two terms, rank and stratification, as distinguished earlier in this chapter.

Indeed, there may be a way to do this, or at least to throw light on the problem: by very careful osteological analysis of the human remains found at sites of uncertain attribution vis-à-vis ranking/stratification. This has been attempted in the New World, for instance, at Tikal, a Maya site, where Havilland (1967) discovered that skeletons found in tombs were significantly taller than those in the same site but not entombed, possibly indicating a superior diet for the former in the period of individual growth. Analysis of a comparable kind has been done in China. A study of human dentition from Shang tombs in An-yang has revealed differences between those given high-status burials and those sacrificed at the grave. The latter may have suffered malnutrition (Mao and Yen 1959; Chang 1976:55). Unfortunately, such work has not been a matter of course since the 1950s. Freeman (1977:90), speaking on the basis of personal observations and conversations in the People's Republic of China in 1975, complains about "the policy of discarding most human skeletal material after excavation."

The complex of problems that attend archaeological investigations of state origins is very serious, but it can be overcome, at least in part, by new archaeological techniques, especially those associated with extensive as well as intensive methods. (For the former, see Streuver 1979; for the latter, see Rathje 1970; Peebles and Kus 1977. For an overview of the situation in archaeology see Haas 1979.) There remains at least one other approach, that which synthesizes whatever historical materials may be available.

For example, K. C. Chang (ch. 16 below) quotes a passage from the work of Fu Ssu-nien (1935:1112, 1117) putting forth the opinion that Hsia shared its environment with various "Yi" tribes which he identifies as Ta Hao 大皞, Shao Hao 少皞, Yu Chi 有濟, and Hsü Fang 徐方. Finding that the Shang were not of Yi ethnicity, Fu asserts that Shang indeed absorbed many aspects of Yi culture and received the help of the Yi people in their conquest of Hsia. There is much of interest in Fu's theory. There is an implication that the Yi people were organized at a reasonable level of complexity—perhaps as worthy of the designation "state" as Hsia or

Shang. If not, their tribal existence is perhaps a consequence of the kinds of interaction to which they were party, involving military and other types of engagement with state-organized societies.

Of course, the existence of the Hsia is not yet verified; much less is anything known of its political structure. Nonetheless, it is significant that such a scholar as Chang seems quite convinced, not only that there was a Hsia state, but that it may have been to some extent contemporary with Shang and perhaps even Chou. The question of the existence of Hsia as a political entity aside, our view of the state/tribe nexus in the political evolution of China requires radical reinterpretation. This is a reaction to the discovery of the Ch'ing-lien-kang culture and the re-evaluation of what used to be the Sheng-wen horizon, now referred to as Ta-p'en-k'eng. What these newer interpretations mean to me is that the illusion of a monocentric emergence of the state in China must be abandoned.

The older interpretation of the rise of the Chinese state located that event somewhere in the north, most likely in modern Honan or nearby. In terms of figure 15.1, the "Hsia tribe" or the "Shang tribe" would have evolved into the first state and would have done so partly as a result of warfare with other discrete tribes of barbarians. But the results of archaeology undermine this interpretation. We are now more inclined to see Chinese culture evolving over a very broad area. Certainly that area includes the region south of the Huai river, for that is the area par excellence of the Ch'ing-lien-kang culture. It is also one of the areas singled out for attention in the *Shih-ching*—in the "Lu Sung," for example, where there are repeated mentions of the subduing of the Huai Yi 淮夷, for which the translation into English is usually "the tribes of the Huai" (as in Legge 1960:618, 620; see also his map, facing p. 127, showing the "Hwae hordes.") Of particular interest are the sixth and seventh stanzas of the fourth ode (Mao 300) of the "Lu Sung" (ibid., pp. 627–628):

> The mountain of T'ae is lofty,
> Looked up to by the State of Loo.
> We grandly possess also Kwei and Mung;
> And we shall extend to the limits of the east,
> Even the States along the sea.
> The tribes of the Hwae will seek our alliance:—
> All will proffer their allegiance:—
> Such shall be the achievements of the marquis of Loo.

> He shall maintain the possession of Hoo and Yih,
> And extend his sway to the regions of Seu,
> Even to the States along the sea.
> The tribes of the Hwae, the Man, and the Mih,
> And those tribes [still more] to the south,

> All will proffer their allegiance:—
> Not one will dare not answer to his call,
> Thus showing their obedience to the marquis of Loo.

We are struck by this seeming stew of tribes (represented in the Chinese text by the character Yi 夷) and states (represented by *pang* 邦). How to explain this concatenation?

Contrary to the argument of this paper, previous scholars have made or accepted the almost automatic assumption that tribes have been in existence from time immemorial. From this assumption flows the view that where states and civilizations emerged and spread, these new expanding forms of society would encroach upon the pre-existing tribes in their hinterland, ultimately over-running and incorporating them. Another scenario exists which supplements the foregoing. Tribes living elsewhere are attracted by the potential spoils of civilization, migrate toward them, and sometimes manage to capture the ruling power of the state. This is a familiar story throughout Chinese history and has also occurred elsewhere, as in the Aztec conquest of the Valley of Mexico. The question, however, remains: Was the non-state society organized as a *tribe* prior to its contact with an already organized state? Perhaps an answer lies in Legge's commentary to the ode "Yin wu" (Mao 305) (Legge 1960:644). Glossing these lines,

> Even from the Këang of Te,
> They dared not but come with their offerings;
> [Their chiefs] dared not but come to seek acknowledgement:—
> Such is the regular rule of Shang,

this explanation is provided by Legge:

> This was the rule laid down anciently for the chiefs of the wild tribes, which lay beyond the nine provinces of the kingdom. Every chief once in his time was required to present himself at court. The rule, in normal periods, was observed by a chief, immediately after he succeeded to the headship of his tribe (ibid., p. 645).

Undoubtedly the *Shih-ching* odes, even those which, like this one, purport to be among the oldest, were composed some time, probably a long time, after the earliest emergence of the state in the region. In that respect, it is like the ancient law codes found on the remains of tablets in Mesopotamia. Framed long after the onset of state polity, they are nonetheless a window on that ancient world, and they can be worked for clues to the process by which the state emerged (Fried 1978). I find the implications of the ancient lines quoted here intelligible in light of a theory that sees the chiefs of "wild tribes" as less the products of an indigenous political process than of installation by an external state. The original creation of such a chief would then be revalidated at appropriate intervals.

In the final analysis, interpretation of the origins of the Chinese state in terms of tribal origins is speculative and based more upon theory than upon hard data. In the current Chinese case, the dominating theory is closely related to that informing comparable efforts elsewhere in the world. All are Hobbesian, seeing the pre-state world in terms of tribal isolates separated by no-man's-lands in which most interactions were violent and brutal. Interestingly, this image is common to non-Marxists and Marxists alike. It may, however, be more of a projection of the antagonistic world that is so familiar to us than an accurate portrayal of the quality of intergroup social relations prior to the emergence of the state as an institution. The notion of the tribe is a historical one—it had a time of origin as a concept, and it has been ascendant for about 150 years. It is not particularly elegant and does not benefit from the action of Occam's Razor when compared with the simpler non-tribal scenario for the origin of the state suggested above. Perhaps this chapter will goad the reader into reviewing the assumptions upon which the notion of a Chinese antiquity filled with ancient, pristine tribes, leading to the emergence of the Chinese state, is based.

REFERENCES

Adams, Richard N.
   1975   *Energy and Structure.* Austin, Tex.

Berndt, Ronald M.
   1962   *Excess and Restraint: Social Control Among a New Guinea Mountain People.* Chicago.

Chagnon, Napoleon A.
   1968   "Yanomamo Social Organization and Warfare." In *War: The Anthropology of Armed Conflict and Aggression*, edited by Morton H. Fried, Robert F. Murphy, and Marvin Harris: pp. 109–159. Garden City, N.Y.

Chang, K. C. [Kwang-chih]
   1976   *Early Chinese Civilization: Anthropological Perspectives.* Cambridge, Mass.
   1977   *The Archaeology of Ancient China.* 3d ed., rev. and enl. New Haven.

Creel, Herrlee Glessner
1970   *The Origins of Statecraft in China*, vol. 1: *The Western Chou Empire*. Chicago.

Engels, Frederick
1892   *Der Ursprung der Familie: Privateigentums und die Staat.* 1884. Reprint, Stuttgart.
1972   *The Origin of the Family: Private Property and the State.* Edited and with an introduction by Eleanor Burke Leacock. New York.

Freeman, Leslie G., Jr.
1977   "Paleolithic Archaeology and Paleoanthropology in China." In *Paleoanthropology in the People's Republic of China*, edited by W. W. Howells and Patricia Jones Tsuchitani: pp. 79–113. Washington, D.C.

Fried, Morton H.
1960   "On the Evolution of Social Stratification and the State." In *Culture in History*, edited by Stanley Diamond: pp. 713–731. New York.
1968   "The State: The Institution." In *International Encyclopedia of the Social Sciences* 15:143–150. New York.
1976   *The Notion of Tribe*. Menlo Park, Ca.
1978   "The State, the Chicken and the Egg: Or, Which Came First?" In *Origins of the State: The Anthropology of Political Evolution*, edited by Ronald Cohen and Elman R. Service: pp. 35–47. Philadelphia.
1980   "A Continent Found, A Universe Lost." In *Theory and Practice: Essays presented to Gene Weltfish*, edited by Stanley Diamond: pp. 263–284. The Hague.

Fu Ssu-nien 傅斯年
1935   "Yi-hsia tung-hsi shuo 夷夏東西說." In *Ch'ing-chu Ts'ai Yüan-p'ei hsien-sheng liu-shih-wu sui lun-wen-chi, hsia ts'e* 慶祝蔡元培先生六十五歲論文集, 下冊: pp. 1093–1134. Peking.

Haas, Jonathan
1979   "The Evolution of the Prehistoric State: Toward an Archaeological Analysis of Political Organization." Ph.D. dissertation, Columbia University.

Havilland, William A.
1967   "Stature at Tikal, Guatemala: Implications for Ancient Maya Demography and Social Organization." *American Antiquity* 36:316–325.

Ho, Ping-ti
1975   *The Cradle of the East: An Inquiry into the Indigenous Origins of Techniques and Ideas of Neolithic and Early Historic China, 5000–1000 B.C.* Hong Kong and Chicago.

Ku Wei-ch'in 顧維勤
1975   *Ts'ung K'ao-ku ts'ai-liao k'an Shang-Chou nu-li she-hui ti chieh-chi ya-p'o* 從考古材料看商周奴隸社會的階級壓迫. Peking.

Lattimore, Owen
1940   *Inner Asian Frontiers of China.* American Geographical Society Research Series no. 21. New York.

Legge, James
1960   *The Chinese Classics*, vol. 4: *The She King.* 1872. Reprint, Hong Kong.

Mao, Hsieh-chün and Yen, Yen
1959   "Dental Condition of the Shang Dynasty Skulls Excavated from Anyang and Hui-xian." *Vertebrata Palasiatica* 3: 79–80.

Maspero, Sir Gaston C. C.
1878   *Histoire ancienne des peuples de l'Orient.* Paris.

Moret, Alexandre and Davy, Georges
1926   *From Tribe to Empire: Social Organization Among Primitives and in the Ancient East.* Translated by V. Gordon Childe. New York.

Peebles, Christopher, and Kus, Susan M.
1977   "Some Archaeological Correlates of Ranked Societies." *American Antiquity* 42: 521–548.

Rappaport, Roy A.
1968   *Pigs for the Ancestors: Ritual in the Ecology of a New Guinea People.* New Haven.

Rathje, William L.
1970   "Socio-Political Implications of Lowland Maya Burials: Methodology and Tentative Hypotheses." *World Archaeology* 1.3: 359–374.

Rousseau, Jean-Jacques
1967   *The Origin of Inequality and the Social Contract.* 1955. Reprint, New York.

Shen-hsi-sheng   Shen-hsi-sheng Hsi-an Pan-p'o po-wu-kuan
陝西省西安半坡博物舘
1977   *Chung-kuo yüan-shih she-hui* 中國原始社會. Peking.

Shih Hsing-pang 石興邦
1962   "Yu kuan Ma-chia-yao wen-hua ti yi-hsieh wen-t'i
有關馬家窰文化的一些問題." *KK* 1962.6 : 318–329.

Spencer, Herbert
1896   *The Principles of Sociology*, vols. 1–2. 1876. Reprint, New
York.
1967   *The Evolution of Society: Selections from Herbert
Spencer's Principles of Sociology*, edited by Robert
Carneiro. Chicago.

Streuver, Stuart
1979   *Koster: Americans in Search of Their Prehistoric Past.* New
York.

Su Ping-ch'i 蘇秉琦
1965   *Kuan-yü Yang-shao wen-hua ti jo-kan wen-t'i* 關於仰韶
文化的若干問題." *KKHP* 1965.1 : 51–82.

T'ung Chu-ch'en 佟柱臣
1975   "Ts'ung k'ao-ku ts'ai-liao shih-t'an wo kuo ti ssu-yu-chih
ho chieh-chi ch'i-yüan 從考古材料試探我國的私有制
和階級起源." *KK* 1975.4 : 213–227.

Turney-High, Harry Holbert
1949   *Primitive War: Its Practice and Concepts.* Columbia.

16

Sandai Archaeology and the Formation of States in Ancient China: Processual Aspects of the Origins of Chinese Civilization

K. C. CHANG

Sandai—the Three (*san*) Dynasties (*dai*), Hsia, Shang, and Chou—
evidently was a crucial period in the ancient history of China: in this period
written records began, the polities that eventually coalesced to form what
we know as China first formed, and the foundations of many customs and
institutions found throughout Chinese history were laid. Since the beginning of scientific archaeology in China in the early decades of this century,
many scholars have expected important contributions to the history of this
period. Some would go so far as to predict that perhaps the most important
contribution archaeology can make in China will be in connection with the
history of Sandai.

The tremendous progress of archaeological work during the past
decade or so in China has indeed led us to a crucial stage in the study of
Sandai history. We are still far from definitive conclusions about most of
the major issues, but I believe we are now at a stage where we can recognize
some of the new directions Sandai studies will be taking. One of the issues
worthy of pursuit that one sees emerging in the currently available data
pertains to the formation of states in ancient China. In my opinion, two
elements that have formed the cornerstone of our understanding of Sandai
history are due for a basic overhaul. These are, first, the emphasis on the

NOTE: Work on this chapter has been part of the research on Shang civilization supported
by a grant from the National Endowment for the Humanities. Portions of the chapter have
been published in Chang 1980:347–362.

495

vertical, successive relationship of the Three Dynasties and, second, the understanding of the developing sequence of the Three Dynasties as an island of civilization in a sea of barbarous contemporaries. Rethinking both old and new archaeological data has led me to conclude that these two views constitute important barriers to a true understanding of the ancient history of China. I am convinced that the horizontal interrelationship of the Three Dynasties was crucial to the formation process of the ancient Chinese states. Pertinent data in this area are, moreover, significant for the comparative study of state formation.

SANDAI INTERRELATIONSHIP IN WRITTEN CHINESE HISTORY

The "Sandai" was a concept that appeared as early as late Chou (*Meng-tzu* 3A.2: "The Sandai shared them [various mourning ceremonies] *san tai kung chih* 三代共之"). Since modern historiography emerged in China, many scholars have discussed the interrelationship of the Three Dynasties, but most have focused on cultural similarities and differences and the resultant issue of ethnic classification. What I emphasize here is, instead, the political interrelationship of Hsia, Shang, and Chou as three parallel or at least overlapping polities. Cultural classification and political classification are not necessarily identical, and both classifications can be considered. One can view the Sandai as follows: Hsia, Shang, and Chou were subcultures of a common—ancient Chinese—culture, but more particularly they were opposed political groups. Their horizontal rather than their sequential interrelationship is the key to understanding their development, and it is, thus, the key to understanding the formation process of ancient Chinese states. As Barnard (1960:488) pointed out more than twenty years ago, one must first of all "take into account the separate but concurrent nature of the so-called Three Dynasties."

Chronology

From the point of view of their relative political eminence, the Three Dynasties were successive: the Shang dynasty began when T'ang "overthrew" the Hsia, and the Chou dynasty began when Wu Wang "overthrew" the Shang. The durations of these two dynasties, according to the *Ku-pen Chu-shu chi-nien* (Fan 1962:17, 24), follow: "[The Hsia dynasty] from Yü 禹 to Chieh 桀 had seventeen kings . . . and lasted 471 years," and "[the Shang dynasty], from T'ang 湯's subjugation of Hsia to Shou 受, had twenty-nine kings and lasted 496 years."[1] The Chou 周 dynasty began with Wu Wang's conquest of King Chou 紂, an event traditionally dated to 1122 B.C.,[2] and ended with Ch'in's subjugation of the royal city in 256 B.C., totaling thirty-seven kings and 867 years. Altogether, the three dynasties lasted more than 1,800 years. But Hsia, Shang, and Chou were not merely three chronological segments. Shang was a powerful political entity prior to its subjugation of Hsia, and Chou was a powerful political entity prior to its subjugation of Shang. In other words, Hsia and Shang were two chronologically parallel—or at least overlapping—political groups, as were Shang and Chou.

For how long during the approximately five hundred years of the Hsia dynasty did Shang exist as a significant political entity? Another way of asking this is: How much did Shang overlap with Hsia during the latter's dynastic reign? According to myths and legends of late Chou and early Han (e.g., those recorded in the *Shih pen* 世本 and the *Ti hsi* 帝繫), Yü 禹, the founding ancestor of the Hsia dynasty, descended from Chuan Hsü 顓頊, a descendant of the Yellow Emperor; and Hsieh 契, founding ancestor of the ruling clan of the Shang dynasty, descended from Ti K'u 帝嚳, another descendant of the Yellow Emperor. The *Shih-chi* records that the ancestors of all three dynasties, Yü 禹, Hsieh 契, and Hou Chi 后稷, served in the royal courts of Ti Yao and Ti Shun. From these accounts, Hsia and Shang, at least, were two political groups with a parallel existence beginning with the Yellow Emperor. On the basis of more reliable data, however, one can say only that the Shang were able to claim a history of their own of considerable glory prior to their conquest of Hsia, a history now often referred to as that of the period of *hsien-kung hsien-wang* 先公先王 or predynastic lords and kings. In the *Shih-ching* ("Ch'ang fa," Mao 304) we read that

> The dark king valiantly ruled;
> The service of small states everywhere he received,
> The service of great States everywhere he received.
> . . . .
> Hsiang-t'u [相土] was very glorious;
> Beyond the seas he ruled.
>
> (Waley 1960:277)

---

1. See the detailed discussion on the various systems of chronology for the duration of the Shang dynasty in Tung 1945: pt. 1, *ch.* 4 ("Yin Chronology"). See Keightley 1978 for a generally skeptical view of the *Chu-shu chi-nien*'s value as a chronological source.

2. For various hypotheses concerning the year of the Wu Wang conquest, see Tung 1951a; 1951b; Chou 1971; Ho 1973. See too, ch. 17, n. 1, below.

The *Shih-chi* and other later texts record fourteen predynastic lords and kings. Ch'en Meng-chia contended that "perhaps the fourteen kings of Hsia were the same fourteen [predynastic] kings of Shang," and that "the so-called T'ang-Wu 湯武 Revolution was in fact only a struggle for power among kinsmen" (Ch'en 1936:491). It is doubtful that Hsia kings were in fact predynastic Shang kings, but Ch'en's contention suggests the possibility that the Shang political group co-existed with the Hsia dynasty throughout the latter's reign. Because of the extreme scarcity of Hsia texts, data which bear on Hsia's direct contact with Shang do not, however, become available until the period of Hsia's Chieh and Shang's T'ang. Nevertheless, according to Fu Ssu-nien, throughout their dynastic reign the Hsia were in constant conflict with eastern states that were Shang's allies.

> Prior to or during Shang and Western Chou periods, there was more than a single ethnic group living in the area that is now Shantung, eastern Honan, northern Kiangsu, the northeastern corner of Anhwei, and perhaps the coast of Hopei on the Gulf of Chihli, and, across the Gulf, the two sides of the Liaotung peninsula and Korea. Those that one can find in textual records included such tribal units as Ta Hao 大皞, Shao Hao 少皞, Yu Chi 有濟, and Hsü Fang 徐方 and such clan names as Feng 風, Ying 盈, and Yen 偃; all of them were referred to as Yi 夷 ... The major events during the Hsia dynasty were the conflicts with these Yi groups (Fu 1935:1112).

The Shang, in Fu's belief, "were not Yi themselves, but they at times dominated the Yi peoples, and they adopted the Yi culture and were supported by the Yi people in their conquest and subjugation of the Hsia. The conquest can thus be said to be an Yi triumph over the Hsia" (ibid., p. 1117). Insofar as the opposition between Yi and Hsia is concerned, Shang was evidently one of the Yi states, and it maintained a certain political status during the whole reign of Hsia.

For the Chou overlap with Shang during the latter's reign of approximately five hundred years, there are better data due to the more abundant textual material. In the older texts the most important information is provided by the *Shih-ching* ("Pi kung," Mao 300), which says

> Descendant of Hou Chi
> Was the Great King
> Who lived on the southern slopes of Mount Ch'i
> And began to trim the Shang.
> (Waley 1960:270)

The Chou's power is seen to rise during the reign of T'ai Wang 太王 (Great King) in the middle Wei river valley. It was during the reign of Chi Li 季歷, T'ai Wang's son, that, according to the *Ku-pen Chu-shu chi-nien*, major contacts and conflicts with the Shang began to take place:

Thirty-fourth year of King Wu Yi 武乙: Chi Li, King of Chou, brought his respects (Fan 1962:22);

Fourth Year of King Ta Ting 大丁: Chi, King of Chou, was appointed a Mu Shih 牧師 of Yin (Fan 1962:23);

King Wen Ting 文丁: The King had Chi Li killed (Fan 1962:23).

Chi Li's son, Wen Wang, was referred to as Ch'ang, the lord of the West, and his son Wu Wang undertook the conquest of Shang in the eleventh year of his reign. Chi Li appeared toward the end of Shang Wu Yi's reign, which makes T'ai Wang a contemporary of Wu Yi, who reigned during Period IV of Tung Tso-pin's oracle-inscription chronology. But the name Chou appeared in oracle-bone inscriptions as early as Period I during Wu Ting's reign, and throughout most of the An-yang period Chou appeared to be a subordinate state of Shang (Shima 1958:411; cf. "State Criteria," ch. 17 below)—although it appears that it was not until Periods IV and V, the reigns of Wu Yi, Wen Wu Ting, Ti Yi, and Ti Hsin of Shang and of T'ai Wang, Chi Li, Wen Wang, and Wu Wang of Chou, that Chou made a significant rise in power and began to have close encounters with the Shang court. On 1 November 1977 a Hsinhua News Agency dispatch reported the discovery of a batch of inscribed oracle bones, considered to date from Chou Wen Wang's reign, at Ching-tang 京當 People's Commune in Ch'i-shan-hsien, Shensi:

> On one piece of oracle shell, a ritual sacrifice to Wen Wu Ti Yi [father of Shang's Chou Wang 紂王], performed by Chou Wen Wang, was recorded. Another piece records the visit of the Shang King to Shensi . . . indicating Western Chou's subordinate relationship with Shang prior to Wu Wang's conquest.

To conclude: both new and old textual data indicate considerable temporal overlap between Hsia and Shang as political powers, and between Shang and Chou as well. In other words, Shang was among the states that existed during the period when Hsia was given supremacy in Chou texts, and Chou was among the states during the period when Shang was given supremacy. Conversely, Ch'i 杞, the direct descendant state of Hsia, was one of the states which existed during both the Shang and Chou dynasties, and the state of Sung 宋, Shang's postdynastic successor, was one of the states which existed during the Chou dynasty. The interrelationship of the Three Dynasties thus was not only one of sequential succession; it was also characterized by their parallel existence as contemporary states. In the context of North China as a whole, the latter must be viewed as the primary relationship, and the sequence of dynastic succession can be regarded as indicating changes in the relative power of the three states (cf. Barnard 1960).

Geography

The geographic dominion of the Three Dynasties, as plotted according to the locations of their capital cities, is generally agreed to have been as follows: Chou was in the west, Hsia in the middle, and Shang in the east. The Hsia, according to Ting Shan,

> began in the southwestern corner of what is now Shansi province. Moving south across the Huang Ho, they first stayed between Hsien-cheng and Mi-hsien, then lived in Lo-yang, and finally moved around in an area bounded to the east by Ch'en-liu in Honan and Kuan-ch'eng in Shantung, to the north by P'u-yang in Hopei [now in Honan], and to the west by eastern Shensi. Their wandering footsteps did not stray far from the course of the Huang Ho (1935:114).

The Hsia locations postulated by Fu Ssu-nien (1935:1111–1112), Hsü Hsü-sheng (1959), and Chao T'ieh-han (1965) do not substantially differ from this view.

The main area of Shang activities, as indicated by the location of the six royal capitals from T'ang to P'an Keng, centered in the following regions: "Po, near Shang-ch'iu, in the south; Ao and Hsing, on both sides of the Huang Ho near Cheng-chou, in the west; Hsiang and Yin, facing each other across the Wei river near An-yang, in the north; Yen, near Ch'ü-fu, in the east" (T'ang 1973:8; cf. Ch'ü 1965). The locations of the predynastic lords and kings of the Shang are impossible to determine. Fu Ssu-nien's view (1935:1106) "that since Hsiang-t'u's eastern capital was under Mount T'ai, his western regions may have reached the western banks of the Chi 濟 river; and since he 'ruled beyond the seas,' his sphere was the Gulf of Chihli" is certainly plausible.

The center of activity for the predynastic Chou has generally been placed in the Wei river valley of Shensi (e.g., Ting 1935:113; Ch'i 1946), but Ch'ien Mu (1931) believes that the Chou, before T'ai Wang and Wang Chi, lived in the Fen river valley of southern Shansi. This disagreement cannot yet be resolved (see Hsü Cho-yun 1968); but there is no question about the middle and lower Wei river valley near Ch'i-shan being the political center of the Chou since T'ai Wang's reign.

Judging from their respective central spheres of activity, Hsia, Shang, and Chou were clearly states with different geographic centers.[3]

3. This refers only to their centers of activity. The territorial definition of the three dynasties is a much more complex problem and cannot be discussed here. The territorial limits of the Hsia dynasty are essentially unknown; but it cannot include all the Nine Provinces described in the "Yü kung." For discussion of the territory directly ruled by the Shang royal house, see Shima 1958; Li 1959; Matsumaru 1963; compare ch. 17 below.

Culture and Society

The Hsia, Shang, and Chou shared the same culture and differed from one another only in matters of detail; such is the general agreement of scholars according to both old and new written records. In *Li chi* ("Li ch'i"), it is stated that "the regulations of the Three Dynasties are the same, and all the people followed them." In the *Lun-yü* ("Wei cheng"), Confucius is quoted as having said that "the Yin dynasty followed the regulations of the Hsia: wherein it took from or added to them may be known; the Chou dynasty followed the regulations of the Yin: wherein it took from or added to them may be known." Some ancient historians have stressed these "takings or addings," maintaining that the Hsia, Shang, and Chou were three different ethnic groups. Ting Shan, for example, basing his views on the differences in ritual practice among the Three Dynasties as recorded in the *Lun-yü*, *Meng-tzu*, *Chou li* ("K'ao kung chi"), and *Li chi*, concludes (1935) that Hsia culture was native to the Central Plains, that the Shang were a northeastern people affiliated with the Yen Po 燕亳 and Shan Jung 山戎, and that the Chou were a northwestern people related to the Jung 戎 and Ti 狄. This view stresses the differences of detail. But "peoples" are classificatory categories based on language and culture characteristics. We do not know the details of the Hsia language, but on the basis of the extant data on the Hsia we have no reason to speculate that it was any different from the language of the Shang or Chou. As to cultural classifications, they are often classifications of degree. To what extent cultures must differ for separate ethnic groups to be recognized is often a subjective judgment made to serve a specific purpose. As pointed out by Yen Yi-p'ing (1952: 394), the sacred trees used for the earth ritual were different among the Three Dynasties—pine for the Hsia, cypress for the Shang, and chestnut for the Chou—but all dynasties performed earth rituals and used sacred trees. Basing himself on broad similarities of culture rather than differences of detail, Yen concludes that Hsia, Shang, and Chou were variations of the same cultural tradition.

In social organization and levels of societal development, the Hsia, Shang, and Chou shared an important feature: lineages ruling from walled towns. The Hsia was a dynasty of the Ssu 姒 clan, the Shang of the Tzu 子 clan, and the Chou of the Chi 姬 clan. All were similarly ruled by dynastic groups within clans, although the Three Dynasties came from different clans. There were also some fundamental similarities in the royal succession rules; this I have discussed in some detail before (Chang 1963; 1973). The Shang kings were referred to posthumously by the ten celestial stems, which indicate the classification scheme of lineages within the ruling dynasty. Members of the ten lineage groups alternated on the throne between two moieties, a system identical with the so-called *chao-mu* system of the Western Chou. The latter had by Eastern Chou all but disappeared as the result of fundamental changes in the Chou society, and its details are no longer clear in extant Eastern Chou texts. Its nature can now be better understood because of our new understanding of the comparable system of the Shang. The Hsia system of succession to kingship is not now clear, but the Hsia also used the ten celestial stems for posthumous names (Yang 1960); and we have good reason to believe that the Hsia system resembles the Shang in important details (Chang 1973). The Hsia, therefore, very possibly also had a *chao-mu* system.

Not only did the Three Dynasties probably have the same system of kingship, but both the Shang and Chou, at least enfeoffed royal lineage members, an institution that cannot be discussed separately from the early history of walled towns in ancient China (Chang 1976a : 68–71). All three dynasties built walled towns. *Shih pen* credits Kun 鯀 with the first building of walled towns, suggesting the importance of this institution in Hsia history. Shang towns have been archaeologically established (in Cheng-chou and Huang-p'i). Chou town-building activities are vividly described in the *Shih-ching* (e.g., "Mien," Mao 237). All these point to a common level of societal development.

ARCHAEOLOGICAL MANIFESTATIONS OF THE SANDAI INTERRELATIONSHIP

The placement of Sandai cultures and history in the archaeological record can be seen as one of the crucial issues of contemporary Chinese archaeology.

For the three dynasties and cultures involved, the archaeology of the Chou has had the longest history, but the culture of the predynastic and Western Chou is, apart from its bronze vessels (many inscribed), the least well known. The fifty years of Shang archaeology, beginning in 1928 with the excavation at An-yang by the Academia Sinica, can be divided into several stages: the first began with the 1928 excavation; the second dawned with the discovery of the Shang town in Cheng-chou in 1950; the excavation of the Erh-li-t'ou site in Yen-shih in 1959 initiated the third; and the fourth can be said to have commenced with the publication of the Ta-wen-k'ou report and the discoveries of Shang sites in the Yangtze valley in the 1970s. As far as Hsia archaeology is concerned, we are still at the stage where we debate whether there is a Hsia culture in the existing archaeological data. My own view is that Hsia archaeology actually began in 1959 with

Hsü Ping-ch'ang's field trip in western Honan for the express purpose of looking for a Hsia-hsü, the ruins of the Hsia. But this is surely not the occasion for a detailed description of Sandai archaeology as it is known to date. The following discussion will be confined to the issue of the Sandai interrelationship from the point of view of available archaeological records.

The Question of Hsia in Chinese Archaeology

When Yang-shao culture was first brought to light in the 1920s, this new prehistoric culture was sometimes identified with the Hsia, whose legendary area of distribution more or less coincided with the known sphere of Yang-shao sites at that time (see, e.g., Hsü Chung-shu 1931). This hypothesis, however, has long since been abandoned in view of the increasingly greater antiquity ascribed to Yang-shao culture (5000–3000 B.C., according to available radiocarbon dates; see Hsia 1977:222), the much greater area of distribution of this culture than that attained by the Hsia, and the incongruence of Yang-shao society with known or presumed Hsia conditions.

Only writing can provide unquestionable identification of archaeological cultures with cultures and peoples known in historical texts—and the best example of such identification is, of course, provided by the oracle-bone inscriptions from Yin-hsü, near modern An-yang, in which we find names of kings and officials identical with, and genealogical relationships almost identical with, those recorded in the *Shih-chi*. When writing is not available, we can appeal to the time and space frames of the cultures concerned. Any archaeological culture (or cultures) that is found to be more or less confined within the geographical borders of the legendary Hsia and that can be dated to the several centuries before and after 2000 B.C. qualifies as a candidate for the Hsia. In the history of Chinese archaeology, the first years of the fifth decade of this century saw the beginning of a strong interest among Chinese archaeologists and ancient historians in a Hsia archaeology. The following comments in the 1962 synthesis of Chinese archaeology are noteworthy:

> Legendary accounts in the texts about the Hsia sphere of activity are important data for the exploration of Hsia culture. Such data point to two areas that were especially close to Hsia: one is the Lo-yang plain and the neighborhoods of Teng-feng and Yü-hsien in Honan, and the other is the middle and lower Fen river valley in southwestern Shansi. Both areas are associated with the legendary capital towns of the Hsia dynasty and with some important historical events.
> Pursuing the above-mentioned clues, we have, in the past several years undertaken extensive surveys and spot excavations in more than twenty counties

and towns in Honan (including Teng-feng, Yü-hsien, Yen-shih, Kung-hsien, Lo-yang, Cheng-chou, and San-men-hsia), as well as in the southwestern parts of Shansi. The results of these surveys and test excavations have disclosed the following facts: In the area of western Honan remains of three different cultures that were earlier than the Early Shang cultures [of Cheng-chou] have been widely found, namely, the Yang-shao culture, the "Honan Lung-shan culture," and culture of the Lo-ta-miao type. Among these three, the Yang-shao culture is located at the bottom stratigraphically, its age is the farthest removed from Early Shang culture, and the distribution of its sites has also far exceeded the sphere of activity of the Hsia dynasty in legendary accounts. With regard to the nature of the society of Yang-shao culture, it does not match the societal conditions of the Hsia dynasty in legendary accounts. For these reasons it cannot possibly be the Hsia dynasty culture. Honan Lung-shan culture is a late Neolithic culture; its area of distribution is relatively extensive, and it is as a rule directly overlaid by the early culture of the Shang dynasty, quite close to the Shang dynasty in age. In terms of the nature of society, Honan Lung-shan culture represents a society of patri-clans, in which the phenomena of poor-rich differentiation had appeared, and it thus resembles some of the legends pertaining to Hsia society. As to the cultural remains of the Lo-ta-miao type, our investigations have shown that stratigraphically they lie between the early culture of the Shang dynasty and Honan Lung-shan culture, corresponding in age possibly to Late Hsia. Therefore, the above-mentioned two cultures deserve our attention in the exploration of Hsia culture.

Remains of the Lo-ta-miao type culture were first discovered in 1956 at Lo-ta-miao, Cheng-chou. Subsequent surveys in a wide area indicate that this kind of cultural remains occurs extensively in the environs of western Honan . . . Whether the Lo-ta-miao type culture was a part of Hsia culture, or whether it was a part of Shang culture of the predynastic lords and kings period, has not yet been generally agreed upon by archaeologists. Some archaeologists believe that the Lo-ta-miao type culture itself could be further subdivided, with its upper strata, which are closer to the Early Shang culture, being of Shang culture before the Early Shang, and its lower strata, which are closer to the Honan Lung-shan culture, being of Hsia culture. Other archaeologists believe that the absolute age of this culture cannot yet be determined and that it has a greater number of Shang culture characteristics, and they believe that the lower strata of the Lo-ta-miao type culture were still part of Shang culture, and that only the earlier Honan Lung-shan culture can be Hsia culture (CKKH 1962b:43–45).

In the decade and a half since the above was published, the Lo-ta-miao type culture has become much better known at the Erh-li-t'ou site in Yen-shih, resulting in a change of the name of the culture to the Erh-li-t'ou type culture or Early Shang. (The Early Shang in the above-quoted passage has now become Middle Shang.) Because Yen-shih has traditionally been regarded as one of the possible locations of Po, Shang's earliest dynastic capital, and because Erh-li-t'ou pottery is typologically intermediate between the pottery of the Honan Lung-shan culture and that of the later Shang culture in Cheng-chou and An-yang, many scholars appear to have gradually inclined toward the view equating Erh-li-t'ou culture with Early

Shang rather than with Hsia. In the 1965 report of an investigation at Erh-li-t'ou we find the observation that "the possibility is great that the Erh-li-t'ou site was the capital city of T'ang of Shang, Hsi Po" (*KK* 1965.5:224). In the 1974 report of the remains of a palatial structure (*KK* 1974.4:248) and the 1975 report of excavations of sections 3 and 8 of Erh-li-t'ou (*KK* 1975.5:308), the authors stated their further belief that new archaeological data have strengthened the identification of Erh-li-t'ou with Po, T'ang's capital. Thus, the Erh-li-t'ou site typifies an Early Shang site, the Shang city at Cheng-chou typifies a Middle Shang site, and Yin-hsü at An-yang typifies a Late Shang site. These three sites are now regarded as constituting the whole sequence of Shang archaeology.

But the judgment of Erh-li-t'ou culture as part of Hsia or as Early Shang must still be based on the fundamental evidence of time and space. In space, Erh-li-t'ou culture is seen

> in Yen-shih at Hui-tsui as well as Erh-li-t'ou, in Lo-yang at Tung-kan-kou, in Kung-hsien at Shao-ch'ai, in Cheng-chou at Lo-ta-miao, in Ying-yang at Ch'i-li-p'u, and dozens of other sites. Sites similar to those in western Honan are also found in southern Shansi . . . Noteworthy is the fact that the area of the geographical distribution of Erh-li-t'ou culture is precisely the area of activity of the Hsia people as given in texts—the area lined by the Yi 伊, the Lo 洛, the Huang Ho, and the Chi 濟 [rivers] (T'ung 1975b:29).

Four corrected radiocarbon dates from the Erh-li-t'ou site have been reported:

ZK–212	Erh-li-t'ou I	1906 ± 104 B.C.
ZK–285	Erh-li-t'ou I	1885 ± 104 B.C.
ZK–286	Erh-li-t'ou IV	1604 ± 101 B.C.
ZK–257	Erh-li-t'ou III	1429 ± 105 B.C.

The two Erh-li-t'ou I samples cluster together well and give a range of 1781–2010 B.C., which falls within the Hsia period. Erh-li-t'ou III represents the site's peak of development, having yielded a "palace" foundation, bronze vessels, and jades. The single sample from this stratum has yielded a chronological range of 1324–1534 B.C. This is the major basis for T'ung Chu-ch'en's opinion (1975b:30–32) that by Erh-li-t'ou III the site had been taken over by Shang and provided the location for their capital, Po. But the fourth sample (unavailable to T'ung at his writing), ZK–286 from Erh-li-t'ou IV, has yielded an earlier date and could fall within latest Hsia or earliest Shang. Either the stratum III sample or the stratum IV sample must be wrong. As Hsia Nai (1977:218) pointed out, "only a series of mutually consistent radiocarbon dates is of value, and one or two isolated samples, in and of themselves, are not particularly significant."

Since the four strata at Erh-li-t'ou represent a continuous development, there is a strong likelihood that Erh-li-t'ou III falls within the period 1781–1534, namely, in the gap between the first two and the third samples.

But these dates are not the only chronological grounds for placing the whole of the Erh-li-t'ou culture in the Hsia column (Chang 1976b). As just stated, the four strata of Erh-li-t'ou represent a continuous development, with level III marking its peak (*KK* 1965.5: 215–224; *KK* 1974.4: 234–248; *KK* 1975.5: 302–309). Chen-hsün 斟鄩, capital of the Hsia during the reign of its final king, Chieh, is identified by many highly respected advocates with the environs of Lo-yang (see the modern synthesis in Chao 1965). The identification of Erh-li-t'ou I and II with Hsia and Erh-li-t'ou III and IV with Hsia's terminal capital site would be consistent with the history of the Erh-li-t'ou site itself. The alternative view, which sees Erh-li-t'ou I and II as Hsia but III as beginning Shang, would call for a much greater degree of archaeological disconformity, due to a dynastic change, than is apparent at the site. In short, according to available data, the identification of Erh-li-t'ou culture as Hsia is consistent with the evidence of both time and space, although we will need many more radiocarbon dates, especially those associated with the remains of Erh-li-t'ou III and IV, before this identification can be firmly established.

Accepting for the time being the hypothesis that Erh-li-t'ou culture was indeed Hsia, what was its origin? Both from the point of view of pottery typology and from the standpoint of societal levels of development, the long-held view that the Honan Lung-shan culture was the predecessor of the Erh-li-t'ou culture is entirely consistent with the evidence. Although this culture is not yet fully known in archaeology, available data contain strong indications. The phalli of clay found at several sites of the Honan Lung-shan culture (Andersson 1943: pl. 30.1; 1947: pl. 31.3) are good evidence of the worship of male ancestors, and the practice of scapulimancy suggests the nature of the religious beliefs and political structure of the time. Wheel-made pottery points to highly specialized handicrafts (CKKH 1959: 92).

In the autumn of 1957, members of the Han-tan Archaeological Excavation Team of the Archaeology Program of Peking University brought to light a house foundation and two wells at a Lung-shan culture site at Chien-kou-ts'un in Han-tan, Hopei.

> Within the house foundation were found four human skulls with signs of blows and scalpings, apparently indicating that these victims were scalped after having been killed . . . The wells were first abandoned and then five layers of human skeletons, including both males and females and both old and young indi-

viduals, were buried in them, some having been decapitated and some showing postures of struggling. From these one postulates that some of the dead were murdered or were buried alive (*KK* 1959.10:531–532).

This is probable evidence of intervillage warfare, indicating that by the time of the Honan Lung-shan culture the society had reached a stage of "penal code internally and armed forces externally" (the *Shang-chün shu's* characterization of Huang Ti), laying a foundation for Hsia civilization of the Erh-li-t'ou type. The earthen wall found encircling the Lung-shan culture site at Hou-kang, An-yang (Shih Chang-ju 1947), points in the same direction.

Even though a Honan Lung-shan culture/Erh-li-t'ou development is a reasonable hypothesis, the origins of a few important new cultural traits of the Erh-li-t'ou culture must still be further studied. The most important of these is, of course, bronze vessels. Four bronze vessels have been brought to light thus far from Erh-li-t'ou III; their manufacture exhibits primitive features and they are all undecorated, but they certainly cannot pass as evidence of a bronze technology in its infancy. We expect that more bronzes will be found not only at a good many additional Erh-li-t'ou sites but also at Honan Lung-shan sites. Another issue of importance that awaits further research concerns the early history of the Erh-li-t'ou III ceramic inscriptions and their exact position in the history of Chinese writing (see ch. 12, item 15, above). If indeed the palace remains at Erh-li-t'ou had anything to do with the Hsia capital under Chieh, we can certainly expect future discoveries of other Hsia capital sites within the confines of the Erh-li-t'ou culture area. The archaeology of the Hsia has only just begun.

"Early Shang" in Shang Archaeology

From the time of the first discovery and excavation of Yin-hsü, at An-yang, to 1950, when the Shang city at Cheng-chou was brought to light, one of the major issues of Shang archaeology has been the question of the origins of the mature civilization of Yin-hsü. When the Shang city at Cheng-chou was discovered, this question was answered in part: Shang civilization was pushed back from "Late Shang" to "Middle Shang"; Middle Shang civilization, as represented by the remains at the Erh-li-kang site in Cheng-chou, was evidently a step closer to the ancestral Lung-shan culture. Middle Shang culture, after close to thirty additional years of discovery and study, is now shown to be found throughout northern and central China, from near Peking in Hopei (*WW* 1977.11) to Kiangsi south of the Yangtze (Chiang-hsi-sheng, Pei-ching ta-hsüeh, and Ch'ing-chiang-hsien 1975). The Middle Shang civilization found in so vast an area obviously manifests the accomplishments of people that belonged to more than a single political unit. The precise territorial limits of the state under Shang dynastic rule is an important problem, but it lies beyond the scope of this paper. The locations of the royal capitals during the Middle Shang period are another important issue. Among the capital towns prior to Yin in An-yang, two are thought to have been in the area of Cheng-chou, namely, Ao and Hsing. The Shang town that has been found archaeologically in Cheng-chou is generally considered identifiable with Ao (An 1961: 73, e.g.).

Can Middle Shang be pushed back further in time? The first Shang dynasty capital, just prior to Ao, was Po 亳. Other than Yin (An-Yang), Po served the longest as royal capital. Where was Po located? Many localities in North China have Po as part of their names, but there is virtual unanimity among scholars that T'ang's Po is located south of Shang-ch'iu in southeastern Honan and north of Po-hsien in northwestern Anhwei (Fu 1935: 1103–1104; Tung 1945; pt. 2, *ch.* 9: 62; Tung 1953; Chao 1965). Many scholars also believe that remains from the earliest segments of the dynastic period of the Shang will be found here. In fact, before the Sino-Japanese War, Li Ching-tan of the Institute of History and Philology, Academia Sinica, went to this area to carry out an archaeological survey precisely for the purpose of locating earlier Shang sites, but he was unsuccessful (Li 1947).

Hsü Hsü-sheng's 1959 expedition to western Honan was undertaken with the goal of finding Hsia ruins, but when he found the Erh-li-t'ou site he immediately identified it with Po, T'ang's capital, basing his identification on the traditional belief that Yen-shih was the location of Hsi (western) Po. But this conclusion was really prompted by a historical accident: sites with similar cultures were first found at Lo-ta-miao in Cheng-chou, where they were regarded as representing an early phase of the Shang. With this preconception, when Hsü and his colleagues saw similar remains at Erh-li-t'ou they referred to them without the slightest hesitation as Early Shang. Hsü stated in his report: "Erh-li-t'ou is nine kilometers west-southwest of Yen-shih . . . Remains here are similar in nature to the remains of Lo-ta-miao of Cheng-chou and Tung-kan-kou of Lo-yang, and are probably Early Shang" (Hsü 1959: 598). Because of this preconception, Hsü and his colleagues, having set out to find the ruins of Hsia, were unable to recognize them when they did find them! They then had to attempt to explain why such a large Shang site should be found in Hsia territory:

> The identification of Yen-shih as the capital of T'ang of Shang was probably made for the first time by Pan Ku in his commentary under the entry for Yen-

shih-hsien, Ho-nan-chün, in the "Ti li chih" chapter of the *Han shu*: "Shih-hsiang, Yin T'ang's capital" . . . Prior to this trip, Hsü Hsü-sheng was rather skeptical of the western Po hypothesis, but he could not completely ignore it because it had been the view of a person of Han times. Because the *Yen-shih chih* (a Ch'ien-lung period compilation) contains clear information about its exact location, we thought we might on this trip check into its validity. Now we have seen this site, which is huge, although we did not attempt to delineate its borders. If what the natives told us [as to its vast area] turns out to be true, it must have been a major city, with a good chance of being the capital city of T'ang of Shang (Hsü 1959 : 598–600).

This is a good example of how presumptions can lead unsuspecting archaeologists astray. But if what I maintained above—that the Erh-li-t'ou site was a Hsia, not a Shang capital—proves true, then this whole Erh-li-t'ou culture must be eliminated from Shang history, and Early Shang sites still remain to be identified.

At the time of the discovery of the Lung-shan culture at Ch'eng-tzu-yai in Shantung, Chinese archaeologists believed that this new culture, with its rammed earth village wall, pottery inscriptions, and oracle bones, which were probable antecedents of similar items in Shang civilization, was directly ancestral to the Shang (e.g., Li Chi 1934: xv–xvi). Afterward, Lung-shan sites were also found in Honan, together with more rammed village walls and scapulimancy; pottery inscriptions have now been found in the even earlier Yang-shao culture sites in Pan-p'o and Chiang-chai in the lower Wei river valley of Shensi. Therefore, when Shang civilization was pushed back from middle Shang to the Honan Lung-shan culture, through the Erh-li-t'ou type, no question was raised about the eligibility of the Honan Lung-shan culture as the Shang's ancestor. But if Erh-li-t'ou is in fact Hsia, not Shang—even though Middle Shang elements could still include items handed down from the Honan Lung-shan and the Erh-li-t'ou cultures (in view of the fact that "the Yin followed the rituals of the Hsia" [*Lun-yü* 2.23])—the question of whether there are elements in Middle and Late Shang directly derived from the east once more becomes highly pertinent.

Any renewed effort to examine the relation of Shang civilization to the prehistorical cultures of the eastern coast will inevitably direct our attention to two points in particular: (1) cultural items shared by the Shang and the coastal Neolithic culture but lacking or rare in the Honan Lung-shan culture, and (2) the question of whether the eastern coastal prehistoric cultures provided both the societal and technological background for the emergence of the Shang state. It will prove fruitful to include in our inquiry both the Ta-wen-k'ou culture, found mostly in the past decade or so and shown to be earlier than the Shantung Lung-shan, and the Lung-shan culture. Regarding the nature of the societal background, several essays published in the past two or three years discussing the nature of Ta-wen-k'ou society agree on the following points: it consisted of rich and poor components (judging from the amount and nature of the furnishings of individual graves); there was specialization of the ceramic industry (wheeled pottery); and marriages were probably monogamous (there were graves with man-woman pairs) (T'ung 1975a; Wei 1975; Chang and Hsü 1976; Chung 1976; Shih Hsin 1975; Shan and Shih 1976; Yü Chung-han 1976; Lu 1976). By Shantung Lung-shan times, additional new cultural elements—scapulimancy, more and better wheel-made pottery, and metal objects[4]—indicate an even higher level of societal and technological development, certainly appropriate to the rise of the Shang state.

As for Shang/east coast cultural connections, in a recent article (Chang 1976b) I listed the following cultural traits and complexes as having been shared by them:

(a) very rich grave furnishings
(b) wooden burial chambers and the second-level platform
(c) use of turtle shells
(d) certain ceramic types and modes, including white pottery
(e) bone spatulas, bone carvings, turquoise inlays, and certain decorative art designs

I refer the reader to my earlier work for detailed description and discussion of these shared features. In addition, I have noticed that there is good evidence, in both the Ta-wen-k'ou culture (Shan-tung-sheng and Chi-nan-shih 1974:12; Han, Lu, and Chang 1974: pl. 3) and the Shantung Lung-shan culture (Kanaseki 1960), for the custom of tooth extraction. According to Kanaseki, tooth extraction has also been found on one Shang skull from An-yang. This is surely one item—among others—worth pursuing. But in any event, "most of the above items had to do with the religion, ritual life, and art of the ruling class" (Chang 1976b:165). This seems to imply that the rulers of the Shang dynasty could have been a political group, and a conquering one, from the east. The implication certainly accords with the legendary beginnings of the Shang dynasty in the east, and it explains very simply the fact that Middle and Late Shang cultures contained elements attributable to both the Honan and the Shantung Lung-shan cultures. In short, the predynastic, early lords/early

---

4. At least two Shantung Lung-shan culture sites have yielded metal objects: Ta-ch'eng-shan, in T'ang-shan, where two copper plates were recovered (Ho-pei-sheng 1959; K'ang 1960), and San-li-ho, in Chiao-hsien, Shantung, which recently yielded two "awl-like" metal objects (Ch'ang-wei and K'ao-ku 1977:266).

kings period of Shang history probably overlaps at least in part with the prehistoric cultures of the eastern coastal areas of North China, and an Early Shang period in Shang archaeology must be postulated for the final stages of the predynastic Shang history and for the early centuries of the Shang dynasty, which we locate in the area of easternmost Honan, western Shantung, and northwestern Anhwei.

> This area has been part of the famous Huang Ho flood region throughout Chinese history, and it has been on the old course of the Huang Ho itself. Ancient remains in the area must be buried deep under the silts deposited during many centuries. For this reason alone, in the archaeology of North China this area—east of K'ai-feng and west of the Grand Canal—has been the most barren in yielding cultural remains. I believe if a real Early Shang can be found here in the future, it will be a culture that, on one hand, bears some fundamental similarities to Hsia culture of the Erh-li-t'ou type and one that, on the other hand, constitutes an intermediate phase between the Ta-wen-k'ou and Lung-shan cultures and the later phases of Shang civilization. Later Shang civilization can thus be said to result from an intermixture of both Eastern and Western cultures" (Chang 1976b: 168–169).

Chou Archaeology Before the Conquest

The pertinent issue here in Chou archaeology concerns the nature of Chou society prior to Wu Wang's conquest of Shang. From the legendary founding of the Chou clan to the conquest, five (or six, in another account) capitals served the Chou ruling house: Yi, Pin, Ch'i, Feng, and Hao (Shih Chang-ju 1952; Ch'ü 1971). Feng and Hao are generally believed to have been located on the two banks of the Feng river near Sian, where they served as the capital seats of Wen Wang and Wu Wang. Ch'i, located in the Chou Plain (Chou Yüan) under Mount Ch'i as described in the *Shih-ching*, to which T'ai Wang moved under pressure from the Ti (according to the *Meng-tzu*, "Liang Hui Wang, hsia"), served as the capital city of T'ai Wang, Wang Chi (Chi Li), and Wen Wang. The newly discovered Wen Wang period inscribed bones and shells mentioned above may testify that Chou was then a subordinate state of the Shang dynasty. The archaeological work here has not yet been described, but it is understood that remains of a "palace" as well as inscribed bones and shells have come to light at Ching-tang. There has been considerable archaeological work undertaken at the sites of Feng and Hao, but remains that can definitely be dated to the preconquest period are rare. Some of the early Western Chou residential remains at the site of Chang-chia-p'o on the west bank of the Feng river are regarded as "possibly having begun to accumulate since the time when Wen Wang built the town of Feng" (CKKH 1962a : 74). Among the early remains at Chang-chia-p'o are bronze artifacts. In 1976 a group of Western

Chou bronze vessels was found on the terrace of the Ling river northeast of
Lin-t'ung, Shensi, among them a *kuei* vessel with an inscription of thirty-
two characters on the inside bottom. The inscription records that "Wu
Wang conquered Shang, in the morning of the day chia-tzu," and it also
states that the vessel was cast following an event that took place on day
hsin-wei, the eighth day after the conquest (Lin-t'ung-hsien 1977:1–7;
T'ang 1977:8–9; Yü Hsing-wu 1977:10–12). This is the earliest existing
Western Chou vessel with a date that can be firmly tied to historical events,
and it proves beyond doubt that at the time of the conquest the Chou
people possessed a bronze technology and a literacy comparable to that of
the Shang. If the new discoveries at Chou Yüan include a palace, scapulimancy, and writing, then clearly this high level of Chou civilization had
been reached by the time the Chou had Ch'i as their ruling seat. How much
further back one can push these Chou cultural elements will depend on
future archaeological work.

Ultimately, however, Chou civilization is believed to have been derived
from the Shensi Lung-shan culture (or the K'o-hsing-chuang II culture).
Some of the burial patterns of this culture (vertical earthen pit-graves as the
rule, with scattered skeletons in storage pits as a variation) may indicate
the beginnings of the differentiation of social status (CKKH 1962a:8), and
its scapulimancy and wheel-made pottery again suggest some degree of
specialization in industry and religion. As with the other Lung-shan cultures, the Shensi variety is capable of providing the basis for a regional
civilization, in this case that of the Chou.

THE PROCESS OF SANDAI STATE FORMATION

This discussion should make it clear that the "insular model" of ancient
Chinese civilizational development that up to now has dominated our
thinking about ancient China—a model in which the Three Dynasties are
seen in sequential order as an island of civilization encircled by barbarous
cultures—is inadequate. Instead, contemporary Sandai archaeology
points to a parallel and interrelated development model for the origins of
Chinese civilization, one that sees a number of civilized states throughout a
large area of northern and central China and that views their formation as
parallel, interrelated, and interactive. The terms Hsia dynasty, Shang
dynasty, and Chou dynasty each have at least two meanings. First, they
refer to a time period, approximately 2200–1750 B.C. for Hsia, 1750–1100
B.C., for Shang, and 1100–220 B.C. for Chou. Second, they refer to a
dynastic reign. The rulers of the Hsia state were believed by late Chou and

subsequent historians to have been accorded supreme status by a number of states during the Hsia dynasty. During the Shang dynasty the Shang state's royal house was accorded that status; and during the Chou dynasty the Chou kings were believed to reign supreme. But at the same time, Hsia, Shang, and Chou were three polities or states, and their interrelationship was parallel: the three states were probably all in existence during all three dynasties, although their relative political powers had shifted. Table 16.1 makes clear the relationships of these various terms.

From a social evolutionary perspective, the formation of the Sandai civilizations can be analyzed according to the following significant stages:

(1) Level of village societies. In the Yang-shao and Ch'ing-lien-kang cultures, individual villages were the primary social unit politically and economically.

(2) Level of intervillage aggregates. At this level villages had developed political, economic, and military bonds that lead us to find the following phenomena in the archaeological record: the beginning of internal differentiation into poor and rich classes; evidence of internal and/or external violence; specialized handicrafts (such as pottery); the existence of religious specialists, probably in the exclusive service of the chieftain class. Under these conditions, intervillage leagues of a more or less permanent nature had formed, administered by full-time rulers. We classify the Shensi, Honan, and Shantung Lung-

TABLE 16.1 **Development model of the parallel and interrelated Sandai civilizations**

	Han			
200 B.C.	Ch'in			
Chou 1100				
Shang 1750	Chou	Hsia		Shang
Hsia 2200				
2500	Shensi Lung-shan culture	Honan Lung-shan culture		Shantung Lung-shan culture
3200	Miao-ti-kou II culture			Ta-wen-k'ou culture
5000	Yang-shao culture			Ch'ing-lien-kang culture

shan cultures at this level; the Ta-wen-k'ou (or Hua-t'ing) culture of the east coast may have reached this degree of development, but we are not certain yet of the classificatory status of the Miao-ti-kou II culture in the interior.

(3) Level of state societies. This is the period of Sandai in ancient Chinese history; archaeologically we refer to the Erh-li-t'ou culture and its contemporaries, Shang civilization, and Chou civilization. At this level, settlements formed complex and permanent networks (often stratified into several levels). The full-time rulerships of such networks became the monopoly of individual clans or lineages, and rulers were assisted by a relatively permanent control and administrative mechanism, including the mechanism to oppress with force, both internally and externally.

The earliest archaeological culture attributable to this last level is the Erh-li-t'ou culture of northwestern Honan. Among the Hsia's contemporary states the Shang was surely a most important one; it is believed that the Shang's earlier segments will be found in the general area of eastern Honan, western Shantung, and northernmost Anhwei. Many Shang sites from Middle Shang onward have been uncovered throughout northern and central China. These sites were not all under the rule of a single state; but of the many contemporary states within the area of distribution of Shang remains, the state of Shang was apparently the most powerful. We do not know exactly what the word "reigned" entailed in terms of the hierarchical relations of Shang with the other states during the Shang "dynasty." The reigning status undoubtedly involved political and ceremonial supremacy; there was probably a kind of tributary network, but whether this network had real economic—aside from ceremonial and symbolic—significance is as yet unclear. After Wu Wang's conquest, the reigning status shifted to Chou. After Chou the contending states were replaced by a higher form of state society, namely, the centralized bureaucratic government of the Ch'in and Han empires

Thus formulated, the evolutionary sequence of ancient Chinese societies may provide scholars of comparative social evolution with important new data. It also makes its own unique contribution. In the past decade or so, American anthropologists have shown increasing interest in theories of social evolution (e.g., Friedman 1975; Service 1962; 1975; Fried 1967), and a number of archaeologists have attempted to apply some of these theories to archaeological sequences in various parts of the world, focusing their attention particularly on the question of the origin of the state (e.g., Carneiro 1970; Flannery 1972; Sanders 1974; Sanders and Price 1968; Trigger 1976; Wright 1977). In such discussions, relatively few have utilized contemporary Chinese data. On the other hand, ancient Chinese historical issues have only rarely been approached from a general, comparative perspective. The time seems ripe for comparativists and Sinologists to join forces.

REFERENCES

An Chin-huai 安金槐
1961   "Shih-lun Cheng-chou Shang-tai ch'eng-chih—Ao-tu 試論鄭州商代城址一隞都." *WW* 1961.4/5:73–80.

Andersson, J. G.
1943   "Researches into the Prehistory of the Chinese." *BMFEA* 15:1–304.
1947   "Prehistoric Sites in Honan." *BMFEA* 19:1–124.

Barnard, Noel
1960   "[Book Review of] Chou Hung-hsiang, *Shang-Yin ti-wang pen-chi*." *Monumenta Serica* 19:486–515.

Carneiro, Robert L.
1970   "A Theory of the Origin of the State." *Science* 169:733–738.

Chang Ch'ing 張青 **and Hsü Yüan-pang** 徐元邦
1976   "Kuan-yü ssu-yu-chih ch'i-yüan ti t'an-t'ao—hsüeh-hsi En-ko-ssu 'Chia-t'ing, ssu-yu-chih ho kuo-chia ti ch'i-yüan' ti yi-tien t'i-hui 關於私有制起源的探討—學習恩格斯《家庭，私有制和國家的起源》的一點體會." *KK* 1976.3:161–164.

Chang Kwang-chih 張光直
1963   "Shang-wang miao-hao hsin-k'ao 商王廟號新考." *Chung-yang yen-chiu-yüan min-tsu-hsüeh yen-chiu-so chi-k'an* 中央研究院民族學研究所集刊 10:125–205.
1973   "T'an Wang Hai yü Yi Yin ti chi-jih ping tsai lun Yin-Shang wang chih 談王亥與伊尹的祭日並再論殷商王制." *Chung-yang yen-chiu-yüan min-tsu-hsüeh yen-chiu-so chi-k'an* 中央研究院民族學研究所集刊 35:111–127.
1976a   *Early Chinese Civilization: Anthropological Perspectives.* Cambridge, Mass.
1976b   "Yin-Shang wen-ming ch'i-yüan yen-chiu shang ti yi-ko kuan-chien wen-t'i 殷商文明起源研究上的一個關鍵問題." In *Shen Kang-po hsien-sheng pa-chih jung-ch'ing lun-wen chi* 沈剛伯先生八秩榮慶論文集: pp. 151–169. Taipei.

1980   *Shang Civilization*. New Haven.

Ch'ang-wei and K'ao-ku   Ch'ang-wei ti-ch'ü yi-shu-kuan
            昌維地區藝術舘 and K'ao-ku yen-chiu-so Shan-tung tui
            考古研究所山東隊.
1977   "Shan-tung Chiao-hsien San-li-ho yi-chih fa-chüeh chien-
            pao 山東胶縣三里河遺址發掘簡報." *KK* 1977.4:262–267.

Chao T'ieh-han 趙鐵寒
1965   *Ku-shih k'ao-shu* 古史考述. Taipei.

Ch'en Meng-chia 陳夢家
1936   "Shang-tai ti shen-hua yü wu-shu 商代的神話與巫術."
            Yen-ching hsüeh-pao 燕京學報 20:485–576.

Ch'i Ssu-ho 齊思和
1946   "Hsi-Chou ti-li k'ao 西周地理考." *Yen-ching hsüeh-pao*
            燕京學報 30:63–106.

Chiang-hsi-sheng, Pei-ching ta-hsüeh, and Ch'ing-chiang-hsien   Chiang-
            hsi-sheng po-wu-kuan 江西省博物舘, Pei-ching ta-hsüeh
            li-shih-hsi k'ao-ku chuan-yeh 北京大學歷史系考古專業,
            and Ch'ing-chiang-hsien po-wu-kuan 清江縣博物舘.
1975   "Chiang-hsi Ch'ing-chiang Wu-ch'eng Shang-tai yi-chih
            fa-chüeh chien-pao 江西清江吳城商代遺址發掘簡報."
            WW 1975.7:51–71.

Ch'ien Mu 錢穆
1931   "Chou ch'u ti-li k'ao 周初地理考." *Yen-ching hsüeh-pao*
            燕京學報 10:1955–2008.

Chou Fa-kao 周法高
1971   "Hsi-Chou nien-tai k'ao 西周年代考." *Hsiang-kang
            chung-wen ta-hsüeh Chung-kuo wen-hua yen-chiu-so
            hsüeh-pao* 香港中文大學中國文化研究所學報 4:173–205.

Ch'ü Wan-li 屈萬里
1965   "Shih-chi Yin-pen-chi chi ch'i-t'a chi-lu chung so-tsai Yin-
            Shang shih-tai ti shih-shih 史記殷本紀及其他紀錄中
            所載殷商時代的史事." *Kuo-li T'ai-wan ta-hsüeh wen-shih-
            che hsüeh-pao* 國立臺灣大學文史哲學報 14:87–118.
1971   "Hsi-Chou shih-shih kai-shu 西周史事概述." *BIHP*
            42:775–802.

Chung Lu 鍾麓
1976   "Ts'ung Chiang-su yüan-shih she-hui hou-ch'i k'ao-ku
            tzu-liao k'an ssu-yu-chih ti ch'an-sheng 從江蘇原始
            社會後期考古資料看私有制的產生." *KK* 1976.3:165–167.

CKKH
1959　　*Miao-ti-kou yü San-li-ch'iao* 廟底溝與三里橋. Chung-kuo
　　　　t'ien-yeh k'ao-ku pao-kao-chi k'ao-ku-hsüeh chuan-k'an
　　　　ting chung ti-chiu-hao 中國田野考古報告集考古學專刊
　　　　丁種第九號. Peking.
1962a　 *Feng-hsi fa-chüeh pao-kao* 灃西發掘報告. Chung-kuo t'ien-
　　　　yeh k'ao-ku pao-kao-chi k'ao-ku-hsüeh chuan-k'an ting
　　　　chung ti-shih-erh hao 中國田野考古報告集考古學
　　　　專刊丁種第十二號. Peking.
1962b　 *Hsin Chung-kuo ti k'ao-ku shou-huo* 新中國的考古收獲.
　　　　K'ao-ku-hsüeh chuan-k'an chia chung ti-liu-hao 考古學
　　　　專刊甲種第六號. Peking.

Fan Hsiang-yung 范祥雍
1962　　*Ku-pen chu-shu chi-nien chi-chiao ting-pu* 古本竹書
　　　　紀年輯校訂補. Shanghai.

Flannery, Kent V.
1972　　"The Cultural Evolution of Civilizations." *Annual Review
　　　　of Ecology and Systematics* 3:399–426.

Fried, Morton H.
1967　　*The Evolution of Political Society*. New York.

Friedman, Jonathan
1975　　"Tribes, States, and Transformations." In *Marxist
　　　　Analysis and Social Anthropology*, edited by Maurice
　　　　Bloch: pp. 161–202. London.

Fu Ssu-nien 傅斯年
1935　　"Yi-Hsia tung-hsi shuo 夷夏東西說." In *Ch'ing-chu Ts'ai
　　　　Yüan-p'ei hsien-sheng liu-shih-wu sui lun-wen-chi
　　　　慶祝蔡元培先生六十五歲論文集*. Part 2:1093–1134.
　　　　Peking.

Han, Lu, and Chang　Han K'ang-hsin 韓康信, Lu Ch'ing-wu 陸慶伍,
　　　　and Chang Chen-piao 張振標
1974　　"Chiang-su P'i-hsien Ta-tun-tzu hsin-shih-ch'i shih-tai jen-
　　　　ku ti yen-chiu 江蘇邳縣大墩子新石器時代人骨的研究."
　　　　KKHP 1974.2:125–141.

Ho Ping-ti 何炳棣
1973　　"Chou-ch'u nien-tai p'ing-yi 周初年代平議." *Hsiang-kang
　　　　chung-wen ta-hsüeh hsüeh-pao* 香港中文大學學報
　　　　1:17–35.

Ho-pei-sheng　Ho-pei-sheng wen-wu kuan-li wei-yuan-hui 河北省文物
　　　　管理委員會

1959   "Ho-pei T'ang-shan-shih Ta-ch'eng-shan yi-chih fa-chüeh
            pao-kao 河北唐山市大城山遺址發掘報告." *KKHP*
            1959.3:17–36.

Hsia Nai 夏鼐
1977   "T'an-14 ts'e-ting nien-tai ho Chung-kuo shih-ch'ien k'ao-
            ku-hsüeh 碳-14測定年代和中國史前考古學." *KK*
            1977.4:217–232. (Partially translated by Nancy Price in
            Early China 3 [Fall 1977]: 87–93.)

Hsü Cho-yun 許倬雲
1968   "Chou-jen ti hsing-ch'i chi Chou wen-hua ti chi-ch'u
            周人的興起及周文化的基礎." *BIHP* 38:435–458.

Hsü Chung-shu 徐中舒
1931   "Tsai-lun Hsiao-t'un yü Yang-shao 再論小屯與仰韶." *An-
            yang fa-chüeh pao-kao* 安陽發掘報告 3:523–557.

Hsü Hsü-sheng 徐旭生
1959   "1959 nien hsia Yü-hsi tiao-ch'a Hsia-hsü ti ch'u-pu pao-
            kao 1959年夏豫西調查夏墟的初步報告." *KK*
            1959.11:592–600.

Kanaseki Takeo
1960   "The Custom of Teeth Extraction in Ancient China."
            *Extrait des actes du VIe Congrès Internationale des
            Sciences Anthropologiques et Ethnologiques, Paris*: vol. 1:
            201–205.

K'ang Chieh 康捷
1960   "Kuan-yü T'ang-shen Ta-ch'eng-shan yi-chih wen-hua
            hsing-chih ti t'ao-lun 關於唐山大城山遺址文化性質的
            討論." *KK* 1960.6:21–23.

Keightley, David N.
1978   "The *Bamboo Annals* and Shang-Chou Chronology."
            Harvard Journal of Asiatic Studies 38:423–438.

KK
1959.10   "1957 nien Han-tan fa-chüeh chien-pao 1957年邯鄲
            發掘簡報": pp. 531–536.
1965.5   "Ho-nan Yen-shih Erh-li-t'ou yi-chih fa-chüeh chien-pao
            河南偃師二里頭遺址發掘簡報": pp. 215–224.
1974.4   "Ho-nan Yen-shih Erh-li-t'ou tsao Shang kung-tien yi-
            chih fa-chüeh chien-pao 河南偃師二里頭早商宮殿遺址
            發掘簡報": pp. 234–248.
1975.5   "Ho-nan Yen-shih Erh-li-t'ou yi-chih san, pa ch'ü fa-

chüeh chien-pao 河南偃師二里頭遺址三, 八區發掘簡報 ":
pp. 302–309.

Li Chi 李濟

1934 "Hsü erh 序二." In *Ch'eng-tzu-yai* 城子崖, edited by Li
Chi: pp. xi–xviii. Nanking.

Li Ching-tan 李景聃

1947 "Yü-tung Shang-ch'iu Yung-ch'eng tiao-ch'a chi Tsao-lü-
t'ai Hei-ku-tui Ts'ao-ch'iao san-ch'u hsiao fa-chüeh
豫東商邱永城調查及造律台黑孤堆曹橋三處小發掘."
KKHP 1947.2 : 83–120.

Li Hsüeh-ch'in 李學勤

1959 *Yin-tai ti-li chien-lun* 殷代地理簡論. Peking.

Lin-t'ung-hsien Lin-t'ung-hsien wen-hua-kuan 臨潼縣文化舘

1977 "Shen-hsi Lin-t'ung fa-hsien Wu Wang cheng Shang kuei
陝西臨潼發現武王征商簋." *WW* 1977.8 : 1–7.

Lu Po 魯波

1976 "Ts'ung Ta-wen-k'ou wen-hua k'an wo kuo ti ssu-yu-chih
ti ch'i-yüan 從大汶口文化看我國的私有制的起源." *WW*
1976.7 : 74–81.

Matsumaru Michio 松丸道雄

1963 "Inkyo bokujichū no denryōchi ni tsuite 殷墟卜辭中
の田猟地について." *Tōyō bunka kenkyū jo kiyō* 東洋
文化研究所紀要 31 : 1–163.

Sanders, William T.

1974 "Chiefdom to State: Political Evolution at Kaminaljuyu,
Guatemala." In *Reconstructing Complex Societies*, edited
by Charlotte B. Moore, Supplement to the Bulletin of the
American School of Oriental Research, no. 20 : 97–121.

Sanders, William T., and Price, Barbara J.

1968 *Mesoamerica: The Evolution of a Civilization*. New York.

Service, Elman R.

1962 *Primitive Social Organization: An Evolutionary
Perspective.* New York.

1975 *Origins of the State and Civilization: The Process of
Cultural Evolution*. New York.

Shan Ta 單達 and Shih Ping 史兵

1976 "Ts'ung Ta-wen-k'ou wen-hua yi-ts'un k'an wo kuo ku-tai

ssu-yu-chih ti yün-yü ho meng-ya 從大汶口文化遺存
看我國古代私有制的孕育和萌芽." *WW* 1976.4:84–88.

Shan-tung-sheng and Chi-nan-shih   Shan-tung-sheng wen-wu kuan-li-
ch'u 山東省文物管理處 and Chi-nan-shih po-wu-kuan
濟南市博物舘.
1974   *Ta-wen-k'ou* 大汶口. Peking.

Shih Chang-ju 石璋如
1947   "Ho-nan An-yang Hou-kang ti Yin-mu 河南安陽後岡的
殷墓." *BIHP* 13:21–48.
1952   "Chou-tu yi-chi yü ts'ai-t'ao yi-ts'un 周都遺蹟與
彩陶遺存." *Ta-lu tsa-chih she t'e-k'an* 大陸雜誌社特刊
1:357–385.

Shih Hsin 施新
1975   "Kuan-yü wo kuo chieh-chi she-hui ch'an-sheng ti yi-hsieh
wen-t'i 關於我國階級社會產生的一些問題 ." *WW*
1975.5:27–34.

Shima Kunio 島邦男
1958   *Inkyo bokuji kenkyū* 殷墟卜辭研究. Hirosaki.

T'ang Lan 唐蘭
1973   "Ts'ung Ho-nan Cheng-chou ch'u-t'u ti Shang-tai ch'ien-
ch'i ch'ing-t'ung-ch'i t'an-ch'i 從河南鄭州出土的
商代前期青銅器談起." *WW* 1973.7:5–14.
1977   "Hsi-Chou shih-tai tsui-tsao ti yi-chien t'ung-ch'i Li kuei
ming-wen chieh-shih 西周時代最早的一件銅器利簋銘文
解釋." *WW* 1977.8:8–9.

Ting Shan 丁山
1935   "Yu San-tai tu-yi lun ch'i min-tsu wen-hua 由三代
都邑論其民族文化." *BIHP* 5:89–129.

Trigger, Bruce
1976   "Inequality and Communication in Early Civilizations."
Anthropologica, n.s. 18:27–52.

Tung Tso-pin 董作賓
1945   *Yin li-p'u* 殷曆譜. 2 vols. Nan-ch'i, Szechwan.
1951a   "Wu Wang fa Chou nien-yüeh-jih chin-k'ao 武王伐紂
年月日今考." *Kuo-li T'ai-wan ta-hsüeh wen-shih-che hsüeh-
pao* 國立臺灣大學文史哲學報 3:177–212.
1951b   "Hsi-Chou nien li-p'u 西周年曆譜." *BIHP* 23:681–760.
1953   "Pu-tz'u chung ti Po yü Shang 卜辭中的亳與商." *Ta-lu
tsa-chih* 大陸雜誌 6:8–12.

T'ung Chu-ch'en 佟柱臣
1975a   "Ts'ung k'ao-ku ts'ai-liao shih-t'an wo kuo ti ssu-yu-chih
ho chieh-chi ti ch'i-yüan 從考古材料試探我國的私有制
和階級的起源."*KK* 1975.4: 213–221.
1975b   "Ts'ung Erh-li-t'ou lei-hsing wen-hua shih-t'an Chung-kuo
ti kuo-chia ch'i-yüan wen-t'i 從二里頭類型文化試談中國的
國家起源問題." *WW* 1975.6: 29–33.

Waley, Arthur
1960   *The Book of Songs.* Rev. ed. New York.

Wei Ch'in 魏勤
1975   "Ts'ung Ta-wen-k'ou wen-hua mu-tsang k'an ssu-yu-chih
ti ch'i-yüan 從大汶口文化墓葬看私有制的起源." *KK*
1975.5:264–270.

Wright, Henry T.
1977   "Recent Research on the Origin of the State." *Annual
Review of Anthropology* 6:379–397.

WW
1977.11 "Pei-ching-shih P'ing-ku-hsien fa-hsien Shang-tai mu-
tsang 北京市平谷縣發現商代墓葬 ": pp. 1–8.

Yang Chün-shih 楊君實
1960   "K'ang Keng yü Hsia hui 康庚與夏諱." *Ta-lu tsa-chih*
大陸雜誌 20.3:83–88.

Yen Yi-p'ing 嚴一萍
1952   "Hsia Shang Chou wen-hua yi-t'ung k'ao 夏商周文化
異同考." *Ta-lu tsa-chih she t'e-k'an* 大陸雜誌社特刊
1:387–421.

Yü Chung-han 于中航
1976   "Ta-wen-k'ou wen-hua ho yüan-shih she-hui ti chieh-t'i
大汶口文化和原始社會的解體." *WW* 1976.5:64–73.

Yü Hsing-wu 于省吾
1977   "Li kuei wen k'ao-shih 利簋文考釋." *WW* 1977.8:10–12.

17

The Late Shang State:
When, Where, and What?

DAVID N. KEIGHTLEY

The increasing richness of the archaeological record, together with the presence of numerous oracle-bone inscriptions, allows us to study the Shang state in action. This provides the opportunity not simply to apply general anthropological theories about early state modules, redistribution, compliance relations, administrative institutionalization, and so on, but to use the Shang evidence to test and perhaps refine those theories.

The state, for our purposes, can be defined as "a geographically delimited segment of human society united by common obedience to a single sovereign," with the term referring "either to the society as a whole or, more specifically, to the sovereign authority that controls it" (Watkins 1968:150). Wheatley (1971:52–63) has provided an elegant and theoretically seductive account of the Shang state that, with certain possible exceptions (Keightley 1973b:527; but see n. 4, below), seems to ring true. There is no doubt, as he and others have noted, that the Shang state was a Bronze Age theocracy. It is hard to separate the activities and interests of the state from those the king and the royal lineage. Politics were dynastic and compliance relations were conceived primarily in terms of dynastic advantage and the ancestral cult that legitimated the dynasty. The state included the various officers and functionaries clustered around the king, the various allied leaders who subscribed to the king's authority, and the populations, associated with these officers and leaders, who were ready to accept the customary ties of obligation, loyalty, and belief that bind all Bronze Age societies together. The endurance of the dynasty, together with the emergence of proto-bureaucratic titles and conceptions of administrative jurisdiction, hierarchy, and authority—in both the religious and political spheres—suggests that there was a rudimentary state structure, and that the Late Shang kings were not merely chiefs but heads of a state that was beginning to assume an institutional existence of its own. (For descriptions in English, based upon the oracle-bone inscriptions, of Shang state and administration, see Chou 1968; Keightley 1969; Chao Lin 1972. For the general model by which primitive chiefdoms are thought to evolve into primitive states, see Service 1975). When I use the term "Shang state," therefore, I shall be referring to the king, his family both alive and dead, his consorts, his officers, and all those associated groups which, on the basis of the inscriptional evidence, can be shown to have accepted more often than not the authority and aspirations of that central dynastic cluster. In referring to the constituent elements of the Shang state I avoid, in the initial analysis, such terms as chief, chiefdom, tribe, clan, and early state module and limit myself to neutral terms such as "leader" and "group." Consideration of the Shang evidence must precede any use of the more specific terms.

THE SHANG STATE: WHEN

In this exploratory study of the Shang state, I refer primarily to the period for which we have inscriptions, the period some archaeologists and art historians call the Late Shang or An-yang phase (Soper 1966; Kane 1973:356–358; Keightley 1978b:xiii). On the basis of (1) four lunar eclipses recorded in the oracle-bone inscriptions of Wu Ting, (2) estimated reign lengths, and (3) two carbon-14 dates (ZK–5, ZK–86) from the Hsiao-t'un area, it is possible to argue that this "historical period," that is, the era of the eight or nine kings from Wu Ting (*not* P'an Keng) to Ti Hsin, ran from circa 1200 to circa 1050–1040 B.C. (Keightley 1978b:xiii, 171–176, 228).[1]

If we accept these dates, if we accept the historicity of the Shang genealogy recorded by the oracle-bone inscriptions, and if we further accept an average reign length of twenty years (or a generation reign of thirty years when fraternal succession occurred), then a count backward from Wu Ting (ca. 1200–1181 B.C.) brings us to circa 1460–1441 B.C. for

---

1. The general accuracy of this chronology is independently supported by several recent papers of David Nivison that, relying upon new insights to date the Western Chou bronze inscriptions, argue that the battle of Mu-yeh, in which the Chou overthrew the Shang, occurred on 15 January 1045 B.C. (See, e.g., Nivison 1980.)

the reign of T'ang or Ta Yi, the dynasty founder. Two more carbon-14 dates—ZK–177 (1573 ± 140 B.C.) and ZK–178 (1598 ± 110 B.C.)—from Cheng-chou, the first from the *hang-t'u* wall, the second from Erh-li-kang, upper level, indicate that, using the outside limits, the Bronze Age occupation probably flourished in Cheng-chou circa 1713–1433 B.C. This suggests—and, in view of the uncertain reliability of the carbon-14 dates and the one-sigma confidence intervals involved (see Keightley 1978b:173, n. 15), it is at present only a suggestion—that T'ang may have founded the Shang dynasty as the main Cheng-chou occupation was ending; it suggests the possibility, in short, that Cheng-chou should not be regarded as a Middle Shang dynastic capital, but as a major urban complex of an earlier group, possibly the Hsia. I advance this only as a hypothesis and to pose a question. If there are now sound reasons for taking the "Early Shang" sites in the Lo-yang area as Hsia (K. C. Chang 1976a; 1978:90; cf. "The Question of Hsia in Chinese Archaeology" in ch. 16 above), on what grounds are the "Middle Shang" sites in the Cheng-chou area to be taken as Shang? A firmer chronology, derived from clusters of carbon-14 dates, may help resolve the issue. It should be noted here that Tsou (1978) argues that the Early Shang occupation at Cheng-chou should be equated with the first five generations of the Shang dynasty, and that the Shang site at Cheng-chou was in fact Po 亳, T'ang's capital. Tsou makes an excellent case for showing that there was a Po located in the Cheng-chou area in Eastern Chou times. But it is far less certain that the Shang settlement was the Po of T'ang, especially since there was no later tradition to that effect.

These considerations raise the possibility that much of the expansion of "Shang civilization" during the Erh-li-kang phase (Chang 1977:271), especially into the middle Yangtze area, may not have taken place under Shang dynastic auspices. The reduced scale of "Shang" activity in a site like P'an-lung-ch'eng, Huang-p'i-hsien, Hupei (114°22′ east, 30°52′ north; latitude and longitude calculated from the maps in Geelan and Twitchett 1974), during the An-yang phase (*WW* 1976.2a:6) supports this conclusion, suggesting perhaps that the settlement had at that time lost its base of support in the north (cf. Bagley 1977:166, 169, 212).

The comparatively late date that I assign the Shang historical period leads me to discuss the geography of the Shang state primarily in terms of those archaeological sites that have been classified by various scholars, depending on the terminology they prefer, as belonging to the Late Shang, Yin-hsü, An-yang, or Hsiao-t'un phases; since the dynastic state existed prior to the historical period, however, I also consider those sites classified as Upper Erh-li-kang or Jen-min Park (for a tentative correlation of these culture phases, see Chang 1977:270, table 13).

THE SHANG STATE: WHERE

The political geography of the Late Shang state is a subject so large and complex that it would require a book, with several years' research, to do it justice. What follows represents only an exploration of methodology and some possible conclusions. In brief, I use the inscriptions (from Period I, the reign of Wu Ting [ca. 1200–1181 B.C.?], unless otherwise noted; for an introduction to Tung Tso-pin's five periods, see Keightley 1978b:92–93, 203, table 14) to look for evidence of the Shang state's sovereignty and territoriality, its powers of coercion, its economic activities, and the legitimizing religious functions that encouraged routine compliance with its authority. Having identified and ranked the places or persons that may be said to have been, to one degree or another, members of the Shang state, I then try to place them on a map, and finally I attempt to relate the key areas of the Shang state as delineated by the inscriptions to a map of the chronologically appropriate Shang cultural sites as revealed by archaeology.

The study is fraught with uncertainties, the most serious of which is the incomplete nature of the inscriptional and archaeological record. If, for example, a cache of oracle-bone inscriptions referring to Shang settlements in X or Y has not yet been found (on the typicality of the present corpus of inscriptions, see Keightley 1978b:137–140), then we are not able to refer to such sites, even though they have been excavated, as part of the state. Similarly, if sites have not been excavated in areas where the inscriptions suggest they should be found (see in particular the discussion of the Hung-kou, below), we cannot yet claim with assurance that the state embraced these areas. But since only the combination of inscriptional and archaeological evidence will enable us to identify elements of the Shang state (as opposed to participants in Shang culture), we must proceed along these lines, provisional though our conclusions will be.

Shang conceptions of territoriality can be documented in the inscriptions. The term "our fields" (wo t'ien 我田) indicates that certain lands— presumably those that had been cleared for agriculture, sometimes by state labor gangs (Keightley 1969:98ff)—were thought to be part of the royal domain. For example, "Crack-making on ping-ch'en, Yung divined: 'Cry out: Inspect our fields'" (Ch'ien-pien 5.26.1); "our northern fields will not perhaps receive harvest" (Yi-pien 5584; both at S353.3–4). References to inspecting the "northern fields" (pei-t'ien) on a bronze (Akatsuka

1977:714), to "center fields" (*chung-t'ien*; S419.4), and to "southern fields" (*nan-t'ien*) receiving harvest (*Jimbun* 1932; S413.3) also confirm that Shang territory was partly conceived in terms of usable land, of fields where crops could be grown. (S numbers refer to page and row in Shima 1971; for full citations to the abbreviations by which oracle-bone collections are cited, see Keightley 1978b:229–231.) It was also conceived in terms of hunting areas where the Shang could "take to the field." (*T'ien* 田, "field," generally has this verbal sense in the inscriptions; see Li Hsiao-ting 1965:4025–4026.)

The term *pi* 鄙, "border, outskirts," further suggests a sense of delimited territory. For example, Kuo of Chih (Chih Kuo 沚馘), a Shang state member (see Keightley 1979–80, criterion 31), reported: "The T'u-fang are besieging in our eastern borders and have harmed two settlements. The Kung(?)�-fang also raided the fields of our western borders" (*Ching-hua* 2; S353.4). Particularly interesting is the term *tien* 奠, apparently used to refer to an administrative area. For example: "Divined: 'Our *tien* areas will receive harvest'" (*T'ieh-yi* 10.2); "on the seventh day, chi-ch'ou, Yu Hua of Ch'ang (? 長友化) called out and reported saying, 'The Kung(?)-fang are besieging in our western *tien*-area (called) Feng'" (*Han-ch'eng*). These areas were also referred to collectively as the *to-tien* 多奠, "the many *tien*". Thus, "Crack-making on ping-wu, Pin divined: 'Cry out: Inspect the bovids in the many *tien* areas'" (*Ping-pien* 353.1; the negative charge pair appears on the other side of the plastron; all at S389.4).

Other groups were conceived as having their own borders. We have already seen Kuo of Chih reporting about attacks on his eastern and western borders in Period I (*Ching-hua* 2, above); in Period V we find: "On kuei-mao, the king, crack-making, divined: 'In the (next) ten days there will be no disaster.' In the first month, when the king came to attack the Jen-fang. In the borders of the Archer Lord Hsi, of Yu" (*Ho-pien* 189; S268.4). Other inscriptions probably from the same campaign appear to refer to "the borders of Tzu(?) Shang (㦰 商)" (*Chin-chang* 728; *Ho-pien* 189; both at S268.4; for a discussion of the names and their possible locations, see Jao 1959:614).

The evidence suggests, in short, that rudimentary conceptions of territorial jurisdiction did exist, but that they were understood largely in terms of land used by particular local groups of whom the Shang were only the most eminent; there is no evidence that Kuo of Chih thought of his borders as being the Shang borders, no evidence that a conception of state territory, as opposed to group or clan or tribe territory, existed. None of the territorial terms above appear frequently in the divination inscriptions, nor are they recorded with sufficient precision to enable us to place them on a map.

State Criteria

The divination inscriptions provide an intermittently detailed, if not sharply focused, record of the king's conceptions of religion and politics. The fact that the king divined about a certain officer carrying out his orders does not prove that the officer obeyed, or had to obey, the order; but the divination record indicates that such obedience was, in the king's mind, a realistic possibility. The thirty-nine criteria listed below, under headings that are general and by no means exclusive, delineate the king's conception of state activity (or, to put it more accurately, our conceptions of the functions that, were we the Shang king, we would expect to find in a Shang state). Most of the criteria represent divination topics, indicating the king's concern with the activities and well-being of his subordinates and allies.

State Criteria

(In all cases the letters X and Y stand for Shang allies, dependencies, or state members; A and B stand for enemies or non-members of the state.

Sovereignty
    1. The king orders (*ling* 令) X.
    2. A Shang state member orders X (Y orders X) or X orders a Shang state member (X orders Y).
    3. The king calls upon or cries out (*hu* 呼) for X to act.
    4. X supports the king's affairs (*ku wang shih* 固王事).
    5. X leads or takes officers or men.
    6. X goes, hunts, catches, or does any activity not covered by other criteria.
    7. X reports news, or the king informs X, or Y reports in X.
    8. X comes (to have audience).
    9. Y does at X something not covered by other criteria.

Territoriality
    10. The king hunts, or inspects, or does some other activity (we cannot decipher) at X.
    11. The king goes to, from, enters into, returns to X.
    12. The king sends men to X, or calls upon officers or men to go to X, or divines about Y going to X.
    13. The king issues orders at X or orders the men of X to do something.
    14. The king divines at X.
    15. The king divines at, or is at, "camp X."
    16. The king receives scapulas, turtle shells, or some other product at X.
    17. The king raises men at X.
    18. The king orders X to lead the men of Y.
    19. A will not reach to, i.e., come as far as, X.
    20. X combined with the title of Hou 侯 (or Po 伯?), Tzu 子, Fu 婦, or more lowly titles.
    21. The term A-fang 方, generally used of non-Shang groups. (A negative criterion.)

Religion and Kinship
  22. The king offers sacrifices to or at X.
  23. The king offers rituals, sacrifices, on behalf of X, or Tzu-X, etc.
  24. X participates in a Shang sacrifice or ritual.
  25. X prepares pyromantic materials.
  26. (Ritual) agriculture by X or at X.
  27. Royal concern about the health of X.
  28. Incantations to ensure X's well-being.
  29. X will receive harvest, rainfall.
  30. Y sacrifices or offers ritual at X.

Alliances and Warfare
  31. The king (or his officers) follows, X, or X follows Y.
  32. The king will destroy A at X.
  33. The king divines that X will perhaps lose *chung* 眾 or *jen* 人.
  34. Divinations of the form A will (or will not) harm, destroy, attack X; or X will (or will not) harm, destroy, attack A; or X will (will not) encounter fang 方.
  35. X will receive assistance, will not be defeated.
  36. Identity of diviners' or recording officials' names with those of other regions.
  37. Marriage alliance.

Exchange: Trade and Tribute(?)
  38. Income notations: X sent in shells and scapulas.
  39. X will supply other goods.

"State Score": The Degree of State Participation

Thirty-eight of the thirty-nine criteria can be taken as positive indications of potential membership in the Shang state (criterion 21 is the sole negative criterion). In certain cases, such as those of X being ordered to do something (criteria 1, 3) or X supporting the king's affairs (criterion 4), the presumption is strong that X was indeed part of the network of command and service exemplifying that "obedience to a single sovereign" which I have proposed defines the state. In numerous other cases, however, the evidence is ambiguous. The fact that X on occasion was considered a possible ally, or that X on occasion sent in some turtle shells, does not of itself require that X have been a member—as opposed to a temporary ally—of the Shang state. Furthermore, it is unlikely that the state itself, however conceived by the Shang, was immutable and stable in its location and functions. It seems most suitable to conceive of the Shang state as a political-religious force-field, stronger in some areas and at some times than in others, whose power to influence events advanced and receded in accordance with a variety of factors such as the personality and energy of the reigning Shang king, his marriage alliances, the successes of his crops and his armies, the strength of the surrounding groups, and so on.

The case of the Chou 周 illustrates how the criteria can be used. Some of the evidence, as indicated, is anomalous; that is, in one case (criterion 21) Chou was referred to as Chou-fang, a non-Shang designation, and in another case (criterion 28) it appears that the Shang wished harm to the Chou. But the rest of the evidence—all from Period I unless otherwise noted—presents a relatively consistent picture of the Chou as members of the Shang state: they received orders from the king (criterion 1) and from another state member (2); they supported the king's affairs (4); the king divined about the Chou leading officers and men (5) and about the Chou hunts (6); the Chou were given the title of archer lord (20) and were generally not called Chou-fang (21); the Chou participated in a Shang sacrifice (24); the Shang king was concerned when Chou was sick (27) and prayed that Chou would suffer no disaster or curse, and in the last case the divination was performed by a diviner of the royal family group (28); the Shang may have sacrificed at Chou (30); the Chou were potential allies (31) and the Shang were concerned that the Chou not suffer in battle (34); marriage relations appear to have existed between Shang and Chou (37); finally, the Chou did send in plastrons for divination (38). In short, the Chou satisfy fourteen of the thirty-eight positive criteria, proposed for state membership.[2]

On the other hand, it is clear that the Chou were not at the core of the Shang state. They were not "called upon" (hu 呼) to do anything (3), suggesting that they were not within earshot; the Chou did not report (7); they did not come to have audience (8), nor did they ritually prepare the turtle shells used by the Shang king (25). Distance, both physical and political, between the Chou and the Shang is also indicated by the following evidence: the king did not hunt, inspect, or go to their area in periods I to IV (10, 11), he did not divine (14) or make camp (15) or raise men (17) in their area, nor did he lead the men of Chou or order other officers to do so (18). In the realm of agriculture, the Chou did not participate in Shang rituals (26), nor did the Shang divine about the success of the Chou harvests (29). In terms of service obligations, the Chou supplied no diviner of that name

2. Given limitations of space, the evidence, presented in an appendix to my original Berkeley conference paper, cannot be detailed here; it has been published separately as Keightley 1979–80. The relevant inscriptions, keyed to their criteria, are: 1. *Kikkō* 1.26.16; *Ch'ien-pien* 6.63.1; 5.7.7 + 6.51.7; *T'ieh-yün* 128.2; *Yi-pien* 6015 (all S299.4). 2. *Shih-to* 2.82 (S299.4). 4. *Ch'ien-pien* 5.7.7 + 6.51.7 and others at S216.1. 5. *Yi-pien* 7312 (S144.2); *Ch'ien-pien* 6.63.1 (S229.4). 6. *Ping-pien* 442.13–14 (S299.3). 20. *Chia-pien* 436.2 (S299.3); Hsinhua-she 1977. 21. *Chui-ho* 181 (S299.3); Hsinhua-she 1977. 24. *Yi-pien* 3408 (S299.4; cf. S244.4); Hsinhua-she 1977. 27. *Yi-ts'un* 129 (S299.4). 28. *T'ieh-yün* 36.1 (S299.3); *Yi-pien* 8896 (S300.1). 30. *Hou-pien* 2.15.2 (S299.4). 31. *Ch'ien-pien* 7.31.4; *Hou-pien* 2.37.4; *T'ung-tsuan* VIII.5 (all S299.4). 34. *T'ieh-yi* 4.12 (S300.1). 37. *Yi-pien* 8854; 8894; *Yeh-ch'u* 2.46.15 (last two at S299.4). 38. *Yi-pien* 5452; *Ping-pien* 274.5 (both S299.3).

to the Shang court (36), nor, with the exception of turtle shells (38), did they send in any other goods (39). These fifteen criteria, in short, suggest by their absence that the Shang had little direct contact with the Chou or their locale.

Anomalies remain. The problem of the -fang suffix (21) has already been alluded to. It is also curious that although the Shang apparently sacrificed at Chou (30) they did not, at least until Period V, inspect, go, divine, or make camp there (10–15). One possible explanation would be that royal divinations performed at that distance (some 625 kilometers from Hsiao-t'un as the crow flies) were less likely to have been returned from the Chou region for storage. A related anomaly, not unique with Chou, is that references to Chou virtually disappear from the divination records after Period I (for the possible significance of this trend, see "The Geography of the Shang State," below). This is particularly striking since it was the Chou who eventually overthrew the Shang at the end of Period V. The 1977 discovery of a large cache of what are said to be Western Chou oracle bones in the Fu-feng Ch'i-shan area (approximately 107°45′ east, 34°23′ north) 100 kilometers west of Sian (Hsinhua-she 1977; *WW* 1979.10) reveals that the Shang king, at least in Period V, did indeed visit and hunt in the region (criteria 10, 11) and that the makers of these oracle inscriptions worshipped the Shang ancestors (24).

On the assumption that anything divined about was of interest to the Shang king, we can estimate the degree to which the Chou were part of the Shang state by counting the number of inscriptions (individual charges and marginal notations) that mention Chou. Shima (S299.3–300.1) lists 70 (plus 12 more fragmentary occurrences of the graph alone). The count of 82 means nothing by itself, but it can be used for making comparisons with other groups.

On the basis of the 14 positive criteria, the 15 criteria which do not apply, and the total of 82 references, it can be concluded that in Period I the Chou were one of the more distant groups that formed part of the Shang state and that Shang control over the Chou was neither strong nor continual, but that the interest and concern were present. To quantify our results in a crude way, we can multiply the 14 criteria by the 82 references to give a "state score" of 1,648. This is a relatively high score, and it is important to notice that its size is not simply due to the number of references—82 is not particularly large—but to the variety of role categories (14) fulfilled by the Chou. Eighty-two references to a hunting area, by contrast, which played no other role in the Shang polity, would result in a score of only 82 times 1 equals 82. Frequency of divination in short does not necessarily imply complexity of state participation; it is the variety of roles that reveals the degree to which a particular group was part of the Shang state, that reveals its relative strength within the Shang force field.

MAPPING THE SHANG STATE

It has been estimated that over 500 place names are recorded in the oracle-bone inscriptions (Huang 1977:148); it would be neither feasible nor useful to calculate the "state score" for each. For this preliminary study, I have limited myself to the approximately 143 place-names discussed and, so far as possible, mapped by Shima (1958:360–442).

It is first necessary to demonstrate how Shang maps can be drawn. Considerable scholarship has been devoted to the question. The major works are those by Kuo Mo-jo (1933), Tung Tso-pin (1945), Ch'en Meng-chia (1956), Shima Kunio (1958), Li Hsüeh-ch'in (1959), Matsumaru Michio (1963), Chung Po-sheng (1972), and Huang Ch'ing-sheng (1977). Chung (1972:1–24) provides an excellent evaluation of the previous studies and the methodology to be employed; Hsü (1977:xxxiii–xxxvi), like Chung, provides cogent criticism of Matsumaru's methods and conclusions. Akatsuka (1977:615–859) attempts to locate place names recorded on Shang bronzes.[3]

Archaeological finds by themselves enable us to map only Shang culture; to map the state we must turn to the inscriptional evidence. And the map of the state must be based, so far as possible, upon the contemporary inscriptions which enable us to determine the relation between the various locations.

Reference Points

At present, no reference point is established without question. Particularly disturbing is the possibility that, in view of the Shang king's frequent peregrinations (see "The Shang State: What" and "Conclusions," below), some of the groups we are attempting to map changed locations. The fact that the bulk of the divinations about Chou, for example, comes from Period I may indicate a shift in the nature of Shang-Chou relations in the later periods. But it may also indicate that the Chou moved further away from the Shang in the later periods. Scholars may eventually be able

---

3. Computer programs may eventually permit us to draw more accurate Shang maps. For an introduction to the statistical methods involved, see Kendall 1971 and the other works cited therein.

to resolve problems of this sort on a period-by-period basis, but present evidence is not sufficiently informative.

The central reference point on any Shang map would presumably be occupied by the capital. We do not yet understand what Shang conceptions of the capital may have been; we are not certain if the capital remained fixed throughout the historical period; we are not certain what phrases in the oracle-bone inscriptions refer to the capital; and we are not sure if the archaeological site of the capital has been discovered.

This is not the place to explore the complex questions involved. In order to establish a reference point, I make the following provisional assumptions:

> 1. The Hsiao-t'un site (36°07′ north, 114°19′ east) was referred to in the inscriptions (S43.1–2) as *tzu-yi* 茲邑, "this settlement."
> 2. Hsiao-t'un was not the capital, but a cult and mortuary center.
> 3. In the oracle-bone inscriptions the Shang capital—to the extent that there was such a conception—was variously called *Shang, ta yi Shang* 大邑商, *chung Shang* 中商, and *ch'iu Shang* 丘商 (S279.2–3).
> 4. This capital was located near modern Shang-ch'iu 商丘 (34°26′ north, 115°39′ east), Honan.

I base these conclusions, in whole or in part, upon Tung (1945), Shima (1958), Miyazaki (1970), and Chung (1972). The latter (pp. 45–58) provides a useful introduction to the issues and evidence. For an introduction to the reasons why Hsiao-t'un was not the capital, see Keightley (1978b: xiv, n. 6).

The choice of Shang-ch'iu is based primarily on (1) Tung's reconstruction of the itineraries of the Period V campaigns, which seem to require a place called "Shang" in Eastern Honan; (2) the similarity between the name *ch'iu-Shang* of the bone inscriptions (S279.3) and the traditional Shang-ch'iu; (3) the fact that the capital of the Shang-successor state of Sung is said to have been established at Shang-ch'iu, which would presumably have been in the Shang heartland; (4) strong Eastern Chou traditions that at least one of the Shang capitals was in this area (Creel [1937: 158–167] summarizes the evidence); and (5) Shang-ch'iu's location at the center of the North China plain, standing at the junction of many modern and presumably also ancient routes. These considerations are not conclusive, but they provide a hypothetical reference point that seems to accord with the rest of the evidence.

The fact that no major Shang sites have yet been excavated in the eastern Honan panhandle around Shang-ch'iu emphasizes the provisional nature of this conclusion. Chang (1977: 260) has suggested other archaeological sites that might have been Shang capitals: Hui-hsien (113°47′ east, 35°27′ north) in Honan, 90 kilometers south-southwest of Hsiao-t'un; Hsing-t'ai (114°30′ east, 37°04′ north) in Hopei, some 80 kilometers north of Hsiao-t'un; and Kao-ch'eng (114°51′ east, 38°02′ north), also in Hopei, some 140 kilometers north of Hsiao-t'un. Miyazaki (1970) has suggested that the Shang capital was located at Hsin-ts'un, Chün-hsien (114°32′ east, 35°40′ north), some 60 kilometers south of Hsiao-t'un, in the region of the old Wei 衞 capital. Till more evidence appears, the capital reference point should probably be treated as a "reference zone" covering southern Hopei and the northern and eastern Honan panhandles.

Chou can be offered as a second reference point. The name appears in the Shang inscriptions, with a state score of 1,648. Shima (1958:410) places Chou in the area of Shensi, Ch'i-shan 岐山 (107°37′ east, 34°27′ north), the traditional Chou homeland. Inscriptional evidence supports this conclusion. "We should not order Chou to go to 戉" (*Hsü-pien* 3.28.3; S299.4) places Chou reasonably close to 戉. Other inscriptions indicate that 戉 was two days' journey north of Fu (甫/甫), which may be located in southwest Shansi (Shima 1958:383 locates it in southwest Shansi, northwest sector; Chung [1972: facing p. 170] locates it in southwest Shansi, southwest sector). Three charges of the form "Chou will lead (the)𢦏" (*Yi-pien* 7312; S299.3) indicate that Chou was near the Ch'in homeland—if, as Shima (1958:410) argues, 𢦏 can be read as Ch'in 嬠 = 秦. Chung (1972: facing p. 170) likewise places Chou in Shensi. The recent find of what appear to be more than fifteen thousand pre-dynastic Chou oracle bones precisely in Ch'i-shan-hsien (Hsinhua-she 1977), together with an increasing number of early Chou bronzes and other artifacts in the middle Wei valley (e.g., *WW* 1977.8:1–7), provides added support for the view that the "Chou" of the oracle-bone inscriptions did indeed refer to the traditional Chou homeland north of the Wei river.

Reference points can also be established by relating the names found in the Shang divination inscriptions to the names and insignia found on Shang and Western Chou bronzes whose place of excavation (and hence, perhaps, place of use) is known. This method is fraught with problems, and no precise or reliable results have yet been obtained (see Weber 1973:4–5 on the difficulties involved in establishing provenance, and thus regional styles, for bronzes). Some examples will indicate the kinds of evidence that have to be assessed.

K'o-tso-hsien (approximately 40°58′ north, 119°40′ east), Liaoning. A group of Shang (or Shang-Chou) bronzes was found in a tomb here on 6 March 1973. A *lei* (no. 2) bore the inscription: 父子𡇡𠕷 (*KK* 1973.4:225). A *fang-lei* in the

Shanghai museum bears the inscription: 督 𠆢 奠 亞. This suggests a link between
督 and 𠆢 (*chu* 竹 [?]; some scholars read the graph as *jan* 冄 —e.g., Akatsuka
1977:776). Chu appears with some frequency in the oracle bones (S453.1–2); it
is hard to assign a state score because too many of the inscriptions are ambiguous, but the role score would be fairly high (Chu satisfies criteria 1, 6, 20, 24, 38).
One inscription indicates that 𡛝, "woman of Chu(?)," lay in the north: "When it
came to the ninth day, hsin-mao, there really was the coming of alarming news
from the north. Yu Ch'i Chu(?串妻𡛝) reported, saying: 'The T'u-fang have
invaded our fields (with) ten men'" (*Ching-hua* 6; S138.2; *KK* 1974.6:368, 370).
Other evidence, as we shall see, locates the T'u-fang in the north. If we are willing
to accept the links between 督 and 𠆢 and 𡛝, and if we are willing to accept that
the Shang (Shang-Chou) bronzes were buried in the tomb by the occupants of
the region (rather than buried as heirlooms or booty by later inhabitants who
might have brought the vessels from elsewhere), then we have some evidence
that the 𠆢 of the bone inscriptions was located in K'o-tso-hsien, Liaoning. (Yen
[1978:5, 134, 136] uses an entry in *Kua-ti-chih* [completed A.D. 642] to argue
that Chu was in the vicinity of Hopei, Fu-ning-hsien [approximately 39°55′
north, 119°15′ east], which is close to K'o-tso.)

Huang-hsien (120°31′ east, 37°39′ north), Shantung. Late Western Chou
bronzes found here bear the name Chi 曩, with a *ting* bearing the title Chi Hou
曩侯 (Ch'i 1972:8–9; *KK* 1974.6:370, nn. 2, 3; cf. Yen 1978:140). The place-
name Chi appears in two oracle-bone inscriptions and Chi Hou appears in one
more, all from Period V (S403.3). This suggests that the Shang place Chi may
have been located in the region of Huang-hsien. The issue is complicated by the
appearance of the four-character inscription Chi Hou Ya Yi 曩侯亞矣 on a
fang-ting excavated from K'o-tso-hsien, Liaoning, which is dated to Late Shang
(*KK* 1974.6:366, 369; the same title appears on a Shang *yu* [Akatsuka
1977:647]). This suggests either that (1) Chi was originally in Liaoning, and a
branch of the clan moved to Shantung during the Western Chou, or (2) even in
Shang times there were at least two branches of the clan, and hence two places,
called Chi.

T'ung-shan (about 117°11′ east, 34°14′ north), Kiangsu. Uninscribed oracle
bones, bronze weapons, and human sacrifices have been found at Ch'iu-wan
(*KK* 1973.2:71–79; Bulling 1977). There is a strong tradition in texts like *Shih-
pen* and *Kua-ti-chih* that the old P'eng-ch'eng 彭城 was in this Hsü-chou 徐州
region. A Shang place 𣄼 (= P'eng 彭) appears in the oracle-bone inscriptions
(S400.3) and in a Shang bronze inscription (Akatsuka 1977:640). It is possible,
therefore, that the P'eng of Shang times was located in T'ung-shan (Wang and
Ch'en 1973:55).

Shih-lou-hsien (110°49′ east, 37°01′ north), Shansi. Late Shang finds include
a bronze *ko* with 𠈌 inscribed on one side and 开 on the other (*WW* 1976.2b).
The name 𠈌 (= Ping 竝) occurs with some frequency in the oracle bones
(S39.4–40.1), the place or person satisfying criteria 1, 5, 6, 7, 11, 24, 28, 31, 33,
34, and 38 for a state score of about 550. It is possible, therefore, that the Ping of
the inscriptions was located in west central Shansi. Divinations such as: "Ch'a of
Ping(? Ping Ch'a 竝 𠈌) attacks the 𦫶-fang, he will receive assistance" (*Ts'ui-pien*
1535; S39.4) suggest a possible connection between Ping and Ch'a, which other
inscriptions locate in northern Shansi (Shima 1958:423). The discovery in Shih-
lou of a *ku* beaker bearing a "Tzu 子" (*WW* 1972.4:2) suggests another possible
link with the Shang royal lineage. The provincial style of the artifacts found in
the Shih-lou region, however, has led Bagley (1977:211–212) to characterize it
as one of the "culturally advanced provincial centers in the years following

Middle Shang." We cannot be certain if the Ping artifact found at Shih-lou is to be associated with the Ping of the inscriptions. But if that association is accepted we have the interesting case of a Shang state member (state score 550) that, on the basis of the archaeological evidence, was perhaps producing its own bronzes and was relatively independent culturally. This would suggest in turn that a high state score would not necessarily imply strong economic or cultural links between the state member and the Shang.

One of the most recent attempts to combine inscriptional and archaeological evidence is that of Chiang (1976: 44–45), who, on the basis of names found on Shang oracle bones and Chou bronzes, and on the basis of the provenance of the bronzes, argues for at least three Shang fiefs or dependencies in the Chiang-Han region, in the area of An-lu-hsien (113°43′ east, 31°15′ north) and Sui-hsien (113°23′ east, 31°42′ north) in Hupei, during the reign of Wu Ting. I would draw rather different conclusions. Only one of the groups mentioned, Tseng 曾 (= 鄫 S299.2–3) had a significant state score (of about 84). The evidence suggests that Wu Ting conducted a campaign in the region (this is supported by later tradition; see *Shih-ching*, "Yin Wu," Mao 305), that he had few allies there, and that the absence of inscriptions about later campaigns suggests that the Late Shang were not able to maintain themselves there. Bagley (1977: 212) likewise takes the inscriptions to show that "the area was no longer a secure possession of the Anyang kings" and notes that "there is so far at least correspondingly little archaeological evidence of Anyang period sites in Hupei." If the Tseng of the Chou inscriptions were successor to the Tseng of the Period I bone inscriptions, it may have maintained itself in the area not as a Shang state member but as an independent statelet. It is worth noting that though the south may not have been under Shang control, it was not, unlike the north and the west, a source of trouble (see the *tzu-nan* 自南, "from the south," inscriptions at S413.2–413.3). There is some evidence of turtle shells arriving from the south (as well as from the east and west; see Keightley 1978b: 12; Yen 1978: 3–5), suggesting peaceful exchange relations, perhaps with the Middle Shang sites in the Yangtze valley and beyond. (For rather similar conclusions, see Kane 1974–75: 102, n. 13, citing Hayashi Minao; Wang, Chang, and Yang 1977: 5, citing Kuo Mojo.)

Whatever differences of opinion may exist about individual cases, the method of relating Shang names found on bronzes in particular areas is clearly important for the reconstruction of Shang geography. (For a detailed study in English, which locates 盂 [S93.1–2] near present Chi-ning [116°36′ east, 35°19′ north], Shantung, see Chow 1968: 166–183). Continuing discoveries of inscription-bearing Shang and early Western Chou bronzes will permit it to be applied more extensively.

Distances and Directions

When two or more place names appear on the same oracle bone it can be assumed that they lay relatively close to one another. If X and Y appear on one bone and Y and Z on another, there is a strong presumption that X and Z were not too distant, and X, Y, and Z can be treated as a geographical cluster (for an example, see Chung 1972:39). More useful are those Period V oracle bones that contain a series of inscriptions recording the cyclical date, the place of divination, and the king's intention to travel to another place. For example:

> Crack-making on ping-hsü (day 23), divined at 亯: "to[day] the king goes to [敦], there will be no disaster."
> Crack-making on keng-yin (day 27), divined at 敦: "The king goes to 盂, there will be no disaster."
> Crack-making on jen-ch'en (day 29), divined at 盂: "Today the king goes to 斝, there will be no disaster."
> Crack-making on chia-wu (day 31), divined at 斝: "The king goes to 杓, there will be no disaster" (*Ch'ien-pien* 2.8.7; S62.3; discussed by Chung 1972:35).

Information like this permits us to chart the king's itinerary and to indicate the *maximum* number of days of travel that separated the places involved: 亯 —4 days— 敦 —2 days— 盂 —2 days— 斝. In one case (*K'u-fang* 981, as reconstructed by Shima 1958:379), it is possible to argue that it took approximately one hundred days to travel between Shu (𣌗/蜀), which Shima (ibid., pp. 380, 383) locates on the Honan-Shensi border just south of T'ung-kuan, and Shang, the capital. In this case the king would have traveled some 520 kilometers, probably along the south bank of the Ho, averaging 5.2 to 5.7 kilometers a day.

It is evident that we cannot always assume that the king in moving, say, from 亯 to 斝 traveled in a straight line or traveled every day; he might have backtracked, zigzagged, or spent several days in one place. And the hundred-day itinerary supposedly required to move from Shu to the capital might have taken no more than ten days (with the king resting, or moving in circles, on the intervening nine days of each week). Our uncertainties are compounded by the failure of most inscriptions to specify if the king traveled north, east, south, or west.

Some inscriptions do refer to directions in a useful way. For example: "When it came to the fifth day, ting-yu, there really was the coming of alarming news from the west. Kuo of Chih (Chih Kuo 沚馘) reporting, said: 'The T'u-fang are besieging in our eastern borders and have harmed two settlements. The Kung(?)-fang also raided the fields of our western borders'" (*Ching-hua* 2; S435.2; for initial glosses on the translation, see Keightley 1978b:44, nn. 80–82). This tells us that Chih lay to the west of

the Shang (capital?) and that the T'u-fang and Kung(?)-fang lay east and
west, respectively, of Chih. Another inscription (*Ching-hua* 6; S23.3) associates the T'u-fang with alarming news "from the north," indicating that
the range of T'u-fang operations—and presumably the locations of Chih
and the Kung(?)-fang—lay not just west, but northwest of Shang (as Shima
1958:423 plots them, in northern Shansi). The fact that the Kung(?)-fang
also harmed and were attacked by Yüeh (�/戉) (*Ch'ien-pien* 7.8.1. and
thirteen other inscriptions at S350.1) places Yüeh in the same area; Yüeh's
wars with the Ch'ien 𢼄/湔-fang (*Ts'ui-pien* 1123 and seven other inscriptions at S350.1) place that group in the same area; and so on. This cluster of
places can thus be located to the northwest of the Shang.

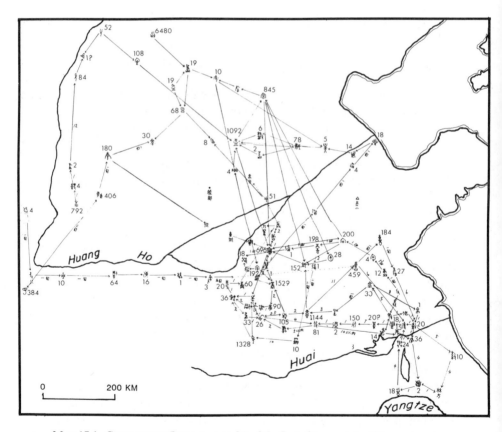

MAP 17.1. **State scores (large numerals) of the Late Shang state. (Place-name map
taken from Shima 1958:382–383; his small numerals near the arrows indicate the
number of days or ten-day periods [*hsün*] required to travel from one place to
another.)**

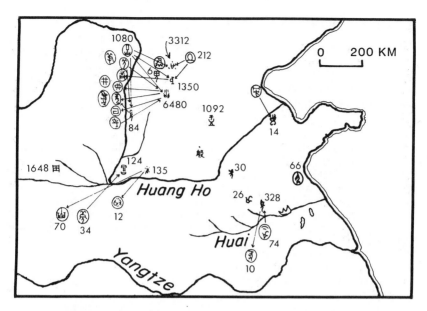

MAP 17.2. **State scores (arabic numerals) of major allies and enemies in Late Shang. (Place-name map taken from Shima 1958:423.)**

The problems involved in mapping the Shang state should not be minimized. Firm reference points are few. Distances are maximal and are expressed in temporal, not linear, measure. Directions are rarely given. The possibility that different places had the same name at the same time (see Chung 1972:45), remains troubling. Nevertheless, it is possible, given the clues we have, to check one piece of evidence against another and, by constantly adjusting our conclusions, to arrive at a consistent, schematic map of approximately 143 Shang place-names (see map 17.1). Precise locations cannot be established, but the general area and the direction and distance from the Shang in which clusters of places must have lain can be determined with some assurance. The fact that Shima (1958:382–383) and Chung (1972: facing 170) have drawn Shang maps that are generally similar encourages us to accept their reconstructions as valid working hypotheses. (The rudimentary map provided by Tung [1945: pt. 2, *ch.* 9, p. 40b], and reproduced by Yen [1978:131] places various Shang allies and enemies from the time of Wu Ting in Shensi; Shima [see map 17.2], by contrast, places most of them in Shansi. The differences involve distance more than direction. I do not find Tung's arguments persuasive.)

THE GEOGRAPHY OF THE SHANG STATE

The state scores for most places mapped by Shima are given in arabic numerals on maps 17.1 and 17.2, and the inscriptional criteria and presumed locations for those places he mapped with a state score of 150 or higher are given in table 17.1. This evidence suggests that major elements of the Late Shang state were clustered in the following areas:

1. The Huang Ho flood plain to the west and south of the Shantung massif, i.e., southern Hopei (Yü, Kung); the capital area in the eastern Honan panhandle (Ch'iu-Shang, Shun); the Hopei-Shantung-Honan junction (Sang); east central Honan (Wang) and north central Anhwei (Wu, Yung); southern Shantung (Wu, T'u, T'an, Hsiang) and possibly northern Kiangsu (Hui).
2. The southwest corner of Shansi (Fu) and up the Fen river (Pei, Sui), this cluster linked perhaps to Shu in the northwest corner of Honan near the Shensi border (Shu).
3. North (Ch'a) and northeast Shansi (Chih, Wu), a border region beset with enemies (Kung[?]-fang, T'u-fang).
4. West central Shensi, north of the Wei valley, i.e., the Chou homelands near Ch'i-shan.

These areas, presented as shaded regions on map 17.3, should be compared with the distribution of the sites or finds contemporary with Upper Erh-li-kang or Late Shang (An-yang) stages indicated on the same map. In general, the fit between the two sets of data is good. The following points should be noted.

1. No Late Shang sites have been found in the Shang-ch'iu region of the eastern Honan panhandle.
2. The inscriptions indicate no major state elements in the northern Honan, Cheng-chou-Lo-yang region. This accords well with the small number of Late Shang occupations that have been identified in this area. If this were indeed the center of Hsia power, it may have been excluded from the system of alliances, sacrifices, royal visits, etc., that comprised the Shang polity.
3. The inscriptions indicate that the Shang state did not extend east of the Huang Ho in Shantung, south of the Huai, or into northern Hopei and Liaoning. The Late Shang sites in these areas were presumably independent statelets—Bagley's "provincial centers," Hsia splinter groups perhaps, with roots in the Erh-li-kang stage—that the Shang had been unable to incorporate in their state. Kane, too (1974–75), has stressed the cultural independence of the Late An-yang bronze industries in the south. The fact that no southern bronzes have any ancestor dedications leads her to suspect that they were not the product of Shang colonies (ibid., p. 85).

The question of ancestor dedications, in fact, raises interesting problems. An inscription on a pot fragment found at Wu-ch'eng, Ch'ing-chiang (approximately 115°31′ east, 28°04′ north), Kiangsi, appears to record that "Chung 仲, being in Ts'ai Mu 材目, makes burnt offering to the ancestors

TABLE 17.1 **Shang Places with a State Score of 150 or More**

Province	Place	Oracle graph	Modern graph	Criteria satisfied	S reference	State score	Approx. location[a]	Period / Comments
Anhwei	Yung	永		1 3 6 11 15 31 36	323.1–2	150	46 B3–C3	I–V
Honan	Wang	璧		1 11 14 17? 28 31 34 39	110.2–111.1	1,328	55 F4–G4, F5–G5	I, III–V. High score due to Wang Ch'eng, Period I general, ally, or group. Shang, or Shang allies, may have fought Wang in I and V.
	Shun	羣		10 11 14 15 16 17 22 26 29 31 39	264.2–4; 265.2–3 seriatim	1,144	55 H3–H4	I–V
	Shang	商		3 11 13 14 20 22 26 28 29 30 31	279.2–280.3	1,529	55 G3	I–V. If one assumes that most divinations (place unrecorded) took place at Shang, the state score would be astronomical. Shang appears on Shang bronzes (Akatsuka 1977:650, 739, 808).
	Wu	牢		6 10 11 14 19	272.3–4	240	55 G3	II–V
	Shu	蜀		4 11 17 24 28 29 31 32	106.4	384	54 B3	I only
Hopei	Kung	宮		10 11 12 14	269.4–270.2	845	31 C6	I, III–V. Mainly a hunt area.
	Yü	盂		7 9 11 14 22 29 31	387.1–4	1,092	31 B7–C7	III–V. Mainly a hunt area. The Yü-fang entries at S387.3 are excluded from the state score; Yü may have become a Shang enemy in V.

TABLE 17.1 *(cont.)*

Province	Place	Oracle graph	Modern graph	Criteria satisfied	S reference	State score	Approx. location[a]	Period / Comments
Shansi	Fu	𤰔	甫	1 3 6 9 10 11 14 26 27 29 30 31	298.4–299.1	792	39 B5–B6, C5–C6	Mainly I. Fu appears on Shang bronzes (Akatsuka 1977:716, 753).
	Ch'a	𣂈	甾	1 2 3 4 5 6 7 8 9 11 12 18 19 20 27 28 29 31 34 35 38 39	98.1–99.3	6,480	38 D2–E2	I–IV. High score due to Ch'a Chih Hua, Period I ally. Ch'a appears on Shang bronzes (Hayashi 1968:35, fig. 14; Akatuska 1977:661, 808).
	Pei	𤕫	詩	9 10 11 12 14 29 30	329.1–2	406	39 C5–D5	I only. Important place of military assembly.
	Sui	繐	繐	10? 11 12 14 15 22	432.3–4	180	39 C5	I, III + IV. Sui-fang in III suggests Sui became Shang enemy.
	Chih	沚	沚	1 7 8 10 11 12 14 19 24 29 31 34	65.4–67.1	3,312	38 E2	Mainly I. High score due to Chih Kuo, Shang general, ally. Chih appears on Shang bronzes (Akatsuka 1977:709, 711).
	Yüeh	戉	戉	1 3 6 8 28 31 33 34 35	349.4	1,350	38 E2	Shang ally in I.

TABLE 17.1 (*cont.*)

Province	Place	Oracle graph	Modern graph	Criteria satisfied	S reference	State score	Approx. location[a]	Period / Comments
Shantung	Sang	桑	喪	10 11 26 31	191.1–191.4	696	31 C7	I to V. Mainly a III–V hunting area.
	Hsiang	向	向	10 11 22? 31	269.3–4	200	34 D4	A hunting and divining area in I, III–V. Hsiang appears on a Shang bronze (Akatsuka 1977:811).
	Wu(?)		unknown	10 14	478.4–479.2	198	34 B4–C4	V. Divining (and hunting) area.
	T'u		徐	10 11	189.1–3	152	34 B4	II–V. Rich hunting area. T'u appears on a Shang bronze (Akatsuka 1977:631).
	Hui(?)		曹	10 14 15	431.2–432.1	459	34 D5	V. Hunting area; fairly long periods of occupation.
	T'an(?)		覃	10 11 14 15	432.2–3	184	34 D4–5	V. Hunting and divining area; scheduled divinations suggest consistent occupation.
Shensi	Chou	周	周	1 2 4 5 6 20 24 27 28 30 31 34 37 38	299.3–300.1	1,648	63 C6	I, II (V?)

[a] Reference is to map square in Geelan and Twitchett 1974.

MAP 17.3. **Major regions (shaded) of the Late Shang state (derived from the oracle-bone inscriptions [see map 17.1]) superimposed upon a map of sites and finds of the Upper Erh-li-kang and An-yang stages. (Site-map adapted from Chang 1977:219.)**

(*tsu* 祖) and(?) to Shang Chia 上甲" (Chao Feng 1976:222–223, fig. 9.1–2 [rubbing illegible at the crucial Shang Chia]). Bagley (1977:210–211) treats the site as one of a series of local Neolithic cultures, "altered or transformed by contact with Shang civilization." The formula *liao tsu chih Shang Chia* 尞祖之上甲 is not found on the oracle bones; the pot may have been imported (together with the bronze lid; Bagley 1977:210, fig. 46); nevertheless, there is here a tenuous hint that Shang Chia, the putative progenitor of the Shang *lineage*, may have been worshipped in the south. Since Shang

Chia was not the founder of the Shang *dynasty*, no political implications about state membership can be drawn from this one record, and indeed, the vagueness of the record "burnt offering to the ancestors and to Shang Chia" suggests no very precise link with An-yang ritual practice.

The ancestral dedications such as those to Fu Chia, Fu Ting, Fu Yi, and Fu Wu that have been found on the bronzes unearthed at K'o-tso-hsien, Liaoning (*WW* 1977.12:26), indicate the extent to which Shang-style lineage designations were used in the north. In the absence of more specific links, however, these can tell us nothing about the extent of the Shang state, for there is no doubt that certain Late Shang bronzes were dedicated to ancestors not recorded in the sacrifice divinations of the royal house, ancestors who may therefore have been associated with elites independent of the state (Akatsuka 1977:728). And there is some evidence that Shang allies had their own extensive genealogies (ibid., pp. 405–407, discussing what may be references to as many as twenty-three ancestral stands for Yi Yin [*Ching-chin* 4101; *Yi-ts'un* 211; both S365.2]). Ancestral titles by themselves, therefore, tell us nothing about the extent of the state.

> 4. One significant appendage of the Shang state extended beyond the political vacuum in northern Honan to the T'ung-kuan bend and into the Wei river valley.
>
> 5. There was a powerful Shang presence in Shansi. The archaeological evidence places this along the banks of the north-south reach of the Ho; the inscriptional evidence, by contrast, places it more in the southwest and northeast corners of the province.

The presence of Shang state elements in the Wei valley and in Shansi, apparently isolated from the core of the state in the Huang Ho plain, suggests that the state functioned in part as an alliance of regional groupings, the descendants perhaps of allies who had once united against or derived from (these alternatives are not exclusive) the Hsia, who had cemented their alliance by ties of marriage, kinship, and religion, and who had continued to maintain themselves in their native regions. To the extent that the virtual disappearance of the Chou from the divination record after Period I may be considered to have real historical (as opposed to mere historiographical) significance (on the issues involved, see Keightley 1978b:132, n. 38), it can be assumed that the Chou ceased to participate actively in the Shang state after the reign of Wu Ting—a situation that could be well explained by distance and the passage of time. Divergence between the style of the An-yang bronzes and that of contemporary vessels found in Shensi (Rawson 1980:88–91) may support such a view. Similar conclusions can be applied to the Shang state elements in Shansi; four of the six groups there (Chih, Fu, Pei, Wu) ceased to play a role after Period I (see table 17.1). And a study of Late Shang bronze styles in general has led Bagley (1977:213) to suggest that, though "an early expansion of dynastic power stimulated the rise of regional bronze-using societies," these regional groups forced "a retrenchment of the dynasty around the beginning of the Anyang period." (Compare Kane 1974–75 on the independence of the southern bronze industries.) The oracular evidence supports such a view of political contraction after the reign of Wu Ting, with the enduring state members concentrated in Honan and Shantung (table 17.1), the core of the state.

Something should be said about the discrepancies between the inscriptional (maps 17.1 and 17.2) and the archaeological (map 17.3) evidence, particularly with regard to Shang-ch'iu (number 1 above), Shansi (5), and the rather unexpected situation in north central Honan (2). There are several possible explanations:

1. The method of reconstruction used by Shima (1958) and Chung (1972) is faulty.
2. The archaeological sites are there but have not yet been discovered.
3. The activities at many of these sites—issuing orders, hunting, fighting, recruiting, meeting—would not have left archaeological remains.
4. The state score is misleading, giving undue emphasis to those areas of the Shang state that were trouble spots, subject to enemy invasion, for instance, and thus divined about out of all proportion to their actual importance in the state.

There is probably an element of truth in all these explanations.

There is nothing to be done about the first; the maps were drawn on the basis of the best criteria, and it would be tendentious to skew them to fit the archaeological evidence—which is frequently ambiguous, if not uninformative, about state affiliations and which will always be incomplete.

With regard to the second explanation, we must await further discoveries of Shang sites, perhaps in the shaded areas of map 17.3. Chang (1978:90) has described the eastern Honan/western Shantung area as "the least archaeologically known within all of North China because it is situated at the heart of the Huang Ho flood plain and its surface is covered with thick deposits of silt." (The total absence of metal-bearing sites in northeastern Honan and the Honan panhandle is amply demonstrated by the blank areas on the distribution maps of Barnard and Satō [1975].) The Hung-kou 鴻溝, a waterway built, according to Ssu-ma Ch'ien, after the labors of the Sage Emperor Yü, was well known in this area by Eastern Chou times. Its original name, I suspect, was not Canal of the Wild Geese, or Far-Flung Conduit (Needham 1971:269), but the homophonous Hung

Kou 洪溝, Flood Ditch, an indication that in antiquity the area was inundated by the Huang Ho, destroying city sites and concealing archaeological remains. The situation was little different in modern times; between 1904 and 1929 the Shang-ch'iu area suffered thirteen floods (Buck 1937:13, table 9).

The third explanation causes us to consider the kind of archaeological evidence we are looking for. There is a natural tendency to think that all sites associated with the Shang state ought to be copies, to some degree, of the classic Hsiao-t'un site, with evidence of bronze casting, rammed earth construction, human sacrifice, large *ya*-shaped burial pits, white ware, and oracle bones. The fact that few, if any, Late Shang sites fully satisfy this model suggests that the greater part of the state (in terms of area and population) consisted of settlements at a Neolithic stage of culture, dominated by the bronze-making center (or centers) and relying upon the center's industrial products, administrative skills, and spiritual powers of intercession. The areas through which the king hunted and fought, where he camped and divined, for which he prayed for rain and harvest, where his officers met and recruited men, and so on, may well have left the lowliest and most plebeian of archaeological records, records to which, in fact, even if they have been noticed, we might be hard put to assign a Shang rather than a Neolithic date. (With the exception of northern Shansi, Lung-shanoid sites have been found over the whole area of the Shang state defined by the inscriptions; see Chang 1977:170, fig. 78.) The Shang state in short was at various stages of development; archaeology is most likely to identify only the advanced, bronze-casting, elite centers, while contemporary Shang inscriptions may have referred to the state at all levels of development. It is not surprising that the inscriptional and archaeological maps do not always match.

The fourth explanation bears in an important way on the nature of inscriptional sources. If the central areas of the state were firmly under Shang control, then the very fact that they were subject to routine, and hence increasingly secular, administration might have led to their being divined about with less frequency. This raises the possibility that many of the Late Shang archaeological sites in map 17.3 were indeed constituent elements of the state—so firmly so, in fact, that it was unnecessary for the king to divine about their assistance, obedience, tribute payments, orders, and so on, with great frequency. In this view, the king would have felt so safe as he traveled to and from Hsiao-t'un and through north-central Honan that he would have felt no need to divine about his route or safety. I am not persuaded by this argument, for the king did not, in my view, divine only when he was in doubt or danger; he divined continually to test the ever-problematical will of the spirits. Nevertheless, it is proper to bear such historiographical cautions in mind, particularly when we consider the reduced scope, and perhaps increasingly secular nature, of Shang divination in Period V.

THE SHANG STATE: WHAT

Map 17.1, whatever its geographical accuracy, suggests that the Late Shang state consisted, in part, of a series of nodal points, with the important ones frequently appearing at crossroads on the king's various journeys. That most of the sites have low scores (of the 88 cases for which I have calculated state scores, 44, or 50 percent, had a state score of 20 or less and 27, or 31 percent, had a state score of 10 or less) indicates that relatively few places (e.g., the 21 places with state scores of 150 or higher listed in table 17.1) were important to the king, or were visited by him frequently. One has the sense, in short, of the state as a thin network of pathways and encampments; the king and information and resources traveled along the pathways, but the network was laid over a hinterland that rarely saw or felt the king's presence and authority. State power would have been generally intermittent and, in areas like Shensi and Shansi, rather transitory. Such a picture, which emphasizes points and journeys, reflects in part the bias of our sources, which tend to divine particularly about the king's peregrinations.

But it is a picture that accords well with the nature of the state criteria revealed by the inscriptions (Keightley, 1979–80). When we consider the role of force and coercion, the evidence (criteria 31–35) suggests that the king relied primarily upon his own armies and the help of a few close supporters.

The coercive power of the state may on occasion have been shared, but it was not widely delegated. In general, only the king, or his immediate family ("it should be Fu Hao whom the king orders to attack Jen [?]" [Yi-ts'un 527; S71.1]) is recorded as actually attacking (correcting, rectifying, cheng 正) an enemy (S70.4–71.3). Similarly, only attacks (fa 伐) by the king or his close officers were divined by the Shang; for example, "Divined: 'Cry out (hu) for the to-ch'en 多臣 to attack the Kung(?)-fang'" (Ho-pien 114; S130.4); "Divined: 'It should be Pi 𢀖 to whom we cry out, "Attack the Kung(?)-(-fang)"''"(Chih-hsü 140; S130.4). There are few if any divinations about other allies or groups attacking the fang countries.

Theology may explain the virtual silence of the inscriptions on this point; that is, the Shang may not have divined such topics because Ti, the high god, could not be persuaded by the Shang ancestors who interceded with him to assist the victories of non-Shang groups. (For an initial sketch of the theology of Shang divination, see Keightley 1978a; the subject will be treated in detail in Keightley, forthcoming [b].) Even if this is true, the theological limits implied by Shang weakness in the spirit world presumably reflected geopolitical realities among the living.

There are numerous divinations about the king joining allies on campaign (criterion 31), but the Shang did not divine about such groups fighting by themselves for the Shang cause, that is, on a campaign whose outcome we expect the Shang would have wished to divine. This indicates that the military power which maintained the Shang state was dynastic. Loyalty to the Shang must have been very much a matter of immediate self-interest and expediency. Neither the Shang nor their allies expected the allies to fight for any Shang "state." They would only fight for the king when he fought beside them.

This view is confirmed by divinations that seek to determine if the king should go on campaign himself, for example: "The Kung(?)-fang are going out, the king himself 'corrects' them, (the spirits from) Hsia (Yi) (to) Shang (Chia) approve and confer (assistance) on us" (*Pai-ken* 25; S115.2); or "It should be the king himself who 'corrects' the Jen-fang" (*Ts'ui-pien* 1185; S115.3; on the king's personal participation see, too, Keightley 1975: 35–42).

The dynastic and ad hoc nature of the state is confirmed by the status of the diviners (to be discussed in detail in Keightley, forthcoming [a]). The evidence (see the discussion of criterion 36 in Keightley 1979–80) makes it likely that the diviners were associated in some way with the surrounding settlements and their bronze-vessel-making, insignia-casting elites. They were particularly likely to appear as diviners when the Shang king had established relations with (or had conferred titles upon?) their leaders, or had married a woman of their group; in the latter case, the diviner might have been among the retainers who accompanied the royal consort to her new home in Shang. Those groups, including some archer lords (criterion 20), which produced diviners in this way were presumably Shang allies and potential members of the state.

Since the post of diviner was highly strategic, it can be further assumed that such groups were trusted and reliable allies. The large number of diviners' names—we know of some 120—and the fact that the diviners tended to flourish for a reign or two and then vanish, suggests further that such alliances were not conceived in institutional terms (i.e., between one state and another) but in dynastic terms: between one ruling lineage and another. In this model, therefore, the composition of the Shang state might have changed quite abruptly as the personal ties of one dynast were replaced by those of his successor.

By Period V the king was virtually the only diviner recorded; this indicates that divination had become a royal monopoly. Divination had also become more routine and perfunctory (Keightley 1978b:35–36). Whether these changes in divination procedure indicate that the nature of the Shang state itself had changed—from a congeries of "federal" groups to a more centralized and autocratic state—cannot yet be determined. It is at least plausible that the putative loss of control over, or contact with, areas in Shansi and Shensi resulted in a tighter, more compact state in which the king no longer needed, or was no longer able to rely upon, the extensive alliances of kin and retainers with which Wu Ting—for whom some eighty-eight "royal women" are recorded (criterion 37)—had bolstered the state.

The provisional or irregular nature of Shang state activity is also suggested by a consideration of exchange relations (criteria 38, 39). Archaeological evidence reveals the extent to which the Shang settlements in An-yang drew upon resources from other areas of China and East Asia. Various routes may have been used for the transport of gold, copper, maritime products, and precious stones (Shih Chang-ju, cited by Wheatley 1971:283); jade may have come from Baikalia along the Amur valley (Watson 1971:59); animal and shell remains argue for extensive trade with the south (Teilhard de Chardin and Young 1936:56; cf. Hu 1944:13a). Chang (1975:216–217) has posited movements of agricultural produce, animals (cattle, sheep, horses), handicraft products, prestige goods (cowries, turtle shells, jade), slaves, and prisoners. The raw materials (turtle shells and bovid scapulas) required for divination were also transported, frequently several hundred at a time. (See Keightley 1978b:15, though the extent of this traffic should not be over-estimated.) Crude calculations (based on ibid., pp. 165–170) suggest that the Shang might have imported the scapulas from approximately nine head of cattle or water buffalo and the plastrons from approximately twenty turtles, every month.

Gifts of cowrie shells, recorded on Late Shang ritual bronzes (e.g., Akatsuka 1977:615, 631, 642, 643) do document the existence of religious and political ties between the donor, frequently the king, and the recipient. But apart from such symbolic exchanges, which might also have involved jade or horses (ibid., pp. 636, 640, 648), there is no evidence that the groups which exchanged with the Shang were members of the state. Turtle shells may have come from the Yangtze valley and cowries may have come from the south and southeast coast, but in neither case did the state extend that far. If the inscription maps are correct, the Shang made no special effort to incorporate the copper and tin deposits that were "comparatively dense . . . in the Shensi-Honan areas" (Barnard and Satō 1975:26; see their map of the sites, p. 25).

The fact that exchanges were a topic of divination (criterion 39) indicates that—in the reign of Wu Ting at least, when the great majority of such charges was recorded—the exchanges were not yet routine, and that the ability of the Shang to extract or invite such payments was by no means assured. The disappearance of such topics from the divination record by Period V may be due to either the general reduction in the scope of Shang divination (Keightley 1978b:35–36, 122), the routinization of such economic exchanges, or their disappearance.

The identification of over a hundred "tribute-paying" areas suggests that exchange was not of itself evidence of membership in the Shang state. As Chou (1970–71:365) has noted, the areas were so numerous "that one cannot presuppose a complex system of supervision and a strong central power holding practically uncontested sway over the Subject States." It is more likely, at least for those cases in which Wu Ting divined about the subject, that the shipments of livestock, prisoners, ivory, and other commodities were the supplementary perquisites that, it was hoped, the power of the Shang state would encourage; they were not yet conceived as integral to the state structure.

CONCLUSIONS: THE INCIPIENT DYNASTIC STATE

The Shang state—at least as pictured in the oracle-bone inscriptions of period I—was defined by a series of dynastic operations. Orders were issued, but they were the king's, frequently transmitted by him orally. Dependents came to have audience with the king, and the king in turn was concerned about their actions and good fortune and the success of their harvests. Royal gifts, at times conferred when the king was on tour (e.g., see the bronze inscriptions at Akatsuka 1977:631, 661, 666, 679, 690), and royal hospitality strengthened ties of mutual obligation. The king displayed his power by frequent travel, hunting, and inspecting along the pathways of his realm, delegating little of his military power and expecting no "legal" or "constitutional" military support in return. The cooperation of subordinates was on occasion problematical (see the discussion of criterion 4 in Keightley 1979–80).

If, as the inscriptions suggest, the state was in origin an alliance of independent groups whose tutelary spirits were incorporated into the genealogy and ritual structure of the court as their leaders joined the Shang federation (Akatsuka 1977:512–513 and passim; Keightley, forthcoming [b]), then the king in his travels would have moved through a landscape pregnant with symbolic meaning, sacrificing to the local spirits, giving and receiving power at each holy place, and thus renewing the religious and kin ties (fictive or not) that bound the state together. And the king, as he traveled, would have been a force for cultural as well as political unification, impressing the local populations with his language, his writing system, his sumptuary displays, his weaponry, his tastes, and his beliefs.

The peripatetic nature of the king's role can be judged from the large number of hunt-plus-place-name divinations that constitute a significant proportion of the total corpus of oracle-bone inscriptions (Chung Po-sheng 1972:6). These divinations remind us that the journeys were not without peril (Keightley 1979–80, criterion 10), and that the king's power and safety were frequently exposed to the dangers, political and spiritual, of travel through potentially unfriendly hinterlands. Tung Tso-pin's reconstruction of the Period V campaigns against the Jen-fang 人方 in the southeast (1945: pt. 2, *ch.* 5:23a; *ch.* 8:7–9), indicates that the last Shang king was away from his capital for some three hundred days. Power so itinerant in nature suggests in turn that the capital may have been a base of operations, a cult center, a necropolis, an industrial and artisanal center, rather than a fixed administrative and redistributive center. It is striking that in map 17.1 all roads do *not* lead to Shang. Shang, like Hsiao-t'un, may have been only a *ta yi* 大邑, a "great settlement," one of the centers to which the king repaired from time to time. There may have been no paramount, central capital. (The fact that no Western Chou capital site has yet been excavated supports such an interpretation.) The term *ta yi Shang*, "the great settlement, Shang" (S279.2–3), which may have referred to a capital, appears only in the Period V inscriptions; this suggests that the very conception of a great settlement was a late development. The traditional capital removals attributed to the Shang, whose former kings, according to *Shang-shu* ("P'an Keng") "did not perpetuate their cities (*pu ch'ang chüeh yi* 不常厥邑)" (Karlgren 1950:20; on this point see Chang 1976b:50–51), may represent a dim memory of periodic shifts in "centers of operation" as the kings exhausted their ability to exploit certain areas. State power traveled with the king and his court of diviners and retainers, who prayed and sacrificed to legitimate the orders and expropriations that he levied on the populations and groups that came into his intermittent view. Any area that did not see the king for a number of years might well have ceased to think itself a member of the Shang state and, given the lack of personal contact with the king, would indeed have ceased to be one.

I am tempted to wonder, parenthetically, if the title of king did not refer to "the one who goes"; *wang* 王 /*gwang* 大 was phonetically and graphically related to *wang* 往 /*gwang* 𢓊 —the latter a picture of a foot above the phonetic for "king." Rather than being, in *Shuo-wen*'s paronamastic terms, "the one to whom the world goes" (*wang t'ien-hsia chih so kuei-wang yeh* 王天下之所歸往也), the Shang king would have been the one who went to the world, the "goer." And be that as it may, the theme of the ritual magic-making journey in later Chinese literature (see Hawkes 1967, esp. pp. 82–83) may well have derived its imaginative power from the tradition of these early royal progresses.

All decisions, alliances, orders were the king's. The heavy burden of personal leadership born by "I the one (or the first) man" (*yü yi-jen* 余一人; on this phrase see Hu 1957:75) was alleviated and justified by continual divinatory and sacrificial appeals to the ancestors and other spirits, appeals that sapped the king's energies in the form of prayers, incantations, and spells and that drained his economic resources. A significant part of his redistributive activities, in fact, probably involved the sharing of large quantities of sacrificial meat with retainers, combining personal hospitality with religious sanctions and economic sustenance (Keightley 1975:32).

The schedule of the royal hunts confirms the relatively undemanding nature of the king's administrative duties at a central place. By Period V the hunts were regularly divined for the same five days out of every ten (Matsumaru 1963). If we assume that the hunt lasted much of the day— and the frequently encountered Period III + IV hunt incantation, "the whole day will be without disaster" (S104.4-105.2), encourages us to do so—it seems that the last rulers of the Late Shang state could routinely consider spending half their time in pursuit of game. The hunts served political, economic, and military purposes; but the maintenance of the royal table and household in this relatively primitive way suggests once again that the king was not directing a sophisticated administrative apparatus that required his constant attendance in a fixed capital. The king's journeys, furthermore, would have meant that he was frequently out of touch with his officers, who would thus have acted not as bureaucrats but as petty rulers, guided by only the most general and intermittent policy directives.

The king's view of the state, in short, was defined by the horizons of his travels, by his continual need to show the flag, by the demands of his numerous campaigns, by his incessant divining, praying, and sacrificing, by the personal and frequently familial nature of his links to subordinates and to the supernatural powers. If it is "characteristic of patrimonialism that the ruler treats all political administration as his personal affair, while the officials, appointed by the ruler on the basis of his personal confidence in them, in turn regard their administrative operations as a personal service to their ruler in a context of duty and respect" (Wheatley 1971:52), then we can affirm with some confidence that the Shang state was a patrimonial one, satisfying, so far as we are able to tell, the Weberian criteria.[4]

It is tempting to assume that other groups that participated in the state were, to the extent that "administrative operations" formed a significant part of their activities, equally patrimonial. As Chang has noted (1976b:54), "the Tzu clan . . . could not have been the sole component of the Shang ruling aristocracy"; and he suggests that "lineage fission within the clans, localization of marriageable partners, and the legitimization of the local powers" would have helped distribute members of the aristocracy all over the state, with the "cities and towns . . . [being] the seats of the lineages at the local level." These plausible suppositions suggest our need to know more about the relations that existed between the center and the periphery.

For the final, and major, question is: are we justified in speaking of the Late Shang as a state at all? Can we distinguish between a Shang chiefdom and a Shang state? Service (1975:304), for example, argues that in general terms "there seems to be no way to discriminate the state from the chiefdom stage." Can we refer to Late Shang as an early state module (Renfrew 1975:24, 26–27) as opposed to what we might characterize as a central person module?

The questions are partly those of definition. Trigger (1974:100–101), though noting that "for transitional societies it may not be possible to determine whether or not a state was present," has listed some classes of archaeological evidence "that definitely suggest the existence of a state." These are: (1) "building programmes of a labour-intensive nature that are specifically designed to affirm the personal glory of high-status individuals or to display the power of the state"; (2) "the emergence of full-time specialists to serve the needs of the elite and the state apparatus which they control. In general, these specialists fall into four classes: artisans, bureauc-

4. On the basis of the evidence presented in this chapter, I am now happy to withdraw the "major caution" I urged upon Wheatley (Keightley 1973b:527) in his use of the term "patrimonial."

rats, soldiers and retainers"—the presence of such "master specialists" is related to the creation of an "elite culture or what Robert Redfield has called a 'Great Tradition'"; (3) "large-scale human sacrifice in connection with high status burials." The Late Shang satisfy most of these criteria. The use of large conscript labor gangs to serve a central elite can be well documented, both archaeologically and in the inscriptions (Keightley 1969:66–144); so can the existence of specialized artisans (ibid., pp. 8–65; Keightley 1970); and so can the lavish human sacrifices (e.g., *KK* 1977.3: 210–214; 1978.1:71–72). Inscriptions about sacrifice to dead kings and ministers(?), together with the appearance of complexly ornamented ritual bronzes, some inscribed with ancestor dedications, afford evidence of an emerging Great Tradition serving the needs of particular lineage groups. The extent to which specialized "bureaucrats, soldiers and retainers" had appeared is less certain, though in my view the *chung* 衆, as dependents permanently attached to the royal house (Keightley 1969:89–97), would probably satisfy the last two categories. In these broad terms, therefore, one can conclude that the Late Shang was indeed a state. Future research must consider the geographical distribution of these state-like elements in the general area of Shang culture.

As archaeological techniques become more refined, particularly with regard to the relative dating of sites, it may be possible to document the evolution of the Shang state. That evolution can also be approached in another way, for the shift in the nature of our inscriptional sources suggests a corresponding shift in the structure of the polity.

> Broad changes can be discerned in the content of the inscriptions. By Period V, emphasis was focused upon divinations about the sacrificial schedule, the ten-day period and the night, and the hunt. Other areas of life, such as dreams, sickness, enemy attacks, requests for harvest, and the issuing of orders were divined far less frequently than they had been in Period I, if at all . . . The forms of Shang divination also changed markedly . . . The trend toward terser, less detailed, and always optimistic prognostications and verifications, the reduced use of crack-notations and complementary pairs of charges, the disappearance of marginal notations, the virtual disappearance of diviners' names, the smaller number of calligraphic variants and divination formulas, the reduced size of the script—these phenomena were related to both the standardization of Shang divination procedures and the general shrinkage in the scope of the topics divined (Keightley 1978b:122).

I have previously discussed the metaphysical and theological implications of this shift (Keightley 1973a:14–17; 1976:14–16). It is tempting to assume—and since the evidence is largely negative we can only make assumptions—that the shift was also related to administrative and political activity. The more tentative and problematical divinations of period I may have reflected a time when institutions, such as they were, were new, when the nature of the succession (i.e., the fraternal succession of Wu Ting's "fathers" and sons) was still uncertain, when the obedience of the king's supporters was conditional. The positive and negative complementarity of the Period I divination charges may have been an expression of the "centralized cajolery of the chiefdom" (Webb 1975:165), and the theocratic cast of Wu Ting's rule may have represented the final and circumscribed stages of the Shang chiefdom rather than the increasingly powerful nature of the emerging Shang state. As Webb (ibid., p. 177) has argued:

> The well-known theocratic cast of early states is more likely to reflect a rapidly vanishing condition in which, in the absence of state controls, only religious public works could be carried out, than to indicate the great force of specifically theocratic sanctions; the later history of states is one of a decreasing role of cultus in governmental affairs.

The reduced scope and routine nature of the late divination record may reflect precisely the increasing secularization of the king's activities, his increasing ability to command rather than cajole.

If it is the "free obedience" of the chiefdom system that prevents the chief from being "a truly effective locus of sovereignty" (ibid., p. 161), then the shift between advanced tribal and incipient state systems of government "entails a basic and total alteration in the manner in which the authority of the leadership is ultimately enforced and upheld" (p. 157). The extensive military campaigns undertaken by the Period V Shang kings, which are well documented in the inscriptions (e.g., Tung 1945: pt. 2, *ch.* 5:23a; *ch.* 8: 7–9), are impressive testimony to their powers of coercion and to institutionalized control of violence. (One can note, for example, that the Period V kings never divine about "raising men" [S1.1–3]; presumably this topic was now non-problematical and secular.)

The shifts in divinatory metaphysics and theology can similarly be seen as shifts in the nature of legitimating authority (Keightley 1975:49–52), an authority that had grown more assured and routine than it had been in Period I. These links need to be documented and explored in more detail (Keightley: forthcoming [a]), but for the moment I am willing to suggest a late Late Shang shift from an advanced tribal to at least an incipient dynastic state. The Period V state, as my analysis of table 17.1 has suggested, may have been smaller than in Period I; but that very smallness, with its implications of tighter control, may help to qualify it as an early state module (Renfrew 1975:14 notes that "the early state module apparently falls within a restricted size range"). But for all the evidence of institutionalized coercive power, of regular dynastic succession, of a more secular decision-making process, we are still dealing with a patrimonial dynastic state.

It is true that proto-bureaucratic forms of administration existed, even in Period. I.

> Written documents certainly played a major role in the organization of the state. The king issued orders to officers by their titles; administration was conducted through group assignments; such groups formed part of a hierarchical administration in which the king ordered individual officers, the officers ordered these groups, and the groups in turn directed the conscripts beneath them. And we can document, in some cases, a filiation between the titles of these Shang groups and the later bureaucratic titles of Chou times (Keightley 1978a:221; for an introduction to Shang proto-bureaucracy, see Ch'en 1956:503–522; Shima 1958: 461–475; Chou 1968; Keightley 1969:10–29; also 1970; Creel 1970:32–40).

But the evidence is sketchy at best, and, as I have argued elsewhere (Keightley 1978a:216–224), the organizing metaphors and institutions of Shang life were those of an ancestor worship that, for all its generational, hierachical, and jurisdictional qualities, was still essentially particularistic and kin-centered rather than non-ascriptive and bureaucratic. The lineage was the source of authority in both government and religion.

The oracle-bone inscriptions indicate the existence of such state-defining institutions as permanent status positions, but they give no indication that their character was essentially bureaucratic rather than, as seems more plausible, patrimonial. Nor, and this is a crucial point, do the inscriptions give firm information about how the Shang appointed (if they did) or controlled their provincial representatives. The silence of the inscriptions about these points may of course be only that: silence. And it is particularly frustrating because such silence is precisely what we would expect as increasing secularization and professionalization of administration removed such topics from the realm of divination and thus from the enduring inscriptional record. The late Late Shang is thus a Cheshire cat; its putative secular body can only be inferred, perhaps quite wrongly and never conclusively, from its dwindling divinatory and theocratic grin.

Creel's conclusion (1970:420) that "from the point of view of strict bureaucratic procedure" the Western Chou was "a Mad Hatter's Tea Party," that "it was, indeed, virtually impossible" for the Western Chou kings "with the resources and techniques available to them, [to] organize and maintain a centralized administration adequate to control the broad territories to which they laid claim" (p. 417), suggests that the Late Shang situation would not have been very different. It is doubtful therefore that the Late Shang state—whatever its claims to large, chiefdom-like hegemony under Wu Ting—was, by Period V, little more than an incipient state, a dynastic lineage ruling in proto-bureaucratic, patrimonial style over a central and perhaps shifting nucleus, and beyond that area operating still by a series of chiefdom-like forays.

The origin of the Chinese state involved a slow and gradual evolution, from "the general kin-based patterns of social interaction that characterize smaller-scale societies" to "professionalized and institutionally-differentiated" political activities (Trigger 1974:96). Shang theocracy created the patrimonial proto-bureaucratic mix from which the more secular Chou and Han states were to emerge. But the fruition, the filling out of the state model—in terms of both geography and effective centralized bureaucratic control—was still far in the future when one incipient dynastic state, the Shang, fell to another, the Chou, in the middle of the eleventh century B.C.

REFERENCES

For full citations to the abbreviations by which oracle-bone collections are cited, see Keightley 1978b:229–231.

Akatsuka Kiyoshi 赤塚忠
   1977   *Chūgoku kodai no shūkyō to bunka—In ōchō no saishi*
                中国古代の宗教と文化 ― 殷王朝の祭祀. Tokyo.

Bagley, Robert W.
   1977   "P'an-lung-ch'eng: A Shang City in Hupei." *Artibus Asiae*
                39.3/4:165–219.

Barnard, Noel, and Satō, Tamotsu
   1975   *Metallurgical Remains of Ancient China*. Tokyo.

Buck, John Lossing
   1937   *Land Utilization in China: Statistics*. Nanking.

Bulling, A. Gutkind
   1977   "A Late Shang Place of Sacrifice and Its Historical
                Significance." *Expedition* 19.4:1–11.

Chang, K. C. [Kwang-chih] 張光直
   1975   "Ancient Trade as Economics or as Ecology." In *Ancient
                Civilization and Trade*, edited by J. A. Sabloff and C. C.
                Lamberg-Karlovsky: pp. 211–224. Albuquerque.
   1976a   "Yin-Shang wen-ming ch'i-yüan yen-chiu shang ti yi-ko
                kuan-chien wen-t'i 殷商文明起源研究上的一個關鍵問題."

In *Shen Kang-po hsien-sheng pa-chih jung-ch'ing lun-wen-chi* 沈剛伯先生八秩榮慶論文集: pp. 1–15. Taipei.

1976b   *Early Chinese Civilization: Anthropological Perspectives.* Cambridge, Mass.

1977   *The Archaeology of Ancient China.* 3d ed., rev. and enl. New Haven.

1978   "The Origins of Chinese Civilization: A Review." *Journal of the American Oriental Society* 98.1:85–91.

Chao Feng 趙峯
1976   "Ch'ing-chiang t'ao-wen chi ch'i so fan-ying ti Yin-tai nung-yeh ho chi-ssu 清江陶文及其所反映的殷代農業和祭祀." *KK* 1976.4:221–228.

Chao Lin
1972   "Shang Government." Ph.D. dissertation, University of Chicago.

Ch'en Meng-chia 陳夢家
1956   *Yin-hsü pu-tz'u tsung-shu* 殷虛卜辭綜述. Peking.

Ch'i Wen-t'ao 齊文濤
1972   "Kai-shu chin-nien lai Shan-tung ch'u-t'u ti Shang-Chou ch'ing-t'ung-ch'i 概述近年來山東出土的商周青銅器." *WW* 1972.5:3–18.

Chiang Hung 江鴻
1976   "P'an-lung-ch'eng yü Shang-ch'ao ti nan-t'u 盤龍城與商朝的南土." *WW* 1976.2:42–46.

Chou, Hung-hsiang
1968   "Some Aspects of Shang Administration: A Survey Based Solely on the Evidence Available in the Oracle Bone Texts." Ph.D. Dissertation, Australian National University.
1970–71 "Fu-X Ladies of the Shang Dynasty." *Monumenta Serica* 29:346–390.

Chow, Tse-tsung
1968   "The Early History of the Chinese Word *Shih* (Poetry)." In *Wen Lin: Studies in the Chinese Humanities*, edited by Chow Tse-tsung: pp. 151–209. Madison, Wis.

Chung Po-sheng 鍾柏生
1972   *Pu-tz'u chung so-chien Yin-wang t'ien-yu ti-ming k'ao— chien-lun t'ien-yu ti-ming yen-chiu fang-fa* 卜辭中所見殷王田游地名考—兼論田游地名研究方法. Taipei.

Creel, Herrlee Glessner
1937   *Studies in Early Chinese Culture, 1st ser.* American
           Council of Learned Societies in Chinese and Related
           Civilizations, no. 3. Baltimore.
1970   *The Origins of Statecraft in China,* vol. 1: *The Western
           Chou Empire.* Chicago.

Geelan, P. J. M., and Twitchett, D. C.
1974   *The Times Atlas of China.* London.

Hawkes, David
1967   "The Quest of the Goddess." *Asia Major,* n.s. 13:71–94.

Hayashi Minao 林巳奈夫
1968   "Inshū jidai no zuzō kigō 殷周時代の図象記号." *Tōhō
           gakuhō* 東方学報 39:1–117.

Hsinhua-she 新華社
1977   "Shen-hsi Chou-yüan fa-hsien chen-kuei chia-ku 陝西周原
           發現珍貴甲骨." *Ta kung-pao* 大公報 17 October: 1.
           (Translated in *Early China* 3 [Fall 1977]: 97–98.)

Hsü, Chin-hsiung
1977   *The Menzies Collection of Shang Dynasty Oracle Bones,*
           vol. 2: *The Text.* Toronto.

Hu Hou-hsüan 胡厚宣
1944   "Yin-tai pu-kuei chih lai-yüan 殷代卜龜之來源." In Hu,
           Chia-ku-hsüeh Shang-shih lun-ts'ung ch'u-chi 甲骨學
           商史論叢初集. Ch'eng-tu.
1957   "Shih 'yü yi-jen' 釋'余一人'." *Li-shih yen-chiu* 歷史研究
           1957.1:75–78.

Huang Ch'ing-sheng 黃慶生
1977   *Yin-tai t'ien-lieh yen-chiu* 殷代田獵研究. Taipei.

Jao Tsung-yi 饒宗頤
1959   *Yin-tai chen-pu jen-wu t'ung-k'ao* 殷代貞卜人物通考. 2
           vols. Hong Kong.

Kane, Virginia C.
1973   "The Chronological Significance of the Inscribed Ancestor
           Dedication in the Periodization of Shang Dynasty Bronze
           Vessels." *Artibus Asiae* 35.4:335–370.
1974–75   "The Independent Bronze Industries in the South of China
           Contemporary with the Shang and Western Chou
           Dynasties." *Archives of Asian Art* 28:77–107.

Karlgren, Bernhard
1950   *The Book of Documents.* Stockholm.

Keightley, David N.
1969   "Public Work in Ancient China: A Study of Forced Labor in the Shang and Western Chou." Ph.D. dissertation, Columbia University.
1970   "The Temple Artisans of Ancient China, Part One: The *Kung* and *To-kung* of Shang." Paper delivered at the Modern Chinese History Project Colloquium, University of Washington, Seattle, 17 December. Mimeographed.
1973a   "Shang Metaphysics." Paper delivered at the Annual Meeting, Association for Asian Studies, Chicago, March.
1973b   "Religion and the Rise of Urbanism." *Journal of the American Oriental Society* 93.4:527–538.
1975   "Legitimation in Shang China." Paper prepared for the Conference on Legitimation of Chinese Imperial Regimes, Asilomar, Ca., 15–24 June. Mimeographed.
1976   "Shang Divination: The Magico-Religious Legacy." Paper prepared for the Workshop on Classical Chinese Thought, Harvard University, 2–13 August. Mimeographed.
1978a   "The Religious Commitment: Shang Theology and the Genesis of Chinese Political Culture." *History of Religions* 17.3–4:211–224.
1978b   *Sources of Shang History: The Oracle-Bone Inscriptions of Bronze Age China.* Berkeley.
1979–80 "The Shang State as Seen in the Oracle-bone Inscriptions." *Early China* 5:25–34.
forthcoming (a)   "The World of the Royal Diviner."
forthcoming (b)   "Akatsuka Kiyoshi and the Culture of Early China: A Study in Historical Method."

Kendall, David G.
1971   "Construction of Maps from 'Odd Bits of Information.'" *Nature* 231:158–159.

KK
1973.2   "Chiang-su T'ung-shan Ch'iu-wan ku yi-chih ti fa-chüeh 江蘇銅山丘灣古遺址的發掘": pp. 71–79.
1973.4   "Liao-ning K'o-tso-hsien Pei-tung-ts'un fa-hsien Yin-tai ch'ing-t'ung-ch'i 遼寧喀左縣北洞村發現殷代青銅器": pp. 225–226, 257.
1974.6   "Liao-ning K'o-tso-hsien Pei-tung-ts'un ch'u-t'u ti Yin-Chou ch'ing-t'ung ch'i 遼寧喀左縣北洞村出土的 殷周青銅器": pp. 364–372.

1977.3   "An-yang Yin-tai chi-ssu k'eng jen-ku ti hsing-pieh nien-
              ling chien-ting 安陽殷代祭祀坑人骨的性別年齡鑒定":
              pp. 210–214.
1978.1   "An-yang Ta-ssu-k'ung-ts'un Yin-tai sha-hsün k'eng
              安陽大司空村殷代殺殉坑": pp. 71–72.

Kuo Mo-jo 郭沫若
1933   *Pu-tz'u t'ung-tsuan* 卜辭通纂. Tokyo. *K'ao-shih* for nos.
              659–663.

Li Hsiao-ting 李孝定
1965   *Chia-ku wen-tzu chi-shih* 甲骨文字集釋. Chung-yang yen-
              chiu-yüan li-shih yü-yen yen-chiu-so chuan-k'an chih wu-
              shih 中央研究院歷史語言研究所專刊之五十. 8 vols.
              Nankang.

Li Hsüeh-ch'in 李學勤
1959   *Yin-tai ti-li chien-lun* 殷代地理簡論. Peking.

Matsumaru Michio 松丸道雄
1963   "Inkyo bokujichū no denryōchi ni tsuite—Indai kokka
              kōzō kenkyū no tame ni 殷墟卜辞中の田猟地について—
              殷代国家構造研究のために." *Tōyō bunka kenkyūjo kiyō*
              東洋文化研究所紀要 31:1–163.

Miyazaki Ichisada 宮崎市定
1970   "Chūgoku kodai no toshi kokka to sono bochi—Shōyū
              wa doko ni attaka 中国古代の都市国家とその墓地—
              商邑は何処にあったか." *Tōyōshi kenkyū* 東洋史研究
              28.4:265–280; also "Hoi 補遺." 29.2:275–280.

Needham, Joseph
1971   *Science and Civilisation in China*, vol. 4: *Physics and
              Physical Technology*, pt. III: "Engineering and Nautics."
              With the collaboration of Wang Ling and Lu Gwei-djen.
              Cambridge, Eng.

Nivison, David S.
1980   "The Dates of Western Chou." Paper prepared for the
              Metropolitan Museum Symposium, "The Great Bronze
              Age of China," New York, 3 June, revised 15 July 1980.

Rawson, Jessica
1980   *Ancient China: Its Art and Archaeology*. London.

Renfrew, Colin
1975   "Trade as Action at a Distance." In *Ancient Civilization*

and Trade, edited by J. A. Sabloff and C. C. Lamberg-Karlovsky: pp. 1–59. Albuquerque.

S   See Shima Kunio 1971.

Service, Elman R.
1975   *Origins of the State and Civilization: The Process of Cultural Evolution*. New York.

Shima Kunio 島邦男
1958   *Inkyo bokuji kenkyū* 殷墟卜辞研究. Hirosaki.
1971   *Inkyo bokuji sōrui* 殷墟卜辞綜類. 2nd rev. ed. Tokyo.

Soper, Alexander C.
1966   "Early, Middle, and Late Shang: A Note." *Artibus Asiae* 28:5–38.

Teilhard de Chardin, P., and Young, C. C.
1936   "On the Mammalian Remains from the Archaeological Site of An-yang." *PS* ser. C, vol. 12.

Trigger, Bruce
1974   "The Archaeology of Government." *World Archaeology* 6.1:95–106.

Tsou Heng 鄒衡
1978   "Cheng-chou Shang-ch'eng chi T'ang-tu Po shuo 鄭州商城即湯都亳說." *WW* 1978.2:69–71.

Tung Tso-pin 董作賓
1945   *Yin-li-p'u* 殷曆譜. 2 vols. Nan-ch'i, Szechwan.

Wang Yü-hsin 王宇信 and Ch'en Shao-ti 陳紹棣
1973   "Kuan-yü Chiang-su T'ung-shan Ch'iu-wan Shang-tai chi-ssu yi-chih 關於江蘇銅山丘灣商代祭祀遺址." *WW* 1973.12:55–58.

Wang Yü-hsin, Chang Yung-shan 張永山, and Yang Sheng-nan 楊升南
1977   "Shih-lun Yin-hsü wu-hao mu ti 'Fu Hao' 試論殷墟五號墓的'婦好.'" *KKHP* 1977.2:1–22.

Watkins, Frederick M.
1968   "State: The Concept." In *International Encyclopedia of the Social Sciences*: vol. 15:150–156. New York.

Watson, William
1971   *Cultural Frontiers in Ancient East Asia*. Edinburgh.

Webb, Malcolm C.
1975   "The Flag Follows Trade: An Essay on the Necessary

Interaction of Military and Commercial Factors in State Formation." In *Ancient Civilization and Trade*, edited by J. A. Sabloff and C. C. Lamberg-Karlovsky: pp. 155–209. Albuquerque.

Weber, George W., Jr.
1973   *The Ornaments of Late Chou Bronzes: A Method of Analysis.* New Brunswick, N.J.

Wheatley, Paul
1971   *The Pivot of the Four Quarters: A Preliminary Enquiry into the Origins and Character of the Ancient Chinese City.* Chicago.

WW
1972.4   "Shan-hsi-sheng shih-nien lai ti wen-wu k'ao-ku hsin shou-huo 山西省十年來的文物考古新收獲 ": pp. 1–4.
1976.2a   "P'an-lung-ch'eng yi-chiu-ch'i-ssu nien-tu t'ien-yeh k'ao-ku chi-yao 盤龍城一九七四年度田野考古紀要 ": pp. 5–15.
1976.2b   "Shan-hsi Shih-lou hsin cheng-chi tao ti chi-chien Shang-tai ch'ing-t'ung-ch'i 山西石樓新征集到的幾件 商代青銅器 ": p. 94.
1977.8   "Shen-hsi Lin-t'ung fa-hsien Wu-wang cheng Shang kuei 陝西臨潼發現武王征商簋 ": pp. 1–7.
1977.12   "Liao-ning-sheng K'o-tso-hsien Shan-wan-tzu ch'u-t'u Yin-Chou ch'ing-t'ung-ch'i 遼寧省喀左縣山灣子 出土殷周青銅器 ": pp. 23–33, 43.
1979.10   "Shen-hsi Ch'i-shan Feng-ch'u-ts'un fa-hsien Chou-ch'u chia-ku-wen 陝西岐山鳳雛村發現周初甲骨文 ": pp. 38–43.

Yen Yi-p'ing 嚴一萍
1978   *Chia-ku hsüeh* 甲骨學. 2 vols. Taipei.

Concluding Remarks

K. C. CHANG

Semantic strictures could make the phrase "the origins of Chinese civilization" almost impossible to define; but we shall simply understand it in the commonsensical way it is understood by the contributors to this volume, as the beginning process of the civilization that we refer to as Chinese—not as Japanese, Indian, Greek, or Mayan. The word "process" here is understood to refer both to systematized history and to abstract pattern or law. It includes, thus, the questions what, when, where, how, and why.

Even so, some simple explanations of the words "Chinese" and "origins" are in order lest we be led astray by possibly diverse interpretations of them. We can probably agree that in the modern world and for much of the historic period Chinese culture is definable in terms of the commonly recognizable characteristics of language, material culture, social organization, behavioral norms, and supernatural ideas and practices (e.g., see Yü 1976). We can probably agree, too, that this modern and historical Chinese culture is the contemporary version of a developmental continuum whose existence can be traced back to distant antiquity. Because that developmental history is long, it has incorporated many changes, which make its tracing far from simple. For one thing, the modern Chinese have incorporated many ethnic components, so that tracing their respective origins requires studying the histories of multiple ethnic groups rather than a single group. As Fried (1973:343) has pointed out, one sense of the word "Chinese" in Chinese folk usage is the Han component. If we were to confine our efforts to the study of the history of the Han component alone, referring to this as the history of Chinese civilization, we would be prejudging the issue and would have defined a "Chinese" history before even beginning to delineate the perimeters of that history.

My suggestion is that we explore our area descriptively at first, going back beyond the period in which a Chinese civilization evidently ancestral to the modern version can clearly be seen—probably to the Ch'in and Han Dynasties during the four or five centuries around the time of Christ. Then, we determine how many earlier recognizable cultures were ancestral to the civilization of that period. If only one culture exclusively or in large part fulfilled that role, then that culture alone would be our earlier "Chinese." If two or more meet the requirement, then all of them are "Chinese."

The above formulation of the issue presupposes an understanding of the word "origins" in terms of the developmental processes of a whole civilization—not just questions of precedence of one or two elements of that civilization relative to similar elements in other civilizations. Understanding the origins of Chinese civilization involves full knowledge of all the major aspects of the Chinese or proto-Chinese development. It must be based on full knowledge of the development of important elements of the proto-Chinese civilization, the history of the interrelationship of all such elements, including their effects on one another, and the history of the natural environment in which the formative process took place.

Such knowledge is above all descriptive knowledge, which accumulates continuously and renders it necessary for students of ancient China to continually examine new facts and formulate new ideas. Such facts are to be unearthed in many fields: environmental sciences, involving ancient as well as modern meteorology, topography, soils, plants, animals, and minerals; archaeology, which brings to light remains of past cultures; historiography, for the study of the early accounts of Chinese lives and their histories; historical linguistics, to reconstruct prehistoric linguistic forms; ethnology, to reconstruct the diverse ethnic components in early China. It is not just that students of these, and other, learned fields must work together to deal with the issue of Chinese origins. Rather, studies in all these fields build up fundamental data necessary for our descriptive knowledge of the period in which Chinese civilization was forming.

The Berkeley conference took the necessary first step toward a fuller understanding of the earliest Chinese developmental process by bringing together scholars from many fields to exchange both descriptive information and current interpretive issues in their respective disciplines. The papers collected in this volume must, then, be integrated by those of us who are interested in the large picture of earlier China. I shall briefly present here some of my own views on how these papers have advanced our understanding of the Chinese developmental process.

BIOGEOGRAPHICAL ENVIRONMENT AND PLANT DOMESTICATION

The first four chapters, by Whyte, Li, Chang, and Fogg, form a unit that deals with the origin of what is possibly the most fundamental element of Chinese civilization: Chinese agriculture.

These chapters complement one another well, although their authors do not agree on every issue. Offering an environmentalist theory of ultimate cause, Whyte describes the uplifting of the Tibetan land mass in the late Tertiary and the resultant desiccation of the eastern part of Asia—seeing in the ecosystemic stress this brought about on the one hand, and the emergence of gramineous and leguminous annuals on the other, the ultimate cause of the origins of agriculture in China. The Tibetan orogeny and its vast effects on much of Asia are now widely recognized geological events, and Whyte's biogeographic arguments in favor of an environmental interpretation of agricultural origins carry much force; his emphasis on the coincidental appearance of annuals is particularly noteworthy. It is now, as he has noted, up to the "archaeologists and anthropologists to decide on the extent to which they are able to accept the interpretation that environment determined the behavior of early man."

That decision in my opinion cannot be made on the level of orogeny, plate tectonics, and upper atmospheric meterology. At that level one's choices are very limited. The decision must be made at the level of man's behavioral interaction within his ecosystem, and it must be made on the basis of empirical evidence. Such evidence, as Whyte pointed out, is as yet inadequate for a definitive interpretation, but available data on climatic and biotic conditions during the crucial period for Chinese agricultural origins, namely, the several millennia on both sides of 10,000 B.C., does not point to conspicuous aridity and resultant stress in any of the areas of China where important early agricultural centers were located (Tsukada 1966, 1967; Chung-kuo k'o-hsüeh-yüan 1977).

Instead, as the last glaciation drew to a close, we begin to see relative abundance and diversity of natural resources, especially in the lower Yangtze area, with its early rice farming, as Li emphatically points out in chapter 2. Moreover, agricultural beginnings in China—as elsewhere—took place at a time when Palaeolithic industries reached their peak of complexity, sophistication, and efficiency. Whatever environmental compulsions toward agriculture may have existed, they could not possibly have achieved the significant result in which we are interested without the active role of man with a particular technology and social station.

Just as Whyte's chapter provides the necessary large setting for our topic involving macrotime and macrospace, Li's brings us down to earth and describes in detail the environmental conditions in different parts of China where early farming cultures subsisted on different plant assemblages, as well as the histories of the important plants in each area. Environmental conditions surely have had a determining effect on styles of cultures, at least insofar as their plants are concerned. At the same time, however, Li points out that, despite environmental barriers, "the use of the products of soybeans, tea, mulberries, hemp, and lacquer, to name only a few, has become a universal and unifying force in the culture that is typically 'Chinese.'" This assemblage gives us a solid beginning for any compilation of Chinese characteristics.

Li's contribution will in my judgment be a classic for years to come, inspiring and guiding future research in historical botany and cultural history alike. Archaeological data unearthed in recent years from various parts of China already take on a special significance and interest when viewed within Li's biogeographic framework.

In chapter 3, Chang focuses on millets, rice, and the soybean, the three plants of greatest importance in early China, and discusses their histories of cultivation, together with information on a few other crops. A plant geneticist himself, Chang nevertheless stresses the need for an interdisciplinary approach in the study of the early history of the major food crops and pays a special compliment to the early Chinese textual records as useful sources of agricultural information. For their part, historians can especially appreciate the assistance of plant scientists in the knotty area of nomenclature. Chang has considerably clarified the nomenclature problem, but the difficulty of the issue is shown in the fact that Chang's and Li's terminologies do not completely coincide. Ancient Chinese terms were folk terms or ethnoscientific categories, and their identification with the Latin nomenclature is not an issue that can be settled by etymological studies. An eventual solution to this problem may, I suspect, be found archaeologically. In a number of Han dynasty tombs, food remains contained in pottery vessels were sometimes identified by inscriptions written on the vessels. Although few if any of the remains have yet been botanically studied, we are confident that such remains will eventually offer us definitive evidence of the true botanical identities of *shu* and *chi*.

Fogg (chapter 4) illustrates some of the problems involved in relating folk taxonomies to scientific taxonomies. He also shows how ethnography and ethnobotany can be used to uncover a domesticating process that may be analogous to similar processes at work thousands of years ago. The choice of the Taiwan aborigines for Fogg's research is particularly fortunate, not only because the mountains of Taiwan are among the few places in the world where varieties of millets are in use in important ways, but also because these mountain peoples may include direct descendants of the earliest millet growers on the mainland of China. But that is yet another controversial topic!

Although ethnobotany and botany may provide boundless inspiration, and historical botany may awe us with the richness of its textual data, the ultimate solution to the problem of Chinese agricultural origins must rest with archaeology—which brings to light cultures in which the initial domesticating process occurred—and palaeobotany, which deals with remains of the cultivated plants. Here knowledge depends not on speculation or theory but on empirical facts. The most important archaeological facts pertaining to both millets and rice—the two most important Chinese food crops—did not come to light until the past few years; and once they appeared, the whole scene suddenly changed with regard to the history of their domestication. The earliest rice found at Ho-mu-tu has been referred to by both Li and Chang; it can safely be dated to the sixth millennium B.C. Millets of equal or greater antiquity have now been reported from sites of the newly discovered P'ei-li-kang culture of central Honan and southern Hopei, dated to the sixth or even the seventh millennium B.C. (An 1979: 336). Any theory about the origins and migrations of rice and millets must now take these finds into account. There will be more finds of this kind from many more sites, especially when techniques for recovering plant macrofossils are widely adopted in Chinese Neolithic excavations. (A most interesting recent find is the remains of a cereal thought to be kaoliang discovered from the third component of the Yang-shao culture site at Ta-ho-ts'un, Cheng-chou, dated to the late fourth millennium B.C.; see Cheng-chou-shih 1979). I do not believe I am overly optimistic in predicting that within another decade, under the combined assault of archaeologists, botanists, and environmental scientists, the whole issue of Chinese agricultural origins will yield significant, even startling, results. I would like to think that the chapters in this volume make a contribution toward these results.

PHYSICAL CHARACTERISTICS OF THE EARLIEST CHINESE

Culture can sometimes be characterized as super-organic, but it is always created by and anchored within flesh-and-blood populations. Chinese civilization may now be manifested in such "things" as pottery, bronzes, and jades, but it was created and left behind by people; and getting acquainted with the people behind the civilization—*any* civilization— must be among our first orders of business.

The early Chinese crania, under Howells' analysis (chapter 11), show a surprising degree of homogeneity. Not only is it the case that "the population of China in [the] northern region has been constant in physique . . . and also surprisingly homogeneous, since the Neolithic," the crania also "provide no significant differentiation of north and south." The Chinese, northern and southern, have proved to be a unified population, but "Mongoloids north and south of China do not readily approach Chinese." This observation from cranial evidence is of tremendous import for students of Chinese culture, and its implications are obvious, though dangerously complicated.

The origin of this Chinese population, homogeneous since the Neolithic, can be tackled only on very slim evidence: three skulls from the Upper Cave, Chou-k'ou-tien, and one skull from Liu-chiang, Kwangsi. Howells seems to think that the Upper Cave crania may be too recent and too undifferentiated to be directly ancestral to the Neolithic Chinese, but he does not think the latter had to immigrate from anywhere over any significant distance. This problem actually is not a problem about Chinese origins alone; it pertains to the origins of the Mongoloids in general. The data are scanty, the area involved is immense; but the new archaeological potential is always excellent. For the time being, we can be content with the evidence dated to after the beginning of agriculture and can see a population continuum within which the cultural developments that led to the high civilizations of the second and first millennia B.C. took place. For the earlier ancestry of this population, the period of 10,000–5,000 B.C. will prove crucial, as it is already proving crucial for cultural evolution.

THE LINGUISTIC PICTURE

The people who inhabited the area that is now China seem to have been a physically homogenous lot; and, as shown archaeologically, they shared a broadly similar culture from a very early time. But they probably did not all speak the same tongue. Li (chapter 13) reconstructs the earliest known Chinese—Archaic Chinese; and Pulleyblank, in his comprehensive review (chapter 14), speculates about the languages (some of which belonged to the same family) spoken in various parts of China. We can agree with Pulleyblank without doubt that the following language families have been spoken in China for a long time, possibly as far back as prehistory, when Chinese civilization was being formed: Sino-Tibetan, Miao-Yao. Tai, Austro-Asiatic, Austronesian, and Altai, and perhaps others. But besides that part of Sino-Tibetan which has a long literate history, none of the others has left enough of a trace to track down. We must look to our linguistic colleagues for more definitive studies in the future. With regard to

Pulleyblank's observation about the lack of any non-Chinese writing system in China, I should like to note that some of the pottery marks found at the Black Pottery site in Liang-chu (Ho T'ien-hsing 1937) and at the Middle Shang site at Wu-ch'eng in Ch'ing-chiang, Kiangsi (T'ang 1975), also seem to indicate something not quite identical with the Han Chinese script.

The word "Chinese" as used by both Li and Pulleyblank leaves one confused. Can we not call the language Han, and the culture Chinese? This terminological confusion seems to lie at the root of many arguments about designating something as Chinese or non-Chinese.

ARCHAEOLOGICAL ENTITIES

The three archaeological chapters by Pearson with the assistance of Lo, Meacham, and Huber deal generally with the earliest farming cultures in Li's three biogeographic regions of China (chapter 2): North China, South China, and southern Asia. In a sense, these cultures make up the backbone of the conference because they provide the basic data for discerning the similarities and differences of cultural entities in early China.

Pearson, Meacham, and Huber demonstrate in two ways the tremendous advances made by Neolithic archaeology in China in the past thirty years. First, the material they discuss is almost overwhelmingly rich compared with the scanty information available prior to 1949. Second, although their chapters clarify the Neolithic archaeology of China in numerous ways, they also raise many questions; and their views sometimes differ, not insignificantly. This is a sign of the increased maturity of our field, but it also presents problems for the commentator. This is a time when diversity of views must be encouraged; and I must allow the reader to confront these three well-researched and stimulating presentations and reach his own conclusions about the best possible case they jointly or separately provide.

Two of the chapters (by Huber and Meacham) take issue strongly and directly with interpretive hypotheses with which I am sometimes, rightly or wrongly, identified. To comment on their proposals I would inevitably be drawn into a defensive posture, which would not be an appropriate use of my position as commentator. I shall instead supplement these three chapters by remarking some important archaeological data, found too recently to have been taken into account at the time of the Berkeley conference, that date from the period 10,000–5,000 B.C., the period before both the Yang-shao and Ho-mu-tu cultures. At about 5,000 B.C., we begin to see well-defined Neolithic cultures with full-fledged agricultural activities, and the bulk of the controversy in the chapters in question concerns the inter-relationship of these cultures. Possibly many of the answers will be found in this earlier 10,000–5,000 B.C. period.

For details I refer to two recent papers, one of my own (1978) and the other by An Chih-min (1979). They discuss archaeological data—with pottery, polished stone implements, and the sometimes convincing evidence of agriculture—that preceded both the Yang-shao culture of North China and the Ho-mu-tu culture of the lower Yangtze. The most important of the new sites and their carbon-14 dates (Chang 1975; Hsia 1977; Chung-kuo she-hui 1979; Barnard 1980) are, from north to south:

```
Tz'u-shan, Wu-an, Hopei
     (ZK–439)          5405 ± 100 b.c.
     (ZK–440)          5285 ± 105 b.c.
P'ei-li-kang, Hsin-cheng, Honan
     (ZK–434)          5935 ± 480 b.c.
Pei-shou-ling (lower stratum), Pao-chi, Shensi
     (ZK–519)          5156 ± 149 b.c.
     (ZK–534)          5023 ± 135 b.c.
Hsien-jen-tung, Wan-nien, Kiangsi
     (ZK–39)           8920 ± 240 b.c.
     (ZK–92–0)         6875 ± 240 b.c.
Fu-kuo-tun, Quemoy, Fukien
     (NTU–65)          4790–ca. 5500 b.c.
Tseng-p'i-yen, Kuei-lin, Kwangsi
     (ZK–279–1)        9360 ± 180 b.c.
```

There are still unresolved problems regarding some of these dates, but it seems certain that the sites belonged to an earlier epoch then either Yang-shao or Ho-mu-tu. Significantly, the northern sites contained pottery types and modes clearly ancestral to Yang-shao forms, and remains of millet grains were found along with querns, grinding stones, and (at some sites) sickles. The southern sites, on the other hand, feature the coarse and distinctive cord-marks that characterize the Ho-mu-tu ceramics. Possibly the cultures distinctive at 5,000 B.C., had already taken shape well before that date. On the other hand, the northern and southern sites shared significant ceramic modes. Cord-marks and incised patterns adorn the exterior surfaces of pottery at all sites, and the presence of a distinctive rocker-stamping and of shell-impressions has been stressed at several of the sites both north and south. It is entirely possible that answers to the question of the cultural interrelationship of East and West and of North and South will be found in the archaeological data of this earlier period. And the exploration of the period is only just beginning.

ORIGINS OF CHINESE BRONZE METALLURGY AND WRITING

Among all the components of early Chinese civilization, the origins of bronze metallurgy and of writing have commanded particular interest. Unquestionably, both played crucial roles in the formation of early Chinese civilization, and they warrant the attention they have received. On the other hand, neither can be isolated from the rest of Chinese culture, and the history of neither can be equated with the history of the whole civilization. These points, I think, are made clear by the two chapters on bronze metallurgy by Franklin and Barnard.

In a recent, posthumously published paper, T'ang (1979) stated that pieces of metal had long been known from Pan-p'o and Chiang-chai, in Yang-shao culture layers dated to the early fifth millennium B.C. The circumstances of both finds had been described to me earlier by archaeologists at the Institute of Archaeology in Peking, and it appears that the Yang-shao context of the Chiang-chai find, at least, is unassailable. The find was a small disc of brass, about 70 percent copper and 30 percent zinc. The metallurgical problems posed by such an alloy at this early date are difficult but not insurmountable (Chang 1980). Small amounts of metal, furthermore, have been known from Ma-chia-yao, Ch'i-chia, and Lung-shan sites. Thus, whatever the Yang-shao situation, one does not feel too out of place in stating that some knowledge of metal working had always been part of the Chinese technological repertoire since sometime in the Neolithic. But there was no full-blown bronze metallurgy until the Bronze Age of Shang and Chou (or of Hsia, Shang, and Chou). The civilization in which bronze metallurgy was to develop was as important to its development as—or even more important than—the role played by bronze metallurgy in the origin of that civilization, as observed by Franklin.

The same is true for the origin of writing. One has to be amazed by the numerous instances of prehistoric potters' marks Cheung has amassed in chapter 12. I am convinced that some of the pottery marks of Pan-p'o and Chiang-chai were, individually, directly ancestral to the same characters in the writing systems of the Shang and the Chou. But was there a written language among the people of the Yang-shao culture? Risky as it is to answer this question on the basis of negative evidence, I do not feel nervous in saying that the Yang-shao culture and a true writing system do not mix. There were written characters in the Yang-shao, just as there was metal working in the Yang-shao, but there was neither a writing system nor bronze metallurgy until a civilizational level had been reached in Chinese development.

What then were the pottery marks in prehistory? Since the discovery of the Pan-p'o marks, many scholars have seen in them the earliest examples of Chinese numerals (Kuo 1972a; Cheng 1973; Ho Ping-ti 1975). I do not find their arguments convincing. They claim to have identified the numerals one, two, three, four, five, seven, and ten. But what we really have are signs that consist of one stroke, two strokes, three strokes, four strokes, an X, a cross, and a vertical stroke that happen to resemble those numerals. For us to accept the numeral status of these signs in their contemporary context, we must be sure that at least one of two conditions is met: that these signs occur in a context unmistakably pointing to a counting of numbers, such as three men, twelve deer, and so forth, or that they occur as a series including the three Chinese numerals that are arbitrarily shaped, namely, six, eight, and nine. None of these three numerals has been found convincingly to occur in any of the prehistoric pottery characters.

Then what were they? Potter's marks are found on pottery throughout the world and in all periods, and everywhere their primary function was often to serve as some kind of identification mark (Savage 1974:897). In later periods, many bronze vessels bear similar marks that are often believed to be clan or lineage emblems; the pottery marks probably served the same purpose. If this is true, writing found its first use in China to identify one's kin group. This would be another proof—if any is needed—of the importance of kinship in Chinese culture.

THE SOCIETAL FRAMEWORK FOR THE FORMATION OF CHINESE CIVILIZATION

The histories of both bronze metallurgy and writing illustrate the absolute necessity, in any discussion of the developmental process of Chinese civilization (i.e., its "origins"), for a discussion of the societal framework of that civilization and *its* developmental process (or social evolution). This latter aspect, in fact, is the only area in which a non-specialist is likely to be interested in the whole topic of Chinese origins. His interest in the developmental process of Chinese civilization might be due only to its bearing on universal patterns that apply to mankind as a whole or to the civilization of *his* special interest. For the same reasons, the only chapter in this volume that will be professionally relevant to most non-Sinologists and comparativists will be, I daresay, Fried's chapter 15, which has truly theoretical originality.

But as Fried has made clear, valid use of the Chinese data for comparative purposes must depend on valid understandings of those data in terms of their internal order. It is this tension between, on the one hand, being truthful to the ever-increasing Chinese data base that requires constantly renewed efforts in its own study and, on the other hand, trying to conform such data to purported universal patterns already formulated elsewhere in the world without the benefit of Chinese experience that has characterized most aspects of many important controversies in Chinese social historiography.

A few examples will show why comparative sociological issues are relevant to a study of China's origins. Ever since the initial application of Marxist historical philosophy to Chinese data, the issue of periodization has been a perennial topic of scholarly polemics; and, insofar as the ancient period is concerned, the uncertainty centers on the beginning and end of the slave society stage. The latest controversy concerns the placement of its beginnings with the Ta-wen-k'ou culture of Shantung or, as the traditionalists would have it, with the Three Dynasties (T'ang 1977; 1978; P'eng 1977); and the placement of its end with the end of Shang, the end of Western Chou, the beginning of the Warring States period, the Ch'in unification, the beginning of Eastern Han, or the end of Eastern Han (*Kuang-ming jih-pao* 1978). Related to this are the issues of the origin of the state in China (e.g., T'ung 1975) and of the Asiatic mode of production (e.g., Hou 1979).

True enough, these are Marxist issues, but that fact does not lessen their general theoretical importance to Marxists and non-Marxists alike. It is well known that in the 1920s, when Kuo Mo-jo was first experimenting with the Marxist interpretation of ancient Chinese history, he placed the Shang society within the primitive society category; but in the late 1940s, confronted with massive new archaeological evidence from the Yin ruins in An-yang, he revised his scheme and assigned Shang to the slave society stage instead (Kuo 1972b). Current disagreements about the beginning and end of slave society in China are clearly recognized as an issue in the general study of social evolution that must depend on continued study of pertinent data, including new archaeological and epigraphical data. The same can be said about the question of the state's origins (Cohen and Service 1978) and the Asiatic mode of production (Anderson 1974), both topics of profound significance and wide interest in comparative sociology and political economics. One fact about the continued study of the Asiatic mode of production that never ceases to amaze me is that students of the question base their arguments on bits and pieces culled from the writings of Marx and Engels a hundred years old but choose to ignore the rich knowledge and new data pertaining to the economy of Shang and Chou China, often characterized as a model for the Asiatic mode!

I must also admit that students of the origins of Chinese civilization, for our part, have achieved more in the study of art, artifacts, and cultural history than in the characterization of ancient economies and politics. Keightley's chapter on the late Shang state is a solid contribution in the latter areas. My own discussion (chapter 16) of the Three Dynasties examines the societal factors in the origins of Chinese civilization.

Where has this volume brought us? And where do we go from here?

I am fascinated by Jettmar's description of recent Soviet scholarship on the question of Chinese origins (chapter 8), especially the symposium volume of M. V. Kriukov, N. V. Sofronov, and N. N. Cheboksarov. Indeed, there are similarities between their volume and ours: Cheboksarov is our Howells, Kriukov our archaeologists, and Sofronov is our Fang Kuei Li and Pulleyblank, although the Soviet views are in many cases quite different from those of their Berkeley counterparts. I wish I could read what they have written—especially since I assume that they can read what I have written.

Relying on Jettmar's summaries, I can at the same time see that our volume differs from some Soviet scholarship in fundamental ways. We have dealt with the origins of Chinese *civilization*, not of the Chinese *people*. If, thanks to Jettmar's characterization, I understand the word "ethnogenesis" correctly, the search for Chinese ethnogenesis requires primarily a study of Chinese statements in the written records, the kind of study pioneered, for example, by Li Chi (1928). The search for the origins of Chinese civilization, on the other hand, is much broader and can be more objective. Prehistoric cultural entities can be characterized as Chinese if their attributes warrant such an appellation, based on either material or stylistic-symbolic grounds, even if the bearers of those cultures were excluded at one time or another from the we-group by bearers of other cultures more legitimately identified as being Chinese at the time, and vice versa. Actually, the Soviet scholars cited by Jettmar follow largely the same lines we have followed in their pursuit of Chinese ethnogenesis, and I am somewhat skeptical of the relevance that many aspects of material history may have for understanding the nature of the Chinese "ethnos," which surely involves a study of mental states as well as their material foundations.

Something else we have not done in this volume is to project politics into our contributions. This is a notable achievement that deserves a comment or two because it is a rare achievement that is permitted by the present environment in the United States. We are a society of diverse origins; we have the same human prejudices found elsewhere, and some of us may have our private reasons for wanting the issue of Chinese origins resolved one way rather than another. But we are also a free-wheeling and rather informal society, and few of us would think of attempting to browbeat the rest into submission with our own age, position, or authority. That means that, at our scholarly presentations and discussions, we have only one criterion with which to judge other people's points of view: the scientific criterion. Any position on an issue that is not meant to be scientifically justified or defended is rarely regarded seriously; and if one takes such a position more than an excusable once or twice, he quickly loses his credibility. No American academic can function in academic communities effectively without scholarly credibility. Therefore, even though the contributors to this volume may have their share of ethnocentric ideas and prejudices about the emotional topic of Chinese origins, these have been so well hidden that they do not for practical purposes exist. When, in the course of the conference, Professor A averred that the Chineseness of Chinese civilization goes back a long way, or when Dr. B ventured that culture trait X came to China from, say, Persia, their colleagues could take their statements at face value and assume the absence of ulterior motives. In short, the motto "seek truth from facts" was practiced at the Berkeley conference, as it is at similar conferences throughout the United States. If anyone had done the kind of transparent flip-flop Jettmar describes in connection with the Amur region, or concerning the west/east and north/south connections, he would have been laughed out of the conference room.

Rather than ask what "truths" we have obtained from the available facts, it may be useful to ask instead, what was our objective in seeking the truth about Chinese origins? Although the subject matter is readily justifiable, our objectives in getting at it may not be apparent or uniform.

Intense interest by much of the populace about the origins of magnificent civilizations is accounted for by fundamental curiosity. A healthy portion of that curiosity stems from the desire to seek or reaffirm one's own ethnical and cultural heritage—"roots"—but most people are curious about the origins of other peoples' civilizations, or of things in general, as well. Historians, archaeologists, and ethnologists are often called upon to satisfy that curiosity.

There is surely no conflict between scholars' civic services and their scholarly pursuits; scholarly research need not be justified by anything other than simple, raw curiosity. But scholars are interested in the origins of Chinese civilization for more specific reasons as well. The beginning of

Chinese history, the history of a civilization that is both qualitatively and quantitatively significant, must be a crucial part of any understanding of that history as a whole. And, because of the obvious importance of that civilization throughout world history, a knowledge of its origins is indispensable for students of historical processes in general—including cultural and social evolution. Any historical theory, including but by no means confined to Marxist historical materialism, enhances its validity with regard to the present and the future, as well as the past, if it explains the process of Chinese development; and it is found wanting if it does not.

Our objectives in seeking to know the origins of Chinese civilization, in short, have everything to do with the detailed developmental process (the what, when, where, how, and why) of Chinese civilization but nothing to do with politics, past or contemporary psychology, or any contest with other civilizations as to who was first in what. As we seek no short or simplistic answers, our objectives are not easy to satisfy because they depend upon factual and interpretive knowledge that is both diversified and cumulative. The contents of this volume testify to our progress so far and indicate the gaps in our knowledge. But in my opinion these chapters establish a landmark in the study of China's origins because, for the first time, they set the whole endeavor on an interdisciplinary course toward calm, systematic, and cumulative understanding.

REFERENCES

An Chih-min 安志敏
  1979   "P'ei-li-kang, Tz'u-shan, ho Yang-shao—shih lun Chung-
              yüan hsin shih-ch'i wen-hua ti yüan-yüan chi fa-chan
              裴李岡、磁山、和仰韶 ── 試論中原新石器文化的淵源及
              發展." *KK* 1979.4:335–346.

Anderson, Perry
  1974   *Lineages of the Absolutist State.* London.

Barnard, Noel
  1980   *Radiocarbon Dates and Their Significance in the Chinese
              Archaeological Scene: A List of 420 Entries Compiled from
              Chinese Sources Published up to Close of 1979.* Canberra.

Chang Kwang-chih 張光直
  1975   "Chung-kuo k'ao-ku-hsüeh shang ti fang-she-hsing t'an-su

nien-tai chi ch'i yi-yi 中國考古學上的放射性碳素年代
及其意義." *Kuo-li T'ai-wan ta-hsüeh k'ao-ku jen-lei hsüeh-
k'an* 國立臺灣大學考古人類學刊 37–38:29–43.

1978 "Kung-yuan ch'ien wu-ch'ien nien tao yi-wan-nien ch'ien
Chung-kuo yüan-ku wen-hua tzu-liao 公元前五千年到
一萬年前中國遠古文化資料." *Chung-yang yen-chiu-yüan
min-tsu-hsüeh yen-chiu-so chi-k'an* 中央研究院民族學
研究所集刊 46:113–120.

1980 "The Chinese Bronze Age: A Modern Synthesis." In *The
Great Bronze Age of China*, edited by Wen Fong: pp.
35–50. New York.

Cheng Te-k'un 鄭德坤
1973 "Chung-kuo shang-ku shu ming ti yen-pien chi ch'i ying-
yung 中國上古數名的演變及其應用." *Hsiang-kang chung-
wen ta-hsüeh hsüeh-pao* 香港中文大學學報 1:37–58.

Cheng-chou-shih Cheng-chou-shih po-wu-kuan 鄭州市博物館
1979 "Cheng-chou Ta-ho-ts'un yi-chih fa-chüeh pao-kao
鄭州大河村遺址發掘報告." *KKHP* 1979.3:301–374.

Chung-kuo k'o-hsüeh-yüan Chung-kuo k'o-hsüeh-yüan, Kuei-yang ti-
ch'iu hua-hsüeh yen-chiu-so, Ti-ssu-chi pao-fen tsu, C 14
tsu 中國科學院貴陽地球化學研究所, 第四紀孢粉組,
C14組
1977 "Liao-ning-sheng nan-pu yi-wan-nien lai tzu-jan huan-
ching ti yen-pien 遼寧省南部一萬年來自然環境的演變."
Chung-kuo k'o-hsüeh 中國科學 1977.6:603–614.

Chung-kuo she-hui Chung-kuo she-hui k'o-hsüeh-yüan k'ao-ku yen-
chiu-so shih-yen-shih 中國社會科學院考古研究所實驗室
1979 "Fang-she-hsing t'an-su ts'e-ting nien-tai pao-kao (liu)
放射性碳素測定年代報告(六)." KK 1979.1:89–96.

Cohen, Ronald, and Service, E. R., eds.
1978 *Origins of the State: The Anthropology of Political
Evolution.* Philadelphia.

Fried, Morton H.
1973 "China: An Anthropological Overview." In *An
Introduction to Chinese Civilization*, edited by John
Meskill: pp. 341–378. New York.

Ho, Ping-ti
1975 *The Cradle of the East: An Inquiry into the Indigenous
Origins of Techniques and Ideas of Neolithic and Early
Historic China, 5000–1000 B.C.* Hong Kong and Chicago.

Ho T'ien-hsing 何天行

1937   *Hang-hsien Liang-chu-chen chih shih-ch'i yü hei-t'ao* 杭縣良渚鎮之石器與黑陶. Shanghai.

Hou Wai-lu 侯外廬

1979   *Chung-kuo ku-tai she-hui shih lun* 中國古代社會史論. Hong Kong (reprint).

Hsia Nai 夏鼐

1977   "T'an-shih-ssu ts'e-ting nien-tai ho Chung-kuo shih-ch'ien k'ao-ku-hsüeh 碳-14測定年代和中國史前考古學." *KK* 1977.4:217–232. (Partially translated by Nancy Price in *Early China* 3 [Fall 1977]:87–93.)

Kuang-ming jih-pao 光明日報

1978   "Yung-yü ch'ung-p'o chin-ch'ü kan-yü pai-chia cheng-ming—Chung-kuo ku-tai shih fen-ch'i wen-t'i hsüeh-shu t'ao-lun hui tsai Ch'ang-ch'un chao-k'ai 勇於衝破禁區，敢於百家爭鳴 —中國古代史分期問題學術討論會在長春召開." 8 November 1978.

Kuo Mo-jo 郭沫若

1972a   "Ku-tai wen-tzu chih pien-cheng ti fa-chan 古代文字之辯証的發展." *KK* 1972.3:2–13.

1972b   *Nu-li-chih shih-tai* 奴隸制時代. Peking.

Li Chi

1928   *The Formation of the Chinese People.* Cambridge, Mass.

P'eng Pang-chiung 彭邦烔

1977   "Shih shih-tsu she-hui pu shih nu-li-chih she-hui—chiu Ta-wen-k'ou wen-hua ho T'ang Lan hsien-sheng shang-ch'üeh 是氏族社會不是奴隸制社會 — 就大汶口文化和唐蘭先生商榷." *Kuang-ming jih-pao* 光明日報 5 December 1977.

Savage, George

1974   "Pottery." In *The New Encyclopaedia Britannica*, 15th ed., 14:892–931. Chicago.

T'ang Lan 唐蘭

1975   "Kuan-yü Chiang-hsi Wu-ch'eng wen-hua yi-chih yü wen-tzu ti ch'u-pu t'an-so 關於江西吳城文化遺址與文字的初步探索." *WW* 1975.7:72–76.

1977   "Ts'ung Ta-wen-k'ou wen-hua ti t'ao-ch'i wen-tzu k'an wo-kuo tsui-tsao wen-hua ti nien-tai 從大汶口文化的陶器文字看我國最早文化的年代." *Kuang-ming jih-pao* 光明日報 14 July 1977.

1978	"Tsai lun Ta-wen-k'ou wen-hua ti she-hui hsing-chih ho Ta-wen-k'ou ti t'ao-ch'i wen-tzu—chien ta P'eng Pang-chiung t'ung-chih 再論大汶口文化的社會性質和大汶口的陶器文字 — 兼答彭邦炯同志." *Kuang-ming jih-Pao* 光明日報 23 February 1978.
1979	"Chung-kuo ch'ing-t'ung-ch'i ti ch'i-yüan yü fa-chan 中國青銅器的起源與發展." *Ku kung po-wu-yuan yüan-k'an* 故宮博物院院刊 1979.1:4–10.

Tsukada, Matsuo 塚田松雄

1966	"Late Pleistocene Vegetation and Climate in Taiwan (Formosa)." *Proceedings of the National Academy of Sciences* 55:543–548.
1967	"Vegetation in Subtropical Formosa during the Pleistocene Glaciations and the Holocene." *Palaeogeography, Palaeoclimatology, Palaeoecology* 3:49–64.

T'ung Chu-ch'en 佟柱臣

1975	"Ts'ung Erh-li-t'ou lei-hsing wen-hua shih-t'an Chung-kuo ti kuo-chia ch'i-yüan wen-t'i 從二里頭類型文化試談中國的國家起源問題." *WW* 1975.6:29–33, 84.

Yü Ying-shih 余英時

1976	"Kuan-yü Chung-kuo li-shih t'e-chih ti yi-hsieh k'an-fa 關於中國歷史特質的一些看法." In his *Li-shih yü ssu-hsiang* 歷史與思想: pp. 271–284. Taipei.

FINDING LIST
OF CARBON-14
DATES CITED

INDEX AND GLOSSARY

Chinese graphs not given here may be found at the first occurrence of a word in the text; homophones are listed according to the radical order of the Chinese graphs. Geographical names in parentheses refer to the *hsien* in which a site is located; the graph(s) for the *hsien* may be found at the glossary entry for its name. Wade-Giles romanizations are supplied in parentheses when they differ from the romanizations used in the text. No graphs are provided for those common names, geographical locations, and book titles that are readily available in standard reference works.

pigweed (*Chenopodium album*), 36

P'i-hsien 丕縣, xxvii. *See also* Liu-lin;
Ta-tun-tzu

pine (*Pinus*), 27, 39, 40, 43;
massioniana, 40; *yunnanensis*, 41

Ping (place), 535

p'ing (vessel), 204

Ping-chou 幷州, 67

P'ing-ku 平谷, xxvii, 248, 290, 291,
544. *See also* Liu-chia-ho

P'ing-ling-ch'eng 平陵城, 330

P'ing-shan 平山. *See* Ling-shou

P'ing-yin 平陰, 544

Pin-hsien 邠縣, xxvii, 544. *See also*
Hsia-meng-ts'un

p'i-p'a (loquat), 46

Piper betle (betel nut), 52

Pistacia, 29

plants: and animals, 9; aquatic,
43–46; and climate, 9; climax
types, 9, 10; cultivated, 29–38,
42–51, 222–223; domestication
of, 21–55, 95–113, 158, 566–569;
evolution of, 9, 13–15; fibrous, 48;
gramineous, 13, 15; heliophilous,
23; industrial, 50; leguminous, 13;
mesophytic, 9, 15; original, 25–
29, 39–42, 52; prehistoric, 7, 9,
11, 24; range of, 54–55; and temperature, 26; xerophytic, 9. *See
also* cereals; crops; and *names of
individual species*

plastromancy, 209, 210 n. *See also*
scapulimancy

plate tectonics, 5

plum, Chinese (*Prunus salicina*), 35

Po 亳 (place), 505, 508, 525

Po (title), 528

po (vessel), 121, 179, 193, 324, 370

po-ch'i (water chestnut), 43

Po-hsien 亳縣. *See* Tiao-yü-t'ai

Po-lao. *See* Pao-lou

pollen analysis. *See* palynology

Polygonum hydropiper (common
smartweed), 36

Polygonum tinctorium (Chinese
indigo), 38

Polynesians, 299, 307–313 passim

pottery: black, 162, 164, 186–187,
199; Chung Yüan, 181–186, 195,
204, 207; Ch'ing-lien-kang, 121,
126, 128, 129–130, 138; designs
on, 181–185, 192–193, 210; early
Neolithic, 572; geometric, 161–
162, 165–166, 167; Ho-mu-
tu, 49, 124, 572; Honan Lung-
shan, 506; Hua-t'ing, 192; inscriptions, 323–383, 413–414, 573–
574; Kiangsu Lung-shan, 187–
195; Liu-lin, 189, 190–191;
manufacture, 282–283; and
metallurgy, xxix, 207, 209, 269–
271; molds for hinges, 256–257,
266; painted, 124, 177–210;
Shantung Lung-shan, 195–202;
wheel-turned, 158, 168, 199,
202, 510; Yüeh, 151, 156–157,
158

Po-wu-chih 博物志, 441

precipitation, 23, 55; and millet
cultivation, 99, 100; in North
China, 25; and rice cultivation,
75; in South China, 39

prickly ash, Chinese (*Zanthoxylum
simulans*), 38

priesthood, 169. *See also* religion;
ritual

*Problemy genezisa kitaiskoi tsivili-
zatsii: Formirovanie osnov
material'noi kul'tury i etnosa*, 218

ch'eng), 329–330, 362, 368, 372, 381, 382

Wan-nien 萬年, xxvi. *See also* Hsien-jen-tung

Ward, Lauriston, xix

warfare: Lung-shan, 507; Shang, 529, 541–543, 548, and state, 479–480, 485–486

water buffalo. *See* animal remains; animals

water-caltrop (*Trapa*), 43, 44, 124, 131

water chestnut (*Eleocharis tuberosa*), 43, 44, 159 n.

water dropwort (*Oenanthe javanica*), 44, 45

water-shield (*Brasenia schreberi*), 44, 45

water spinach (*Ipomoea aquatica*), 44, 45

Watson, William, 178

Wei (barbarians), 442–446

Wei-fang 濰坊, xxvii, 199–201

Wei-hsien 濰縣. *See* Lu-chia-k'ou

Weng-yüan 翁源, xxvi, 121, 161

Wen-hsien 溫縣, 544

Western origins of Chinese culture, xix, 170, 232, 383

wetland agriculture, 54

wheat, 30, 67, 77, 78–79

wind, 8, 23

wine, 98

woodland, 23, 27. *See also* forests

Woolley, Sir Leonard, 280–281

wormwood (*Artemisia*), 10, 27–28

wrought metal hypothesis. *See* metal, wrought; *see also* metal, sheet

Wu (state), 75

Wu (place), 541

Wu (?) (place), 543

Wu-an 武安. *See* Tz'u-shan

Wu-ch'eng 吳城 (Ch'ing-chiang): pottery inscriptions at, 338–341, 363, 370–371, 372, 376, 381, 382, 540, 571. *See also* Liu-shu-kou

Wu Chiang. *See* Wu-sung Chiang

Wu-chieh (people), 456

Wu-chin 武進. *See* Yen-ch'eng

wu-chiu (Chinese tallow tree), 50

Wu-hsien 吳縣. *See* Ts'ao-hsieh-shan

Wu-hsing 吳興. *See* Ch'ien-shan-yang

Wu-huan 烏桓 (people), 446, 453, 454

wu-lan (*Canarium pimela*), 52

Wu-ling 武陵, 426

Wu-lou 五樓 (Sian): pottery inscriptions at, 325, 362, 372, 380, 381

Wu-p'ing 武平, 356

Wu Shan-ching 吳山菁, 128, 181 n.

Wu-sun 烏孫 (people), 7, 457–458

Wu-sung Chiang 吳淞江 (river), 439

Wu Ting 武丁 (Shang king), 499, 524, 536

Wu-Yüeh ch'un-ch'iu 吳越春秋, 411

Xanthium strumarium (cocklebur), 36

ya 亞 (shape), 547

ya 牙 "tooth," 439

yam (*Dioscorea opposita*), 48, 51, 102, 111, 155

Yami (Ya-mei) 雅美. *See* Taiwan aborigines

yang-mei (*Myrica rubra*), 46

Yang-shao culture: and agriculture, 66, 95, 110, 119; and Ch'ing-lien-kang, 127, 140, 164; and climate, 4; dates, 239, 240; and Hsia, 503; and Lung-shan, 177–210; and

Designer: Randall Goodall
Compositor: Asco Trade Typesetting Ltd.
Printer: Vail-Ballou Press
Binder: Vail-Ballou Press
Text: Times Roman
Display: Trump Medieval bold italic and Times Roman